# THE DUTY OF DELIGHT

Dorothy Day at Maryfarm, Easton, PA, ca. 1937

# THE DUTY OF DELIGHT

*The Diaries of Dorothy Day*

EDITED BY

## ROBERT ELLSBERG

MARQUETTE UNIVERSITY PRESS

MARQUETTE
UNIVERSITY

PRESS

LIBRARY OF CONGRESS CATALOGING-IN-PUBLICATION DATA

Day, Dorothy, 1897-1980.
  The duty of delight : the diaries of Dorothy Day / edited by Robert Ellsberg.
    p. cm.
  Includes bibliographical references and index.
  ISBN-13: 978-0-87462-023-8 (clothbound : alk. paper)
  ISBN-10: 0-87462-023-6 (clothbound : alk. paper)
  1. Day, Dorothy, 1897-1980—Diaries. 2. Catholics—United States—Diaries. I.
Ellsberg, Robert. II. Title.
  BX4705.D283A3 2008
  267'.182092—dc22
  [B]

                                                                    2008007883

Copyright © 2008 by Marquette University

Introduction © 2008 by Robert Ellsberg

Cover photo: Dorothy Day on the beach at Spanish Camp, Staten Island,
ca. August 1977 (from slide by Stanley Vishnewski)

www.marquette.edu/mupress/

**FOUNDED 1916**

MARQUETTE UNIVERSITY PRESS
MILWAUKEE

The Association of Jesuit University Presses

"Today I thought of a title for my book, *The Duty of Delight,* as a sequel to *The Long Loneliness.* I was thinking how, as one gets older, we are tempted to sadness, knowing life as it is here on earth, the suffering, the Cross. And how we must overcome it daily, growing in love, and the joy which goes with loving."

Dorothy Day, February 24, 1961

# Contents

# PREFACE

Dorothy Day's diaries are part of the special Dorothy Day-Catholic Worker Collection housed at Marquette University's Raynor Memorial Libraries in Milwaukee, Wisconsin. According to Day's wishes, these personal papers were to be sealed for twenty-five years after her death. As that anniversary approached in November 2005, I received an invitation from the University to serve as editor of these writings—both her diaries, and the letters that will be the focus of a future volume. Over the course of the next year I received a total of eleven CDs containing scanned versions of all of Day's extant journals from 1934-1979. These disks contained many thousands of files—each consisting of a single scanned page of handwritten text. When transcribed, this material amounted to over a thousand single-spaced pages, which I subsequently reduced by about half to arrive at the present volume.

The opportunity to read and work on this text has been a great privilege, for which I owe special thanks to Matt Blessing, Head of Special Collections and Archives at Marquette and Phil Runkel, the redoubtable Marquette archivist, who has devoted thirty years to this collection. My own engagement with this work has felt, at times, like the culmination of an assignment that began over thirty years ago when Dorothy Day asked me to serve as managing editor of the *Catholic Worker* newspaper. Although I performed that job for only two years (1976-1978), it was an appointment that would prove decisive for the rest of my life.

Embarking on this project, I was grateful for my early familiarity with Dorothy's handwriting. But the task of deciphering and transcribing her minuscule script was only the beginning. The greater challenge was selecting what to omit. This was relatively easy in the case of shorthand notes on her travels, random lists of facts (especially the comings and goings of her fellow Catholic Workers), quotations from books, and summaries of retreats and lectures. A good deal of what remained was simply a kind of log: a record of what time she rose; the temperature and weather forecast (a subject of exceptional interest); what time she went to Mass; what she ate for breakfast; who she met (though rarely what they discussed); what she read; if she traveled, the timetable of her departure and arrival and notes on the conditions of the road. For the most part this was of limited interest.

And yet the very *dailiness* of this record tells an important story of its own. Dorothy Day's life at the Catholic Worker was marked by a number of remarkable episodes, and she was a witness or participant in many of the most significant social movements of the twentieth century. But by and large, her life was spent in very ordinary ways. Her sanctity—if one wishes to call it that—was expressed not just in heroic deeds but in the mundane duties of everyday life. Her "spirituality" was rooted in a constant effort to be more charitable toward those closest at hand. And she was sustained in this practice—as her diaries make clear—by a regular discipline of prayer and worship.

These diaries provide a unique window on Dorothy's inner life, her ruminations, and even her dreams. And yet they are not a complete reflection of her life and times. Writing for herself alone, she did not bother to describe or introduce most of the people she wrote about, and she made only passing reference to the headlines of the day. To help put these writings in context, I have found it necessary to fill in some of the gaps, whether through footnotes, parenthetical asides, or occasional insertions from *The Catholic Worker*. Nevertheless, the writing here—intimate, at times confessional—conveys an impression not always present in her public writing. Even readers intimately familiar with her books and her CW columns are likely to encounter new and unfamiliar dimensions to her personality. At least they may come to a better appreciation of what was implied in her favorite phrase, "the duty of delight."

My thanks are due to many people, including Patrick Jordan, Frank Donovan, Jim Forest, and Tom Cornell, who clarified a number of references; my son Nicholas, and my wife, Peggy Ellsberg; Jim Martin; Rachelle Linner; Andrew Tallon, director of Marquette University Press (the only publisher I know who also designs and typesets his books), for his excellent management of this project; Matt Blessing of the Raynor Memorial Libraries; the Archdiocese of New York and Marquette University's Edward Simmons Religious Commitment Fund, both of which provided generous support. I want to emphasize my debt to Phil Runkel for his painstaking corrections of my transcription and his careful attention to detail. His dedication and unparalleled knowledge of the Dorothy Day-Catholic Worker Collection have made him an invaluable resource.

I noted that the original diaries, as I received them from Marquette, extended only through 1979. As Phil Runkel explained, regretfully, the Archives had never received any diary for 1980, the last year of Dorothy's life. This was disappointing, though I doubted there was anything to be done about it. Dorothy's room at Maryhouse had already been swept several times for her personal papers, and it seemed unlikely that anything had been overlooked. Nevertheless, I consulted Frank Donovan, the longtime CW office manager and, toward the end of Dorothy's life, her most devoted assistant. My query prompted him to look in the drawer of Dorothy's bedside table. And there he found it: a small red-leather diary from 1980, unread by anyone for more than twenty-five years, the final entries written just a week before she died.

To hold that small book and to transcribe its contents brought this project to a fitting conclusion. But for me it closed a more personal circle, recalling memories of her voice, and of the stories she told, and of our last meeting in that room—which marked both an end and a beginning.

# INTRODUCTION

❦

In *The Long Loneliness* Dorothy Day described her early habit of keeping
a diary: "When I was a child, my sister and I kept notebooks; recording
happiness made it last longer, we felt, and recording sorrow dramatized it
and took away its bitterness; and often we settled some problem which beset
us, even while we wrote about it." Though somewhat irregularly, she maintained this habit throughout her life. Sometimes her reflections were prompted by happiness, and sometimes by sorrow. But mostly her diary entries were
an expression of her intense interest in life, her need to observe and take note
of what was happening around her and to track her own responses.

Unfortunately, the diaries from her early life were lost. Thus we have no
contemporary record of the years described in her memoirs or in an earlier
(and much regretted) autobiographical novel. That part of her life included a
mostly happy childhood in New York, Oakland, and Chicago; a brief college
career; a return to New York in 1916, which put her in touch with many of
the leading radical journalists and activists of the day; her arrest with suffragists in Washington and her friendship with an assorted lot of socialists,
anarchists, and literary Bohemians; her association with the playwright Eugene O'Neill; an unhappy love affair; and what she later described as years
of restless searching. She acknowledged, in her books, that there was much
that she left out. As she later noted in her diary, "Aside from drug addiction,
I committed all the sins young people commit today." Though that story lies
outside the scope of this volume, the memories and associations from her
early years would continue to surface and shape the rest of her life.

In her first memoir, *From Union Square to Rome* (1938), she quoted verbatim from a journal she kept while living on Staten Island in 1925 with her
"common-law husband," Forster Batterham. From that text, later revised in
*The Long Loneliness* (1952), we get an immediate impression of the peace and
happiness that preceded her conversion to Catholicism.

> I have been passing through some years of fret and strife, beauty and ugli-
> ness, days and even weeks of sadness and despair, but seldom has there been
> the quiet beauty and happiness I have now. I thought all those years I had

freedom, but now I feel that I had neither real freedom nor even a sense of freedom.

She wrote particularly about her experience of pregnancy and the feelings of gratitude she felt—a gratitude so large that only God could receive it.

But that happiness was not to endure. Her decision to have her daughter Tamar baptized in the Catholic Church, followed by her own conversion in 1927, involved a wrenching separation from Forster, who would have nothing to do with marriage or religion. That sacrifice was the decisive turning point in her life. But it left open the question of just what she was supposed to do next. She had found a new home in the Catholic Church, but little sense of community. For five years she struggled to support Tamar on her earnings as a writer, but all the while she yearned to find some way of connecting her new faith with her abiding commitment to social justice.

In December 1932 she went to Washington, D.C. to cover a Communist-inspired "Hunger March of the Unemployed." On the Feast of the Immaculate Conception she visited the National Shrine and there prayed that "some way would be opened up for me to work for the poor and the oppressed." And when she returned to her apartment in New York she found Peter Maurin waiting for her. Maurin, a French-born peasant-philosopher, twenty years her senior, had learned her name from the editor of *Commonweal* magazine. Even before their meeting he had determined that Dorothy Day would be the one to implement his vision.

Dorothy often described their encounter and her debt to Peter Maurin, noting that it took some while for her to comprehend that his plan was the answer to her prayer. Maurin proposed a movement that would implement the radical social message of the gospels. Without awaiting funding or authorization from the bishops, they would start a newspaper and begin at once to build "a new society within the shell of the old."

Five months later *The Catholic Worker* newspaper was launched. At a Communist rally in Union Square on May 1, 1933 Dorothy and a few volunteers handed out papers to demonstrators and curious passersby. In an editorial she described the paper's mission:

> For those who are sitting on park benches in the warm spring sunlight.
> For those who are huddling in shelters trying to escape the rain.
> For those who are walking the streets in the all but futile search for work.
> For those who think that there is no hope for the future, no recognition of their plight—this little paper is addressed.

It is printed to call their attention to the fact that the Catholic Church has a social program—to let them know that there are men of God who are working not only for their spiritual but for their material welfare.

Peter Maurin, typically, was not on hand for this occasion. His role, as he conceived it, was to enunciate principles, leaving the practical implementation to others—that is, to Dorothy. But his vision shaped the emerging movement in many ways, not least by his positive vision of an alternative society—a future that would be different, as he put it, "if we make the present different."

The present certainly cried out for an alternative. This was the heart of the Depression when millions around the country were uprooted, unemployed, or hanging on by their fingertips. New York City was filled with hungry, hopeless people "walking the streets in the all but futile search for work." For Dorothy this represented not just an economic problem but a profound spiritual crisis—for each one of these people bore the image of Christ.

Before long the Catholic Worker opened a soup kitchen, and then a shelter for the homeless. Maurin had challenged the U.S. bishops to open "houses of hospitality" in every diocese to meet the needs of the vast numbers of unemployed and homeless. When a homeless woman arrived at the Catholic Worker office one day asking where to find these houses of hospitality, Dorothy's response was to rent an apartment, and then a house. This was the first of many such houses of hospitality around the country. They became the heart of the Catholic Worker—centers for practicing the "Works of Mercy": feeding the hungry, sheltering the homeless, clothing the naked. It was a program drawn from the gospels. As Jesus said, "Inasmuch as you did these things to the least of my brethren you did them to me."

It is at this point, in 1934, that Dorothy's diaries begin. Already the Catholic Worker was becoming a movement; the paper's circulation was steadily climbing and new houses were emerging around the country. There turned out to be quite a large audience eager for a paper addressing social issues from a Catholic perspective. Seminaries and churches around the country ordered bundles. Idealistic young people, unemployed workers, and a wide assortment of colorful characters were drawn to the cause, attracted perhaps by the spirit of community, or Maurin's philosophy of voluntary poverty, or by the sense of adventure that Dorothy conveyed in her columns. Her diaries from these early days reflect the giddy, improvisational atmosphere of the Worker, when Providence, chance, or a knock on the door might determine what would happen next.

There was no formal "Rule" to life in a Catholic Worker house. Dorothy likened it to a family—sometimes offering a foretaste of heaven, and at other times just the opposite. And over this sometimes fractious family Dorothy was the unquestioned matriarch. Everyone looked to her for leadership, sympathy, and inspiration, while readily blaming her for anything that went wrong. Meanwhile she promoted an ethic of personal responsibility, recalling Peter Maurin's exhortation to "be what you want the other person to be." Because the Worker's doors were open to everyone—the poor, the crazed, the needy in every sense—community life was frequently marked by disorder and confusion. At one point, she writes,

> In town the usual crosses, Carney calling us all racketeers, calling the spiritual reading pious twaddle; Mr. Breen with his vile accusations; the misery of Minas and the Professor; Kate's illness; the suit against us, the bills piling up and the unconscious discouragement in people like Frank and Jim—these things to be topped by such a lack of understanding of the personalist idea from those you expect the most from, lays me low.

And yet things got done. The paper was published and mailed out. Thousands of meals were served each week. And the world received a remarkable spectacle of the Gospel in action.

In its early years the *Catholic Worker* featured a good deal of topical reporting about strikes, evictions, and labor struggles. Almost every issue contained a number of Peter Maurin's lapidary "Easy Essays." Often there might be excerpts from one of the pope's social encyclicals. And there were always a number of talented writers. But it was Dorothy's writing—personal, engaged, rooted in the everyday—that defined the spirit of the paper.

Her literary influences ranged from Jack London to Chekhov. But ultimately the style was her own. She described it as "epistolary." Her column, she wrote, was "a letter to friends." "Writing," as she explained, "is an act of community. It is a letter, it is comforting, consoling, helping, advising on our part, as well as asking it on yours. It is a part of our human association with each other. It is an expression of our love and concern for each other."

Meanwhile, in her diaries, she wrote a different kind of letter—addressed to herself—describing the events of the day as well as her own personal struggles. In the beginning, these private ruminations overlapped a good deal with her articles in the paper. But over time the public and private voices began to diverge. For long stretches her diary—written in spare moments—might consist of little more than a log of her daily activities. But at other times it offered an opportunity to work out problems or to reflect on matters of private concern. In these diaries she might confide her loneliness and discouragement, or describe her physical ailments, scold herself for a failure of charity, or note some insight or an act of kindness that reminded her of God.

For those who have studied Dorothy Day's published writings, the voice in these diaries is mostly familiar. In her column, "On Pilgrimage," she regularly described her travels, her activities, and her reading of the "signs of the times." And yet certain themes stand out here, such as the intense discipline of her spiritual and sacramental life. She attended daily Mass, which usually meant rising at dawn. She prayed the monastic hours from a breviary, a practice she adopted even before becoming a Benedictine oblate in 1955. She devoted time each day to meditating on scripture, saying the rosary, or other spiritual exercises. None of this is particularly remarkable. And yet the matter-of-fact recital of such habits underscores the fact that her daily life was spent in continuous reference to God. As she writes, "Without the sacraments of the church, I certainly do not think that I could go on."

At the same time her diaries reflect her often complicated relationship with church authorities. In one of her early entries she describes a visit from a monsignor who reported the Cardinal's approval of the Catholic Worker ("a modern miracle"). The archdiocese, he reported, "would give us an Imprimatur if they thought it would not hinder us in our work." But later, as the Worker's pacifist and anarchist tendencies emerged, there was no more talk of an Imprimatur. In fact, in 1951 she describes being called to the chancery and informed that "we would either have to cease publication or change our name." (She finessed that ultimatum by noting that ceasing publication "would be a grave scandal to our readers and would put into the hands of our enemies, the enemies of the Church, a formidable weapon.")

Among the more personal themes in her diaries is the relationship with family members, such as her younger sister Della, her daughter Tamar, and her many grandchildren. Though she had limited contact with other members of her immediate family (who disapproved of her religion, her radicalism, and her notoriety), she remained constantly in touch with Della, who lived within easy visiting range. Despite their differences (Della was a dedicated proponent of Planned Parenthood), Dorothy called on her sister nearly every week, often staying overnight to enjoy some rest and recuperation.

The most significant relationship in her life was undoubtedly with her daughter Tamar, who was seven when the Catholic Worker was founded. Dorothy's diaries show her anxiety about raising a child in this uncertain environment, and the difficulty of balancing the needs of her daughter and the demands of the larger household. When Tamar married at 18 and began her own family, Dorothy took naturally to the role of mother-in-law and grandmother. She was a frequent visitor in Tamar's home—often for months at a time—in West Virginia or later in Vermont.

One year, while Tamar pursued a degree in practical nursing which took her away from home, Dorothy moved in and cared for her grandchildren for four months. And so her days were spent in getting children to school, driving them to football practice, helping them with their homework, confronting them about their chores or their adolescent moods, and putting them to bed—in other words, the daily work of any parent or grandparent. She worried about their welfare and happiness; she suffered terribly when her grandson Eric was drafted and sent to Vietnam; she was "prostrate" with grief when one of her great-grandsons was killed in a car accident. Such episodes belie the common impression that Dorothy's unusual life in the Catholic Worker placed her outside the concerns of "ordinary" family life.

At the same time her diaries cast new light on her relationship with Tamar's father, Forster Batterham. In her published memoirs she wrote of him with respect and enduring affection. She credited him with a major role in her conversion to a faith he could not share. But there was no indication that they ever saw one another again. In fact, over time, Forster began to reappear in her life.

In 1959, remarkably, he asked for her help in caring for his long-time companion, Nanette, who was dying of cancer. And so, for several months, Dorothy spent much of each day with the couple on Staten Island, helping with housework, offering companionship and consolation. On the day before she died, Nanette asked to be baptized—an ironic and poignant repetition of the summer of 1927 that had ended with Dorothy's own conversion. And once again, after Nanette's death, Dorothy and Forster went their separate ways.

But now they stayed in closer touch. Forster would call to inquire after their "progeny." She would visit him when he was in the hospital. He gave her a radio for her room. In later years he would frame art prints to decorate the walls of the Catholic Worker. And toward the end of her life, as she notes in her diary, he took to calling her every day.

These are a few of the personal stories that emerge in these diaries. They are set against the daily domestic dramas of the Catholic Worker that occupied so much of her life. Her public activities, already well-documented in her other writings, receive less attention. And yet her diaries do reflect her response, over a period of nearly five decades, to the vast changes in America, the church, and the wider world.

As the diaries begin, in the 1930s, we see her vital interest in strikes and labor struggles and the problems of the Depression. She met with union leaders, labor priests, and bishops who undoubtedly saw in the Worker a Catholic counterweight to the appeal of Communism. Later, as her pacifist convictions became a defining feature of the Catholic Worker, she would occupy a more marginal position, far outside the Catholic mainstream. In the 1940s, as the world went to war, Dorothy devoted more attention to her own spiritual life. But then in the 1950s, facing the perils of the Cold War, she embarked on a new style of activism, courting arrest several times (and serving jail sentences of up to thirty days) for her protests against civil defense drills in New York City. With the publication of *The Long Loneliness* she began to achieve a new profile as a voice of conscience crying in the wilderness.

Her journals from the 1960s reflect the turbulence of the times. We see her traveling to Cuba on the eve of the Missile Crisis, fasting for peace in Rome during the Second Vatican Council, facing bullets with an interracial community in Georgia, and standing in solidarity with young men burning their draft cards. Suddenly Dorothy had become the spiritual godmother to a new generation standing up against war and the established disorder. Despite her age, Dorothy understood the idealism of youth, the yearning for freedom, and the instinct for the heroic. And yet she recoiled from the spirit of nihilism and the self-indulgence of the "counter-culture."

With the 1970s she welcomed signs of a renewed interest in community and the efforts to build a society, as Peter Maurin used to say, "where it is easier for people to be good." As she grew old, she prepared to let go, to entrust the vision to a new generation. And yet her old feistiness remained. We see her staring down the IRS with her refusal either to pay taxes or to register as a charitable organization. We see her, at the age of 75, being arrested on a picket line with the United Farmworkers.

And through her diaries we see her gradually slowing down, adjusting, after a heart attack, to the end of her restless travels, eventually settling into the confinement of her room at the CW shelter for homeless women on East Third St. In her youth she had received a great "revelation"—that for anyone attuned to the life of the mind, the future held the promise of unending fascination. And now she could observe, "No matter how old I get ... no matter how feeble, short of breath, incapable of walking more than a few blocks, what with heart murmurs, heart failures, emphysema perhaps, arthritis in feet and knees, with all these symptoms of age and decrepitude, my heart can still leap for joy as I read and suddenly assent to some great truth enunciated by some great mind and heart."

That intense interest in life continued, as she took in the world around her and rummaged increasingly in the "rag-bag" of memory. She had always been a "compulsive" writer, "ever since I was 8 years old when I wrote a serial story on a little pad of pink paper for my younger sister's entertainment." And writing was virtually the last thing to go. Toward the end her newspaper columns reverted to short, breathless excerpts from her diary—just enough, she said, "to let people know I am still alive." She kept writing until a few days before her death on November 29, 1980.

David O'Brien, writing in *Commonweal* after her death, famously called Dorothy Day "the most significant, interesting, and influential person in the history of American Catholicism." The truth of that pronouncement has become clearer with the passage of time. She has been the subject of biographies, plays, documentaries, a Hollywood film, and even a number of children's books. She has been inducted into the "Women's Hall of Fame," and is widely recognized as the radical conscience of the Catholic Church in America. But certainly a significant measure of her legacy came in 2000 when the Vatican officially accepted her cause for canonization, and she received the formal title "Servant of God."

If Dorothy Day is one day formally canonized, this diary will offer something quite unusual in the annals of the saints—an opportunity to follow, almost day by day, in the footsteps of a holy person. Through these writings we can trace the movements of her spirit and her quest for God. We can see her praying for wisdom and courage in meeting the challenges of her day. But we also join her as she watches television, devours mystery novels, goes to the movies, plays with her grandchildren, and listens to the opera.

Many people tend to think of saints as otherworldly heroes, close to God but not exactly human. These diaries confirm Thomas Merton's observation that sanctity is a matter of being more fully human: "This implies a greater capacity for concern, for suffering, for understanding, for sympathy, and also for humor, for joy, for appreciation for the good and beautiful things of life."

To be human is constantly to fall short of the ideals one sets for oneself. Dorothy Day was no exception. There are frequent reminders in these pages of her capacity for impatience, anger, judgment, and self-righteousness. We are reminded of these things because she herself points them out. ("Thinking gloomily of the sins and shortcomings of others," she writes, "it suddenly came to me to remember my own offenses, just as heinous as those of others. If I concern myself with my own sins and lament them, if I remember my own failures and lapses, I will not be resentful of others. This was most cheering and lifted the load of gloom from my mind. It makes one unhappy to judge people and happy to love them.") And so we are reminded too that holiness is not a state of perfection, but a faithful striving that lasts a lifetime. It is expressed primarily in small ways, day after day, through the practice of forgiveness, patience, self-sacrifice, and compassion.

Dorothy's favorite saint was Therese of Lisieux, popularly known as the "Little Flower." St. Therese died at the age of 24 in 1897—the year of Dorothy's birth—in a small Carmelite convent in Normandy. At first glance these two women, the contemplative and the activist, would appear to have little in common. Nevertheless, Dorothy was powerfully attracted to her story and even wrote an account of her life. St. Therese taught the value of the "Little Way"—a path to holiness that lay in performing all our daily tasks and duties in a spirit of love and in the presence of God. Dorothy embraced this teaching. She believed that each act of love, each work of mercy might increase the balance of love in the world. And she extended this principle to the social sphere. Each act of protest or witness for peace—though apparently foolish and ineffective, no more than a pebble in a pond—might send forth ripples that could transform the world.

The title of this book, "the duty of delight," comes from John Ruskin, the nineteenth-century English critic. Dorothy incorporated his phrase in the epilogue to *The Long Loneliness* and later considered using it as the title for one of her books. She repeated it frequently in her diaries—often after a recital of drudgery or disappointment. It served as a reminder to find God in all things—the sorrows of daily life and the moments of joy, both of which she experienced in abundance.

As for sorrows, these included: ill health; the aches and pains of aging; the loss of old friends; the struggles to pay the bills and put out a monthly paper; real estate woes and the ordeals of home maintenance; loneliness and anxiety; squabbling amongst community members. After returning from one trip, she writes, "I have had this completely alone feeling.... A time when the memory and understanding fail one completely and only the will remains, so that I feel hard and rigid, and at the same time ready to sit like a soft fool and weep my eyes out."

Then there were the sorrows of poverty: noise, foul odors, poor food, and the outbreak of violence amongst the drunk or insane; the various kinds of lice and bedbugs; constant insecurity and the world's disdain. ("In this groaning of spirit, everything is irksome to me. The dirt, the garbage heaped in the gutters, the flies, the hopelessness of the human beings around me, all oppress me.") And then there were the sorrows of the world, which weighed so heavily: war and hatred, fear, corruption, the despair and cynicism of the young, the contempt for life, and other offenses against human dignity. All these things are noted in her diary.

But there were also the moments of joy: the Saturday afternoon opera; the magic spell of a book; "the soft sound of waves on the beach"; the chatter of happy children; the sights and solitude of a long bus trip; the beauty of church and the liturgy, with its appeal to all the senses; the language of Scripture; the experience of community at its best; the excitement of a new venture; signs that a new generation was responding to the vision of Peter Maurin and to the faith on which she had staked her life.

I knew Dorothy Day in the last five years of her life, 1975-80, when I came to live at the Catholic Worker in New York City. I was nineteen at the time of our meeting, and my first impression was that I had never met someone so "old" who showed such apparent interest in me and my opinions. I was immediately won. After one of our conversations I dared to show her some notes from my own diary. (Did I suppose she would be edified by my two-week-old impressions of life at the Catholic Worker?) The next day I missed her; she had gone back to the farm upstate. But she had left me a note: "Good thing to keep a journal," she wrote. "Please ask Frank [Donovan] to find you a copy of a book in my room, *Prayer is a Hunger,* which describes writing as a form of prayer. Love, Dorothy."

St. Teresa of Avila defined prayer as "nothing but friendly intercourse, and frequent solitary converse, with Him Who we know loves us." Certainly, for Dorothy, writing was a form of prayer. That is especially evident in the writing published here for the first time. It is striking how many entries in her diaries refer specifically to prayer and how often she directly addresses God as the intended reader of her heart. After years of reciting the prayers of the Office the language of the Psalms had become her daily bread.

But ultimately her words, whether written or spoken, derived their meaning from the consistency, courage, and faithfulness of her life. These diaries provide a unique window on that life, and on the witness of a woman for whom, in the end, everything was a form of prayer.

# CHRONOLOGY

## 1932

December      Dorothy Day travels to Washington, D.C. to cover the "Hunger March of the Unemployed," a Communist-organized demonstration. On December 8 she prays at the crypt of the Shrine of the Immaculate Conception that some way will open for her to combine her Catholic faith and her commitment to social justice. When she returns to New York she meets Peter Maurin, who inspires her to start a newspaper.

## 1933

*President Franklin D. Roosevelt introduces the New Deal to respond to the Depression.*

May 1      The first issue of *The Catholic Worker* is distributed in Union Square. Catholic Worker office at 436 East 15th St.

## 1934

March      Ade Bethune, a young art student, visits the Catholic Worker and begins contributing to the paper. Among her contributions: the design of the CW masthead.

May      Peter Maurin opens a short-lived house in Harlem.

## 1935

March      CW moves to 144 Charles Street.

May      Circulation of the paper reaches 100,000.

June      CW rents a house on Staten Island.

Summer      CW pickets the German ship, Bremen, protesting Nazi policies.

# 1936

April          CW moves to 115 Mott St., headquarters for the next 14 years.

               Farm established outside of Easton, Pennsylvania.

May            New York seamen go on strike. CW offers support to National
               Maritime Union. Circulation reaches 110,000.

June           Sheed & Ward publishes Peter Maurin's *Easy Essays.*

July           *Francisco Franco leads a coup against the leftist-dominated government
               in Spain. The Spanish Civil War ensues. In the United States most
               Catholic publications support Franco.* The Catholic Worker *and* The
               Commonweal *are exceptions.*

# 1937

February       DD visits sit-down strikers at General Motors plant in Flint, Michi-
               gan.

               Catholic Worker John Cort helps found the Association of Catholic
               Trade Unionists.

# 1938

               Publication of *From Union Square to Rome.*

November       *Kristallnacht—Nazi assault on Jewish synagogues and businesses in
               Germany.*

# 1939

January        Publication of *House of Hospitality.*

March          *Fascist victory in Spanish Civil War.*

May            Dorothy Day among founders of the Committee of Catholics to
               Fight Anti-Semitism.

               Death of Dorothy's father, John Day.

September      *Hitler invades Poland. Beginning of World War II.*
               Dorothy meets Fr. Pacifique Roy, a Canadian Josephite priest, who
               becomes one of her closest spiritual advisors.

# 1940

Feb-May        Long trip down West Coast.

| | |
|---|---|
| July | Dorothy testifies before Congressional Committee on Conscription. |
| September | *Beginning of the Blitz of London.* |
| October | *Draft registration begins in the U.S.* |

## 1941

| | |
|---|---|
| July | Attends a retreat with Fr. John J. Hugo. |
| August | Fr. Hugo leads CW retreat in Oakmont, Pennsylvania. |
| October | CW opens a women's house at 104 Bayard St. |
| December 7 | *Japanese attack on Pearl Harbor. U.S. declares war.* |

## 1942

| | |
|---|---|
| January | CW appears with banner headline reading: "We continue our Christian Pacifist Stand." |
| December | *Beginning of the Manhattan Project to devise an atomic bomb.* |

## 1943

| | |
|---|---|
| March | Women's house on Bayard is condemned. Women move back to Mott St. |
| September | Dorothy plans to take a year's leave from the Catholic Worker. She spends six months away, first at the Grail in Libertyville, Illinois, then in Farmingdale, Long Island. In March she returns to the CW. |

## 1944

| | |
|---|---|
| April 19 | Dorothy's daughter Tamar marries David Hennessy, soon after her 18th birthday. |
| June | Allied invasion of Europe begins. |
| August 7 | *Franz Jagerstatter, an Austrian peasant, is the sole Catholic layman in Austria killed by the Nazis for refusing to serve in Hitler's army.* |

## 1945

| | |
|---|---|
| August | *On August 6, Feast of the Transfiguration. U.S. drops first atomic bomb on Hiroshima. Three days later, another atomic bomb on Nagasaki. On August 14 Japan surrenders. World War II is over.* |

October 24          Dorothy's mother, Grace Satterlee Day, dies.

## 1946

January             *First meeting of the United Nations.*

February            Dorothy chooses a new name for her CW column: "On Pilgrim-age."

## 1947

CW gives up the farm at Easton; purchases new farm in Newburgh, New York.

Tamar and David Hennessy move to West Virginia.

## 1948

January             *Death of Mahatma Gandhi in India.*

July                *Publication of Thomas Merton's autobiography,* The Seven Storey Mountain.

December            CW publishes *On Pilgrimage*, Dorothy's account of a single year.

## 1949

March               Catholic Worker supports the cause of cemetery workers on strike against the Archdiocese of New York. Cardinal Spellman accuses the workers of being under the influence of Communist agitators.

May 15              Death of Peter Maurin.

October             *Victory of Communist forces of Mao Zedong in China.*

## 1950

April               Dorothy to Washington for one-week fast for peace.

Easter              Ammon Hennacy pays his first visit to the Catholic Worker. He returns in 1952 and remains part of the community for the next 8 years.

June 25             *Korean War begins.*

Summer              Notice of eviction from 115 Mott St.

August              Move to new Peter Maurin farm on Staten Island. Hennessys move to Westminster, Maryland.

September        CW moves to 221 Chrystie St.

*The Internal Security (McCarran) Act is passed, ordering the registration of all Communist organizations and the internment of Communists in times of national emergency.*

November 1       *Pope Pius XII defines the dogma of the Assumption of the Blessed Virgin Mary.*

## 1951

May              Tamar Hennessy and family move to Staten Island, living for first six months at Peter Maurin Farm.

## 1952

January          Publication of *The Long Loneliness.*

March            DD speaks at Carnegie Hall in a meeting against the Smith Act.

*First test of Hydrogen bomb.*

October          Two-part profile of DD by Dwight Macdonald appears in *The New Yorker.*

November         Ammon Hennacy received into the Catholic church.

## 1953

June 19          *Communists Ethel and Julius Rosenberg, charged as Russian spies, are executed in New York. Dorothy publishes a Meditation on their death.*

July 27          *Korean War ends with signing of armistice.*

## 1954

May              *Defeat of French forces at Dien Bien Phu, signals end of first Indochina War. DD comments in an article, "Theophane Venard and Ho Chi Minh."*

*In Brown v. Board of Education case, Supreme Court overturns segregation in public schools, setting off a new chapter in the civil rights struggle.*

## 1955

June 15          Dorothy Day, Ammon Hennacy, A.J. Muste and others are arrested for refusing to participate in mandatory civil defense drills. She is released without sentence or fine.

| | |
|---|---|
| October | Dorothy called before Workman's Compensation Board and charged with being a "slum landlord." |
| December 1 | *Rosa Parks is arrested in Montgomery Alabama after refusing to give up her seat on a public bus to a white passenger. Her action sparks a bus boycott under the leadership of Rev. Martin Luther King, Jr.* |

## 1956

| | |
|---|---|
| July 20 | Civil Defense drill. Dorothy is arrested and this time jailed for five days in January. |

## 1957

| | |
|---|---|
| April | Dorothy travels to Georgia to support the interracial Koinonia community. She is shot at while taking a turn as sentry at the front gate. |
| July 12 | DD again defies civil defense drill. Sentenced to thirty days in jail. |
| September | Tamar and her family move to Perkinsville, Vermont. |
| August | City announces plan to seize Chrystie St. house by right of eminent domain to build a subway line. |

## 1958

| | |
|---|---|
| January | DD undertakes pilgrimage to Shrine of Our Lady of Guadalupe in Mexico City. |
| May 6 | Civil Defense drill. Dorothy arrested, though her 30-day sentence is suspended. |
| August | Ammon Hennacy undertakes a 40-day fast in front of the Atomic Energy Commission in Washington. |
| October 28 | *Angelo Giuseppe Roncalli is elected Pope and takes the name John XXIII.* |
| December | *Fidel Castro leads guerrilla army in Cuba to victory over dictator Fulgencio Batista.* |
| December | Forced to give up Chrystie St. house, CW community disperses to apartments. Rents store-front at 39 Spring St. for office and soup kitchen. |

# 1959

| | |
|---|---|
| January 25 | *Pope John XXIII announces intention to convoke an ecumenical Council in Rome.* |
| April 17 | Civil Defense drill. Dorothy arrested and sentenced to ten days in jail. |
| Sept-Jan 60 | Dorothy nurses Nanette (Forster's companion) on Staten Island. |

# 1960

| | |
|---|---|
| May 3 | New York Air Raid Drill. 28 arrested, but not Dorothy. |
| September | DD publishes an open letter to the City, returning $3,579.39 interest on the payment for Chrystie St. building. |
| October | Publication of *Therese.* |
| November | *Election of John F. Kennedy, first Catholic president of the United States.* |

# 1961

| | |
|---|---|
| January 29 | Catholic Workers participate in sit-in at the Atomic Energy Commission building in New York City. |
| April 17 | *U.S.-sponsored Bay of Pigs invasion of Cuba ends in failure.* |
| August | CW prints Thomas Merton's "Chant To Be Used in Processions Around a Site with Furnaces." <br> CW moves to 175 Chrystie St. |

# 1962

| | |
|---|---|
| Sept 5-Oct 5 | DD travels to Cuba. |
| October | *Announcement of the formation of an American Pax Association.* |
| October 11 | *Second Vatican Council is convened.* |
| Oct 22-29 | *Cuban Missile crisis prompted by discovery of Soviet missile sites in Cuba. Nuclear war narrowly averted.* |

# 1963

| | |
|---|---|
| April 11 | *Pope John XXIII issues his encyclical* Pacem in Terris. |
| April-May | Dorothy travels on peace pilgrimage to Rome. She sees Pope John in a public appearance at the Vatican. |

| | |
|---|---|
| June 3 | *Death of Pope John XXIII.* |
| | *Election of Giovanni Battista Montini as Pope Paul VI.* |
| August 28 | *Martin Luther King delivers his famous "I Have a Dream" speech at a March in Washington for Civil Rights.* |
| October | Dorothy travels to England for conference on peace at Spode House, a Dominican retreat house. |
| November | Publication of *Loaves and Fishes.* |
| November 22 | *President John F. Kennedy is assassinated. Lyndon Johnson becomes president.* |

## 1964

| | |
|---|---|
| April | New CW farm at Tivoli, New York. |
| August | *Congress passes the Tonkin Gulf Resolution authorizing the President to "take all necessary measures to repel any armed attacks against the forces of the United States and to prevent future aggression."* |
| Aug-Dec | Dorothy stays in Perkinsville, looking after Tamar's family while she is taking a nursing degree. |
| October | Catholic Peace Fellowship founded by Jim Forest and Tom Cornell, former CW editors. |
| November 4 | *Lyndon Johnson wins presidential election.* |
| December 19 | CW joins other peace groups in sponsoring protests against the Vietnam war. |

## 1965

| | |
|---|---|
| February 21 | *Malcolm X, black Muslim leader, is assassinated in New York City.* |
| February 28 | *President Johnson announces a policy of continuous air strikes against North Vietnam.* |
| March | *Martin Luther King leads a procession of 4,000 civil rights demonstrators from Selma to Montgomery, Alabama.* |
| August | *Riots in Watts district of Los Angeles.* |
| | Special Issue of the CW: "War and Peace at the Vatican Council." |

| | |
|---|---|
| Sept-Oct | Dorothy sails to Rome for final session of Vatican II and takes part in a ten-day fast by international women to encourage the Council to make a clear statement on war and peace. |
| October 15 | David Miller of the Catholic Worker defies the Selective Service Law by burning his draft card. He is arrested. |
| November 6 | Five young men burn draft cards in Union Square. Dorothy Day and A.J. Muste, two elders of the peace movement, speak and lend their support. |
| November 9 | Roger LaPorte, a young Catholic Worker, immolates himself on the steps of the United Nations as a protest against the Vietnam War. |

## 1966

| | |
|---|---|
| April | *U.S. troops in Vietnam number 250,000.* |
| May 16 | *Martin Luther King, Jr. makes his first public statement opposing the war.* |
| August | *Cesar Chavez founds the United Farm Workers union.* |

## 1967

| | |
|---|---|
| October | Dorothy travels to Rome for the International Congress of the Laity. She is one of two Americans invited to receive Communion from the hands of Pope Paul VI. Visits Danilo Dolci in Italy and returns through England. |
| December | *Anti-war march on the Pentagon.* |

## 1968

| | |
|---|---|
| April 4 | *Martin Luther King, Jr. assassinated in Memphis, Tennessee.* |
| May 17 | *Catonsville Nine, including Frs. Daniel and Philip Berrigan, burn draft files in Catonsville, Maryland.* |
| June 5 | *Robert F. Kennedy is assassinated in Los Angeles.* |
| July | CW moves to St. Joseph House, 36 East First St. |
| | *Pope Paul VI issues encyclical* Humanae Vitae *upholding the church's prohibition against all artificial means of birth control.* |
| Sept 24 | *Milwaukee 14, including former CW editor Jim Forest, arrested for burning draft files.* |

November        *Richard M. Nixon is elected president of the United States.*

Dec 10          *Thomas Merton accidentally electrocuted at monastic conference in Bangkok, Thailand.*

## 1969

May             Dorothy visits the headquarters of the United Farm Workers in Delano, California. She takes part in a memorial service for Robert F. Kennedy. The next day, while picketing with striking farmworkers, she has to jump to avoid a speeding car that swerves toward her.

October 15      *Moratorium against the War.*

## 1970

January 14      Death of Ammon Hennacy in Salt Lake City. Dorothy attends his funeral.

April           *U.S. invasion of Cambodia. National Guard shootings at Kent State and Jackson State Universities.*

August          DD undertakes extensive trip to Australia, Hong Kong, India, Tanzania, Rome and England. In Calcutta she spends several days with Mother Teresa and her community.

## 1971

May             *Demonstrations against war. Massive arrests in Washington, D.C.*

June            *Publication of the Pentagon Papers in the* New York Times *and other papers.*

July            Traveling with Nina Polcyn and a tour group, DD visits Eastern Europe and Russia.

September       *Uprising at Attica State prison, suppressed at the cost of 39 lives.*

## 1972

January         DD visits UFW headquarters in La Paz, California.

April           IRS addresses the CW demanding payment of $296,359 in supposedly unpaid taxes. In July, in the face of widespread protest, and DD's own intransigence, the IRS withdraws its claim.

November 2      *Richard Nixon reelected president.*

November 8      Dorothy's 75th birthday. *America* magazine devotes a special issue to her. Notre Dame awards her the Laetare Medal.

December        *Christmas week, massive bombing campaign in North Vietnam.*

## 1973

January         *"Ceasefire" in Vietnam. But war continues.*

August          Joins picketing farmworkers in California. Dorothy is arrested, spends nearly two weeks in a prison farm.

October         Founding of Pax Christi-USA. Dorothy addresses Assembly in Washington.

Fall            Travels to England and Northern Ireland.

## 1974

January         Accepts the Isaac Hecker award from the Paulists in Boston.

July            Catholic Worker purchases a music school at 55 E. Third St. Maryhouse is intended as a shelter for homeless women.

August          *President Richard Nixon resigns.*

## 1975

April           *War ends in Indochina.*

## 1976

January         Maryhouse opens on East Third St.

August 6        Invited to address the Eucharistic Congress in Philadelphia on the Feast of the Transfiguration (Hiroshima Day). Soon after, she suffers a heart attack.

## 1977

May             CW celebrates 100th anniversary of birth of Peter Maurin.

October         DD hospitalized for chest pains, Beth Israel Hospital.

November 8      Dorothy's 80th birthday. Receives personal greeting from Pope Paul VI.

## 1978

August 6        *Death of Pope Paul VI.*

October 16      *Election of Pope John Paul II.*

## 1979

January        DD's great-grandson, Justin, is killed in a car accident.

June 17        Mother Teresa of Calcutta visits Maryhouse.

October        Closing of CW Farm in Tivoli. Peter Maurin Farm opens in Marl-
               boro, N.Y.

November       Death of Stanley Vishnewski.

## 1980

April          Death of Dorothy's sister Della.

November 8     Dorothy's 83rd birthday.

November 29    Dorothy Day dies at Maryhouse.

PART I

# THE THIRTIES

Dorothy Day's diaries begin in early 1934, nearly a year after the launching of the Catholic Worker on May 1, 1933. By this time the main features of the movement were already in place: the newspaper, selling as it always would for "a penny a copy"; houses of hospitality for the practice of the Works of Mercy; and round-table discussions for the clarification of thought. By the next year, with the establishment of the first farming communes on Staten Island, and then in Easton, Pennsylvania, all the elements of Peter Maurin's original vision would be in place.

Dorothy's diaries for this period, intermittent and fairly random, are mostly written on loose sheets of lined paper—in some cases seemingly torn from a notebook. She evidently drew little distinction between these private writings and the relatively personal reportage and reflection that she contributed to the paper. Indeed, many of these entries were reproduced, verbatim, in her early book, House of Hospitality, a chronicle of the early years of the Catholic Worker.

These early diaries, set against the social struggles and hard times of the Depression, document the steady growth of the movement. Within two years the circulation of the paper had risen to over 100,000. New houses were springing up around the country. All this posed increasing demands on Dorothy's time, energy, and presence. She was the one who raised the money, who set the tone, who settled disputes, and responded to frequent requests for clarification from the Chancery. Through her extensive trips around the country she helped spread the vision, and united the movement through her monthly columns in the paper.

Travel would remain a constant feature of her life over the decades to come. She frankly welcomed a long bus trip as an occasion for solitude, a chance to collect her thoughts, and to find refreshment in a change of scene. But always upon returning she faced complaints and reproaches: "You are always away!" Community life was marked by many joys. But in a community made up, to such an extent, by the walking wounded, Catholic Worker life was always marked by disputes, bickering, and rivalries. Desperately trying to inculcate a spirit of personal responsibility and "self-organization" Dorothy referred to herself at one point as "being in the position of a dictator trying to legislate herself out of existence."

*While struggling with the demands of the CW family, there was also the matter of her own family—in particular, her daughter Tamar, who was only seven when the Catholic Worker was launched. These early diaries reflect Dorothy's efforts to raise her child in the midst of an unconventional family, always wondering—as any parent does—whether she was doing enough or doing it right.*

*Many significant events are overlooked in these diaries. For example, while there are many references to Dorothy's involvement with the labor movement, she does not describe the Worker's extensive involvement in the seamen's strike in 1936. Nor does she write about the Worker's pacifist response to the Spanish Civil War, and the opposition this drew both from Catholic allies and friends on the Left. There is relatively little reflection here on the gathering clouds in Europe, or any anticipation of the storm to come.*

*But for all that they leave out or elide, these early diaries certainly document Dorothy's spiritual struggles—her sense of loneliness, even in the midst of community, her efforts to maintain her equilibrium amidst the constant responsibilities and burdens of leadership, and her ongoing efforts to see Christ in those around her—not just in the saints, but in "the poor lost ones, the abandoned ones, the sick, the crazed, the solitary human beings whom Christ so loved, in whom I see, with a terrible anguish, the body of this death."*

*As the decade comes to a close, she concludes her final entry with these resolutions: "To pay no attention to health of body but only that of soul. To plan day on arising and evening examination of conscience. More spiritual reading… To waste no time. More conscientious about letters, visits, about these records. More charity."*

# 1934

Thursday, March 14, 1934[1]

We are an international household. Yesterday afternoon Peter [Maurin] brought in his Turkish [*Armenian*] friend Mr. Minas and asked if he could put up a bed for him. So we went out and got a camp cot to put up in the kitchen after the meetings are over in the evening. Tamar and I each had two blankets so I took one off each bed for him, one for under and one for over, since a camp cot has no mattress. Now we sit down to table, Turkish, French, Irish, Polish Jew, Lithuanian, Italian, and American.

As for the meetings there are all nationalities there too—Ukrainian, Spanish, Italian, German, Belgian, Swiss, English, Scotch, Irish, Russian, Negro, French, Lithuanian, Jew, and now Turkish. I do not know what his religion is.

---

1 Some of these entries appear almost verbatim in Dorothy Day's *House of Hospitality* (New York: Sheed & Ward, 1939), henceforth *HH*. For this entry, see p. 30.

I have not asked him. Peter says he was educated in a Jesuit school in Egypt and writes poetry.

Right now he is sitting down in the kitchen, getting quotations—the pronouncements of various priests against Fascism. He is also going to distribute our daily supplement through the streets.

Last night Frank [O'Donnell][2] took the supplement around to various saloons in the neighborhood, most of which are run by Catholics and one of which down by Tompkins Square is frequented by Communists. At this, the last place he visited, he said they were all in a most affable mood, and after reading the sheet gravely, registered their approval by singing "*Proschai, proschai.*"

Eileen [Corridon][3] went over to Sheed and Ward's last night to their monthly disputation and distributed there. She says that cars and chauffeurs were lined up in front of the door. They should have been invited inside to partake of Catholic culture.

It is hard to put over the idea of Catholic culture because people are afraid of the word culture in America. They think at once of Shakespeare clubs and Browning societies and they are repelled.

Speaking of Mr. [Frank] Sheed,[4] one of the things he said when speaking here the other night was this:

"The Christians in Russia—and there are Christians in Russia who are allowed to practice their religion after a fashion—say: 'Do not try to save us from the Bolsheviks. They are materialists with material aims, ignoring and denying God—and they say so. But Western Christians are also materialists with material aims, denying God—but they don't say so. Leave us alone and perhaps a new Christianity will arise in Russia.'"

March 21[5]

Last night I went up to the Mothers' Club at St. Barnabas (243rd St.) parish to talk to the women who all live in snug warm houses with their husbands and children around them, their times filled and their life sweetened by the good works their concerted means permit them to do.

---

2 Of Frank O'Donnell, the CW's first business manager, Dorothy wrote: "He had been working as a salesman, selling people things they didn't really want, and who had a guilty conscience about it." *Loaves and Fishes* (New York: Harper & Row, 1963; Maryknoll, NY: Orbis Books, 1997), 25. Henceforth, *LF*.

3 Eileen Corridon was "a fierce worker like her cousin (the priest who was portrayed in the film *Waterfront*)." *LF*, 138.

4 Frank Sheed was co-founder, with his wife Maisie Ward, of the Catholic publishing house, Sheed & Ward.

5 See *HH*, 35-38.

They had contributed before ($34) to the work of the Teresa-Joseph Cooperative and they took up a collection again of ten dollars.

This morning a contrast. Margaret [Polk][6] came in to find a letter from her mother saying that her six-year-old child had been committed to an institution. Her mother is running a boarding home for miners (it is a small mining town in Pennsylvania, and she neglected to watch over or care for the child). We were considering what we could do in the way of getting the child out of the institution when Mrs. [Carleton] Hayes called up and told us she was sending a check for twenty dollars which she had collected from among her friends. This would about cover the trip down. We shall see what can be done.

Little duties pile up. I get up at seven-thirty, go to eight o'clock Mass, have breakfast, and prepare breakfast for Peter, Mr. Minas, Tamar, and myself; go through the mail, do bookkeeping, hand the orders over to Frank and put the letters inside to be answered; read some of the liturgy of the day and write the daily page to be mimeographed. All the while there are interruptions of people coming in and the telephone. Frank and Eileen come in about 10-11. Peter and Mr. Minas go out. Margaret comes in. Tamar and Freddy [Rubino] play about. Sometimes Tamar does her arithmetic by playing with the money in the cash box and sometimes in the big graphic arithmetic book I bought her. She reads about a page and a half a day, also some prayers. The rest of the time she plays outside these warm spring days.

Then the Home Relief worker, wanting a Confirmation outfit for a twelve-year-old girl; then Charlie Rich, a convert from Judaism, to type some of his deeply spiritual writings. Then Tessa[7] with her dialectic materialism and her baby, which is baptized a Catholic but who she insists is going to grow up a "Daily Worker" and not a "Catholic Worker."

Mr. Minas returns to take out the papers. A Fascist drops in to try to whip up hatred amongst us for the Jews.

At four I went to meet Della[8] at Hearn's for coffee. Then Ade Bethune[9] in with some of her lovely drawings of Don Bosco, St. Catherine of Siena, her second Corporal Work of Mercy, and her Labor Guild head. She stayed to

---

6 When Margaret Polk, "a Lithuanian girl from the mining regions of Pennsylvania came to us and took over the cooking, we were happy indeed... She loved being propagandist as well as cook." *LL*, 185.

7 Tessa [De Aragon] was the wife of Dorothy's younger brother John. Both she and her husband remained close to Dorothy, though their sympathies lay with the Communist Party.

8 Della [Spier] was Dorothy's older sister, a close friend and confidante throughout her life.

9 Ade Bethune was a young art student who became part of the CW family after sending in some drawings of saints. She went on to redesign the CW's masthead and her art for many years virtually defined the CW aesthetic.

make an impression on the stencil of Don Bosco for the Italian kids in the neighborhood for Easter Monday, the day after his canonization.

After meeting Della and walking until my legs ached grievously, I went into Lily's[10] for supper, heard all about Kenneth Burke's work for the *New Masses,* and how Horace Greeley thinks he will go further and complete Marx. Edward Stahlberg came in and talked about fascism in America and asked me to send him exchanges in relation to this subject. It is regrettable to state that whereas I can give him many excellent articles, I should have to acknowledge to myself that many secular and Jesuit priests throughout the country are fascist in sympathy. I have heard them rave against the Jews and I have heard Salesian fathers boast that Mussolini was a product of one of their institutions.

It is eleven-thirty p.m. Father Donnelly from *America* spoke tonight for us at the school and we had a very good crowd. He spoke on the Mass and the best way of assisting at it, and I shall make it the subject of our sheet tomorrow.

Eileen in a temper again all day. Her emotional friendship, which is a mixture of love and hate, helpfulness and obstructive tactics, is a trial indeed, but evidently one God has sent. I get so impatient at times that I have to go off by myself and read St. Francis de Sales' letters to calm myself. Sometimes it seems much easier to work alone. Dorothy [Weston][11] continues [to be] sick and we see little of her except as she comes to draw out money to sustain life.

Meanwhile the letters pile up and it will just mean that while Eileen sulks and Dorothy suffers I shall have to answer them.

## March 23

A sincere repentance for my sins—the result of turning my eyes inward on myself, instead of regarding the faults of others—this is what is most necessary for me. And having come to this conclusion matters straighten themselves out. When people fasten themselves to you with an emotional friendship it is hard, though. One is driven to a slightly strained reserve and the atmosphere is not a natural one.

The weather is very cold again and I have spent the better part of the day upstairs in my room with a fire and with books. The paper must go to press

---

10   Lily Burke, the first wife of the literary critic Kenneth Burke, was the sister of Forster Batterham (Tamar's father).

11   Dorothy Weston was "a dainty young Irish girl with black hair and bright blue eyes, just out of school…She was more scholar than journalist, and when she prepared a paper on birth control or on the Ohrback strike she made a thorough job of it." *LF,* 138.

Monday morning so that means a good deal of work... Why can't people let each other alone and not obtrude on each other?

Margaret is not well and is worrying over her little girl who is living with her mother down in a mining village in Virginia. She wants to get her up here because the child is neglected and neighbors want to have her put in an institution which is what Margaret's mother is always threatening to do. After the paper comes out perhaps Eileen can drive down there with her and settle it.

Eileen has a car now, borrowing fifty dollars from her roommate to pay for it, which the paper can pay off ten a month. The license plates took the last fifteen in the bank and we have not quite enough now for stamps. However these needs are taken care of from day to day, some way or other.

John [Day][12] came in last night and we all went over to Dorothy's for drinks and sandwiches. John has joined the C.P. [Communist Party], he and Tessa, and today I've been going around feeling rather shocked and miserable. Also I awoke too late for Mass and that spoiled my day. I always feel sad at keeping Lent so badly. I keep resolving and failing miserably and starting in again. Tonight I feel weak and miserable, totally incapable of attending the lecture. Prof Vaughn was to come and didn't show up and Peter [Maurin] is taking his place and the heckling is trying to the nerves. But I feel a quitter for that too. So I shall read Conrad and forget my troubles.

Monday, April 8

Tonight there was no speaker announced so I got Florence Schwartz on the phone and asked her if she would not come up and take dictation while Peter and [Steve] Hergenhan[13] talked. She is here now, sitting at the talk, and they are suffering from stage fright and speaking as though in a dream, so slowly, so heavily that the half dozen or so who have dropped in are nodding. The night is conspiring against them too, warm, mild, and breezy, conducive to physical and mental languor.

All day it has been so, warm and sunny, a happy day, with the buds swelling in the parks. I was down in City Hall Park this afternoon on the way to Barclay Street and I surveyed every tree, searching for swelling buds.

Now in the night the streets are swarming with people and there is a liveliness, a surge, a vitality in the air which is almost unendurable.

---

12   John Day was Dorothy's younger brother.

13   Steve Hergenhan earned an extended treatment in *The Long Loneliness*. "He was a German carpenter, a skilled workman who after forty years of frugal living had bought himself a plot of ground near Suffern, New York." He often served as a foil for Peter Maurin's street-corner disquisitions. See *The Long Loneliness* (New York: Harper & Row, 1952), 193ff. Henceforth *LL*.

Mr. Minas sits out here writing poetry and laughing over the efforts of Peter and Hergenhan. "They are not making points," he says very truly.

John Geis just came in, our Brother Juniper.[14] He is applying again for a soap box in Columbus Circle and invites us all to come up and see it.

## April 14

Saturday morning and I am hard up with a cold and toothache, and Dorothy has had to go up to New Haven and take my place at the luncheon. Peter and Herg are scrubbing the floor downstairs, Eileen is out distributing papers. The other night she gave Peter a very good hair cut, so now he looks very well-groomed.

## May 18[15]

John's three objections to religion.

1. It is morbid.
2. It is cannibalistic.
3. How can an all-powerful, all-loving God permit evil?

I must write about these objections.

Last month I sent out an appeal which brought in enough money to pay all the bills so aside from seventy dollars we owe for the printer we are all clear. God is good.

We put an appeal in the paper also for a store in Harlem for a branch office and a lawyer. Mr. Daley has donated us a store rent free to which Peter and Herg will move next Monday.

## Saturday, May 19, Eve of Pentecost

Such magnificent weather yesterday and today and I have been feeling very happy. God rewards us for so little effort. Just a resolute turning to Him of our wills. I have felt so low these last weeks—so sad at being away from Tamar that everything was distasteful to me—all spiritual duties too so that my heart was in nothing and my mind was restless and confused. But just the keeping myself apart and the resolute attempt to read was of great help. So now everything is easier. We depend so much on the Holy Spirit.

---

14   A reference to one of St. Francis' more eccentric followers.

15   Dorothy addressed her brother John's objections to religion (without identifying their source) in *From Union Square to Rome* (Silver Springs, MD: Preservation of the Faith Press, 1938; Maryknoll, NY: Orbis Books, 2006), 156-177. Henceforth, *FUSR*.

May 21

If a brother or sister be naked and destitute of daily food, and one of you say unto them, Depart in peace, be ye warmed and filled; notwithstanding ye give them not those things which are needful to the body: what doth it profit? Even so faith, if it hath not works, is dead belong alone. James II 15. Also James V.

Be ready always to give an answer to every man that asketh you a reason of the hope that is in you. I Peter 3:5

Wednesday, June 6. Staten Island

Tamar and I have been down here on the beach for the last ten days except for a Thursday and a Friday night. I had to go in to see about the paper's coming out. Due to writing it hurriedly and making it up hurriedly it is a careless and slovenly job and I have not wanted to look at it all week,

A daily telephone call puts me in touch with the office every day at four.

Peter was at the office when I called up and said all was going well at Harlem. Father [John] La Farge[16] had been to see him there and Negro men beginning to drop in. He is trying to get chairs but the priest at the parish to which he applied could not spare them. They cost $6 a night for 60 and it is too much. He had just spent $10 on blackboards for his Harlem store and wasted some money. But we have none.

July 24

Up for the seven o'clock this morning and after coffee went to the 8 at Twelfth Street, since Mr. Minas was not up yet. Father Zaline is expressing more interest in our work. We need to reach the Italians with so many of them turning Communist.

As soon as I got home and opened the office at nine people started coming in for clothes—shoes, pants, dresses.

Down to the assay office at noon to sell the old gold donated to the paper by Mrs. Biller. It will help tremendously toward paying the printing bill.

Sept 22[17]

Overcast, drizzling, warm. "The ear is not content with hearing nor the eye with seeing." I'm thinking of this because I'm listening to the Symphonic Hour on the radio—Brahms's 1st Symphony—and enjoying it very much, though Margaret bothers me with remarks about there being no butter, Tom

---

16   Father La Farge, a Jesuit priest, was an editor of *America* magazine, and one of the leading Catholic champions of racial justice.

17   See *HH*, 77-88.

asks for stencils, the baby frets, etc. Even so I enjoy it. But we cannot depend on our senses at all for enjoyment. What gives us keen enjoyment one day we listen to with indifference the next, the beauties of the beach arouse us to thanksgiving and exultation at one time and at another leave us lonely and miserable. "It is vanity to mind this present life, and not to look forward unto those things which are to come."

It is hard for me to look forward or to have any conception of future happiness. Sometimes I am afraid of this being lack of faith. On the other hand it makes it easier for me to live in the present moment as Caussade[18] advises, and, let us hope, adds to the merit of endurance.

Hardships to offer up. Going to bed at night with the foul smell of unwashed bodies in my nostrils. Lack of privacy. But Christ was born in a stable and a stable is apt to be unclean and odorous. If the Blessed Mother could endure it, why not I. Also, Christ had no place to lay His head in the years of His public life. The birds of the air have their nests and the foxes their holes but the Son of Man has no place to lay His head.

Yesterday Monsignor [Arthur J.] Scanlon [Rector of the Diocesan Seminary and the Censor of the diocese] honored us with a visit to tell us about his and the Cardinal's approval of our work (which they call a modern miracle). He says he wishes to appoint a spiritual advisor for us to be consulted on doctrinal matters only, and not on such subjects as strikes or labor in general. He seemed to think we would not like this (though we are glad) and assured us it is only to facilitate our progress—that they would give us an Imprimatur if they thought it would not hinder us in our work.

Margaret coming in with the carriage full of baby and vegetables, he blessed the baby and incidentally our food for the evening. Margaret did not put the tomatoes on the table because they had not been blessed and she wanted this to be an entirely blessed meal.

October 25, Friday, 11:30 p.m.[19]

I suppose it is a grace not to be able to have time to take or derive satisfaction in the work we are doing. What time I have my impulse is to self-criticism and examination of conscience, and I am constantly humiliated at my own imperfections and at my halting progress. Perhaps I deceive myself here too and excuse my lack of recollection. But I do know how small I am and

---

18   Jean-Pierre de Caussade (1675-1751), a French Jesuit, analyzed the "sacrament of the present moment" in his classic work (one of Dorothy's favorites), *Abandonment to Divine Providence*.

19   See *HH*, 78-79.

how little I can do and I beg You, Lord, to help me for I cannot help myself. Touch my heart and help me to be ever mindful of Thee.

Dec 14[20]

A quiet evening. Mr. Minas and I have just finished our usual evening late repast. Some evenings, if Frank or Peter is here, we have wine. Otherwise cocoa. And bread and mustard or black olives. Mr. Minas sprinkles his with red pepper.

He is a little thin man with long white hair, a yellow face, greenish eyes with immense pupils and a predatory nose. The men get very well fitted out with suits somehow or other but the shoes are not so good. Mr. Minas' turn up at the toes, which somehow fits in with his Oriental appearance. He is very clean always and before he uses cups or spoons, always carefully rinses them. He is always on the lookout for bugs, and the funny little silverfish which run around the kitchen drive him frantic. Always too, red ants are getting into the ice box. Right now the cockroaches are under cover and not a bedbug has been seen for months. So at present he is at peace. A month ago we had fleas in my side of the house. They are gone, after Tom went around with the spray gun. Now there are only centipedes on my side of the house and the funny silver bugs on Mr. Minas'.

He is very fond of our black cat, whom Mary Sheehan[21] calls Social Justice. He washes her face and paws carefully every day and finds her a little bit of everything, just now Parmesan cheese for instance, and she is thirsty and drinking the goldfish water, terrifying the three fish.

He writes poetry in beautiful Armenian script and carries around his notebook pinned with a safety pin to his pocket ever since he lost it this summer. That was a terrific tragedy—we all felt that his poetry represented everything to him, all that our faith means to us. We all started praying and the next day a young Episcopalian boy came in with the manuscript. Margaret insisted it was St. Anthony in disguise.

We had been reading Dostoevsky, Mr. Minas and I, for the last few months. I've been at *Crime and Punishment* and he *The Idiot*, both of us rereading them. I had only Sundays and late evenings, but he went around with his under his arm continually, trying to find a quiet corner, which is always difficult around here.

---

20   See *HH*, 79.

21   Mary Sheehan was "an unemployed girl...who joined our group [and had] a taste for badinage." *LF*, 27.

# 1935

Feb 19[22]

It is just after midnight and I have been sitting in the outer office alone with two mad creatures with God in their hearts. All three of us tormented in our various ways, all three of us alone, so completely alone too. Karl's madness consists of going in for astrology—it is his passion and it must be regarded seriously. He is young, good looking in a very German way, and very solitary and inarticulate except on the question of astrology.

The other, Bernard Adelson, we met when I spoke at Father Rothlauf's last month. He came down the next night and has been with us ever since, off and on, one time speaking in inspired fashion of the Mystical Body, of other Christs, of the Psalms, quoting them in Hebrew, and then going off into a perfect mania of persecution talk, holding his head and speaking of madness and death.

As I sit I am weeping—I have been torn recently by people, by things that happen. Surely we are, here in our community, made up of poor lost ones, the abandoned ones, the sick, the crazed and the solitary human beings whom Christ so loved and in whom I see, with a terrible anguish, the body of this death. And out in the streets wandering somewhere, is Mr. Minas, solitary among a multitude, surrounded by us all day long, but not one of us save in his humanity, denying, not knowing—yet clinging to some dream, some ideal of beauty which he tries to express in his poetry which no one but he can read.

Catherine is tossing in her bed, unable to sleep what with the wailing of cats in the backyard who act as though all the devils were in them—Catherine, too, with the misery of her illness hanging over her, with the uncertainty, the pain and nerve-racking treatments she undergoes.

I have seen too much of suffering recently what with visiting the girl who is in Woonsocket that Father Michael sent me to visit, who suffers in her skeleton body the torments Christ suffered. I cannot write about her—it is impossible to talk about these supernatural manifestations which are beyond my comprehension.

March 8—First Friday in Lent

Lent is teaching me a great deal through the lessons at hand—teaching me not to be surprised at the foolishness, even the treachery of creatures. It really

---

22  See *HH*, 87-88.

has nothing to do with them—it is something outside themselves—it is for my good.

New Year's Eve[23]

Stanley [Vishnewski][24] is down for these days to help with the wood chopping and gathering driftwood. Even so we have just had to buy two cartons of coal which make five for this year already. It will be good when we are all on the farming commune and the expense is concentrated in one place. One of the best things people can do—the very people who are with you—is to criticize the management and lack of economy, though God knows what else you can do.

The difficulty to look forward to is everybody living under the same roof and getting along together, so strange a conglomeration of people as we all are. There is the Professor now, who has been down here for the past few months. The only manual labor he has ever done has been to cart wood from the beach and it is indeed inspiring to see him pushing the wheel barrow briskly down the road on his way to and from the beach. But he collects at the same time old shoes, tarpaulin, weeds, and bottles. The bottles, he says, are to build a house with. It would take several million, but you can construct a house with the necks all turned inward and the chinks filled up with cement and you will have a cool and light house. He read about it somewhere! He also has ideas about food and the waste of time there is in cooking and eating.

He spends his time trying to figure out an international language and claims knowledge of all languages. When Francis, who is Lithuanian, tried to check up on him, he insisted that everyone spoke Lithuanian differently. He is however a linguist and has taught languages. It has been drink which has been his curse, making him lose employment as a teacher and degraded him to the Welfare Island hospital. Peter picked him up on the street and brought him to us and he has been with us a year and a half.

Francis took offense last night at sleeping in another room from Stanley and walked out this morning without breakfast. So there are general grievances in the air. And general grievances against me for having such people around.

---

23   See *HH*, 127-28.

24   Dorothy described Stanley Vishnewski as "a seventeen-year-old Lithuanian boy from the Williamsburg section of Brooklyn who used to walk to New York over the bridge every day... He sold the paper, too, and ran errands and worked without wages despite the urging of his father, a tailor, that he ought to be looking for a job. (Stanley has remained with us ever since)." *LF*, 25. Indeed, Stanley remained at the CW until his death in 1979, although, according to his longest-running joke, he had not yet decided whether he planned to stay.

Talk of the farming commune and the place at Gillette. "And what are you going to do on the farming commune?" although that had been gone over many times before. Past failures are never forgotten or excused.

If you *are* discouraged, everyone would relapse into a state of discouragement and hopeless anger at circumstances and everyone else. And if you are not discouraged everyone tries to make you be and are angry because you are not. It is hard to know what tack to take. The only thing is to be oblivious, as Peter is, and go right on and on.

I am going to keep a notebook faithfully this year for my own encouragement. For one thing, I am always able to get rid of depression by writing it all out. For another thing, I forget things so easily—people I meet, suggestions that are made, information I am given. I shall try to keep it up completely.

Friday night[25] Father [Paul Hanly] Furfey[26] was in town from Washington and we had an impromptu meeting which lasted until 12. We had already had a roundtable discussion starting at the dinner table, continuing through the dishes and on until nine when he came.

The discussion was heated as it usually is, everyone speaking with vehemence and bobbing up and down from the floor. And Dr. Furfey not having heard Peter before thought it was necessary to calm people and began reminding us that we must not pay so much attention to the economic side of things, that spirituality was all that mattered after all. So I hopped up and said that you can't preach the Gospel to men with empty stomachs and that if he had been down to the Municipal Lodging house and seen 12,000 men being fed at South Ferry, he would think it was necessary to put some emphasis on the material. Which convinced him that I also was an externalist I am sure.

He treated me with sweetness and charity during the rest of his visit when I encountered him, but he spent most of his time with Tom and Dorothy, in their neat, comfortable, and orderly home, reciting the Office, singing the hours, and discussing spiritual things. Meanwhile, we at our cluttered office were feeding the hungry that came in. I am afraid my indignation at Peter's ideas being slighted had an element of self-love and pride in it, but just the same, there is ground for indignation. The crowd at the office get to Mass every morning, and are translating their spirituality into the natural order from morning to night. But it is true we are not "respectable," we are criticized for our dress, our enthusiasm, and for the very works of mercy we

---

25   See *HH*, 129-130.

26   Paul Hanly Furfey, a priest and sociologist from Catholic University, was a good friend, and sometime critic, of the Worker.

are doing. Outside criticism is not so bad, but the criticism from within, the grumbling, the complaints, the insidious discontent spread around—these things are hard to bear.

However, the thing is to bear it patiently, to take it lightly, not to let it interfere with one's own work. The very fact that it is hard shows how much self-love and pride I have, what a deposit of meanness there is at the base of everything I do. I really am ashamed of myself, and shall try to do better. And I shall be happy too to think that God thinks I am strong enough to bear these trials, otherwise we would not be having them. Someone said we must beware when everything is going along smoothly. That is when there is no progress made.

Yesterday Bill Callahan [a recent graduate of City College] and I went out to Gillette to see the farm and it is perfect—everything we could wish for a farming commune. I shall pray to God real hard for it, because considering the difficult personalities, and their spirit of self-sacrifice, perhaps God wishes the first one to be a little easy just to encourage us to go on. It is in his hands, after all.

In the evening there was a meeting in the office—Saturday night and all day Sunday, the meeting at Tom's, and as a visitor said, by that time they were all talked out. Fr. Furfey said a few more words about "spirituality" and to beware of "wordy ones," as St. Paul said; and I had a feeling he meant Peter, and probably me too, as I could be called a wordy one.

Oh dear, I am remembered of St. Teresa who said, "The devil sends me so offensive a bad spirit of temper that at times I think I could eat people up."

I am glad that she felt that way too. St. Thomas said that there is no sin in having a righteous wrath provided there is no undue desire for revenge.

I am afraid I am very stiff-necked. I shall read the Office and go to sleep. But first to concoct a rule for the coming year. It is a thing about which I have been meditating for quite some time—for two months to be exact.

I read in Tanqueray [The Spiritual Life] while on the trip that a rule of life was necessary for all, lay as [well as] cleric. So I resolved then to be more careful not to omit certain devotions that I let myself off from on account of my irregular life and fatigue. After all when I have been working from seven until twelve at night, or traveling fifteen hours by bus, I can realize all the more these words, "Can you not watch with me one hour?" That I have resolved is to be my motto for the coming year, in order to foster recollection.

I have written just as I felt this evening, so as to hide nothing of my mood. I shall look at it next year and try to find if I have gotten rid of any fault. This last year I at last kept the pledge which was something.

## RULE FOR 1936[27]

The Catholic Worker to be in the hands of St. Joseph, and Tamar and I to continue under our novice mistress, the little St. Teresa, who alone can teach us how to do the little things and cultivate a spirit of humility. St. Joseph is also taking care of me this year as I asked him up at Montreal at the shrine.

"Can you not watch with me one hour?"

I shall remember this whenever I am tired and want to omit prayer, the extra prayers I shall set myself. Because after all I am going to try to pray the simplest, humblest way, with no spiritual ambition

Morning prayers, in my room before going to Mass. I always omit them, rushing out of the house just in time as I do. If I were less slothful it would be better. Remember what Leon Bloy said about health in this month's *Coliseum*. Not try too hard to catch up on sleep, but to be sensible about sleep nevertheless.

Around the middle of the day to take, even though it be to snatch, fifteen minutes of absolute quiet, thinking about God and talking to God.

Read the Office as much as I can, if only Prime and Compline, but all whenever possible.

One visit during the day always without fail.

The rosary daily.

I do plenty of spiritual reading to refresh myself and to encourage myself so I do not have to remind myself of that.

The thing to remember is not to read so much or talk so much about God, but to talk to God.

To practice the presence of God.

A nightly examination as to this rule and not just about faults.

To be gentle and charitable in thought, word, and deed.

# 1936

May 21, Ascension Day. Easton farm

On the hillside writing letters. Hot but with a breeze. We all went to 8 Mass. Last Sunday Carney got the professor to go for the first time in years. Gibson is going to confession this Saturday for the first time in 19 years. I am very happy. The boys don't know how much good they can do by translating the spiritual into the material as they are doing.

---

27   See *HH*, 131.

June 3, Wednesday[28]

Last night we said rosary out under the trees, praying for rain. The moon was coming up, there was a smell of sweet clover in the air, and it was very quiet. Carney led. Now there are 19 of us... .

Still very dry and a lot of planting and transplanting to do yet. Seed potatoes have gone up to five dollars a bushel. The work is coming along fine and the place is beginning to look as though people lived there who loved it.

July 12, Sunday, Mott St.

For the last four days an awful spell of heat, the worst in forty years they say. All night people sit out on the streets, mothers holding their heavy, sleeping babies. Sprinkling trucks spray the garbage up from the gutters onto the sidewalks and steamy fetid odors rise and choke one. The heat does not bother me as the smell does.

We have a houseful of invalids. Charlie Rich is sick with the heat. Never well at any time what with his stomach ulcers, he goes around reading the Office of the Dead, his eyes heavy and his face drawn.

The Professor has been out on a drunk and is lying trembling in his room while he is here. He has just stolen five dollars from me, the money we had to send the sharecropper packages of clothes, and he must be tormented in soul as in body.

Mr. Breen has also been sick this last week, alternately cursing out damn niggers and miscegenationists (as he calls us all, when it isn't "nigger-lovers") and weeping over his sins and begging forgiveness in a most maudlin manner. He comes down at least a score of times in the course of the morning while I am working and breathes foully at me while he mumbles in my ear his great love and desire to serve me; and he alternates this senile tenderness by sudden changes of mood into a frenzy of hate at the Professor or Russin. He has deliriums constantly.

"They are making fun of the church," he screamed suddenly, yesterday. "They are pretending to perform a baptism in the speakeasy in front." (The speakeasy where they sell wine night and day to singing, roistering laborers who all but murder each other when they are not bawling out Sardinian songs, adds to the general unrest!)

August 8, Saturday noon. Farm[29]

Fish soup is cooking also, but had greens for one o'clock lunch. I have been canning tomatoes all morning—12 quarts—and my hands are so tired I can

---

28 See *HH*, 164-65.
29 See *HH*, 165-66.

scarcely write. A perfect day for working, good breeze. I'm sitting out under the old apple tree on a very good but not very handsome bench that John Griffin[30] made out of an unused shutter. The three ducks are trying to take a bath in front of me. The drake is constantly biting at the neck of one of the ducks and she turns and returns his caress. Then they both lift themselves preeningly and raise their wings and flutter. The rooster and one hen are sharing a worm and murmuring together.

Monday Aug 10. Mott St.

Ten p.m. and I am most comfortably settled in the extra apartment in the front house [on Mott St.] which Miss [Gertrude] Burke turned over to us. It will be good to be able to sit up and work in the evening and not worry about waking Kate Smith up.

Today was very full. First of all a long discussion with John Cort[31] about personalism, hospitality, state responsibility, and organized charity. (He was objecting to caring for such people as Prof. La Valle, etc.). It was a long one. He is very conscientious, sticks to the job of being in the office, cleaning house, seeing people, indoctrinating, spiritual reading at table, etc. I am very critical with him, but I do think he's a good worker.

Then Carney—and I told him he could not go down to Easton now, and I think it came as a great shock to him. He told John later very threateningly that he was going to write letters to certain people about us, that we were racketeers and not doing our duty by him (one of the duties is to provide him with clothes, a commutation ticket to Easton, which costs $80, better food, and security from persecution).

Mr. Minas came next, telling me of his hunger and suffering, his quarrel with Rosemary over taking stuff from the kitchen. I must give Knut Hamsun's *Hunger* to Rosemary to read. She manages beautifully with normal people but with our special charges like the Prof. and Minas there is conflict.

---

30   John Griffin was "a convalescent from pneumonia," who "just came to us off the Bowery, and slept out in the wagon shed." *LF,* 53.

31   John Cort was "a tall, blond, argumentative [young man], not long out of Harvard … who was so interested in labor that it was through his efforts that a Catholic Association of Trade Unionists got under way." *LF,* 139. According to Cort's own account, he was attracted to the CW after hearing Dorothy speak: "I was captured by her sense of humor. And by her laugh, which was rather infectious and attractive. I remember saying to myself, 'This woman is getting a lot of fun out of life. And I'd like to get some of that for myself, so maybe I'd better try that same kind of life.'" (Rosalie Riegle, *Dorothy Day: Portraits by Those Who Knew Her* [Maryknoll, NY: Orbis Books, 2003, 2]).

Then came Joe Hughes.[32] He was to have sailed Saturday but before sailing the entire ship got drunk and he fell off the wagon too and was fired. He was feeling like hell about it and swears he won't go to sea again, it will be the same thing over again. He was too confident, after going to daily Mass and Communion. It is always the way. Thank God he came back right away. I would have felt bad if he had not. He's all right now, is going down to the farm tomorrow and will help with the farm and road mending, and thence to Bethlehem to try for a job as a steel worker. (Breaking out like that probably did him good. Better have it happen here than in New Orleans where he would be far away from us.)

Sunday Aug 16, Mott Street, 5 p.m.[33]

Downstairs in the yard there are a dozen men sitting at long tables drinking wine. The yard is decorated with branches and electric lights, as is all the street in front for blocks around. Today is the last day of the fiesta celebrating the Assumption.

This feast day a happy one for me and filled with resolutions. First to pay every possible attention to my own soul, as Father Lallemant stresses. Again a rule of life to be determined on; more time spent in prayer. I shall start again trying to make that 6 a.m. Mass so that I can have time for thanksgiving, meditation, and reading early in the morning. There is so much to do, people require so much of one, there are always callers and letters, and in this neighborhood constant noise. And in the country, the same demands made upon one, work to participate in, etc. So I must do more to guard every moment and keep recollected. I can help people far more then, anyway.

Mass today at 10 and eleven; cleaning office; wrote ten letters, talked to a Coughlinite[34] visitor, and so the day goes.

Friday, Aug 18, Farm[35]

Low in mind all day, full of tears. Got up at 6 to wash leftover milk pails and get breakfast; talked to Bill about the *Newman News* and [Hazen] Ordway about marriage and jobs and Mass at 7:40.

---

32   Joe Hughes, a former seaman, became attached to the Worker during the seaman's strike. He married Marge Crowe [Hughes], who became one of Dorothy's closest companions.

33   See *HH,* 169.

34   A follower of Fr. Charles Coughlin, a demagogic priest in Detroit who exerted wide influence through his newspaper and radio broadcasts. His populist message took an increasingly anti-Semitic, if not fascist, turn, and his influence declined after the attack on Pearl Harbor.

35   See *HH,* 170-72.

Bill and John Curran,[36] Bergen and Ordway went in to New York to distribute papers at a Communist rally at Madison Square Garden. Mary got fifty from her sister and contributes it to the grocery fund.

Aside from a few ill-timed jokes about Steve going and getting a job because I was lecturing the boys on the lay apostolate and the need of our not becoming top heavy, jokes which had a grain of bitter feeling as always, she is getting along well and cheerfully, and working prodigiously at jam-making and canning.

But Jim so low and bitter in spirits, oppressed at the work to be done, lack of funds, too many visitors and children, waste of food which is rotting on the vines, the uselessness of eating corn, because it uses so much butter, and it all comes down to his objection to responsibility which he takes out on me, letting me know in little ways that he thinks I ought to do other than I am doing.

What with him, John Curran and his discourses on daily Mass and orderliness, and John Cort in town, not to speak of the Boston group, Ottawa, Toronto, Missouri, all discouraged, all looking for organization instead of self-organization, all of them weary of the idea of freedom and personal responsibility—I feel bitterly oppressed, yet confirmed in my conviction that we have to emphasize personal responsibility at all costs. It is most certainly at the price of bitter suffering for myself. For I am just in the position of a dictator trying to legislate himself out of existence. They accept my regime, which emphasizes freedom and personal responsibility, but under protest. They all complain at the idea of there being this freedom in town and here, that there is no boss.

Today I just happened to light on Dostoevsky's "Grand Inquisitor," which was most apropos. Freedom—how men hate it and chafe under it; how unhappy they are with it.

Also I read Sunday night in town [Jacques] Maritain's use of pure means in his *Freedom and the Modern World*. I read while the Italians outside sang and shouted their allegiance to Mussolini. It was hard concentrating then, just as it is hard now with all the disturbances incidental to life in a community.

---

36   John Curran was a veteran of the Navy who quit his job as a night guard to join the CW. According to Stanley Vishnewski, Curran considered himself a follower of Peter Maurin—not Dorothy. When he was put in charge of the petty cash, "we discovered an unpleasant aspect of John's character." While always generous with his own money, "he became completely tight-fisted with the house money." As Stanley recalled, "We would be forced to beg to get a dime for a cup of coffee and piece of pie." See Vishnewski's memoir, *Wings of the Dawn*, published by the Catholic Worker.

This week Eleanor and Bernice, two colored children, and Mary and Annie Giogas are down and they are singing and dancing all the day. I should be happy to see them ... But I have satisfaction in nothing.

"Are we trying to make a farm here or aren't we?"

A statement of that kind, an attitude of criticism of all that Peter and I stand for, has the power to down me completely so that I feel utterly incapable of going to Boston and meeting the opposition there and all their trials and discouragements. Nothing but the grace of God can help me but I feel utterly lacking, ineffective, my strength failing.

In town the usual crosses, Carney calling us all racketeers, calling the spiritual reading pious twaddle; Mr. Breen with his vile accusations; the misery of Minas and the Professor; Kate's illness; the suit against us, the bills piling up and the unconscious discouragement in people like Frank and Jim—these things to be topped by such a lack of understanding of the personalist idea from those you expect the most from, lays me low.

Since I got back from Pittsburgh I have had this completely alone feeling. A temptation of the devil, doubtless, and to succumb to it is a lack of faith and hope. There is nothing to do but bear it, but my heart is as heavy as lead, and my mind dull and uninspired. A time when the memory and understanding fail one completely and only the will remains, so that I feel hard and rigid, and at the same time ready to sit like a soft fool and weep my eyes out.

Tonight Tamar had a nose bleed, a headache, and a stomachache, and although the latter probably came from eating green pears, as she confessed, still to think of the little time I have with her, constantly to be on the go, leaving her to the care of others, sending her away so that she can lead a regular life and not be subject to the moods and vagaries of the crowd of us, this is probably the cruelest hardship of all. She is happy, she does not feel torn constantly as I do, and then the doubt arises, probably she too feels that I am failing her just as the crowd on Mott St. and the crowd down here feel it.

"You are always away." "You are never down here."

And then when I get to Boston—"This is your work, why are you not up here more often?"

Never before have I had such a compete sense of failure, of utter misery.

"O spiritual soul, when thou seest thy desire obscured, thy will arid and constrained, and thy faculties incapable of any interior act, be not grieved at this, but look upon it rather as a great good, for God is delivering thee from thy self, taking the matter out of thy hands... The way of suffering is safer and also more profitable than that of rejoicing and of action. In suffering God gives strength, but in action and in joy the soul does but show its own weakness and imperfections."—St. John of the Cross

In Boston for three days.

Took boat at 5 for N.Y. Still low and dragged out. Feeling nothing accomplished. Mr. Schwartz drove me down here where the atmosphere is morose and the weather does not help. Reading Caussade and New Testament does help, and hiding my own sadness.

Oct 6

The October issue will be out tomorrow night. All of the copy is done except the "Day by Day" [*Dorothy's column*] and what unions ought to be. John is downstairs doing letters, and I, ill, am taking it easy on my couch. What with seeing the censor, Fr. McSorley, getting a letter off to the Cardinal yesterday and the Catechetical Congress, the last week has been very full.

Tuesday Oct 27

Mass at nine, a requiem. Solemn high. Communion. Talked with John [Cort] over the *Globe* strike...

Returned to office to go over mail, write letters, while John G. put up radiators and Mr. Breen stomped in and out, shouting "Nigger lover" at me. Mr. A in to say goodbye. Left $100 for poor. About 50 men came in destitute. We need clothes horribly. Nine women today got coats. Four more couldn't get any.

*The outbreak of the Spanish Civil War in 1936 posed a test for the CW. Most Catholics identified with the cause of General Franco and regarded his rebellion against the Republican government as a virtual holy war against godless atheism.* The Commonweal *and* The Catholic Worker *were notable exceptions to this rule. In November 1936 the CW ran an editorial "On the Use of Force," making plain the movement's pacifist position:*

> And now the whole world is turning to "force" to conquer. Fascist and Communist alike believe that only by the shedding of blood can they achieve victory. Catholics, too, believe that suffering and the shedding of blood "must needs be," as Our Lord said to the disciples at Emmaus. But their teaching, their hard saying is, that they must be willing to shed every drop of their own blood, and not take the blood of their brothers. They are willing to die for their faith, believing that the blood of martyrs is the seed of the Church...
>
> Our Lord said, "Destroy this temple and in three days I will raise it up." And do not His words apply not only to Him as Head of his Church but to His members? How can the Head be separated from the members? The Catholic Church cannot be destroyed in Spain or in Mexico. But we do not believe that force of arms can save it. We believe that if Our Lord were alive *today he would say as He said to St. Peter, "Put up thy sword."*

Christians, when they are seeking to defend their faith by arms, by force and violence, are like those who said to Our Lord, "Come down from the Cross. If you are the Son of God, save Yourself."

But Christ did not come down from the Cross. He drank to the last drop the agony of His suffering, and was not part of the agony the hopelessness, the unbelief, of His own disciples?

Christ is being crucified today, every day. Shall we ask Him with the unbelieving world to come down from the Cross? Or shall we joyfully, as His brothers, "complete the sufferings of Christ"? ... [37]

Dec 6, Sunday. On the train, 9 p.m.

Up for 6:00 Mass this a.m. Then back to 115 [Mott St.] to have coffee and talk to Evans, the unemployed mechanic, who stayed there over night. A steeplejack, a sand hog, carpenter, restaurant worker, and I engaged in a discussion of our industrial civilization, the machine and unemployment, the land and cooperatives. The wage system can be discussed thus with the unemployed, when you get half dozen at a time. When they come in in a crowd it is hard to talk. But those you do reach go out and talk to others.

In the afternoon to Fr. Ford's where Chapman and [Kenneth] Burke talked on Communism and Catholicism. We brought the seamen up to the meeting and they took up a collection after the meeting. We have planned to get a group of Catholic seamen together to indoctrinate them and prepare them to combat Communist tactics.

Such a situation drives Peter [Maurin] crazy because the men are interested in wages and hours and he, being opposed to the wage system and strikes, finds it hard to start in with such elementals and get in his stuff. He sees history, the philosophy of labor, the long view, but he does not see immediate tactics, strategy....

Went to confession last night and Communion this a.m. but feel a great sense of conflict, almost a beginning of the struggle all over again...

Reading St. Bernard, [Thomas] à Kempis.

# 1937

May 8, Saturday. St. Elizabeth rectory, Chicago

What with being sick this week, felt very low tonight. Read, prayed, wept, and then thought—why do we expect any happiness? God wills for us the present moment. We must take it with a joyful will at least. Never let our moods affect others. Hide any sadness. We are suffering sadness and fatigue

---

37   See Robert Ellsberg, ed., *Dorothy Day: Selected Writings* (Maryknoll, NY: Orbis Books, 1992), 77-88. Henceforth, *SW.*

just because our will is painfully struggling. Our Lord must teach me, I cannot learn by myself to give up my will completely, to accept the present moment, to live in the presence of God. I should be happy that this struggle is going on, that I am not content. A paradox. I was just reading over the last pages herein for my help. It serves to convince me that nothing depends on me, I can do nothing. Moods, discouragement, bickerings pass and the work proceeds, the influence is far-reaching.

It is a great privilege to be here in a rectory in this slum.

Downtown this afternoon for a hat, also to the Calvert Library. Home to meeting of group with Fr. [Martin] Carrabine which I almost missed.

May 30, Sunday

A new resolution, to write these few lines every day.

Today was beautiful. 9 a.m. Mass and communion. Coffee at the office and up to the farm. Long talk with O'Connell, Elias, Eddie, Herg, John Curran and all in general. Everybody very happy, even Hergenhan, tho he says he is going to leave on completion of the house unless I change my "fundamental ideals." He has the foundation finished and is starting on the lumber work and chimney. Lunch at 2:30 and dishes. The house very clean and pleasant and whole farm looking wonderful.

May 31

Slept in the afternoon, very tired, and in the evening wrote. Five steel strikers killed in Chicago and 105 injured, 28 by bullets.

June 3, Thursday

After 9 Mass to the chancery office, then Fr. McSorley.[38] Msgr. [Francis] McIntyre[39] fine about the Rochester conference. Fr. McS. all against CIO.

Went down to S.I. to see Tamar at 3:30. She is fine and wants to stay to be in play. Only two more weeks of school but she is well content. These are always exciting days at school.

---

38   Fr. Joseph McSorley, a Paulist priest, was Dorothy's first spiritual advisor. It was he who suggested that she approach the Paulists about printing the first issue of the CW. For a time, after the Chancery urged Dorothy to seek a spiritual advisor, he agreed to serve informally in this capacity. He often accompanied her on meetings with church authorities.

39   Msgr. Francis McIntyre was one of Dorothy's principal contacts at the Chancery. Years before he had been helpful to her during the time of her conversion. In later years, as Cardinal McIntyre, Archbishop of Los Angeles, he became something of a scourge to liberal Catholics in his archdiocese. Dorothy would challenge his support for the Vietnam War, but she always remembered him with gratitude for his kindness.

Friday, June 4

Luke, Maurice, Bill and Elias all stumbling drunk at all hours. No sleep for hours. John Filliger[40] the only reliable one drinking and he stopped yesterday.

Today after I stated that no one could stay and drink, Elias left. Then Bill. O'Connell went to bed sick. Then with B and baker arriving we discovered Elias had been trying to cash a CW check. He couldn't but he borrowed 5 from the baker. Then Luke disappeared.

Frank came up in the evening to say Elias had broken in the store. But no Luke.

Wrote letters all p.m. Eddie and Ray cleaned the kitchen. Supper peaceful and read *Resurrection* before bed.

Sat. June 5

Up at 9. Lauds, Angelus, read Little Flower.

All is peaceful. Put on my bathing suit and went down to the spring to bathe after supper. Then we sat out by the barn and played with the dogs, the goat until dusk. Cocoa and to bed at 10.

Sun, June 6

Frank M. & I walked to the station at 6:30 & I got 7:30 train. Found telegram from Chicago saying they were suppressing our June number there on account of our calling police murderers. In the afternoon Mary, Helen, and I down to see Tamar in the annual entertainment and picnic afterward. Home at 9:30.

Tuesday June 15

Mr. O'Connell is 70, a descendent of [Irish patriot] Daniel O'Connell. He says there are no saints like the Irish, that none of them would have betrayed our Lord. He has worn ten uniforms—police, fireman, army and navy and Boer. And then telling me how he went bootless for 7 months and had to take the boots off the feet of an Irishman in the English army. He got no further in his tale of the uniforms he wore. He is really a great old man, still hearty—a fine carpenter and he can work and drink with the best of them. But he cannot work with others and he must go on his solitary drunks.

Yesterday and today have been so quiet and happy. Reading and writing and putting all trouble out of mind.

---

40   John Filliger, a former seaman, stayed on at the CW after the seamen's strike. (He liked to say he had been shanghaied while he was drunk.) The CW's most competent farmer, he settled on the various farms until his death. He was known as "Farmer John."

Wrote editorial. "Religion is opium of people." On daily communion.

Reading *Bread and Wine* by [Ignacio] Silone. Very good. Finished *Resurrection* last week. Also very good.

CIO in big battle with Republic Steel. *Times* constantly pointing out how they are losing. Either morale is low or else they are successful. Impossible to get real truth in papers.

Roses all in bloom in front of the house.

Wednesday June 16

There has been great reform going on up at the farm. Joe Zarrella[41] has made it his job to express the idea of leadership and personalism.

Meditation. August 6. Friday

Mass and communion at the Syrian church down in Easton. On the conversion of sinners. While I was praying I thought—these men, these workers, these leaders of labor, may turn toward God in their hearts through the things we recall to them in the *Catholic Worker*. They may continue fallen away, outside the faith, not professing any particular creed, and yet their hearts may be turned to God. Either now or in the future. The world will never know of their inner conversion, nor will their followers. They will no more proclaim themselves Catholics than they do now proclaim themselves Communist. They are good leaders now. See Scully's letter in the *Tablet*. They are following Catholic principles of social justice. Our work will probably make them continue good leaders.... The big fight is against violence more than it is against atheism. These men are not atheists, and if they are bitter Catholics there is reason for it.

The attributes of the soul are, according to St. Teresa, memory, understanding, and will. If you use these three, you can bring to life again your love for your husband, your memory of your first love for him, your understanding of his difficulties and the troubles that have come between you; your will to love him now. If only for self preservation you must use the will as you cannot go on in this state of unhappiness and friction. Love is a matter of the will anyway, when it isn't just a biological urge that beclouds every other issue. If you will to love someone (even the most repulsive and wicked), and try to serve him as an expression of that love,—then you soon come to *feel* love. And God will hear your prayers. "Enlarge Thou my heart that Thou mayest enter in!" You can pray the same way, that your heart may be enlarged to love again.

---

41   Joe Zarrella came upon members of the Catholic Worker handing out papers in a May Day parade in 1935. He asked if he could help and stayed on to become a mainstay of the movement.

It is true that we cannot be happy unless we love, so it is worth making every effort to love. It is a question of deepest obligation for you since as a Catholic you have made this promise and you knew what you were doing. If your husband had been a Catholic these things would have come up too.

The union between man and woman is the closest analogy in this moral life to the union between God and man. One cannot properly be said to understand the love of God without understanding the deepest fleshly as well as spiritual love between man and woman. The two should go hand in hand. You cannot separate the soul from the body. Even throughout the psalms you find the union of the two. "My heart and my flesh cry out for the living God." "The love of God should quicken the body as well as the soul."

August 7. St. Cajetan

On suffering. Joe has hay fever and he works so hard and we need him so I found myself praying that he be cured immediately. And then I thought that his misery was probably worth more to the work than his ease. (Easy to judge for others). We do not make enough of suffering, we do not rejoice in this coin that is given us to pay our debts and those of others. I should welcome my sick headaches, but usually I rebel, thinking how if I had been a bit more sensible I could have avoided it. But then often it cannot be avoided, it just descends on one. So it should be welcomed in those cases at least as an opportunity of quietly enduring without complaint and submitting and accepting the will of God. The sacrament of the present moment.

One of the objections to suffering which we do not admit is that it is undignified. It is not a wound heroically received in battle. Hay fever, colds in the head, bilious attacks, poison ivy, such like irritations which are sometimes even worse than a severe illness are to say the least petty and undignified. But in reality it takes heroic virtue to practice patience in little things, things which seem little to others but which afflict one with unrest and misery. Patience with each other and with each other's bickerings. We can even offer up, however, our own lack of peace, our own worry. Since I offered all the distractions, turmoil and unrest I felt at things going askew a few weeks ago, my petty fretting over this one and that one, I have felt much better and more able to cope with everything.

Toothaches, bruised faces even, received in street fighting are ugly and grotesque. It is hard to heroically receive blows in the face from a policeman, for instance, and take it like a Christian, in the spirit of non-resistance. A spirit of hatred and a fierce desire for retaliation seems more manly, more human. Moral force being hard to see, is a thousand times harder than physical force. Strength of spirit is not so often felt to be apparent as strength of body. And we in our vanity wish this strength to be apparent. Human respect again. And yet moral force is always felt.

# 1938

*Dorothy's diary jumps from August 1937 to June 1938.*

June 25. St. William. Saturday

Today we moved down to the beach and Tamar, Steve, and I went swimming. He says he likes Coney Island better than Atlantic City, it is more genuine.

Thinking about the farm at Mass. It will always be necessary to have a central farm, a communal farm. At present there is no prospect of families. Those who have married or wanting to be, will not accept voluntary poverty to that extent, nor have they the humility or patience to accept manual labor or share in it with others. Also they wish too immediate results. They haven't the vision and get discouraged at the prospect of collecting stones and digging.

The farm is progressing well. There is growth. There is every reason to be encouraged. All at the farm are unemployed workers, now busy building for their own and the Common Good.

Peter is down there for the summer so I am free to travel and write.

June 29. Harrisburg

Meditation on the bus. Rainy and cold. Thinking gloomily of the sins and shortcomings of others, it suddenly came to me to remember my own offenses, just as heinous as those of others. If I concern myself with my own sins and lament them, if I remember my own failures and lapses, I will not be resentful of others. This was most cheering and lifted the load of gloom from my mind. It makes one unhappy to judge people and happy to love them.

We had a meeting of the friends of the CW and there was an equal number of colored and white. The colored confessed to giving up when they discovered the new housing appropriations were not going to reach them. A great need for people to unite and work for their poorer fellows. They can be meek for themselves but not for others. St. Thomas says a man cannot lead a good life without a certain amount of goods. It is impossible for people to keep straight, living under such conditions. Whole families crowded in one room, people living in shacks in the open, vice rampant, it is a miracle if children remain uncontaminated. I would suggest the tenants go on a sit-down strike against paying rent, and so call attention to their situation. The first small step is to get water for them.

Housing, interracial justice and cooperation are the three things the friends of the CW in Harrisburg are interested in. And they have already done much along these lines. Along with this work, they are also talking about a farm to settle about five young men, two married and with families, the others working to make marriage possible. With an auxiliary group to help them, with those who are working helping those who are not working, much can be done. Mutual aid, without help or interference from the government. Working along both lines is necessary.

Pittsburgh, July 2. Visitation

Got in last night by bus. Still damp and rainy. The halls of St. Joseph's house smell of cats. They have cleaned up one wing and about thirty men are being housed and fed three meals a day, and about 500 their lunch of stew. A man donates $100 worth of meat a month which is a godsend and they get vegetables from the produce market. Someone gave a truck. They are all drinking sassafras tea since one of the merchants at the market gave them a big basket of the root bark for brewing. I had some for supper last night and it was good. It is supposed to thin the blood and be good in the spring time. Mr. Lenz who is the head of the house, is a nurse and he recommends it. It is good we have a nurse here. Also that we have a large house. One of the men has mumps and he is segregated down the hall from me. My room is on the second floor, very clean and comfortable. For breakfast, oatmeal, dry toast, and very weak coffee. We talked of raising pigs and chickens and bacon and eggs for breakfast. Everyone's face lit up. Prayers in the little chapel morning and evening and grace at meals.

Read the end of *Resurrection* on the bus yesterday, and the analysis of revolutionary types was very interesting. Also Tolstoi's solution of living the Gospel, not judging or punishing our neighbor.

July 3. Sunday

Warm, sunny. Great depression of spirits. Job is to hide it from others, to accept it as penance, reparation, and to pray constantly for an increase in my heart of the love of God and man.

The epistle today: I reckon the sufferings of this time are not worthy to be compared with the glory to come that shall be revealed in us.... . For we know now that every creature groaneth, and travaileth in pain, even till now; and not only it, but ourselves also, who have the first fruits of the spirit, even we ourselves groan within ourselves, waiting for the adoption of the sons of God, redemption of our body. Rom VIII

In this groaning of spirit everything is irksome to me. The dirt, the garbage heaped in the gutters, the flies, the hopelessness of the human beings around me, all oppress me. In my comforting Charles Rich the other day, when he stated he was surprised that anyone could keep going, I told him that others did not have his capacity for suffering, also that his health was poor which made the outlook dark. Fortunately people do live from day to day, and God lifts their spirits to help them endure. There is a supernatural reason for our lack of consolation and we should endure it gratefully. If God didn't think we could stand it we wouldn't be visited with this pain.

Faber's pamphlet, "Weariness in Well Doing" is good. It is a good check and states reasons, usually our own fault, for our sadnesses. But sometimes we can find no reason and must just accept the cross. My natural reasons right now are a separation from Tamar and the difficulties of keeping the work going with no money. But sadness can come for other reasons too.

Speaking of being hypercritical, while I ate this noon I remembered the set up at the Archbishop's palace, the delicate wines, the delicious food, the abundance of delicacies and exquisite service. And I wished the princes of the church were living voluntarily down in a place like this where the food is scarce and often bad. Today for instance for breakfast was coffee so weak that the skim milk, slightly soured, took from it any color it had. The oatmeal was tasteless, but the toast, dry, was good. For lunch a very greasy lamb stew, plain lettuce, and boiled parsnips. No one ate any parsnips but the stew was cleaned up. It was a good stew. But there is nothing in the house for the coming week to make soup out of. The cellar is full of baskets of radishes, parsnips, and woody turnips, slimy lettuce, and spinach.

The place is full of flies as a result of the decaying vegetables and the cellar is half flooded with water which makes it worse. Also dirty baskets covered with slime are piled ceiling high, and the garbage is heaped up in the yard in cans uncovered and haunted with flies.

There is plenty of work here to do, getting plumbing fixed, getting the cellar cleaned up, and disposing of the stuff we cannot use. And getting some supplies in that can be used, such as beans for soup.

Tomorrow the soup line will get a concoction of turnips and parsnips and lamb fat. God knows what kind of a concoction that will be, but not very appetizing. I shall concentrate on the food problem and drag in the lay apostolate on that basis.

It is an insult to St. Joseph, our provider, to serve such meals.

Fr. Rice was just in—he has been ill and is still weak, but feeling better after his retreat. The trouble is the lay people have left the work to him, thinking three priests are at the head of this Alliance. It should be the work of the laity. Most of the money comes from young curates who can ill afford to help.

I'm going over to John Brophy's [national director of the CIO] for supper now, the afternoon having already passed.

Thursday July 7

After writing the previous I was too occupied to feel low, and the prayers I had said lifted my spirits.

Enjoyed the evening at Brophy's. Borrowed *The Stars Look Down* by Cronin from him and read until 3 a.m. A very good book about the coal country in England.

The quietest Fourth I ever spent.

Meeting in East Pittsburgh, chief of police and wife present. Many steel workers. Supper at McCune's. Picked an armload of sweet clover which has made my room smell lovely.

Saw Bishop Boyle and we talked for 2 hours about the land movement. About the colonizations in French Canada. Bishop worries about next generation in this homestead business. Opportunities for youth. I quoted St. Francis, "We do not know what we haven't practiced." We will have to take those problems as we come to them. Pray for more leaders. Meanwhile the unemployed are being given work, fed, housed, clothed. And people's minds are being turned landward by this living vital indoctrination.

Sunday July 17, Coney Island

Our greatest need is mutual charity, love, and loyalty to each other. It is the only way to solve problems, get cooperation, and have peace. To see the good in our neighbor, and develop it. To forgive and not to judge. Never to speak ill of one another. Not to be upset at others doing so, but change the conversation or walk away.

Peter's example at the farm should be felt this summer. He walks to Mass daily, communicates…So many hours of manual labor and time for reading and discussion. He is mending the roads, making flowerbeds, and the whole lower farm is improved.

My problem is not to become upset at people's discontent and criticism but to keep myself peaceful, kind, and patient. My great fault when one person is criticizing another to me is to point out their faults and that only makes things worse.

Last Thursday night I arrived in Phil. at 6:50 from Pittsburgh after riding all day on the bus. There were 2 children next to me who were sick off and on all day. In between they ate some more bananas, cake, and candy. I had some perfume which I could use so I sat with my handkerchief pressed to my nose but my mouth kept watering sickly. Nothing to help ward off the flies. But the trip was beautiful nevertheless.

Visited Bishop Eustace of Camden in the afternoon. Talked to him about Christian associations of workers in parishes, to raise up leaders in union movement. They are beginning to organize Campbell's Soup factories and 5 workers were arrested for giving out handbills. We talked too of Bridgeton and the Seabrook farms, so huge they must be sprayed by aeroplane, where transient workers, whole families are forced to work all day in the fields for bare subsistence. A propertyless and even homeless population living on starvation wages.

Tuesday, July 19

Signed papers, Peter and I, for farm. Mass 7:30. P & I had breakfast together and lawyers at 9:15. On 2:20 bus for N.Y. Conversation with Bill, Gerry [Griffin][42] walking out, on farm and his oppositions. He asked me to stay on Mott St. for a year, which I will gladly do beginning Sept 1, after Nova Scotia trip. So I shall accept no more speaking engagements out of town. I offered this last Aug but he wished full authority then, thinking he could handle situations. Now he recognizes he cannot manage a House, so will only do what he wants. The tragedy is he refuses to try to. He insists he is a realist. What he is refusing to try to do is be a saint.

July 31, Sunday, Coney Island

Came down last night at 5 with Mary who had come in town for meat. Still scorching weather. Went to 10 a.m. Mass. *Tablet* has another attack in its letters columns. Two weeks ago one signed "Dominican." Four years ago this summer the *Tablet* was carrying a series of letters against us. I finally was requested to answer them.

The Little Office is a very present help in trouble. For months I've been debating joining Dominican Tertiaries. Very tired over weekend. T came back exhausted.

---

42   Gerry Griffin, according to Dorothy, was "an irascible, hard-working young man who endeared himself to me by loving Dostoevsky." *LF*, 139.

Wed, Aug 10. Feast of St. Lawrence

Since last writing much peace of mind, tho situations remain the same. But constant pain in my right hand, arm and shoulder so it is hard to write.

Saw Mother and Pop [July 23]. Very happy meeting. Tamar, Mother, and I had lunch together at Grand Central and saw her off on noon train.

Miss Mullen's criticisms. Lack of charity and too heavy indoctrination. I believe that it is that which is getting John down. Peter wishes everyone to read and become articulate regardless of his nature. John Curran's emphasis (wrong) on justice. "If the other fellow does this, why not I?" Peter's stand: "If they ask for my cloak, let them have my coat too." He has given up eggs and milk because there is quarreling over it.

In spite of all these things and constant pain, I have had great peace of mind. The regular recitation of the Little Office has helped much.

Aug 14, Sunday. Hospital, Sisters of St. Martha [Antigonish, Nova Scotia]

When we arrived Wed., met at 1:30 by Peter Nearing and A.B. MacDonald and taken to Mt. St. Bernard where we have stayed till today, coming over daily to the hospital for treatment for my arm.

Thursday drove to Truro with Fr. Coady to speak to the miners in convention. Friday spoke to Sisters at Bethany, the mother house and today to Notre Dame Sisters at four and here at 7:30. It has rained every day until today. Now it is warm and sunny again. Tamar has been reading constantly, *Little Lord Fauntleroy, Pollyanna*, and such like fiction. She is enjoying herself very much, breakfasting in bed what with her cold which has hung on a week now.

My reading has been slight. [Vincent] McNabb on prayer. Importance of keeping to regular prayer. Even one Our Father morning and evening. Little Office. Rosary. Today we had much. Mass, 2 Benedictions, Little Office, and now before bed the rosary. [Abbot Columba] Marmion on the Way of the Cross. I must add this to my devotions to gain the grace of fortitude in suffering. I must accept this pain in my shoulder as penance for my sins. The other day at the communion rail, it was as tho the Lord held my shoulder tightly in his clasp.

I met here at the hospital a Miss O'Brien who is suffering most horrible affliction after sleeping sickness, crippling paralysis, and a constant grotesque tremor of her tongue which hangs out of her open mouth. I don't know when the sight of suffering has affected me so painfully. I went up to read to her today. I feel she is doing penance for our sins. I must remember to read her that poem on sickness which someone sent me when I was sick. She was a brilliant student and a school teacher.

All are Scotch hereabouts. Very silent people. They just sit. Tamar finds it hard to get used to two or three just sitting and looking at you while eating. I cannot get used to it myself.

Aug 15, Monday. Feast of the Assumption
Slept last night at St. Martha's Hospital. At Bethany this morning watched carding wool to make comforters, spinning, weaving. They have also a printing press, bookbinding, many sewing rooms.

Now at 2 p.m. we are down here at the shore—Tamar playing in the water with a little boat she found. Very still and calm, but with a constant murmur of wind in the pines. A few sea gulls, the mooing of a cow in the distance, a crow, but no other sounds. Tamar's splashing is the loudest. Not a house in sight, tho there is a neighbor vacationing down the shore with a sailboat. Some small boys hammering now and then. Silence and complete calm.

At Mott St. now they are celebrating the feast of the Assumption and Sam, Rocco, and the hubbub will be like that of a market place for the entire summer. Only when school reopens will there be comparative quiet again. But there is never quiet there in that most congested area of New York City. I shall remember this scene often with much refreshment.

Sat Sept 10. 1 p.m.
Yesterday I drove in from the farm with John Curran and Tamar, the latter very much crowded by baskets of vegetables and fruits. I drove most of the way down the day before, getting off at the circle and going on to Allentown. I had read a book on Therese Neumann [*modern mystic*] the night before until 2 a.m. and was very tired all day. Went to bed before dark.

We are having so many visitors now we have to put them up at a lodging house on the Bowery.

Visiting a friend at jail. Bars, screens, separation of two feet from the visitor. A 15-minute visit once a week allowed. No bananas, oranges, meat. No Mass on Sunday. A priest comes every two weeks and preaches a sermon and a few girls sing a few hymns. No confession, communion, no visits—though the man may be in 90 days. I thought how the men would be facing a sermon from being present, assisting at Mass. I noticed how different they are visiting their friends at the screen.

As I came down the street afterward a well dressed priest drove by in a big car. Then I passed another—also well dressed, comfortable…Then still another out in front of a most luxurious mansion, the parish house, playing with a dog on a leash. All of them well fed, well housed, comfortable, caring for the safe people like themselves. And where are the priests for the poor, the down and out, the sick in city hospitals, in jails. It is the little of God's children who do not get cared for. God help them and God help the priest who is caught in the bourgeois system and cannot get out.

Sunday Sept 11, 6:30 p.m.

Tamar and I are just home from visiting Mother and Pop up at the Hotel. We had dinner which Tamar enjoyed mightily. Yesterday we went to the 5 & 10 to get paper and had lunch. There, 25¢ a plate and she said it was the best meal she had had since her return from Nova Scotia. We have enough to eat but meals prepared for forty are never as good as those prepared for a family. Tamar is crocheting an afghan—Mother just is finishing one for her. We are certainly very happy at the new plan of being together and her going to school down here on Mott St. The only reason I ever sent her away was because with all my speaking trips I could not take proper care of her. But now I am to be at home for a year. I am grieved always at this talk of not raising one's children in these surroundings. I am going to write on Holy Poverty and the family....

A priest (Josephite) came in for help. Had left his house last Tuesday, quarrel with Superior. Said he did not blame him for kicking him out. Drinking since and his clothes were in a hotel, he said. He seemed most unhappy and miserable. Sent him over to St. Joseph's Clergy House, Stirling, to Brother Joseph.

As I write I am thinking, venal soul that I am—St. Joseph, you must help us, we "have given an onion"[43] to a priest of an order named in your honor. And then I think that really, that is all we did. We are leaving it to Fr. Joachim's order to do the rest—the really hard job.

St. Bernadette compared herself to a broom standing in a corner. We are just insignificant instruments and we do very little... but we are in such terrible need just now. We just have to keep on praying and praying for help.

In this last two years we have sent out appeals which would not have been enough to pay our bills if it had not been for two large benefactors, both of whom gave us a thousand each time. But I don't think they will continue to help. Miss Gage was approached by the Labor Leader and helped, and C.S. was approached by several of our friends who came to know that he had

---

43    In *From Union Square to Rome* Dorothy relates a story from Dostoevsky's *Brothers Karamazov* about a mean old woman who claimed she deserved salvation because she once "gave away an onion."

helped us. Both wished their benefactions to remain secret but somehow it got around. Not that they told us not to mention it but I feel they think us indiscreet. We are too open about everything—everyone knows our business. In a way that cannot be helped.... Also I do not think people like to be asked personally. They do not mind appeals. They are mimeographed and in a way impersonal. They leave a person free to help or not to help...

Reading *Pelle the Conqueror*, a good proletarian novel.

Last night after confession I was talking to Joe, Gerry, John Cogley, John Cort, Larry and Ray and was uncharitable about some around the Labor Leader who are in the Labor movement as a career. John Cort said they were better than the Communists anyway, and I quoted "The lukewarm I will spew out of my mouth." The trouble is I want them extremist, as Catholics, so I judge harshly. It would not be so bad if I did not descend to personalities. I went to bed resolved to try to keep silence—to keep to my cell. Every time I come out I am less a man.

Thursday Sept 15. 10:15 p.m.

Had supper with Ade [Bethune], her mother, father, André, and a pleasant evening. This afternoon a woman came in, left a box for me and rushed out. In it there was $41 in coins. Joe rushed after her to thank her but she was gone. St. Joseph is answering our prayers. This evening Mr. Bethune gave me a check for $50 for the farm to be put towards a truck. He had been much upset at our wrecking ours. "Like an artery being cut," he said. I was so touched by his generosity. He had been ill all summer too.

This afternoon down to Kenedy's [Catholic publisher] where I sat reading *Pope Pius XI and World Peace* for 2 hrs. On Spain and Italy. It did not impress me. The fact that the Phalangists feed 800 children daily does not prove that they are not fascist in tendency. Here the Catholic Charities through the parochial schools feed many thousand and say little of it.

A morning at letters. Mass at 8:30 and the children sing beautifully. Feast of the Seven Sorrows of the Blessed Virgin.

Sunday Sept 18

Went to 9 Mass and communion and Tamar and I had breakfast in a happy and leisurely manner. Afterward house cleaning and now she and Arthur [Sheehan] are out in the barn watching the new pigs born last night. There were ten and she lay on two. But the others are beauties.

Grey and showery today. Typically fall. The trees are beginning to change tho there has been no frost yet and it is warm today...

Wednesday. St. Matthew. First fall day. Sept 21

Up at 5:00 after going to sleep at nine. Helped Scotty on the line and went to 7 Mass. Letters all morning with Walter. Another from Pittsburgh in, drunk and talking about "giving himself up." We put him to bed in Mr. Breen's room and gave him bromides. Headache all p.m.

Walter came in at five to tell me Dan Russell died this morning. And I did not get to see him yesterday, what with being ill and just forgetting it. Arranged for his funeral with Graciano. We have not a penny in the house. Fr. O'Connor gave us the deed to the cemetery plot he owns but it costs $25 to open the grave. The money goes to the Cathedral, Graciano said, and the gravediggers are not paid a living wage. Dan is to have a hundred dollar funeral in death when in life he starved and suffered.

Sept 28. Wednesday. 9:30 p.m.

Up until one thirty last night reading [Richard] Gregg's book [*The Power of Nonviolence*]. So up at 7:30 this morning.

In the afternoon Fr. Bertrand in with David Gordon, most peculiar Jewish convert—somewhat like a Grand Inquisitor. Wanting to shed his own and other's blood for his faith. He does not believe that man is little lower than the angels. He does not believe we should love our enemies, and considers us dangerous heretics. Me especially. He tells me I am eaten up with pride and self-love. On this point one might as well look upon him as a voice of conscience accusing one, for how hard it is to detect these sins in oneself.

The house is very crowded right now. A Japanese woman on the top floor. First she was with Kate and Caroline because we were cleaning up there. The controversy was bitter. She is a Buddhist and Kate Irish. Neither Christian in that they were unkind to each other. Kate the worst. They finally rioted last week over an open door, the Japanese woman wanting it closed. I had to help Jim move the latter back upstairs at 11:30 at night. Jim is an ever-present help.

Night before last there was a murder on the Bowery, one man crushing the skull of another with a cleaver. Jim got it out of his hand and held him down until the police came.

There was another murder last month. A man just out of Sing Sing caught up with by a gang and shot many times. John Cort was in on that, getting both the license numbers of the "murder car" and the priest for the dying man.

Sat Oct 1. Farm

St. Augustine's *City of God*. Quoting Horace:
"The liquor that new vessels first contains
Behind them leave a taste that long remains."

At first reading I thought of my early Communism, but since he said *new* vessels, I can look back on my early religious fervor which underlay my radicalism and finally saved me.

Monday Oct 3. Feast of the Little Flower

Today an epileptic on the line. Twice he had convulsions and twice we called the ambulance but they refused to take him.

Tamar and I to eight o'clock Mass and Communion. Breakfast at a little Chinese coffee shop.

A girl in, Jewish convert, who several times has tried to take her life, her home conditions are so hard. A rebellion against suffering. Little we can do.

Thoughts at Mass. During the day I get so tied up with such a multitude of things to do, and people to see and always that sense of being able to do so little, and that so badly. And after all the Mass is the most important work of the day. Praying for the work will make up all the lack. If I can just remember to do that well—as well as I am able, everything else will take care of itself.

The priests have to depend mostly on prayer and faith in the Sacraments. How can they give personal attention to the 10,000 or 15,000 people in their parishes, for instance. They have to do what they can—dispense the Sacraments and leave most of the work to God.

Tamar suffering with headaches and weeping over her homework because it is so hard and the teacher cranky. It is hard too; hard even for me to do.

Now it is 10:30. No Office said today. So I'll say the Office of the Dead for the Cardinal and Dan Russell.

# 1939

*Dorothy's diary skips from November 1938 to February 1939*

Feb 27. Monday[44]

They are having a mission at Transfiguration Church on Mott St. It began last night, a Jesuit, Fr. McGrath conducting it. He is very good, preaching in popular fashion yet dealing with profound ideas. Last night—the desire we all have for life, knowledge and love. Tonight, mortal sin.

---

44   See Dorothy's column, "Day after Day," March 1938.

The men from the Bowery were there, ragged, dirty, jobless, most of them. Longshore workers, teamsters, gandy dancers, sand hogs, restaurant workers, men who had led hard and dangerous lives. There were Irish, Italian, mostly, but other nationalities too. Poles, Croatians, Hungarians. There were young and old, men and women, single and married.

Tonight and last night I sat next to some of the Bowery men, living on relief in lodging houses or sleeping in doorways. They were as poor, as destitute, as "down and out" as man can get. And yet how close they are to our Lord!

"He was a man so much like other men that it took the kiss of a Judas to single him out," [François] Mauriac wrote.

He was like that man in the pew beside me. He was as like him as his brother. He was his brother. And I felt Christ in that man beside me and loved him.

Every morning I break my fast with the men in the breadline. Some of them speak to me. Many of them do not. But they know me and I know them. And there is a sense of comradeship there. We know each other in the breaking of bread.

It was good to see some of the men there at the Mission…

St. Teresa said she so loved to hear the Word of God preached, that she could listen with enjoyment to the poorest preacher. I know what she meant. Just as long as it is the word of God and not politics, finances, labor discussions. On the first Sunday in Lent our Italian priest [Fr. Fiorentino] spoke to us on "too much eatings, too much drinkings," and how we should work to make our souls strong. He was very simple and very good. And this mission priest is very good indeed. It is an exceptionally good mission and my heart is filled with gratitude that God has so blessed us this Lent.

He spoke tonight on free will and mortal sin. And I thought what a giant and enabling gift. I thanked God for giving us a "strong conflict." I thought too "how terrible a thing it was to fall into the hands of a living God." A "living God." That very phrase makes me realize Him as a living God…

I have a very bad habit of conversing with the preacher in my mind as I listen to him, and sometimes contradicting him.

Tonight, for instance, he told a story of sudden death to a person in mortal sin, and the hopelessness of the loved ones left behind.

And I thought suddenly of a young boy I knew who committed suicide. I asked a priest afterward as to the efficacy of praying for him. He said, "There is no time with God, and perhaps he foresees the prayers you will say and so gave him time to turn to Him at that last moment with love and longing and repentance." That has comforted me much. It makes me pray daily for Sacco and Vanzetti, for Alexander Berkman, for others who died to all intents and purposes estranged from God.[45]

And I thought tonight, as I listened, "The mothers in this congregation know that hope in the mercy of God. Some of them perhaps have sons who have met with sudden and violent deaths. There have been two murders that we know of on this street this past year. And there was that longshoreman crushed to death last month by a falling load of iron. There was our old janitor who died of gas poisoning last week. Their mothers, their loved ones know that God will hear their prayers. This strong hope, this boundless faith, no loving God can withstand."

I too clung to this assurance in my heart as I listened and as I prayed.

Today we had to send Mary O'Connor away to Bellevue. She had been with us since last April, almost a year. She wandered in from the streets, a poor unbalanced creature, pale and dirty and distraught. She wore a high wig, set on top of a dirty tangled mass of grey hair. Her arms and legs were like pipe stems, and her skin like parchment. She got better for a while. She had been living on 25¢ a day when she could get it for scrubbing. She used to go around the East Side, knocking on doors asking for work. She had been going hungry for some time when she came to us and finally she had been evicted from her skylight room. For a while regular meals and security helped her. But not for long.

For the last four months, she has been keeping us up nights chasing imaginary pursuers with a broom. She liked to start cleaning her room at two in the morning, running a carpet sweeper over the floor diligently. Lately she has taken to attacking people, stepping on their feet, kicking them, spitting at them, throwing a plate with very poor aim.

We took broom handle and scissors away from her. One night at one thirty I went upstairs ... *[left unfinished]*

Ember Wednesday, March 1
"The cares of my heart are multiplied; from my necessities deliver me, O Lord. Consider my lowliness and my burden and pardon all my sins." Ps 24

Meeting last night. I spoke: Ade, Harry, Fr. Nelson. Meeting not over till 12:30 really.

---

45   "There is no time with God": judging by the number of times Dorothy cited this statement over the years, it must be counted among the most important bits of spiritual counsel she ever received.

Best thought: Fr. Nelson on prayer. He was saying as he went out the door, being on one's knees not entirely necessary. Attitude of reverence from courtly days. Jews stood. When our Lord went into the desert or up on the mountain to pray, not necessarily always on his knees. One can walk with the Lord. I remember how I used to pray, walking on the beach. Tamar and I love to say the rosary while walking.

I do not have to retire to my room to pray. It is enough to get out and walk in the wilderness of the streets.

March 9, Thursday
*Memories of Lenin.* Krupskaya [*Lenin's widow*].
Most of the volume which I have just finished reading is about this struggle between philosophies. I finished the book last night. I had been in bed sick with headache all day which passes at nightfall. When I slept I dreamed of revolution and a poem, the last line of each stanza, "Be kind, Cain!"[46] It was almost in a tone of satire, directed at me. Helen had said I was too kind to the Communists in my book and the attitude taken by our opponents is that we do not realize what they are capable of. Indeed we do! Revolution, terror, mob-spirit makes murderers. But still, in spite of the poem, our stand has to be "Love your enemies, overcome evil with good."

Human touches in the book: her housekeeping efforts; her mother; cigarettes, religion; the sense of comradeship, not only between husband and wife, but mother; the love of nature, woods, mountains. Lenin missing train to pick mushrooms; time spent in study and libraries, loneliness, need of fiction, going to movies. Krupskaya helping with relief work in Switzerland.

Lessons for us. Study, constant study.

Palm Sunday, April 2, 1939
(Passion Sunday, Matins)
Jeremiah: "And I said: The Lord God, I cannot speak for I am a child. And the Lord said to me: say not: I am a child: for thou shalt go to all that I shall send thee, and whatsoever I shall command thee, thou shalt speak. Be not afraid at their presence: for I am with thee to deliver thee saith the Lord. And the Lord put forth his hand and touched my mouth. And the Lord said to me: Behold, I have given my words in thy mouth."

---

46   Dorothy remembered this dream thirty years later: "I remember having a nightmare [before] World War II in which, thinking of our pacifist position, I heard a voice saying 'Be kind, Cain,' as if such words could ward off the blow that was about to fall. I know what human fear is and how often it keeps us from following our conscience." ("Fear in Our Time," April 1968)

Tonight I have to speak at Labor Temple and I am so fatigued by a two weeks' speaking trip that I was miserable about it. The above words from the breviary are a comfort. I dislike speaking. It is only with the greatest effort that I speak. The idea depresses me for a day beforehand. I get physically sick from it. But it must be done.

John Ryder died March 31, his heart failing him. He'd been sick with asthma these last few years. He was a sea captain and had been with us since the strike. He helped on "the line" at first but working in a steamy, hot kitchen in a draft made him worse and he had to give it up. He took charge of the Catholic Union of Unemployed meetings on Monday afternoons, leading in the rosary, giving literature to the men.

Tues May 16
Met J[ohn Day] at restaurant. Home at 11:30. Telephone call, Pop ill.

Wed May 17
Pop died this morning 7:30.

Thurs.
Met mother at train.

Fri.
Funeral.[47]

Sat May 20
Mr. Breen died at 5:30 p.m.[48]

---

47   Dorothy and her father did not enjoy a close relationship. A newspaperman most of his life, John I. Day ended his days as an inspector for the New York State racing commission. (He asked to have his ashes scattered over the Hialeah track in Miami.) His attitude toward his elder daughter may be gauged from his remarks in a letter to a family friend: "Dorothy, the oldest girl, is the nut of the family. When she came out of the university she was a Communist. Now she's a Catholic crusader. She owns and runs a Catholic paper and skyhoots all over the country, delivering lectures. She has one girl in a Catholic school and is separated from her husband. You'll probably hear of her if you have any Catholic friends. She was in Miami last winter and lived out with Clem and Kate. I wouldn't have her around me." Cited in William D. Miller, *Dorothy Day: A Biography* (New York: Doubleday, 1982), p. 311.

48   "Mr. Breen is someone we will not soon forget.... [He] remained with us until he died. As the end drew near, we all sat around his bedside, taking turns saying the rosary. In his last moments, Mr. Breen looked up at us and said, 'I have only one possession left in the world—my cane. I want you to have it. Take it—take it and wrap it around the necks of some of these bastards around here.' Then he turned on a beatific smile. In his weak voice he whispered, 'God has been good to me.' And smiling, he died." *LF*, 38-39.

May 28. Pentecost.

Yesterday Cenacle. Fr. McSorley, "Love is rarest and highest of virtues…
The devil shows you worst of a man, the Holy Ghost the best." Went to confession. Long talk. Voluntary poverty of new archbishop.

I was thinking afterward how everyone dwells on our poverty. But we are
not nearly poor enough. Read Steinbeck's article on squatters in California. It
is not enough to present a picture of conditions. One must go there to share
that poverty. Then others will help. Immediate works of mercy shows what
can be done now, not waiting for the revolution or for the state. Strip oneself
here first. We are going to the bean fields this summer.

Some people are scapegoats. Thinking in St. Michael's church the other day.
They hear our sins. They are punished for our sins. They are always deceived.
Their most secret sins laid bare. How we should love them for their suffering!
How grateful we should be to them for their even unconscious bearing of sin
and remorse and shame. They endure, not understanding. I was thinking of
Michael.

Beach, Phillipsburg, July 8, 5:30

A broiling hot day. Came back last night after 24 hours in the city. We have
been a week in the country now. I returned from month's trip June 28.

Everything is very peaceful this year, aside from Bernard leaving, Roddy
disappearing last night, and Fr. losing money. But compared to last year, or
even any year so far things are far more settled. Last year Fr. Duffy and Joe
both made the place uncomfortable, also John Curran. Conflict often is grave,
means growth, clarification, but it is damn uncomfortable.

While I was in heard that Joe had been around drunk.

About others' sins. Drunkenness and all the sins which follow in its wake
are so obviously ugly and monstrous, and mean such unhappiness for the
poor sinner that it is all the more important that we do not judge or condemn. In the eyes of God the hidden subtle sins must be far worse. We must
make every effort of will to love more and more—to hang on to each other
with love. They should serve to show us the hideousness of our own sins so
that we truly repent and abhor them.

July 30. Sunday. 11 a.m.

Have been working all month at proofs of the new book and a last chapter
[*House of Hospitality*]. Articles for the paper (Ben Joe Labray)[49] and letters.

---

49   For some years the CW ran a column under the byline "Ben Joe Labray"—actually written by Dorothy and other members of the staff. It described the adventures of a character like

Article "Tale of Two Capitals" printed in the *Commonweal*.[50] Spent month between Easton, Staten Island, and New York. Also F[orster] is transferring hut in Princess Bay to Tamar and we are going to build a camp there for children next year. If I can do it this fall I will.

All this month Fr. Woods and Fr. Palmer at the farm and next month a retreat Aug 26-29. The place will be blessed.

Aug 28. Feast of St. Augustine. 9 a.m.

So far everything has gone beautifully. Conferences on Compassion, exam of conscience, contrition, Faith, Hope, the Mass. All keeping silence. Seventy-two here today from 14 groups. All our prayers for peace.

Sunday Sept 24

Mass at 7:30. A perfect morning, misty, but warm. Easy to get up. I sat up late reading a detective story. Rather depressed at first what with dirty house, children, Mrs. B, and general effusiveness. But meditated on "living with God." We are not living with Mellas or Buleys but with God. Most adorable, true, beautiful, lovable, and our place is in Heaven, of refreshment light and peace. Here our life is but "a night spent in an uncomfortable inn," as St. Teresa says. Even so we have Him with us, my companion, friend, Lover—more my master. What are hardships endured for Him? Where he wants me to be, there I must be happy.

The poor. To love to be with the poor is of course hard. There are not all poor among us, and only one poor family. Of course dirt, inefficiency, dullness, lack of taste, beauty, culture—all these are a part of poverty. Are they poor because of this lack in them, or do these characteristics grow out of their poverty? Who can say? It will be hard to change them because we are poor now ourselves. Are we letting it get us? Are there those amongst us who are becoming dull, dirty, lethargic, listless, indolent, slothful?

October 21 Saturday

A warm bright day at the farm. The trees are still in all their glory. This afternoon the children were going with John up the hill in the hay wagon and Nancy's head of curls was like a flame. I thought, seeing how her hair matched some of the tees, of the blind man whom Christ healed who said, "I see men, like trees walking."

St. Benedict Joseph Labre (d. 1783), a poor, holy man who was often given "the bum's rush."
50 "A Tale of Two Capitals," *Commonweal,* July 14, 1959. Reprinted in Patrick Jordan, ed., *Dorothy Day: Writings from Commonweal* (Collegeville, MN: Liturgical, 2002), 67-73. She describes the Catholic Worker houses in Washington, D.C. and Harrisburg, Penn.

The children are sweet but wild. There is not much discipline in the family, and they are much retarded. The two youngest look very badly nourished, though Nancy, the oldest, is a big strong girl, big for her years. Billy, four, is toothless in front and his new teeth have not yet grown in. Pretty early to have lost teeth. Raymond had his hair cut today and looks a thousand times better. His face beamed and he kept looking at himself in the mirror, pleased and surprised. They need good food and plenty of milk and it makes you heartsick to see them being stinted.

Mrs. Buley said today, "I don't let Nancy sit down because she criticizes how much her father eats. She is always checking up on him." I made them sit down with us instead of making them wait to eat the leftovers. Also they are given tea instead of milk, and their father, a huge fellow sits with a big bowl of bread and milk to top off with. I'm going to make them sit at the table with the others, at least while I am here to check up on it. Of course when a man is working out of doors on the WPA he has an appetite, but Nancy is huge and like him and I can see how there would be trouble. But how heartbreaking it is when a mother has never enough food to go around! She is a little withered thing but full of energy, and always stinting herself so that others can have more.

The children are very imitative. When Tamar and I blessed ourselves, Nancy carefully followed suit, and the Professor looked at her with astonishment. They need care, and love and good food, and they will be brighter. But they do need to be taught to work. Unfortunately, school is so far, and they are gone from dawn to dark, so there is only Saturday. If I could just get out Saturdays with some energy so that we could have a regime of housecleaning that day. Here is this girl coming from Wisconsin to help in the work. If she would only come out and help Mrs. Buley and try to train her in working more slowly and efficiently. Of course that is much to ask, but our work is made up of all the little things having to do with daily life.

Nov 24. Friday. Day after Thanksgiving.

In a few days Advent starts. To us who use our missals every day it is the beginning of the new year. It always makes me happy—beginnings—the opportunity constantly to make fresh starts. One resolution: to write daily. So many things happen, so many people, so many places. For instance, I do not want to forget our landlord in Burlington (House of Hospitality in Burlington), a Mohammedan, who prays five times daily and since there is no mosque prays in his own heart. When he fasts, he fasts from 4 a.m. to 6 in the evening, if I am not mistaken, every day for thirty days—a period corresponding to our Lent...

Finished *In the Footsteps of St. Francis*. Reading *In the Footsteps of St. Paul* and *Public Life of Our Lord*. New Testament. Last night read *Crime and Punishment*. Reflected on past life, seeking satisfaction in material pleasures, sense of sin also.

Days are taken up with troubles of others. The need to be withdrawn and at the same time unselfish. Strengthening of the will.

December 4. Biscayne Bay. 3 p.m.

Arose at nine, wrote letters. Call from Della and K. Mella. Left at 11:30 for the boat to meet Kate. It anchors above Second Ave. bridge at a beautiful cocoanut grove. The boat is a ferry, like a raft with a cabin on it.

The ferry comes over Tuesdays and Thursdays, and the first and third Saturdays and Sundays. It takes an hour to get over to the island—a beautiful sail. There are two harbors—Hacienda and Hurricane Harbors—and we entered the former, which was lined with palms like a park. The island is seven miles long and a mile wide, so a station wagon took us and our bundles to the ocean side, where Kate and Clem [*cousins on her father's side*] live.

Last night I read in the *Imitation* the chapter on idle conversations in the First Book aloud to Tamar and myself, taking it much to heart. We had been down to Jesu church in the afternoon and made the stations. Mother is much better, so I am at ease about her. As to myself, I believe it is my own shortcomings rather than ill health or low blood pressure which keeps me in a listless and exhausted state. A vigorous effort this coming year will result in benefit to myself and the whole movement. Then I shall more easily be able to stand the work. Of course, this rest, this breathing spell, is good, and I shall take full advantage of it.

The year has been hard. Many speaking engagements, visits to Milwaukee, Chicago, twice to St. Louis, Springfield, Ramsey, Toledo, Cleveland, Akron, Canton, Detroit, Pittsburgh, Buffalo, Rochester, Washington, Baltimore, Virginia, Philadelphia. Burlington, Worcester, Boston, Providence, Harrisburg—all these houses and groups; the finishing up of *House of Hospitality*; at least a thousand letters and hundreds of speaking engagements; sicknesses and deaths in the house; the death of my father; the day by day work at Mott Street, the farm; what care I can give a thirteen-year-old child; all these occupations and works have indeed worn me down so that it is good to rest quietly and read and write and meditate for a month. I shall do letters and keep this notebook, but aside from that, try to keep myself quiet.

Coffee now with Kate—then the beach....

December 5

Up at eight. We had awakened for the sunrise, Tamar and I, but went back
to sleep again. A perfectly calm day, no breeze, so I do not see how Pat can get
over for me in his sailboat. Sun and sea and palm trees. The only sound is the
pump for the water supply and the little chicks and the occasional announcement of a hen who has laid an egg. Kate puts a teaspoonful of black molasses
in the water (1 quart) for the new chicks to counterbalance the change of diet
and scene. The air is full of little midges which sting.

Little Office. *Imitation.*

December 6

Again to bed early last night at 9:30. A wonderful place to sleep and rest.
So still—the only sounds those of airplanes going in and out of the airport at
Cocoanut Grove, five and a half miles across the bay. No birds here, strangely
enough, except down in the zoo, where canaries, doves and parrots are kept.
Also about five monkeys and two alligators and a goat. Tamar and I went for
a walk through the little Negro village. There are twenty-five Negroes on the
island and about fifteen whites.

December 11, Monday. Miami

Sunny hot day. Yesterday it was cloudy and an occasional shower. At sunset
I walked down to the trail. Philharmonic concert yesterday—Mozart 41 in
C, and Beethoven's Fifth. Saturday, "Boris Goudonoff," but it made Mother
nervous, so at the end of the second act I went downtown and got a Kathleen Norris at Sardine's circulating library, which Aunt Jenny is enjoying im-
mensely. I am going to start *Gone with the Wind.*

I am doing a few letters a day. Just knitting, reading, meals and rest.

Wednesday, December 13. The Island

Came back yesterday going downtown early to buy Tamar a skirt and to get
Kate some stuff at the Five and Ten. Boat left at 12:30—a lovely ride. And I
was thinking as I came over, how little we appreciate the beauties under our
noses. The ferry ride to Staten Island is a lovely one, any season, and that walk
along the river park. I shall enjoy them the more when I go back.

On the Feast of the Immaculate Conception I got up at seven and before
the others were up, went downtown to Jesu church. I was there by 7:30 and
made the stations and went to confession and Mass at 8. The church was
crowded. At nine, over to the dock to meet Tamar, and back again to the
ten o'clock Mass. We were early enough to read the Office. Then home to
lunch and back to the boat by 2, and Tamar came back alone. While home,

P prepared the meals and did dishes, so that Aunt Jenny could rest. She went shopping Saturday and Monday.

### Sunday, December 17

Symphony No. 5 in C-Minor—Mahler. Mother and Aunt Jane are sitting on the porch, Tamar reading one of the Montgomery books, and I have just finished the dishes and reading *The Imitation*. Aunty Jenny cooked the chicken dinner, and Tamar and I have been doing the rest of the kitchen work. Last night, to confession, and this morning, to 8 o'clock Mass. We were home to breakfast by 9:15. The weather is lovely and warm—too warm for walking. Kate, Clem, Allen, Tamar and I came over yesterday afternoon. It was the anniversary of Fred Brown's death, and I read the Office of the Dead for him.

### Christmas Day—3 p.m.

Last night Tamar, Aunt Jenny and I went to Midnight Mass. It was Tamar's first, and she had a hard time staying awake. We left at 11:30, and drove with Mary Bee and her husband, Tom Hallgan, over to see the new church of St. Peter and Paul, a church with the walls up, but only a roof of steel girders and the sky, flowered with stars and bright with a full moon directly overhead, just about us. Soft breezes stirred the pines with which the sanctuary was lined, and the altar was blazing with scarlet poinsettia flowers. Planks were laid out, a foot above the plank floor, for benches, and although the church was crowded when we got there, we got seated in the second row.

Before the Mass there were Christmas carols, and promptly at the stroke of twelve the Mass began. It was the most beautiful Christmas Mass I have ever assisted at. Tamar was not at all sleepy, nor was I. It was beautiful to receive Communion out there under the sky. We stopped at Mary Bee's for a little refreshment, and then to bed by 2. This morning we were up by 10, and had a happy Christmas, opening Tamar's Christmas packages.

### Dec 26

Bus for Mobile, left at 2:30. Crowded but not hot. Beautiful thru Everglades. Two flats. 2 hrs late. No lunch stops. Changed at Tallahassee. Cloudburst. Changed at Marianna 7:00. In Mobile by noon since this is Central time. Met friend of Peter's on bus. Arrived Dec 27. Saw Bishop Tonlin. Slept. Bed nine.

### Dec 29

There is much to be thankful for this past year.

The growth of the C.U.U. [Catholic Union of Unemployed]

The retreat on the farm.
Publication of *H. of H.* [*House of Hospitality*]
Reorganization of business office.
Growth of groups and houses.
Much too of hardships and sadness in the past year.

Resolution this year. To pay no attention to health of body but only that of soul. To plan day on arising and evening examination of conscience. More spiritual reading. (Like *In Footsteps of St. Francis.*) More letters to groups. To waste no time. More conscientious about letters, visits, about these records. More charity.

For God: "Can you not watch one hour with me?"
For neighbor: "Little children, love one another."

# PART II

# THE FORTIES

Dorothy's diaries for the 1940s are relatively sparse, in several years falling virtually silent (most likely lost). By this time she usually carried a spiral notebook for jotting down thoughts as they occurred to her. In addition, she sometimes used a daily pocket diary that allowed room every day for a sentence or two (or more in her miniscule script).

For Dorothy and the CW, these years of war, marked by enormous suffering and drama on the global stage, were a time of relative quiet and introspection. Many CW houses closed. The paper's circulation dropped by half. There were enough Catholic conscientious objectors to fill one labor camp in New Hampshire—supported (just barely) by the Catholic Worker. A few men were imprisoned for draft resistance. But despite the paper's pacifist line—on which Dorothy was firm—many CW members served overseas in the military.

As usual, Dorothy traveled widely. But it was the interior journey that largely occupied her. In 1939 she attended her first retreat with Fr. Pacifique Roy, a French Canadian Josephite priest, and experienced what she called "a foretaste of heaven." He in turn led her to Fr. John Hugo of Pittsburgh, who became one of her principal spiritual advisors. His retreats permanently enlarged her spiritual outlook, convincing her that holiness is the ordinary vocation of all Christians—a steady process of "putting off the old man and putting on Christ."

During this time Dorothy briefly contemplated leaving the movement, perhaps embracing some anonymous life as a hospital orderly. "The world is too much with me in the Catholic Worker," she wrote during a retreat. "The world is suffering and dying. I am not suffering and dying in the CW, I am writing and talking about it." She announced plans to take a year's leave of absence but returned after six months. She had clarified her vocation to community life and her place in the Catholic Worker. She would never again be tempted to leave.

In 1944 her daughter Tamar, age 18, married David Hennessy. With this Dorothy assumed a new role as mother-in-law, and soon grandmother to Tamar's growing family (nine children, eventually). Henceforth a good deal of her time *over the years would be spent with the Hennessy family in their various, mostly rural, homesteads.*

*Dorothy welcomed the end of the war, but recognized in the dropping of the atomic bomb the beginning of a terrible era of fear, one that would pose new challenges for the Christian conscience. Fortunately, the end of the war also brought a new wave of dedicated workers. Some, like Robert Ludlow, had spent time in c.o. camps, while others, like Jack English and Tom Sullivan, had served in the military overseas. In either case, they brought a fresh vision, confident leadership, and a Catholic zeal to match Dorothy's own.*

*But this fresh start was accompanied by loss. For some years Peter Maurin had been a more or less passive member of the community. Following a stroke, and finding himself "no longer able to think," he had largely fallen silent. His death in 1949 marked the end of an era.*

*Significantly, it was in these years that Dorothy settled on a new name for her column: "On Pilgrimage." There was a literal basis to this, as her column often described her far-reaching comings and goings. But it also represented a spiritual attitude, reflected in the words of St. Catherine of Siena, which she liked to quote: "All the way to Heaven is Heaven, because He said 'I am the Way.'"*

# 1940

Jan 2. The Holy Family

For each family that is with us, and each family we come in contact with, let us pray, keeping in mind the Holy Family which dwelt in peace and poverty and love and joy. Sometimes it is hard to see Christ in his poor. Sometimes it is hard to see the Blessed Mother in women we come in contact with. But if we minister to each other, as we would want to serve the Holy Family, not judging the faults of others, but serving them with joy and with respect, then that is the true way of seeing Christ in our neighbor. If He thought them worth dying for, who are we to judge?

I remember one family on the west side, a longshoreman who got only a day or so on the docks every few weeks. He drank, his wife drank, and their children were growing up disorderly and dishonest. No one would help them. They sold the clothes they were given for liquor. The relief people said the man had work and didn't report it to them. Consequently often the family went hungry. We spent all one winter giving food and clothing to this family. It was indeed hard to see Christ in these poor. Yet for no other reason could we help them. Without the religious motive, it was a waste of time. With this motive, not one crumb of our help was wasted. Provided we did it with love. And of course if you help people, you soon begin to love them. Just as gratitude makes you love people.

Jan 2

At 7 to Mass, served beautifully by a young seminarian who made one feel the beauty and the dignity and drama of the Mass.

Jan 17—Baltimore[51]

Omissions. Need to emphasize our fellowship in the work. I should have liked to gather together the group in the [CW] house on S. Paca St, 25 of them and talk to them about what the whole work is, their part in it; that they are truly playing a part in it though perhaps they do not see it. The men who cook, wash dishes, scrub, clean, launder, ministering to others, are part of a movement. To try to convey to them the glimpse of the "whole." They see only part. We all see thru a glass darkly. Some see more clearly than others. Our joy in the work increases with our vision of the whole. Just as when a man uses his whole body he is in better health. Not just head or hand. Workers must be scholars and scholars workers, as Peter says.

Heaven is when we see God face to face, when we shall see Him as He is. Now it is only a glimpse, a suggestion of light, of joy, of unity, of completion...

Reading the Little Office on the train. Strange how repetition, faithfulness in reading the same Little Office each day, instead of becoming stale with repetition, becomes ever fresher. Verses stand out, a light glows on what was obscure and hidden. There is an increase of understanding.

It is very cold tonight. Writing on the train between Baltimore and Philadelphia there is a cold wind sweeping thru the car. Outside the snow is falling. I wonder how they are keeping warm in the other houses—up in Burlington for instance. There was already snow in the mountains when I was up there in November. Donald and Norman Langlois, one feels, are always ready for any hardship, and no amount of cold can dampen their ardent spirits.

I recall, on a night like this, the story of a saint who was so filled with a burning love of God that he melted the snow around him, and others were warmed by the flame of his love. A model for all our fellow workers, these winter days.

---

51   See "Day After Day," February 1940.

Jan 18.

Paid a call on Joe Curran up at the National Maritime Union headquarters on Eleventh Ave. today bringing with me Prof. Downing from Fordham University who teaches history (and labor history at the Labor School). He had spoken at our Tuesday night forum a few days before.

He was much impressed at the growth of the union.

It would be a good thing if all those who taught in our Catholic Labor Schools or in our colleges in the depts. of sociology and economics, in N.Y. (priests and laymen) would visit this union hall to see what organization can mean.

Feb 24

The first few days in Portland were days of suffering of mind and body. Fatigue, nervous indigestion, sleeplessness, worry over Jim and Grace, and Fr. Reinhold's desire for his $16,000 house—these things had me down and nervous to the extreme. There was a reaction too, to the stimulation of the Seattle group. I enjoyed every moment of my visit, and here in Portland there is no young crowd but two or three older women who have many obligations.

We must constantly return to a sense of the necessity of keeping our own integrity. We are each one us alone, and can only try to change ourselves first of all. How far we are going to reach others and effect others is something we cannot know. To have faith in others to the extent of always seeing them as creatures of body and soul.

Spoke at 11 to the Holy Name nuns.

Monday Feb 25[52]

Yesterday Mass at 8. Then to the Good Shepherds to speak to the girls, a gay, simple responsive group. We drove past Sullivan's Gulch on the way back, a deep rut, flooded right now, where little shacks and gardens struggle up and down, most of them in water now, inhabited as we could see from the wisps of smoke which came from the dizzy looking chimneys. Fr. McDermot says that it is part of his parish and he goes down there to visit the sick.

The afternoon I spent in bed, resting, not even reading. But I heard "The Catholic Hour" and enjoyed Msgr. [Fulton] Sheen's talk on the Blessed Mother.

Last night I spoke at a little Methodist church on Mt. Tabor. Probably I was the first Catholic to ever speak there, and I spoke simply on the love of God and the love of one's neighbor, as the dominant force in the work of rebuilding the social order.

---

52   See "CW Editor on West Coast," May 1940.

I told of the little Methodist churches I had seen in the South in the share-cropper district, and in one of them the windows were broken by mobs try-ing to prevent the organizing of the workers, and in the other were evicted sharecroppers living in every corner.

Some of the people left the church when I began to speak. The young people were laughing and talking among themselves, and it was difficult.

Today it is raining steadily, more than just Oregon mist. But on the way down to the shelter I saw daffodils, crocus, hepatica, heather, all in bloom, and the grass and some of the shrubs are green. It is truly spring here with buds coming on the rose bushes and other shrubs and trees that do not stay green all winter. Fruit trees also are beginning to bloom.

### Thurs. Feb 29

To Mt. Angel Benedictine College and Seminary. Monastery burned 1926. By the light of fire the monks sang their office. They had managed to save choir books, little else. Spoke to students.

In the evening to St. Vincent's Hospital, Providence nuns. Afterward to "Grapes of Wrath."

### Monday, March 4

All day yesterday on the bus from Portland and Spokane, and a terrifying and awe-inspiring trip through the mountains and along the Columbia River highway, then through waste lands, and vast wheat country which made me realize more than ever the industrial, factory system of farming. Arrived at eight and meeting with a priest from Pullman where Washington State Col-lege is situated, dinner and conversation with the Sisters, and so to bed. Today a meeting with Bishop White, a luncheon with the social workers of the city, a meeting at Marycliff at two, with the sisters at the parochial schools at four-thirty, a priest from Belgium, and dinner with Mrs. Nelson, a friend of the sisters.

Mrs. Nelson has left her husband and wishes to enter a convent.

### March 5

It has been a fearful winter. Even nature itself travaileth and groaneth since the fall. Seeming to reflect man's perversity. War in Finland, war in Eastern Europe, war in China and Japan.

And down in Shenandoah, Pennsylvania, half a town sinking, buildings cracking, schools closed, homes evacuated, due to the sinking of the center of the town into the old anthracite diggings that honeycomb the mountain be-neath the town. The same condition of danger exists in many another of the

Pennsylvania towns, Scranton especially, where there are fissures and houses and roads sinking. Again the greed of man, in ravishing the treasures of the earth. The mining companies did not see to it that safety props were left in the mines, they explained to us once in Scranton. The fault is laid at the door of the owners of the vast mines which underlay Pennsylvania.

Friday Mar 15. Feast of Seven Sorrows
    On train for San Francisco from Portland.
    Up at six and Catherine and I paid a visit to the Sisters at the Precious Blood Monastery after Mass. Bertha called for us and took us to the train.
    Bertha says I am gruff and indifferent to people (she means when I come off the platform or am meeting a mass of them at a time.) She rightly points out we are trying to change people's attitudes, to create understanding, to combat class war. So I must learn to be more cordial to people and overcome that immense sense of weariness and even impatience when people, quite sincerely, tell me how they enjoy my books, how interested they are in my work. Miss Jordan told me I look at people as tho they were going to steal 5 minutes of my time! It makes me unhappy to give such an impression, I feel as tho I had failed people again and again, not only on trips, but at Mott St. I must do better, guard myself rigidly, control my fatigue, not mention it. But oh, it is so hard, I'll just have to work every day at it.
    These hours on trains or bus are so precious—to be alone for a short while, it is a complete relaxation, a joy. I am a weak and faulty vessel to be freighted with so valuable a message as cargo. I am an unprofitable servant and must begin over again right now to change myself. God help me.

Palm Sunday, March 17. San Francisco
    Today woke up with bad headache so slept until 10:30. Salesian high Mass, the gospel sung. Stayed in church until twelve with much joy. A beautiful spring day, sunny and warm.
    The smells of spring, the sound of birds, the grounds around the seminary were beautiful. We heard Vespers, kneeling behind a grill directly over the altar. The Sisters came in at the sides. But ours was a position of vantage and I was overwhelmed at being right over the altar, the Blessed Sacrament out of my sight but so near, and the strong sound of Gregorian rising in waves of adoration and praise, which seemed to fling themselves joyfully against the altar.
    We got in Oakland at 7 and I was able to offer up Mass at 8 at St. Boniface. Fr. Paul away so a quiet day. Hair done, bought blouse, slept, went to confes-

sion and to newsreel theater to see Finland at peace and March of Time. Read *Anna Karenina* and bed at eleven.

Account of my speech before Portland longshoremen in *Voice of Federation* this week.

## Monday, March 18

Mass at 8:00. Talked to Fr. Paul until 11:30. He told me of [Harry] Bridges[53] coming to him to get straightened out so he can receive the Sacraments. He came twice and again with wife, sister-in-law, and daughter. I had just prayed so hard at Mass for him, that this news was overwhelming and yet no surprise. Certainly prayer can accomplish all things. God has touched his heart and his will being good the result is inevitable. Now to redouble prayers! I will offer the Little Office too every day I am here.

Father has been at death's door and lost his leg. He has been thru frightful suffering. But he goes on with his work.

## March 29, San Francisco

The union man reads the paper because it deals with things that concern him, poverty, unemployment, war, injustice in industry.

In traveling, I find the workers know the paper, like the paper. But they like to emphasize our work for the "dispossessed" and feel themselves apart, sure in their power. In time of trouble they are most anxious and grateful for our help, but when there is no crisis, they are condescending. We are missionaries. They are confident that we are not going to enter into factional fights or use the word "Catholic" to swing votes. That in itself is a victory. But they are afraid of us too, because we extend the spiritual.

They still think, as they have always thought, that church and schools, church and state, church and unions cannot be mixed. In other words, they distrust Catholics because of the aims of Catholics. It is not because of a lack of recognition of the need to correlate the material and the spiritual. But because they fear the Catholic as a pressure group.

## April 1, Salinas

On the drive down from S.F. Mrs. [Carey] McWilliams told me of the early Salinas strike. They were organized Filipino and American in an AF of L union, had good conditions but the grocers, packers, and shippers were determined to break the union, not to renew the contract when it expired. A

---

53  Harry Bridges, a naturalized citizen from Australia, was the militant leader of the longshoreman's union. The U.S. government tried unsuccessfully to have him deported on the charge that he was a Communist, but they could never prove their case.

violent strike started, scabs imported, tents put up for thousands of workers within riot fences, which surround the scabs' sheds. They still remain. I saw them this afternoon as a threat, a reminder, a preparation.

Vigilantes were formed, citizens committees, everyone was deputized. People were afraid, not of the thousands of agricultural workers but that Harry Bridges—his longshoremen were going to come one hundred miles down the valley and take over the fields and the town.

They organized all shopkeepers not to sell to those thousands living in camps around the town. They would starve them out. Even a little tobacconist, when they tried to enlist him and failed, was assaulted. A tear gas bomb lodged in his arm. No doctor or nurse could be procured. Mrs. McWilliams had to dig it out herself. She told of treating the workers' eyes with a solution of paregoric—water on compresses to ease their pain after tear gas attacks. An old woman was in the line of fire and was injured. Ax handles were brought in and the boys in the manual training school given the job of weighting them with iron to use as weapons. Mrs. McWilliams took this matter to the governor.

It was a time of terror for three weeks. Then an agreement was signed for the Americans, not for the Filipinos. They were left out on a limb. Another strike occurred a few years later and then the union was smashed completely.

Dear Fellow workers at Pittsburgh:

This is to repeat again some of the things I talked to you about.

Urging you to build up a feeling of fellowship among yourselves, to try each one of you to be what you would have the other fellow be, to help each other and to love each other, because Christ loves each one of you.

Living as we are in a time of emergency, thrown together in a companionship with others of different races and creeds, let us try to think of ourselves as a community, in thirty-three houses of unemployed.

Let us live in peace, and then we are a little oasis of peace in a war-torn world. Let us have no bitterness, no class strife, so that we can build up our strength to work for justice and love. Let us pray together, no matter what our faith is, for each other and for the whole world. Pray for the unemployed, for steelworkers, for auto workers, rubber workers, textile workers, stockyard workers, lumber workers, maritime workers, migratory workers in the fields, cannery workers—for all the workers in our own country.

God uses the simple and ignorant and powerless ones in this world such as we are to confound the wise.

June 4

Paper went to press yesterday, a peace edition.[54] A headache this morning, but it disappeared later. But I stayed in bed just the same, the first time I have had a chance since coming home.

Read *The Labyrinthine Ways* [also known as *The Power and the Glory*] by Graham Greene, one of the best books I've come across for a long time. It cuts like a knife into any complacency. I wept while I was reading it. A tremendous book, better than *The Diary of a Country Priest* [by Georges Bernanos], more human, and yet closer to God.

Met Fr. Ward at the printers yesterday, a venomous, sour character. He accused us of cheating the government in getting our second class mailing permit. He also has accused me to our friends of not living here in the house, but in a private apartment. We were reserved with each other and I pretended not to notice his accusation in regard to the P.O. I resolved not to repeat it to the others and did not—a small victory. If I could only control my tongue.

Terrible times this week. The battle of the withdrawal from Flanders, Paris bombed. If one could realize it at all one would go mad.

June 17. Monday

4:30 p.m. Most irregular hours. Got in from Altoona at 3 a.m. after speaking engagement. A priest from Australia and three seminarians at the farm on their way to Vancouver to sail on July 10. All from Rome and home on account of the war.

All these seminarians love the work so much, they see the dream of a Christian life in the world. It is the field in which they wish to work.

I am so tired I can't write except bare facts. Mass at seven but I had broken my fast at the bus station at three before I knew the priest was here. We talked until 12 when the boys left. Then I slept until 4. One feels weaker after sleep then before.

Tamar and Helen and I came down Friday; Tamar's school was out Thursday.

Sunday June 9 she graduated. The day before we went over to see mother at Garden City. She was sick.

---

54   In this "peace edition" of June 1940 Dorothy renewed the pacifist position of the CW in relation to the war in Europe: "Many of our readers ask, 'What is the stand of the CATHOLIC WORKER in regard to the present war?' They are thinking as they ask the question, of course, of the stand we took during the Spanish Civil War. We repeat that, as in the Ethiopian war, the Spanish war, the Japanese and Chinese war, the Russian-Finnish war—so in the present war we stand unalterably opposed to war as a means of saving 'Christianity,' 'civilization,' 'democracy.' We do not believe that they can be saved by these means." ("Our Stand," June 1940)

I was thinking this morning about our neighbors' attitudes toward us, their respect for the ideas of the paper. I do not think however that they have respect for us personally for trying to live these ideals. They respect our "success"—that we keep going, and probably suspect we have backing or rich friends. They respect us because "important" people come to see us. But if we should be suppressed, and could not pay our bills, they would be just as contemptuous, or rather much more contemptuous than they are to the poor around us. They would despise us for our failure.

We have yet to learn what voluntary poverty really means.

### Sat. July 6. Princess Bay [Staten Island]

Our first night on the beach. Fortunately too cold for mosquitoes. Not enough blankets. An hour ago I woke up cold and desolate. Now I am sitting in the camp with hot coffee and black bread, all alone, the birds singing all around, the sun just coming up warm, and I am appreciating to the full my peace and solitude and happy it will not be disturbed for some time. Hours alone, especially in such beauty, are precious.

Eve and I came down yesterday, bringing Mrs. Sheed and Alma Savage to see the beginnings of the camp and farm. We stayed up late at Sharrott Rd. until eleven, and it took me hours to get to sleep. I miss Tamar terribly, unhappily at night, but in the day not sadly. My nights are always in sadness and desolation and it seems as tho as soon as I lie down I am on a rack of bitterness and pain. Then in the day I am again strong enough to make an act of faith and love and go on in peace and joy.

### Monday July 22

Last Monday I spoke at Baroness [Catherine] de Hueck's[55] [Friendship House] and tonight at Fr. Ford's.

After being down in Washington last week to testify before the Senate Com. against conscription bill[56] (three very good days) I got home to face the situation of Bill. He left last week and is staying at his sister's. Now there is the [Easton] farm to settle.

---

55   The Baroness Catherine de Hueck was a Russian émigrée who established a community in Toronto, and later in Harlem (Friendship House), along similar lines as the Catholic Worker, except, as Dorothy noted, "Their place is much cleaner and quieter."

56   With Joe Zarrella Dorothy traveled to Washington to testify in hearings before the Military Affairs Committee of Congress, which was discussing the adoption of the Compulsory Military Training Law. She noted that the proposed law made no provision for Catholic conscientious objectors and warned that if an unjust law were passed she would consider it her duty to resist it.

Tuesday July 23. 11 p.m.

Today the telephone was turned off. Gas and electric next. No Mass, ankle an excuse. It does get very badly swollen at night and pains. Visitors all morning—lunch with John. Visit at St. Francis. Work on paper. Frank in filled with grievances against Joe and me. I am so often shocked at the positive venom in the majority around me against me and Joe [Zarrella]. He is called a young punk, a stooge, a yes man, and God knows what else. I probably don't hear the worst.

Victor says the conflict comes over the spiritual program. But the charges are mismanagement of funds, self-glorification, God knows why the whole thing does not fall apart. The only indication (for me) of the will of God can come thru the Archbishop. Fr. Joachim is on my side, also Fr. McSorley, but they can be assured of not knowing the facts. God permits it for my sins of course.

July 24

To be hated and scorned by one's very own—this is poverty. This is perfect joy.[57]

The man of the family, out of work thru no fault of his own, scorned, heaped with recriminations by wife, children. This happens daily. It is part of the world's sorrow. Again due to their hard hearts, more than to poverty.

F. O'D. to breakfast last night. Only an hour in church saved me from much anguish. I worry about not having true poverty. Then a scene occurs with recriminations because we are broke, accusing me of bad management, bad judgment, and I realize how the father of a family feels. So I could rejoice in suffering poverty.

Wrote editorial and conscription article. Read "This then is perfect joy" for lunch.

Maryfarm, Aug 27, Wednesday

Cold and steady rain since Sunday. Temperature lowest in 70 years. 50° Sunday. I am sitting down in the cabin with Tamar, and we are wearing wool dresses and have an oil stove lit. Outside it is windless but every now and then it starts drizzling again.

---

57  In *The Little Flowers of St. Francis* there is an account of how St. Francis once asked his friars to tell him the meaning of "perfect joy." After dismissing in turn their various suggestions, Francis described a hypothetical instance of unmerited abuse and humiliation at the hands of their own brethren. "This then is perfect joy," he observed. Life at the Catholic Worker often brought this story to mind.

Father Woods left Sunday and the retreat begins on Friday night. If this weather keeps up it will be terrible. Tamar and I are snug enough down in the little cabin and there is privacy and peace down there.

It always makes me feel selfish but I must confess my weakness that I cannot do without. Always when I come down to the farm there are so many problems, so much unrest which seems to center around me since everyone wishes me to settle something, that I need some time alone for prayer and reading so that I can attain some proper perspective and peace of spirit to deal with myself and others. I need to overcome a sense of my own impotence, my own failure, and an impatience at others that goes with it. I must remember not to judge myself, as St. Paul says. Such a sense of defeat comes from expecting too much of one's self, also from a sense of pride. More and more I realize how good God is to me to send me discouragements, failures, antagonisms.

The only way to proceed is to remember that God's ways are not our ways. To bear our own burdens, do our own work as best we can, and not fret because we cannot do more or do another's work. To be in that state of mind is to get nothing done.

P.m. Tamar and I went downtown; saw Shirley Temple, walked almost home. Reading *War and Peace*.

## Sept 26. Newport

Left at eight this a.m. It was Ade [Bethune's] day at Portsmouth Priory so I went directly to Ade's new house, where I slept in a delightful little attic room.[58] Had supper here at the studio and now we are all working for a bit before bedtime. It is delightful out, cold for the first time and clear. Yesterday it poured all day. Very warm for week past. Missed Mass this morning in getting Tamar off. Headache besides, still with me.

## Sept 27[59]

Mass at the Cenacle at 7:15 and back to the house for a few hrs. reading. John Cort and Fr. Joseph [Woods] came over to the studio from the Priory. John is staying there this term finishing a labor novel. We had a good morning discussing the war, conscription, labor unions, and meanwhile cutting up rags for rugs. After all, now that the [conscription] act is passed it is easier not to be heated. We would not be in any case but it is hard not to be impatient

---

58   Ade Bethune ran an arts and crafts school in Newport, Rhode Island. Dorothy sent her daughter Tamar there to study for much of 1942-1943.
59   See "Short Trip to Nearby CW Groups," October 1940.

or at least not to be over-vigorous and even exhausting in opposing others in what we consider false and harmful convictions.

Ade has a very good library. There is a good selection of music so that classes this year include folk dancing. Once a week a professor from Portsmouth Priory teaches metaphysics.

Here, surrounding Ade is one of the most interesting cells of the CW. And it is closely attached to Portsmouth Priory (our Fr. Joseph is there who spends his summers at Maryfarm at Easton). So the ideal of the Benedictines of work and prayer prevail.

This group too has close contact with other CW groups. Ade travels a good deal (in spite of her teaching one day a week at the Priory) so she has been able to decorate many of the CW houses.

Although the works of mercy are performed individually by the persons making up the group—there is no bread line or hospice—the emphasis is placed on the craft school idea. Since the finances are not exhausted by spending everything for food, there is some money for paint and everything presents a scrubbed and painted appearance. After all there are only a dozen working together, not hundreds. But these will be teachers, craftsmen, indoctrinators by example. In the short hours I was there I had a lesson in lettering and learned how to make a hooked rug, an accomplishment I will pass on to others at Mott Street. Already we have a knitting class.

Thirty houses and eleven farms! And thru them all, despite differences of opinion, is a sense of fundamental unity, a sense of community, of common striving, of sharing a common crust.

## Sept 28

Last night the Boston group held a meeting at Pius XI hall which is behind the Pius XI cooperative book store. Clare McGrath is in charge of the store which sponsors a series of lectures this winter on Saturday afternoons. There was a good crowd and a friendly one. I spoke on peace and conscientious objection, and as I spoke I was thinking what a duty it was for all of us to speak and write now while there is no declared war. There are so many who hate war and peacetime conscription, who do not know what they can do, who have no sense of united effort, and who will sit back and accept with resignation the evils which are imposed upon us. This is not working for God's will to be done on earth as it is in Heaven. It is the pie in the sky attitude.

Books in Wartime: *Labyrinthine Ways. To the End of the World. Kristin Lavransdatter. Master of Hestviken.* Jeremiah. 1 Kings.

People live, eat, sleep, love, worship, marry, have children, and somehow live in the midst of war, in the midst of anguish. The sun continues to shine, the leaves flaunt their vivid color, there is a serene warmth in the day and an invigorating cold at night.

Turn off your radio. Put away your daily paper. Read one review of events a week and spend some time reading such books as the above. They tell too of days of striving and of strife. They are of other centuries and also of our own. They make us realize that all times are perilous, that men live in a dangerous world, in peril constantly of losing or maiming soul and body.

We get some sense of perspective reading such books. Renewed courage and faith and even joy to live. And man cannot live long without joy, without some vestige of happiness to light up his days.

Last week:

Oct 2. Took Nancy to Philadelphia and Easton. Weather marvelous

Oct 4. Spoke Capitol Hotel.

Oct 9. Press.

Oct 16. [Draft] Registration Day. Many of us fasted on bread and water until 5. Or bread and coffee.

Nov 7

Detroit yesterday and today. Visited River Rouge plant of Ford with Marie and Lou. A terrifying experience.[60]

Nazareth shop at St. Francis house Meeting Fr. Weyand, Univ. Detroit, argument on war. Fr. Kern spiritual advisor, Holy House, which was a good way to end this year of my life. Forty-three tomorrow.

Monday, Nov 11

Fr. Luke from Lisle, [Ill.], St. Procopius [Abbey] picked me up for meeting there. Bohemian Benedictines. Magnificent work. They certainly follow Christ in poverty, hard work. The nuns too put us to shame. I love most specially those little foreign sisters who work in kitchens and laundries, who wear away their youth and beauty for Christ, their spouse, and who are so completely happy.

I had wanted to stay at St. Procopius, especially in the storm which was raging. The monastery stands out on the plain on the prairie and the winds howled around it. The sisters did not have their storm windows up and even with all the heat on that 65-mile-an-hour gale made the place cold. But Joan

---

60    The River Rouge plant of the Ford Motor Company in Dearborn, Michigan was at that time the largest factory in the world.

Quilty, a young crippled girl, very active in the youth movement in spite of being in a wheel chair, invited me to her home and I went there.[61]

Atlantic City. Nov 23

Reading Little Office on the beach. Sea gulls, high, piercing notes, chirping sparrows. The thunder of waves, muffled because it is an offshore wind. Not a sound of humans tho there are plenty on boardwalk. Horses galloping and the seagulls pay no attention. But a ragged old man starts throwing grain to them and from up and down the beach they take off running before they fold their legs under them to fly.

Beginning of Advent. Nov 30, Sat. Midnight

Tamar and I to Brooklyn to look at Xmas windows, shop for paper, go to movies. Della over with jacket and candy. We had a good visit for an hour.

For the last three days I have stayed in bed with a feeling of cramped pains in the heart (now gone, however). I wrote letters, worked on the book but kept physically quiet. I enjoyed myself.

Sat. Dec 7. Eve of Feast. Midnight

Today to Della's. Mother there. Warm and spring-like, sunny until evening and then a warm rain. Now home in bed and sound of river boats very clear. Child crying, occasional auto horn, people talking. As soon as weather clears everyone is on the streets again.

When I become too comfortable I feel guilty. Have had such a good rest in bed, I feel much better, tho still with some pain around heart and headache.

"Heaven had better be good."—Joe Zarrella.

Dec 29. Sunday. Farm

A beautiful Christmas.

An hysterical scene at Loretta's in which she accused me of kicking out all Irish and for reasons of my own keeping on Joe [Zarrella] who got Damien drunk at age of 3. Of being responsible for bums and loafers on farm and making a bum out of Frank.

A New Year's resolution to say nothing; repeat nothing. The most difficult of mortifications.

Tonight the president spoke. America an arsenal. We are at war, undeclared.

---

61   In 1955 Dorothy became a Benedictine Oblate of St. Procopius Abbey, Lisle, Illinois, and she often returned there for retreats.

# 1941

*Few of Dorothy's notes or journals for the next several years have survived.*

May 5. Mott St.
   Cool and sunny. The farm needs rain. Tonight at 10:30 Sec of War Stimson asked for use of Navy for Britain. For convoys, but act of war. Undeclared.
   Tamar and I to supper with Forster, he sad and speechless with the war.

May 20, Tuesday
   Up till one last night reading *Studs Lonergan*. A terrible indictment of Catholic education. Visit earlier in the evening to Transfiguration [parish]. Saw Polish priest there. Up this morning at 7:30. Mass 8 a.m. Will see Bishop tomorrow.
   Sigrid Undset [author of *Kristin Lavrandsdatter*] wants to come to dinner this week or next.

Aug 12. Tuesday, noon
   Staying in bed. Just exhausted after two months traveling. Since June 11. See date book. Marge says "Write in your notebook. It does more good than reading." How often I have done that.
   Breakfast a thick slice of dry bread and some very bad coffee. I dictate a dozen letters. My brain is in a fog. I feel too weak to climb stairs. I have prescribed for myself this day in bed but I keep thinking it is my spirit that is all wrong. I am surrounded by repellent disorder, noise, people, and have no spirit of inner solitude or poverty.

*December 7, 1941, the Japanese attack Pearl Harbor. The United States is at war.*

# 1942

*The January 1942 issue of the CW, the first to appear after the declaration of war, displays this headline:*

## Our Country Passes from Undeclared War to Declared War We Continue Our Christian Pacifist Stand

We are still pacifists. Our manifesto is the Sermon on the Mount, which means that we will try to be peacemakers. Speaking for many of our conscientious objectors, we will not participate in armed warfare or in making munitions, or by buying government bonds to prosecute the war, or in urging others to these efforts.

But neither will we be carping in our criticism. We love our country and we love our President. We have been the only country in the world where men of all nations have taken refuge from oppression. We recognize that while in the order of intention we have tried to stand for peace, for love of our brother, in the order of execution we have failed as Americans in living up to our principles.

Because of our refusal to assist in the prosecution of war and our insistence that our collaboration be one for peace, we may find ourselves in difficulties. But we trust in the generosity and understanding of our government and our friends, to permit us to continue, to use our paper to "preach Christ crucified."

May the Blessed Mary, Mother of love, of faith, of knowledge and of hope, pray for us.[62]

# 1943

*The January 1943 issue carried an editorial by Dorothy entitled "If Conscription Comes for Women":*

I will not register for conscription, if conscription comes for women, nor will I make a statement to the government on registration day as to my stand, lest this be used as involuntary registration on my part. Instead, I publish my statement here, my declaration of purpose, and if it encourages other women not to register, I shall be glad at such increase in our numbers

I shall not register because I believe modern war to be murder, incompatible with a religion of love. I shall not register because registration is the first step towards conscription, and I agree with Cardinal Gasparri, that the only way to do away with war is to do away with conscription.

*Elsewhere in this issue, she supplied a synopsis of recent events at the CW:*

As I write this, it is the end of the year (and the end of our first ten years!) and it is good to give a general summary of the work. Our paper has gone down in circulation, mostly on account of the cancellation of bundle orders, but the single subscribers have increased daily. The circulation now stands at 55,000…

In connection with THE CATHOLIC WORKER, we have continued to maintain houses of hospitality where the works of mercy can be practiced through voluntary poverty (none of us or our helpers receiving pay), and the help of readers of the paper and our kind neighbors. Clothes and food are provided to all who come, and lodging is provided for as many as the house

---

62   See *SW,* 262-63.

will hold… A sum total of sixteen houses [are] still open, and sixteen closed. Six farms connected with houses of hospitality are operating … Houses and farms are imperfect expressions of our personalist, communitarian philosophy. As St. Francis said, "You do not know what you have not practiced."

During this one year there have been seven marriages. Eddie Priest, Joe Zarrella, Bill Callahan, Marjorie Crowe, Margaret Bingham, Hazen Ordway, Ann Mack, all of whom have been closely associated with the New York house… Marjorie Crowe Hughes had a baby girl Joanna, at the Easton Hospital in mid-December, and Dorothy Gauchat had a baby girl, Anita, in mid-October on Our Lady of the Wayside Farm at Avon, Ohio.

During the year there were two deaths, that of Steve Hergenhan at St. Rose's Cancer Home down on the East River, and of James McGovern, first mate of a tanker, torpedoed last winter. There was an account of Steve's death in the paper, and a further account of his life and contribution to our work in New York and on the Easton farm. But we have not talked of Mac's death. It was so hard, so cruel, we could not write about it at the time. Mac's body was washed up in an open boat with that of a number of others on the coast of Panama, dead of hunger and thirst, some months after the torpedoing of his boat…

In listing houses of hospitality that have been closed, I should state that the reason for the closing was lack of workers rather than lack of need for the houses. There are always the poor, as our Lord reminded us. There are always the lame, the halt and the blind, people being discharged from hospitals, unemployables, vagrants. There are always these, "our least brethren," in whom we may see Christ as he told us to. And the harder it is to see him under dirt and drink and vermin, the more we are exercising our faith. "Love is surrender," we had been told on our retreat in July. "Give yourself to God in the poor." And how else can we show our love for God? …

But due to war, our workers are scattered. Gerry Griffin is somewhere in Palestine right now in training before launching off on a career of ambulance driving around Tunisia. Lou Murphy and Joe Zarrella are accepted by the Field Service and will be going to Africa soon. The whole Chicago crowd, and some of the Milwaukee crowd, are scattered in camps or on islands in the Pacific. Jack English of Cleveland, and Ossie Bondy of Windsor, are somewhere in England. Others of our movement are in our conscientious objector camp at Warner, New Hampshire, enduring the isolation and detachment of what is practically a concentration camp. Others are working in the Alexian Brothers Hospital in Chicago, some as nurses, some as maintenance men around the hospital.

During the last month, F.B.I. representatives came to Mott Street and picked up David Mason, one of the three leaders of the Philadelphia Catholic Worker activities, for refusing induction. He is forty-four years old, but is protesting conscription by his refusal. At present he is held over on West Street at a Federal Detention headquarters until his trial, or until we raise

$1,000 bail and get him out until the trial, so that he can enjoy a bit more freedom.

During the last year, I have spent five months away from Mott Street in travel and in visiting our houses and farms around the country. Three of those months were on a trip to the West Coast. The time away was distributed as follows: January, one week; February, three days; March, three days; all of April, May and half of June; October, three weeks; November, one week; December, two weeks. During the summer I was away a week for our yearly retreat at Pittsburgh. Seven months out of the twelve I have spent at St. Joseph's house, Maryhouse and a few weekends at Maryfarm.

Now I am away again, accompanying my mother South, for she was not well and no other member of the family was free to go. Here I can finish up the Peter Maurin book,[63] and on my way home, I shall visit reader friends in Southern cities which have seemed so inaccessible, due to lack of finances and lack of supporters. Peter Maurin is in New York, and so are Arthur Sheehan, Jack Thornton, and Charlie O'Rourke, so the work will get done, the houses will go on, the paper will come out, and, God willing, I will be home in February.

*From her "Day after Day" column in the July 1943 issue:*

We last went to press June 23, and looking through my date book to find out what has been happening since then, I find I spoke on the 24th at the Yorkville Vocational High School, at their graduation exercises, and was happy to see a goodly crowd of colored and white girls, and colored and white families, gathered together amicably on this good occasion. I spoke about cooperatives and farming communes as expressions of our brotherhood in Christ, and in general tried to convey an idea of the philosophy of work which is Peter's pet subject.

July 1—Father Joseph Woods of Portsmouth Priory happened in, and since he is stationed for the summer at Malvern, Long Island, we immediately asked him to give us weekly talks in the dining room of St. Joseph's House. The talks have been crowded, though the nights have been sweltering.

July 2—Jack Thornton, who has been in charge of the House of Hospitality for the past year, reported for his physical, since he is going into the army as an [non-combatant] "objector." Immediately after being accepted he went to Pittsburgh with Dwight Larrowe for his retreat.

Monday, July 12— I spoke at Friendship House on Negro conditions in the South as I saw them last winter, and ended up talking of retreats and the use of the weapons of the spirit.

---

63   Dorothy worked on and off for several years on a book about Peter Maurin. Several chapters were published in the CW, but it never amounted to a finished book. An historian, Francis Sicius, later fleshed out the manuscript and saw to its publication: *Peter Maurin: Apostle to the World* by Dorothy Day and Francis Sicius (Maryknoll, NY: Orbis Books, 2004).

Thursday, July 15— I started out for Rosewood Training School, outside of Baltimore, where the Association of Catholic Conscientious Objectors has one of its two camps. The other is at the Alexian Brothers Hospital, in Chicago.

Saturday, July 17— A conference of the Association of Catholic Conscientious objectors was held in Washington, at Pilgrimage Hall, near the Franciscan Monastery. It is a lovely place to hold such a meeting. We had lunch there. It was quiet, and all around the heat shimmered and the birds were still, and the grass smelled fresh and sweet outside the windows.

The following week was the week of the retreat.

Sunday, July 25—Was spent on a picnic thirty miles out of Kittanning, Pa., with Fr. Hugo and his genial pastor...

*Notes from a retreat in Oakmont, Pennsylvania:*

July 19

Fr. Hugo said once, quoting from somewhere, that the best thing to do with the best of things is to give them up. Well, I have long since "given up," "offered up" the field, the shore, for the city slums. "Why are you staying here?" Fr. [Vincent] McNabb's friends asked him, he who lived in London but was forever talking about "Nazareth or Social Chaos." "To get people out of here," he replied.

So it is my vocation to agitate, to be a journalist, a pamphleteer, and now my time must be spent in these cities, these slums. But how wonderful it is to be out here in this Christian community, set up in the midst of fields, atop a hill, and to have samples of Heaven all about, not hell. I truly love sweet clover in God and thank Him. "All ye works of the Lord—bless ye the Lord."

The children are having their holy hour in the chapel. They have the sweetest voices, singing hymns. It is a perfect day, clear, just cool enough, dry and sunny. I've been fasting all day and feel slightly light with hunger. Last night we had a Holy Hour from 11-12.

For the last days I have felt a stronger determination, a resolution to spend more time in prayer and work. And suddenly there crystallized in my mind an idea that had been working there for some time, even for some years. I more or less expressed it when I talked of going off to be a "desert father." It is that idea Lallemant [*The Spiritual Doctrine*] expresses, and is quoted by Huxley. It long since terrified me in [Jean-Baptiste] Chautard [*Soul of the Apostolate*] when he spoke of the heresy of good works.

I always felt God would indicate his will for me by some exterior act—by the paper being suppressed, by the Archbishop suggesting that I leave. Now it suddenly comes to me, Why do I not just hand the paper over to Peter and Arthur, Dave and Fr. Duffy, and leave? I no longer feel I can save my soul by this work; no, more, I am in danger of losing it. I am in danger of becoming like that woman in *Bleak House* who worked so hard for foreign missions and neglected her family. Or like that woman in *The Possessed*, the Governor's wife, who had a finger in every pie and felt important. St. Paul defines woman's place. Sister Peter Claver says woman's place is to love and to suffer.

What I want to do is get a job, in some hospital as ward-maid, get a room, preferably next door to a church; and there in the solitude of the city, living and working with the poor; to learn to pray, to work, to suffer, to be silent.

The world is too much with me in the Catholic Worker. The world is suffering and dying. I am not suffering and dying in the CW, I am writing and talking about it.

Of course I will not save my soul alone. Wherever we are we are with people. We drag them down, or pull them up. Or we get dragged down or pulled up. And in recognition of this latter fact, I recognize also the need for aids and counsel in the path to God.

That is why as soon as possible I will try to organize days of recollection—primarily for myself. I will not be able to stand the impact of the world otherwise. Primarily for myself. But that will mean others—how many, who can tell? And later, retreats! We can do nothing today without saints; big ones and little ones. The only weapons we will develop will be those of prayer and penance. And the world will leave us alone, saying—after all, they are not doing anything. Just a bunch of smug fools praying. We will not be as tormented by its scorn as we are by the praise of the world for works of mercy, houses of hospitality, and farming communes. They are necessary—they are the results of the work we are beginning. It is only by the grace of God they have sprung up and prospered.

But we need thousands of hospices after the war—thousands of refuges, thousands of "farming communes." And we need saints to start them and to operate them.

Hence this new move. Hence this running away, to seek a hidden life.

I have always been so sure I was right, that I was being led by God—that is, in the main outlines of my life—that I confidently expected Him to show His will by external events.

And I looked for some unmistakable sign. I disregarded all the little signs. I begin now to see them and with such clearness that I have to beg not to be shown too much, for fear I cannot bear it.

I need strength to do what I have to do—strength and joy and peace and vision.

Lord, that I may see! That prayer is certainly answered most overwhelmingly on this retreat. It shows one has to make at least three retreats before you slough off the thick skin, so as to become sensitive enough to feel the breath of his inspirations.

August 27

Thinking of Peter [Maurin] book and move and hardness of solitude, and goodness of poverty. Streets quiet. Canary, dogs. Morning glories, peppers, fire escape.

We have 3 kittens. Shorty talks about great big men with great big feet endangering them, indeed stepping on them. They show no evidence. They are beautiful. Man is ugly. Celia with her slow huge mouthfuls. Mr. Walsh, like a fat slug, talking about pyorrhea, complaining that someone accused him of urinating in the sink in the office. Coughings, spittings, Smoky Joe weeping. Man with long beard for supper. Statue of Blessed Mother and flowers.

*Over the summer Dorothy determined to take some time away from the CW. In the September CW she announced her plan to take a year's leave of absence:*

> For the last few years I've been thinking a great deal of putting aside the responsibility of the Catholic Worker ... but every time that idea came to me I put it aside as a temptation. It was during my retreat this summer that the conviction came to me that I should take this step.

*She spent the first month at the Grail, a center for training women for the lay apostolate, in Libertyville, Illinois. In October she moved to Farmingdale, Long Island, where Tamar had enrolled in an agricultural school. Dorothy lived nearby in a Dominican convent. She had an apartment of her own and spent much of the time alone.*

November 8-9

Exam conscience. It is good to have visitors. One's faults stand out. Also to show how hard it is to establish regular habits. For instance, forget reading rule at breakfast.

1. Gluttony, remedy fasting.

2. Speaking ill of neighbor C. Remedy silence.

3. Self-will, desire not to be corrected. Being sure one is right, i.e., dishtowels. Oatmeal.

4. Desire to correct others when wrong (little things don't matter).

5. Impatience in thought, speech. Remedy, recollection, silence. Practice presence of God. Repetitive prayers to establish habits.

Breaking solitude by writing letters (cards). Meanness about my time to Mrs. Mooney and the wasting it myself. Selfishness, looking to my own comfort.

Nov 14

With Della—resenting criticism, impatience. Criticizing others to others.

# 1944

February 1944. Farmingdale, Long Island

What is poverty? I sit here on a clear cold winter's afternoon down on Long Island surrounded by a snow-covered countryside and listen to the Philharmonic Symphony. At the same time I darn stockings, three pairs, all I possess, heavy cotton, grey, tan, and one brown wool, and reflect that these come to me from the cancerous poor, entering a hospital to die. For ten years I have worn stockings which an old lady, a dear friend, who is spending her declining years in this hospital, has collected for me and carefully darned and patched. Often these have come to me soiled, or with that heavy hospital smell which never seemed to leave them even after many washings. And the wearing of these stockings and other second-hand clothes has saved me much money to use for the running of our houses of hospitality and the publishing of a paper.

But the fact remains that I have stockings to cover me when others go cold and naked. The fact remains that I am now listening to a concert—Brahms' 2nd Symphony, joyful music to heal my sadness. All day I have felt sad. But even tho I feel the need of recreation I get afflicted by scruples. What right have I got to recreation? What need have I of recreation? "The best thing to do with the best of things is to give them up" [Fr. Hugo]. Most recreation is worldly, music, plays, painting, writing.

I am sad on account of Dwight [Larrowe], a heavy sadness, an oppressive sense of shock and failure. He has left his leadership of the conscientious objectors and has gone into the army, one more Christian fighting other Christians, accepting conscription, the army, because of *obedience*. Fr. Hugo started him off reflecting on the meaning of obedience and abandonment and Herbert Schwartz finished him off. He is going to make a week's retreat with Schwartz before leaving.

I too accepted obedience. I regard it as a virtue of most profound importance for our time. So important that I sometimes wonder if it were not better to leave Fr. Hugo and his direction rather than sin against obedience. Can I take it? Or am I getting scrupulous and uneasy?

He is generous. He tells me to keep my spiritual liberty. But do I not take too much liberty?

Some priests refuse to let a penitent for instance take a pledge for a long period for fear of his breaking it and so being guilty of mortal sin.

I think the virtue of obedience to my spiritual director is so important that either I should ask him to moderate his severity in order to give me more ease of mind and less scrupulosity, or I should change my director.

For instance, I am to practice solitude and silence. Especially I was thinking of this in regard to the work. Not to go near the office, nor to advise and consult and influence others, to devote myself to prayer and penance and silence.

Primarily I was thinking of solitude in its figurative sense, in regard to the Catholic Worker and all its parts, not in a literal sense. I intended to see my brothers, sister, mother, and child. To be as close to the latter as possible, as a matter of fact, because she wishes to marry soon and this will be my last year with her. I suggested my mother living with me, to make up to her somewhat for my neglect in the past but Fr. Hugo vetoed that. I agreed but said I must visit her. (She is in Florida now so I shall not see her for three months). Fr. Hugo quoted "He who does not leave father or mother for my sake cannot be my disciple." But mother is old, 74, she does not cling to me or dote on me as a mother does on a son. I have been uneasy about these visits.

Then in regard to Tamar, Fr. said I did have an obligation there, so we have been together pretty steadily, as much as possible, considering she has to live half a mile away in a dormitory. But when she comes to see me she brings her roommate. They come for brief visits and drink cocoa and eat bread and honey. When she goes to the dentist she wants me with her. One weekend there was to be a painful new brace and after her grueling time in the chair I took her to "Jane Eyre" to distract her mind. Then we had supper with her friend and mine, Marjorie, at the station before we came back.

Tuesday I was called into the Chancery (the Bishop was not there and I must go again next Tuesday). On my way to the station after two Masses at the Cathedral and a Holy Hour at St. Francis' church, I met Fr. Joachim, MSST, who used to be my spiritual advisor, and we talked for two hours. I had not seen him since last March.

These contacts, though I have not been able to help them, though I have not brought them about, give me a sense of guilt. Of course, in that I talk too much I deserve a sense of guilt.

I am oppressed in general by a sense of failure, of sin. Abbot [Columba] Marmion advised one of his penitents to cultivate a sense of compunction so I am indeed blessed in having this. The sins of my entire past life from earliest childhood come often to my mind to fill me with a sense of iniquity. St. Augustine was right when he talked of the wickedness there is even in children. One does not wonder then at the punishment that descends on the entire world, men, women, and children, as a result of sin. I only regret I do not have to suffer more of this punishment myself. Perhaps God does not think me strong enough. I can remember the deep sense of peace I had some years ago in the midst of an ugly illness, an abscessed throat. I rejoiced to think God took matters out of my hands—"whom the Lord loveth He chasteneth." No penances voluntarily undertaken can equal what the Lord sends us. There is always the sting of self.

Yes, compunction is good, and the desire for penance, instructive in every human heart. I think it is in the encyclical of Pius XI, quoted in the Breviary as one of the lessons for the feast of the Sacred Heart, that brings this out. One *desires* to share in the sufferings of Christ. One desires to share in the hardships of the beloved, hunger, thirst, vigils, and this means self-imposed mortifications, self-imposed dying to self. (That this can lead to Jansenism, Catharism, individualism, is the charge of some priests when one talks of penance, mortification, detachment from creatures.) But it is *love* that gives these desires, and love is a glowing, happy thing, a radiant, warming fire. We want to strip ourselves to clothe our beloved. We want to fast because of his hunger even if we cannot feed him, since we cannot feed the hungry of India, China, Europe—we will share his sufferings and rejoice in this cross.

This blindness of love, this folly of love—this seeing Christ in others, everywhere and not seeing the ugly, the obvious, the dirty, the sinful—this means we do not see the faults of others,—only our own. We see only Christ in them. We have eyes only for our beloved, ears for His voice.

This is what caused the saints to go to what writers like Aldous Huxley (not to speak of our own Catholics) called repulsive extremes. Perhaps hagiographers were too prone to wallow in vomit, pus, sputum, the utterly repulsive—all to make their "point," as Peter would say, showing how the saints rose *above* the natural, the human, and became supernatural, superhuman, in their love. Nothing was difficult to them, all was clear, shining and beautiful on the pathway of love.

There is that prayer of St. Bonaventure in most missals as a thanksgiving after communion prayer. There is that chapter in the [*Imitation*] of *Christ*— Book III chap v.

What mother ever considers the ugliness of cleaning up after her baby, or sick child or sick husband? These things are not mentioned by critics. But to the saints everyone is child and lover.

One of the troubles with the rigorous retreat we make each year is that it sets the retreatants to criticizing everyone, including themselves of course. Criticizing spiritual writers, orders, clergy, the running of rectories and convents, education, Catholic Action and Catholic activities. Instead of seeking concordances, agreements, only disagreements are seen. Discouragement sets in and discouragement is a temptation of the devil.

What I must do is cultivate a joyful silence and not criticize others for criticizing; to confess my sins in confession and not to explain or justify myself. Let others accuse, criticize as they will, I must maintain a cheerful silence.

I feel sick? I must keep silent.

I am sad? I must keep silent.

I have had bad news? I must keep silent.

Monday, Feb. 14. St. Valentine's day

"I have said to the Lord, Thou hast no need of my good deeds." Ps XV.2

I want to write about our enemy the flesh, which is also our dear companion on this pilgrimage, our body, thru which we receive our greatest joys of body and spirit. Our senses convey to us knowledge of the truth; we hear of the faith with our ears, we see and understand things invisible thru things visible; we speak words of earthly and eternal love (alas, also words of ugliness and hate).

Our dear flesh, our good bodies, which God made, which begin to die even as we begin to live, ever dying, ever renewing and finally decaying and being put into the ground like grains of wheat to rise again with new life at the last day. "I believe in the resurrection of the body and life everlasting."

Brother Ass, St. Francis called our bodies, and what burdens it must bear of joy and sorrow, what torrents of pleasure pass over it, into what an abyss of pain it can fall.

A woman contemplates her body, "that earthen vessel," that temple of the Holy Ghost, and young or old it is always holy. Young, it is as fresh and fragrant as flowers. Old, it is worn and stale, there is the smell of age and corruption.

But this aging flesh, I love it, I treat it tenderly, but also I rejoice that it has been well used. That was my vocation—a wife and mother, I gave myself to husband and children, my flesh well used, droops, my breasts sag, my face withers, but my eyes and lips rejoice and love and laugh with happiness.

Am I a virgin, a single woman, have I willingly cast myself into the arms of God or have I longed for earthly love, and it has passed me by? Then God has chosen me and "blessed are those who have not seen but believed" in this love, this terrible, overwhelming, cruelly demanding love of the living God.

We give ourselves with our bodies, we become one flesh with our mate (it is not good for man to live alone). I am bone of his bone, flesh of his flesh.

But how much more so of Christ. We are espoused to Him. We are members of His Mystical Body. We are fed by Him, one "puts on Christ."

Man is to know, love and serve God, and how shall we know Him save thru Christ, who was Man: The flesh of Jesus was the flesh of Mary, so how close we should feel to her, our Mother.

"Behold thy Mother."

We do not dwell upon the pleasures of the body, nor talk of them. There is barrack's room talk of wine, women, and song, of course—the talk of starved men, seeking an anodyne from pain. This is not the kind of remembrance even the most gross woman wishes of herself, in the memory and conversation of those she loves.

"Pin-up girls"—flesh in the abstract, tempting the memory to the grossest and most fruitless of pleasures, to still the fearful expectation of the most useless pain.

St. Francis de Sales in his conference on marriage in *The Devout Life* describes the salacious mind which gloats on the remembrance of past pleasures and the anticipation of those to come. This disassociation of the flesh from the Spirit is evil and is bitter fruit in the mouth.

As with pleasure, so in regard to passing sickness, women would well ponder the evils of concentrating on their bodily infirmities, symptoms, pains, operations, and make it a rule never to mention them.

We are so subject to our bodies. At their slightest bidding we make ourselves warm, cool, fed, refreshed, and we count ourselves most spiritual when we are never conscious of them because they are so well cared for they are perfectly comfortable and never bother us.

The bourgeois, the material, fights for abstractions like freedom, democracy, because he has the material things of this life (which he is most fearful of being deprived of). The poor fight for bread, for increase in wages, for time to rest, for warmth, for privacy.

Have you ever been in the two-room shacks of poor Negroes in the South, or of miners in Pennsylvania, Kentucky and West Virginia, of steel workers, have you seen the slums of Washington, D.C. or Harrisburg, Pa. and seen people living ten in a room?

No one talking about the spiritual here in hovels. Keep that locked in our own breasts. Here we cannot show our love for them by talking retreats, the spiritual life. "A certain amount of goods is necessary to lead a good life"—St. Thomas. Privacy above all. A certain freedom from nagging hunger and anxiety and pain.

We cannot make a Christian social order without Christians. It is impossible save by heroic charity to live in the present social order and be Christians.

### Feb 16

Voluntary poverty again. My Bible says the Hebrews did not consider Daniel one of the prophets because he lived in kings' household. (But our Lord quotes him as a prophet. He lived and studied in the kings' households but lived on "pulse and water," he and three companions. How much easier to do things in community. Nor did they become lean and embarrass the king's servants who were put in charge of them.

Yesterday, after a visit at the chancery office, I went to the Metropolitan Museum and saw slabs of pavement with beautiful rug patterns which perhaps were trodden on by the feet of Daniel. I saw Babylonian and Assyrian antiquities, lions, winged beings worshipping and fertilizing the sacred tree, carvings in alabaster.

Reading Dom Van Zeller's book on Daniel brought about this visit. Such bright glowing writing on the major and minor prophets as the Benedictine monk has done has lighted up the entire Old Testament for me.

How I came across this writer from Downside Abbey, England. I was lamenting the fall of a young girl in our midst who had fallen in love and eloped with a conscienceless character. (He stole; he had been living with a woman on relief whose husband was in jail. She had four children and died giving birth to a fifth begotten in adultery. He begged me to go to the wake and as I prayed over the coffin he nudged me, pointing to a string of rosary beads in her hands. "I gave her that; I was always doing little things like that for her," he sniffed. He was the nearest to Studs Lonergan I have ever met.)

Fr. Joseph, who is also a Benedictine, began telling me the story of Osee, or Hosea. He was a prophet, a holy man, but the Lord commanded him to marry a harlot, who deceived him again and again and whom he yet received back into his bosom. He was a disgrace in all likelihood, to his day and age, scoffed at and despised, and yet he remains to this day a figure of God's love for his people, who are fornicators and adulterers, turning to other gods.

I was looking thru Wm Lyons Phelps' memoirs the other day and reading his interview with George Moore, who salaciously spoke of adultery as the ordinary thing. Prof. Phelps, with his evidently usual friendly forthrightness, that never offended, insisted it was not *usual,* stating that he knew those who had never so offended. But he was thinking of it in its literal sense.

Over and over again union with God was described as a marriage, faithlessness to God as adultery. We are all adulterers, fornicators, impure in the sight of God.

Fr. Joseph was not justifying the young girl but he was showing how in the long view we could trust that all things would work together for good to them that love God.

Feb 18. St. Bernadette. Also St. Simeon

A beautiful day. The sky heavy with clouds. The sun coming and going, wondrous patches of blue sky, intense against the lavender and purple and warm rose of the clouds. The trees black and silvery from recent rain, branches filled with starlings, sparrows, bluebirds. The bush in back of the shed where apples are stored (a fragrant place) is rose-tipped. Out in the fields, the cover crop shows pale green against the black soil, and scattered are quicksilver pools reflecting the sky.

There is always color, life, thru the winter; under the grass the dead leaves and the snow, green plants stay alive.

Down in the chicken house the incubator chicks are hatching out. Mr. Lang showed me the sharp steel-like points on their beaks which grew there just to release them from the shell and afterward fall off. Day old chicks can go without food and water for some days—and so be shipped, because the yolk forms their stomachs and its absorption suffices them for food, Mr. Lang says.

Such miracles we see all around us, which we accept so readily, yet no one can explain or produce life. Yet so many will not accept transubstantiation.

Here are two beautiful quotations:

"Understanding is the reward of faith. Therefore seek not to understand that thou mayest believe, but believe that thou mayest understand." St. Augustine.

"Unless you believe you shall not understand." Isaiah 7:9

"What is wisdom indeed if not the rational understanding of faith? But again what is it to understand?" Etienne Gilson

I do not remember the name of the Gilson book which had these quotations, but they convinced me of the necessity for praying for those without faith rather than indulging in the futile attempt to make them understand.

In the Van Zeller book there are very good comments on the prayers of Daniel. Whenever I get discouraged and say to the Lord, "Teach me to pray," as the disciples did, I am driven to the example of prayer in the Bible, both Old and New Testament.

Here I have the opportunity to spend hours every day in the chapel and am usually there three hours a day. The comfort of such quiet, such solitude, helps much in relieving the dryness and even pain of prayer.

When, because of travel, or the press of work, I cannot be there, I feel it. Fr. Matteo has preached the Holy Hour (nocturnal) in the house for years. He says all the churches and schools can be left, etc, but take Christ out of the home and the people are lost. And it is true that today our churches may be crowded for devotions, people going by themselves and losing themselves in the comfortable anonymity of a crowd, but the family does not pray *together* at home. The sense of *community* is lost, even that most basic of all communities, the family. Such salutary church going may give comfort, but Fr. Lallemant says to beware of being comfortable. Another instance of religion becoming the opium of the people.

In the book of Daniel the idea of penance is brought out. It was because he "afflicted himself" that his prayers were heard. Yet it is a cheerful book on the whole and though Daniel had a hard time with his own people he got four foreign kings to acknowledge the one true God.

What spasmodic writing I have done this last six months—with plenty of time to write in. I have written a number of new chapters for the book about Peter [Maurin] and rewritten a good deal of it. I have written five articles which have been published and five not published. Some in this note book.

I have got quite out of the habit of diary keeping but since my spiritual adviser counsels against writing for some months save for meditations, I shall try to be more regular about this and write some every day, whether just to keep track of events or to write "reflections" as I am so fond of doing. The trouble is that being editor and journalist I write always with a view to publication and leave out all sorts of inconsequential happenings, which are very significant to me, and which also would be helpful to refresh my memory for future writings. I'm going to try to be more regular in future.

Today is a typical one. Arose at 5:45, Mass at 6:30. Breakfast 7:30. Reading Van Zeller's Isaiah and pouring over maps of the Assyrian Empire until 8:30. Dishwashing, listening to the news. I have just resumed this once this last month in my worry over my brother [Donald] in Helsinki[64] and Gerry and Joe and Lou at [Monte] Cassino. (God only knows where Tom, Jim, Jack, and John, Arthur and others of our crowd are. Jack English in prison camp in Rumania, and the Russians now at the border.)

In chapel to practice in my use of the weapons of the spirit for an hour and a half. It is too hard, I accomplish nothing, I tell myself every day. Like St. Teresa I hold on to a book so as not to be utterly bare before Him. My mind like an idiot wanders, converses, debates, argues, flounders. If I get in 15 minutes of honest to God praying, I'm doing well. It is an act of will being there, knowing I'll have to keep up this struggle thru life and yet proceeding "at the pace of a hen."

The chapel was hot too. And I felt irritated at a Sister who makes the Stations at least four times while I am there, round and round the chapel. I beat my breast for judging my neighbor in my thoughts.

Last night Sister Nurse was walking rapidly up and down the walk between the buildings with one of the old Sisters who has lost her mind. "Three times today, she has run away from me," she said to me thru the window. "I am trying to tire her out. She is a bad girl." And taking her patient's hand in her arm, she hurried her up and down the paths, their habits flying in the March wind. I love the Sisters, all of them. They work hard, they pray, they keep going from day to day and keep faith alive in the world.

Coming back to my room I found Tamar there reading Sutherland's *Laws of Life*. [Tamar's] marriage [to David Hennessy] is set for April 19. Eight o'clock Mass, St. Bernard's church. She is calm and peaceful, finishing up her term exams, going to her barn duty. To pass dairy barn the students must milk six cows in an hour, plough five acres, etc., besides all the class and book and laboratory work. Tamar of course is missing a lot by not finishing her course, but she figures marriage comes first these war times. She is 18, has had one year high school, one term in Canada where she learned spinning and weaving and sewing, ten months apprenticed to Ade Bethune where she learned much from housework, cooking, carpentry, garden work, and care of chickens, rabbits, folk dancing, and liturgy.

She is marrying someone who accepts poverty, manual labor, loves country life and literature and, of course, first of all, loves her. They are much alike in virtues and faults.

This year is turning out differently than I planned, as all things do. Instead of staying in one place here I am going to the Easton farm a week from now,

---

64  Dorothy's brother Donald had gone in 1939 to cover the Russian invasion of Finland for the *Chicago Tribune*. When the paper called him back he resigned and enlisted in the Finnish army.

and ten days later leaving there for Ohio. However, I shall practice solitude and silence as much as I can wherever I am.

Tamar stayed to lunch and we had carrots, bacon, bread and tea. At two I walked as far as the corner to get my milk and came back to listen to the Chicago Symphony, Sibelius 2nd Symphony in D Major.

"As deceivers, yet true." [2 Cor 6:8]
This came to my mind this morning when I began to reflect on the virtues of silence as opposed to "truthful speaking out," which usually means telling another what you think of him—wherein you differ from him, where he is wrong, etc. A good part of this impulse is under the guise of honesty, frankness, truthfulness. Also *duty*. If one is in charge of a house, for instance, in a position of authority as teacher, etc.

But the best rule is also to wait, consider, ponder, before judging and acting. Err on the side of gentleness. Be a *sower*, not a *weeder*. But if one does not weed, the weeds choke the good plants. (Perhaps also the good plants will choke out the weeds.) It depends also on one's position. Another good reason for being in the *least* place, not taking on *authority*. (This does not mean avoiding *responsibility* and *work*.)

Anyway, silence: We cannot have too much of it, especially from women. We all talk too much and too often. (Just because men do it is no excuse for our doing it.) We should mollify, reconcile, pacify. We should not be "disagreeable." But if you don't speak out you will be considered a hypocrite? Never mind about public opinion. If we speak out we are misjudged; if we are silent, we are misjudged.

So what difference does it make? "As deceivers, yet true." St. Paul. "I come not to judge." Jesus … "Women's part is to love."—Sister Peter Claver[65]

*In the end, Dorothy's "year" away from the CW lasted only six months. By March she was back on Mott St. Solitude, she had concluded, was not for her. At some point she wrote this account of her solitary retreat:*

> Every Friday afternoon I walked the mile to the village and took the train, getting off a few stops along the line and then walking another mile or so [to see her mother, Grace Day] and then sat and sewed and chatted with her…

---

65    Sister Peter Claver (1899-2004), a member of the Mission Servants of the Most Blessed Trinity played a tremendous role in Dorothy's life and the history of the CW. As recounted in *The Long Loneliness*, it was Sister who provided Dorothy with the first contribution—$1—toward publication of the CW. And it was later she who introduced Dorothy to Fr. Roy and his retreats.

But most of the week, those seven long days, I was alone. I got up at 6:30 for a seven o'clock Mass. The Sisters, of course, were already in the chapel for their meditation and morning prayers. Then after a solitary breakfast, the only meal I enjoyed during the day, I returned to the chapel for another hour of praying and meditative reading

During the month of October I read St. Teresa's treatises on prayer, or some of them. Mostly I labored at watering the garden of my soul, with much toil. The litanies, the rosary, repetitive prayer always helped to put me in an attitude of adoration and thanksgiving and petition.

Sometimes I prayed with joy and delight. Other times each bead of my rosary was heavy as lead. My steps dragged, my lips were numb. I felt a dead weight. I could do nothing but make an act of will and sit or kneel, and sigh in an agony of boredom. Taking refuge in St. Benedict's advice to pray often and in short prayers, I took flight on these occasions and walked, or went back to my room and read or tried to work. I well discovered what acedia was, that noonday devil, so well described in Helen Waddell's translation of The Desert Fathers.

In the afternoon I tried to rest but restlessness was often my portion. I read also two hours daily on Goodier's *Life of Jesus Christ*, which I have found unequalled...

I came to the conclusion during those months that such a hermit's life for a woman was impossible. Man is not meant to live alone... To cook for one's self, to eat by one's self, to sew, wash, clean for one's self is a sterile joy. Community, whether of the family, or convent, or boarding house, is absolutely necessary...

From that "year" I spent away from my work, I began to understand the greatness of the Little Flower [St. Therese of Lisieux]. By doing nothing she did everything. She let loose powers, consolations, a stream of faith, hope and love that will never cease to flow. How much richer we are because of her.[66]

Palm Sunday

The birds awoke me with their singing today. It is light now at 6:20 a.m. (wartime). It is warm and cloudy and probably it will rain. Two Masses today, and Julia stayed to breakfast (a feast) and for the nine o'clock. The young Dominican said the Mass prayers and the Gospel slowly, distinctly, so one could reflect as one followed him. A day of rejoicing and of sorrow. Again the twofold aspect of the Cross.

I shall always have a bright red cross in my room to be reminded of this. One can see why last Friday was the "feast" of Our Lady of Sorrows, and so celebrated by the Mexicans.

---

66    This text appears in William Miller, *All is Grace: The Spirituality of Dorothy Day* (Garden City, NJ: Doubleday, 1986), 105-106.

Monday in Holy Week

The Gospel in the Mass today is about Mary Magdalene anointing Jesus with the costly ointment at the dinner party, and Judas saying sourly that it should have been sold and the money given to the poor.

How unjudging Jesus was, and how appreciative and grateful. Mary Magdalene had been forgiven some time before, had reformed her life, had gone back to live with her sister Martha, but evidently she had not as yet "stripped herself"—gotten rid of all her possessions, even her most unnecessary ones like precious ointments, since she had some on hand to anoint our Lord with. "By little and by little" we go on, and if we accept the deprivations that come about month by month, year by year, with joy, as coming from God's hand, He is evidently patient and rewarding of this abandonment.

Not that we must not do our share too in generous sowing. Especially of all unnecessary things. But food and clothing we need and we must consider our state in life, as mother, wife—a member of a family. It is good to cook a good meal for others, to wear an attractive, modest dress for others—and for oneself too.

But people are horrified at the idea of giving up cigarettes, candy, liquor, movies, radio, newspapers—and all these things are so unnecessary. Without them we would be so rich, our family life would be so full. We deprive ourselves of so much in order to have these anodynes, these means of forgetfulness. When we should be sitting down and meditating in our heart on the richness and glory and generosity of God.

Tom [Sullivan] writes from the Pacific that heaven for him at that moment is in a cigarette, a piece of candy—"tho of course letters come first." If I could I'd overwhelm him with cigarettes and candy, deprived as he is, prisoner of conscription, of every normal joy of family, of peace, surrounded by hardship and making light of it.

Tuesday in Holy Week

Last night I had boiled chicken feed, cracked corn, wheat and oats, dandelion greens and a piece of bacon and tea with lemon. Before collecting my supper (there was a cold wind) I had spent an hour in chapel with rosary and vespers. Darned stockings all evening. I listen to the news morning and evening so anxious I am about Donald. Finland is not going to make peace with Russia!

Friday in Easter Week. Easton

A beautiful sunny day. I went up the hill at 8:30 to stay with the children, Eve's two and Helen's 10 mos., Celia, whom Eve is taking care of. I stopped on the way up to rest, sitting on the hayrack which stands by the side of the road, and reading Matins and Lauds while I rested. These hills are steeper than I remember them.

I had no sooner settled to write a few notes when Father Magee (pastor of what used to be the Syrian Church) came up for a brief visit. Peter Maurin soon followed and as they sat and drank "wheat coffee," which Victor calls "satzy," they talked of Benedictinism, the Rural Life Movement, authority and freedom, while I sat and practiced holy silence when I felt like bursting in with disagreements.

Tamar and I went up to the highest alfalfa field to see the goats and it was hazy gold all over the Jersey fields far down below us, and the Delaware River sparkled in the sun. It winds in a complete and sharp semi-circle around our Catholic Worker hill-top farm.

After we came down the hill we worked at house cleaning the cabin where Tamar and Dave will live after their marriage. It is vermin-ridden now.

Then suddenly in the midst of the bright sunny afternoon, while Helen and her other four babies and Tamar and I were resting on a sunny bank, tragedy came. Vic arrived to tell us wild dogs had attacked all the goats after we had left—killed one outright and fatally wounded three others whom he would have to kill. The scrawniest, poorest one of the lot was left, with a tiny white buck, and the buck and doe of the best goat, only two weeks old, and not likely to survive the death of the mother.

Tamar is nursing them now, feeding them out of a bottle every few hours, and they are living with us in the kitchen where it is warm.

I felt so sorry for Vic and Eve after their years of tender care of all the goats, and the expense too of feeding them when they were unproductive. They are having to buy milk from the dairy for their babies and it is constant drain.

*Tamar's wedding to David Hennessy took place on April 19. Peter Maurin delivered a speech on "pigs for profit," an event Dorothy described in* The Long Loneliness.

May 5. The Grail, Foster, Ohio

I am sitting at the window of my room at 3:45 p.m. swathed in sweater and blanket, looking out at a rainy landscape and sipping a glass of hot milk. That very hot glass of milk warming my hands typifies the loving, warm, generous spirit all around me. "Filled with the milk of human kindness," are these Grail workers.

Day before yesterday, I arrived at 7:53, getting off the greyhound bus right at the edge of a meadow on the other side of a long bridge over the Miami

River. The two houses stand on the hilltop and look down on the river. There is the sound of rushing water over a dam and now the river is swollen and turbulent from much rain. Stairs (Jacob's ladder) lead down to the road which runs thru the little town, and leads around the corner to the Church where we have Mass three days a week. Other mornings we recite Prime and read the Prayer of the Mass of that day. Both mornings now it has poured and we have knelt wet in the Church. I prayed the Blessed Mother not to let me get a cold and the rheumatic pains I'm so subject to.

There is one full day:
    Arise 6:45
    Prime
    Mass
    Breakfast
    Manual labor 10-12
    Meditation 12-1:15
    Lunch
    Rest
    Meditation 3-4
    Work 4-6
    Supper
    Practice singing
    Compline. Bed.

And the entire day in silence! Which is hard at meals, a real mortification in the true sense of the word, but a joy at all other times. So much to think about. So much work to do. "My lines have fallen in goodly places."

Meditation on the immensity of God. When I was a child in California (mother and the wind).

Our meditations this week are on the practice of the presence of God.[67]

Saturday. St. John at Latin Gate. May 6.

This morning we arose at 6:45, recited prime in the parlor downstairs and then went for a good walk before going to the Church, which, by the way, is named St. John's. We crossed the high bridge, walked a half mile down the highway, turned down a side road and came back by another bridge and down the river road to the church. There was a man out in a flat boat in the river, examining his lines which extended across the stream.

---

67  A reference to one of Dorothy's favorite books, *The Practice of the Presence of God* by Brother Lawrence of the Resurrection (1611-1691).

After my hours of meditation down in the Church I came back to find a huge tub of hot water laid out on a canvas mat, covered with bath towels. Also hot milk, so welcome on these cold rainy days. It must have been a terrific job to carry that tubful up the stairs. But these things are done unobtrusively, so quietly, invisibly! While we were in the parlor to make our preparation for Mass for an hour before supper, the tub and accoutrements as quietly and mysteriously were wafted over.

How intensely grateful I am for these lovely, hospitable acts. My room, bright, freshly painted, filled with tulips and lilacs, plenty of soft warm blankets; a raincoat to cover me, Joan [Overboss] taking my shoes tonight to clean them! Country shoes are dirty!

There is little furniture so the place is easy to clean. Not enough chairs, so three or four have to kneel at the table.

Rosary comes directly after and today Joan knelt with her arms outstretched thru the whole rosary. Others did the same for a decade at a time.

They are generous to others, unsparing of themselves. There is plenty of food and rest, but they never stop working until five on Saturday when they begin to prepare for the Sabbath, which they truly keep.

Meditation: The difference between a dead-weight knowledge and a living rich experience can never be enough expressed. Everyone knows too much, feels too little. St. Paul—the new man. Seeing all things new (Chesterton). St. Ignatius: obedience. St. Francis: poverty. St. Dominic: truth. Pray that some great thought will click. Pray to become aware, to will to live in Presence. Necessary to continually renew your intentions—pure intention: kneel down every now and then. Or stand, eyes closed before a new job, etc. To pray always, to create the propitious atmosphere. Let the men give the lecture, women create atmosphere.

June 10

This last week has been a week of war. The invasion of Europe started Tues. Fr. Magee announced it at Mass. Since then the Syrians have been three times a day in church. There has been conflict on the farm too, but not serious— over private vs. communal property. I do not rightly understand the issue. I only know it is best to keep silence and wait and things straighten out. To overcome my own temptation to impatience and anger, I went to confession, Corpus Christi, and shall go again when anything impends.

Thurs Nov 30. Fr. Roy SSJ[68]

On retreat we are with God. Do not put Him to one side. Are you alive supernaturally? Are you dead or alive? Are we alive as sons of God? All nations have turned away from God. The only visible sign of Christianity is *brotherly love.* Where is it now? We must be convinced of Jesus. Try to reproduce His life.

Texts of St. Paul: Time will come when people will not endure sound doctrine. People will come from all over to hear good sermons. But they leave out fundamental teaching of Christianity: The Cross. If we really understood what it means to be a son of God, it would be next to impossible to offend God. The fable they believe is "as long as there is no sin it, it is all right." The cause of sin is to act from *natural motive,* for self. It is not *sufficient* to lead a good natural life. Greater difference between God and man and man and dog.

Up here in the chapel conference room, twelve of us listen to Fr. Roy talking of faith and the supernatural life.

# 1945

*Dorothy's diary skips from November 1944 to February 1945.*

Tuesday, Feb 20

Snow, cold. No coal or oil. Burning boxes downstairs and in the guest apartment, old linoleum, layers of it torn up from the floor. Painting almost done.

Tonight there was a reception in honor of Jacques Maritain, given at the New School of Social Research to which I was invited. Some eleven years ago when M. Maritain was on his way back to France, our Lithuanian miner's daughter cook made him some candy as a parting gift. So tonight to keep up the tradition I brought him and Raissa Maritain a loaf of unleavened bread, a pair of hand-knitted socks, and (for the Holy Father, since M. Maritain has been appointed Ambassador from France to the Vatican) some copies of the *Catholic Worker.* He was very happy, he said, to receive them and promised to put some copies, which he would select, into the hands of the Holy Father. He was so cordial that I was very happy I went, though it had not been with-

---

68  Fr. Pacifique Roy, a saintly French-Canadian priest, became one of Dorothy's closest spiritual advisors. He came to live for some years at Maryfarm, where he set an example by his capacity for work, his joyfulness, and his ability to make the gospel come alive. When he lost his memory one day and had to be hospitalized, Dorothy asked him whether he had possibly offered himself as a victim. Suddenly lucid, he replied, "We are always saying to God things we don't really mean, and He takes us at our word." (*LF,* 128-34)

out much misgiving and much prayer. God help him in the most critical and trying days ahead.

Sunday March 4

Today is Tamar's 19th birthday. It was so warm she planted radishes, picked chickweed for the sick hen, and cherry branches for the Easter altar. David put the cow out for the second time. It looks as though this most severe winter (worst in 20 years) is over. And Tamar has been warm in her tarpapered shack which she and David call Cobbett Cottage. Last year at this time she was worrying about the cold and squalor of poverty and I was reading Newman to comfort myself about her marriage which began most certainly with much hardship. Their honeymoon was taken up with using sulpher candles, kerosene and carbolic on the little house which had been lived in by the Buleys. On her wedding eve she planted a rose bush. There was neither mirror nor bath to prepare her for her wedding. She bathed in a pail the night before, and never did see how lovely she looked in her wedding dress, made by Mrs. De Aragon.[69]

David and I talk history—[William] Cobbett, [G.K.] Chesterton, [Hilaire] Belloc, and [Eric] Gill.[70] Today Peter and I have been talking [Léon] Bloy and [Charles] Péguy. Jon T. is reading the former's "Letters to his Fiancé."

I must speak Wednesday to a high school assembly together with a Protestant and a Jew. We present 3 religions and the students we address have no faith, the majority. Their leaders are Marx, Freud, Darwin. It is in the air they breathe. What was most daring to believe and live by a generation ago now is a commonplace.

A friend of mine worked with a group of socialists back in 1918 who were much interested in Freud. They used to tell her seriously her health would be endangered if she did not get rid of some of her inhibitions—in other words succumb to the advances of one or another of them. That was the talk of the intellectuals in those days. Now this present day there is M., a former nun of a contemplative order, who after 7 years or so in the convent is out these past 5 years or so earning a living. She is working right now in a government loft at a power machine mending army and navy clothes. Her companions are colored, Puerto Ricans, Italians, the poor from our neighborhood. And they are talking the same way. They discuss their weekend amours with a horrifying frankness. They live for their gluttony and their lust. And they assure her

---

69   The mother of Tessa Day, Dorothy's sister-in-law.

70   David Hennessy was a devotee of the English Distributists, and later tried to conduct a mail-order business in their books and pamphlets.

she will have a nervous breakdown if she does not live in the same way. One generation the intellectuals, the next generation the poor, the workers.

What am I to talk of to these young high school students for 15 minutes at their nine o'clock assembly? Mutual tolerance, the brotherhood of man? There is no brotherhood unless we recognize each other as creatures of body and soul.

Mike Gold[71] in his *Jews Without Money* used to say he was chased on the streets of the East Side with the taunt "Christ-Killer." Now we are all Christ killers. Shall I read them Léon Bloy on the Jew, or Péguy, or Maritain, or St. Paul?

Or shall I ask them if they have any faith, Protestant, Catholic, or Jew and what do they know of that faith? Do you believe, I would like to ask them, that we are fighting, Catholic, Protestant, and Jew, for the right to worship God as we choose? That is what a billboard I saw in Brooklyn the other day said. Do you believe it? In what do you believe? What do you read? Do you read the seething ironies, the satires of Aldous Huxley? Do you read Franz Werfel, Ignazio Silone, Arthur Koestler? All non-Catholic, but men of faith. Or Bernanos, [François] Mauriac, [Emmanuel] Mounier, [Etienne] Gilson, [Jacques] Maritain, Gill or Belloc or Chesterton—all Catholic thinkers.

In many countries students have been the revolutionaries interested in ideas, plotting, planning, revolting for them. In this country has education spread out over the millions meant a lowering of every standard of thought? A giving up of ideals? Perhaps it is only the Communist youth who has retained a belief with the zeal to work for it, using any means that comes to hand, to work for the order in which they believe. The rest, are they stupefied with bread and circuses, as so many of their elders?

Every one must go through something analogous to a conversion—conversion to an idea, a thought, a desire, a dream, a vision—without vision the people perish. In my teens I read Upton Sinclair's *The Jungle*, and Jack London's *The Road*, and became converted to the poor, to a love for and desire to be always with the poor and suffering—the workers of the world. I was converted to the idea of the Messianic mission of the proletariat. Ten years later I was converted to Christ because I found him in the people, though hidden.

In the people, not in the masses. The pope has pointed out in his Christmas message this year '44 the distinction between the masses and the people and these words called down the wrath of Stalin. The masses, insensate, unthink-

---

71   Mike Gold, a leading Communist journalist and the author of *Jews Without Money*, was one of Dorothy's oldest friends.

ing, moved by propaganda, by unscrupulous rulers, by Stalins and Hitlers, are quite a different thing from the people, temples of the Holy Ghost, made to the image and likeness of God.

But the term "the masses" had become a holy term, part of the opiate of the people. It was a holy idea, the dictatorship of the proletariat. The masses had the idea of the masses—something which moved this insensate mass to emotion, to holy wrath, to zeal, frenzy. It gave them faith in themselves—a belief that representatives of that inchoate mass were representing them, a living, breathing, collective soul. The idea dispelled the loneliness with which each one of us is afflicted, it dispelled the sense of our helplessness, our hopelessness.

And the Holy Father has pointed once again to the responsibility of each one of us, has reminded us of our free will when we have been looking to selling our inheritance for a mess of pottage, when we have been asking that Christ turn stones into bread. "Security, security," we cry, and the answer is "Not by bread alone do men live but by every word which falleth from the mouth of God."

*

When a man has to kill a dog by beating him over the head—he stops beating him when he is dead.

The same with us. When we are dead we no longer suffer, we are no longer chastised. When we are dead to ourselves.

Meditate on some aspect of the passion. For me Agony in the Garden, desertion of friends, aloneness, lack of love on the part of others—on my own part. The greatest suffering of Christ was the Temptation, not to love his fellows any more.

The preceding paragraph was written two months ago and a few weeks ago a very hard experience began. Michael [Kovalak][72] first, then Cyril [Carney], began tormenting me with demands for the impossible—Michael that I get him back in the seminary from which he was dismissed five years ago, and Cyril that I take him to Easton and give him a private room for his mind's health. He has recently been released from Rockland State Hospital for the Insane, where he had been confined for trying to kill his brother (for the last nine years). This persecution lasted weeks—on Michael's part it had been recurrent for years, but this was his worst attack.

---

72   Mike Kovalak was a loyal member of the CW household from before the War until his death in 1977. He always wore a black suit and he had the long features, beard, and wide eyes of a Byzantine icon. He was forever in mourning for his failed vocation as a monk.

He would come in and stand over me and with livid face—sweat rolling down his face—call down curses from heaven upon me, damning my soul to the lowest hell for interfering, as he said, with his vocation. He was going to see to it, he protested, that I was going to be punished, and all who worked with me. I was afraid for a time that he would set fire to the house. I was afraid, coming and going. It was bad enough to be pestered by one, but two! And then Polly [Holladay, *Greenwich Village restaurant owner*], who came out of Manhattan State Hospital also came to the office and, according to Dave and Fr. Duffy, was very abusive. She wrote me a very mysterious letter and asked that she come down and cook for us. Three!

In the country it had been almost as bad with scenes on the part of Jon [Thornton], his wife, Maurice [O'Connell], and a few months before another mental case whose mother joined in abusing me for my lack of charity in not keeping her. Then H.G. added her voice to those others with letters. Thief, hypocrite, lacking in hospitality, charity, and brotherly love, lazy, a malingerer, expecting others to do all the work while I went traveling around the country, a liar, cheat, deceiver, perverter of Peter's teaching. People have so trembled with rage as they approached me, shaking their fists, shouting, beating on the table, that I have literally expected to be assaulted, beaten.

One night I dreamt that I was struck. I have a haunting memory of having read somewhere of a woman being torn to pieces by a mob and I have felt so surrounded by hatred that I was afraid. I wrote to Fr. Hugo and without telling him details, told him of my feeling surrounded by hate but he did not reply, answering only about his own work, his own complaints. We are all so alone. I wrote to the Abbot of Gethsemane to whom I have gone before and told him of my cold and desolate fear and he wrote a very reassuring letter.

But how fearful a work this is. I wonder at my presumption and yet I have to go on. I pray for love—that I may learn to love God, and I am surrounded by such human hatred and dislike that all natural love and companionship is taken from me. Certainly all the joy one has in loving others is taken from me. "Hell is not to love any more."[73] "Love in practice is a harsh and dreadful thing compared to love in dreams."[74] I can only comfort myself by remembering that vines must be pruned to bear fruit. Love is being cut away to bear more love. I prayed to understand some aspect of the Passion and am oppressed with fear. Which, after all, is what I have prayed for. In the Garden, He began to be afraid. He was "sorrowful and dismayed. My soul, he said, is

---

73   A line from Georges Bernanos's novel, *Diary of a Country Priest.*

74   One of Dorothy's favorite lines, spoken by the saintly Father Zossima in Dostoevsky's *Brothers Karamazov.* William Miller took this for the title of his history of the Catholic Worker movement, *A Harsh and Dreadful Love.*

ready to die with sorrow. He began to be bewildered and dismayed." ([Ronald] Knox)

Another thing—when these accusations begin to rain down upon me, I can see all too clearly that though immediately and specifically not applicable, they are generally true, of the past if not of the present. Like the character in Koestler's *Darkness at Noon* I can see how I have been guilty and am suffering only for my sins, past and present.

St. Joseph's Day

Today we tried to sing the Mass. A dismal failure, first pitched too low, then too high. Fr. Roy, sad at our singing, took the girls to the train. Hans, too, and then picked up Fr. Magee's organ that he had offered us. Which means more noise. I wonder whether my sense of hearing or smell torments me most. Washing all morning. The machine is wonderful. More organ practice. I fled to Tamar. I had had a horrible dream last night, from thinking of Selma Bjorno, in the psychopathic ward, and from thinking about Al and Frank and their tragedies. I dreamed all Frank's children were imbeciles—little old men such as I had seen at Rosewood.

March 22

Tamar went to the hospital today for her clinic visit and they kept her.

March 23. Feast of the Seven Sorrows. No word yet

"Blessed is the fruit of thy womb."

"From the sweet blossom of thy womb." Out of the depths have I cried unto thee O Lord. Out of the depths of my heart and understanding. It is not understanding, however. How can one understand the mysteries of life and birth? What a wonderful time to have a child. Tomorrow is the feast of the Annunciation usually but this year it is transferred to April 9.

April 3

Tamar came home that time and this a.m. at 10:30 went again.

Baby Rebecca born at 7:30.

June 24

Last Thurs 21 Jon [Thornton] left for Philadelphia to begin to serve his four-year sentence for refusal of conscription. He left without saying goodbye to any of us here on the lower farm.

Since last writing Rebecca has grown and become very much a person. Tamar and I go out walking with her in the evening. What joy.

Tuesday June 26

We should hunger and thirst after holiness.

Too few even desire holiness. "Make us desire to walk in the way of Thy commandments."

Fr. Urban Gerhart is giving us this first summer retreat. Yesterday it was very hot, ninety, but today is cool and comfortable.

Pius XI in Encyclical on Christ the King says evils of the world due to secularism.

So far since we started this retreat house last Fall we have had four retreats, Sept., Thanksgiving, Xmas, Easter. So far four more are slated for the summer.

Our life-long fight as a Christian is to get off the natural level and on the supernatural. Our lives must be a pure act of love, repeated many times over. We are invited to a life of infinitely higher level, union with God. Baptistry a few steps down signifying burial, death with Christ. We cultivate our human powers only as they help us reach God. We have manhood, we are given Christhood.

We always act out of motives—animal, human, or divine. There are 3 lives in us all seeking their loves. As long as we keep the lower subservient we have harmony. All day long we should keep on saying, "O my God I love you," or "I am loving God."

Tho we are given a share of divine life, we have no natural liking for it. Here is source of all our difficulty and all our merit too. Fr. Nelson calls our life a testing, a temptation. These are they who continue with me in my temptations.

St. John 3.5. Unless a man be born again. Adam life, natural life must be brought under complete control. St. Paul 3:17. Whatever you do in word or work do all in name of Lord Jesus. Work for Lord, not for men.

1 Cor. 10.31. Definition of supernatural life. Whatever you do—do all for glory of God. Use all—as a train, to get someplace. Creatures are steps. In this way we have a true love for creatures—an instrument in service of God. No wishes of my own passion, own self-life. Every action has an infinite value.

Grace is communicated life of God. Soul takes on divine life but does not change its identity. Like iron in the fire, transformed but still iron.

If you live the life of faith, it is non-sense. The Cross is non-sense. We must give over our faculties to God. "Thy meat is to do the will of Him who sent me" Matt 22.20.

St. Thomas. Perfection of Christian life consists in charity, to man, to God first.

*From Dorothy's column in the July-August 1945 CW, "Notes by the Way":*

June 29th

Today, two FBI men came in to see Fr. Duffy about a draft evader. He knew Father and had talked to him on a number of occasions. With the stand he is taking, this is the last place that he would hang out, with us fighting conscription as we are, issuing articles on its immorality, etc. These two men, a Mr. Walsh and a Mr. Seccor, used first a bullying tone, then an emotional appeal, and then threats, trying to make Father Duffy promise that he would let them know if he came across the young man they were looking for. We have had many a man from the FBI come in to interview us but none so stupid in their behavior as these two.

July 4

Reading Raissa Maritain's *Adventures in Grace* and was much interested in her account of Père Clerrisac's spiritual direction. He had a great admiration for primitive Christianity and the works of the early Fathers. Jacques and Raissa were reading St. John of the Cross at the time and were intensely desirous of sanctity, and conscious of the need for effort to attain it. Père Clerrisac emphasized God's grace rather than personal effort. A point which I well understand. It interests me much to see this struggle of two points of view which goes on still, and I do not see why there should be any opposition between emphasizing the need for effort toward personal sanctification and at the same time the calm faith that God can do all things. "Love God and do as you will" [St. Augustine]. I love the Maritains for their love for St. John of the Cross.

July 21. Sat eve

It is still light enough to sit outside and write. An almost full moon is coming up over the hill. I am sitting on Tamar's front step between the forsythia bush and the mulberry tree, watching the kittens. The mother cat is chasing crickets. It is clear up here but over the town is a pall of smoke. An airplane flies overhead, a night bird cries out in the trees, the ewe under the cherry trees cries out for her two adventurous lambs, almost as big as she is, and they pay no attention to her. They can frolic around, she is tied. The other sheep, which Father Magee gave David and Tamar for a wedding present, runs around loose too. Also Monsie, the kid of the Angora goat. They have a very good time together. Every now and then they come up on the porch of the little cabin I inhabit on the farm and stampede around. The other night I was reading Vespers and the big round sheep with the long solemn face and the tiny kid both stood at the door and looked in at me solemnly.

We owe a great debt of gratitude to that sheep. First for the lbs of wool she gave us which we put in a burlap sack and sent to Bartlett, Harmony, Maine to be carded and spun. It cost only $1.80 for the fleece and we have skeins of beautiful strong wool. Now we have three more sheep which cost 8 a piece and we will have wool for suits, blankets, socks, etc. We have not yet bought a loom but are looking for a small one, easy to handle and to move about.

We are grateful too for the older sheep bringing back the three new ones when they had wandered away. They stayed in the woods for several weeks, and finally wandered down the hill and into the barn one stormy evening.

Since the June issue of the paper came out Gerry Griffin has come home after 3 years in Syria, Africa, Italy, and Holland. We don't know how long we will have him with us. Dwight Larrowe is back on a 35-day furlough and will have to go on to the Pacific. (Gerry is with the American Field Service, a lieutenant, in charge of thirty ambulances). John Givens from the Seattle group, a seaman, is in between trips. Previously he had been shipping out from the West Coast but now from Baltimore. He was on his way to France and will bring greetings from us to [Emmanuel] Mounier, and his group in Paris.

Jack English, back from a Rumanian prison camp. Martie Rooney, of the Rochester group, back from a German prison camp.

Jack, who was with one of our Cleveland groups, stayed a weekend with Richard Strachan, not long out of prison, where he had served his third term for being an objector to the draft, cleaned St. Joseph's House of Hospitality in preparation for some thirty beds and mattresses sent us from Maryknoll. (They are always helping us outfit our houses.)

During this past six weeks Jon Thornton, who with his wife and two children have been living on Maryfarm (he was formerly one of the Baltimore group which was solidly C.O.), was sentenced to four years and has started to serve his term at Danbury.

So far this summer we have had three retreats. There will be three more.

July 22. Sunday. Feast of St. Mary Magdalene
Today Fr. Myron beginning his retreat, we have our Lord with us all day, all night, thru all this week in His humanity and His divinity, in the Blessed Sacrament of the altar.

July 23
Thinking of a difficult friend. Probably it is a devotion to truth which makes her so critical in speech. She *must* tell what she sees as the truth about people, their motives, their actions, their lives. Fr. Faber says we must control our thoughts as well as our tongues. "Thought, word, and deed."

*On August 6, Feast of the Transfiguration, the United States dropped an atomic bomb on the city of Hiroshima. Dorothy responded to this event in the September issue ("We Go on Record"):*

> Mr. Truman was jubilant. President Truman. True man; what a strange name, come to think of it. We refer to Jesus Christ as true God and true Man. Truman is a true man of his time in that he was jubilant. He was not a son of God, brother of Christ, brother of the Japanese, jubilating as he did. He went from table to table on the cruiser which was bringing him home from the Big Three conference, telling the great news; "jubilant" the newspapers said. Jubilate Deo. We have killed 318,000 Japanese.
>
> That is, we hope we have killed them, the Associated Press, on page one, column one of the *Herald Tribune,* says. The effect is hoped for, not known. It is to be hoped they are vaporized, our Japanese brothers — scattered, men, women and babies, to the four winds, over the seven seas. Perhaps we will breathe their dust into our nostrils, feel them in the fog of New York on our faces, feel them in the rain on the hills of Easton... .
>
> Everyone says, "I wonder what the Pope thinks of it?" How everyone turns to the Vatican for judgment, even though they do not seem to listen to the voice there! But our Lord Himself has already pronounced judgment on the atomic bomb. When James and John (John the beloved) wished to call down fire from heaven on their enemies, Jesus said: "You know not of what spirit you are. The Son of Man came not to destroy souls but to save." He said also, "What you do unto the least of these my brethren, you do unto me."[75]

*The war ended on August 14.*

*From "Notes by the Way," September 1945:*

> The last line of the last "Notes by the Way" announced that we were going to make a pilgrimage for peace. And now peace is here, thank God, and our pilgrimage will be in thanksgiving as well as in penance for having used the atomic bomb.
>
> We heard the whistles blow when we were on the farm, and all the group gathered together to sing the Te Deum.
>
> In New York, on Mott Street, the joyful festivities continued for several weeks. We thought at first there would be an octave of rejoicing, as the noise, the confetti, the street dancing went on and on. It began on the feast of the Assumption, continued during the feast of San Rocco, and block after block had dancing and parties. There was no drinking, no disorder. Grandmothers and two-year-olds danced, and the juke boxes were pulled out into the

---

75   See *SW,* 266-69.

streets, and firecrackers were set off from housetops, and bands played, and the atmosphere was one of joy.

The flags are still flying in the streets right now because within a week another feast, that of San Gennaro, not celebrated during the war, will begin and continue for five days. Then the Chinese down the block will have some more victory parades, as they did during the first rejoicings, and it is hard to see how the feastings and the paradings can be any more elaborate. By the end of September we will begin to settle down hereabouts for the fall and winter, digging ourselves in, one might say, to face coal shortages, more unemployment, and the illness and hardship that come with poverty and breadlines. The poor know how to rejoice, we are glad to say, just as profoundly as they know how to suffer.

## Sept 3

In my first book [*From Union Square to Rome*] (and how I hate that journalistic title) I dealt at the end with some objections made by my brother to religion. One of the objections was that religion is *morbid*. To be religious is to be morbid. And I can see so well what he means.

One has to *die* to oneself. One has to put off the old man, the Adam life, and put on the Christ life. One has to mortify oneself, mortify one's members. In other words it is morbid to think of death, or dying. It is an end to which all are drifting, but it inclines to melancholy to think of it.

No one wants to die. No one wants to think of dying, save those in intolerable fatigue or agony who look toward rest from their labors.

When one is "in love" one feels a renewal, a sense of being thoroughly alive, a feeling, a consciousness of every sense, alert, keen, and functioning normally to its fullest extent. Or rather, one might also say an expectation of fulfillment, an expectation of flowering, a hunger and thirst for the ineffable where death is swallowed up in victory when we will be dissolved and be with the beloved.

We look for happiness in sex, for pleasure, for ease, for fulfillment; and we lose it or spoil it in two ways: first by not accepting it all as from God, as a sample of God's love, as a foretaste of a new heaven and a new earth, by seeking such happiness as an end in itself; and second by frittering away our taste for true happiness. If we eat always between meals, we have no taste for the banquet. If we listen all day to cheap claptrap on the radio we have no taste for the symphony. Our ears, our tastes are dulled. And in these days, when all the senses are indulged and catered to, there is a living on the surface, a surface excitement, a titillation, which never goes below to the great depths of passion. Even Catholics are affected by these attitudes toward sex. They indulge in all the pleasures of the day. Music is savage, stirring the blood, movements of the dance are provocative, dress is immodest, pictures are suggestive. And if you speak... [*no further text*]

*From "Notes by the Way," October 1945:*

Tom Sullivan, formerly of the Chicago Catholic Worker, is staying here for a while, just back from the Pacific. Jack English, formerly from the Cleveland Catholic Worker is staying, too. Gerry Griffin is back for good now and in charge of the house. That will give Dave Mason[76] more time for writing, makeup, printing, and a good deal of that work can be done on the farm.

He used to love the Philadelphia farm and spent a good deal of his time there. He'll be able to get more to the country now after being tied in New York for the past three years. Charles O'Rourke beams to see the gang coming back, and Father Duffy keeps thinking his labors are going to be lightened, but somehow they never are.

Thanks to such a crew around, there has been a lot of painting going on. The office is painted throughout. Also the front of the building painted green. The halls are washed, and part of the rear house painted red. The back fence is a brilliant green. We begin to look festive, and by the time Christmas is here, we'll probably have Christmas trees blooming in the back yard.

What I've always wanted is ailanthus trees.

*Dorothy's mother, Grace Satterlee Day, died on October 24. She described this event in "Notes by the Way," November 1945:*

"My soul hath thirsted after the strong living God; when shall I come and appear before the face of God?"

But the psalmist also says, "In death there is no one that is mindful of Thee." So it made me happy that I could be with my mother the last few weeks of her life, and for the last ten days at her bedside daily and hourly. Sometimes I thought to myself that it was like being present at a birth to sit by a dying person and see their intentness on what is happening to them. It almost seems that one is absorbed in a struggle, a fearful, grim, physical struggle, to breathe, to swallow, to live.

And so, I kept thinking to myself, how necessary it is for one of their loved ones to be beside them, to pray for them, to offer up prayers for them unceasingly, as well as to do all those little offices one can. When my daughter was a little tiny girl, she said to me once, "When I get to be a great big woman and you are a little tiny girl, I'll take care of you," and I thought of that when I had to feed my mother by the spoonful and urge her to eat her custard.

---

76 Dorothy described David Mason as "a large, slow-moving friend ... who had been a proofreader on a Philadelphia paper. He had also run the house of hospitality in Philadelphia and came to us after it was closed down by the war... No crisis was too much for him, and there were many of them." *LF,* 65.

How good God was to me, to let me be there. I had prayed so constantly
that I would be beside her when she died; for years, I had offered up that
prayer. And God granted it quite literally. I was there, holding her hand,
and she just turned her head and sighed. That was her last breath, that little
sigh: and her hand was warm in mine for a long time after…

One morning I prayed to the Little Flower, whose picture is over the foot
of my bed, that she would especially look after my mother. I reminded her
of her own grief at her father's long dying. That night Julia Porcelli brought
me in some dried blessed roses. The next day, a friend brought a tiny bouquet
with lace paper about it made up of roses and carnations, and my mother
greeted it with a smile and held it in her hands a few times that afternoon.
And it was that evening that she died, so quietly, so gently, saying but a few
moments before to my brother, "Kiss me goodnight and run along, because
I want to go to sleep."

### Christmas 1945

Trees were selling at $35 dollars. Msgr. Nelson bought the Xmas dinner for
200 at the CW. On Maryfarm we had a day of recollection. Pouring rain. Rebecca angelic. My resolution at New Year or rather Dec 26—to sow family.
Toothache.

# 1946

### January 1. Circumcision

Last night we kept vigil at the Cenacle, Sister Peter Claver and I until after
twelve. The nuns were singing *Parce, Domine, parce populo*, before the clamor
started which ushered in the New Year.

Resolution, sowing family.

### January 2

First rabid anti-Semitism in neighborhood. Anti-foreign in general. Two
Jewish shops and two Chinese (one the *Chinese Daily News*) had their windows smashed.

Toothaches and infection in the jaw for over a week.

### January 3

Today read most of the Office traveling on the subway between dentists.
A cold clear day and the house is out of coal again. Visited Julia [Porcelli] at
the Art Student's League and saw her limestone, Mary and Joseph's Betrothal.
Very Jewish—warm, tender. I spoke to her about letting me have it for Mother's gave.

January 4
Seven o'clock at St. Andrew's. Msgr. did not hear confessions. Writing all day, letters, called to be saints. Five other stores have broken windows, now Italian.

January 5
A mild spring-like day so that we could let the fires go out in the apartment. All morning we moved coal, three tons, which Msgr. Nelson gave us. In the afternoon letters, things for the paper. Opera "El Tabarro" and "Don Pasquale."

January 6. Epiphany
A leisurely day. Spring weather. Bath and head wash at John [Day's] (Della there last night), noonday Mass at St. Elizabeth's, a bus downtown at two, writing on textiles, housing, poverty, etc, before bed.

January 7. Press day. Warm
The paper went to press. The place all stripped for action. No fires needed in the house. Walked this evening thru East Side to buy herring and hair brushes. Home at ten.

January 8
Dwight got paper with station wagon. Della and I met at Beulah's to go over mother's things. Drove back to her house where I spent the night.

January 9
Leisurely breakfast, symphony while I washed dishes. Della drove me down with all mother's things at noon—it threatened snow.

January 10
No lunch, no tea, no hot water, no use of sinks in kitchen.

January 12
Jane down so stayed in bed for the day, a good rest. Read Evelyn Waugh's *Brideshead Revisited*, not a satire; a search for God thru creatures. Hound of Heaven. Took care of Rebecca while Tamar and Dave went shopping and to confession. To bed after supper again.

January 13

Masses at seven and ten. I took care of Rebecca for the 10 o'clock. In the afternoon a ride down the Lehigh thru Glendon and around the other side of the river. Rosary, supper, music, burning Xmas greens. Very happy evening. Bed at nine.

January 14. 16°

Letters tonight, writing till late before the fireplace. Supper at Tamar's, she sick with chills. A walk with Rebecca and she none too warmly dressed. We are reading Newman's *Idea of a University* at meals.

January 15. St. Paul hermit. 20° Farm

There was a smell of snow in the air, but by nightfall a beautiful sunset. Arose at six, Mass at St. Mary's chapel. Wrote during my meditation on marriage. Walk with Tamar thru the Italian cemetery, rosary on the way. A cold wind. Attack in *Ecclesiastical Review*.[77]

January 17

Dentist at 11. Reading review of [Ignazio] Silone and [André] Malraux in *New Yorker*—Edmund Wilson. Spent evening marking "Day by Day" and stories in paper for Dave M. to paste up for book—typing.

January 18. 25°

Stanley and David selling papers on Times Square. Letters for me all day—to Archbishop Spellman also. Lunch at Penn Station with Sister Peter Claver and family, Marjorie too. She will come with friend to give us lessons in letters. (A new pen, present from Grace Maguire.)

January 19

Opera upstairs because Jack still not well—"Madame Butterfly." Charlie's birthday and Syrian pastry and tea. Left on 6:50 train with John Ryder and Stanley for farm, laden with type, paper, etc. Arrived at 8:30 and met by Father who is giving a retreat to Joe Connell.

January 20

Two Masses at 7:45 and 8:30. I stayed with Rebecca for 8:30. It breaks her heart to be left alone.

---

77   An essay in the *ER* charged Fr. Hugo with Jansenistic tendencies.

January 21. Cold, rainy

Slaughter of the hog. Great preparations, Raymond and Floyd, Harold, Joe—all bringing water, wood, and heating water in the big bath tub. John Filliger and Joe Cotter worked valiantly with some of Father's good wine to keep off the cold.

January 22

Bitter cold still. Others walking to Mass say that crust sounds like broken glass as you walk over it. Cutting up of pig today, and salting down most of it. Much work on head and hams, and much lard rendered. Washed 24 diapers and other things. Very good for waist line. T. not particularly well. The cold has her down.

January 23. 5°

All walked to Mass but Stanley, John Daly, Peter and me. Letters, reading de Rougemont's *Devil's Share*. Napped. Went sleighing with Rebecca and the poor darling had two spills. Made supper and washed dishes for T. Read, toasted wheat. Bed at 9:30.

January 25

A futile day of many people, all wanting to talk, and talk sad to hear. A fallen priest, young, smug, well dressed, quite fat. Had become involved with a woman as well as with drink. Someone who wished to boost our circulation. Bill Banning just out of jail for c.o. who wished to do big things but not little ones.

January 28

Carpentry done. Great and luxurious feeling of privacy, in my one room where I can leave my papers about, letters, etc. I hate to have anyone read anything I write while I am writing it.

January 31

From Providence to Boston. Bing Crosby in "Bells of St. Mary's." Mediocre.

February 1. Boston

Saw Archbishop [Richard] Cushing this morning. Mass at the Cathedral.

Bus at 3:30. The ride was horrible with drunken and obscene sailors from Portsmouth urinating on the floor.

As deceivers, yet true: "I say what I think." "If I do not like her I'm not going to act as tho I did." The world calls this honesty. But in the supernatural life, in the life of faith, we must see Christ in others—talk as tho we liked all, think well, speak well, do well to others.

How much land does a man need?[78]

Thank God for giving me this practical light.

Means and ends amplified. Peter [Maurin] and Fr. Roy typical.

Now Peter has gotten suddenly old, relaxed physically. He sits by the fire, a continual source of irritation to Fr. [Duffy]. "Peter loves the stove," he will say. "Peter's love is the stove." And there is an acrid note of criticism.

But Peter does not answer. He never justifies himself. His silence is perfect.

Fr. is always justifying himself. I have his same faults so we are very good for each other. I criticize, I justify myself, etc. My particular examen every day is on holy silence.

Only solution is to see every man as better than oneself. Which means hunting for good points, seeing Christ in them, sowing one's judgment, loving even unto folly

Men—each one seeks only his own even thought it is his particular service to Christ, his particular method of drawing all men, of showing his love for them.

Again it is *loving in general.* "Love in practice is a harsh and dreadful thing compared to love in dreams." It is a sword sundering bones and marrow. It reaches down into the depths. It means suffering. Passion is suffering. It is selfless. It seeks to lose self in God.

Friends of the family. The man who came to dinner.[79] Ann, the woman who desires to be beaten, subjugated, so she is a shrew.

Everyone goes thru something analogous to a conversion. They see God. A great light has fallen upon them. They must communicate this good.

Every virtue has its vice. The bottle smells of wine it once contained. [St. Augustine]

Enthusiasm, single-mindedness, also selfish. Never listen to others. Critical of others.

---

78   A reference to a story by Leo Tolstoy. Ultimately a man needs as much land as it takes to bury him.

79   References to a story by Dostoevsky and a popular film about guests who overstay their welcome.

Fear. The courage of converts. No fear in the blood. State & Church. Persecution.

## Feb 6

Titus 3.14. It would be well if our brethren would learn to find honorable employment, so as to meet what necessity demands of them, instead of having nothing to contribute.

This applies so much to the leaders (not the workers) who come to the CW. So many wish to take a "leading" part, instead of considering themselves "servants" of all, as our Lord said. They wish to be leaders of men. Ralph Templin, formerly head of the "School of Living" at Suffern, N.Y., and formerly missionary to India, has expressed these ideas forcibly in a recent letter sent out to friends of the personalist and communitarian movements. He is resigning his work at Suffern to further this idea of brotherhood.

## February 7

Bed. Arrived home last night at one. It was good to get home to be sick. Stopped at Muni for coffee and bagel. Would have telegraphed for someone to meet me but Western Union strike.

## February 8

Bed. Letter from Della. News from [brother] Donald thru a soldier who visited Beulah and Sam [Day]. Donald and Edit are living in a little inn in the Alps. I have read over all his letters—he never mentions names—or very seldom. But he does mention that he and Edit have many friends in Germany.[80]

## February 10

Too ill for Mass. Some friends delivered 6 tons coal, friends of Sister Dulcinia.

## February 13

My first day up. Nine a.m. Mass. Letters, exchanges, two seminarians from Maryknoll.

After lunch, Marge and I foolishly went looking at dresses, it being her birthday. It started to rain and my fever went up. Joe stayed home baking his ham (his birthday present from Kay).

---

80  In 1944, Donald Day and his wife fled Finland for Germany, where he made broadcasts urging resistance against the Bolsheviks. As a result, after the War, he was detained by the Americans and prohibited from returning to the United States.

February 14

9 a.m. Mass. Stayed up till noon but Smokey Joe's intimate insistence on being in the bosom of the family discouraged me so I went back to bed. I am greatly lacking in charity these days.

February 15. 10°

Letters all day. Bitter wind. Put car in garage. Mass at nine. Crippled sacristan tried to make woman with cancerous face stop begging in church. Loud commotion.

March 25. Annunciation. Boston

Mass at Immaculate Conception Jesuit parish with Jane [O'Donnell]. Pouring rain and we got soaked. Jane interested in book shop. Hope we can have it.

March 27 *[writing in capital letters—practicing calligraphy]*

DROVE TO FARM WITH JOE WHO DID ALL ERRANDS. GARDENS ARE BEGINNING TO LOOK BEAUTIFUL. PLOUGHING BEGUN.

March 28

Spring cleaning.
*[Sketch of goats—look more like foxes.]*
Trying to sketch goats. Chloe died today. Three kids born yesterday. Outside my porch 6 hogs grunt. Today planting onion sets.

April 1

Press day. Fr. O'Loughlin visiting. Dutch doctor, two years in Buchenwald.

April 2

LETTERS. SHOPPING FOR OVERALLS FOR REBECCA (ONE MUST PRACTICE LETTERING FIRST WITH CAPITALS).

April 3

Rebecca's birthday. A very happy day and a very gay baby.

April 4

Farm. 5:30. Sent flax seed to our farms. Letters. Father Grace put up the Cross and a shrine to St. Joseph.

Yesterday Rebecca's birthday. A very happy day all around. She is really most adorable.

April 5

Rose 5:30. I meditate on Tamar's future. Probably I shall spend much time baby tending and begin to know real poverty. If I am to do any writing I should begin now.

April 14. Palm Sunday

Low Mass at 8:00. Chapel full. The group with Jane sang the 10 o'clock at Fr. Magee's Syrian Church. I read *Martin Chuzzlewit* [Dickens].

April 15. Warm.

Mass at 7. Washing, arranging chapel, planting onion sets, fencing, etc. Jane & I left after lunch. Stanley has leaflet "Called to be saints" ready.

June 2. New York

A leisurely breakfast in bed, what with Marge pampering me. Mass at noon at Transfiguration Wrote all afternoon "On Pilgrimage."[81]

June 3

Missed Mass what with sleeping late at Tamar's. Arrived at 11 last night,— she was waiting up for me, very lonely without Dave.

June 4

Mass and communion. We are practicing the Veni Sancta and the Te Deum for Pentecost. The sheep are all sheered, thank God. The new fence up—the cattle changed.

June 5

Missed communion. Drove in town, leaving at four with Duncan. Flat tire. Arrived at 7 anyway. Dave back from Washington. Father slightly easier. These have been pleasant days at the farm housecleaning and helping care for Becky. I'm making an afghan for Joanna. Tamar is making a hooked rug.

---

81  In the February 1946 issue Dorothy introduced a new title for her column: "On Pilgrimage." "We should always be thinking of ourselves as pilgrims anyway. When things get tough, I like to recall St. Teresa's 'Life is a night spent in an uncomfortable inn.' And from the gay way she wrote of her adventures, she agreed also with St. Catherine of Siena, who said: 'All the Way to Heaven is Heaven, for He said, I am the Way.'"

Sunday July 14. Meditation on the bus, 7:30

How happy I am in Tamar's happiness. I was thinking of human love and divine love as I came down and how good God has been to us—and a great thankfulness filled my heart. Dave's father just died and I was so thankful it was a quick and not too lingering a death. He had suffered much as it was, two operations in the last 3 years. I prayed the rosary for him all the way in Thurs night and the next night he died.

I remember two things Tamar saying that indicate her happiness. One was when I had a little visit with her on the bus platform as I passed them on my way to the Grail two years ago. She had just been married a week and she looked so proud and happy. She said with a warm note of joy—"He does just what I ask him to do,"—so happy in her power over him, the power of love. And I was thinking God often shows His love for us so much that way, giving us what we ask for so distinctly—like my prayer that mother would not die alone, and then her dying with her hand in mine!

Just last week Tamar said in relation to some zinnia seeds David had bought for her—proudly, confidently—"He always gets just the right things." She talks so little that these remarks are indicative.

I thought on the bus that this is the joyful, confident way we should regard our dear Lord, our spouse.

Another thought, too, when I was considering the great amount of company we are having and the difficulty of seeing so many people. These are the guests of our husband, say, and we wish to do them all honor, make them comfortable and happy. If I keep these thoughts in mind, how much easier to do everything for *love* of Him!

I prayed God at Mass this 5th Sunday after Pentecost to give me the grace to suffer pain gladly. Since I have to suffer it, it would be too bad to waste this precious coin.

I was healed this day of hemorrhoids which I have had several years.

*Meanwhile, Peter Maurin was failing. From "On Pilgrimage," July-August 1946:*

During the month Peter Maurin was anointed. He has been sick for the past couple of years and staying down at the farm at Easton. He is no worse than he has been, but when one is nearly seventy and with heart trouble, it is not good to take chances. The doctor has said that he might die in his sleep and how would we feel if we had never had him anointed. When I asked the pastor to send Fr. Gibson up to the farm, he told me sternly that I should have done it long before, and I felt he was right. What a habit we have of looking at the Last Sacrament as the end. And we do not like to think the end has come for our dear ones. And yet anointing is for the health of the soul and body. Often people rally after being anointed. We should have more instruction on it.

### Aug 2

Blessed are the pure in heart, the single-minded. Men are more that way than women. Duncan in the kitchen sets his mind just on what he is doing. Women think of a million other things.

So many come to the office with their many ideas.

Fr.—Lithuanian with passion plays. Fr. Jones with his colonizing. Fr. [Don] Hessler[82] with his discussion groups. Catholic Action. Fr. Roy—retreats and only retreats.

### Aug 8. Fr. Ott. 7:30 Conference

So many comings and going, yet the silence is kept very well, all seems very quiet and peaceful.

Yet troubles too. Eva nearly died last night with her asthma. And when I went up to see her today there was little Catherine in bed with her, also sick with a cold, and it looked to me as tho she had asthma too. It is heartbreaking. Yesterday I went to see Eileen. She is much better, very much in control of herself. I told her she could come to Mott St. by Thanksgiving. God help me, I do these things unwillingly. I find it hard always. My love of peace and quiet inclines me always to want to do nothing. This drag to take my ease is like the pull of gravity. Will it always be so? My first impulse is always to say *no*. God forgive me for this unwillingness which pollutes all my actions.

Tonight pulled flax, and laid it out on my lawn to rot. Two of the women on this retreat have teased the remainder of Tamar's wool, so it is ready for carding and spinning.

### Sept.

In an article in the *Times* book review there is an article of intellectual and literary trends in Paris today. Marxists, existentialists, and Catholics. Some of the latter are in the middle school it said. I don't see how. The E. are mostly atheists whose faith is a noble despair. They profess to follow Kierkegaard and Dostoevsky and Nietzsche. How they can omit the faith of the first two it is hard to see. "I cannot conceive of life without Him," Dostoevsky said.

---

82    Fr. Don Hessler, a Maryknoll priest, was an early friend of the CW. He was in Hong Kong at the outset of the war and spent several years in a Japanese prison camp. Later he worked in Latin America. He claimed always that Dorothy Day was the most significant influence in his life.

Sept 15 Sunday Feast of the Seven Sorrows of the Blessed Virgin Mary
    The priest to give the retreat showed up with a heavy smell of liquor on his breath. Perhaps he had a cold.
    "The ways of the Lord are unscrupulous."

Sept 16. Monday
    Smiddy out of his mind and the Trappists hastily sent him to us. Unholy haste. He was filled with drugs, acted drunken. There was a psychiatrist there but they only advise drugs and a change of environment. "Fortunately," the father who brought him to us said, "he had not yet taken vows, so they were not responsible for him." To have kept him would have scandalized the monks.

Thurs.
    Smiddy disappeared.

Fri.
    Eileen is ready to come out of the mental hospital. She also was sent us by a priest. We are renting a little flat for her around the corner. She announced to all that she is going to run the office, answer the phone, receive visitors, etc. God forbid.

Dec 10. Tuesday
    Some of these preceding notes were written last year, some the year before. My diaries are scattered in many books.
    Today after the nine o'clock I visited the chancery office. Saw Msgr. Nelson and Gaffney. Must go tomorrow to see Archbishop Spellman about the women's retreat house. Fr. Fiorentino is sick with grippe. He wants us to have a woman's retreat house in his parish. Also another farm.
    Last month we decided to leave Maryfarm, to give up the struggle against all the families there against a retreat house. The farm… [*missing text*]

Wednesday—Dec 11. 9 a.m.
    I'm staying in bed an extra hour because of my usual complaints. Female trouble!
    I would like to write more of the miseries of the flesh which women must bear, to pay for their vanity and their misuse of their bodies for generations.
    The breasts and womb of the Virgin Mary are praised but how silent we are about the dried up dugs of modern women. When I nursed at King's County Hospital during 1918, it was horrifying to see the case of "fallen womb"

of poor old Negro women who had worked hard, stood on their feet over washboard and ironing board and never had proper or sufficient care after childbirth.

# 1947

*From "On Pilgrimage," April 1947:*

Peter [Maurin] gave us a great scare this month. He had been spending the winter in Rochester, in the warmth and comfort of Teresa Weider's home, and in order that he might spend the last half of Lent in town, I went up to fetch him in the middle of the month. He stood the trip well, visited the Newburgh farm, arrived in New York safely, and then after a day at Mott Street disappeared! ...

Everyone began scattering in all directions looking for him. Cabot sat up in the office all night, hoping for a call; the police were notified; Gallivan and Rocco made a tour along the Bowery, visiting the "horse markets" and some of the lodging houses; and we all sat and conjectured and worried. Could he have visited some former friends? His memory was failing him often, and he used to refer to Easton as Kingston, where he had lived and worked before he met me. Could he have gone to Kingston by bus? Could he have gone to Easton?

When we had notified the police, the cloistered Maryknoll Sisters, the Carmelites of Newport, and Abbot Dunn of the Trappist Monastery at Gethsemani, begging them to start offering up prayers for his safe return, we had done all we could...

We slept uneasily. We dreamed of hearing his footsteps on the stair, of hearing his cough, of his call. "Dorrity," he always called me. But there was no sign of him. His accent was so thick, and had become thicker these recent years, so if he did ask directions, falteringly, would people take the trouble to wait patiently until they understood him, and answer him? Or would he be too independent to inquire? There are strong streaks of the anarchist in Peter.

Yes, Peter is bearing his cross now, not being able to use the mind in which he used to take such keen delight. "I can no longer think," he says now and then, sadly. Because he has thought so clearly and so well in the past, we do what no journal has done before. We keep reprinting his little essays from month to month. There are always new readers, always those whose eyes are more opened now to read and understand...

But then, suddenly one noon, after he had been gone four days, he returned. He was thinner, but his color was better. He had been lost, he said, and he was smiling happily to be back. He had been riding on buses up to the Bronx and down to South Ferry... What the human frame can endure in the way of fatigue and hunger! Strangely enough, Peter looks all the better for his adventure...

And just to see that he does not get lost again, we will put notes in all his pockets. "I am Peter Maurin, founder of the Catholic Worker movement... I live at 115 Mott Street, half a block north of Canal." And we ask any of our friends and readers, if they see him wandering ever, to bring him home.

At the end of Lent, we will have his room fixed for him at Maryfarm, Newburgh, and he can sit on the porch in the sun and watch John spreading manure over the fields ready for plowing.

# 1948

*Most of Dorothy's journal for 1948 appeared in the CW and was published in book form as* On Pilgrimage.[83] *A good part of the year—January to March to begin with—she spent with Tamar and her family in their new home in rural West Virginia. Notes on the domestic details of daily life (awaiting the birth of a new baby, for instance), were combined with reflections on her reading, on the lives of the saints, the challenge of love, and the call to holiness. "Meditations for women, these notes should be called," Dorothy observed, "jumping as I do from the profane to the sacred over and over. But then, living in the country, with little children, with growing things, one has the sacramental view of life. All things are His and all are holy."*

June 17, 1948. St. Ephraim

Every now and then I have a delightful dream, warm, full of love, of the body as well as the soul, a dream so rich and pervasive that it remains with me for a few days and it is my real life, and my ordinary life but a dream.

Everyone instinctively tries to seek meanings and the first and most obvious meaning of my dream was that on these spring and early summer days the sap is flowing even in those of fifty. The air is full of sweet smells, the ears rejoice in the sound of birds, the eyes—all the senses are delighted. Everything springs up overnight all around one. And so I suddenly found myself in a dream with a child—it must have been mine since I was nursing it, but the child was not real to me. I did not have my joy in it until I suddenly realized I had another baby too, a little colored child to nurse, and I thought, "How wonderful to be a foster mother to a colored baby—to give it my milk even though I do not seem to have too much!" In my dream I was most conscious of my aged breasts—but somehow they had milk for both, and I woke with

---

83   The original edition was published by the Catholic Worker. It has been reprinted: Dorothy Day, *On Pilgrimage* (Grand Rapids: Eerdmans, 1999).

a sweet joy—that particularly tender, warm peace one feels when nursing a baby.

That happiness stayed with me thru a few days so that I wanted to write it down, not to lose it. For even the remembrance of joys is a taste of the joy itself, and gives strength. So I was thinking, and then the more obvious ideas began to haunt me. My breasts were lean, I remembered to have felt them, as I had seen my daughter do, to see at which breast my own baby had nursed last. I began to fret—was such a dream a sign of my presumption? Was I an empty cistern, trying to refresh others? Was it self-aggrandizement—this generosity? Was I neglecting my own to help others?

I had the thought—in my first flush of joy at the sweetness of the dream—that my dreams certainly were direct, not hidden. But perhaps there are hidden meanings after all.

St. John's day. June 24

Sad rainy weather, heavy making, physically and mentally. Letter from Tamar—loneliness there. I must send her [Willa Cather's] *My Antonia*—stories of pioneers will give her courage. Certainly she is very well off compared to those homeless families in the Municipal Lodging House Irene [Naughton][84] and I visited. And well off compared to the few mental cases we have here now.

A sad world. We are surrounded by sadness. Michael grim and resentful, Carney drunk as well as mad. It is time of full moon.

One must will to rejoice. Wish Father Conway was here to give a conference on Heaven.

*From her column in the July-August 1948 issue:*

> "Your column will not be a pilgrimage this month," one of the men on the farm says, "since you have not been off the place for two months almost." I had begun to feel not only that life was like a "night spent in an uncomfortable inn," as St. Teresa has it (and the weather has been so very hot that the group of us who sleep up under the roof have felt that our inn is indeed not what it should be in the way of comfort), but I also had begun to feel like an innkeeper.

---

84  Dorothy described Irene Naughton as "one of the brightest writers we ever had on the paper." She "wrote many keen analyses of unemployment, corruption in unions, chain store business techniques, and decentralization... She had bright red hair and a warm laugh, and she could write nothing that did not have an Irish lilt to it." *LF*, 141.

*Reflecting on the ideals of her youth:*

> Well, now at fifty, I cannot say that I have been disillusioned. But I cannot say either that I yet share the poverty and the suffering of the poor. No matter how much I may live in a slum, I can never be poor as the mother of three, six, ten children is poor (or rich either). I can never give up enough. I have always to struggle against self. I am not disillusioned with myself either. I know my talents and abilities as well as failures. But I have done woefully little. I am fifty, and more than half of my adult life is past. Who knows how much time is left after fifty? Newman says the tragedy is never to have begun.

## Nov 6. Sat. 4 p.m.

Tamar and Dave in the woods getting persimmons. Steady rain, but very warm. The children in wading all day. Trees are all bare and the black walnuts are harvested. A good year for them.

## Dec. 17—Friday. Della's

For years whenever I am asked at schools and colleges about the opposition between communism and Catholicism I have tried to be as simple as possible and quote from one of the Queen's Work pamphlets. There are three points. The atheism which is an integral part of Marxism, the use of violence to achieve social change, and the abolition of private property. And I used to quote Eric Gill who said "property is proper to man." And by the time I had pointed out our own use of force, our acceptance of modern war, our acceptance of a proletariat, propertyless, irresponsible status, our denial of Christ in those of other race or color, I had not only convinced my audience that I was opposed to finance capitalism, a capitalism founded on usury, but that I must still be a communist. Trying to talk about these things is not so simple. The entire last issue of *Blackfriars* is about property. A supplement has been issued about property with much quotation from St. Thomas.

We who live on Mott St. have much to say on the necessity of property for the average man. When family possesses nothing, and children are coming along and there are old people to care for one thinks longingly of a "house" rather than a flat, a home owned, not mortgaged, a plot of ground for fruit trees (there is a Russian saying that if a man plants 3 trees in his life he will never go to hell).

How can we teach our children about creation and a creator when there are only man-made streets about. How about life and death and resurrection unless they see the seed fall into the ground and die and yet bring forth fruit. A place to live, a home of one's own, 5 acres and liberty, 3 acres and a cow. And yet St. Gertrude said, "Property, the more common it is the more holy it is." And Proudhon said, "Property is theft."

And the success of the communism of religious orders. "Possessing nothing yet possessing all things." It would sound like anti-clericalism to list the acreage of many monasteries in America, tax exempt, always extending, buying up farms and properties round about until entire villages are owned by an Order. "How much land does a man need?" How much land does an order need, one might say. On the one hand, it does not seem becoming in an order which has achieved the temporal security of ownership to decry private property for the masses, for the people who own nothing. Nevertheless (in the bitterness of spirit which life in the slums—the life of the family in the slums brings), I am happy to see this issue of *Blackfriars* supplement on Property.

The present vast possessions of the Robber Barons need to be overthrown, cast down, appropriated, decentralized, distributed, etc. A vast reform is needed. The power of the great corporations, Standard Oil, U.S. Steel, General Motors, the great banks, will all be overthrown and that is something to be looked forward to.

"He has put down the mighty from their seat, and the rich he hath sent empty away."

Communists love to allude to the communism of the early Church. And in the *Layman's New Testament* I saw a quotation from St. Thomas, an explanation, that it was because of the prophecy that Jerusalem was to be destroyed that all the new converts, numbering thousands, sold all that they had and gave their possessions to the apostles to be distributed.

And now it is with great joy that I read in Fr. [John] Osterreicher's booklet another explanation: "Salvation is from the Jews" he reminds us, St. John writes. He quotes Msgr. Chas Journet saying of the infant church: "Never again on earth will the church be so fervent, so loving, so pure as when she was wholly Jewish. Never again in the course of the ages will she find sanctity like that of the BV or even like that of the Apostles." St. Augustine wrote in wonder that "it has not been recorded that any Church of pagan nations did this (sell all that they had and distribute to all), because those who had as their gods idols made by hands were not found so near the truth."

I was thinking while I was in the hospital, how hard those doctors worked—looking after the bodies of all the patients who came in. Dr. Pressley, the one who operated on me, was on hand at 7 a.m. each day to do dressings. He works all day—operated afternoons, visited wards evenings—often he was still around at ten at night.

And where are the priests visiting the sick? Only when they are called definitely for the dying, to anoint or bring viaticum, often when people are unconscious. A priest came in to see me, and gave me his blessing—and the sight was so extraordinary and unusual that everyone was remarking on it.

What a tremendous amount priests could do at these serious times in our lives. Just to be there—to bless, to remind the patients of God. His very presence lifts their hearts to God, so that because of him just so many more prayers rise to Heaven. The Little Flower said her mission was to make God more loved. A priest's presence and kindness always makes God more loved.

In a ward of 12 there were two of us who had our missals, rosaries. A Christian Scientist prayed aloud and with tears. An old colored woman read a Fr. Frey psalm book. And these were four of us praying out of 12 and I have no doubt the others did too.

Oh, to be so zealous for God, to love Him, praise Him, make Him more loved!

Fr. Oesterreicher's booklet emphasizes the zeal of the Jew in praising God, in putting first things first.

4th Sunday in Advent. Woke up to a steady snow. Sue off to Church but I cannot get there. At this time of the year one longs for song and carol.

Dec 21. Tues.

Came home from Della's yesterday.

Operation was on octave of feast of Immaculate Conception. Still hurts, drains.

Dec 23. Newburgh

Saw Lily. Forster's store had been robbed—all fountain pens and watches. Gave F. pictures of three children framed.

Trimmed tree tonight and it looks beautiful. Last night had dinner with Caroline Gordon[85] and two young men, one a teacher from Univ. of Mo., the other a kid from Norfolk. Borrowed two of his books and a booklet of Gypsy recipes for herb medicines from Columbia Univ. library. I shall copy for Tamar.

News this Xmas:

All went to Communion Xmas day.

---

85   Caroline Gordon, the novelist, was married to the writer Allen Tate. In the 1920s they were part of the same New York literary set in which Dorothy traveled. For many years she and Dorothy were out of touch, but in 1947 Caroline converted to Catholicism and their friendship resumed. She and Tate divorced in 1959.

# 1949

Jan 11, '49. Cloudy, 40°. Stotler's Crossroads [West Virginia]

A good day to rest, cloudy and mild, I got here yesterday afternoon at four. Father Ballard driving me from Hagerstown, about thirty-two miles away. Our next-door neighbor here works at Fairchild's, the airplane factory, where eight thousand are employed. He works nights and tries to farm days. He has one son in the army in Japan and two young ones in school.

I'm staying here for a month and on my way home I think I'll ask Mr. Wagner if he cannot arrange that I visit the factory. I've been thru Ford's and seen the assembly line there, but never an airplane plant.

It is raining out now and there is a soft fall that I hope it will clear up by morning so we can have another good walk. We hung out a line full of clothes today and the extra rinsing will do them good. Half the wash we hung inside to have it dry.

Now I am having a cup of catnip tea which I hope will settle my cough for the night. I know it's a sedative anyway.

Wednesday

When we woke up this morning the ground was covered with snow. The branches of the trees were covered because it was that heavy, wet, clinging snow, not the dry fine kind.

Thursday

This morning they went to town at ten and were back at noon with whiting for lunch. That is the cheapest fish there is but even that is thirty cents a pound inland. We saved the heads for soup Friday. Tamar baked, and then we went for a long walk up through the woods to the topmost corner of the farm, looking down on the Webers on one side and the Hennessy place on this. It was a lovely walk through pine woods and there was such a thaw that the ground was soggy underfoot. The babies had their galoshes on, but Tamar and I had just our walking shoes so we did not come home with dry feet. I guess it was about forty in the afternoon but in the morning it was 27.

Sunday, Jan 16

It is so warm out we are sitting outdoors, the children without coats—at least Becky, the hardiest. David left this noon for Washington for the inauguration. He had never missed one yet, he said. We went to the nine o'clock Mass and Father Kealey preached on marriage. He reads both epistle and gospel with a good strong voice, and is filled with zeal for his wide-flung parish, full of Irish names, and all Protestant. He has only a few hundred parishioners.

David has put a wire fence around the garden and it is a garden enclosed. Around the house and this he has put up still another fence to enclose the whole house, flower and vegetable garden, to keep out the chickens, who root up everything. Right now there are no gates, so the chickens are all inside, scratching and clucking and crowing. There is also the sound of the cowbell from Red down by the brook, and the three goats wander on the hillside.

There is Susie, three years old, born the day Becky was, a welcome distraction from worry. There is Nancy and another goat, shaggy and un-doe-ish, they are not sure yet whether she is male or female. Meanwhile we can call it Hermie.

Feb. 15. 70° at 3 p.m.

I am much saddened these days by the lack of meekness on the part of Catholics to persecution. Loving one's enemy, blessing those that persecute, the whole teaching of love. Cardinal Spellman's speech, the Holy Father's, etc., all an incitement to war.

Friendship House in Harlem has started a bread-line and feeds about a hundred men a day. Now they will begin to suffer the rebukes of many friends for "contributing to delinquency," for helping "the unworthy poor."

*In March the Catholic Worker lent its support to a strike by cemetery workers employed by the Archdiocese of New York. Cardinal Spellman, who charged that the workers were under the influence of Communist agitators, brought in Catholic seminarians to dig the graves. He was "proud," he said, "to be a strikebreaker." In the April 1949 issue Dorothy wrote:*

> The story of the strike is told elsewhere; to me its terrible significance lay in the fact that at one end of the world Cardinal Mindszenty and Archbishop Stepinac are lying in jail suffering at the hands of the masses, and, here in our present peaceful New York, a Cardinal [Spellman], ill-advised, exercised so overwhelming a show of force against a handful of poor working men. It was a temptation of the devil to that most awful of all wars, the war between the clergy and the laity, a heightening of the tension which is there and which it is the work of both to try to overcome…
>
> Our pacifism must be a complete pacifism, and our love must grow in strength to overcome bitterness and resentments… What more foolish a love is there than that portrayed in the gospel—the father for the prodigal son,

the love of the shepherd for his sheep, the love which asked the servants to sit down so that the master could minister to them, wait upon them, wash their feet in a gesture of total and utter abandonment of love! And how far we are from it all!

Such a struggle going on shows how far we are from it, and how near to the surface class war is here in this country. There need be no Communist influence to fan the flame of resentment, the sense of injury which working men have been feeling over the years.

And in this struggle as in all the other varieties of war we have known, our job is to build up techniques of nonviolent resistance, using the force of love to overcome hatred, praying and suffering with our brothers in their conflicts.

*Peter Maurin, co-founder of the Catholic Worker, died on May 15, 1949. Dorothy wrote an account of his final days in the June 1949 issue:*

John Filliger had shaved him Saturday, he remembered, and Michael Kovalak had dressed and cared for him on Sunday, conducting him to the Chapel for Mass that morning, taking him to and from his room to rest. He had looked in again at Peter at nine Sunday night and found him sleeping rather restlessly on his side instead of on his back as he usually did. Eileen McCarthy had given him, as she did every night, a glass of wine, and I suppose Hans made his usual facetious gesture with the water pitcher, asking her to fill it for him. It makes me happy to think how everyone was caring for him. And honored to do so, Jane always said, when she spoke of Peter's needs. He was surrounded by loving care. Fr. Faley brought him communion the days he could not get up, and it was impressive, day after day at that sick bed, to hear those prayers, to witness that slow dying. A King, a Pope, could have no more devoted attention, than Fr. John Faley, who has been with us this past year, gave Peter.

At eleven that night, Hans said, Peter began coughing, and it went on for some minutes. Then he tried to rise, and fell over on his pillow, breathing heavily. Hans put on the light and called Father Faley and Jane. Michael, Eileen and others came too, and there were prayers for the dying about the bedside. He died immediately, there was no struggle, no pain. He was laid out at Newburgh the first night, in the conference room where he had sat so often, trying to understand the discussions and lectures. Flowers were all about him from shrubs in our garden and from our neighbors. He wore for shroud a suit which had been sent in for the poor. There was no rouge on his grey face which looked like granite, strong, contemplative, set toward eternity. There was a requiem Mass in our chapel sung by Michael and Alan and the rest...

Peter was buried in St. John's Cemetery, Queens, in a grave given us by Fr. Pierre Conway, the Dominican. Peter was another St. John, a voice crying in the wilderness, and a voice too, saying, "My little children, love one another." As the body was carried out of the church those great and triumphant words rang out, the *In Paradisum.*

"May the angels lead thee into paradise; may the martyrs receive thee at thy coming, and lead thee into the holy city of Jerusalem. May the choir of angels receive thee, and mayest thou have eternal rest with Lazarus, who once was poor."[86]

## June 12

These following two weeks I spent with Tamar. It was very hot except for a day of rain, a downpour which led to floods in W. Va. Later in the month a flood which led to their door. Tamar is pregnant and not feeling too well—dragged out and lonely. Fortunately when I left Mrs. Hennessy arrived and stayed 2 weeks so T had a month of visitors. I sent her *Gone with the Wind, Soul of Woman, Rainbow,* and *Women in Love* to keep her company. It is something to have a good book to look forward to at night. We washed and cleaned and cooked and it is amazing how the time sped by. Haymaking, cooking, cleaning, washing.

There is so much talk of community and so many who desire to share your life, who look at you with wistful eyes, who want from you what you cannot give—companionship. Less hard work, security. Class barriers. They want to move in with you, crawl into your skin. This awful intimacy. Tamar is appalled. Is this what I have to look forward to? she thinks. Loneliness, Freda, Irene, Mrs. Livingston at 80, all young girls with them, longing for love—all in fact who are not working for others. WORK IS ANSWER.

## July 26

All this week Irene and Helen making scenes, wanting to be loved rather than to love, to be appreciated, etc. My turn next. I had better watch for self-deceit. Recite St. Francis prayer daily. Read St. John of the Cross. Fr. Faber's Conferences.

## Within the Octave of Corpus Christi, '49

Haying season, and we got one field in before a 3-day rain. It is hot as ever now but a steamy heat. David is helping the neighbors, Betty Fearnow, get theirs in the barn. The evening chores: Feed chickens, collect eggs; pig; milk and feed cow; goat; draw water from well for washing; water from spring for drinking; fill lamps; wash children and put to bed. And tonight weeding and planting tomatoes and finishing a tub of wash.

---

86   See *SW,* 123-27.

To dry up a cow: milk her on the ground, the neighbors say. The fact that her milk is going to waste, is not being used, causes her to cease giving.

We come to love by knowing.

We know God thru creatures—samples—man made to image of God. Love of neighbor and God so closely linked in one virtue, charity. Reduced all in practice to love of neighbor. This is law and prophets. Man's love for God can be measured by his love for the one he loves least. "For the same measure shall be meted to him." A man loves himself without limit. St. Thomas. As I have loved you (unto death). We should prefer our neighbor's welfare to all except our own soul's welfare. We are all one flesh.

July 7. St. Cyril and Methodius

When I told Fr. Fiorentino that [Tamar] having 4th child: "Not much self-control there," he said.[87]

Having heard this many times from many other Jansenist Catholics I could control myself to a certain extent. But for a priest to say such things. Oh, the cleavage between priest and people, the comfortable and the destitute!

"Do you know the facts of life?" I wanted to say. Instead I said meekly, "Once a year may produce such a result."

That's right, he said. The trouble is he always thinks before he speaks. He says the first thing that comes into his head and reconsiders it afterward.

St. Paul said, 1 Cor 7.

When we were taking care of Helen's 5 while she had her 6th, M. said: "What strong curbs God has put on man's passions by family life. How it moderates them, tones them down." Another time he said, "I am convinced we know nothing of the love of God until we know human love."

By the time a woman is having her 4th child the call of the flesh is far less acute.

One of the troubles with love is that it gets buried in the debris of life, the hardships of child-bearing, the drain and drag of children on the mother is such that she is apt to neglect her husband and lose that love of body and soul so that she has to explore and search in her depths and seek it and pray for it, wooing it and caressing it again into life, seeking it in the body of her husband, bone of his bone and flesh of his flesh, breathing life into what seems dead, as Elias did to the widow's son.

D. H. Lawrence had this concept of love, of sex love, and you find it in *The Rainbow* and *Women in Love.*

---

87  This comment evidently stung. Dorothy adverted to it bitterly until the end of her life. See, for example, May 15, 1969.

Things missed: The last look of the dying, a baby's first smile.

Aug 3. Tues.

A day in our lives. Our alarm clocks do not work. They are always out of order. But the sun rising at the foot of Hester St. awakens one. If it did not, then the bells from Precious Blood Church around on Baxter Street begin to ring at six o'clock, then at six-thirty, then at quarter of seven. By this time one is sure it is time to get up. Aside from the bells, it is usually quiet at this time of the morning. The neighborhood has quieted down by two o'clock in the morning. It is like living in Coney Island on Mott Street.

In Chinatown the streets are crowded below Canal, with tourists as well as the people who live in the crowded tenements. Nowhere else is there such congestion, not even in Harlem, as there is in Chinatown. Families live, eat, sleep in their stores, laundries, and one can look in from the street and watch the mother giving a baby a bath. Some years ago there was a fire and a huge rat-ridden tenement went up like a Christmas tree. Men were sleeping in bunks, in tiers, in conditions approaching those of Buchenwald, and many of them lost their lives. Every fire is a five alarm fire down here.

Noise! But one would rather have this noise of children than be without it.

Trucks—juke boxes, radios, the "L" from Third Ave two blocks away. The house itself trembles with the din.

Monday, Aug 8

Today Tamar and I are canning tomatoes. Seven quarts are on the stove now and when they have boiled 45 minutes I must take them off. Can't go out with the children, under the black walnut tree because the oil stove, as all oil stoves after a year, may literally go up in smoke. So I must sit in the kitchen and watch it. Dave has left for Washington for the week to look around for work, a place to live, etc. If he would only find work around here! Of course there is the loneliness too. They need to be nearer people.

Yesterday we went swimming and it is wonderful how the brook bed has changed—it is shallower where we swim, deeper in the channel. Becky saw a snapping turtle and screamed but Eric wanted to go after it.

These hot August days when we are so tired I wake up wondering what we will do in the dead of winter—it seems to get harder in anticipation and yet I know by experience how one should take the hardships as they come, day by day, one by one, rather than look forward, or backward either. To live in the *now* is to be like little children. To be utterly dependent on our Father is to be like little children.

Alexis Carel says man needs extremes of heat and cold, hardship and ease, rest and work, tension and relaxation, to keep him fit. One has that in such surroundings as these, so utterly different from the city, from the lives of others we know. It is like a "shock treatment," these extremes Carel talks of. I remember reading in Tolstoi of the tremendous work of the peasant, the long hours at planting and harvesting, when he worked night and day. And then his idleness, slackness, at other periods. I wonder if there are many nervous breakdowns among the Russians.

Today it is such a disease with us, our hospitals full, suicides, even amongst Catholics. Fr. Palmer talked of nervous breakdowns in his parish. Fr. Judge said there were ten suicides in his parish in the short time he was there in the most fertile country, in the most prosperous parish in the state. One young girl of nineteen hung herself over a door on a piece of cord and so the cord would not hurt her neck she knotted a silk handkerchief around it.

This breakdown business is prevalent among young mothers too, with young children, and I have heard of two recently whose husbands, as the saying goes, were good providers, held good secure jobs, and well equipped homes. One reads of the prevalence of leprosy in the middle ages when there were leper houses to care for them. Now it is mental hospitals which are an ever-increasing drain on the state. The Church does not feel her responsibility here. It is Holy Mother the State.

Aug 14. Sunday

The feast of St. Lawrence. He sold the estates of the Church when they were in danger of confiscation and gave the money to the poor.

John Curran in a dying condition. Went up there this morning and he was half paralyzed. Cecilia and I had a hard time with him.

From 11-8 I was out at Newton for Jack [English's] "clothing," ten young men starting the novitiate. It was a night of the fiesta and opera singers, men and women with loud speakers to increase their already gargantuan voices, were on the bandstand which is built for this feast each year right across the street.

I got back to find Cecilia in despair, not able to move John. With the help of Kay Brinkworth who has worked at St. Francis home for the aged, we got him changed, up on a stool for a brief moment, rubbed his back and neck with alcohol, and made him comfortable for the night. He cannot hold anything in his stomach at all, tho we tried to give him lemonade.

At one time when I was talking to him he said, "I have not Peter's sanctity," and I reflected on his humility last night as I saw him so uncomplaining, in the midst of such complete poverty—poverty which he had lived with for fifteen years, imposed upon him in a way by ill health and the unemployment of the times, but none the less, joyfully accepted.[88]

No ice in the house, in the midst of this terrible heat, so we had to go over for it to the Hughes's who are luxuriating in a secondhand gas-ice box this summer, purchased for $20 and set up by Joe.

## Amarillo, Texas. Dec 27

Left Tulsa at 5 p.m. Monday. Arrived 6:30 a.m. at Amarillo. Here I am visiting the Blessed Martin Mission which is in charge of Fr. Lux, O.P. who was chaplain to the Blessed Martin Center in Chicago. There is the beauty of the sky but unutterably desolate wastes on all sides—the endless prairies of Texas which have their own wild natural beauty until the hand of man touches them. Father's mission is on the edge of town and the tiny houses of the Negro population straggle along for miles with never a tree or bush to break the monotony.

They are evidently not too willing to give relief here. Fr. says the quickest way to get a man out of jail is to say you are going to put his wife and children on relief.

## Dec 29. St. Thomas

Mary Ann Green had us to supper last night. A friend served. The little girl she is caring for has been with her 2 years. She was found eating from garbage cans. Her mother, a prostitute, was given life for murder. The child's legs were scarred with cigarette burns from the drunken men who frequented her mother's cabin. The sufferings of children.

This afternoon I leave for Phoenix.

---

88  Dorothy's obituary for John Curran, "a most ardent disciple of Peter Maurin," appeared in the September 1949 CW.

# PART III

# THE FIFTIES

❧❧❧

The decade of the Fifties is largely remembered as a time of Cold War fears, McCarthyism, and general conformism. Not so for the Catholic Worker, where the post-war years were marked by a new era of public activism and dissent. The defiant attitude was expressed in a banner headline in the CW: "We are Un-American; We are Catholics." Dorothy's willingness to stand beside Communists and other targets of the Red Scare was not lost on J. Edgar Hoover, director of the FBI. In a note in her files he observed that Dorothy Day "has engaged in activities which strongly suggest that she is consciously or unconsciously being used by communist groups."

Much of this new activism coincided with the arrival of a new actor on the Catholic Worker scene. Ammon Hennacy, who called himself a "one-man revolution," had honed his convictions while serving a prison term as a conscientious objector during World War I. Having decided that Dorothy was the most consistent radical and Christian he had ever met, he decided to become a Catholic and join her cause.

It was Hennacy who organized the Worker's first public foray into civil disobedience. When the City announced plans for a mandatory civil defense drill he seized the opportunity to raise a witness for peace. While thousands obediently responded to the planned siren by taking shelter, he and Dorothy and a band of assorted pacifists stayed put. In what became an annual ritual, they were regularly arrested and jailed—but not without making their point. Within a few years, the small group had grown to thousands, putting an end to the city's foolish "rehearsal for death."

By this time Dorothy was attracting attention beyond Catholic circles. Her autobiography, The Long Loneliness (published in 1952), was widely reviewed. It prompted a two-part profile in The New Yorker magazine. Meanwhile new volunteers arrived to take up the vision. And, as always, there were the perennial worries about family, real estate, new houses opening and closing, and the daily challenge of the Works of Mercy.

*As the decade ended, Dorothy was called to perform a very personal work of mercy—thereby, in a curious way, revisiting the site and the circumstances of her conversion many years before.*

# 1950

From Phoenix to San Diego. Took the All American bus because of the crowds on New Year's and at 2 a.m. ours broke down 20 miles out of Yuma in the desert just over the Mexican border. It was cold, the bus was crowded with sailors trying to get back on duty. Sailors in peacetime are something else from sailors in wartime, I must say. The driver and one of them walked several miles down the road to find help. No one would pick them up. Fortunately, the driver did not tell us we had to wait until another bus from San Diego arrived, [and] we would have to wait. We mostly slept that night and then an unsavory character in a desert shack with a harried wife made us coffee, which was wonderful.

Los Angeles, January 9. Monday

Since I arrived I have had a splitting head—the old migraine headache. It is just fading out today. That afternoon spent with Eleanor Tracy and Miss Price. They work with the Negroes and are not in good standing with the Bishop who has withdrawn their support from them. They are eager for more lay apostles.

Spoke Saturday night before interracial council here.

Sunday it poured. Mass at 10. Could not receive because of my head.

Tomorrow I must see Archbishop [Francis] McIntyre.[89]

Tuesday Jan 10

Wrote all morning, headache continuing. Have been to Mass every morning notwithstanding, missing Communion Sat and Sun. Today it is brightening.

This a.m. saw Archbishop McIntyre, who was most touchingly cordial. People love him here. They say he is humble and holy and that is the way I have always felt about him. He warmed my heart and increased my devotion to the church and the hierarchy. How the heart *wants* to love. How grateful it is to be able to love, to find people loveable. The archbishop asked after Fr. Duffy, said he wanted to see him, how much he cared for him, how much

---

89   James Francis McIntyre, formerly Dorothy's contact at the N.Y. Chancery, was now the archbishop of Los Angeles.

we had all gone thru together. How much he loved the work.[90] He called in Bishop McGuckin and Bishop Manning.[91] The latter is young. I did not realize he was a bishop.

In the evening to the Sisters of Social Service where I spoke on our retreat house and the vision of Peter—anarchism, etc.

Wednesday—I am better, thank God. It rains and is cold.

Whatever is true, by whomsoever it is spoken, proceeds from the Holy Ghost.—St. Thomas.

Dan Marshall, a radical Catholic, was reprimanded by the Archbishop. He was responsible for changing the law on interracial marriage in California. No help from churchmen who should have spoken out. I do not understand the Archbishop and his friendliness to me and enmity, expressed hostility, toward those who are working for justice. He acts as tho he thought I were holding people down instead of trying to stir them up. He told Dan he would be forced to reprimand him, doing it as a citizen, not as an archbishop, as tho he could![92]

Fr. Forrestal of San Diego said Cardinal Newman opposed the promulgation of the dogma of the infallibility of the Pope on those grounds—that there would be misunderstanding of when the Pope spoke infallibly.

Fr. Phillips said no one felt they could advise young mothers so expertly as old maids and young priests—that he had always disagreed with the Pope when it came to his attitude toward capital. It has no rights, only the right to serve, to provide means, tools, direction. True capital is the labor of men.

---

90   Father Clarence Duffy was an Irish priest who had lived with the CW off and on since the late 1930s. Recently, he had run afoul of the New York archdiocese because of his outspokenness on matters of social justice, particularly his willingness to appear on platforms with Communist-front groups. Dorothy devoted two columns to his situation and the dilemmas it posed—the demands of obedience to authority vs. conscience: "Beyond Politics," November 1949, and "The Case of Father Duffy," December 1949: "Fr. Duffy is ... suffering in a great and terrible anguish, living with the poor as he has always done, and he is not patient with his suffering, because ... he is not a patient man.. . We accept the authority of the Church but we wonder why it shows itself in such strange ways."

91   Bishop Timothy Manning would later succeed Cardinal McIntyre as Archbishop of Los Angeles in 1970.

92   The contrast between McIntyre's friendliness toward Dorothy and his attitude toward activists in his own diocese was indeed remarkable. In a column in May 1950 ("Poverty Incorporated") she fondly recalled his comments in this interview: "When I saw Archbishop McIntyre on my January trip to the coast, he told me then never to give up the work we had started, that it was a difficult and delicate and dangerous work which God evidently wanted us to do. I quote this, and I am sure he would not mind, to show that many Bishops as well as priests are dear friends of the work and wish us to continue."

Spoke to women's group—colored and white, all ages, under patronage of Our Lady of Mercy—on the works of mercy.

Monday, March 20. St. Joseph's Mass. Farm. Newburgh, N.Y.

No sale yet and we hope St. Joseph will send us a message today. Fr. [Faley] had removed the Blessed Sacrament 2 weeks ago thinking we were going to move. I persuaded him to let us have it. It will take us at least 3 weeks to move *after* sale.

St. Benedict's. March 21. First day of Spring

Agnes on our floor putting up her hair in curl papers each night. Judy with a bow in her hair. Agnes must be 65. Suzanne very drunk. I tried to persuade her to go home—she agreed but wanted me to kiss her—horrible lustful woman. Toothless wet mouth. To see the ugliness of passion.[93] They are removing the doors from between the rooms by our women's apartments. We are a lodging house!

Feast of the Annunciation. March 25

Dear God, I thank Thee, the farm is sold—to Charlie, who runs the fruit stand across the road. Yesterday morning I took the 10 o'clock bus into N.Y. A beautiful and cold day. Went to the bank to talk about a loan but it does not look as though it would be easy to get. Got to the office in time to meet Mike Gold and his wife who had just gotten in from France and Italy. It was the first time I had seen him in 15 years. They had 2 boys, 13 and 10. The first Nicolai, named after Lenin. They are staying at present at Brattleboro, Vermont with Mannie [*Mike Gold's brother*].[94]

It was a spring-like night tho cold. All were gay and Elinor, Marge [Hughes],[95] and I stayed up talking till 12. Then at 1 a man and women came

---

93   This is one of the incidents referred to in Dorothy's comment, "The older I get, the more I see that life is made up of many steps, and they are very small affairs, not giant strides. I have 'kissed a leper,' not once but twice—consciously—and I cannot say I am much the better for it." ("On Pilgrimage, April 1953)

94   Years later, recalling this visit from her old comrade, Dorothy wrote: "One day in the fifties... Mike, his wife Elizabeth, and their two sons...visited us on our farm on Staten Island. They had brought me a gift, an old print with a painted representation of a pilgrimage to the shrine of St. Anne of Brittany... We still talked of how man's freedom could be protected, how man's basic needs could be provided for through collectives, or cooperatives, or farming communes, as Peter Maurin always called them. But we always came back to the problem of the use of force in bringing about the common good."

95   "Marge Hughes is as much of a secretary as I have ever had. She first came in the early days of the work, when she was twenty-one, and helped me with our already enormous correspondence... In the early days she often accompanied Peter on his forays." (*LF* 142-143) She

bringing a drunken woman in and I was very harsh in not taking her. As Tom said, before dawn came, I had denied our Lord in her. I felt very guilty—more for my manner than for doing it, as we could not have all the other women in the house disturbed.

At the 9 o'clock Mass and a man there so foul in smell that the congregation had to stay on one side of the church. In complete rags and filth. Then at lunch 2 men from St. Francis Church, Third Order members, the kind like California George, talking constantly of miracles, confraternities, dangling with crucifixes, difficult, but their minds set on the honor and glory of God. Certainly thinking always of him—still, unbalanced, needing help. If I ever go off in the head, I hope I go in that way, haunting churches, saying beads, etc. A happy way to be.

Monday
"God is nearer to us than our own soul, for he is the Ground on whom our soul standeth."—Julian [of Norwich]

Last night we were kept awake till one by Mike D. having epileptic fits one after another. Poor fellow. He is getting worse. The other Mike [Kovalak] was in a worse state, mourning Helen Butterfield and his lost vocation.

Now I must write on the book—also articles for the next issue.

Today it is mild, sun, birds, no wind. Still snow and ice on slopes here. The sap is rising. But then I have been having trouble all winter.

Thursday March 30
Today we went to press. A cold day. Just when we had finished the makeup Jack came down to tell us we had been notified we had to move by July. Time to get a note in the paper.[96]

Agnes took home my book last night [*The Long Loneliness*] and finished it at 3 in the morning. And liked it. Della will come down for it tomorrow and read it over the weekend, delivering it to Harpers.

What with Newburgh farm sale which has not gone thru and fear of Staten Island tenants not being out on time, the book, sickness, the fast ahead—and now in bed with a heavy head cold—general misery.

---

married Joe Hughes, a former seaman and volunteer at the CW, and raised several children, including Dorothy's goddaughter Johannah.

96   In the midst of real estate transactions involving the CW farms, Dorothy learned that the owners of the CW house on Mott St. wished to sell the property. ("On Pilgrimage," May 1950)

Monday April 3

The fast started Saturday at midnight.[97] I took the train down, feeling guilty of extravagance—$8.75 with tax, feeling too very much alone in this experience. But then one needs to do penance alone. That is part of it. Meeting at Inspiration House stated at 8 and lasted until 11:30. Then Ammon [Hennacy][98] and I and the Halls went out for coffee and toast. I had egg beside. Not much sleep as reporters came in at 2 insisting on rousing a few fasters. Three of us were sleeping in a parlor so no privacy all day. Up at 7, and after a period of meditation, a walk. Mary [Houston] and Mabel [Knight] called for me to go to the Shrine for Mass. It was wonderful to be there for the blessing of palms, procession, as well as Mass. Distributed leaflets afterward and the girls helped bless them. Slept fitfully in p.m. Short walk and meeting—too many meetings.

A half dozen from [Friendship House] here. I had a bad headache and nausea by evening, so could not speak. Hoarse still from my cold, eyes dim, etc. The first day was bad. Bed at 9:30 and up at 7, to 8 o'clock Mass with Ammon at Sacred Heart church, and feeling much better since. It is presumption to think of being sustained by the host but nevertheless a great increase of strength and peace after communion. It is a dull day, threatening showers. I must go by car to Mass and walk 3 blocks. There are 40 or so here. Mabel came in in the afternoon and we went to a little convent near St. Paul's Church for Benediction. Stopped at the Center for a crucifix and statue of the Blessed Mother for my desk.

Tuesday, April 4

Bright sunny days. Very warm so that most people are going without coats. Mass at 8 with Ammon and Joe Craigmyle—the latter driving us in his truck. He has been in jail for the last year for refusing to register... The hardship of the fast is not so much the fast as in being away from all family, friends, and

---

97  "During Holy Week this year a group gathered in Washington at a settlement hospice called Inspiration House, to fast for peace for the week. It was a time of intense penance and prayer. Many of those fasting engaged in demonstration and distribution of literature. Aside from distributing hand bills at the Shrine of the Immaculate Conception on Palm Sunday, I spent my time in the penance we set out to do." (May 1950)

98  This is the first reference in Dorothy's diaries to Ammon Hennacy, who would become one of the great influences in her life and the life of the CW. Hennacy, who liked to call himself a "one-man revolution," was an anarchist-pacifist who strove to live out his convictions with utter consistency. Their acquaintance began after Hennacy approached Dorothy after a talk: "He wanted me to know that, though he was not a Catholic and thought the Catholic Church one of the most evil institutions in the world, he *was* a Tolstoian Christian, having become one in prison" (in solitary confinement in Atlanta Penitentiary as a conscientious objector during World War I). In 1952 he moved to New York and joined the CW community, where he remained the next eight years.

associates. Feeling of great solitude. It hurts me terribly to be so near Tamar and Dave and the babies, yet so far. And so little chance of going soon, what with the moving... The book too, much work remains to be done on that and it can be done only in spare time. I should be including all these worries in my intentions yet am too abstract and fuzzy minded to think, read, or do anything but the necessities—steady headache. I do not think of food as yet. No desire for water. I have to remember to drink it. Across the street my desk faces a window—there is a lovely little park. Forsythia is all in bloom. Am reading *Kristin [Lavransdatter]*. I shall write letters today. I am not participating in the demonstrations—yesterday before the White House and today the Soviet Embassy. Ammon is visiting the Indian Commissioner with his friends. There are many letters I should [write], so I will try to catch up on them.

Wednesday April 5

Last night a telegram from Bob saying Chas. [O'Rourke] in a serious condition—to return... I was not aware how far their solicitude for my condition moved them to send it so I phoned NY. ... who said he had had heart attacks during the day. When Tom returned from the hospital he called again at eleven and said he had rallied and would call me at 10 this morning. So I await the call now.

It seems to me easier to do a big fast of six days than to discipline and restrain oneself daily. It makes me so ashamed of my lack of mortification in little things, eating between meals, or from habit when it is put before one, and one does not need it. Today Ammon, Ann and Lloyd from the Peacemakers went to Mass with me. What strength and joy in Mass and Communion. The church is packed. As in Canada they have to start giving Communion right after the consecration. A. J. Muste[99] very ill and weak. Also Pearl Hall. They are thin to start with. Very holy.

April 11. Tuesday. N.Y.

Advice: To efface ourselves and diminish our wants more and more...Dead calm in spiritual life is dangerous. Water & food run short. "Use every means to shake it off." A simple exercise: sign of cross even. St. Ignatius says never omit 2 examens, 15 minutes each.

1. Thank God for favors.
2. Beg for light.

---

99   A.J. Muste, executive secretary of the Fellowship of Reconciliation, was one of the outstanding American exponents of Christian nonviolence in the twentieth century. He and Dorothy shared many platforms and picket lines, right until his death in 1967.

3. Survey
4. Repent
5. Resolve
Object to correct faults.

Chambers called [from Harper's]. Likes book which was handed in April 3. All in all, as to moving—time to practice abandonment.

## Thursday April 20

Sick in bed with a temp and cramps—a form of intestinal flu, I think. Anyway, just when I was planning again to visit Tamar—this weekend would be a convenient time—I get sick. Just cleared my room a bit—washed my underthings, etc. A rainy day, not cold.

Went to see Forster—he left just before I got there. Had a good talk with Lily [Burke]. Thru the mail *Godly Prayers*, an old ragged book of Peter's, thin and worn with a bookmark dated '33 and an outline of one of his talks, just listing the topics.

Anabelle brought word from Msgr. Betowski of a Paulist property for sale, a former convent which the nuns only vacated a month ago to move into a new building. A wonderful location for us. The building really suitable—kitchen, laundry, backyard, library, meeting room, chapel, and dormitory space. Price $30,000 at least. Fr. McMahon the pastor very cordial, wanting us. A beautiful church.

The place is ideal, so suitable as to neighborhood, parish, etc. that I shall just cease looking further and pray instead. I have started again the rosary novena, a powerful prayer. Also will make my appeal in the May issue. God grant that this business of finding a new home in town and country be worked out. Peter, pray for us. Sts. Peter and Paul, Blessed Mother, and Mother Cabrini, St. Joseph, pray for us.

No word from Irene. Chas is better. Tom and Eleanor suddenly much attracted. They would be a good and happy couple. He really should choose now, at 37. She is 28.

I feel calm, still, immobilized by being ill. As in "The Cocktail Party": "Wait and do nothing." This morning read a pamphlet on Silence by Sister Elizabeth of the Trinity. Very important. That is so emphasized in the retreats.

Friday April 21. A cold gray day—50°

I am still in bed, grippish. John McKeon[100] very pessimistic about the farm and everyone's condition there. The uncertainty of the moving has them all down.

Stanley brought me stock, spicily sweet. Helen Leary just sent up ice cream. Tom brought me oranges and Marie my meals. Everyone is so good. Marge and Eleanor run in late at night with a delicious plate and I am reading over our last 10 May Day issues.

I am praying but not working. Seeing people takes much time and I do not even do that well. Had dinner with Katherine Burton[101] the other night and visited the Maryknoll Sisters.

Tuesday April 25. Still cold, grey

Jane said the mortgage had gone thru, and the bank called to tell her. We had a fine visit to the farm [on Staten Island] Sunday. The place looks better every time. Frank said it could really pay, what with fruit and asparagus all in. He envied us.

Sitting by Aunt Jenny's[102] bed. She had a stroke Saturday and Grace has been up every night with her since. I came yesterday morning. Della could not come.

Friday—an awful day. Everyone quarrelling. Irene talked, and well, but everyone too disturbed to appreciate.... Chancery office—saw Msgr. [Edward] Gaffney (and Archbishop Mitty). We can buy the 61 St. place subject to Cardinal's approval for $25,000 cash. We have $9,000 toward it. So we must appeal for $6,000.

Saturday a.m.

Confession at Precious Blood. Could not sleep until 4 a.m. Everything smooth today, after everyone blew his top last night. Natalie, Agnes, Eleanor, Tom. Bob and I innocent bystanders. Jack full of conspiracy. Chas better. Aunt Jenny in the hospital. Della went up yesterday.

---

100 John McKeon, who came to the CW in the late 1940s, was one of the best writers the paper ever had. Apart from his series "Poverty's Progress," he wrote Peter Maurin's obituary.

101 Katherine Burton specialized in writing biographies of foundresses of religious orders. Dorothy was reading her biography of Rose Hawthorne, *Sorrow Built a Bridge*, when she decided to start *The Catholic Worker*.

102 Aunt Jenny—the sister of Dorothy's mother—was her only Catholic relative.

Sunday April 30

Bill Duffy died. Red Miller found him dead on the floor when he woke. We called the priest and the police. He lay there on the floor completely stiff and rigid—one arm half up as tho frozen in one position just as he started to move. His face was like wax and blood had come from his nose and dried on his upper lip and chin.

The police went through his suitcase and clothes for papers and found discharge papers—he was a member of the Dublin fusiliers and had fought in the Boer war. One of the younger policemen looked around the room and commented on its squalor. "You should teach these old men to be clean," he said. "You take them off the Bowery."

There was the dirt of poverty there, dingy, but clean-swept floor, the bed painted white, sink clean, mirror over it also clean, both other beds in the room neatly made. Bill's bed also was made but the police had uncovered the soiled blankets and pillow slip which had been hidden by the dark blue woolen blanket.

Bill had been with us for years—twelve or more—and no one meddled with his clothes or bed. He had charge of the hot water heater in the cellar which was jocularly called Duffy's tavern. Many of his friends have spent the night there, and there too he had held forth the nights he was drinking. He took upon himself the job of our water heater. But he earned pocket money and wine from the janitor, Joe, who in turn was receiving free rent for the services he had delegated to Bill, who dragged out the ashes and garbage cans several times a day, swept the halls, hosed out the yard, etc.

Fred the German cook thoughtfully swept out the yard when he heard of Bill's death. Because it was Sunday morning his death was not discovered until noon just before lunch, which is always eggs on Sunday. Everyone came in as usual and in the awed hush over the death, two strangers, battered and odorous from their last night's dissipations, sneaked in and relished much the extra meal they had filched before the breadline started at one-thirty. It is terrible to have to serve two sets of meals—one for the house (about 75) and another for the line (300). We always have the same for breakfast, so no one crashes the door then.

Today it is raining and cold once again.

No spring yet at all. Press tomorrow. I still have "On Pilgrimage" to do. Listening to the radio instead.

Must call Della about Aunt Jenny next.

(Aunt J. sleeping most of the time. Does not recognize people.)

Monday, May 1. St. Philip and James

Rainy, cold. For the first time paper not distributed. Irene ill with shingles. Just the same she got up at 5:30 and we went to 6 a.m. Mass and we both wrote until 9. She had to go to clinic afterward. Bed rest of day. In mail Mary Fabili writes of closing of Oakland house, and breakdown of Chas, his public confession like a Dostoyevsky scene. Glad I did not mention Archbishop Mitty in our meeting in "On Pilgrimage."

Paper went off well today—anniversary issue with Peter on front page.

More difficulties about sale of farm. Rosary novena goes on. Wednesday funeral 9:30, missa cantata. The charge will be $10, the brother at the Franciscan Church said. The funeral from Andrews will be $125. He will be wrapped in a shroud, the coffin will be a black covered pine box, and he will be buried in a free grave in Calvary, set aside for "worthy poor." To open a grave for the worthy poor costs $15. $50 for others.

Reading Martin Buber's *Paths to Utopia*. Wonderful book. Also *Drama of Atheist Humanism* by Father [Henri] de Lubac, S.J.


Sunday May 7

Today Johannah [Hughes] made her first Holy Communion at Transfiguration. A lovely May morning, hot in sun. Yesterday Della moved to Cos Cob. Yesterday I came down from 2 days and 3 nights on the farm. Made a day of recollection. Read [St.] Catherine of Genoa.


Thursday, Ascension Day. May 18

Yesterday, Dave [Mason], Helen Crowe and I started at 8:15 and arrived at Tamar's at 7:30 p.m. Still light. We had trouble with one tire, and it was shot—also the front left, so bought two winter retreads for $25.50.

A good trip aside from fearful storm and no windshield wiper. One storm after another then thru the mountains and lightning and thunder and the rain in sheets. There is no window in one side of the car and it leaked under the windshield on our feet. I just kept going. Electric storms made me too nervous to stop as many of the trucks were doing. We ate in the car, liverwurst and whole wheat bread, and Helen drank buttermilk. For dessert bananas. We received Communion, Dave and I, at Transfiguration before we left.

The electric lines are thru from Stotlers Crossroads to Rock Gap but Tamar would of course have to have her house wired. Will ask Forster to help.


Saturday, May 20

Finally sun came out after two days rain. We have worked so hard as usual. Dave M. washed up living room yesterday and today the kitchen. Yesterday we went to Winchester and got Tamar glasses. Beautiful drive. Rained all the way and D. M. had to work windshield wiper by hand. Got shoes, phonograph needles, fish. Took wrong road to get there. Easy coming back.

Monday May 22. 11 a.m.

Helen and I sitting under the pear tree with the cousins. Becky runs around, Eric and Susie cracking black walnuts with a hammer. They play with real tools. Dave M. is trying to fix rear seat of the car. Sunny and windy. Today bread making, washing, and a visit to the brook. Split pea soup for dinner. Some of Tamar's bacon for breakfast.

It is so beautiful that I cannot even think, only breathe and bask in the sun. The baby Nicky sleeps and wakes, laughs and sings all day. The children eat well, sleep well, and entertain each other all day.

Tamar looks wonderful—weighs 135 lbs. I weigh 180, a disgrace—partly my age and also I should not eat fats. Down here we have been having milk, cream, butter, and cheese—truly a luxurious diet. The children demand pictures so here is a copy of an Eric Gill Xmas card which Tamar sent to announce the baby. *[Drawing of Madonna and child]*

Monday May 29, cold, rainy

Today saw Msgr. Gaffney about the house. We cannot have the house on 62 St. The consulters [of the archdiocese] met and passed judgment against us. Afraid of fire, trouble with the city, of sponsoring us, etc. I am glad it was not Fr. McMahon's fault.

So here we are with $23,000 and no house. We must just wait. Msgr. G. advises against the place next door.

Over the weekend a retreat at the farm. Fr. Faley gave it. Much time in prayer. How hard it is for brothers to dwell together in unity. I write down all the troubles to see them evaporate by next year. We grow thru these struggles.

Saturday June 3

A great sense of restlessness what with still no home for the CW. Tom just rushed up and told of the Barat settlement on Chrystie St., which had belonged to the Jesuits and now to a theater, which is up again for sale. He is over there now looking it over to see whether it was ever used for living quarters. Price asked $33,000. We have $25,000 including a $3,000 loan. Also no bills paid. So we need $10,000 more within a month. It is preposterous—these amounts. I must take to reading Mother Cabrini again to get in the mood for asking. Our Father's business in N.Y. seems to demand a fortune.

We talk of compassion, of suffering *with* others. Here we have a little taste of homelessness and hostility. The reality of scheming, planning, wondering, planning, uncertainty as to what to do. The lot of most people. It occupies so much of one's thoughts, one can well see how people can think these days so little of God. One can well see why St. Thomas counsels one never to make a change until forced to it—it occupies so much time,

And yet last night in the midst of this turmoil of living and responsibility, we had our regular Friday night meting in the backyard, the first of the year and there was a gentle breeze after a hot day and there was room for the fifty who were there to listen to good talk on Augustine and Thomas and the soul and heart expanded in joy and worship and thankfulness that even here now, in the midst of stress and anguish, one can hold fast to goodness, truth, beauty ineffable.

Visited chancery office this week and saw Msgr. Gaffney who told me that consulters of the diocese did not want us to buy—that we were recognized as a Catholic group and yet they had no supervision over us. If it were only the works of mercy it would be all right but our ideas as to Christian anarchism and pacifism are so opposed to theirs. They will concede our rightness in the long view but not yet. Like St. Augustine, "Give me purity, but not yet."

St. Anthony's Day, June 13

End of the festa, a lovely one, good concerts as usual across the street. Tonight Irene and I took a long walk down to our new house. The old Barat settlement, which we obtained miraculously the last day of the rosary novena. We need a few thousand more and I am continuing the novena. We said it on a park bench while we watched the children play, under the green plane trees. The Blessed Mother is compared to a plane tree. Then we walked over Houston almost to the river—around Hamilton Fish Park and went to Benediction at Our Lady of Sorrows, the Capuchin church. There is a beautiful outdoor shrine to Our Lady of Fatima there in the schoolyard. On the way home we stopped for a bite of supper, for shoes and stockings, and then home for the last concert—the folksingers—the part I always enjoy the most.

Wednesday, June 14. St. Basil. Rain, cold

Today worked with resolution after reading St. Athanasius' *Life of St. Anthony* and at once after Mass a message from Mrs. Brown on Staten Island indicating we would lose the house there unless we could get $8,000 (the owners would take a $7,000 mortgage) before the end of the month. There is so little sympathy with farm and retreat movement from Tom and Bob that all day I have been quite in despair about it all. Then tonight at 9:30, Fr. Joachim called up (he had gotten out of bed to do so) to comfort me by saying God is nearest when He seems furthest off. Mass at nine. 10:15-11:30 reading St. Teresa's *Foundations*.

Retreat June 18. Sunday. 7:30 p.m. Fr. Brown
  "Come apart now and rest awhile." Our Lord to the apostles.
  Two preliminaries. Silence. Accept challenge. Work for metanoia.
  Obstacles in the way. Fr. Brown's voice and inflections, dramatic like Fr. Betowsky. That and my terrible preoccupations about property, mortgages, law, movings, are an almost insuperable obstacle to a good retreat. Best retreat masters were Fr. Roy, Fr. Farina, Hugo, Meenan—these men are natural, sincere, earnest, intense. Much easier to listen to.
  I have been making monthly days of recollection, daily hours of reading and recollection, rosary novenas, fasting from meat, trying for a more disciplined life.
  Theme of retreat. Love: positive side. Detachment from the world: negative side.
  Fatigue, mental, physical, is not a good beginning for a retreat.
  Here are my obstacles. I can only pray that God will enable me to make a good retreat.
  Need strong affirmation of supernatural aspect of our religion. No matter how much we may use natural means, we must stress supernatural. What use blueprints if building is never begun?
  We must cease to be ruled by reason, good as it is but begin to live by faith.

Monday—9:30
  Saturday night Tony [Aratari], Fr. Hessler and I went to Helene Iswolsky's[103] to meet Fr. [Jean] Danielou. Very vigorous, alive. Also a Jesuit. His book *Salvation of the Nations* only one translated. Speaks English well but some difficulty. Fr. [William] Lynch, editor of *Thought*, Carol [Jackson] of *Integrity*, Fr. [John] Oesterreicher. Fr. O. seemed hostile. He said he needed

---

103 Helene Iswolsky, daughter of the last Russian ambassador to France under the Czar, was a remarkable woman: a scholar, writer, and advocate of ecumenical dialogue. She emigrated to the U.S. in 1941 and soon became friends with Dorothy, whom she recruited to be part of the The Third Hour, a group to promote dialogue among Orthodox, Catholic, and Protestant intellectuals (including the poet W.H. Auden). In the 1960s Helene moved to the Catholic Worker farm at Tivoli, where she lived until her death in 1975.

to exorcise us from our bad thoughts. He is infuriated by our pacifism. Fr. O. said he recognized need of nonviolent resistance, but also of violent.

To be written about: The fantastic things that are happening. Troubles at Upton. The spirit of anger, fear, contention. Maryfarm breaking up. "Property is theft."[104]

The things we are writing and talking about and the things which are happening. Do they contradict? How can we continue to have faith in the face of such contradictions? A hard school. A bitter school. Given the fact we have bad material to work with. God can take even this? To Him be glory. We can take no credit. We have great natural talents, but great passions, great obstacles in the way of our work.

Tuesday p.m. 4

A letter from Tamar today. They are going to have a bricklayer come fix the chimney and close in the spring. Her garden is fine, she says. Good seeds make all the difference. She discourages Marge from coming or Dave from buying materials. It is far better to let them work things out for themselves.

Just now a knock came at the door and a young man wanted to spend the night. I told him to go eat but that we could not put him up. Always this impulse to say no. Yet each such encounter is an opportunity to see Christ in the other. Our brother. So I left the conference and told him to stay. He will make the conference tonight, Benediction, Mass in the morning. Who knows but that God would miss these prayers that might have been said, this praise, this thanks, this glory, no matter how inarticulate our brother is.

Where in the world did these words come from: "The saddest words of tongue or pen are those few words, what might have been."[105] Doggerel, but true. All the kindness we might do, but don't.

These grey days I have been sleeping in the p.m. Gerald Heard gave me a great deal when he talked of the creative powers of sleep. It is true. I wake around four just before dawn. Vigil.

What to do about this place, Staten Island, etc. What is God's will? What does He want me to do?

---

104 A famous phrase by the French utopian-anarchist, Pierre-Joseph Proudhon. Dorothy often paired this, dialectically, with Eric Gill's saying, "Property is proper to man."
105 From John Greenleaf Whittier's poem, "Maud Miller."

Frank Coyle, Mr. Walsh, the real estate man, both advise for S.I. at least to see how it works out. It could be sold later, Tom says, if we cannot sell Mary-farm, Newburgh. It will be an expensive testing—this seeing what is God's will by trial and error, is hard. The trials which come with property. What it brings out in people—the suffering which is intense, bitter. Then too are we losing our poverty?

Love of God is love of preference. When we choose him before all creatures.

Ten—20—30 times a day we have opportunity to choose him before creatures. We should be delighted at opportunity, by deed, effort, it is hard.

We glory in tribulation for the trial of our faith worketh hope.

Visit from Christine Ell this last week. Romany Marie wants to see me. Helen Crowe writes that Peggy (Cowley) Baird's husband has just died. Here is news from four women I knew 25 years or more ago.[106] All alone, childless, and poor. I see where I will have a beguinage. Only those were places of hard work—these groups of women, there is nothing new under the sun.

Wednesday June 21. 9:30

Last night looking thru the files for Helen Crowe's research on St. Patrick, I came across Peter's letters to me.

In spite of damp my rheumatism is much better. Since visit to Holy Redeemer Church Thurs—devotions to Our Lady of Perpetual Help. My fasting from meat for a year was an act of thanksgiving—also for Tom's health.

If I could only make up my mind about S.I. If I cannot by Friday, I'll call Fr. Meenan and see if he can make it up for me.

It is beautiful here, plenty of room for growth of a community if God so wills it and if any builders can come.

Today it is the first day of summer, June 21. One half of the year 1950 is gone. Outside a watery sun is trying to shine. King barks, trucks roll by, children on a bicycle. At this stage of retreat, one is fatigued, tired of attention especially to so much that one has heard before. A retreat of this kind becomes an act of will, of mortification. Silence, prayer, two Masses, Prime, Compline, rosary, 4 hours of conferences, 4 15-minute periods of prayer in

---

106 These were all women from Dorothy's past in the New York radical and literary scene. One of them, Peggy Baird (former wife of the writer Malcolm Cowley), her cell-mate in Washington when they were jailed for a suffragist protest, would later spend her final years at the Catholic Worker farm at Tivoli.

the chapel. This is a strain, and I am breaking it by working a bit on the files, weeding, thinning out, making room for new.

Sister Peter Claver arrived home from her pilgrimage to Rome. She told me of the Pope's Mass, Lourdes, where she left part of her heart. It was she who first gave me the retreat notes of Fr. [Onesimus] Lacouture, introduced me to Father Roy, and he in turn to Fr. Hugo.

I must write of the retreat in my book. Just thought of three titles/subtitles: Childhood; Life of Nature; The Unwilling Celibate.[107]

Wed. 4 p.m. The sun is shining, now the wind has blown away all the clouds. We are sitting down by the pond which is full of bulrushes right now. We sit by Joe's shrine to the Little Flower in the shade and all around is the smell of wild red clover, also grape blossoms, and the sound of birds and even the croaking of some frogs in the pond.

Powers of self-deceit persuading us things are necessary that are not. We can sow all unnecessary. Samples.[108] All faults, however petty, can be traced to capital sins.

Such sorrow and heartbreak in the world. Maureen is so saddened by no children, no farm. And she gives way to it, this sadness; how we should cultivate joy, thankfulness.

Thurs June 22

This morning Mary Roberts became violently ill and had to go into the hospital. She is home now. Joe Gil and Eileen Egan[109] came last night to take Maureen back to the hospital. So much sickness and so much psychosomatic.

Eileen Egan suggests that where a saint [*Peter Maurin*] has lived and died should be held sacred. Another reason for staying here [*Maryfarm in Newburgh*]. My own will has to be upset. At any rate, if God lets me lose that

---

107 The final part titles for *The Long Loneliness* are Searching; Natural Happiness; Love is the Measure.

108 One of the points of Fr. Roy's retreat was that all pleasures or happiness in this life are simply "samples" of our eternal happiness.

109 Eileen Egan, who worked for Catholic Relief Services, would become one of the most important figures in the American Catholic peace movement. Although she never lived at the Worker, she was a prolific contributor to the paper. For years she chaired the Worker's Friday night meetings "for the clarification of thought," and she became Dorothy's frequent traveling companion.

thousand we put down, he has seen to it we have $30,000 for the new house. It has resulted in getting rid of two houses, a cow, a calf, pigs, the feed bills which were enormous.

This 11 a.m. conference is not at all pleasing to me. It is not well balanced, reasoned, planned. St. Teresa who spoke and wrote much on obedience in starting her reformed order seemed to go against the spirit of obedience. Her immediate superiors considered her a trouble maker.

Aunt Jenny has been very ill—a stroke, etc. I was up there for a few days so Grace could go back to work. She was taken to St. Francis Hospital. She was not there two days before she was removed to the City Home with no notification of the family. Another example of Catholic Charity. Now they have moved and I must visit them again next week.

### Friday June 23

This morning during the conference I looked out the window to see above a pigeon on the roof. Then later in the morning while we were in chapel there it was under the crabapple tree, then in a cleft in the rock wall, then again it flew up to the roof of the cement house right over Peter [Maurin's] room, resting there, and aside from some hoppings and preenings, it stayed right there for a few hours. Eileen said she fed it—that it was a carrier pigeon.

### Sunday July 2. Visitation

Very hot these days. Have been in town since the retreat except for a weekend at Della's. Deed for Chrystie St. not signed yet.

Dave [Hennessy] called to tell about his new job in Westminster, Md. on the Newman Press. So they must find a home. Marge [Hughes] also. We will stay at Newburgh.

A shattering headache last 24 hours. Today better.

### Monday July 3

Mass and Confession 7 a.m. with Marge and Irene. Irene to W. Va. Marge this a.m. to Gouvernor hospital with Mary who was complaining of her leg. Dave M. making scene over injustice of not being allowed to work. Johanna wrote on the table: "I hate Dorothy, I love Dave."

Much telephoning—Sandy Katz—Dave Dellinger[110] about peace demonstration [*in response to the outbreak of the Korean War*]. We are not announcing

---

110 David Dellinger, a former World War II draft resister, became one of the leading peace activists of the post-war period. He would achieve a certain notoriety in the late 1960s as one of the Chicago 7, a group of anti-war activists charged with conspiracy.

our world citizenship. We might renounce our primary allegiance to U.S. State. In p.m. Dorothy Chang came in. Husband in Shanghai, daughter in Salvation Army camp, boy on farm and a 19-year-old just dead. Found drowned last month in Hudson. Suicide, perhaps. Terrible grief. A woman my age. An anarchist, Tolstoian, sent to us by Resistance group. Joe Cuellar knows her.

Typed Episcopalian speech. Sent food over to Dave [Mason] tonight as peace offering.

## July 4

Last night 10:45 Cyril Carney ran into Michael Kovalak. Showed him a *Soviet Literary Review* and said it was only there he found some inspiration. Christianity no longer appealed to him. So Michael talked to him for 2 hours and invited him down for further discussion. M. is always doing things like that for others. Every time I get impatient with him he does something which arouses my admiration.

## Friday July 7

Mass these last few days at Transfiguration and the music lifts the heart. I do love that little church best of all. Jane & I had coffee and toast after.

## Our Lady of Carmel

Last night we all walked to 115 St. and First Ave to Our Lady of Mt. Carmel on pilgrimage. We started at 11:15 and arrived at 1:30. Had to wait till four for a Mass. It showered heavily. Bed at 6:15. Slept till 2.00. Then to Coney Island with the children. We picked sweet clover and I have a bouquet before me.

## Sunday July 22 morning

This week Chas O'Rourke died and was buried.[111] He was staying at Mott St. while Tom [Sullivan][112] was in the hospital and when Tom came home last

---

111 Charles O'Rourke had been part of the CW since the mid-thirties, when he was active in the National Maritime Union strike. "There was something godlike about Charlie, this large interest he showed in everyone, this genial charity. He was kindly and friendly to all, pacifist and militarist and to those who 'just went,' drafted in the forces. He was never one to be dogmatic, to press his point on others. He was silent, gentle, and one would be tempted to call him a rather amused spectator of the goings on of the Catholic Worker, if he had not worked so hard at the mailing list, to whom, after all, our pacifist literature was going out." ("Charles O'Rourke: The Death of a Beloved Apostle," July-August 1950)

112 Tom Sullivan, originally of the Chicago Catholic Worker, served in the army during the war, and then returned to join the New York CW staff. He became house manager and wrote a popular column for the paper until his departure in 1955.

Sat he waited until after clinic on Wed to take Chas to the farm. Thurs. 9 a.m. we had a jovial breakfast, poached eggs on toasted Italian bread, coffee, and Jack [English][113] was dashing around trying to find strawberries (frozen) and came in with melons instead. I drove them to the Hudson River Day Line and there they met Agnes [Bird]. They had a lovely day, Chas visited around at the farm and went to bed at 10:30. He awoke at four with a heart attack and after a struggle for half an hour to breathe he died. Fr. Faley was there. He was in Peter's room. Tom was telephoning the doctor at the moment. Fr. Faley had just heard his confession. Chas's family—nephews, nieces—took over then, and he was buried at St. Stephen's Church the next morning at a missa cantata which Fr. Boyton, S.J., his boyhood friend, sang. We went out to the cemetery with him. Tom went back to the farm.

As one grows older one wants to hear the details of the last days of old friends. I put a death notice in the *Herald Tribune* and *Times* and when I was telephoning it, saying how Chas had chosen to devote the last fifteen years of his life to the poor and that tho he was a lover of all beauty, he chose to spend his last days in the slums. In this notice I said he was the circulation manager of the CW. I was trying to speak in terms people would understand.

Peter Maurin's indoctrination has affected people more than they realize— so that those who come to give themselves to the CW try to ask nothing for themselves. Beginning with doing without salary, they do without title also.

Wednesday—Aug 2

Communion at six. Fr. Hessler said Mass 7 a.m. Bob, Jack, Tom, Tony, Roger, Elinor and I at Mass. Fr. Hessler talked to us last night on the need to restrain any activism. Let our souls catch up with us. Press today. July-Aug [issue]. David [Hennessy] called up. They are moving Friday to Westminster. I'll go down Sat. Very happy about it.

Aug 24, Thursday

Since last writing the paper has gone to press, I have visited Tamar for 4 days and 2 visits to Newburgh, one a retreat. Marge went to Newburgh for a week, so I used her apartment—have slept in Irene's bed while she was away and in several other beds, whatever happened to be empty. It will be good to be in one spot instead of scattered over 115-116 Mott and 221-223 Chrystie. We are going to lose much of our appearance of poverty in moving into our new quarters with its larger rooms, baths, hot water, heat, etc. We must all the

---

113 Jack English had worked at the Cleveland CW before joining the air force. He was shot down in a bomber and spent much of the war in a prison camp. Afterward he joined the New York CW, later quitting to become a Trappist monk (and priest) at Conyers, Georgia.

more cultivate the austerity, the detachment, the self-discipline, the interior poverty we so lack. It is our greatest message. To be poor with the poor.[114]

I am reading [Louis] Fischer's *Gandhi*. Most interesting. Here is an old Indian poem:

> I died as a mineral and became a plant,
> I died as a plant and became an animal.
> I died as an animal and was a man.
> When should I fear? When was I less by dying?

Sept 1. St. Giles

Deborah, Eileen and I moved into the Peter Maurin Farm [on Staten Island], Aug 30. The place was purchased on the feast of St. Augustine. We now have taxes, interest, and mortgage payments due. Taxes also in N.Y. and Newburgh. Interest of $200 a year in Newburgh.

Fr. McGrath, our parish priest, called this a.m. Very friendly. Deb and I to Mass at 6:45 at St. Louis Academy.

Visited neighbors with bread and got vegetables next door. Fish man comes Tues and Friday to door. We got a 5-lb codfish for a dollar which we are baking. We are begging and he said he would bring us cuttings from filets for chowder.

We are all so happy and comfortable after a first night of great misery. Eileen is a great help, cleaning, baking.

Sunday Sept 17

Today at 6 I must go in to town so as to be at clinic tomorrow morning at Memorial. Last Sunday Tessa took me to her doctor and he said I had a tumor. Went to Westminster Sunday. Spoke Monday in Washington. Tues to Tamar again. Wed p.m. to N.Y. Thurs & Friday in Chrystie St. Sat & Sun here. Much traveling. Got a good many letters written here. Tom in Chicago, perhaps to get Fr. [John] Cordes.

---

114 In the September 1950 issue, Dorothy provided a chronicle of the deliberations and struggles in deciding to purchase Peter Maurin Farm while also purchasing a new house on Chrystie St. "Then one morning like the importunate widow, I asked for a sign of the Lord. It was at Mass, and I kept saying to myself, 'If I don't hear something by eleven o'clock this morning, I am going to drop the whole idea and put it out of my mind altogether.' It was a promise to the Lord. Before eleven o'clock a friend had called and offered to lend us several thousand dollars, the old owners had come down in their initial payment and offered to take the mortgage themselves, and I had my sign. Within another two weeks, I was able to obtain two thousand dollars more from friends, and the papers are now all signed."

Fri Sept 29. St. Michael's Day

Fr. Cordes arrived from Chicago with Tom Tues and came to S.I. with us. It is always so good to write our problems down so that in reading them over 6 months or a year later one can see them evaporate.

I go to the clinic again Wed to get a final verdict as to operation. Fr. C. is very sad this morning, wailing right now in his misery in the kitchen and being comforted by Eileen and Dave. They are wonderfully kind to him. Poor man, he wanders so restlessly about, so expectantly, looking to me as tho I could do anything except to try to reassure him, make him comfortable here. We can feast him, feed him up, give him music and some companionship.[115]

John Givens came out. Told me of Eileen, her refusal of him finally—how if I had been younger or he older ten years ago when he met me he would have asked me to marry him. Men do not consider your work. Also it shows what a human aspect there is in this work. Human love does warm us and predispose us to the love of God.

Monday, October 2. Guardian Angels

Sunny and bright and very hot with that beautiful autumn stillness. Crickets, an occasional rooster, a car going by now and then, these disturb the stillness only to make me appreciate it the more.

Up at seven—light since 5:30. The sun rises over the trees right at my window. Prayers facing it.

Sat Oct 7. PM Farm. Holy Rosary

Meditation at Mass and after. On Peter's silence with others. On "better that one man should die." My article was on human relationships for this issue. That difficult issue of the common good. For instance, a family who wishes to put away an epileptic child for the common good of the family. Or put an old person in a home because the others will have more peace and quiet. Or those in the CW movement, who fear that this one or that one like M. Sheehan or D. will misinterpret the movement, give a wrong impression or drive others away. It was the high priest who said, Better one should die—shall we put Jesus to death?

I got news on feast of St. Francis no operation needed.

---

115 Among the many priests who passed through the Catholic Worker over the years, a number were alcoholics or were otherwise psychologically wounded. Dorothy welcomed them with respect and reverence, even as she acknowledged their human weaknesses.

Tues. Oct 10. PM Farm

Bright and warm, no coat. To S.I. at 10:30. Paper arrived to be mailed out. Pear trees are getting barer, what with a wind. But the cherry tree outside my window is full of foliage. Fields never seemed greener in contrast to yellow patches of sedge and colorful woods. Crickets make sleepy sounds, but no birds. Plane trees on Chrystie St. in full leaf yet but they are yellowing and falling and you can smell them under foot.

Father Cordes has been here two weeks now and he is sitting out today enjoying the sun and air. Eileen, Dave, and Hans [Tunnesen] are working hard.

This is a wonderful neighborhood for us to be in.

Caroline Gordon and I had lunch Thurs. She will speak in 2 weeks. Lent her Buber's [Tales of the] Hasidim.

Thurs Oct 12. S.I.

Rain and mist. J.W. gave us a cabinet radio and I have a little one in my room. Such joy in being here. Father getting better. Hans and Dave working. Letters all day.

Yesterday I was reading an article on sex education for children in *Integrity*. It was on the Feast of the Maternity and emphasis was laid throughout on the virginity of the Blessed Mother.

"All you who are married," says St. Bernard, "revere this integrity of the flesh in corruptible flesh. You holy virgins, revere the motherhood of the Virgin. All humanity, imitate the humility of the Mother of God."

St. Leo talks of the taint of human flesh, so although we recognize that the flesh of Jesus is the flesh of Mary, we know that both were without stain. Theirs alone is holy. Ours has that taint, that tendency left by original sin.

Of course there is embarrassment for the mother and father in talking of it. Why would there not be? "Christ was begotten by a new birth, conceived by a virgin, born of a virgin, without the cooperation of a human father, without injury to the maternal virginity." —St. Leo

Fri Oct 13

Spoke at Chrystie St. Peace. Too crowded. Mae Bellucci there and Carmen Mathews.[116] Brilliant women. Carmen in television. Came to S.I. at 11 with Jane.

---

116 Carmen Mathews, an actress, was a loyal friend of the Worker. At Christmas time each year she would often offer a performance, perhaps a dramatic reading of "A Christmas Carol," or some other work.

Sat Oct 14

Beautiful day. Sun rises 5:45. Mass at 6:45. Jane left at 11. Visited the Sisters at St. Louis Academy.

It is too late now to weed the asparagus. The seeds have already fallen so we all went to the beach and got a load of seaweed to mulch the field. Supper at 6. Compline. Fr. Cordes joined us. Reading *Villette* [Charlotte Brontë]. Finished *Far from the Madding Crowd* [Thomas Hardy]. Sunny day. Warm.

Sunday quiet and grey. Eileen walked to church with us. No visitors. Fr. Cordes read Gerard Manly Hopkins aloud all afternoon. Mending rosaries.

Monday. Letters. Chancery office a.m. Msgr. Gaffney very nice. Advises against Jefferson School attendance.[117]

Vigil of St. Simon and Jude

Today Fr. [John] Schutz offered the Holy Sacrifice at Peter Maurin Farm on the altar which Hans built and Michael varnished. The altar stone was the one from the Philadelphia house on which Fr. Jos. Woods and Fr. Pacifique Roy had offered Mass. The chalice came from the Maryknoll cloister. (Also ciborium and linens). Tabernacle from Msgr. Corrigan at the Mission of the Immaculate Conception, monstrance, Hosts and candlesticks from St. Louis Academy. Prie Dieu (altar rail) from Marists. Vestments from Mde. de Bethune. We sang the Mass and Jane intoned the proper. Fr. Cordes also received.

Nov 14. St. Josaphat

Still undecided as to Rome trip. Frances and Mary left Sat. Made me promise I would still try for passport. So I will write letter; get the other affidavit needed and try again. There is still time to join them in Rome.

Still think of selling Maryfarm since we owe.

Thanksgiving Day '50. Nov 23. 9:30

At the beginning of every new venture upheavals. Eileen has been in a state for exactly one week—leaving the house last Monday.

Very quiet with Eileen gone—much less tension, tho Dave got upset tonight because I claim there is too much heat on. We should learn to regulate the steam. I must get Joe to teach me. Fr. Chrysostom at Newburgh for the retreat. A Muscovite and Michael also there to sing the liturgy.

---

117 The Jefferson School of Social Science was a Marxist adult education institute in New York associated with the Communist Party.

If Eileen comes back she will have to go back to the farm where she cannot take over or build cliques. Dave and she are a combination. If she can hold a job it will be wonderful.

Visited Tamar two weeks ago—hot weather, the last week in October, and we had a lovely time canning, driving, picnicking. A real rainstorm the day I left. A river running down the road. All are well.

All summer I had miserable rheumatic pains—now they are much less. Now I have waves of heat (I suppose these are the hot flashes people speak of) and these, combined with the heat of our new houses, are terrible.

To the opera last Saturday—"The Flying Dutchman"—and met Forster there. Then Isabel MacRae in and she wanted me to go to *La Traviata*. It reminded me of the *Tannhauser*—hell is too much pleasure.

Isabel is talking of the virtues of molasses, sunflower seed and vinegar for health. (Forster did not mention his health once. I had been writing about him in my book [*The Long Loneliness*]. Will we ever get peacefully settled so I can write? Must there always be people tearing each other, and incidentally me, apart?)

Nov 26, Sunday

All day yesterday a frightful storm. Electric off and 400,000 homes without heat and light. An argument for coal and wood—the old-fashioned range and oil lamp.

This the last Sunday of Pentecost is a sad one. Woeful.

Next Sunday a day of recollection at Father [Louis] Farina's in Oakmont, near Pittsburgh. I shall spend the rest of the evening reading *Three Who Made a Revolution* by Bertram Wolfe.

Monday Nov 27

A beautiful day full of fragrance. One would think all the broken trees in the woods were exuding a delightful smell of their sap.

Mass at 6:45. It is a dusky dawn as we leave at 6:15 and the sun is coming up as we get out. After breakfast Dave and Joe went to the beach to gather lumber from the storm and Chas McCormack drove down to haul it. They got a ladder, a lifesaving stand, and many beams and planks, 2 x 4s and other expensive pieces. They ate lunch of cabbage soup on the beach, and were gone until four. For me there was baking, cooking, writing. Today the water was like glass and many boats out fishing. We had a good supper of creamed onions, salad, homemade bread and plum pudding with hard sauce, which delighted the men. A Brahms symphony—Compline.

Gertrude Burke is dead. Funeral tomorrow. God bless her. May she rest in peace. It was her uncle Kerrigan who built 115 Mott St. and who stood on the steps of old St. Patrick's with a gun in his hands warding off the Know Nothings. Miss Burke gave the building to the House of Calvary where she stayed after her mother's death but we were given the use of them these last 14 years and just for fun, adding up 500 meals a day, an understatement since for some years there were more, for 365 days a year for 14 years, that makes 2,555,000 meals served. As for nights lodging at the rate of 50¢ a night, and that does not count all the "flops" at Bowery hotels we've paid for, that amounts to 255,500 nights lodging.

What untold good can be done by generous Christians like the widows who run the House of Calvary and maids like Miss Burke who aided them! None of this was state aid, these 255,500 nights lodging. In that tiny kitchen it seems scarcely possible 2,555,000 meals were served. Chalked up like this it must look strange to Shorty, Slim, Leo, Robert, Fred, and others who helped to serve them. They don't do any counting up, any more than Miss Gertrude Sarah Burke did, who was shy and diffident and a bit frightened of our work, I am sure, but who helped us to the end. God bless her mightily, and may she enjoy a place of refreshment, light, and peace.

Vigil of the Immaculate Conception. Super Flumina, Foster

Arrived last night at 7:35, leaving Pittsburgh at 11. Fr. Farina took me to the bus. I had been to confession the night before and felt much consoled with his help. I must visit Bishop Deardon to ask again that he may give a retreat to us.

It rained on the way down and the glare of lights on the black pavement was hard on the eyes. It was like getting home to get off at Foster, the first time I've been here since the year of Tamar's marriage, 1944. They are reading and meditating on love. Rodriguez; St. Therese; St. Bernard. The great weapons of the spirit. This a.m. pouring, turned to snow. Arose at 6:30. Lauds, then sung Mass. Breakfast at 9:30. Every Thursday a special loaf is served for breakfast and this prayer is said:

> "O Lord, Jesus Christ, bread of angels, Living bread unto eternal life, bless this bread as thou didst bless the five loaves in the wilderness; that all who eat it with reverence may thru it attain the corporal and spiritual help they desire. Who livest and reignest eternally. Amen."

The bread is then sprinkled with holy water.

Saturday Dec 10

The day after the feast of the Immaculate Conception and the day before the Second Sunday in Advent.

We spent the afternoon of the vigil peeling apples at Super Flumina and reading the life of St. Therese. It is so beautiful here, the fields and hills all white, the river rushing on thru the valley and lights of the cars on the bridge. Sheep, goats, rabbits, chickens—a warm cozy farm. Pumps for water, outside toilets, wood stoves, bare, scrubbed, and beautiful.

In the morning of the feast I got up at seven instead of six, as I have on all my trip, and had coffee and came by cab to the Grail. Mass was at 7:45, a beautiful sung Mass with an offertory procession.

Much prayer here now. Up at 5:30. Lauds—then to church for an hour of mental prayer. Mass at 7:45. Breakfast at nine. Rosary with a five-minute or seven meditation after each decade. Solemn vespers. I spoke on poverty and love. Bed at 9.

Stayed in bed today, resting and reading *Glories of Grace* [Matthias Scheeben], tremendous lifting of the heart.

Dec 20. Wednesday. Ember Day. Westminster

It is ten a.m. and Tamar is resting after the first four hours of work. What with ironing shirts before breakfast, she has to get up early. Dave must be at work at 8. It has been very cold. Arrived last Saturday. It had been a grueling trek, but thanks to my day in bed on Sat before I got along well. Sunday a.m. I had spoken again at the Grail for breakfast. Saw the girls in the afternoon.

Monday at 2:45 started for Pittsburgh, snowing. Arrived at 1:30. Stayed at Fort Pitt. Visited Bishop Deardon on Tues. Left on 4:20 bus and arrived in New York at 4:30. First Mass at St. Francis is at 5. Had breakfast and then slept till 1:30.

Went to Peter Maurin Farm with Vincenza.

Wrote an answer to the *Commonweal* editorial, "Blood, Sweat, and Tears."[118] Bed at 12. Up at 3:45 to catch 4:10 bus to Baltimore since there was a railroad strike on. Sat. noon spoke at Hoffman House. Home to Tamar at 5 down an icy hill. It has been a week of icy weather 10-15°. No Mass Sunday

---

118 Dorothy was critical of a *Commonweal* editorial supporting a strong national defense. She wrote: "We shall of course be called defeatists and appeasers. Nevertheless I would say that our way of life, as we are living it, is not worth saving. Let us lay down our way of life, our life itself, rather than go on with this senseless slaughter." See Patrick Jordan, ed., *Dorothy Day: Writings from* Commonweal, 117-120.

Friday

Very threatening—looks like snow or rain. Last night Tamar went shopping and to the movies with Dave. Home at ten. I bathed the children. Much exuberance. The baby is very grand, eats well. Tamar and I are going to make candy popcorn balls.

We were talking about the need of a good Christmas story—and I was thinking what fun it would be to embody many of ourselves in a story of the West Virginia farm for children—all very cheerful. It is one of those new days when the baby cries and the house won't get warm and there is washing, housecleaning, and cooking to do and it is an ember day.

Sunday, Christmas Eve

Tamar and I went to 7:45 Mass. They heard confessions before. The hill still impossible. We climbed up thru the field. No pleasure in going out. The children run out and play however. They are very good. Tamar and I trimmed the tree and set out the toys. The children went to bed at six, like angels.

Monday, Christmas day

I went early to Christmas Mass, a bitter walk, so Tamar and Dave could go later together.

Attack in *Commonweal.*[119]

# 1951

January 12. Friday night

Fritz Eichenberg spoke tonight, wonderfully. He is truly a great teacher.[120]

---

119 In the same issue of *The Commonweal* as Dorothy's letter (December 29th, 1950), there appeared an unsigned editorial (evidently by John Cogley) which stated, in part: "In the Communications section of this issue we are publishing a letter from Dorothy Day. Miss Day takes *The Commonweal* to task for an editorial, on the present world crisis, which she describes as 'a perfect example of that secularism which the bishops of the United States...deplore as a greater danger than Communism.' These are harsh words and seem to call for some kind of answer, though it is doubtful if anything other than complete pacifism, on the part of *The Commonweal*, and the nation at large, would satisfy Miss Day." The editorial continued, "In short, if we believed that pure Christianity and pacifism were identical, then we should be forced by logic to take the position *The Catholic Worker* has held for so long and bravely. But we do not believe these things..."

120 Fritz Eichenberg, a German-born Quaker convert, was one of the master wood-engravers of the twentieth century, famous for his illustrations of literary classics by Dostoevsky and Tolstoy. Dorothy and Eichenberg met at a Quaker retreat house and became fast friends. His illustrations for the CW, donated freely, redefined the appearance of the paper. Some, like his "Christ of the Breadlines," visually exemplified the spiritual message of the Worker.

Came in this morning after 6:30 Mass.

Walked up to 12th St. to get [Alexander] Berkman's *Prison Memoirs [of an Anarchist]*. (Last night Paula and I at S.I. read aloud from *Three Who Made a Revolution* by Bertram Wolfe.) Also got Conrad's *Victory* and Dreiser's *The Genius* to read at Aunt Jenny's where I go tomorrow.

All this week I have been at Peter Farm working on my book, helping there. A cold, a headache, bad eyes—it may be smog or oil burners.

Jan 15 Monday. Poughkeepsie. St. Paul, hermit. St. Maurus

Yesterday Jane, Philip and Molly, Hans and I drove up to Aunt Jenny's. Just as we got to the bridge it began to snow, and soon we could scarcely see.

This is the pen Tom [Sullivan] gave me for my birthday, already ruined. A Parker. How hard to work with bum tools. Fritz Eichenberg spoke to us on Eric Gill, work and time, the sacramentality of things, etc. A good meeting. He will come later to speak on Peace. I am to go to the Tuckahoe Quaker meeting to speak on Peace Feb 4.

How the winter begins to fly. Much snow and cold, but we are very snug. Peter [Maurin] Farm, Maryfarm, and St. Joseph's House. The oil burner at the latter place bothers my eyes, a clear indication from the Lord to stay at the farms. Now I am here for two weeks and will work at my book, please God.

Here at Aunt Jenny's they are on a hillside and ice made it hard to get out. I have only rubbers, no galoshes. Must get some. It is so beautiful and white, with trees black against the snow. Pines are beautiful.

Thursday Jan 18. St. Peter's Chair

Great joy in Scheeben's *Glories of Divine Grace*. Bad eyes yet. Over a month. Evidently not oil burners.

Letter from Tamar and Dave. Car fixed. Children well. F. gave them tricycles for Christmas.

Reading Office every day. Not much time for letters or book. Aunt J. not too well. Letter from [John] Cogley.[121] My article hurt him. He is in a state. I shall try to say nothing about it. Writing is hard.

Mild weather. Thawing all week. Snow almost gone. Aunt J. says we will have 30 snow storms this winter.

Reading a book by Dorothy Canfield in which mention is made of a woman's empty arms. They need never be empty. Nor hands idle. There are always sick, the old, the children to be cared for. And with love.

---

121 Before becoming the editor of *The Commonweal*, John Cogley had been a leader of the Chicago Catholic Worker and a frequent contributor to the CW. He differed from Dorothy's position on pacifism and served in the army during the war. Despite their differences, Cogley remained an admirer, and strongly defended her protests during the Civil Defense drills in New York.

We must express it with sweetness, with tenderness. When I saw the altar boy kiss the cruet I felt how necessary ritual is. To kiss the earth. To lift the arms, to embrace the lonely, etc.

Sat. Jan 20. Maryfarm

In the chapel. Whenever I am here I am overwhelmed with gratitude for God's goodness to us. The order, the peace here, the beauty, are an oasis. We cannot give up this place. We must try to make Peter Farm like it in silence, order, work—everything so ordered that people will be enabled to praise God in peace and rest.

Now I must be at Aunt Jane's another week and I am praying Veronica returns to her so I may leave with a free mind. Aunt J. may have another five or ten years this way—she has great vitality. On the other hand she may go in her sleep. We can pray together, read together, talk about heaven together for these weeks anyway. I love being there. It is a rest and joy for me.

I am reading Scheeben's *Glories of Grace,* which St. Meinrad's put out in 5 pamphlets. I am in pamphlet three and the theological virtues of faith, hope, and charity are described so beautifully that one realizes the immense riches we possess.

Ammon Hennacy says that when he is working in the fields he stops at the end of a furrow and prays for grace for himself, and for us all. What would we do without these prayers which bind us together! Since, as St. Ignatius said, love is an exchange of gifts, we must remember him too in our prayers.

Tues Jan 22. Poughkeepsie 11:30 a.m.

Bad cold and in eyes, nose, throat. Can scarcely talk or sleep with coughing. Reading *Mao Tse Tung* by Robert Payne.

"It was out of such things, legends, the peasant's desire to own his land, the broad masses of the people—that Mao brought about the revolution...the tragic failure of the Kuomintang lay in the absence of any point of contact with the people."

I have taken these copious notes for peace talks. When we know our enemy, we are more able to love him.

Wednesday Feb 14. 9:30 p.m.

To Bellevue, to Dr. Fonda for eye treatment. He says infection of tear glands. He douched them out with salt water—got me eye drops and salve. Hot compresses night and morning.

Mid-day Mass, Stations, novena, Benediction at Carmelite Church.

Tues Feb 20. Grey day. Mild. Peter [Maurin] Farm

I am in bed with head cold. Irene is studying pruning. Hans is hammering in the attic. Ray and Isadore are making flats to plant salads. Albert is cleaning around and has discovered a cistern under the sacristy (house). Father Konrad gave the first of his talks on the sacraments Sunday. Very fine. This is the time of year for pruning—Lent—natural and supernatural.

Saturday—Feb 24

On train for Stamford to meet Della. 8:30 Mass. Today's Gospel the Prodigal Son. The folly of such love. Such a Father. We must be servants. The implications of that thought. It means we would never put anyone out. We would nurse them thru such seizures. The problem of contributing to delinquency.

I spoke last night on China. Half a dozen Chinese present. Mostly disagreed. The old problem. No one is convinced of poverty. They think it is a man's own fault.

*Dorothy was frequently asked what she would do if the Archdiocese ordered her to close the Catholic Worker. This remained a hypothetical question. There did come a day, however, when she was confronted with the choice: cease publication, or change the name of the* Catholic Worker.

March 4 Sunday. Laetare. 9:45 p.m.

Friday Bob [Ludlow][122] took to his bed with measles. Sat. I was called to chancery office where Msgr. Gaffney told me we would have to cease publication or change our name.

I have flu and a headache and infected eye.

Mrs. Dechsli called and wants payment on the Staten Island house.

All last two weeks Mary, Judy, Ann, Jean and Hatty have been drunk.

Jane—Billy—John all having trouble, which landed Billy in jail for 10 days. Fr. Faley is leaving.

I cannot think of any other immediate troubles right now. Except not being able to work on "The Long Loneliness."

"Our troubles were multiplied. Afterward we made haste."

---

122 Bob Ludlow, a Catholic convert and one of the most intellectually gifted editors of the CW, was the principal theorist of the Worker's pacifism. As Dorothy noted in *The Long Loneliness,* "Robert is doctrinaire and dogmatic, sometimes belligerent in tone so that we find ourselves in hot water and are forced to reconsider and re-present our positions. And yet he is the mildest of mortals, meek and disciplined in his personal life, ready to withdraw or subside, to hold his position alone, if need be…His writings have aroused the conscience, have spotlighted attention on the grave questions of freedom and authority." (*LL,* 267)

Tomorrow we go to press. Tues I am supposed to speak at Muhlenberg College. Today is Tamar's birthday and I long to visit her. I stayed in the office all day after 11 a.m. Mass.

Joe Monroe and I are fasting from meat in view of all our troubles. Tony [Aratari] found me quotations from [Friedrich] von Hugel to sustain me— about the suppression of an Italian paper in 1907. Michael [Harrington][123] urges me to fortitude and the fighting against obscurantism in the Church. Jack comes out with hopeful suggestions about adding a box to the paper, "published without ecclesiastical approval."

March 8. Thurs.

Mike Harrington took the talk at Muhlenberg College and relieved Bob [Ludlow] and me on Tues. Wed. I felt better—wrote appeal and letter to Monsignor. No one liked it.[124] Read [Nicolai] Berdyaev.

"The greatest mystery of life is that satisfaction is felt not by those who take and make demands but by those who give and make sacrifices. In them alone the energy of life does not fail and this is precisely what is meant by creativeness."

March 15. Thurs. Westminster

8:30 a.m. Home from 7 a.m. Mass with firm determination to work in spite of everything, babies, housework, the troubles about Dave's job, etc.[125] Used last *Welcome* this a.m. as preparation for communion and was inspired

---

123  Michael Harrington would become one of the best-known alumni of the Catholic Worker. Recognizing his intellectual gifts, Dorothy often sent him to speaking engagements in her place. He later recalled, "To someone who had never heard of Michael Harrington, I'm not sure how happy they were. Here they are trying to get this famous Catholic woman and instead they get a twenty-three year old." Harrington left the CW when he left the Catholic church. His book *The Other America* is said to have inspired President Johnson to launch the War on Poverty, and he became a prominent exponent of democratic socialism.

124  In response to the Chancery's instruction to drop the word *Catholic* from the name of the CW, Dorothy replied: "First of all I wish to assure you of our love and respectful obedience to the Church, and our gratitude to this Archdiocese, which has so often and so generously defended us from many who attack us..." She noted that none of the staff wished to change the name of the CW, which had operated under that name for 18 years. "I am sure none thinks the Catholic War Veterans (who also use the name Catholic) represents the point of view of the Archdiocese any more than they think the CW does." While she stood ready to receive criticism or disciplinary censure for any theological errors, she noted that ceasing publication "would be a grave scandal to our readers and would put into the hands of our enemies, the enemies of the Church, a formidable weapon." She resolved to be "less dogmatic, more persuasive, less irritating, more winning." The matter was not raised again. (See Miller, *Dorothy Day,* 247-28)

125  David Hennessy lost his job at the Newman bookshop.

to think of writing a story of all those on my lists of the dead—all of whom have such extraordinary stories.

I want to write too a life of the Little Flower [St. Therese of Lisieux] from the mother and woman's standpoint.[126]

Also the story of nine months.

Today the ground is covered with snow, 30°. But the birds sing. The tulips and daffodils are pushing up. We know it is Spring. Though we are just moved in here at 32 E. Green, we are forced to think of finding another place already. How utterly helpless the worker these days with living quarters so scarce. Everything against the family.

Notes: What did our poverty consist of? Insecurity—loss of jobs—no ownership—no property—no responsibility—lack of a philosophy of work.

Paradox: We are pilgrims here. We have here no abiding city. We should live as travelers, not attached to baggage which weights us down. Not accumulating.

And yet—a certain amount of goods is necessary. What kind? Property. The land. Earth to grow food in—to learn from, to walk on. House so we can carry our responsibilities and learn to fulfill the commandment of God to earn our living with the sweat of our brow.

Traveled by night. Very bad train. Very stiff still. Bus travel is better than those older trains.

This afternoon, glimpses of my own ugliness, vanity, pride, cruelty, contempt of others, levity, jeering, carping. Too sensitive to criticism, showing self-seeking love.

I am trying to collect all I can of St. Therese.

Friday April 6. Chrystie St.

Back to N.Y. Wed. morning. Mass at St. Francis at five. House in time for breadline where we now serve our own bread. We use 500 lbs a week, a ton a month of flour. Isadore [Fazio] and Michael Harrington on the house. Dave H. arrives tonight from Westminster. His mother is there with Tamar. He is looking for a job up here, and a place to stay in S.I.

This morning visited Msgr. Schilthuis at Cardinal's residence today to have him read me a letter from the archbishop of Manila on the subject of the war criminals' execution. Promised bread to the Cardinal. St. Francis after. Con-

---

126 Dorothy worked for several years on her book on St. Therese of Lisieux. It was originally to be published by Harper & Row, but they were unhappy with the results. Eventually, in 1960, *Therese* was published by Fides Press.

fession and met Dan Sullivan and had lunch. Great discussion all day—paper was being mailed out—on [Milton] Mayer's letter about funds from the Ford Foundation for the CW. Most against it.[127] Tried to work on my book but much discouraged. The third part will not get along. Will try to keep log but no other writing.

### Sat. April 7
Warm, sunny. Mass 7.30. Breakfast with Dave H. who came last night from Westminster.

Forster gave me a radio for my room. Much joy.

Marge was talking of guilt. She said if people did more penance they would free themselves from subconscious guilt. St. Teresa said when she did more penance she had better health.

### Sun April 22
Cousin Grace just called me that Aunt Jenny died in her sleep. It was just a year ago she had a stroke. Poor Grace is overcome. Funeral Wed. A long wait—it seems to me it should be half-way between the Jewish idea of burying before sundown and the 3 full day and night wakes of the Irish. Aunt Jenny was as sweet and innocent a soul as ever lived—a gentle person. The phrase "happy release" is a good one. I know how she suffered at not being able to move about.

Yesterday moved into the rear room with running water, two windows—much room to move about, to receive guests, to work, wash, clean, write. What joy. Tom [Sullivan], hating all change, and desirous of fitting me into his particular pattern of sanctity for me, in a coal bin perhaps, is grouchy. "Where will the men wash?" They never washed in here anyway. Fred and Andy would not let them. Later in the evening he poked his head in—"Where will Fred sleep?" tho it was obvious the small room was empty. Andy is in the hospital. He had a hemorrhage night before. Chas and one of the men went up to give him blood. He will have to go to the t.b. hospital. Fred also should go but will not. So I was putting no one out as Tom would try to make it appear.

I scrubbed the room and beds and windows with Mary's help, and moved in my own mattress and bedding. The place was filthy. Empty bottles everywhere—sputum behind the bed. A revolting task. A terrible disease, and people are so careless who have it. A white plague. One can't talk to Jack or

---

127  Milton Mayer of *The Progressive* magazine had suggested that the Ford Foundation would be happy to extend a grant to the CW. Dorothy declined, citing her commitment to personal responsibility.

Tom but it does seem to me with two new cases of t.b. in the kitchen Lee should be suspect. Jack and Shorty should be examined.

Last night a peculiar dream. Before going to bed I had gone to Benediction, to confession, spent my hour, troubled it is true, with Tom's attitude. This is my dream. I was on a street car going along a waterfront. It might have been a bus, like the one going along Front Street. Two policemen in the crowded car leaned out the window to shout to some passersby, "The marina is on fire. Put in the alarm." Then when they got off at the next stop they had a visible conflict. They wanted to go back to the marina but their job was to capture two or three thugs in the terminal. It was like a car barn, or like the Jersey City terminal. The thugs came swaggering out to meet them, dressed loudly in stripes or checks. That is all I remember of my dream.

O yes, just before going to bed, Sharkey was engaged in altercation downstairs with a well dressed man who came in loudly proclaiming that he had just stopped a woman from slapping her child—had he done right? Was he all right in his heart? What if he should come in and strike Sharkey? "No one ever tried it yet," said Sharkey, who was half his size and looked like a little terrier. He got him out very tactfully and firmly. It was hard to tell whether he was drunk or mad. As I write other things come into my mind. My conversation with Agnes about Joe M. and pacifism. My conversation with Michael H. in the morning. The lips speak what is in the heart so this business of violence and force must be much in my heart.

(Tina [De Aragon—*the sister of Dorothy's sister-in-law Tessa*] says her Spanish friend who came from a Franco concentration camp and a whole childhood of suffering and poverty says that what this country lacks is joy! And song, a physical expression of joy and sorrow.)

Friday I visited St. Rose's cancer home to see about a bed for a friend's brother who has not long to live. There was an atmosphere of peace and joy there—"the little house of poverty and pain," as Msgr. Betowski called it. It houses only a few hundred patients, a contrast to Ward's Island where there are 5,000, and on one side the wards and rooms look out over the river. Across the street there are trees and children playing and alongside is the river with boats passing all day and a glorious view of the Manhattan Bridge.[128]

A bed was available and after half an hour and visit to the chapel, which is an oasis of beauty, I walked home across Pitt St. to Stanton and then west to Chrystie. The streets were narrow and the buildings high—and everywhere it was quiet for it was almost time for the Passover supper and all the East Side was hushed.

---

128 St. Rose's home for terminal cancer patients was run by an order of Dominican Sisters, founded by Rose Hawthorne, daughter of Nathaniel Hawthorne.

May 20. Sunday. Misty and cold

Tamar and Dave have moved up to Staten Island and are living in the barn which leaks since the hurricane. Hans, bless him, walled in one end and the loft so the bedroom is upstairs and they have a dining room and kitchen downstairs. The children are all well but it is hard on Tamar.

A cold, grey day. Last Sunday a Communion breakfast in Poughkeepsie, for which I was not paid! Money very low. A cold ever since May first. Sinus, eyes. Mary Lese is a good doctor and is bathing them at night. Also using castor oil. Salt water wash, pinch to glass of hot water. No other medicine.

Dave H. starts work at Sheed and Ward [publishers] tomorrow. Since they sold their W. Va. place they have a down payment, and have paid $100 down on a little farm, 4 acres, near us. Hope they can get immediate possession.

Wrote all month on book. Finished to my satisfaction. Now am doing an extra chapter on Tamar. Eleanor typing it in triplicate. They have one copy besides which she did without making any carbon. Jim Shaw made wonderful suggestions all through. Nothing like a good editor who knows what you are writing about.

June 8. Friday

Approaching at things indirectly. I have to speak tonight at Chrystie St., so instead of preparing my talk (I did some yesterday) I am reading Scheeben's *Mysteries of Christianity*. I am so happy that Tamar and family are settled in the house.

I dreamed of Franklin [Spier, *Della's husband*] last night—that he was attempting suicide by cutting his wrists. A beggar came in who needed to be fed and this occupation prevented him. He had been seeking recreation with a display of outboard motors all around the living room. He was still living with Della. I had visited recently while he was recuperating from a lame knee. He is separated from Della now but still demands her care. My problems with her, Tamar, Irene, the book and the work, much on my mind. And yet people do not need you as much as they think they do. It is necessary to be more careful and withdraw.

A beautiful book from William Everson.[129] It makes me more zealous in calligraphy.

Much difficulty about book. Harpers says it is parochial, will be offensive to Catholics.

---

129 William Everson of the Oakland CW, later known as Brother Antoninus, became a famous poet.

June. Peter Maurin Farm

St. Basil day. Caroline Gordon and [Brainard] Cheney from Tennessee to lunch.

Tamar at P.M. farm. Baby due.

June 16

If daily Mass and Communion do not make people kinder, milder, gentler, it must be very saddening to our Lord. The problem of Tom [Sullivan]. Power corrupts. Men become bullies when they hold the purse strings very often. They are rude, angry, overbearing, making others suffer around them. I have seen this all my life with a father and brother like Sam. How to handle it? My belief is with gentleness, silence, withdrawal. People seldom mean all they say.

Anger is momentary. Some people will never apologize tho they may feel sorry. Everything is bottled up inside and it is unseemly, to say the least, to be always trying to pry people open, to make them open (as I consider myself to be, for instance). When I reproached Tom once, he said, "I've always been that way." Meaning his anger, his sulking. He gets over it in a couple of days. There is the element of the spoiled child, having his way. However, can he be changed at 38? Certainly all the chisels and hammers in the house do it little by little. I seem angry when I am silent very often just because of an expression of eye strain. All the more reason to speak gently. My problem is to try and be gentle and kind to *all*. Even, equable, never startling and saddening people by changes of mood. Lifting an atmosphere instead of lowering it.

The women always feel I am favoring the men because I do not publicly espouse their cause, do not take up the issue as it takes place. It is true I am more on the side of the men. All women are. But I expect more from women. More gentleness, subtlety, guile, perception, techniques in making things run smoother.

Women want to be recognized as persons. (Jane, Irene, Helen, all say this.) I think this is one of the things they must sow. And they are not the meek, humble, retiring sort, any of them. So head on collisions. We get men afraid of women, marriage, responsibility, afraid of sex, of love, like Tom who is like a clam, tight shut, withdrawn. Their defense is bullying, shouting, blustering. Not a pretty picture. But are we the ones to "tell them off"? To judge?

I must to a certain extent. But my problem is—I have always done this quietly, secretly, after the event when things are calmed down. The women do not believe I do anything. They want it public, a public upholding. And they must just suffer these public humiliations, many of which they bring on themselves and I must many times be silent. When I flare up, it does no good. Only adds to the flame, the disorder.

I have a hard enough job to curb the anger in my own heart which I sometimes even wake up with, go to sleep with,—a giant to strive with, an ugliness, a sorrow to me—a mighty struggle to love. As long as there is any resentment, bitterness, lack of love in my own heart I am powerless. God must help me. I can safely leave Tom to his guardian angel, to God, the Blessed Mother.

The talk with Jane was good because it made me see my own faults, flippancy, criticalness, gibing attitude, lack of respect and love for others.

July 1, Sunday

No baby yet. Difficult days. 3 Masses.

I was ill again with a cold one day last week. Lesson of St. Jerome on David's old age and feebleness. I feel ancient at 53. Reading Emma Goldman and her experiences in Russia, Sweden, and Germany at that age! But helping care for 4 children, anxiety over Tamar, Veronica's call on me, Jim's irascibility and selfishness, *[text lost]*

July 3

Still no baby. How happy we will be when the new little one is here and all is well.

Yesterday on the feast of the Visitation I awoke ill—depressed, worrying about the question of my own operation. It had been a close night and Rita had not slept with her poison ivy, nor had Jean, and others had been up in and out of the bathroom. The car worked (it did not today) so we got to Mass early. But I felt low indeed. To cook for 15, help Tamar with four children, try to work on my book, see visitors, put up with mental cases and the entire weight of woe around me. It was too much. The children were pettish and whiny as they get on occasion. Everything seemed just too much. Somehow we got by.

July 4

When your hands are tired from peeling potatoes, washing clothes, it is hard to write. Tamar has been gone 24 hours and all is well. There are scratches, bruises, and blisters, but they are happy.

When she left yesterday I probably felt more homesick for her than the children did. She had finished a wash, buried the garbage, mopped the floors, taken a bath, fed all the children, and finally she was ready.

The children were very excited about all the preparations. When she started shining her shoes they all wanted to help. "David will hate these loafers," she said, "but they are so comfortable. There isn't room in my suitcase for my good black shoes. They were donated—not too good a fit."

Her suitcase was packed. Only an inexperienced traveler would have carried so much. Two skirts, 4 blouses, a change of underwear and stockings, a comb and brush, handkerchiefs, and goodness knows what else. She wore a lovely pink nylon crepe which she could wash out and put on again. The other two skirts were cotton seersucker and rather heavy for this weather. While I write, Becky comes to sit beside me, and Nickie comes out of his cold tub where he has been playing to show me his boats made of walnut shells. Eric and Susie are playing Indians in the tent dressing themselves up in ferns which they have discovered resemble feathers.

It is wonderful the scope of their play. Instead of a cage of climbing bars they have the mulberry and cherry trees to climb. There is a swing and there was a seesaw.

Eric, not longer after he was four, did a remarkable thing. He wanted to seesaw when the girls were in school and arranged a ballast of a heavy board on one side to balance himself. This was so satisfactory an arrangement that he continued to seesaw by himself until in a burst of energy he used a new saw to cut the long board in two.

It has been a busy day. The children are awake at seven. The sun was already high and it was very hot. There was only one shade in the living room and the eastern sun was blazing into the room, so I rigged up an old dark blanket to fit the upper part of the other window.

There are so many needs around this house. Screening, shades, linoleum, and paint—all things that cost money. It is no use saying hard work is enough. Materials are needed, tools to work with. It is a part of poverty to be doing without these things. It is a part of poverty to have insufficient physical strength to take care of five children, wash, cook, clean, garden. It is part of destitution to have no philosophy of work; and so to accept manual labor as part of a penitential and creative life. It is wonderful to get those first immediate chores done that enable one to settle down for a few prayers.

When I was visiting John and Helen Cort recently I woke up to the sound of Helen's praying with the children. They prayed at the table as they sat down to breakfast. They say the Office together, John and Helen, and John says Helen falls asleep over her prayers at night. She has five children too.

Another thing to be said in favor of the *Layman's Short Breviary*—Matins is just long enough to hold the attention of the children when it is read aloud. They keep a complete and attentive silence, the oldest three, and even Nicky is hushed by the others.

I find the English translation of the hymn suitable for singing to the Gregorian music.

When the children sing to me it is in a shouting monotone, and none of them seem able to keep a tune yet. Neither Tamar nor Dave sing, nor have I a voice either, tho a true enough ear. The point of Gregorian is that it is to be sung by everyone, as one voice, so that none stands out. Everyone should sing, as a prayer sung is twice said, St. Augustine said. Children sing, or try to, mothers sing lullabies—we all want to sing.

While we sit under the mulberry trees which are still loaded with fruit, Nickie goes into ecstasies over "girls" in the trees, meaning squirrels. This is a bird paradise too and one can lean back in a deck chair and watch flickers, wrens, song sparrows.

The children eat ravenously. It certainly takes time filling up five.

And yet how much easier it all is than it was in West Virginia. There it was chiefly the loneliness—no neighbors but Mrs. Fearnon, no visitors. Three years of that, with primitive conditions, no plumbing, bath, running water. All water to be fetched from the well or cistern or spring, according to the use to which it was to be put. A defective kerosene heater, a wood stove, low ceilings, small windows—and yet incomparable beauty of scene. Groceries cost as much as in New York. There never was any ice to keep the food fresh. But there was an abundance of food from garden—chickens, eggs, butter, milk, and cream. It is a delight to think of.

"Peasants never starve," A Frenchman wrote me recently, "in spite of wars, etc."

The children were all babies then, and the loneliness was bitter.

July 5

No baby. Dave worries much. Wintry weather, high winds, grey clouds, depressing.

Today Father Carrabine called up and said Tom had said I was down in the country having a baby. He laughed as he said it but Tom said his face was startled when Tom pulled his foolish statement with a straight face. What with Tamar and that, my state, and a love letter after a fashion from Ammon [Hennacy] I went to sleep and dreamed I was having a baby in Nov. I even had the date figured out. It was all most casual! A great relief to me when I woke up to find it a dream.

Eric ill these nights and I have had to go to sleep in their room on the floor. St. Jerome has something to say on that and age.

No reading of any consequences. Just finished *The Mayor of Casterbridge*. Read Hardy so long go that it is all fresh for me.

Mon July 9. No baby

This diary could start with the chronicling of aches and pains—rheumatism, lumbago, etc., every day. It also could go on to list work done and that would give satisfaction. So many hours at the ms., letter-writing, talking to visitors, odds and ends of housework, wash, caring for the children, so much that does not show, that does not give one a sense of things accomplished.

And now another disaster, the Heaney baby, 2 years old, drowned.

The duty of delight—as Ruskin says.[130]

Today we have a picnic in the woods. The air is sweet with milkweed in bloom. The honeysuckle is past, the sweet clover goes on all summer.

Yesterday the waves at the beach were delightful. I went to three Masses, to St. Joseph on Rossville for the first time.

Thurs 12. No baby yet

Yesterday sent Parts One and Two to Chambers [at Harper]. Dull work.

July 22. St. Mary Magdalene

Baby born 5:30 a.m. this Sunday. Mary Elizabeth a little beauty. Doctor arrived in ten minutes, the baby in ten more. Tamar is such a wonder. No false alarms, taking everything calmly. Dave far more excited. Children happy and good all day.

Feast of St. Ann

We have just finished saying the rosary at the Peter Maurin Farm. There is Rita, Mary, Bill, and Becky, Susie and Eric and me. Eric weaves his rosary in and out of the back of a chair. Becky counts medals in a letter box and Sue ends by winding her rosary in and out between her toes and saying her beads very seriously in that position. The rest of us kneel decorously. Finished writing for July-Aug paper.

Aug 2 Thurs.

Part III to Harper.

Today very tired after 4-hour meeting. Slept till 8:30. *Life of Jesus,* [François] Mauriac in mail. Sent Harp. ms. Made hour in church on Eliz. St.

Tragic letter from Mary Durnin. Her little Mary dying of leukemia. Praying for them both.

---

130 "The duty of delight," a phrase from John Ruskin, came to serve for Dorothy as a call to mindfulness in the face of drudgery and sorrow. She was at this time completing *The Long Loneliness* and used this line in the book's Postscript: "It is not easy always to be joyful, to keep in mind the duty of delight." Later she contemplated using it as the title for her book *Loaves and Fishes* (see February 24, 1961).

Aug 5.  Our Lady of the Snows

Mary Elizabeth's baptism. Fr. Hyland who baptized me and Tamar, baptized the 5th grandchild. Returned to the farm for vespers and supper, a lovely day. All well and happy, thank God.

Aug 10, Friday

Mary Lisi cooking squash vine soup for me who have been sick all week since Monday with what I diagnose as intestinal flu. Fever, headache, bone ache, etc. Lettuce as dressing for infected cuts, olive oil massages, steam baths, mother's milk for sore eyes, etc.

Fritz [Eichenberg] called about the 3 [wood] cuts for the book.[131] All week Ammon has been fasting and picketing in Phoenix in penance for the atom bomb.[132] My illness was a penance not self-imposed. I am too cowardly.

Fr. Fiorentino, Fr. Mooney, Fr. Hugo, Fr. Farina, all in town together after a visit to Fr. Lacouture.[133] Not a call to us. I feel abandoned by them. They had hoped we would espouse their cause—in a way expected us to be disobedient while they were obedient—all of them, even Fr. Roy. The laity are of so little worth. Fr. Hugo has abandoned the problem of pacifism and distributism for that of nature and the supernatural. Inflexible. Afraid the interest in one will distract from the interest in the other. First things first, yes, but for the laity the question of bread, home, and peace is first.

Sat. Aug 11

Busy all day. Mass at 8. Tamar and Dave to lawyer. She very irritable. He at meeting night before called Bob [Ludlow] a viper. Over [Hilaire] Belloc and the Jews. Words at bedtime. Wrote letters till one. Mary tells me she is leaving to go with the Sisters. The trouble with the truly holy. "I will stay as long as you need me." (But it means, as long as I think you need me… You do not really need me because you have all these bums around who could work but won't. They are not mental, not sick. They are putting something over.) However she has given us 2 ½ months! I sure am grateful.

Monday Aug 13

Slept like one dead after the long drive. Fr. Faley's Mass at seven. Then I went downstairs and had a cup of coffee. First there were flies in the milk.

---

131 Fritz Eichenberg supplied the cover art ("The Annunciation") and three wood-cuts for each part opening of *The Long Loneliness*.

132 Ammon Hennacy fasted one additional day for every year since the dropping of the atomic bomb in 1945.

133 Fr. Onesimus Lacouture, a French Canadian Jesuit, originated "the retreat" that Dorothy experienced through Fr. Roy and Fr. Hugo.

Then it was sour. Poured it out and got another cup. Put canned milk in that. It was sour. Poured it out, then with the next the goat's milk tasted goaty indeed. Everything looked rough, sloppy. Bread cut in huge wedges, kitchen damp, hot and full of flies! And ashamed of my delicacy I thought with content we were like a peasant family—rude, rough, yet comfortable, food plentiful and wholesome.

Thank God there are the poor with us, men of the road stopping over. Sunday Sue and her children and her half-witted brother trying to commit suicide by walking in the middle of the road. Frs. Masterson and Cordes, a man and his wife, unemployable, drifters; old Joe Davin with his broken hip. Veronica, mental. Not to speak of our regular staff, and Fr. Faley, serving them all.

It is a wonderful place, Maryfarm.

Sung Mass at 8 after prime. All girls, voices none very good, but it was correctly done anyway. And I enjoyed singing again. One comes alive in the Mass, is a living part of it.

I feel very happy, in spite of trouble about Tamar and Dave. There will always be that. If there were not, I would be too happy, too attached. As it is, I am glad to get away for a time. Also I am driven to leave them to God.

To do: Send Ammon extracts from St. Paul. He has the liberal's unreasoning hatred of him.

White, *The True Anarchist*. Anarchism based on love not hate. Self-government rather than an imposed government. Recognizing dignity and glory of our sonship and what it entails, what abilities it confers. Our capacities to work, physically, mentally, spiritually. To expect everything of ourselves, with God's grace, and not to judge others. Measure ourselves as to what God wants of us, what talents he has given us to use and not to compare ourselves or judge ourselves by others, whether better or worse. In that way to stand alone, in self-reliance. On the other hand, to be so far from dominating others or wanting to influence others as to 1) not judge (this seems to be folly, but it is the folly of the cross, it is sowing one's judgment); 2) to serve all men, to obey all men, to wash the feet of all men, in love, recognizing our common humanity—we are one flesh, as is said of husbands and wives. And what love surpasses that love? To love our brothers because Christ is our brother. Because we are all children of Mary, Mother of God. To love our brother because Jesus, Son of God, gave us a picture of that love in the story of the prodigal son. That is the kind of Father we have. No judgment there. Only the madness of love, deep, profound, as profligate in its way as the son's tawdry loves had been profligate.

The true anarchist asks nothing for himself, he is self-disciplined, self denying, accepting the Cross, without asking sympathy, without complaint.

The true anarchist loves his brother, according to the new law, ready to die rather than compel his brother to go his totalitarian way, no matter how convinced he may be that his way is the only way.

There are the silent ones, using the weapons of prayer, and work, because in their love they wish others to be happy, and free, as St. Francis was free.

There are many of these silent, humble little people in the world and out of the world. I have met them all over the country. If you used the word anarchist they would be disturbed, not knowing what the word meant, thinking only of its negative aspects—to be against the State. They do not question the status quo, only to see that the world is awry. They do their work, they support and help others physically, spiritually. They know things are wrong but not why they are wrong. Save that men are prone to evil. They do not judge others, but live on poverty and hard work, "being what they want the other fellow to be." If you love, you hunger to serve, to be of use, to give yourself.

Then there are the ones who know, but are afraid to act on their knowledge. They distrust their capacities. They know with their heads but not their hearts. They do not love enough to crave sacrifice. Then there are the articulate ones who cry out like the prophets and they know that revolution begins with themselves. And they try to explain their position. Their love stands by the use of the pen, not the sword, and they have suffered imprisonment and death knowing that in giving their lives they are saving them, and eventually the lives of countless others.

Scorn, bitterness, scoffing, these are no weapons. Belittling others, not seeing Christ in them—this too is to inflict wounds—is to do to Christ what we are doing to the least around us. This is an expression of fear—fear of being laughed at and scorned in turn. If we scorn others we will not win them. There is no love in scorn.

Aug 19

Folly of the Cross.

You cannot serve God and Mammon.

Contempt of world. Detach ourselves. Love God with whole heart and neighbor. Measure one by other. Since I am trying to do without meat in thanksgiving for Ed's generosity and God's care of us, dinner was not enough, cabbage and tomato, so I stopped to ask Jack for cheese. He talked of his difficulties and I told him of the two stories in Acts—of the two who sold what they had and then, lying to St. Peter, held something back. And the other, the servant of Eliseus who ran after Naaman the cured leper, asking for some gold and garments for the young prophets after the Prophet had refused them. The first were struck dead, the second with leprosy. Both were associated with the saints and while making pretension of being detached from the world, held on to it. The terrible danger in this work of ours. God help us all.

Reading from autobiography of St. Therese. One could write a whole chapter on her being patroness of the mentally afflicted. Her illness. Her samples. It is a most amazing story. Its frankness, truth, what a family. Pauline, Marie—the love and yet detachment.

The world—means to an end. Christ prayed for us as He did for his apostles.

Our brothers—to be loved as we love God, in Christ.

Dec 6. St. Nicholas Day

Reading St. Therese. Also *Humiliated Christ in Russian Thought* by Gorodetzky. Must read more Gogol and Turgenev. No Mass this a.m. Fatigue, sprained wrist and sloth.

It has often been a taunt thrown at us that our CW farms were not farms, or farming communes, or agronomic universities, all of which were dear to the heart of Peter Maurin, peasant founder of the CW.

What are they then? Originally they were farms. As such they are known. In some cases with us they have become little communities of 2 or 3 or 4 families, restoring property to the family, a certain amount remaining in common—ready there for other families to come and build and settle. In Michigan there is a retreat house at Marybrook and St. Benedict's is in a way a house of hospitality on the land.

Here in N.Y. there is Maryfarm at Newburgh, a retreat house and house of hospitality. At Peter Maurin Farm at Pleasant Plains, on Staten Island we had as our intention "to restore Sunday," but so far, in the year we have been here it has not been much of a success. The score of conferences we have had have all started so late, priests arriving for the evening rather than the afternoon, that half the participants have had to go home.

Dec 26. Chrystie St.

In Frankfort, Ill., 199 miners lost their lives in a deep pit. Only rescued after 60 hrs. work. Some had just died, their bodies still warm when crews reached them. One miner had written a last note to his wife. "I love you all way. I go tonight with Christ. I love him too."

# 1952

Jan 4. Friday

Sick with headache today. This morning Ade Bethune visited. She may go to Mexico—Yucatan—to see about helping build a church on a mahogany plantation.

We start the year with Mass at P.M. Farm. Fr. Joseph Kiely. The Dellingers [David and Betty] will arrive this week for a few months' visit.

Sunday Jan 13. Octave Epiphany

O God, give me the grace ever to alleviate the crosses of those around me, never to add to them.

Last night I attended the pageant at Nativity Church and was much moved thereby. The church was in darkness and filled with the poor, the old, the young and struggling. There was complete silence. With a man in the pulpit reading the story, a host of young parishioners acted out in pantomime the Christmas story, the Annunciation, Visitation, Birth of Our Lord, Coming of the Angels, the Shepherds, the Kings to adore. Between readings there were carols, sung unaccompanied by organ. The shepherds were especially good. One played a simple gay tune on the clarinet. It was all very simple and moving. It took an hour. Father Dino preached beforehand about the St. Nicholas (Santy Claus) legend and the birth of Christ. The evening ended with Benediction.

Our house will hold just so many, we can feed just so many, and after that we must say no. It makes us realize how little we can do. It is a constant grief, and a humbling of our pride. One woman said to me, "If I knew how sensitive you were, I would not have told you my troubles." So we cannot show how we suffer with them either. We make them feel we are adding to the sum total of suffering instead of lightening it.

A day like yesterday is like life. Much work, much worry. Yet when I took Dave and Tamar to visit Eric at the hospital [with pneumonia], Sue, Becky and I had our breathing spell on the beach and walking out on the little pier at Princess Bay. Later in the day when I sat on a bench at the foot of Sharrot Rd. waiting for a bus to take me in to the ferry, the winter night was wonderful with its clear cold, the sky sparkling, the river sounds, tankers on the Kill van Kull, the hum of the industrial plants a mile away on the Jersey shore. What joy in winter. We can sit out on the garden chairs under the mulberry trees while the children grub in the dirt.

We always write on the great events later. When we live we do not write.

Mass at the Peter Maurin Farm. It is so unspeakably joyful an event that I cannot bear to go away from there. Every morning Hans, John Murray, John McKeon, Kenneth Little, Joe Cuellar, Rita, Mary and I, are there in the strange old pews St. Francis home gave us when they left their old place at 5th St. to move uptown. Fr. Kiely offers the holy sacrifice, and Ed Foerster serves.

Baby Dellinger born last Monday, Rita and Dave Dellinger assisting. All well. The Sissons loaned the baby book—advice to midwives, gov. pamphlets issued during World War II when there was a scarcity of doctors.

My book [*The Long Loneliness*] came out Jan 19.[134] Good reviews. *Newsweek, N.Y. Times,* and *Herald Tribune.* Dwight Macdonald around interviewing for a profile for *New Yorker.*[135]

Sunday Feb 17. P.M. Farm

Yesterday there was spring in the air, then at night a strong east wind and rain came and today is raw and cold. Last week I moved all my belongings down here from Chrystie St. A sign having come from the Little Flower, I canceled my trip. I will write each day and help Tamar.

Radio, typewriter, latest acquisitions. Must work hard on Therese's book. Sent 50 pages in to Sister M. Irene.

Ash Wednesday, Feb 27

Retreat at the Cenacle, at the invitation of Sally Schilthuis. A wonderful way to begin Lent.

We started Susie to kindergarten Tues, and Becky went back after her illness. The writing and finishing my copy of the account of Mr. O'Connell's death and burial Monday took me the rest of the day, Tues, what with driving the children to and from school, so I arrived here at 9:40 last night, which seems like midnight in a convent.[136]

---

134 "I called my last book *The Long Loneliness* because I tried to point out, with St. Augustine, that no matter how crowded life was with activity and joy, family and work, the human heart was never satisfied until it rested in God, the absolute Good, absolute Beauty, absolute Love" ("Month of the Dead, November 1959). In *The Long Loneliness* itself, Dorothy wrote, "Tamar is partly responsible for the title of this book," for having pointed out the loneliness of a mother of young children, thus prompting this reflection: "The only answer in this life, to the loneliness we are all bound to feel, is community. The living together, working together, sharing together, loving God and loving our brother, and living close to him in community so we can show our love for Him." *LL,* 243.

135 Dwight Macdonald's two-part profile of Dorothy appeared in the October 4 and 11, 1952 issues of *The New Yorker.*

136 "A Friend of the Family: Mr. O'Connell is Dead," March 1952. This portrait was also reprised in *Loaves and Fishes.* "There was never a time when we did not have living with us what Dostoevsky calls a 'friend of the family,' one who moves in meekly and temporarily as a

The retreat master is Fr. Philip Berrigan,[137] a Josephite, missioner to the Negro. His first conference was very good. Who we are—a creature of body and soul and the will and mind are evidences of the soul; a creature, what a tender sound that word has. And God created us to return to him. We owe him reverence, and obedience to his will. To obey the will of another is to enter into his life. Mass is showing our dependence on God by offering him what is his, a worthy offering, God to God. We offer him in the Mass and God offers himself to us. We become partakers of the divine life.

I feel hollow with Lenten fasting already. I hope I get into the swing of it these 3 days.

It is very crowded—this day of the retreat—and rather noisy too since many women are making a day of recollection. Dinner at one, a good meal of creamed tuna fish with potato chips mixed in. How one does dwell on food on fast days. But I was thinking too from the standpoint of our own retreats, our own feeding. Also string beans and salad. Another conference at 2:30, then Benediction and I was very sleepy indeed. Now after a nap, there is another conference at 4:30. Then I will walk in the garden. Retreat days are hard.

March 11—Tues on Staten Island

Last night I spoke at Carnegie Hall. Why? To oppose repressive laws. McCarran Act, Smith Act, Feinberg Law with two men lawyers about to go to jail and a splendid Negro who risks her life in working for her race in South Carolina. All communists unfortunately. Also Fowler Harper of Yale, Mr. Fairchild of NYU, I.F. Stone, and Corliss Lamont. Who knows what they are? Wrote my speech and so was not afraid.[138]

Reading *Butler's Lives of the Saints*. I like to pick out the lay saints. Santa Fina, March 12, 1253, and Bd. Nicholas Owen, 1606, was a builder of priest's holes—camouflage escapes.

Wish I had notes on Gerta Blumenthal's talk Friday March 21 on the Christian Hero [and the Saint]. It was magnificent. Mike Harrington says he could enjoy just listening to her read the telephone book, she is so lovely.

---

guest, and who remains permanently, to become an implacable tyrant in the household. One such friend of our family was old Maurice O'Connell, who lived to be eighty-four and who stayed with us for ten years at Maryfarm." See *SW*, 127-132.

137  Fr. Philip Berrigan and his brother Daniel, a Jesuit priest, would become leading figures in the Catholic peace movement.

138  Dorothy justified her willingness to speak on behalf of Communists in an article in the April 1952 issue: "No Party Line." See *SW*, 273-275.

March 22 Sat.

Was invited to speak by the Archbishop in Boston. Also New London and Providence and Concord. May 1. Atlanta and Trappist Abbey Easter Monday. Must accept Archbishop's invitations. And Tom Sullivan is so worried about money. It is staying home and speaking too little that is hard. Traveling is easier.

S.I. Laetare Sunday. March 23

Rain all day but not cold. Hard to drag oneself, heartburn from fatigue. I can remember having this before—before mother died. So now at six I am in bed, listening to the Cathedral choristers.

Prayer of the Little Flower:

"I would willingly hear Thee, and so I beseech of Thee to answer me what I humbly ask: what is truth? Grant that I may see things as they truly are, and never be dazzled by them."

Sunday—Rain pouring. Third Hour meeting

Joe the cook walked out and Jane is doing the cooking. Several women are upset about food, plumbing, etc. Several others about the arrogance of the Catholic Church. Yet all goes well somehow.

I talked this morning about Peter and how he had enlarged our horizons, what he had meant to us as a teacher. And Helene Iswolsky talked of how when she came to U.S. from France, thinking of herself as being all alone, Peter knew her book *Soviet Man Now* and commended her, and how much it meant to her.

Thinking of the Peter [Maurin] book. My writing about him—explaining him. All in one book? When—oh when is there time to write? The art of human contacts.[139] The discipline of writing, of work. It will get done.

Sunday the conference is called "Dialogue with Karl Barth."

Fr. Alex Schmemann on Liturgy

John Cogley. St. Bede—Tuesday

Friday night—May 30. Frederick Loher

A very good meeting which began at 8:15 and went on until 12. But it began badly with Dick Donnelly announcing he would not announce the speaker, that he was anti-Semitic and Fascist (so he had heard). Only Roger and Bob were supposed to have heard his statement about Jewish responsibility but he was prejudged in the minds of the audience. Mr. Penner tried to

---

139 One of Peter Maurin's terms.

bring it out of him by accusing him of being pro-German. But his entire talk and answers were both brilliant, frank, and gentle. I wish Michael Harrington had been there.

Mary and her miracles are a source of amusement to Hatty. The former has a little piece of wood from a boat which came into Naples, given to her by her brother, which has some miraculous properties, Mary claims, over the weather. It rains in the morning when she is about to set out for Mass, she lifts the relic, it stops. "You remember the hurricane year before last? I said the Litany, held up the relic, and it stopped," she told us. But not until it had done millions of dollars worth of damage. Mary's accent is indescribable. She says "summas" for summer. "Status Island" for Staten Island.

Mary is the healer, always ready to go out and beg oranges and grapefruit for anyone ill. Fasting, fruit are her remedies usually. For my eyes, hot applications and drops of pure castor oil. Massage for strain and stiffness—always she is the ministering angel. We will miss her.

Tuesday. June 10. St. Margaret of Scotland

Saturday in bed all day. Sunday at Della's and Franklin sick. Next morning very hot and we left early for Greenwich for conference at Seabrook House of ELSA (Episcopal League for Social Action). Many CP-liners. Most astounding.

Reverend Mellish and Fletcher—Brooklyn and Boston, not pacifist yet all for disarmament. Did not bring up question of non-payment of taxes. I believe they all pay. The meeting held at great estate. Not many there. Slurs at those who wore high church collars, Franciscan garb, or who talked of "being"—Fletcher said they meant "talking." He sneers at prayer rather than action. He said the only peace groups were secular, not Christian. I spoke of immediate action, works of mercy. Not much response.

July 1

Lunch with John Chambers [Harper editor]. [*Long Loneliness*] sold only 9,500 copies. Which means royalties should amount to only $2,375 when the $1,000 advance is taken out. Half to Tamar means $1,137. It is good to reckon it up—take count. And then it is always less than one figured on. Royalties for strange reason amounted to $1,600. Tamar got $500. $500 for P.M. farm. $400 to repay Mae Bellucci, who gave $200 to Willock and $200 to Tom.

July 2

I came down to Staten Island last night so that I would be more ready for my visit—so that Tamar could tell me what Mary should eat, what her schedule is, and so on. Mary is eleven months old, Nickie is 2 ½; Eric is 4 ½; Sue six in August and Becky 7 ½.

The children all woke up bright and early, afraid their mother would start out before they were up. David had already left for work at 6:45, taking the suitcase. Tamar is to leave at three which will get her in town in time to meet David at five.

Tamar says she is so excited she could hardly sleep these last two nights. She wanted to make everything easier for me so she started in mopping floors—living room, kitchen, bath, and the two bedrooms, which the children had previously swept out. They are really efficient those children, and love to help in the garden and house.

The grocer was called and an order left with him, the milkman delivers night at the door. "And what about gas?" Tamar asked. "Do you know how to turn the new tank on? We have used the old one since Dec 10."

She kept remembering things in the course of the morning. "The Clorox is under the tub in the bathroom. The mouse poison and poison ivy powder are all in the back hall under the stairs."

Then she went out to water the two geese who were grazing outside the door. They are a grazing animal, she explained, "and must run loose." But if you go away you must pen them up or they will follow you. "And if you pen them up you must leave alfalfa pellets for them. There are 15 lbs. of them in the kitchen. Cost a dollar."

It has been so dry these last days that leaves on the sassafras trees were turning and dropping, so she spent most of the morning in the garden watering. The children love to help in this. Then the tomato vines had to be tied up and the garbage buried and she was finished.

"This used to be an orchard," Becky said. "There are three peach trees, a plum, two cherries, a pear, 4 mulberry trees, and there are four more in the woods, one beach, plum, and lots of wild cherries."

"There is carrots and lettuce in my garden," said Sue, "and hollyhocks, pansies, and dandelions and a 'balloon' flower and a blanket flower. Marigolds too."

Eric had to give his report. "I got only lettuce and Nickie pulled it all up. I got blue flowers and little fruit trees coming up, out of a grape fruit. And marigolds and dandelions That's all I got."

Aug 8. Sins and offenses

Disclosing sins of another. And why should sins of M. Marr offend me or surprise me? Why is one sin more irritating than another? For instance, M. is a trained nurse and can get work whenever she wants it. She is also a pleasing personality. She comes back again and again after her "benders" to get food, clothing, shelter. Yet if anyone asks her help, she is "not working for nothing"... Then J. Mc., his standard of living, which he will not lower, even if it means borrowing from women, widows, and orphans, to keep it up. It is almost impossible for me to be nice to him, to show him any human sympathy and love. And yet all of us are guilty of the same faults, same ingratitude, the same sense of our own importance and worth.

I fail people daily, God help me, when they come to me for aid and sympathy. There are too many of them, whichever way I turn. Mike K. again tonight. It is not that I can do anything. I must always disappoint them and arouse their bitterness, especially when it is material things they want. But I deny them the Christ in me when I do not show them tenderness, love. God forgive me, and make up to them for it.

Human respect enters in. In the case of J. it is the attitude, "I am not going to be thought to be another of these women falling for his so-conscious charm." My sex is insulted by the injuries he has wrought on others.

And Stanley reminded me, "A bruised reed thou shalt not break." But there is something in a woman that wants to take down that male pride in having begotten a child. Especially when he leaves it to others to bear the brunt of the mother and child's care.

But to disclose the faults of others, even by the slightest word. There is a Russian saying, "For every sin of another which we conceal, three of our own are forgiven."

Wednesday, Aug 20 [Maryfarm retreat]

Slept thru Fr. F's Mass and Compline and felt much better. Last night Father C. was too long—Fr. F. was impatient with the poor Jack who tries so hard to serve and I felt nerve-racked and collapsed and wept. But having my room alone again, despite its stuffiness, I was able to pull myself together.

All the men are invalids so cleaning up was hard. But Kenneth and Gallivan were here and could have helped, and were willing if they were told. The failure in people's interest, the inconstant heart! Perseverance is the greatest of all virtues.

But then God uses these failures to take people away to other work. This work is no longer for them. They have played their part. "Press on, pay no attention to past," Fr. C. is just saying.

Tuesday 7:30

All day in a state of unrest, feeling how M. "had the women hypnotized," as John said, so that they did nothing. Fascinated with conversation. No screen found for chapel and Fr. Faley has been protesting flies all summer. Barns in a state of filth and confusion, thanks to the children. Finally found the screen in a very obvious place—it had just not been looked for. Meals bad. Men sad and resentful and Jane going around in a state about men.

Dear God—I'll try as an exercise, to write my meditations since I am side-tracked in your presence. I find myself saying over and over with my lips— Oh God, O Lord, make haste to help me. O Lord Jesus, have mercy, with every breath I draw. But how much of it is surface, and how much is deep? You know. Only You. Fr. Buckley told us how important it was to direct our intention (a Roman Catholic expression which becomes a cliché). But what I am sure he meant was for us to be very direct, and say to You, I believe You are a personal God, and hear me when I speak, even my trivial petty speech. So I will tell You personally over and over I love You, I adore You, I worship you. Make me mean it in my life. Make me show it by my choices. Make me show it from my waking thought to my sleeping.

When I write, it is because I want to hold my attention to You, now during these 15 minutes before lunch. I want to pray now for Ammon [Hennacy] that You give him light to come with humility to the baptism font, to be confirmed a perfect Christian. How much he would learn to bring strength and comfort to others, to turn from the world and turn to You, to love You and their brothers for love of You. I am very hopeless and pessimistic about asking this, so forgive this too, in me, my unbelief, my lack of faith. I am so surrounded by the poor in interior and exterior goods, they are so gaunt, I can see their faults clearly. So I don't expect too much from them. I know too that only You know the heart. I don't know how good or bad people are. How much vanity, willfulness, pride there may be. And then all this new teaching of psychiatry, Catholic psychiatrists and theologians too, point out how we cannot judge. But I do know that I want with a great longing that Ammon become a Catholic, and I ask You this now, here on the eve of the feast of your mother's Immaculate Heart, to soften his heart and convert him now.

Still, not as I will but as You will, be it done.

I am quite content, tho it makes me feel low at times, to see so many failures in our work. A humiliation too, for us all, to see one outside the Sacraments, without their help, do the things we should be doing, what we write about.

Yes, Thy will be done, and I will continue to love Ammon and have faith in him, and look up to him, and count on him, whether or not he ever becomes a Catholic. And I won't say anything to him about it because I want You to do all the work.[140]

Dear God, forgive me, my failures, my lack of prayer. I have not begun to learn how. You will have to teach me, draw me, and I will run after the odor of Thy garments.

This morning at Mass when Dorothy Willock sat out of weakness, all the children sat. That is the way it is at the CW. I do not give a good example, so the others do not do better.

I do not want to be presumptuous. I did not want so many children, but You sent them. So you must care for them. My very weakness, I will try not to worry so much about. I accept my backaches, headaches, torment of mind as penance for my sins.

Help me to be patient.


Thursday 3:30 p.m.

Ammon is having a very hard time not talking. He runs up to Father after each conference, like a child bursting with some thought. He reminds me of Peter, in a way, full of himself, his mission. "He sure loves to talk about himself," Helen says, but he wins people. Somehow people do take you at your own estimate of yourself. If you believe you are made in God's image and likeness, if you believe you are a brother of Christ, if you believe you can do all things in Him who strengthens you, then you are bound to boast. He goes to an extreme as others go to an extreme of futility. "We can do nothing."

"How can I stand out against the State, the world?"

The Cross is not primarily for sin, but to raise us to the highest level. "If any man will be my disciple, let him deny himself, his human nature, his ego, so he can take up a higher nature, take up his cross *daily* and follow me."

[Ignazio] Silone says we are made in form of a Cross.

In order to possess goods of supernatural order. In order to be a saint. We must die to nature. Does not follow from sin. Not connected primarily with sin; even if sin had not happened it would have been necessary.

---

140  Dorothy's prayer was answered in September when Ammon decided to seek baptism: "In him is no class war, no hatred of any kind. He tosses the word 'pipsqueak,' a Shakespearean word, around rather freely, which is jarring to many, and he himself says of himself that he is a braggart. But he must speak of what he knows, and what he himself has done and can do. Now he has been made a child of God and heir to the kingdom, and he is going to daily Communion to increase the grace that is in him, he will indeed exult like a giant to run the race. May he work more wonders than Gregory the Wonderworker." ("The Conversion of Ammon Hennacy," January 1953)

Transition involves a sacrifice. Redemptive incarnation. Suffering—glory. Cross-Christ. This is never gloomy because we are with Christ. To avoid sin is reasonable. To renounce natural attachments is supranatural. "Love your relatives relatively."

Dear Lord: We pray for peace, peace in the world. We pray for Stalin, for Truman. Forgive our suffering hearts! (We are always afraid people will think us deadly serious, without a sense of humor.)

So when one speaks heavily, awkwardly, from the heart, from the depths, others scoff. We are always failing one another. No mutual charity, no union. Like the husband and wife who are inconsiderate of each other's emotional needs. F. says that S. comes to her casually, picking her up as one would pick up a daily paper. "Like reading the *New York Times*. Casual."

When I say, Lord, that I am too sensitive, it is truly that—my senses, exterior and interior are too thin-skinned. I am tormented by people's moods, their unhappiness. I must live more in my own heart, with Thee. Then when I go forth I have at least serenity. I believe, Dear God. I hope, I love. Teach me.

Dear Lord, Fr. Fiorentino and Msgr. Betowsky were here yesterday and Fr. F. asked my prayers. He gave us $2,000 for this retreat house when we bought it in 1947 and we owe him a great debt of gratitude. He is a hard man to love, a Savonarola, preaching hellfire. "Eating and drinking," he says scornfully. And when I told him T. was having another baby, her fourth, "Not much self control there." How hard to forgive these things, to forget them.[141]

Yet he struggles against a passionate love of his relatives. A bitter struggle. He seems sometimes unbalanced from it. God bless him, love him, comfort him. He is doing penance, suffering for the sins of pastors. Unloved, unappreciated by many because of his rigor.

Dear Lord—old injuries crop up in my mind while I try to pray. I come before you. I am thinking of Ammon and his proposal that we pray at midnight for Bartolomeo Vanzetti and Nicola Sacco who were put to death Aug. 22 [*August 23, 1927*]. I think of him with love and pray for him; then I shudder a bit at his proposal of a holy hour like tonight—almost as tho he were putting Sacco and Vanzetti on a par with Christ. But they were baptized men. They were following their conscience. They were put to death on a false charge. There was Christ in them.[142]

---

141 See entry for July 7, 1949.

142 Dorothy remembered well the summer of 1927 when the Italian anarchists Sacco and Vanzetti were executed in Boston. She was at that moment summoning up her courage to have her daughter Tamar baptized, though this would mean separation from her "common-law husband." "The day they died, the papers had headlines as large as those which proclaimed the

My mind then goes to the volume of letters which they wrote from jail, which Bob has now. I had found it being used as a door stop, a wedge! under a door to hold it open—all battered by wind and rain! And my St. John of the Cross left out under an apple tree to be rain soaked! And my Halgren's catechism, stolen. I know by whom, because he thought I, aspiring to be poor, must be kept poor. My autographed Maritain, Eric Gill!

Natural mysteries—pruning—afflictions for atonement, higher fruitfulness.

Friday

The night conference lasted till after nine beginning at 7:30. Then Compline, and everyone was too tired to rest much. At 11 the Holy Hour was to begin. Caroline Gordon came during the 7:30 conference and she stopped up to have bread and milk. (My bread is beginning to be very good.) She wears a dress like a bathing suit, short, backless. And she brings a lovely statue of the Virgin and Child. Earlier in the week she brought a friend, non-Catholic, "a nymphomaniac," she said blithely, who started at once to flirt with Bud and John.

When Father saw her in dungarees he came to tell her she could not go to the chapel that way. She did not want to go at all. In looking at Caroline's dress, he was reminded of an old lush pastor, "If they bare their bosoms at the communion rail I'll take out my handkerchief and cover them," he roared.

The night vigil 11-12 lasted over. It was supposed to be ½ hour silent prayer, Matins and Benediction. But Fr. was so absorbed he went over an hour. Just as I was thinking of the saint who warmed all around him, and was settling down to read them the entire Psalter (O the blessing of Fr. Frey's little psalm books) and keep vigil all night there was a knocking on the wall. I thought it was the devil (thinking of the Curé d'Ars) but a second rapping came and it was Jane. This finally roused him and he began Matins.

Friday 5 p.m. Aug 22

So often guilty of some faults I should correct in others. Waste of time, idle talk, neglect of others. Here it is the end of the week and I have not made a good retreat. As usual with all the family around, I have fretted over this and that, the mother, the hostess, not accepting the crosses of which there were many, frustrations, pains, lack of rest, headache, strain, impatience, etc. Fiat. Fiat. Fiat.

---

outbreak of war. All the nation mourned. All the nation, I mean, that is made up of the poor, the worker, the trade unionist—those who felt most keenly the sense of solidarity—that very sense of solidarity which made me gradually understand the doctrine of the Mystical Body of Christ whereby we are the members one of another." (LL, 147)

Sat. 10

Last night Joe Monroe, Ammon, Kenneth Little, Fr. [Marion] Casey and I had a Sacco-Vanzetti memorial meeting in the chapel. We said Matins (one nocturn and lessons).

11:15. Last Conference

Went in at 10:45 to say goodbye to Fr. Faley and he kept me until 12 giving me a conference and a very good one, on the life, death, resurrection, in the Mass, rosary, etc. He can confess priests now who come here—a great joy to him.

He looks well but looked nervous at beginning of week. Whole message is Be ye Perfect. Act supernaturally—avoid imperfections, natural motives.

Sept 18.

Sitting in Church at Tottenville while Thelma, Diana and Tamar are at the clinic across the street. (Their names show the unconquered romantic spirit of their mothers.)

Reading *Path of Eternal Wisdom* by [Evelyn] Underhill. Comment on the Stations. It is one thing to have far-off and rapturous vision of Reality. It is another to live in this world of corruption, deformity, vice, disease. Three times, not once, Christ falls, as tho to show us what walking the way of the Cross means—publicly, shamefully, must of necessity be too strong for our bodies if it is to be strong enough to raise our souls to God.

Ruysbroeck: "The love of Jesus is at once avid and generous. All that he has, all that he is, he gives: all that we are, all that we have he takes." We live in the midst of every circumstance of squalor, sin, failure, human disease, perversity. We must play Mary's part as well as Christ's part in the Way of the Cross, looking upon the sufferings of others. We all must have maternal love as well as manly energy. Simon of Cyrene: our kinship with the ordinary and unspiritual. Mission could not be performed without help of other men. Solidarity of all men. "God needs me as much as I need Him"—Meister Eckhart— "to take up every opportunity of service, however trivial."

Friday—Sept 19. St. Januarius

Came in from S.I. Ammon, Stanley and I. Mike K. a nuisance all day. Children home from school. Colds. Yesterday beach. Rough. Supper picnic. They seined, caught baby fish. Sue collected mussel shells. Eric horseshoe crabs. A cork raft floated up on beach made an ideal play pen for Mary and a good backrest for me.

Thought today of short book. The Rosary. At P.M. farm. Fr. Kiely upstairs
ill. Fr. Cordes kneeling by door in his bright plaid shirt and itching. Fr. Duffy
and Cyril, sideways away from crucifix, bent over couch, rumps in air. How
unselfconscious men are.

*Meditation on bus.* Now we have a growing farm. It begins to look very
beautiful. But often before, our farms have grown up and then when people
have gone away weeds have grown, everything looks abandoned and unloved.
Up and down—no progress seemingly. We have here no abiding city. All our
houses and farms are like inns with people coming and going. Very hard for
people to get used to.

# 1953

Feb. 1. Sunday

Over a year has passed. Misplaced my other note book. Or Peggy or Mary
Baker took it

Fr. Duffy sang Mass. Septuagesima.

Fr. Cordes did not get up. Flu? Got up for dinner and supper.

Fr. Kiely still missing. Two and a half weeks now. Fr. Duffy has been working on the farm all summer and the place begins to look like something.
Today he is visiting his brother. If he will only stay! Tamar says she has seen
farms go up and down so many times since '36.

Feb 24

Up till 12, Tom [Sullivan] preparing copy, complaining that Eileen Fantino,
Annabel, the women at Maryfarm writing piously. Women can't help writing that way. Born teachers of children the best of them. Felt grippy—sore
throat all today. Wrote my copy. Read a little of Fr. Doyle. Little sacrifices.
Such as not complaining of the radio last night (and it went off right after).
Not eating a donut on the ferry. Accepting the closing of the Syrian store with
equanimity. Said 15 decades. Prayer of Jesus.

April 23. Wednesday. St. Joseph

"So that the body does not grow tired of keeping alert at prayer, all occa-
sion of grumbling must be kept from it." "He who sleeps, hasn't slept," Fr.
Farina used to say. Discipline of early hours, regular meals. Fasting necessary.
Yesterday they refused to take my blood for Jack Sims. High blood pressure.
Also they said I had just enough for myself. Strange thing to say.

April 25
Dave [Hennessy] resigned [Sheed & Ward], but was practically asked to, his family was getting too big.

Thurs. Feast of Corpus Christi
For the last week I have been saddened first by the departure of Dorothy McMahon and Mildred Shadey and Pat. Pat will be back July first but the others maybe never. They came last September and I've never been so content with fellow workers before. The same spiritual outlook—no criticism, the wonderful devotion of slaves of Mary, serving others, Christ in others.

Went to confession to Fr. Farina, speaking of my cowardice, lack of charity in deed and speech, my sloth in doing penance for others, and I asked him for penance. He told me to keep the church fast on Fridays and on first Fridays to make a 24-hour bread and water fast. He urged a rule of life—so I shall try to be more regular. I get up at 7. Mass at 8. Correspondence—too much talk, too little writing. So back to *Therese* again.

I am reading *Life of Christ* (Papini) and *I Want to See God* (Fides Press). Synthesis of Carmelite teaching. It is deserted on the beach—supper time. Tamar looks so young in her pale yellow seersucker coverall apron. She is six months pregnant now and quite heavy.

Becky made her first Holy Communion Sat May 30. A grey rainy day, but the rain held off until after the May crowning. David worked from 1-9 but got off at 8 on account of the rain. She read in her prayer book, said the rosary the day before—and was recollected both before and after. A very lovely communion breakfast after.

St. Anthony's Day. June 13
Newburgh. Fr. Hannefin's retreat. Rain and cold.
Fr. H. is trying to give the essential for the retreat in 2 days. These first 2 conferences are on the natural motive. Five conferences a day, 45 minutes and 15 in chapel, meditation. He is reading too much.

Wrote Cardinal Spellman on the [Julius and Ethel] Rosenberg case Wednesday. They are to be executed Thursday. We will have a meeting Monday at the C.W.[143]

---

143 The Rosenbergs were members of the Communist Party, convicted of espionage for their supposed role in passing atomic secrets to the Soviets. Despite calls for clemency by many people, including Pope Pius XII, they were executed on June 19, 1953. Dorothy responded in the July 1953 issue with her "Meditation on the Death of the Rosenbergs": "Both went to their deaths firmly, quietly, with no comment. At the last Ethel turned to one of the two police matrons who accompanied her and, clasping her by the hand, pulled her toward her and kissed her warmly. Her last gesture was a gesture of love." See *SW*, 275-277.

Dear God, here are our problems—right now, too fast reading, trying to cram others instead of making a few points slowly, repeating, emphasizing, illustrating. Too theological—as tho addressed to priests who are arguing about single natural motives, etc. The priests are thinking in terms of converting each other. What can Hector make of this or John Rogan?

After lunch. I talked to Fr. H. about not reading the last six conferences! He was very kind, a great man. He said he was so worried about giving the retreat that all week he fretted.

Resolutions: to do more writing. Not to allow others to oppress me so with their problems. Yesterday R. talked to me for 2 ½ hours and after lunch I slept for 2 hours. Utterly exhausted. Have not been sleeping well these last months.

At P.M. farm. Fr. Cordes, Fr. K. and their drink! I worry that I do not give them enough attention and yet each one would absorb you completely—your time and energy, if you would let them. And now Fr. Wenceslas. Persecuted he thinks, by Betty Lou and Roger. He writes bitter sarcastic letters to Bob, inviting him to psychoanalyze him.

Withdraw. Need to be alone. Retreats show how. Silence. Fr. Faley's charity to men. Bowery a place for the poor.

Duty of Delight.


June 29. Sunday 6:20 a.m. Peter Maurin Farm

I awake thinking how easy my life is compared to that of the workers, so much time for the life of the spirit, the life of the mind. And my feeling of guilt, and the necessity of using my talents as God wants me to use them came over me. Then, thinking of Alice Casper's letter, emphasizing the primacy of the spiritual. But we must emphasize justice, must constantly call attention to the condition of the poor.

The Pope said "The masses are lost to the Church." Why? Because Christianity in high places is identified with exploitation. Any attempt to gain a minimum of goods (land, home, tools) for workers is associated with radicalism. Which it is, because it is getting at the roots. We are creatures of *body* and soul. That body and its needs are holy. Christ took on our *humanity*, and we must never lose sight of the humanity of Christ, St. Teresa said.

Reading over all my notes before sending the retreat on to Alice Kathryn. She analyzes constantly; maybe that is why Fr. Farina does not try to explain things to her. I had the good luck this time of making a simple statement in confession of my hot flashes, and fear and trembling, and he took it out of the realm of the natural and put it in the spiritual at once.

July 3. Chrystie St.

Last night I dreamed of Peter—with such love and affection. But the dream was terrible. It was that he was about to be electrocuted like the Rosenbergs, and that after elaborate preparation—he was all geared up in an iron harness, and witnesses' chairs had all been prepared like for our Friday night meetings—there was then a release. He was not to be executed after all. I had been clinging to him, with fear too, lest by this close contact with his harness, I too should be killed. Afterwards I was with someone I did not know, sitting by the river, trying to find a place to be alone with him.

July 26. St. Ann's Day. 11:30 p.m.

Armistice signed in Korea. Thank God. To take effect 12 hrs later? What does that mean? It all sounded very flat over the radio, the President, Rep of the UN speaking as tho it had been a victory against aggression and yet as tho they knew it was a stalemate. But thank God the killing ceases.

There was a sung Mass today—very good. Time only for the prayer of Jesus—always time for that. Waiting, traveling, at any time, in any place, that murmur of the heart. My Lord and my God, my Lord Jesus Christ, Son of God, have mercy on me, a sinner.

Reading in Second Book of Kings now. One loves Saul and Samuel, David and Jonathan. What women, Abigail and her hospitality! Michal and her scorn! And what prayers!

"What am I, O Lord God, and what is my house, that Thou hast brought me thus far?

"I will both play, and make myself meaner than I have done. And I will be little in my own eyes," David said to Michal.

As to armaments, it is easy for the Lord to save by many or by few. The evil of asking for a king. How God's anointing changed Saul, and yet he could still go his own way. The mystery of God's grace and man's freedom.

It is intensely interesting to read the Old Testament.

This last week Fr. Paul Judge gave a retreat at Maryfarm. Tomorrow we go to press and I must then be much closer to Tamar while she awaits her sixth.

A hot hard summer thus far.

Notes for Sept. Conf.

Faith, loyalty, respect for authority. How is this to be reconciled with c.o. and pacifism?

To see Christ in others, especially those in authority, as David saw it in Saul even when Saul kept trying to kill him. Even as Uriah did when he must have known the gossip of the court. To see Christ and only Christ even when following one's conscience incurs what looks like defiance and disobedience. To guard the spirit in which one resists. The spirit of a child, combined with the judgment of a man. "To be subject to every living creature." We obey when we go to jail. Either register or go to jail. We are, after all, given a choice.

I'm afraid I have not kept this spirit of respect towards Senator [Joseph] McCarthy.

There is no room for contempt of others in the Christian life.

I speak and write so much better than I perform. But we can never lower the ideal because we fail in living up to it.

What a great blessing that teaching of [St. Louis] de Montfort is in work like ours. Yesterday Betty Lou said how the painting at Chrystie St. griped her. But a servant is not consulted nor is he to have likes and dislikes. Nor criticism. Just to serve others, because we see Christ in them, with no criticism. To sow our judgments in this respect. To criticize the social order is one thing, people another.

I am writing in chapel. Yesterday was so desperately hard. I had to come down here to S.I. last night even before the meeting to hold myself together. Cannot sleep. Nerves and fatigue. An empty cistern. I must rest here quietly spending hours in the chapel—beyond the sound of human voices.

It had gotten to the point that I did not know, literally, "whether I was coming or going." These people's sayings are so literally true, so descriptive. I was on the ferry reading, and suddenly looking up, the whole bay was turned around, the Statue of Liberty was in the wrong place—I did not know where I was. Suddenly I realized I was going to the Island, not from it, hence my confusion. Too much coming and going.

I was thinking how all our life here should be centered around the altar. Two Masses a day here! What a magnificent privilege. Everything should be done for the chapel, for the priests here. Three now, but only 2 saying Mass.

I have three articles to write:

"The Prayer of Jesus," for *Third Hour.*

"The CW" for *Plough.*

"Peter" for *Jubilee.*

And will I ever get the story of Therese done? Perhaps if I would stay here and write for a year.

Caroline [Gordon] Tate gave me a relic of St. Anthony. I think it is very old, a first class relic but without papers, which she got from Stark Young. I met him only a few times when Norma Millay was playing at the Provincetown Players and lived next door to him.

### At Tamar's. Friday Aug 8

Fasting today with Ammon.

Meditating on pomp and ritual. Since we learn thru our senses, all that shows the glory of and honor in which we hold God, makes us realize His Transcendence. Cardinal Suhard[144] in writing of the meaning of God. Makes one realize the Creator. Mountains, seas, great rivers, storms, winds—these too lift one's heart. John said his first sight of the mountains rising up out of the plains did this to him.

God wishes us to feel His Immanence. He is near as the breath we draw. We have Him present in the Blessed Sacrament of the altar, and if our faith were as a grain of mustard seed, we would be prostrate as we entered His presence. We take His Presence so much for granted!

### Sat. Aug 9. Birth of Margaret [Hennessy]

After my all-day fast—by then it was 36 hours. I was sleeping well when Betty Lou burst into the room to say "Tamar is having her baby. David wants you to come right over." I was dressed in a moment and Betty Lou too, and we went right over at 5:30 a.m. David and Tamar were drinking coffee and she was all dressed, ready to go to the hospital as the doctor had insisted. It was beautiful driving thru the dawn, and we were so happy to be getting her there on time.

Little Margaret was born at 8:30 p.m. I went to see Tamar in the afternoon and David and I in the evening, and half an hour after our visit, the baby was born.

So I have had a beautiful week being with the children. The noisy ones are Mary and Nick. He kept yelling one evening after I had gone downstairs, "God was not ever a little baby." And then it went to his never having been a little baby either. He falls asleep so suddenly. He is shouting, pugnacious, aggressive, and then suddenly he is asleep, like as not with a toad beneath his pillow. Tomato and cabbage worms are also a passion with him and Eric, and even little Mary.

One evening last week—it was the Feast of St. Clare—Stanley was reading to me from Sister Mary of the Trinity, a Poor Clare of Jerusalem, and Becky and Susie were engrossed in listening, when the giggles which had been com-

---

144 Cardinal Suhard, Archbishop of Paris and a sponsor of the Worker Priest movement, died in 1949.

ing pretty continuously from the couch finally attracted our attention. Nick
and Eric were convulsed at the amusing spectacle of each other with a huge
tomato worm lying along the bridge of their noses.

We have been visiting the cemetery several times a week because Friday
next, Aug 21, the Smiths are moving to Brooklyn. I never thought it would
be a happy occasion, visiting cemeteries, but the little cemetery on a gentle
hill back of St. Joseph's Church is a happy spot.

Little Charlie Smith's grave is in the far left hand corner in the southeast
corner. There is a park bench beside the Catholic Worker plot, and when we
have arranged our vases of flower, we sit on the bench and eat the pears we
have gathered from the next field and say the rosary.

I used not to be able to understand Clotilde's predilection for the cemetery
in Leon Bloy's *The Woman Who Was Poor*, but now I do. Life and death—they
are so close together. Little Charlie Smith was drowned July 11. Baby Margaret was born exactly four weeks later. "The spaces of our life, set over against
eternity, are brief and poor."

Feast of St. Bernard. Aug 20

No Mass today. Kenneth down last night drinking. Father K. too. And the
house full with Mary and Dorothy and a friend. Three Maryknoll seminarians coming today. An hour's meditation in chapel.

On St. Bernard preaching a crusade.

And St. Francis preaching peace.

Men most usually are of their time. St. Francis timeless.

T.S. Eliot wrote in "Murder in the Cathedral" that the greatest of all trea-
sons was to do the right thing for the wrong reason. They did the wrong thing
for the right reason: they all had the right reason, the glory of God.

We do not have to follow the saints blindly. Newman, whom we all dearly
love and who is so close to us, who wrote so sublimely in his historical essays, wrote like any insular Englishman of the Turk, the Hun, the Mongol.
He wrote as tho they were scarcely men, scarcely capable of conversion, the
way so many in the Catholic press write of the communist. St. Vincent Ferrer
backed the wrong pope. St. Catherine who backed the right one at the time
also preached a crusade.

When, as a pacifist, I am asked, "What about the crusades?" I must humbly
reply, first that I only answer because St. Peter says we must give a reason for
the faith that is in us, and then that it is hard to see that we gained much by
them. The Middle East and Africa are lost to the faith; those people who used
to be Christian are now Mohammedan. If we had been truly Christian and

let them overcome Europe perhaps (after an initial slaughter, which always takes place anyway) the conqueror could have been conquered, overcome by the Sermon on the Mount.

The Crusades were second best, and we are told to aim at perfection. This is the will of God, your sanctification. Be ye therefore perfect, as your Heavenly Father is perfect, not as St. Bernard was perfect.

He was a man of his time. He tried to correlate the spiritual and the material and he tried to impregnate the temporal. He did not retreat into an ivory tower, tho he was a Cistercian. He wrote in heavenly tomes on love, on the Blessed Mother. Still, there is the paradox—a man who withdrew in the heat of battle and caused others to withdraw.

## Sunday Aug 23

I am keeping the children with me for a week so Tamar can catch up on rest. Mary and Margaret seem like nothing after the 4 others are out.

Reading Edmund Wilson, *To the Finland Station.*

## Sept 20. Sunday

Sung Mass at 8 very good and the sermon beautiful, finished, clear, on faith.

At 11 a picnic on the beach tho rain threatened. Tamar and the little ones came over too. The older 3 on the beach. A crowded, confused day with a great desire on my part to write on love and the strange things that happen to you in growing in the love of God.

## Nov 2. All Soul's Day

Press day. Went to N.Y. after 7 a.m. Mass. Now at 9:15 in bed, not as tired as after one of our usual days of writing, people, and manual labor—and all the children. Today Dave [Hennessy] got a job at the Nassau brass works where Bill McAndrews works.

Returned to PM farm to find a new priest as guest. When Fr. Elias comes back that will be five here. And 3 at Maryfarm. The Little Flower is handing us work to do. Deo gratias.

Fr. Elias has been 10 years in a mental hospital on Long Island, put there by his wife. Also in Chicago, put there by Bishop Sheil. Michael claims Fr. Elias charged a priest with breaking the seal of the confessional when he confessed to suicidal plans. He says he is living to see God's vengeance on those who have persecuted him. M. says to me that those who mistreat God's anointed are in a terrible danger. Mental cases always denounce, threaten.

Friday Nov 13. 6:30 a.m.

When I got home from Roebling where I spoke yesterday, I found my room all carpeted, swept, and garnished, beds made up, by Linda and carpet laid and fire made by Hans! It was a joy. God bless them both.

David's first day of work at the Nassau plant. Salvaging brass, copper, lead, making ingots to be sold to plumbing concerns.

Thurs Nov 19. 10 a.m.

Cold and hemorrhoids making me increasingly miserable. I am remaining in bed today, off my feet. Della said she would come down—she can divide her visit between me and Tamar.

Too much running around again. Too many speaking engagements to no purpose. Marymount, St. Clare's, Young Quakers, Riverside Church. Little writing. The conflict and the strain.

I record it to see if it will pass or grow worse. Had such an attack 10 years ago and it passed.

I always feel guilty at this idleness. But it is better to go to bed and recover than try to keep up and accomplish nothing and be cranky besides. One is too filled with sense of being indispensable. But also, too, seeing others keep up who are worse off.[145]

Dec 12. St. Lucy

Eugene O'Neill died.[146] Eulogy in *Times*. Also Dan Cleary, also Greg Walsh's sister. Also Alice Kathryn's mother. May they rest in peace.

---

145 Dorothy referred to her convalescence in the December 1953 issue: "As for me, illness and a doctor's ultimatum decrees that I stay home for the next months anyway. Riding all night on buses, over the last twenty years, has caught up with me. There are various aspects to being sick. There is the first miserable aspect when one is feverish, nightmarish, depressed, full of pain and suddenly conscious of one's mortality. In the midst of pain one has occasional flashes of insight that at least one is not doing one's own will, and that saying 'Thy will be done,' and 'Be it done unto me according to Thy word,' is something! An act of the will, to say it, even if one may be afraid of not really meaning it... .The second aspect of sickness is the blissful 'taking things easy,' staying off one's feet, leaving 'activity' to others. Not so easy as it sounds in one way, when there is so much to do, and one sees others groaning under their hard work. 'So much to do, so few to do it. Everybody sitting around doing nothing, leaving it to me to do.' This is so general an attitude of mind amongst workers that one longs to plunge into the cleaning, washing, cooking, dishes, or whatever else is at hand, and heartily enjoy doing it. It is hard to remember that those people who groan the most and are the most critical of others are really happy working and would be most unhappy if their work were taken from them. If people would only remember 'the duty of delight,' as Ruskin said."

146 In *The Long Loneliness* Dorothy offered a discrete description of her companionship with the playwright Eugene O'Neill in the winter of 1918. She credited him with teaching her Francis Thompson's poem "The Hound of Heaven," and until the end of her life she continued to remember him in her prayers.

Mass at 8. Have been having a hard time sleeping—a bundle of nerves, so have ceased coffee from noon on. Ammon here, with rose, *Jubilee*, and story of Benedictine ashram, and Christmas cards for prisoners, forty of them in Federal Camps for not registering. We are signing them, mailing tomorrow.

Nothing is more beautiful than the soft sound of waves on the beach.

Today the wind is offshore and quite rough. There are hundreds of gulls black against the slate grey water. The sky is heavy and murky white, and every tree is black, soaked from the rain last night. There are always willows along the beach, straggly sprawling. And yellow plummet marsh grass bordering the fields of Mt. Loretto.

I hope and pray someday to have a house looking out on the bay, a little up off the beach so it will be away from the danger of the tide.

## Sunday within Octave of Christmas

A wonderful Christmas, peaceful and joyful and no dread of upset. We all worked hard Christmas Eve and I felt very guilty vetoing midnight Mass. Will not do that again.

Feel so much better after my 2 months illness—it is like a Christmas gift. Many letters, so cannot get at Therese yet.

## Monday Dec 28. Holy Innocents

Arose at 7 a.m. Mass 7:30. breakfast with Ammon, Fr. Wenceslas, etc. discussion of [John] Cassian and the typing of his Conferences by Stanley and myself.

Fr. Walls and niece arrived bearing popcorn, in a Cadillac. I told him due to my illness, Fr. Kiely's last outbreak, and our crowded condition I would no longer try to handle problems such as his which I was not able to cope with—that it would be spiritual presumption. Then Fr. Elias showed up quite the worse for wear after a wet Christmas in town. He will have to go to Newburgh. He can beg too easily around the metropolitan area.

During the newspaper strike last month Fr. Elias came in before breakfast announcing that Churchill was dead—a way to distract our attention from his condition.

## Retreat, New Year's Eve

Fr. O'Loughlin is a slight thin middle-aged priest with a deeply lined face, black hair, sprinkled with grey—eyeglasses and what one might call an almost consciously uncultured way of talking. His conference tonight was extremely simple—do we choose God's way or Satan? Do we believe in Satan?

On the other hand John is consciously cultured, in voice, gesture, etc. He has a clipped accent, a beard, when serves Mass he enunciates clearly, slowly. *Ad Deum, qui laetificat juventutem meum.* He prostrates himself for the Confiteor. When he hands the priest the cruets he bows deeply from the waist.

Fr. Duffy looks at him quizzically, himself smelling of manure, chicken and cow, very often as he comes on the altar in the morning. Fr. Barney, a Bowery priest with a broken nose and confidential husky voice, used to be enraged by John.

# 1954

New Year's morning

Marty [Corbin][147] arrived bringing Christmas edition of NY *Times* with Pope Pius XII message.[148] Christmas, the broadcast said, always conveys "the finest cherished hopes of plain people and their deep-rooted faith in the possibility of a peaceful happy life, but at no time in the past few years has the conversion of that possibility into reality been so close and so real as at the present time." The broadcast added that "certain governments of the West have been forced to pay heed to the popular demand that the spirit of negotiation prevail over decisions based on force."

The NY *Times* just printed excerpts but they were most provocative of thought. About work and leisure, and the nature of man, the need for and the blessings of technology, but also the futility in placing our hopes in these, the danger of men becoming spiritual pygmies. The need to do away with inequalities in living standards, the folly of hoping in peace from high living standards. He said many of the things we have said before in the CW but the concluding paragraph, dealing as it does with Utopias, authority and the State, might seem to be aimed at us, as at the Soviets, and so I am sure it will be so construed by our friends and enemies.

As we are told by St. Peter to be ready to give reason for the faith that is in us, I must in all humility, as publisher of the *Catholic Worker*, try to comment on it, and explain again, what "anarchism" means to me and what I think it meant to Peter Maurin.

---

147 Martin Corbin and his wife Rita became mainstays of the Catholic Worker over the next decades. Marty served as an editor of the paper, while Rita became one of the regular CW artists.

148 See "The Pope and Peace," February 1954.

We have often enough been accused of taking the Pope's words out of context or of ignoring other words. The Christmas Pope Pius message ran 5,000 words. Here are the words I will comment on.

Our Lord said, "He who will be a leader among you, let him be a servant." On washing the feet of the apostles, "As I have done, so do ye also."

Christ became obedient unto death, even to the death of the Cross. "Be ye subject to every living creature," St. Paul said.

To be a follower of Jesus, one certainly would not seek after authority, or if it were thrust upon one by ability and recognition of that ability by others, as it was in St. Peter, St. Ambrose, Pius XII, and so on, and in Christian statements where there are such then it would seem necessary to cultivate humility, courage, holy indifference, holy poverty, in order to fulfill one's high office. To lead by example. Even St. Francis, humblest, poorest of saints, was thrust into a position of authority.

The problem of authority and freedom is one of the greatest problems of the day.

Russia certainly cannot be accused of lack of authoritarianism. Tho they are "experimenting with the social order," they are certainly "resolved to make the authority of the state and observance of the law prevail among all classes of society." (The Soviet Union is no longer a classless society when it admits to a "middle class." There is a good society, however, where classes are functional rather than acquisitive, as Tawney said.)

How obey the laws of the State when to a man's conscience they run counter to the Divine Law? Thou shalt not kill. "A new precept I give unto you, that you love your neighbor as I have loved you." (And Jesus laid down His life for us.) St. Peter disobeyed the law and said he had to obey God rather than man.

Wars today involve total destruction, obliteration bombing, killing of the innocent, the use of atom and hydrogen bombs.

When one is drafted for such war, when one registers for a draft for such a war, when one pays income tax, 80% of which goes to support such war, or works where armaments are made for such war, one is assenting to take the steps towards this war.

War involves hatred and fear.

Love casts out fear.

The social order which depends on profits, which does not consider men's needs, as to living space, food, is a bad social order and we must work "to make that kind of society where it is easier for men to be good."

The modern States which build up a Hitler, which did not depopulate concentration camps and gas chambers by giving asylum, by imposing economic sanctions, are monstrosities.

We need to look back to the city states of Italy (all their good aspects); to the guilds; to our own early American principles ("He governs best who governs least"); we need to study such a teacher as Don Luigi Sturzo, who held political office [in Italy] and was a founder of a political party who worked toward credit unions, cooperatives, labor unions, as the beginning of man's expression of his dignity and responsibility. We need to consider the principle of subsidiarity when we talk of authority and freedom.

Everything needs to be broken down into smaller units to be workable according to man's nature, including States, factories, cities.

A union is no better than the individuals in it, the individual locals, cells, etc. Man must be responsible, to exercise his freedom, God's greatest gift to him.

The greatest message Peter Maurin had for us was this reminder of man's freedom, and his corresponding philosophy.

That is why he never used the words pacifist or anarchist. Privately, he admitted to both positions. Letters from his brother point out his pacifism as early as his emergence into social action. But was he a pacifist? Tom Sullivan and Jack English asked him once during the last years of his life on the occasion of his spending a few days in the hospital. He answered on that occasion, "No." A year later in regard to registering for the draft, when I asked him what he would do, he said, "I would resist."

How to square those two answers? I have thought a great deal about it these last years especially since reading Brendan O'Grady's thesis on Peter as agitator and going over his essays. Peter's greatest message for us, greater even than his message of poverty, was man's freedom and responsibility. It was a timeless problem. It was a problem a better social order would help to make easier to solve, but it is a problem which will always remain with us "until the day dawn and the shadows rise and the Desire of the everlasting hills shall come."

Peter did not want to be fragmented, if we can use that word, by being labeled pacifist or anarchist. First of all we are Catholics, children of our Holy Father Pius XII in this temporal order. First of all we are Catholics, then Americans, Germans, French, Russian, or Chinese. We are members of the Body of Christ, or potential members. We are sons of God.

A great and terrible thought setting us free, and also making us realize our responsibility.

Ammon Hennacy is an individual anarchist and a well-ordered and peaceful man, subjecting himself in all good things to others around him, whether his army captain boss, his daughters' needs, his duties to his Church, which he has voluntarily chosen in a time of metanoia.

Robert Ludlow has proclaimed himself anarchist; writing as clearly as he could on this thorny subject. He too is a responsible person, faithful to duty, responding to the needs of others.

In thinking of Peter and Ammon and Robert, I think of men meek and humble of heart, desiring no power over others, no position of authority, yet forced to speak out by the exigencies of their time with authority. Loving poverty, content with little, stripping themselves.

I remember Peter when we picketed the German embassy down at the Battery, picking up the leaflets we were handing out which had been strewn around. He was obeying authority. He thought of authority and laws in relation to the "Thomistic doctrine of the Common Good." (He had a book on the subject which he was always urging people to read. Have we read half the books on his list?)

I think of Ammon removing boulders and broken glass from the roadway, not because he uses a car, but to evidence his conviction of man's responsibility which goes with his freedom.

I think of Bob, having no money, asking for carfare, taking upon himself the responsibility of mail, visiting the sick, and never swerving from his self-appointed duties.

These are men so responsible, so conscious of the common good, that perhaps their use of the word anarchist may provoke a study of Statism, totalitarianism, as well as of rightful authority, and man's freedom.

Jan 11. Monday. 8:30 a.m.

Snowed all day yesterday and now 20° in my room when I awoke. Built a fire and now, here by my bed it is 40°. Radio says it will be zero tonight. Five inches of snow expected. Near blizzard they call it.

John Stanley brought in my coffee. He says [Thomas] Merton's message is always the same. The need for seeking prayer and Scriptures as means of reaching God.

Feb. 12. 7 Holy Servites. Also Lincoln's birthday

Home again yesterday afternoon on the Feast of Our Lady of Lourdes. The operation was Monday, Feb 1, German doctor, Chinese and Filipino assistants—the latter had very comfortingly assured me it was not a fistula but a polyp—not a prolapsis but simple hemorrhoid. But just the same it was as painful a week as I ever hope to spend, and I'd never advise anyone to have the operation if they can get out of it in any way. What with Ammon and Jonas, both nature cure men; I am with them, after the event. But now I feel fine, all well and ready for work, to finish the book.

I got most wonderful care when I came out Thurs. p.m. Della, Tamar, Lily and Forster came to see me, also Father Faley and Fr. Duffy.

Worked on make-up Sat. and Sun evenings, in a state of nervous pain, but the paper looks good.

Two teeth pulled Monday at a filthy hole on the Bowery. Too weak to go further.

A horrible tragedy happened last Sunday or Sat night. Max and Ruth Bodenheim were murdered in a dingy furnished room on Third Ave. by a demented friend, Weinberg, whom they caught three days later.[149]

How often I feel that a solid tide of evil is held off from us by the Blessed Sacrament in our midst here at the farms and by our daily Communion at St. Joseph. We hold it back, it is dissolved like a mist by the Sun of Justice.

We each one of us could say, "There but for the grace of God, go I." Poor Ruth and Max—they were with us about 3 months, and Max got to Mass here at Easter. Ruth said she believed only in love, but she was in love only with her own body, and used it to enflame others. Max was tortured by jealousy, and we saw her give him cause at Maryfarm.

The horrible part of it is, I have seen young and sincere girls playing with men's feelings, playing with their own, using their dark deep forces of sex.

Their kindness was particular kindness, particular friendship. As St. Augustine says—we need to love all as tho we loved each one of them particularly. I must get the exact quote.

But in spite of their jealousies, each one must see that we love *all, all* the others, most dearly. And it is so hard to love *some*, and so often whatever we do is repaid with bitterness, hatred and reproach. This is a good pruning for us, of self love. By the pain we feel, we know the measure of our pride and self-love. If people turn against us and accuse us, and we can take it gently, without rancor, how our prayers for them must be listened to, since it is so obvious to us now that we have no influence, we can do nothing to make them love God. He alone, then, will, for the sake of our suffering, soften their hard hearts and comfort them with His love, which is all we want, after all.

Oh how much we want to influence, we want to bring the light and joy and warmth to others. It is good, it is fine to have these noble desires, but it is

---

149 See "Max Bodenheim," March 1954. Dorothy also included this story in *Loaves and Fishes.*

only a beginning in the spiritual life. Our hard hearts must be broken by our failures, by our hurt feelings, by our loss of friends, by our realization that we can do nothing but leave it to God, who has after all done it all, repaired the damage, died on the Cross for us, wiped away our sins—Ruth's sins, Max's sins, and in some miraculous, beautiful, glorious way, opened up for them the gates of eternal life. I see this thru a glass, darkly.

And poor Weinberg, child of no home, placed in an orphanage, kept in a mental hospital for 17 years, never once visited by his mother, taken into the army for one month, released as incapable of public service, shut off from life, from people, without faith, without hope, without love. Earning miserable meals by miserable work—dishwashing, that only job open for the unskilled, the unorganized, the weakling, the crippled, mentally and physically, and taking the only kind of love he knew, bodily love, from wherever he could find it, in this case from a woman as mentally clouded as he himself.

There was violence in Ruth—she wanted men to fight over her. It is an instinct in many women, to want to be so desired that men will pay any price. Where there is no money, then blood takes the place of money. Blood is the money of the poor, Leon Bloy said.

The murderer cried out yesterday, "I have killed two Communists. I should get a medal." There was malice in the smile he turned on the reporters.

But Max was only a poet and his sympathies with Communism were because they had succumbed to the temptation to turn stones into bread and he had known that temptation because he lived with hunger. Drink was his refuge, because drink was easier to come by often than bread.

Ruth, however, went to libertarian social groups and spoke at their meetings, and studied the story of labor on the designs for a new social order.

When she left us in the spring, there were a half dozen pamphlets among her ragged clothes, and one of them is with us still with her name up in one corner: Ruth Fagin. A graduate of the University of Michigan, she said, a teacher of crafts—she was always going to teach us, she said, how to cane chairs. She had suffered a breakdown some time or other in her recent past, and she could not hold any job too long. She came to NY from Detroit, went to the Village which represents the tattered culture of our machine age, and there, one rainy night, encountered Max.

Their meeting is recorded in a poem he wrote to her, a sonnet, beautiful and formal and wistful. His earliest verse had been at a time when he led a most disciplined life (he wrote 14 paperback novels, and several books of verse), had been "free," and as he got older, and most disorganized, his verse became formal and stylized. Every day he was with us he worked on a series of sonnets, dedicated to each one of us, polished, stately, courteous, tho sometimes obscure, and he came to meals, happily reading them aloud to our applause.

I remember one especially to Agnes, widow of a barge captain, who has been helping us for some years, and his delicate appreciation of her sweetness and diligence, her care for us and our comfort, delighted me. Agnes has charge of the second floor bedrooms and the linens and bathroom, and never a word of criticism comes from her lips for such wild disorder as accompanied such guests as Max and Ruth. No matter how comfortable a room, how tidy when they entered, it was soon a shambles of dirty clothes, rags, dust, cigarette butts, newspapers, bits of food, onions, bread, apple cores, empty cups, paper bags, scuffed shoes, dirty socks.

The newspapers commented on the sordid, unheated room on Third Ave, and I thought as I read, how over and over again, in our houses of hospitality, I have seen just such rooms, reflecting the grim and cheerless chaos of the minds of its occupants. There is a comfortable disorder, and the sordid disorder of people who do not love the material, tho they seek all their pleasure in it. In trying to save their lives they lost them. In trying to live the life of the flesh, they have been most hideously tricked.

Ruth said she could cane chairs, but she could not cook, she could not make a home. She kept her own beautiful body neatly clothed, in one or the other of the two dresses she possessed. She was always looking for a job, or trying to sell Max's poetry for him, or seeing his publishers who had taken advantage of his poverty and clouded mental state to cheat him of royalties when his second wife was dying of a heart condition. He had nursed her and buried her, and used the last of his resources to do it, and Ruth, his third wife, who had taken up with him on that rainy night, enamored of his reputation as a writer, and Village character, as well as being fond of him as a person, tried to care for him as he had cared for his previous wife.

They were companions in misery. He was 65, she 35, and she could not forego the admiration, the desire of others. So their association was marked by constant quarrels which led, doubtless, to the final tragedy.

They had known the poverty-stricken dishwasher who had led a vagrant life these last 8 years for some months. They asked shelter of him. Poor souls— why didn't they come to us? And there, in that miserable room, in a section so rough that no one would pay attention to sounds of violence, they were murdered and left, beaten and stabbed, padlocked in the desolate bedroom, to be found by a landlord looking for his rent.

We had been able to do nothing for them but give them shelter for a few months at Maryfarm and Peter Maurin Farm, while Max's broken leg healed. As soon as it was out of the cast, they left. While Max was with us he never drank, he sat stretched out on his bed, smoking his pipe, and thinking of his poems.

He came to meals, he read his poems to us. He was unfailingly grateful, too grateful, for any kindness. He stood with us for the Angelus before meals, he came with us on Easter Sunday, and on some other days, to Mass.

Ruth never came. "I believe only in love," she said.

Everyone who knew them at Maryfarm and Peter Maurin farm remembers them at Mass. May their poor dark tormented souls rest in peace.

Tamar and David need a bigger house so that there is more room for their manifold activities—their plants, collections of shells and specimens, their books, desks, piano, loom, spinning wheel, hooked rug—there are so many things they are interested in—even aside from cooking, washing, sewing, that make a home a place of joy and delight to be in.

Wednesday Feb 17

Tom got back last night much shocked at Bob [Ludlow's] moving to Forsyth St. and taking a job. I don't care what Bob does provided he frequents the sacraments. That is the only important thing. He is following doctor's orders. We will manage. We always have.

March 7. St. Thomas Aquinas. Sunday. 10:30 a.m.

As usual before a retreat or day of recollection all hell broke loose. Molly and Norma fighting in the night—guests arrived Sat night. More scenes. Norma sat up all night because she had to give up the attic to men. Linda is sleeping in dining room.

Thank God we can have conferences in the chapel. The first 15 minutes were interrupted by cow mooing.

Rita [Ham] and Marty [Corbin] engaged.

Bob [Ludlow] left us after Feb issue was mailed—middle of month.

March 16. Tues in bed

Last two days in bed with bad cold, fever, hoarseness. One has time to think. Last chapter of Therese book on Love planned. Finished reading *Man on a Donkey* [H.F.M. Prescott].

Friday March 20. PM Farm

In town all week. Monday to Friday got new bifocals and reading glasses today.

Fritz [Eichenberg] came in for supper too and we went over to see Bob, who seems well and enjoying his work. Letters till 12:30. Some nights I am too tired to sleep.

Holy Week '54

Monday—helping Tamar. Went into town with car and bread after supper, but missing Helene Iswolsky's dinner with Mrs. Reinhold Niebuhr, Fr. [William] Lynch, [W.H.] Auden, and others.

Tuesday—Day of Recollection. Exceptionally good. To the Island after supper.

Wed—Linda and I to Tamar's after lunch. I did letters all morning—helped clean in p.m., made supper.

Thurs—Mass at 8 at Huguenot. A very good sermon from Fr. Hyland on the Repository being the garden of olives, hence made to look like a garden with all its flowers. A beautiful procession and several very good voices in the choir, though there were only hymns at Mass, no Gloria sung. A great pity. Mostly women and children, many babies, and somewhat noisy.

After breakfast I went to Tamar's and took the 3 oldest children with me for visits to St. Joseph's—a very poor little garden, no hymns, no procession, just a low Mass, a score attending.

Then to Our Lady Help of Christians at Tottenville, where I was baptized. Then Immaculate Conception at Mt. Loretto—where we just missed High Mass and procession.

Then Huguenot—Our Lady Star of the Sea, where a little crowd of women and children were keeping watch and reciting prayers. The entire parish had signed up for hours day and night, and they recite the rosary. Litany of the saints, consecration to the Sacred Heart, renewal of baptismal vows, etc. We stayed for half an hour.

At dinner we had lamb as usual, salad, and Ralph piled on creamed onions, string beans, potatoes, etc. I read the Last Supper, the washing of the disciple's feet, the agony in the garden.

Norma said it was sacrilegious to read the story of the Last Supper while we feasted. When she ran out of the room I don't know whether it was to weep or get a handkerchief for a cold. But she ate heartily, much meat. She was very much upset because the children ate her 2 slices of protein bread. Oh community! as Betty says.

"That they may be one," our Lord wanted. The very purpose of his suffering and death. Teach us to love.

Saturday [June 26]

Two men from Boston University, G.I.'s, one wishes to be labor organizer, the other industrial consultant. Formerly transit worker. I was too harsh as usual talking of "piecard artists" and doing the least work for most money. I am ashamed.

Irish gypsy-poet came in, drunk. Told how he came in with 2 broken arms on Mott St. and was tenderly fed. There was a picture of Blessed Martin [de Porres] feeding an old man with a spoon. Then he sang a Yiddish song or a pretended one and told a story of Hassidim, very incoherent and ended up with a poem. When Tom arrived he put him out.

Sunday [June 27]

Mass at 10:30. Glorious. Received Fr. Martin's blessing, also Fr. Tom, his brother. S.J. from Rome. Great occasions in life of individual, much attention paid to each member of order.

This is where we CW all fall down. Do not pay enough attention to each other because of tremendous pressure of visitors, house, breadline, mail, etc. I am conscious daily of erring in this regard. To Betty for instance. Some need it more than others. Often I wonder at her hostility and then realize how much it is my fault.

Visiting psychiatric ward to see Fr. Cordes. He embraced me fervently. Kissing me so hard his bristles scraped my chin. All because I kissed him on the forehead when I first visited him last Sunday. Any little affection brings such tremendous response—it shows how the human heart longs for love.

Monday August 2. St. Alphonsus Liguori. 2:30 p.m.

Tamar and the children, including Ann Fitzgerald and Paul Yamamato, are sieving for shiners and getting plenty of jelly fish. Eric just came and brought me a fish. They just brought in a net-full. It is grey and glassy calm, a good day for fishing. The lovely sound of little waves on the shore.

Ammon pickets Friday, Aug 6. The others too from 4:30-5:30 at Japanese consulate.

Jonas made sassafras tea again tonight. Tastes like root beer. The bark of the root is the most aromatic part.

Aug 8. Nativity of Blessed Mother

7:30 Mass. Beach with children, a cloudy day. The children uncovered a mass of horseshoe crab eggs, each an eighth of an inch in diameter, opalescent, green, transparent, though a little milky, and inside a twisting and turning little crab, perfectly formed, even to all the little squirming legs, the tiny tail, the joint on the back, some free of the egg, some still enclosed. A great marvel, so beautiful to see. They become so huge, too. If one were cast on a desert isle one could have a grand feast of caviar of sorts. Tamar had the children cover them up again and the little shell-full we took out to observe later dried up, but not until we had the joy of watching the little eggs hatch under a magnifying glass.

Susie's baptismal day.

Sept 28. St. Wenceslas Day
Anniversary of day Ammon decided to be a Catholic.

Sept 29. St. Michael
This morning after Mass, as I left the church, I saw a man, dirty and coat-less approaching. He could walk straight but he was shambling. When he got in front of the church he stopped, kicked off his lace-less shoes in a violent gesture which landed them in the middle of Second Ave, and turned and went into the church in his stocking feet. The street cleaner looked after him and then went out—swept up the shoes into his dustpan and dumping them in his cart, trundled them away. He would probably be on our clothes line, which forms at 8 o'clock when we give out all the clothes we have on hand.

Little Flower begged God to let her always see *reality*. Things as they *really* were, so her love would be true and real.

Bad angels can attack us thru our imagination. But they cannot reach our will—our intellect.

Wed. Feast of Immaculate Conception
Mass at 9, sung, at parish church. Letter from Tamar saying she was having another baby. A beautiful day to get such news. Letter writing, dinner, rest, hour at Holy Spirit, supper, 8 p.m. Pontifical Mass at Cathedral and the papal blessing. Bed at 12.

# 1955

Jan. 16. At Tortes
Strange to be reading Jung now between St. Paul and St. Anthony. Desert and beasts. Dark night. Could not get to sleep until 2 what with it. The Little Flower's picture on the wall looks down on me. So I say God, Father, I will take what you send to nourish me, whether it is Caroline with her circles and her delightful pictures of animals, lions and unicorns, or the books she

gave me to look into—or the missal, the breviary and the scriptures, and be content with these glimpses of insight and knowledge you give me, but not trouble too much about it.

May 14. Sat.

My pamphlet published by the Catechetical Guild, "Gospel in Action," with imprimatur, is out. They doctored it, modifying such sentences as that quotation from Fr. Vincent McNabb—St. Peter could go back to his nets but St. Matthew could not go back to his tax gathering, putting in a "possibly" before could not.

Sunday May 15

Anniversary of Peter.

8 a.m. Read Guardini, *The Lord.*

10 breakfast.

10:30 St. Michael's for Russian Mass. Met Helene Iswolsky there, and we had coffee with Lyons Carr and wife and children after Helene came over to Chrystie St.

Reading Von Hugel: *Letters to His Niece.* "Live all you can, as complete and full a life as you can find—do as much as you can for others. Read, work, enjoy—love and help as many souls, do all this. Yes, but remember, be alone, be remote, be away from the world, be desolate. Then you will be near God!"

*Dorothy did not describe in her diary the most significant event of the month: the CW's historic civil disobedience against a statewide compulsory Civil Defense drill. On June 15, at the sound of a siren, all inhabitants of the city were required to take shelter in buildings or subways, in a mock rehearsal for a possible nuclear attack. It was Ammon Hennacy who suggested the protest. On the day of the drill he, Dorothy, and 27 other pacifists, including A.J. Muste, and Julian Beck and Judith Malina of the Living Theater, sat down in City Hall Park and refused to move at the sound of the siren. They were arrested. According to the CW leaflet:*

We make this demonstration, not only to voice our opposition to war, not only to refuse to participate in psychological warfare, which this air raid drill is, but also as an act of public penance for having been the first people in the world to drop the atom bomb, to make the hydrogen bomb. We are engaging only ourselves in this action, not the Church. We are acting as individual Catholics. Jacques Maritain, the French philosopher has written, "We are turning towards men, to speak and act among them, on the temporal plane, because, by our faith, by our baptism, by our confirmation, tiny as we are, we have the vocation of infusing into the world, wheresoever we are, the sap and savor of Christianity."

*An article the next day in the* New York Mirror *described the day this way:*

> *As 679 warning sirens wailed, millions of New Yorkers took shelter in the city's greatest air raid drill—an exercise marred only by 29 arrests and, in spots, by errors, lethargy and defiance, but hailed nonetheless as a "complete success" by authorities.*
>
> *An imaginary H-bomb fell at the corner of N. 7ᵗʰ St. and Kent Ave. in Brooklyn, "wiping out" vast areas of the city and claiming 2,991,185 "fatalities"! Another 1,776,899 men, women and children were listed as "injured" as imaginary flames roared through the area. Robert Condon, City Civil Defense Director, called the drill "a complete success as far as public reaction goes."*

*Those who had "marred" this otherwise successful exercise were brought before a Judge Kaplan who denounced the protesters as "murderers" who "by their conduct and behavior contributed to the utter destruction of these three million theoretically killed in our city." Despite the gravity of these charges—theoretical homicide?— the protestors were released on $1,500 bail. Later, a different judge released them with suspended sentences. The drills became an annual event, and with them, the protests.*[150]

June 20. Retreat. Fr. Casey

To plunge into the supernatural.

No one has seen God at any time until Christ showed himself to us. In our approach to God we can see symbols.

God raises us up to something superior to human nature. What is supernatural destiny of man? Human nature—body and soul—brought together with a marvelous unity. Beyond this God gives us further powers—to share in God's own nature, activity, life. We are divinized. We can know, love God as He knows Himself, by faith here. Reason perfected by faith. "We shall be like to God; we shall see Him as He is. New man, created in grace. Therefore we must be made like to Him."

Aug 17. Wednesday

Last night at Della's. Went up at 5. Drunken woman on Third Ave with a broken bottle got 2 men to lift her to "L." Felt like those who passed by in Good Samaritan story.

---

150 See "Where Are the Poor? They Are in Prisons, Too," July-August 1955, and "The 'Cold Turkey' Cure" in *Loaves and Fishes*. See also *SW,* 277-93.

Working on Therese on train. Headache. Anyway, slept well and awoke feeling fine. It is really these two months' heat, 90° weather, which has us down. Humidity 90 also.

August 28. Sunday
Mark McNamara brought me Russian rosary— black wool. The kind used by St. Basil.

Chiding letters from Mildred O'Toole and Henrietta Hroneck about lack of charity to Judge Kaplan, use of words "stoolie," etc.

Sept 8. Nativity of the Blessed Virgin Mary
Bed last night at one, rose at 7. Reading office and Job. Mass at 9. Met Rita Corbin and came to S.I. by noon. Rest, went to Tamar's, cleaning, dishwashing swiftly and back to farm with children for supper and haircut for Eric. To Oechsli's for tax receipts and accounting. We owe $7,500 on Peter Maurin Farm and must from now on pay off $750 and interest twice yearly—all to be paid in 5 years.

*Dorothy's encounters with the law were not confined to the Civil Defense protests. In October she found herself accused of being a slum landlord.*

Oct 7. Friday. Feast of the Most Holy Rosary. 12 midnight
I must write of occurrences of this week. One day I was summoned to the Workman's Compensation Board.

Our experience with the Tax Dept. was easy and agreeable. They were courteous, both very young, not bullying, as was the judge at the WCB. This board is at 80 Center St. The room was like a little courtroom with a man presiding, a stenographer, a young woman clerk, all sitting behind a long table. Against the wall facing them were two rows of chairs occupied by lawyers and clients, employees and employers, perhaps.

I sat there for an hour listening to the cases called. A butler working in Glen Cove was told the court had no jurisdiction because he was a domestic working in a city of under 40,000. A Negro woman doing a day's work once a week for one employer was ruled out because she had not worked 48 hours a week, etc.

With me it was quite different. The judge presiding was aggressive—acting as tho I were an exploiter of labor. He asked me if the CW were a charitable agency, then ruling we were not, determined we were a private enterprise running for profit, even if the profits accruing to Chas. [McCormack],[151] Ammon and me were used in feeding a thousand others. He wanted to know if we had a license to solicit funds, who did all the work, Chas., Ammon and I? When I said we had volunteer labor he stated that if a man did any work for us and was paid by a meal, we were responsible for any injuries to him while he was with us, and when I asked him about the bread line, he said anyone who did any work around the place, and received meals in exchange. His questions were put in such a way that I had a hard time answering before he cut me short with another question. I was put under oath and everything I said was taken down by a stenographer in his little machine. The final words of the judge were that I had better consult a lawyer or I would find myself in a great deal of trouble.

Between court experiences of this past summer which impressed on us all the sad fact that a man was a criminal if he begged, a criminal if he tried to earn his living by selling on the streets without a license, a criminal if he helped his brother in need without being an accredited charitable organization, we are beginning to feel like the character in *The Trial* by Kafka, an author whom, by the way, Charlie is very fond of.

I have written the appeal for Fall 1955 and I am wondering if we will be permitted to send it out. Also I have written another appeal for the paper, longer, stating the fundamental positions, the reasons for our work. All this trouble forces us to state and restate what we stand for, which is good, of course. Things which could happen if we cannot send out the appeal, we cannot pay our bills. If the paper which could print an appeal is stopped we further could not pay our bills. If the house is condemned by building, health, or fire departments we would have to sell and move. Where to store our accumulated belongings? We could go on living here until put out.

Who knows what the year will bring forth, what scattering of forces, what compelled decentralization.

Tamar's Dave very much upset. Also he is not sending out orders [*for his mail-order business in Distributist literature*] and we are getting complaints. Our using the mails to defraud is another charge that can be brought against me.

It is a hard year. Tom [Sullivan's] departure,[152] and leaving things in a mess, all this trial, which is a witness to our pacifism. Bob [Ludlow's] defection

---

151 Charles McCormack, a salesman "not very happy" with his work, found a copy of the CW in Corpus Christi Church. He visited the house, took the retreat at Newburgh, and joined the staff. He became the CW business manager.

152 An article in the May 1955 issue announced that Tom Sullivan would be taking "an indefinite leave of absence." He briefly entered the Trappist monastery in Conyers, Georgia, but quickly returned to New York, where he became a school teacher and later a principal.

last year and his turning against us this year,[153] Ammon's judging, the lack of helpers—and in other parts of the country, the suffering… Life gets harder. I must read [Jean Pierre de] Caussade again [*Abandonment to Divine Providence*].

I talked to Ammon about not judging others. He doesn't see it. He quotes Jesus: "Woe unto you lawyers, whited sepulchers, etc. Black is black and white, white."

Fr. Roy used to say, "God sees only His Son." We must see Christ in others. We must put love, and strength, and courage where there is none, and we will find it, as St. John of the Cross says.

Friday, Nov 4

Mike Harrington spoke tonight on Marxism and community. Two Jesuits present. Wild discussion.

Mike Kovalak acting up—threatening to jump bail. An article this month in *Life of the Spirit* on how to live with neurotics. We went to press Monday. Aside from that day I have been helping Tamar while Dave was in the hospital with his broken wrist.

Sent ms. of Little Flower (unfinished) to Harpers.

Dec 18. Fourth Sunday of Advent

This last week an infected heel, poison ivy in one eye, flu, arthritis in the feet. Miserable and more so because I could not help Tamar who has her hands full with Dave and his broken arm and the children. Slept in the children's play room and read Conrad's *Chance*. I do like him.

To see "The Prisoner" (Alec Guinness) with Bill Oleksak and Ammon. Confession last night. Saw Chas Mac there and then he was not here all day. It worries me. Is he too planning to leave? And just in this crisis too? Who knows. I have no wisdom, no ability to run things and manage a household.

---

153 Ludlow had abruptly withdrawn from the CW, and publicly renounced his previous "anarchism." In later years he occasionally contributed to the paper, though he had long since rejected Catholicism.

# 1956

Sunday Feb 26

Letter from Bayard Rustin about work in Montgomery where bus boycott is going on. Helene Iswolsky on *Malefactors*.[154] My troubles are multiplied." Housing trial tomorrow.

Just returning from Syracuse. Cecil Hinshaw, Owen Lattimore, Homer Jack and I speaking on Geneva Bandung.[155] What now? I read *[John] Woolman's Journal* on the way back and felt that he would have considered our weekend full of worldly talk. One minute of silence before each meeting was good. Half hour would have been better.

Tuesday Feb 27. Monday

Trial at 155 Court St., with Dorothy Tully [*CW attorney*] there and Charlie [McCormack]. Wednesday again. Paid $200 retainer fee. She has already saved us much time and wear and tear. She knows the law. To printers at twelve.

Letter from Harpers. Called and Eugene Exman wants me to go to Lisieux for more background [on St. Therese] this summer!

Anne Marie Stokes and Elizabeth Mayer in. The former about Abbé Pierre.[156] Poor Abbé Pierre! We must pray hard for him. The devil as a roaring lion goeth about.

How we need to pray and study! It is 10:45 p.m. now and I shall say today's office for him now. God help me and keep me mindful always of prayer.

There was a little story of a Russian woman in the *Russian Observer* giving alms to a beggar on the road who turned out to be a priest just released from a concentration camp. "Wait, I will pray for you!" And she then and there addressed herself to God. What faith!

Wednesday Feb 28

To Mass at 8. Breakfast with Tom [Sullivan]. To Judge Jack Nichols at quarter of ten. Met Dorothy Tully there. Judge was very severe. As soon as he heard there had been a "fatal" fire, he fined me first $500, then changed it

---

154 Dorothy was upset by the publication of *The Malefactors*, a novel by her friend Caroline Gordon, which included characters apparently based on herself and Peter Maurin.

155 The Bandung Conference in Indonesia in April 1955 led to the formation of the Non-aligned Movement of African and Asian countries.

156 Anne Marie Stokes, a learned Frenchwoman, was widely connected in Catholic intellectual circles. She was a frequent contributor to the CW. Abbé Pierre, a French priest, was founder of the Emmaus movement to help the homeless and refugees. See "Priest of the Immediate," *Writings from* Commonweal, 127-131.

to $250. There was no opportunity given to speak. The very fact that people who were lodged were "charity" cases meant a heavier penalty. It was "no charity to house people in a fire trap." He ordered an immediate vacate notice. I had no money to pay my fine so they gave me notice to pay by Friday. I thought it over carefully and then in the hall notified Miss Tully I was going to jail rather than pay my fine. She persuaded me to come to no decision until I could see whether she could get a delay in executing the order to vacate.

Later in the day a *Times* reporter called up and asked if it were true that we had refused Ford Foundation money and why. I told him of the recommendation of Milton Mayer to apply for the money, and of our own emphasis on personal responsibility and dislike of organization and grants for this type of work. I went on to tell him how I had been fined this morning and our imminent eviction. He came right down to see us. Telephoned Judge Nichols and the housing commissioner, with the result that we are to go back up to court tomorrow morning.

Not much chance of getting to France, even if I could get a passport without taking the oath.

Della showed me the review of Caroline Gordon's book appearing in the *NY Times* book section this Sunday. That book *The Malefactors* and the *Nation* article and all this disgrace of court certainly makes you feel guilty. I do not feel injured, but guilty and doing penance. All this moving will be hard, but change is often good. We are anything but static. But right now it is so hard on all the old, the crippled mentally, who are in the house. St. Joseph must find a way. And St. Therese too.

Wednesday March 6
Rainy, Cloudy but not cold. Mass at nine. Sprinkler men in at 9:30 to give estimates.

(Auden's contribution too.)[157]

To begin with last week. Thurs there was a good story in the *Times* on my fine and Judge Nichols telephoned me and Miss Tully to appear before him Thurs again. He remitted fine but the building inspectors said a vacate notice was already out. The judge ordered us to get together with the building dept. Tues March 5, and continued the case until March 21. We also got that day our eviction notice for March 13. An AP man was there and sent out the story and that afternoon the *Herald Tribune*, the *News*, *Time* and *Newsweek* all

---

157 The humiliating court ordeal began to take a positive turn when a *Times* reporter called and interviewed Dorothy. His article apparently caused the judge to revise his harsh attitude. It also prompted an outpouring of financial support from many sources, including the poet W.H. Auden, who walked up to Dorothy and pressed a check into her hand. Only later did she realize it was for $250, the exact amount of her fine.

came over to take pictures. Also calls came inviting me to appear on "Strike it Rich," "On Your Account," "Big Joe," and "John Daly's News Events." I went to the ABC station for the last.

Friday very good stories in *Times* and *News*. Then a disaster. Larry O'Donnell the painter, who was drinking, fell down the front stairs, broke 8 ribs and pierced a lung. (We did not know this till after.) We called the ambulance and Bellevue refused to take him because Larry, in his daze, refused to go—also because he was drunk. Charlie and Roger drove him over half an hour later to St. Vincent's where he had an emergency operation. He was on critical list but is recovering now.

Publicity has brought in funds from old friends. Also from Joint Board of the Amalgamated Clothing Workers, Pres of the Senate at Albany, Mrs. Lewis Mumford, Msgr. Frey, etc. etc.

Tuesday we went to the H&B Commissioner, were shuttled from floor to floor, finally sent direct to the Commissioner Bernard Gibray, who refused to see us on the grounds we were a delegation and saw only Abraham Fisher, our architect (who now demands $500 for his services, saying it is usually $1,500). He summoned also the inspectors. Result: sign contract for overall sprinkler system, for which a law is going thru next year. All to be started in 24 hours, which was a physical impossibility. However in this 24 hours we have found a sprinkler system man, Mr. Block of Aqua Co., the contract is being drawn to sign tomorrow. Difficulties over union labor, steam filters inside which will bring the cost up 25%. The whole question of principle had to be gone into over and over again. It was a day spent in telephoning lawyer, architect, contractors, etc.

Now it is raining—it is 4 p.m. and having had a bath I feel relaxed. Listening to "Rigoletto" on WQXR. In all this week's excitement Tom Sullivan returned from Conyers. All on day of going to court, going to press, etc. Tonight he is at John Cogley's. Tomorrow he may go to Chicago. Then a job and rooms in Yonkers.

Yesterday's epistle was the widow's oil, and our donations equal $7,500, just the estimate of the sprinkler system.

Today's was Jesus' words on the commandment "honor thy father and thy mother," and his comments where he says he who gives to the church what should go to father or mother is voiding the commandment. It seemed to apply to Tom. But there is much talk as to where his duty lies. Fritz is going to Europe next week and he had dinner with him last night. He is suffering at leaving his family.

Sunday was Tamar's birthday. 30 years old and already what a full, what a fulfilled life. She has had much and is a happy woman in spite of all her burdens.

The children are all fine. Last night I dreamed of Becky who with some friend jumped off the old pier at Huguenot to swim a great distance to shore. I was very fearful but could not climb down the pier to the water, which the children had been able to do so easily, because of my age and lack of agility. There was no conclusion to my dream except that I seemed to be on the beach looking for her.

Another dream I suddenly recalled was of being in one of those vast fields in California where grapes grew so thick and closely packed on their stem that one could not pick one without disturbing the symmetry of the whole bunch.

March 9. Friday

This a.m. Miss Seuss from near Buffalo who gave us $5,000 last summer came in for lunch. A quiet little person with a very sweet smile. She takes care of her mother who has arthritis. Wrote appeal.

Mozart Requiem in D Minor.

Friday March 16

A blizzard today and all the city white.

Tomorrow there is to be a weekend conference at Pendle Hill on Community. I must go and write it up for the paper. Appeal came in today and we have started already to get ready to mail it out.

This morning Della called and we went to the flower show in spite of weather. It was not far from either of us, at Wanamaker's. David had insisted and she did not want to go alone. So I missed Auden on television on the "Strike It Rich" program. All here said he was very good and it was not at all undignified. They asked him questions about Franz Werfel, Galileo, and had him identify the "Blue Danube Waltz" and his reward was $315. And also he asked the audience to send each a dollar [*to the CW*]. There is a regular theater for these shows. Mrs. Mayer came down to bring me the check, dear generous souls both of them.

So the judge did me a favor by fining me the two hundred and fifty dollars. I must appear before him again Wed. March 21. These affairs are long drawn out and an ordeal. The fine is held over me, suspended. So it is as tho I stand convicted as a slum landlord, violating the building code.

Monday March 19. St. Joseph's

Today a most beautiful book has come in, almost as a gift from St. Joseph on this his feast day. It is a *Pictorial Life of St. Francis*—with magnificent photographs by Leonard von Matt, text by Walter Hauser, and it is as moving in its way as *The Story of Man*, also a great collection of photographs. It is all about Assisi, its streets, St. Francis tradition, its churches, some of which he rebuilt. Strange that a merchant prince's son, a troubadour, a warrior, should also have known stone work. But all the citizens evidently were called upon to build walls, churches, roads, as well as monasteries and homes. One wonders, seeing the pictures, how all this got done without modern machinery, for hoisting for instance.

There are reproductions of paintings, crucifixes, statues, before which St. Francis prayed. Of the script even of his rule, of two autographs of St. Francis, the early shelter of cave and thatched hut. It is a precious book, unutterably beautiful, and the text fits the pictures. Assisi has but one song to sing, and that song is Francis. The world cannot have enough of it, and the name of Francis is the only echo that the traveler brings away.

I was hearing the children's prayers a few weeks ago and had asked them what they wanted to be. Mary (4) said, "a police lady." Nickie (6) a fireman. Susie didn't know. Becky wanted to be a "mother just like mommy," and Eric (8), woe is me, wanted to be a hobo!

A holy old priest with heart trouble who said he loved St. Joseph and could not let the day go by without honoring him, called up to tell us he is giving us $500 toward the fireproofing! How heartwarming such gifts. May Jesus, Mary, and Joseph bless him.

Help came from an old cellmate, the leader of the suffragists, Lucy Burns. From Army, Navy, chaplains, from people on old age pensions, from Italy, California, etc.

Wed.

Wednesday we went to court again, Miss Tully and I, she having to come in all the way from Great Kills, not stopping at her office on Wall St., but going directly to 151st St. Magistrate's Court.

There the judge wanted to know how things were coming, how much money we had raised for the repairs, and ordered us back again April 17. We had waited in a blistering hot court room from 9:30-12:30. I began to feel great sympathy for the judges with the multitude of cases before them, building code violations, city sanitary code, traffic, etc. Just before we appeared before the judge he was handling 50 cases or so of janitors or superintendents of buildings who had left their garbage can lids off. Each was fined three dollars. I notice by the papers that a bill pending in the state legislature would permit people to pay their fines by mail, as many traffic tickets are paid.

At Mass this morning I prayed for the dead. Gene O'Neill and his black despair and tragic death; a lack of trust which would almost make him refuse to believe if he were faced with the Beatific vision.

Friday June 8. Sacred Heart

Dave [Hennessy] off today and yesterday. Went to work tonight. Would not let me drive him to work. His hostility, his hurt, hurts me. His quarrel with his own mother is bothering him, I know. Best thing I can do is keep away. I am very fond of him and admire him too. Tamar is enjoying her weaving and spinning but is troubled too. School over soon and life will be a bit more relaxed.

Tues June 19

Things that stood in the way of my getting here. Saturday night. Late meeting in Bronx. Driven home by mad Italian who kept assuring me Jesus was married to Mary Magdalene. Bed at 3. Very hot. Could not get to Mass.

June 20

Up at 6:15. Mass, Msgr. Betowsky, 7 a.m., Stanley serving.

God runs the world, not Hitler, Stalin. We know He can bring good out of evil. Pride of life—despising authority. God permits—so we must obey? (I do not agree—how unclear! Are we to stand aside and allow a Buchenwald because duly constituted authority decrees it? What a need of clarifying concepts of authority and obedience! I know that war is evil and there is no such thing as an armed peace. So I must oppose war and all that makes for war even if it goes against duly constituted authority.)

Our sense of values must be right.

Thursday June 21. 8 p.m.

It is a dull, warm evening. The last night of our retreat under Fr. Guerin, Marist. Tomorrow at 11 a.m. there is a final conference, then renewal of baptismal vows.

Veronica drinking—Mildred in a hostile and aggressive mood and another woman drinking too. I had a hard harsh day—in which I felt so uncharitable, denying whatever was asked of me.

Friday June 22

Retreat ends at noon. Fr. Guerin much disturbed by our "anarchism." Blast the word. Ammon started the argument on the First Sunday of June and he took it up in retreat, emphasizing "duly constituted authority"—only our duty to the State—no mitigating words, no definition of the State, as it is now, as it could be. When in confession, I confessed to a critical spirit, he very excitedly began talking about "half-truths" in the CW and the danger of our movement. He becomes so excited it is hard to speak to him, and I am afraid we have made an enemy, not a friend. O, the gulf between priest and people. And how little principles are applied to concrete experience.

I must read and study more on this problem of obedience and authority.

*Dorothy's diary for this year was interrupted, leaving out mention of her arrest at the second annual Civil Defense Drill on July 20. Aside from Dorothy, the CW protesters included Ammon Hennacy, Deane Mary Mowrer, and Stanley Borowski. They all pleaded guilty and were sentenced to five days in jail.*

Nov. 3 Blessed Martin's day

Trial yesterday of Jim Peck and 13 others [*who pleaded not-guilty for the civil defense protest*].

Walked down from W. 21st St. Arthur Sheehan talked on Peter. Very good and peaceful meeting—as always when we talk of Peter. Greatly determined to get right on with Peter's book.[158]

Dec 18 Tues night 11:15

Last week E.I. Watkin, founder of Pax, author of *The Catholic Center, The Bow in the Clouds* and many lives of the saints, was our guest both in New York and on Staten Island. He loved the beach, the wood carvings on the farm, the weaving, the Indian blanket I gave him.

Christmas Eve

Misty and warm. Very foggy on bay. Came over to the Island at three to take Becky and Sue to confession. Dave had already been.

A good supper of herring and now out again to confession.

---

158 Arthur Sheehan, a World War II c.o., took a great interest in Peter Maurin. He wrote Maurin's first biography.

# 1957

**March 3**

One thing I kept thinking of when I was in jail *[five days for civil disobedience in January]*, Fr. Hugo's ministry in Pittsburgh, as chaplain of the workhouse and the city jail. I have heard that he begs for the choirs in the city to sing the Mass for the prisoners. "A prayer sung is twice said." St. Augustine wrote. So there in prison great praise, honor, glory is offered to God, great thanksgiving, great supplication for the poor and for sinners.

*"Last night I was shot at for the first time in my life," Dorothy wrote in her May 1957 column, recounting her visit in April to the courageous Koinonia Community in Americus, Georgia. Koinonia, an interracial Baptist community founded by Clarence Jordan, his wife, and several other families, had been subjected to economic boycott and terrorist attacks for their defiance of segregation. Each night members of the community kept watch in a parked car at the entrance. One night Dorothy and another woman took the 12 to 3 a.m. shift: "Elizabeth with her accordion, to while away the night watches with hymns, and me with my breviary, remembering the Trappists rising at two." Half-way through their shift a passing car peppered their car with gunshots. The two were unharmed, but shaken. Recalling the event some years later, she remarked: "It is strange how the fear always comes afterward, your bones turn to water, and your whole body seems to melt away with fear."*

**Saturday, May 25**

Today was Nick's first holy communion. Stanley baby-sat with Martha, Margaret and Eric and Tamar, Beth, Becky, Sue and Mary and I went to Our Lady Help of Christians to the 8 a.m. Mass. The Church was not crowded and it was a beautiful Mass. St. Greg or St. Mad. Sophie. Afterwards we went to the Tottenville Station and the children had chocolate sundaes and doughnuts for their communion breakfast.

Read C.S. Lewis, *Surprised by Joy.*

**Wednesday May 29**

Today meetings. 9 a.m. Mass. 10 AFSC Stop the Tests Committee. [A.J.] Muste asked me to speak at Community Church June 12. Visited St. Rose's new hospital. St. Stanislaus devotions. Third Hour meeting. An exhausting day. Very warm. Since they said I had high blood pressure at the hospital when I offered my blood I am taking garlic tablets.

Thursday May 30. Ascension Day

Last night I dreamed that one of the women from Koinonia came and brought us an abundance of farm goods. There was a family of migrants in the house, the man much younger than the woman. I knew he was not her husband and started talking to him, wanting to rebuke him in some way. He told me he was much older than he looked. Then later in my dream I was on a train for Montreal, and had misplaced my luggage and found myself going to make a speech in an un-pressed dress and shabby stockings. (Wedding garment?)

Now reading *Applied Christianity* again.

Tues June 11

Death always takes us by surprise. And we never give people credit for being as sick as they are. We can't realize death for them either. It is beyond our imagining. Philip's death was a shock last month and now Catherine Odlivak's this morning.[159] Kieran [Dugan], Bob [Ludlow] and Smoky Joe went to the hospital at 8 to give their blood.

*This year's Civil Defense drill took place on July 12. In advance of the annual protest, Dorothy published this explanation of their motives (July-August 1957):*

> We know what we are in for, the risk we run in openly setting ourselves against this most powerful country in the world. It is a tiny Christian gesture, the gesture of a David against a Goliath in an infinitesimal way.
>
> We do not wish to be defiant, we do not wish to antagonize. We love our country and are only saddened to see its great virtues matched by equally great faults. We are a part of it, we are responsible too.
>
> We do not wish to be defiant, we atone in some way, with this small gesture, for what we did in Hiroshima, and what we are still doing by the manufacture and testing of such weapons

*The protesters, this time, were sentenced to 30 days in jail, which Dorothy, Deane Mary Mowrer, and Judith Malina spent in the Women's House of Detention. She later wrote a long account of her experience in* Loaves and Fishes.

*In September the Hennessy family moved to a new home in Perkinsville, Vermont.*

---

159 Dorothy remembered Catherine Odlivak, a beloved member of the CW family, as someone who excelled at prayer and the works of mercy. "The last words she wrote were on a little tablet by her bed. 'Be kind to the sick, and you are being kind to God.'" ("Catherine Odlivak," November 1957)

Sept 11. Perkinsville, Vermont [*Tamar's new home*]

What a contrast life is. Two months ago tomorrow I was on my way to jail. Last month at this time we were awaiting the baby. Now the baby, Hilaire Peter is here, 3 weeks old and the move of the Hennessy family to Vermont is an accomplished fact.

Tamar and Dave are out to the post office and to a secondhand store and I am alone with the 3 youngest. Margaret is eating cornflakes. Margaret is the fatty. Martha the tiny one is reading (?) and bouncing in a baby chair. The infant is sleeping and I have found one loud station on the feeble radio, which is also a phonograph which does not work. We are cooking on an electric plate, one burner, and today will have a one-pot meal of string beans, potatoes, and bacon. The children started to school yesterday and are not sure if they like it.

The house and meadows in back of it are beautiful. The children and I climbed the hill last night and they raced up and down—a terrific slope. It will be wonderful sledding in winter and I'll be praying their guardian angels to keep them from broken limbs.

The house here is beautifully large but the kitchen and living room only get sun in the morning. The three bedrooms on the side get the afternoon sun.

8 p.m. Children are just in bed. Tamar is also in bed—pretty well worn out. David is still unpacking books. They bought two book cases, one big one for the loom room, which has three windows facing S. and W. Her loom is set up, there is also a rocking chair, a chest of drawers. A stove has arrived, wood and gas, and will be installed tomorrow. When coal, wood, a cow and chicken feed and flour are in they will feel secure for the winter.

Then the problem will be David's job. They say, very discouragingly, that a depression has set in around here, which means that men have only 40 hours work a week instead of all the overtime they are used to. Everyone has bought so much, on time, and has so many payments to make, he feels hard-pressed. Women working also deprive men of jobs. We will just have to have a campaign of prayer.

Monday Sept 23. 11 p.m. Chrystie St.

Getting copy ready for next issue. Chas back after 2 weeks in South. [School integration] crisis in Little Rock. Peggy said she was praying about it.

Last week saw "Round the World in 80 Days."

Thurs. Sept 26

Clear and windy. Mass at 9. Beforehand read Guardini, *Prayer in Practice*. To Eliz. Mayer's. A Jewish holiday so streets were very quiet. We went to her husband's friend, Dr. Brown at 79 St. for a heart examination. He found everything normal. The doctors in jail had told me my heart was enlarged, irregular, etc. I thought at the time they were trying to find some excuse to pardon me, to be rid of me.

The other night at Eliz.'s she played me some of Benjamin Brittan's opera "Turn of the Screw" which she had heard at Ontario this summer. It was engrossing. She tells me he loves the sea and always lives by it. Which makes me like him more.

Our troubles in the house now are on account of Catherine Tarengal and her son John. We are repairing their room and have decided to move them elsewhere. It is a group judgment. The house can stand no more of her quarrels and the boy's screaming, which she so often deliberately provokes.

Catherine and John lived with us for 2 years and the screaming is a daily, especially a nightly occurrence. Catherine is called "the Weasel" by men in kitchen who swear they cannot work with her around. She is in and out, calling them drunken bums, and other names; she is accused of stealing all the clothes from the clothes' line unless she is watched and every few days she is seen going out with sacks of clothes to sell. She gets money from everyone, and Hank and others insist she pummels the boy to make him put on a scene, especially when we have a good deal of company.

Now she tells me she will consent to go on relief after she gets settled in an apartment.[160]

Saturday 3:30 p.m. Boston [October 5]

In the last two days I have attended 20 talks of the two days of talks of the Conference on New Knowledge in Human Values, held in Kresge Auditorium at MIT in Cambridge, which is just across the Charles River basin from Boston proper. The auditorium rises like a mushroom from an unadorned newly planted acre of grass. On the four sides, glass falls like a sheet of rain from the edge of the mushroom. Inside there are 2 telephones, 2 drinking fountains, no comfortable lounges or chairs and not too comfortable seats

---

160 "The Weasel" was the subject of a famous story told of Dorothy. Someone had donated a diamond ring to the Worker. Dorothy gave it to Catherine Tarengal, a woman (as Jim Forest remembers) whose voice "could strip paint off the wall...the kind of person who made you wonder if you were cut out for life in a house of hospitality." When asked if it wouldn't have been wiser to sell the ring and use the money, perhaps, to pay the Weasel's rent, Dorothy replied: "She has her dignity. If she wants to sell the ring, she is free to do so... But if she wants to take a cruise to Bermuda, she can do that, too... Or she can wear the ring, just like the woman who gave it to us. Do you suppose God made diamonds just for the rich?" Jim Forest's account appears in Rosalie G. Riegle, *Dorothy Day: Portraits by Those Who Knew Her* (Maryknoll, NY: Orbis Books, 2003), 145-46.

for 1000 people. It is too warm today, it is hard to understand the speakers, sometimes, but the auditorium is filled with listening people.

Sociologists, philosophers, physicists, biologists, psychologists, physiologists, economists, anthropologists, artists, statesmen, theologians, and mystics—a most extraordinary concourse of human beings give the best they have, limiting themselves to 30-minute written talks with 15-minute question periods, talking of man's loneliness, his fears, his needs, the meaning of value, where it comes from, inside or outside, and so on, making a science of values, axiology, self-realization.... .

Detroit CW, St. Martha [October 12-13]

Always, for 20 years, the Detroit House, thru all controversies, has remained the CW, which makes me very happy.

Here at Martha House they put up both families, i.e., mothers and children, and single women. The men went to the St. Francis House. Right now the men's house is full. There are 400 men served daily, but the women's house is going thru a siege of Asian flu and so closed to families.

I share a room with Bryan and he lies there, deaf-dumb-blind, a beautiful little child, pale and fragile, who suffered from a brain virus infection just after birth and has never developed since, mentally. When he is sick and fretty he can be comforted, Justine says, if she puts her lips against his cheek and sings to him and he feels the vibrations.

The children help feed him and he is nourished too with love. What a mystery such physical afflictions are, and how ardently scientists try to solve these problems of disease. What respect for life and growth. It reminds me of Fr. Hugo's saying how we should not be contented with just a state of grace, of just remaining in a state of grace, and then not growing in grace. "It is as tho a mother were being comforted by someone saying, 'Well, the child has life, anyway,' while the child lies there, deaf, dumb, blind and an imbecile."

The room is cheerful here, a bright setting for this little jewel, this innocent, stainless soul. The room is blue, the woodwork white, blue and white linoleum on the floor. Every now and then a little cooing sound, a gentle murmur comes from the opposite bed. Kevin usually shares the room, but has given his bed the four nights I am here.

People are always talking about how there used to be 30 houses of hospitality. Those were depression days when there were many young men unemployed. Where are they now? Married, living on farms, raising families. John Thornton, Gerry Griffin teaching in Queens college. Tom Sullivan, Bob Ludlow teaching in predominately colored schools. Jim O'Gara editing the *Commonweal*. John Cogley—Fund for Republic.

Sunday Nov 3

Exam of conscience for the week.

Stayed up until 3 and read Camus' *The Fall,* which is an examination into conscience but with despair. How guilty each one of us is—how many people ... [*missing text*]

...order to keep going and do my work. I did not miss Mass and Communion tho I did confession. I must do much more in the way of voluntary poverty and manual labor for health of body and soul. Also not waste my time with idle reading. We have so much, we are so rich in interests, books, music, friends, ideas. God gives us such lights that it is a temptation to rest in them. "One thing is necessary."

Devout and thankful and joyous Masses on All Saints and All Soul's Days.

Friday Dec 27. St. John's day

Was ill last night what with the day's driving when I was too tired. Otherwise slept well. This morning I got up at 8:30 and Matins. Napped till two-thirty. When I woke up we all went for a walk to the top of the hill, a tremendous pull. Even 2-year old Martha went along. Streams rushed down over the rocks at either side of the road and the road itself was caved in many places. Myrtle, ferns, mosses all made a green carpet and overhead the pine and spruce and balsam were beautiful against a blue and sunny sky.

We got home at 4 and had hot chocolate and coffee and Tamar, Dave, and Stanley went shopping for fish for supper. Raw carrots, celery, fried potatoes—fish. We got some washing done. Now at 8:30 the children are all going strong.

Becky wants clothes—she has outgrown everything. She has outgrown rock and roll too—not putting the radio on once. School is hard, Susie says, but Becky says she likes social studies and math, but not biology or English.

Sat. Dec 28. Holy Innocents

Stan Jacobs just came in with a week's growth of beard and half drunk. Bearing a box of sugar which his children had given him for his horses. He wanted coffee and sociability. Dave and Tamar both seem to be in a state of raw nerves tho everyone's health is good and he is getting his unemployment insurance. $36 a week for 35 weeks.

# 1958

**Wednesday, Jan 1**

Fr. McCoy gave me a relic of St. Therese thinking it was Pius X. I had loaned mine to Eleanor at St. Vincent's.

**January 2**

Copy to printer. This morning Charlie [McCormack] called me into his room to tell me he was leaving. A great shock. It was easier to see the others go—they had some definite plan. These situations are heartbreaking. There is no one to take his place.

**January 3**

Tom Cornell in.[161]

Betty [Bartelme] over for dinner and took ms. of CW reader.[162] Beth, Stanley, Roy and Magda in for meeting which was on [Gerard Manley Hopkins'] "The Wreck of the Deutschland" by a Jesuit scholar.

**January 4**

A very tiring day what with mail, copy to read, clothes to get ready and ticket. The whole house was desolated by Charles going. I kept thinking of him wandering as he does, and in such bitter weather. Inside it was cozy and warm but it was as tho he were rejecting us all. Nothing seemed settled. Bed at 12.

*Ascent of Mt. Carmel* [St. Teresa of Avila]—Chap IX. "He that touches pitch shall be defiled with it. A man touches pitch when he allows the desire of his will to be satisfied by any creature."

*In January Dorothy set off on a pilgrimage to the shrine of Our Lady of Guadalupe in Mexico City.*

**January 5. Traveling**

Mass at 9. Tony woke Deane [Mary Mowrer][163] to tell her of my early start and she came at 8 with little loaves of whole wheat bread for my pilgrimage.

---

161 Tom Cornell first visited the CW while still a student at Fairfield. He joined the community full-time in 1962 and edited the paper for two years.

162 Betty Bartelme, a religious books editor at Macmillan, was a frequent contributor to the CW.

163 Deane Mary Mowrer was a highly educated woman of refined tastes. She came to the CW in the late 1950s, and participated in the annual civil defense drills, despite the fact that

Veronica had my clothes ready and hot coffee in a thermos and I left at ten with Chas. [McCormack]. His news—engagement to Agnes [Bird]—delighted me. I can set out with a joyful heart. My prayers are heard.

I telephoned Tamar goodbye. There is snow in Vt. The temp is zero and the car does not work. I had no copy ready for the Jan. issue. The first time, I think. On train now for Chicago: a night sitting up.

January 6. Epiphany

All day on train to Kansas City. At 4:30 called Maryknoll nuns at Our Lady, Queen of the World Hospital and am staying there. A 96-bed, well equipped, beautifully decorated hospital in a Negro section. It is an integrated hospital but because of the neighborhood serves mostly Negroes. Only 10 or 15% Catholic in Kansas City. Very hilly.

January 7

Mass at 6:15. Dominican. Train 9. All day and night to San Antonio. Many stops, a freight train derailed, 3 ½ hours late. Comfortable seats however. Reading *Dark Virgin* by Demerest. Also *One Front Across the World*, by Douglas Hyde. Excellent journalist, but from viewpoint of world. Spiritual weapons and preparedness and force. One canceling out the other.

January 8. Deadly cold on train.

South of Laredo. I thought our car very primitive with its upright seats and filthy toilets but the 3 rear cars with wooden seats, open windows, made this look like luxury. They are a beautiful people. But revolution which was to free them from poverty has made it worse.

Mass at the Cathedral. Bishop Levan met us at train

January 9

A terrible night—real penance goes with a pilgrimage. No heat in car, front and back door would not close, packed with Mexican families who also travel to celebrate the holidays. At San Luis Potosi at 11. Mass at 12. Nothing substantial to eat since noon before. So a good dinner, bacon and eggs. Arriving at 6:30. Unutterably beautiful place.

January 10

Warm, sunny. Mass at 7 a.m. Breakfast 9 a.m. Then to the Mt. of Cristo Rey, and our car broke down so I have a mile and a half of a climbing road

---

she was going steadily blind. She eventually settled on the CW farms and carefully dictated a monthly column, "A Farm with a View."

up the last part of the trip, altitude 7000 or more feet. Then to a shrine where there is perpetual adoration, Benedictine nuns of Christ the King in a convent down the mountain.

## January 11

Mass at 7 at Basilica.

We started promptly at 9. Mrs. K. sick all night. She is 69 but a world traveler. We drove in our 3 cars to San Miguel d'Allende, named not only for St. Michael but for Allende, a national hero who pushed Fr. Hidalgo into revolution when he hesitated, so said the guards.

## January 12

This morning to Our Lady of Guadalupe—out to the hill of Tepeyac and the crowds there were so great it was all but impossible to get to Communion. Pilgrimages on foot, on knees, and whole families camped out in the square, cooking their meals over a tiny charcoal fire, crouching on the ground. No trouble with babies. They are always held. They are almost part of the mother's body. They only leave her arms and breast when they begin to toddle away. I am so moved by the people here, their simplicity, their joy and their melancholy. A day of worship. One is all but stunned by impressions.

## January 13

Mass at the Cathedral, in chapel of the King. Named first in honor of King of Spain but later Christ the King. Mexico never had a king, the guide said.

## January 14

To the seminary of Mr. Martinez, where 80 boys were busy studying. Very poor section, rutted streets, mud shacks, church being built.

## January 15

Today was a long drive to Puebla, starting at nine and following a road up to 10,000 feet over the mountains, around the 2 volcanoes, the sleeping woman and Popocatapetl. Fragrant heat, lizards in the sun.

## January 16

Mass at 8 at San Fernando where Fr. Junipero Serra had his headquarters. All the indulgences granted at St. John Lateran's are gained here. Larry and Maria came and drove me to Pantheon Dolores where we visited the grave of Fr. [Miguel] Pro [*Jesuit martyr*]. We said a decade for his canonization. He was arrested when Obregon was assassinated, because one conspirator was driving his car. There were mourners at his grave besides us and one of our party, Mrs. Kennedy, said it was some time before she could compose herself.

January 17

In the afternoon I visited the Shrine again, but always terribly distracted by people. It is good we are all one Body.

January 18

Audience with Archbishop Miranda this morning at 9 a.m. He kept us until 4:30.

January 20

All day in bus from Durango. Comfortable. 2 drivers go all way from Mexico City to border. Spell each other. 5 min. and 25 mini-stops—no more. People almost got left. Flowers and shrine in bus. Radio blaring. Full but not crowded. Stops desolate—terrible plumbing. Mashed beans, salad best.

January 21

Cold. Rode all day from El Paso in very comfortable bus. Mormon child would not drink coffee. Separated parents. She was being left with mother. Lack of love of stepmother palpable.

January 26. To Phoenix

Too much traffic. Rain. Dreamt of accident last night, being pinned under car. Saw 4 today—collisions.

January 29. Albuquerque

Up at seven, reading *Requiem for a Nun* [Faulkner].

Reading in Exodus about the manna. "Gather for one day only." If you try to provide for 2 days, except for the Sabbath, the food will rot and become wormy. How we must live by faith, according to both Old and New Testament.

February 2. St. Louis. Purification. Bl. Theophane

On bus until 4:30. East Mo covered with snow—very cold. Hoped for evening Mass but there was none. Hotel Baden $2 a night. Blessings of the candles at 7:30.

February 5

Priest at Cardijn Center gave me St. Augustine, Meridian books, and reading Fr. Martindale's essay I thought of my own life, how Forster stabilized it. The need to write a Confession in view of things that have been written.[164]

Spoke at St. Louis U to students, at 12:30 after Mass until 2.

February 7

Mass 8. Library, Marquette.

Visited Betty Cuda at County Hospital. Florence Weinfurter and John Van Ells, her husband, were there. He has diabetes, thin as a rail. The children are in a home. I never liked him so well. We had supper. She is from North Carolina. He from Germany. She obliquely insulting—talking of my dualism, dichotomy, body and soul, good and evil. "At your best when writing of your children."

February 11. Our Lady of Lourdes

Evening Mass at Our Lady of Lourdes Church. A.K. in her most desperate mood—obsessed by obedience and want of a spiritual director and disobedient to her simple duty of kindness to father, aunt, or me. "You can't do this, go there, hear this, read that." In a state of torment and talking ceaselessly. She has a devil perched on her shoulder, she says.

February 13. [Abbey of] Gethsemane

Up at 3:30. Mass at 4:30. Fr. Urban. Breakfast with the Gannons who have a son in Trappists in California. Slept, prayed the Jerusalem Psalms. Community Mass at 8. Fr. U. saw us from 9-11.

February 14

Could not sleep. Read *Miss Lonelyhearts* [Nathanael West]. Did not help any. It was written in 1930. Strong resemblance to the beat generation of S.F. "Why are so many members of the Beat Generation bums and tramps?" "Christ says—go out and find the bums…Find the blind and crippled. Christ invites everyone, including the outcasts."

February 16

Sung Mass at 8, all the Congregation joining. Janet read us some of Cardinal Montini's [*future Pope Paul VI*] talk at Lay Apostolate Congress in Rome in Oct. "The genius of the lay apostolate is love," he said.

---

164  See below, April 22.

Took bus at 2. Arrived in a blizzard in Pittsburgh at 12:30. Zero weather. All ye ice and snow bless the Lord.

February 19. Home. Ash Wednesday
Mass 7. Train. Beautiful scene along the river. Everything cold and dead. What natural faith we have, and in our brothers too. "On this road not to go forward is to turn back." Eccl 19:1. By little and little.

February 20. Eric's birthday.
Could not sleep what with bugs, mice, and other vermin until 4.

February 22
Chas [Butterworth] told me he thought his vocation was the CW, with jail and whatever it might entail.[165] CD drill set for May 3.

February 27
Sue Jenkins called about Agnes O'Neill's book [*Part of a Long Story: Eugene O'Neill as a Young Man in Love*].[166] I should rejoice. Expiation. Remember St. Francis with chicken around his neck.[167]

March 2. Della's. Spring-like
Up at 8. Mass at 12 noon. We talked of [Jacques] Maritain and his new book on America. We kept intending to go out but were too lazy. The sun came and went.
"They saw only Jesus." In gospel of Transfiguration.

March 8
Mass—letters until 12. Opera, "Othello." Short ride after supper. Our poverty lies in lack of room or privacy, never knowing which bed you're going to sleep in. Sheila is feeling it.
Fr. K. told of children in St. Louis breaking into tabernacle and strewing the hosts over the floor and throwing the chalice out the window. So when the boys went into our chapel, Hans chased them. "We only wanted to pray," they said. So Sheila went in and prayed with them.

---

165 Charles Butterworth, a graduate of Harvard Law School, joined the CW community and came to serve as business manager.
166 Agnes O'Neill was the second wife of Eugene O'Neill. They married in 1918, soon after Dorothy's association with him, and divorced in 1929.
167 A reference to self-imposed, and public, mortification. See April 22 below.

March 11

To New York at 9 to visit Kenedy's to read the [Ronald] Knox ms., the new translation of the Littler Flower's autobiography. It is a magnificent translation. Bright, fresh, vigorous, like her picture as a young girl. Such joy of life. Such a loving home. I read 100 pages from 2-5 and Betty came home to supper. Sheila helped mail the papers. She is such a good worker.

March 16. Laetare Sunday

Could not make the day of recollection as Sheila and I had a heavy day cooking and entertaining. We had chicken, fried, and there was enough for supper too. The Lambs came, a fine good family and the doctor likes Ammon, so we like him. His father helped deport [Alexander] Berkman and [Emma] Goldman.

March 18. To town

Sunny and cold. Visited beach house with Mrs. Brown and Stanley. It is perfect for our purposes. Saw Forster there. He is trying to sell to go to Florida. Helene Iswolsky called and said she had a $400 grant to write her memoirs. Wonderful news. Ammon and I visited Pike St. house which was for sale—also the tenement and settlement and St. Teresa's church where we encountered a Brighton Rock episode—a child threatening an old woman with a knife, and he and a little Negro girl teasing and striking her in the church. A terrible neighborhood.

March 19. St. Joseph's Day

A.J. Muste invited me to make a tour of Russia, all expenses paid. A congressional junket, Ammon says.

March 23

Weather bad. Mass at St. Joseph's and a very fine sermon. But a strange accident—the ciborium cover was tight, and when he got it off the hosts spilled all over floor.

Driving in p.m. with Magda to Russian farm for a pig. Will get it next week, too young yet. Then to beach. I am praying for the house there but am waiting for a sign.

March 24

Father could not say Mass so we went to Tottenville. The church was crowded. Corned beef hash for lunch. Wrote my copy for CW. Not very good. But explaining our desperate plight.[168]

March 28. Seven Sorrows

Charlie [Butterworth] called this morning and said he would contribute $500 to the beach house. Wrote to McSorley in Philadelphia about the Easton money to make up the rest of a $1000 deposit. I am certainly asking a great deal of St. Joseph. Arthur Sheehan called. He is working on getting Peter [Maurin's] body moved. Gilligan came drinking and I would not let him in the house. Joe and Hans were the only ones to drink with him.

April 1

Rainy and cold. Hard to write with cooking and yet I love to plan meals, make cornbread, try to economize. Dorothy Tully, our lawyer, says we probably have till Christmas to move and then not to get out till we are forced. The city is broke, asking a billion dollars. Taxes in real estate going up.

April 2

Fritz [Eichenberg], 6 p.m. dinner at little Jewish restaurant. Afterwards to see "Little Flowers of St. Francis," Rossellini's picture. An attempt made to show the grotesque, foolish, brutal face of evil, and the triumph of the fool for Christ, Brother Juniper. Otherwise not a success. Fritz says everyone he knows is under the care of psychiatrists. It is not enough to say Love or perish. Everyone wants to love. But "willingness to bear discomfort," willingness to suffer is the need. There is no love without it. Silence–suffering. God does the rest.

April 3. Holy Thurs.

If I could only learn silence, exterior and interior. I know from my own hasty speech that people do not mean what they say.

April 7

Beautiful Masses these days. Fr. K and B went in to movies. "Brothers Karamazov." Pat, Mike, Magda and children to "Snow White." A very quiet

---

168 The city had announced plans to seize the property on Chrystie St. in order to build a subway line. Thus, the CW faced eviction and, once again, the need to find a new home.

day. Reading Stanley's book which is very good but too pious for non-Catholic publisher.[169]

## April 22

So it is time to write an article about that period—4 months of my life, 40 years ago, when I walked the streets of NY with Gene O'Neill and sat out the nights in taverns—Jimmy Wallace's, nicknamed Hell Hole, and waterfront backrooms. There are so many books being written about Gene—and that winter figures in them too, and so many articles—Malcolm [Cowley's] among them, tho he was a student at Harvard that winter so knew nothing of my capacities or Gene's philosophy.

There is the story of St. Francis and the roast chicken around his neck going thru town saying "I am a glutton." Malcolm Cowley's remark in *Exile's Return* is my roast chicken.[170] When Fr. Rogers who had invited me to speak at Fordham asked me what I drink—"Your drink is wine?" in preparing a little reception. When Dr. [Karl] Stern wanted to know whether I was an alcoholic, when Dwight Macdonald asked me seriously whether I drank longshoremen under the table—I can only confess that yes, I did "fling roses with the throng."

## May 3

[CW] Anniversary supper at house.

Chas [McCormack] and Agnes wedding 10:30. Lou Murphy, Nina Polcyn,[171] Helen Butterfield, Oleksak from out of town. John Cogley and Marty [Corbin] talking pacifism by the hour, but peaceably. Quite a crowd, including Eileen Corridan and Dorothy Weston Coddington.[172] I'm glad Stanley was there because no one else there knew them.

Gerry Griffin too. Joe Zarrella had visited earlier in the month. So crowded a day what with wedding which was beautiful, breakfast at CW, and another at the Midston that I do not know who is were there.

---

169 For many years Stanley Vishnewski worked on a memoir of the early years of the Catholic Worker. It was universally rejected—"by some of the finest publishing houses in America!" he boasted. After his death in 1979 *Wings of the Dawn* was finally printed by the Catholic Worker.

170 In his memoir of Village life in the twenties, Cowley reported that Dorothy earned the admiration of all the gangsters "because she could drink them under the table." Dorothy bitterly resented this remark. Cowley, who ended up marrying Dorothy's good friend Peggy Baird, had also shown an interest in her sister Della.

171 Nina Polcyn spent a summer at the Worker in the 1930s and then helped found the Milwaukee CW. She became one of Dorothy's closest friends.

172 Dorothy Weston was one of the original staff members of the CW.

May 6

Air raid drill, 10:30.

Nina Polcyn called for me at 7:15 and we went to Mass at Nativity. Bob, Ammon, Chas [Butterworth] there. A good breakfast of oatmeal—the kitchen force assured me of their prayers. Bob [Steed][173] drove us up with the signs Kerran [Dugan] had stayed up all night making (he went to 9 o'clock Mass). Bob Gilmore, [Stewart] Meacham, Walker, were the ones from the AFSC [*American Friends Service Committee*]. Deane and I, Ammon, Kerran and Karl Meyer from CW.[174] Judge Kenneth Phipps, a Negro, gave us 30 days and suspended the sentence.

We were until 3 in a cell and read Thoreau's essay on civil disobedience.

May 10. St. Therese send us a house!

We must start praying to the Little Flower for a suitable building for our work and that will be a miracle to start off my book with.

May 13

Working on Therese but I feel a nervous wreck with so many neurotic people, women, etc.

May 16

Stanley [Vishnewski] and I spoke frankly of our grievances one to another. He has always wanted to be put on masthead and I did not know it. He has seemed in too much disagreement—too fearful of the State. How one injures people without knowing it.

May 18

Fr. Daniel Berrigan, SJ, LeMoyne College, and his brother Jerry and wife Carol drove us down thru Cortland—Dryden, past Borden St. RR tracks to right up the hill. Fr. is Karl Meyer's advisor. He gave conferences at Christ the King.[175]

---

173 Bob Steed, a young man from Memphis, would become an editor and house manager at the CW.

174 Karl Meyer, then nineteen, had joined the CW at the previous year's civil disobedience. He stayed on and became a lifelong peace activist.

175 This marked Dorothy's introduction to Fr. Daniel Berrigan, a Jesuit priest and poet who would come to play a major role in her life.

May 24. McKeesport

Confession. To Cecilia's to dinner—a distraught family. Oh for holy silence and holy indifference. Fritz has done us a wonderful picture of a hermit for this issue of the CW. Silence, solitude, prayer.

May 25. Pentecost

To 9 a.m. Mass at St. Peter's, McKeesport. Story in *Register* comparing our "private interpretation" to snake fondling.

May 26

Chas B. contributed $2,000 to beach house. Clare [Boothe] Luce $100.

May 29

Worked all day—reading Therese. Went to see Peg after supper and walked on the beach. It was beautiful and warm. Collected shells. Asked Stanley to be on paper and write Farm column. We will try harder to understand each other.

June 6

Fr. Ganey's meeting was wonderful except that Chas B. brought the meeting to a close at 10 sharp. But people stayed till midnight. Fr. gave me a fan from the Fiji islands where he works, starting credit unions. He is a wonderful speaker and held us entranced, tho it was a very cold night for a meeting in the yard. Afterward he told me he met [J.D.] Salinger and that he said he read the CW every month. He also receives the paper in the Islands. He goes back by Honolulu and will visit Huntington, Willoughby and the 2 others in jail who sailed "The Golden Rule" into forbidden waters [*protesting nuclear testing in the Pacific*].

June 11. Day of recollection

Today I got Fr. Regamy's book, *Nonviolence and the Christian Conscience*, which he inscribes to me, "In very profound communion in the heart of the Prince of Peace and in hope against all hope."

June 13. St. Anthony. Sacred Heart feast

Opportunities to grow in spiritual life—parakeet screaming while symphony is on radio. Mice; coughing; fragments of food; cockroaches; chatter.

June 14. Susie's wedding

A beautiful day for a wedding, but windy. We all met at the Pennington. Charlie B and I going from here. A.J. Muste witnessed the ceremony, which was a public exchange of vows.

A wonderful Quaker ceremony of silences, reading of an excerpt from Chesterton, a poem of Vaughn and a benediction.

June 21

Meditation about Little Brothers. 3 points. Their life work with poor, lack of privacy, no room of their own. Devotion to Blessed Sac; mutual love between them. How this works out with us. Latter point. How Beth [Rogers], Stanley, Bob [Steed], Ammon and I who now make up staff must love each other and help each other by prayers. Much can be written about poverty, work and we have done that. Rule at farm. Mass, visits, Compline. We are already living according to their rule, if we conscientiously try to lead CW life. It is better *now* than it has ever been. My problem. We are kept up so late at night—it is hard to get to an earlier Mass than 8:30 or 9. The day seems half gone. Even that is sharing life with cities, tho our Italian and PR friends are up early enough. Must read Gospels regularly, prayerfully. I read the *Seeds of the Desert* [René Voillaume] or *Imitation* [*of Christ*] before Mass.

June 28. Perkinsville

Auction at 10 and Dave and Tamar and Agnes and Teresa and the older children went and stayed till two. Teresa made the supper. Tamar most depressed, always on the verge of tears. Perhaps it is from having to wean the baby, Hilaire Peter.

July 2. Beach. Visitation

Bob [Steed] brought mail. Two very good letters from Ammon, one from Jack English and one from sale to Image books of *The Long Loneliness*.

July 3. Beach

Closing. God be thanked. Therese has helped us. Blessed Mother too. Smell of privet hedge in bloom. Bees seem to love it.

July 4

Fritz Eichenberg spoke on the face of man and the face of Christ—a beautiful lecture with slides.

Forster promised children a ride yesterday but did not show up to give it to them.

July 10

The theme of a teenager is "nothing to do." Sister Jean Marie at Mt. Loretto said that in spite of planned recreation it is the same. Isadore says he is unhappy. Tony says that tho he is unhappy he has supernatural joy.

Dear God, send us a little wine. Dearest Mary, tell Him we have no wine. One thing we can always do is study to grow in worship, thankfulness.

July 20

These last days with the [Hennessy] children very melancholy. I will miss them so. They too would like to stay. They have enjoyed being with Hughes children so.

July 22

Mass at nine. Very humid day and pouring rain. Headachy and depressed. Pius X was depressed by the misfortunes of family and friends, it is said. Some comfort. Nevertheless, we must try to reflect the happiness God intends for us. I miss the children. Cannot reach Tamar because phone is out of order there.

July 24. Ammon's birthday

Went into town at 5. Saw Russian movie and "The Counterfeiters" with A. Got rolls and bread at public bakery on the way home, 2nd St., also avocados, and had midnight feast. Marge had bought pizzas.

July 25. St. James

Letter from Tamar wanting to give up Vermont house. She is lonely for S.I. and David cannot find work. Started rosary novena.

July 29

Hot day, sunny, calm. Full moon. At the beach tonight and Stanley staying in Maryhouse with the Hughes. He brought my mail—nothing very important. No money and expenses high. How we keep going I do not know. God's Providence.

I sat on a boat on the beach with Forster. They are moving Sept 1. Flight of great north loons overhead. They are divers.

July 31

Notice of Court, Aug 13 about eviction [*from Chrystie St.*].

Bed till noon. Confession at St. Francis with great sense of gratitude and the need to be unjudging of injustice. A greater control of tongue—less criticism.

## August 2

Lily [Burke, *Forster's sister*] came down to visit Forster. She is writing a book and terribly interested in it. About interracial problems. She is wonderfully alive. A Marxist, working still for the Jefferson Library on 15 St., the only Marxist library in the country. Letter from Tamar—very unhappy, which makes me unhappy, which does not help. The only solution is work, even if it is only housework, cooking, etc. but work for *others*. And that does not mean one's family which is just an extension of self. But the pain is there of separation, rejection—I felt it in F. and his attitude towards the children.

## August 4. Press

Arthur Miller in *Harper's*. Reason for writing: to bring news to others of an inner world. Still suffering from my ailment. Took taxi home and to bed.

## August 5

Ammon starts fasting again. [*A forty-day fast in front of Atomic Energy Commission in Washington, D.C.*]

## August 6

Better today. Dreamed I was a novice in a religious order in which there were also children. A happy communal life.

## August 12

Wrote about Gene O'Neill all a.m.

## August 30

Sheila [Johnson] and Kerran [Dugan's] wedding, 10 a.m.

Drove in at seven and got there in plenty of time for wedding. Breakfast a well ordered affair—ham and egg breakfast to 1:00. Then the line, and the party went on in the yard, dancing. It lasted all day. Stanley and I drove Kerran and Sheila down to the beach house for their honeymoon. Slept myself at farm.

## August 31. Perth Amboy

Much paper work. Letters to do and writing. Too many distractions with moving to contemplate paper going to press. And so many deaths and weddings. At the farm, children very noisy. Jim's very distraught over new baby, locking himself in and going into almost a coma.

## September 2

Hunting for house. Very hot. Old bathhouse on Allan St., filthy and decrepit tho only vacant 4 months. Tramps sleeping there. The owner said 400 blankets stolen. Street being torn up. Michael distraught about Magda who is reverting to her former life. How one must live in presence of these problems as tho unmoved. It is so hard. "To care and not to care," as Tom Sullivan headed one of my articles.

God alone, St. John of the Cross used to say. Littler Flower's message on brotherly love! The importance of *this world*.

## September 3

Teilhard de Chardin, S.J. (discoverer of Peking Man). "Man is the crown of God's creation; not the static center of the world, as was long believed, but the axis and point of evolution, which is far more beautiful." Evolution is no blind Darwinian form but the constant creativity of God. The peak of all is God's greatest activity, Christ's presence, the principle of universal vitality.

## September 8

Reading over the beginning of this notebook—sad endings to community begun with such hope.

I looked at all these mothers and children this morning and all the men working at jobs, trying to move their families in the suburbs, and get their children in Catholic school—so normal yet so harried by installment plan buying and insecurity in job, cost of living, etc.

How important to keep the dream to study and plan for the future. "If a thing is worth doing, it is worth doing badly," Chesterton says.

And in another place—"Just because a thing has failed does not prove it wrong." "Unless a seed fall into the ground and die it remains alone, but if it dies it bears much fruit." "Take up your cross and follow Me."

Community is surely a cross.

We are not even the seed. We are the dung, preparing the land to receive the seed.

## September 11

It is a sad time of year and I miss the children. I must remember how engrossed they are in their own life and how happy. I must "desire to be forgotten," "desire to be neglected," etc. The one thing needful. Seek ye first the Kingdom. There is no end to that.

September 15
 In bed, cold.
 Della with so many complaints, ending with "too many children," so I rang off. It will teach me a lesson not to complain. Reading Newman's sermons. "Stewards and also Sons of God." "All flesh is grass…The power and promise of grace." I dreamed (after Mass bell) of going to a barn with great open loft doors on a river and an eagle pushing himself against an open loft window. Then Fr. Faley came and said, "I'm late. I'll sing Mass now."

Sept 22
 Picked grapes with Marge and Tom Cain. Found orchid. Music of the crickets, frogs.
 To be ready to give up the work if God wills.

October 1
 Forster left today for Florida. He left me lamps and irons and knives, left-over stock, all good. I missed seeing him.

October 3
 We are all agreed—this present staff but former, like Chas McC thinks to do without an owned house is impossible. But now we have poverty and precarity. If our Lord wants us to have a house he will send it.
 The old guard thinks I am too old and Bob [Steed] is too young to know what we are doing. But Bob feels this is his chance to reorganize more along old Petrine tradition, dencentralization, personalism.

October 9
 Into town today to Dr. Perera about my eyes. Conjunctivitis and infection of lids too. Most miserable. Chas B. and I to see apartments on Houston, and Elizabeth St. A German and Dutch girl in from Grail, helping with the paper. Too many questions.

October 13
 Pope [Pius XII] buried.
 Marge, Hans, Andy and I spent day at beach. She taking dictation. We walked on beach, very low tide. A seagull had a large sea-bass and could not manage it, kept dropping it so we took it.

October 22

Ms. THERESE delivered to Harpers.

Eyes still bad. Slept all a.m. Then moved bed in from porch. Cold at night may be bad. Too much heat is worse, as in NY. Bob is getting on well without me and it gives him a chance. People cannot appeal to me. Chas B. is over-worked however. Today he is bathing Jim Columbo from whom I had already caught lice. Anne Marie [Stokes] makes light of it. All Breton peasants have them!

N.D. October

How is our spiritual life now? Not much time to analyze it. This can be a Sunday occupation.

My day begins with Mass and Communion. Or rather, our day—all of us dedicated to CW. For me, I try to wake early enough to get in half an hour of Office. I thank God and Pius XII for a hot cup of black coffee from my thermos, which helps to wake me. Rev. Louis Bouyer of the Oratory, *Liturgical Piety*, is my greatest help in understanding the Mass and Office. Père Voillaume is the greatest help in living it. His *Seeds of the Desert* are an inspiration.

Sometimes Fr. Faley is late, but usually on the stroke of seven Mass begins. The sun is coming up and shines on him at the altar. He is slow, deliberate. Since he has returned from the hospital stay of two years, he no longer stutters at the Consecration. This used to be a most painful distraction to me, so I wanted to put my fingers in my ears. Now I have another, or rather several others. The server is either a mild spastic or has St. Vitus dance. He jerks, gulps, hiccups, etc., and sometimes his whole body jerks. Fr. Faley is infinitely patient. The server is very devout, a truly holy young man, with a great desire, a real longing for the religious life. He was with the Franciscans, a brother, in the southwest. He is a convert. Reading history, and seeing someone make the sign of the Cross, the sight of a crucifix, the Corpus, was what brought about his conversion.

Another distraction—several men who do not bathe. All my senses are affronted. This of course comes and goes. Sometimes I notice nothing.

There is time for a brief Thanksgiving—Lauds, and Prime from the Short Breviary. On Sundays I like to read a sermon of Newman or Faber later, since we don't get one at Mass, since Father was sick.

Community life takes time. Breakfast begins with the Angelus and grace. Stanley says the Angelus and Fr. says grace. Conversation is dangerous. I must begin to learn to control my tongue for the day. Tom Cain is at my right. He is always obscure, pedantic, convoluted, roundabout in everything he says.

Voice deep, resonant, and he knows it. Since this is not for publication, I can say he neither shaves nor washes. He has been with us for years with an interim of a year in a t.b. hospital. He has done a wonderful job, clearing around the brook, making paths, enjoying birds, frogs, plants, stars, and making others enjoy them.

At my left Bro. Isaac who does not twitch so much as talk. He is clean and good, But he told me that he has almost a compulsion toward using foul language—it is as tho he had to keep swallowing them. It is as though they gave him convulsions.

Yesterday I mentioned Fr. Furfey saying that if we prayed Compline we would know 21 psalms. Fr. F. said, "The psalms are Hebrew, totally foreign to our way of thinking. Most priests look upon them as a bore. The breviary needs reforming. We should go in for private prayer," etc.!

Such is breakfast. Oatmeal, bread and coffee, maybe prunes. Agnes puts toast in front of Father F and me. And a saucer for our cups and plate under our bowls. No one else rates this. I make up for this by serving her coffee in bed when I share her room in cold weather.

It is said that Eric Gill read the Office at the proper time of day for the various hours. As for me, work takes up the morning. If there were not the Angelus and grace I would not pray again till evening. Of course, the Jesus Prayer of the Russian Pilgrim tides me over the day. I could not do without it.[176]

October 23

All week I have had conjunctivitis. Mortification of eyes. Complications this week—pediculosis [*head lice*]. Jim Colombo is alive, in a bad sense. I caught them also. Marge and I have kept at him, baths, larkspur, various other lotions and sprays. I cleaned his bed, but it has to be done over again a few times. A hairshirt. I evidently need more voluntary penance—fasting, since I am getting so much involuntary.

I finished the *Jubilee* article on our eviction. The chapter rewritten for *Therese.* "So great and so simple."

October 26

Helene Iswolsky at the beach. "What chiefly characterizes Eastern thought is that for it the spiritual and eternal world is most real." "The role of the angels is primarily one of praise." Angels in the Mass. We use their speech.

---

176 The Jesus Prayer ("Lord Jesus Christ, Son of the living God, have mercy on me, a sinner") plays a featured role in the Russian classic, *The Way of a Pilgrim*, which J.D. Salinger later popularized in his novel, *Franny and Zooey.*

Secondary function, to preserve, defend, keep all that is of God. Angels surrounded God as a screen for his holiness, just as clothes surround our body
as a screen for its holiness. One could write on this and so make modesty be
understood.

October 31. Halloween
   While meeting goes on Larry is drunk in office. Ellen fighting in hall, Dan
and Ramon shouting in hall. Anna sweeping the hall. Friday nights are getting to be hell.

November 1
   Whenever I write as I did yesterday it clears up beautifully. Now Isadore
is cooking, Smokey in clothes room. Ammon is back tonight. Bob is happy,
Chas too in spite of my arguments with him over obedience. All is well. We
have a better, more unified group than we ever did before, more conscientious
and hardworking. I feel very happy about it all—it is as it should be.

November 6. Boston College
   Meeting in afternoon at 3 with Father Casey, S.J. He asked me if I would
accept an honorary degree if he could persuade board of Trustees to give it.

November 8. Perkinsville
   It was dark when we got home. The children had slicked up. Sue is always
happy to give up her room. A gracious child at 10. Becky very grownup.
13½. She wanted to know what a virgin was. A boy had asked her if she was
a virgin. What kind of instruction to give?

November 10
   Reading *Nicholas Nickleby*. What a help Dickens is in time of trouble. Tamar disconsolate. Hilaire adorable but cries at night and so she misses sleep.
They are all so good. Not whiney. Sue and Eric are great helps. We cut up pig
for lard. Picked mushrooms in the woods. A grey day.

November 15. Day of Recollection
   In the afternoon I took a little walk and telephoned NY to find we had to
be out Dec 15 at the latest or the marshal would put us on the street.

November 18

Dreamed last night that we were given a hotel! Or even a choice between two. Also of John Stanley who came to me and asked if I felt shame for my past and I said I must look up those words, remorse, contrition.

November 21. NY

Arrived 5 p.m. Sent tights and letters to Tamar. Sent Mrs. Carleton Hayes check to David for books. Home to good news about another house which sounds very good but we will need the loft for some months to come.

Meeting tonight on [G.K.] Chesterton.

November 23. S.I.

Spent day at beach. Stanley too. He is afraid mental illness is "catching." Ed wanted to talk over his domestic tribulations. He is certainly hard pressed. Drove in with Bob. Found Isadore [Fazio] has left over stolen soup.

November 24

A long hard day of seeing people. Mr. Duffey of Transit Authority in a.m. Dorothy Tully came back to lunch and rosary. Then we met Fisher and real estate firm. Complications about house. Cost over all $60,000. Madness.

Bob stands around trying to correct others instead of doing positive work of running house. No plumber. No materials for cleaning. No toilet paper. Much resentment, which paralyzes Bob.

November 30

This morning I met A.J. Muste at the U.N. to present letters of protest about imprisonment of C.O.'s all over the world.

December 2

All day in bed. Dizzy and vague. A bug going around I guess. Read old diaries trying to figure out all that happened the last eight years. So much and yet so much remains the same. What is different? With me, I am now past 60, just 61, to be exact. I feel strong but somewhat stiffened up. Tamar has had 4 more children, has moved from the Island to Vermont. They think they have moved a great deal but the children have only attended 2 schools. We Days attended 5 before we finished 8th grade.

December 4

Tonight I called Tamar and she said they were without water. Had to carry from the spring and melt snow for animals. They have too many animals.

Very icy there. The children are happy. Allen [Tate] has filed suit for divorce against Caroline [Gordon].

December 9
Worked all day at last chapter [of *Therese*]. Freda typing. Veronica very drunk again. We have one or two apartments for women now. We will have to get a room for Millie. Abraham Fisher sent bill for $100.

December 12
Reading Scott Nearing, *Living the Good Life.* "The plain, practical account of a 20-year project in a self-subsistent homestead in Vermont. Together with remarks on how to live sanely and imply in a troubled world."

December 14
Tamar had miscarriage. In hospital.

December 15
For 2 days doctors would not come!

December 16
Fr. McGrath died Sunday
Day of Reparation at St. Elizabeth's in Gramercy Park. The priest is on prayer. Yesterday morning woke with the most certain understanding that all in this life is surely a preparation for the next, a practice, a study, to pass our exams. Also a sense of the real work of that hour of prayer. That feat of endurance, that hour in the desert, that hour of suffering that the Little Sisters make that our Lord can transform so easily into joy.

December 19
Mr. Dido spoke. Ammon was chairman, arguing about will of God and obedience. Mr. Dido is a blind Italian and Ammon could not understand his emphasis was because he *needed* that affirmation because of his affliction. Men are so *obtuse* in their single-mindedness.

December 20
Mass at 9:30. At farm we played Fr. Higgins' closing conference of one of his Recovery retreats on commending ourselves, "endorsing" our little acts to ease the way for further acts. Not to be wiser than God who provided the two duties of procreation (sex) and sustaining life (eating) with pleasure.

December 23

Met Fritz at noon after Mass at Blessed Sacrament church. Saw art exhibit of Grail. Then to Harpers where Eugene Exman said he could not print "Therese." The intellectual Catholic readers were against it. Just another book. The Pantheon book was coming out, etc. So he offered to help in getting it out under our imprint, and advancing us money to publish it. So we could sell it for $1.50, when they would have to charge $5.00. So it is better for us. Also Delaney does not want the last chapter.[177] Wants another brief one, bringing up to date.

After the Harper visit met Ammon at 12th St. and visited [Elizabeth] Gurley Flynn[178] and her sister who has been ill.

December 24

Serenading jail. The officer in charge called the police saying a disorderly crowd were around the jail. The police came but refused to disperse us.

December 25. Christmas

Ammon said he felt not at all peaceful as he sang in front of the jail. He wanted to break down the walls.

When I tried to go to sleep at one I was kept awake by a carousing group on the corner who kept it up until 5:30 and I suffered the agonizing wish for a patrol wagon to drive up to take them all away to forcibly clean them up and sober them. What conflicts in us. What contradictions. "To make the kind of society where it is easier for men to be good," as Peter said. This is what we can keep on doing—and endure the rest. To be present, to suffer, this is *work*, too. Endure, be constant, good words.

Finally got up at 5:30, had a sandwich and coffee.

December 26

Ammon's pamphlet on anarchism returned and we are thinking of writing one or printing one with Peter's essays and his pamphlet and with my introduction, my ideas of anarchism and apologia for Ammon. Also I want to write on spiritual advisors—priests I have known, such as Fr. McKenna, Fr. Zachary, Fr. Lacouture, Fr. Carey, Fr. Roy, Fr. Judge. Ammon sees only good in his former radical friends, ignores rest, but sees ill in clergy—their omis-

---

177  John Delaney was an editor at Image Books (Doubleday), which published the first paperback edition of *The Long Loneliness* in 1959. The chapter referred to, "The Abyss of Faith" (on her jail experiences), later formed the basis of Chapter 16 of *Loaves and Fishes*.

178  Elizabeth Gurley Flynn was a long-time radical, an organizer for the I.W.W. (Industrial Workers of the World) and later a leader in the Communist Party. Earlier in the 1950s she had been imprisoned for several years for violation of the Smith Act.

sions and commissions. I shall try to see only good in them and write book on them.

December 30

We discontinued the bread line after 22 years of continuous service. The bricks falling to the street were a continuous hazard from the house next door.

Transitions are so hard.

December 31

After Mass bought Ammon's Christmas present—scrapbooks and 3 refills which took all morning. The din outside the house is very bad—flying brick and plaster dust.

Then to gas company to have gas turned on at Spring St. [*new office for CW*].

# 1959

## THE NOTEBOOK OF DOROTHY DAY · JANUARY-DECEMBER 1959

"To aim at illuminating the universal through an examination of the particular." (Kibbutz)

January 1. Rainy. Peter Maurin Farm. Feast of Circumcision

Up at nine, rheumatic in knees so went to 12 Mass. Beth [Rogers] and I reading about anarchism in *Encyclopedia Britannica*, 1911 edition, Kropotkin's article. Beth will review Kibbutz book, and will write about anarchism for a leaflet. She is a good editor—good balance, clear writing. New on staff this month: Arthur Sheehan and Chas Butterworth—a good round staff now. Ammon, 49, Chas, 32, Arthur, 49, Stanley, 42, Beth, 38, Bob Steed, 26. We start our moving to our new headquarters at 39 Spring Street on Monday. More rain is forecast for tomorrow.

Today Battista, Cuban dictator, fled to the Dominican Republic. Fidel Castro has taken over.

January 2. Sunny and windy, like March

In town. Out of oil—no heat, no hot water. Fortunately it is not freezing. Bob spending all his time cleaning up loft [*on Spring St.*]. The paper got finished at 5:30. All mailed out. Arthur Sheehan spoke at the meeting on the

Irish. A good crowd for our last meeting on Chrystie St. Even tonight a load of clothes brought in. Also a young girl, a nurse, who made the retreat, came with a pearl ring and $100, some of which I gave to Arthur, who has sickness at home. All the files are over to the loft and my books from my room to the farm library. All day they drilled holes in the street and the farm was so quiet.

January 3

Went to Mass and Benediction at Nativity Church. At ten Bob had not yet started work and I was angry. God forgive me—he worked all the rest of the day. All the small stuff being moved. Father Kay in. Very drunk. I refused to let him stay. To "A Touch of the Poet" by O'Neill with [Bill] Oleksak.

Sunday, January 4

A gray day but not too cold, I imagine around forty. I came down to the farm last night… tired after the bit of moving we had done for the few days before. It will take a week to do it all, and legally we do not have to be out until the 15th. It will save about $300 in rents to keep people in the house until then. But we will be moving the kitchen soon, and the office is almost all moved. The next meeting will be in St. Joseph's loft on Spring Street. Bob is writing "The death of a house." There has been a young fellow around taking pictures of the demolition going on around us. We will have a record of it.

Everyone in the house is much disturbed. Shorty keeps following me around, his face contracted like that of a grief-stricken clown, asking whether we are going to leave him behind. Hatty has been drunk for the last three days, laying in her bed, drinking Muscatel, Sneaky Pete, as the men on the Bowery call it. Bob goes up and hunts around for bottles and takes them away from her and pours them down the sink. But somehow another appears. It is only 35¢ a pint. What an atmosphere. Certainly the loft all open and with windows on three sides, will be clear and clean and fresh and we will start anew. The two-room apartments will be so small that one might just as well be living in a Pullman berth. Any port in a storm, and we are living in a storm, a storm of destruction and rebuilding. The city is changing, and no one seems to think of war but builds and builds just as though there were no danger to cities.

I have come down on the beach for the first time in a month, and after some housecleaning, am sitting in the window, looking out at the birds on the water, a great flock of them, a long black rim, rather like those currents of driftwood one sees coming toward the shore. But these are birds, thousands of them, and just now they suddenly rose from the water, with what seemed to be a dragging of wings and feet, a slow start, and soon they wheeled and turned and were on their way south. I wonder what kind of birds.

Reading Newman's sermon, "Purity and love." St. John is the saint of purity and St. Peter the saint of love, he writes.

January 6. 15°. High wind

Beth and I to Mass at Huguenot. In town by noon and all afternoon packing. To Deane's for supper at seven for Anne Marie [Stokes's] birthday feast. With Helene Iswolsky, Mike Kovalak, and Bob. Deane is a wonderful cook and her house looked lovely.

Helene told us about her grandfather, quite a radical, who was governor of Irkutsk in Siberia. His name was Peter Iswolsky. Bakunin was exiled there, forbidden to leave the city. And he used to call at the governor's mansion. Quite the playboy, Helene said, and charmed his host and hostess. He played the piano and was a brilliant talker. Anyway, Bakunin charmed Madame Iswolsky and tricked Peter Iswolsky into giving him a pass to do some business out of the city and so escaped. But the governor seems not to have been reprimanded.

"Did you travel with a samovar?" we asked Helene. "But no, with a teapot, and when you get to the station you ask for boiling water." She told her mother's story—in Germany when they asked for boiling water the German porter asked, "What degree Fahrenheit?" Helene was on her way to Combermere to spend some wintry months with Catherine de Hueck, also a Russian, who conducts her famous Madonna House Training Center there.

January 7

Reading Boswell's [Life of Samuel] Johnson. He had a friend who was put away for praying all the time, "But those who do not pray and do not worship are the mad ones," Johnson said. "He is more sane than they." And he went on to say the poor man did no one harm and should be released. He made me think of Manny and Jeanette.

January 15. Perkinsville

Awoke today at three a.m. with Hilaire awake and complaining and talking to himself alternately. He kept at it, so at 4:30 I got some hot milk and coffee and began to read Maurice Baring's *Darby and Joan*, a strange Victorian novel, where people are "poor" but manage to live in the country and winter in Malta, etc. Tangled lives, and Joan does her duty or is led to do what she thinks is her duty because people would think her slightly less nice a "person." She is without faith though she would like to believe. Her father "looked upon Catholicism as an interesting historical institution founded on dogma in which no reasonable person could believe, but offering a sensible code of morals and overlaid with a mass of superstitions, which though possibly regrettable, were picturesque, a boon to art; and not more silly and less changeable then the superstitions of men of science."

January 16. Icy. 38°

We woke this morning and the roads were so icy that the schools were closed and all the children are home. It is still raining, and snow and colder is the forecast. Even the cats are sliding down the road. Eric had a few good rides on his sled. Stanley and David are working on the wood. Tamar is spinning. I lie in bed writing letters. Even little Hilaire, seventeen months, tries to help carry wood as they load it into the cellar. Eric and Nick worked all morning. The cow is sick—had pneumonia. They will have to call the vet for the other cow. Dave works very hard—I do not see how Tamar can do without him if he gets a job. They can get by on a little—he has raised so much food. I worry about Sue. Tamar says she is not as gay as she used to be. They are all inarticulate, Irish and English, Hennessy and Batterham as they are. One does not know what they are feeling or thinking. With the silent I am silent, with the articulate and talkative I am stimulated to talk.

January 18

Mass at St. Clement's where the Russian liturgy was celebrated and a sermon preached about the great schism, but very little said about love of our separated brethren, or of Christ on the altars in Russia. Drove to the Fontbonne Academy where the St. Joseph Sisters have monthly meetings with Father Leonard SJ, secretary of liturgical conference. Bishop Wright spoke first on education and charity. I spoke on world poverty and the state's manner of dealing with it and the Church's—the works of mercy.

January 20. Rain. 45°

At six I spoke to Bellevue's student nurses at Newman Club on the Church behind the iron curtain. I told what I knew and quoted from Helene Iswolsky's article in current *Jubilee* and about the religious attitudes in Russian literature. They gave me $10. The Sheeds go out for no less than $200. Barbara Ward asks a thousand. But if I can make anyone think in terms of "love of enemy" in such a talk as tonight it is well worth going out.

January 21

Cardinal Cushing [of Boston] sent us a hundred dollars and a gay letter. A Dominican sister, order of Bethany, who is here to start a foundation in Boston, visited us. One third of the order are from prisons and no one knows which are which. A former prostitute might be a Mother Superior. Father [Franziskus] Stratmann OP, took refuge in their Flemish convent during World War II and wrote, "Neither will I condemn thee."

Now in bed at seven writing and it's good to leave the office and its cares behind. We are still a community, but diffused in a wider community. Martin Buber says the state should be a community of communities.

January 22

A much better sleep last night and up at six. There is such peace in regularity of hours. Here I am in bed at nine with an hour to read and write and no liberty to dawdle away my time staying up late, limited by the common good.

Sat January 31, 1959

Last night I sat up reading *Lolita* [Nabokov], a truly terrible tale, a horrible picture of American life, a vicious tale, reminding me of *Notes from the Underground*.

Reading: *Blackfriars* about Père Pire, OP, who won the Nobel Peace Prize this year; article on [J.D.] Salinger in *Harpers*.

I called Mr. Elliot at Harpers, to tell him I am withdrawing my Therese book.

What a good staff we have now. If I could only get over my knee pains which I've had since Christmas carol singing at the jail. The cold, the tension, and the diet will have to do with it.

Sunday February 1

Our problems now, or rather mine, especially: Tamar and Della's health. They both have good doctors (and my own arthritis and upset stomach too). Here at farm—Stanley's need for comforting, for a job. For a change of view. Also Mike's, Ammon's attitudes. Vivian, who has been married 4 years and now wants a divorce.

Smokey—his drinking, but he is better now. An apartment to live in N.Y. It takes so long to get down here.

Our trial now is no car for the country.

February 2, Monday

Today we went to press. Last night it was fearfully cold. down to zero, but the car started and Beth and I drove in and got there at 9. The work went easily, tho my copy was badly and hastily written because I had gone to the doctor with Della at 4:30. The whole day was spent in writing it but another day would be needed for polishing. How much time a little writing takes. I feel much happier in having scrapped my Therese book. It was just not adequate even as a personal tribute. I had been so harried by so many criticisms that I no longer had perspective.

I called Tamar who has been having pneumonia, the doctor said. My prayers are so much a personal thing—Oh God, my Father, take care of Tamar and her family. Mary our Mother, I gave her to you at her birth,[179] watch over her. St. Joseph—she has no father to protect or comfort her, be to her a father too. And then prayers for all our problems follow—I do not mind writing them out just to see how they are taken care of later.

Tuesday, Feb 3

Called Tamar again tonight and David says the neighbors have been helping—washing, baking. Tonight they took some apples to make pies for them!

So many troubles, And Stanley's depression. He got his manuscript back from Sheed & Ward with a very friendly letter but feels badly. He is so withdrawn.

All day I read Arthur Sheehan's ms. on Peter, which is very good.[180] Must finish tonight. He works hard and has much family trouble besides with a wife ill.

Friday, February 6

Today is my name day and spent in bed with sore throat, cold, rheumatism, but very happily. Finished *Of Whales and Men* by Dr. R. B. Robertson—a fascinating book. Best chapter: South Atlantic Slum (South Georgia) about Ernest Shackleton and an Antarctic expedition and an experience they had when at the extremity of their strength, had the constant delusion that there was one more member than could actually be counted. T.S. Eliot in a poem called "The Wasteland," "Who is the third who walks always besides you?

---

179 In an article for *Commonweal*, "About Mary" (November 5, 1943), Dorothy described this prayer, entrusting Tamar to the care of the Blessed Mother. "You will have to be her mother. Under the best of circumstances I'm a failure as a homemaker. I'm untidy, inconsistent, undisciplined, temperamental, and I have to pray hard every day for final perseverance." See *SW,* 159-162.

180 Arthur Sheehan, *Peter Maurin: Gay Believer* (New York: Hanover House, 1959).

When I count there are only you and I together. But when I look ahead up the white road there is always another one walking beside you gliding wrapt in a brown mantel, hooded..."

February 7. Saturday

Again, the problem of the children in the neighborhood—locked out by their sisters who are left to care for the home, looking for mischief. Last night they came after dark to slash the screens on Marge's porch—to get even for having been sent home. There are two destructive boys in the neighborhood. They steal for stealing's sake. They don't skate or play games, just roam about getting into trouble. The ugliness and desolation of sin. And they are so sinned against. Over and over you hear the parents say, "I'm not going to let my children suffer as I did from poverty, from being laughed at." What injury we are doing our children by our standards.

The new book on Therese is out—*The Hidden Face* by Ida Goerres. It is a marvelous book. Eight years ago when I told Louise Wynhausen I wanted to write a book on Therese, she said the very best book had been written. And now I agree, it is as satisfying as everyone said. Now that I have finished it I am going to start in again, writing a series of essays, trying to cover what I do not think has been thoroughly covered yet (the family itself, for instance, as a whole).

February 8. Sunday

Problems—Keith and his throwing George's coat out the window. Smokey's resentment at being on Bowery. Isadore may take him in? Ammon left Friday—he begins a 40-day fast Wednesday.

February 10. Tuesday

Opera—"Macbeth." So icy underfoot neither Beth nor I could go in.

Argument over phone with Bob about breadline which he is trying to keep out until 5:45. They have been gathering at 4:30. Having Tommy put them out, they hung around anyway, the neighbors complained and landlord called, said inside was large enough. We should let circumstances guide us. Certainly put benches around, reading matter, pictures, murals, music—make an atmosphere for them. After all, I wrote in last issue about our present closeness to the unemployed, the man on the street. Bob goes ahead, his own impulsive way. I suggested he take his vacation now instead of March. Have Charlie also write checks and share in the decisions of the house.

February 11

A happy day—the first of daily Masses at St. Thomas and St. Joseph's in Pleasant Plains and Rossville. A hard day at the office with such an increased soup line. Strange, they do not come in the morning for coffee, but in increasing numbers for lunch and dinner. Unemployment growing.

Called Harpers—Nel Arnold, about Doubleday money—60% of advance royalties on 50,000 copies of *The Long Loneliness*—$350. It will only cover taxes on Tamar's Staten Island place.

February 12

It is hard to convince anyone, priest or people, that Charity must forgive seventy times seven, and that we must not judge. The bitterness with which people regard the poor and down-and-out. Drink, profligate living, laziness, everything is suspected. They help them once, the man who comes to the door, but they come back! They want more help. "Where will it end? Can I accomplish anything? Aren't there poorer people whom I should be helping?" These are the questions they ask themselves which paralyzes all charity, chills it, stops all good work. If we start in by admitting that what we can do is very small—a drop in the bucket—and try to do that very well, it is a beginning and really a great deal.

Here I am, 61 years old, and I can remember three incidents of people with very sweet expressions, happy smiles, welcoming looks, among all my casual encounters, who quite warmed my heart for the rest of the day. People who are in our position, where many calls are made on them, are apt to get a guarded expression, a suspicious look, or even an angry look when they feel frustrated at not being able to help as they wish. Oh! to start out each day and greet each encounter with open arms—a message from our dear Lord, a friend of His, someone He sent, His guest, not ours. The Sacrament of the Present Moment, Father McSorley calls it. He gave me Caussade's *Abandonment [to Divine Providence]* to read, to fill out these ideas.

Bob drove me to the train to Trenton. Later a good audience. Questions on birth control. Population.

February 14. Conyers [Georgia, Trappist Abbey]

Got in late last night thru heavy fog that stopped all airlines. We are staying in the gatehouse and although the Abbey is about finished and will be ready for occupancy in a few months, there is a sea of mud all around it from the recent heavy showers. The heavy red mud of Georgia is covered, however, with a gravel path or wooden plank path from chapel and dining room. There are 100 here now—still living in barns, very crowded. The frogs are croaking; the air is alive with Spring peepers. I even saw a forsythia bush in bloom.

February 15. First Sunday of Lent
    This is Jack English's ordination day and also his birthday. The sun is just setting and there is ridge upon ridge of glorious colors in the sky. The birds are twittering away, a retiring song, and it is too cold tonight for the Spring peepers in the hollows. Jack is the fist CW editor to be ordained a priest—Father Mary Charles. We received communion at the 6 a.m. Mass. Dinner and supper were served in the great refectory of the new monastery which won't be opened for some months.

February 16
    Up at 5. Jack's Mass, a requiem, was at 6 and he took ¾ of an hour. Mockingbirds singing, bright sunny days. It was a rejoicing day
    On the Road by [Jack] Kerouac—such a contrast to this—a sad search for "kicks."
    Drove down to Conyers and called Ammon, who is fasting all of Lent. More trouble at home with Catherine calling police on Mike.

February 18. Koinonia
    135 miles from Atlanta. Crocuses, narcissus, red bud, magnolia, forsythia, etc. all in bloom. Clarence [Jordan] was in Texas. Florence gave me 5 lbs. of nuts after showing me the plant which is very well organized and employs 20 colored women. So they and some men are not afraid to work in spite of threats from neighbors.

February 20
    Have been reading On the Road by Kerouac, somewhat suitable while traveling by bus. A most unhappy book and showing the poor at their desperate worst, the occasional wild outbreak, the reckless search for joy through liquor and sex. Also read Marjorie Morningstar, a paean to the comfort of the bourgeois way of life—what a contrast.

February 21
    Up at 6 for Mass and felt very sick in church which was airless. Had to go out, but how good it was to fast completely on Ember Friday and Saturday. A good long time in the sun. Hoped to get the opera, but I guess they have stopped broadcasting it. Read Marjorie Morningstar—trash.

The diocesan papers are full of stories about atrocities in China and the sufferings of the Church and I get a letter from Betty Chang from Tientsin about the communes and the full-employment, etc. When we see the migrant camps, and our factories in the fields, our system does not offer much.

February 22

Mass at 8, driven by a young man who was going with an intelligent young Lutheran girl, and kept telling me how he argued with her. Did the Protestants have any saints? No. Did the Blessed Mother visit any of them? No, etc. I felt like saying the Catholics needed it more.

A very quiet day, reading [Thomas Merton's] *The Seven Storey Mountain*, the last part—he has plunged himself so deeply in religion that his view of the world and its problems is superficial and scornful.

Dr. Esser said I must break my fast today. So two glasses of orange juice and one of vegetable juice. This is as much of an ordeal as fasting. My tastes running to cereals and bread and eggs and coffee. No more headaches or knee pains, but still general pains in my legs.

March. Sunday. 3rd of Lent

My trip was a good one—life seems to simple traveling, living out of a suitcase, duties well defined. Here at home the paperwork—immeasurable letters and telephone calls chopping up the day, so that nothing gets done or done well. This overall work, "in charge"—so complicated. John [Filliger] with his animals and farm, Hans [Tunnesen] with his carpentry and baking and Sunday cooking—all seems so much simpler.

Here it is noon and already have just arrived home last night I fall victim to selfishness, hopelessness, despondency.

Marge and I sat and discussed income tax, Federal and State, and people's ways of evading it, filing returns in order to get returns from the withholding tax. And here we have never filed, over all the years, and truly vast amounts of money have passed thru our hands.

Ammon is on his 19th day of fasting—and when he worked and ate his one-dish meals in Arizona, how beautifully simple his life is, and here in New York he keeps it simple too.

March 4, Wed.

Reading Gerald Vann, *The Paradox Tree*. He talks of myths—the myth of the hero's struggles with powers of darkness, serpents, dragons, giants, eventual victory, rescues the princess, makes atonement to God, or returns with the elixir of life. Always the tragedy of man ends in victory in all the old stories.

The comedy should have a higher rank then tragedy. "The story of the hero expresses the deep longing for life; immortal or divine."

The reality, the optimism of Catholic Workers. "Starry eyed," *The Nation* called us some years ago. But they recognized this quality.

Wednesday March 11

While I was resting after lunch a Max Sosky called me up from an Automat and told Marge he had just composed music for one of Blake's "Songs of Innocence" and wanted me to hear it because I loved beauty too—poetry and music. He wants me to call him back. Then Harriet Goldstein called up weeping hysterically and saying her child in the foster home was being mistreated, his foot was injured. She has been in a mental hospital for the last few months and is out on a pass. Poor desperate soul. We did her no good. She kept the child up all night, and he lived on coffee and aspirin at six years old. A call from Bob that Larry had been arrested for dressing up like a clown and begging in front of the Penn Station. A *Journal American* reporter called about that. And Bob said he was a crazy person out of a mental hospital and we paid his rent but did not authorize him to beg. Bob in his rough diagnosis was as bad as Larry. Then while Bob was talking someone fell down the stairs, the top flight with the Loft. He called back later and said the man was so limp with drink he was not injured. Ammon also called saying the hoodlums of the neighborhood had yanked our front door off its hinges.

There surely is an apostolate of the telephones—so often we are impulsive and trying to avoid one more responsibility being thrust on us, when if men were gentler, more considerate, we could comfort and advise and cheer a little. St. Therese said we must refuse in such a way that the person went away happy.

Last night Père [René] Voillaume[181] talked at Holy Souls convent and stressed the need of friendship to the most abandoned. Making oneself a brother, not a benefactor.

March 11

It was a cold and dreary day, and we were tired from the meeting last night. Max Sosky's voice over the phone sounded happy.

"I've come across your wonderful paper and I love the whole tone of it. And to think it sells for a penny. I bought a copy from a man on the street and I asked him if you liked music and he said yes, so I thought you'd like to know

---

181 Founder of the Little Brothers of Jesus, based on the spirituality of Charles de Foucauld.

I've made a musical arrangement of Blake's Songs of Innocence and wouldn't you like to have me sing it to you? No—well I can come down to play it to you on the organ you say you have. How much is the fare? I'm not working. Don't worry about feeding me, I'm a vegetarian—just some coffee and cake. It doesn't matter about the weather. Bloomingdale is such a beautiful name. I'll come and play you folk songs."

Another conversation with Mr. Guiddoti—undertaker on Spring Street—black-eyed, bald, big nose. He kept insisting our Bowery men were loitering in doorway, drinking, smashing bottles, urinating, molesting women and children, blocking the sidewalk, keeping women and children from entering their homes, interfering with his business, horrifying and frightening his customers, the relatives who came to "wake" their dear ones at his undertaking parlor. He himself lived upstairs from and owned his building and his home was being invaded by these bums. Our landlord had rented his loft to us out of spite that he would get even with him, that there were hundreds of violations in the buildings he owned.

We were not as bad as the Villagers he had rented to before who ran a dance school and little theater and kept the neighborhood awake with their noise, but just the same we were molesting women and children.

He himself knew what it was to give to the poor—he often gave 15 cents or a quarter. But our breadline he could not stand. Couldn't we just ask them to walk on the other side of the street?

He had talked to Mrs. Black at the Spring Street clinic, which was not really a clinic but a center where mothers were advised as to how to raise and feed their children, and she too said our men were terrifying the women and children.

Couldn't we station a watchman at the door to make the men cross the street and not pass his undertaking establishment?

When I asked him why he should make such a suggestion since the children's playground and welfare center were on that side and that he did not seem to concern himself about their safety in such a suggestion, he said, "Well, everyone must look out for himself—for his own business, and you people are going to spoil my business."

Daily since my conversations with Miss Black, who trembled all over as she talked to me, we have been plagued by broken glass and garbage strewed in our doorway. All our windows have been broken across the front of the house, a firecracker has been thrown at Ammon by children who called him an old stew bum and—blasphemy—the face of Christ our Brother, painted by Mr.

Drewett of the Ave Maria shop on tin and nailed on our door, has been defaced by vandals.

We can only read over again the story of St. Francis, "This then is perfect joy," which we are reprinting in the CW.

March 12. Thursday. Heavy snow

In spite of the weather, high winds. Max Sosky came out to see us, saying he liked to walk. He lives in the Brownsville section of Brooklyn, well dressed, clean-cut face, pleasant and enthusiastic. A delicate soul, and the musical settings he has composed for Blake's Lamb and Tiger are truly impressive. He played on our battered piano in the Hall, then on the organ in the chapel and there he insisted on playing Stephen Foster's "Dolly Day." Not at all suitable. But his Laudate and Hymn of Thanksgiving were lovely. Deane came out yesterday and she enjoyed him very much.

Ammon called. A woman from Wisconsin after reading his book called long distance and talked $50 worth to him. "What better way to spend the money," he said, "when she was taking instruction and needed help—the Church so appalled her." It will appall her worse, Ammon said, when she's in it. But faith's the thing.

March 19. St. Joseph

Stayed in bed today till 11 since I had a heavy schedule in town. To municipal building with Beth and Bob to get $27,000 of money due on the house on Chrystie Street. To start building when we get a permit.

March 20

Manhattan College at 10:30—meeting at noon until 2. In spite of warm day their auditorium was crowded. They are not lukewarm—strongly opposed to pacifism, our voluntary poverty. All ready to take jobs on guided missiles. But they listened.

March 30. Easter Monday

Reading *Warriors of God* by Walter Nigo. Purpose of book to call for a new transfigured monasticism. A new "brotherhood of those marked by pain," as Schweitzer said. Courage to remain small. Silence. A brotherhood of Alyoshas [*the holy hero of* The Brothers Karamazov].

March 31. Tuesday

Every day now since last Thursday I have had a fever of 101 or 2, and finally one of those head colds which make seeing and breathing hard. Humidity has been 95 per cent and no sun to dispel it. Everybody lying around. I had to miss all my engagements today in Boston. Could not even write. Ammon phoned.

## April 2

Ammon just called to say April 17 is date of air raid drill this year. We will have the appeal out and the paper mailed by then.

## April 5

To 8 a.m. Mass at St. Joseph's. My first communion since Holy Thursday. I cannot remember having had such a siege of fever for many years.

## April 7

Finally wrote the appeal, with great effort. Ammon called to say Charles [Butterworth] had been indicted for harboring a deserter and Bob [Steed] got him out on $15,000 bail. Hearing is set for April 21st.[182] Bob was threatened with prosecution for tearing up his draft card.

In ten days the Civil Defense Drill. Stayed at farm tonight. Full chorus of frogs—geese, etc.

## April 9

Deane drove down with Beth last night for a few days of fresh air before jail next week. She gathered dandelions and shells and walked on the beach. I wrote letters. Sent Therese ms. to Jenny Moore.

## April 17. AIR RAID DRILL 1:30 PM City Hall Park

Ammon had wanted Times Square. There were other picketers there—taxi drivers, teachers, bringing their grievances to City Hall and to the public. We had no idea who would be there, but it was so beautiful a day that 18 joined us, including Sheldon Weeks, and three college students, who being under age meant that when we were put under arrest, we were held for the adolescent court in the Tombs, under Judge Roe. The usual procedure.

We were put in separate bull pens, Deane and me and the other 16, and held there until brought to court before Judge Levy. We made a very long line before the judge. He accused me of being ringleader, and instead of saying

---

182 "For a long time it bothered Charles's conscience that he had not yet been to jail," Dorothy wrote in *Loaves and Fishes* (*LF,* 146). And then one day some FBI men came to the CW looking for an Army deserter. Charles went back to the kitchen, where he found the man and told him there were a couple of visitors whom he might not wish to see. The deserter escaped out the back way, and Charles was arrested. He later received a six-month suspended sentence.

we each followed our consciences, as I should have, I said Ammon was also an editor. Whereupon he questioned him—did he not believe in law and order?—and Ammon said he did not. The judge asked him if he had been in a mental hospital. He then put us under $1,000 bail and put trial to Wednesday, April 22nd.

Deane and I went through the usual procedure, taken in a van to the House of Detention.

How to write about this subject—shall we call it particular friendships? Or is that term used by writers of religious treatises too delicate for so heavily evil a subject? St. Paul said, "Let these things be not so much as mentioned among you." But wars, slave labor camps, concentration of those of one sex together have led to the return of black paganism, a playing around, perhaps innocently at first, perhaps with a hunger for affection, for love, with dark forces which... [*break in line*]

JAIL DIARY 1959

There are no gongs, no bells, as in a school or convent. There is the telephone, of course, and gentle as its ring is, we all listen for it because it may mean clinic, roof, linen room, library, commissary, or visitor. We are awakened here in this House of Detention by the words, "It's time to get up, ladies." It was "girls" once and a tart "we are all ladies here," corrected the jailor. She in turn does not like to be called guard or jailor. There are no bells, but there is the jingling of keys. The big gate at the end of the corridor is opened, there is another clank as a lever is thrown which releases the gates of the individual cells and as the key is heard to unlock the two showers, there is a mad clanging of gates as girls rush to be there first. On our corridor there are six charged with homicide, two with kidnapping, and two with cheating the Relief of anything from $75 to $2,000. There are also assault cases, armed robbery, forgery, possession of drugs. It is one corridor on one of the three detention floors, and there are four corridors of, perhaps, sixteen cells, each made for one cot, but containing two. Sometimes one is trundled under the other which also can be hung up on the wall to get it out of the way, but most often both cots are made up because the most comfortable posture is lying down. When both cots are up, the aisle between is perhaps six inches wide. One kneels on one cot to press the stiff buttons over a small sink, usually stopped up, to get hot or cold water. One must drink from cupped hand since when one is entered, she is most completely bereft of all things. "Fail not to put far from you all things until you are alone with God," St. Bernard says. All things are put far from you, but there is not the silence of solitude. Conversation goes on continually.

We were over the worst, Deane and I congratulated ourselves—over the ordeal of picketing, of submitting to arrest, of the ride in the police van which is brutal and inhuman, and actually dangerous to old brittle limbs, to young pregnant women. Yesterday a girl was taken to Bellevue after a miscarriage. She was four months pregnant and they could say the miscarriage was a result of drugs. On the detention floor, the Puerto Rican girls sang in their cells at night—serenely and then last of all, Jean, accused of kidnapping a baby, sang the Our Father. When we were sentenced after ten days, and put on the eleventh floor in the dormitory, the girls never sang. They were too close to each other and felt self-conscious.

Styles—a priest said once they originate in brothels and in Hollywood; women all try to dress like sirens—housewives and business and factory girls do. Dress is not functional. We could also say styles originate in jails. Two years ago the girls were taking in and shaping the seams of their dresses to outline their buttocks. In court I saw many women officers with the same styles, even to the bleached strands of their hair. Powder. They only sold Nat Brown powder in the commissary that mixed with talcum made a rachel shade. One Irish girl said she used Bon Ami cleaning powder—"And it never scratched."

Sentimentalism—in trying to see Christ in our sisters and loving them in their suffering, we are not oblivious to their faults, their sins. This is true love because primarily we love them because Jesus loved them—He came to call sinners, to find the lost sheep. He even left the ninety-nine. He said to forgive seven times seventy. So we love them. We do not overlook the fact that in the natural order they are beautiful, very often, brown skinned, young, tall, of good carriage, strong, graceful, etc. They are also sober. I recognize the fact that outside, stupefied with drugs or ugly with drink, they would be hard to love. They showed us pictures of their children and their faces were alive with love and longing. Afterwards, they lay sorrowful on their beds. But many times too they were triggered by some affront or injustice, screaming or flaring into temper or foul language, and their rage was such that others kept silent until their mutterings died down like the thunder of a summer storm. Arguments, shouting, cursing, laughter. Some nights the arguments on the ward were hideous, sometimes there was wild gaiety, and most vulgar humor.

On our detention floor (half the women are on these floors) there were six women waiting trial for homicide. They had stabbed or shot drunken husbands. One somber woman hired another man to kill her husband for $100. There were those accused of forgery, kidnapping, shoplifting, assault, robbery, possession of drugs, etc. But there, mingling with them, all the day with gates open and corridor free, we were sisters—we saw in ourselves our own capacity for sin, violence, and hatred. We recalled occasions of temper, of throwing things, that might well have led by "accident" to death—theologians and psychiatrists say there are no accidents—and we ourselves being charged with homicides. And what dishonesty are we not capable of? All men are liars, the Bible says. Victor Gollancz in a recent book which deals with man's capacity to oppose nuclear weapons with spiritual ones, also Father Darcy, S.J., quote me when I wrote about my first jail experience. My identification of myself with the other person was so complete that I shared even their despair. The memory of that black hopelessness was still so present to me that this year I made the stations as Abbot Marmion advised us to do to increase my fortitude, and to my petitions I added that Christian joy would also strengthen me. If you want to help others, you cannot convey to others what you do not possess and who can help wanting to bring a little light into so dark a place as a city prison. I would be guilty of lack of gratitude if I did not show in my whole behavior the peace and happiness and joy which is in the foretaste of the well-being of heaven.

So God, knowing my weakness, tempering the wind to the shorn lamb, strengthening the back for the burden made our fifteen days this year easier for us. We were put the last 8 days of our sentence in the large dormitory—airy, tiled with old rose waxed floor covering with pink bedside tables, center tables, potted plants, showers (with curtains) toilets (with doors), etc. There are only twenty-two in the dorm ward which adjoined a dining room where some graciousness was attempted by table cloths, seldom used however. Some girls missed the privacy of the cells, however, for good reasons, desire for some hours of isolation, and also for some other evil reasons. On the detention floors there were two cells one could not pass without carefully averted head. At recreation on the roof when there were also game rooms for rainy days, and on the crowded elevators going to clinic, roof, work assignment, one could not help but see examples of utter depravity. There was one young, very small mulatto girl with short pinafore effect dress, with a brown face and bright yellow, bleached, straight hair—a Lolita—and her companion who looked like a 14-year-old boy, with a sparkling pink and white complexion, jet black hair, waved in ducktail hair-do. Of course, she was twenty-one or she would not be there. There are three detention floors where there are many adolescents who are always supposed to be kept apart, but who have many opportunities of coming in contact with the sentenced prisoners. The flagrant petting that went on in public between these two, the times I saw them wrapped in embraces, "he" with his face buried in the neck of the little bleached blonde, were innumerable and one would think would call for reprimand, or the giving of "infractions," which the prisoners dread very much as they lengthen the days in jail. Though guards are present, these things seem to be ignored. Commissioner Cross says she cannot have an officer outside of each cell, but as long as these actions are ignored, they seem to be tolerated, or even condoned.

Indeed many officers seem to find these actions amusing and laugh at them just as male female impersonators used to be laughed at on Broadway. These conditions are of course aggravated by overcrowding, since practically all cells contain two which should contain only one. The perverse cannot be isolated. Then too there is so often so little kindness and gentleness, that much play is like the playing of young animals, a teasing or affection, and not a guilty play. Still it is dangerous. There is also "friendship." One young girl, who obviously had a schoolgirl crush on a sturdy young married woman who had two children, hung around her a great deal, begging for friendship. When the latter brushed her off, she complained mournfully—"I have nothing; they have taken everything from me, even a friend. One needs a friend." I thought of a little pamphlet of St. Aelred on friendship, published by St. Anthony's Press, also of the friendships of David and Jonathan.

All love is a reflection of the love of God, just as all sin is perversion, a turning from God and a turning to creatures. All love must be respected. But evil is very close. The devil likes to simulate the good. He likes to offer what God truly offers. To make my point clear, I must be very personal and say that on one occasion in prison, I felt myself assaulted by memories of my own sex life, my life with Forster, of the sins of my past life. They were so pertinacious that one could almost be scrupulous in Confession as to whether or not there was "delectation in temptation," as St. Francis de Sales said. Then I suddenly realized that this was in the air and if I, a woman of 61, felt this at a time of life where, as Huysmans said, temptations are of the mind more than of the flesh, how much more so in these young ones, whose flesh must cry out fiercely for consummation and fruition.

May 1
   Release from House of Detention at 11:30.

May 7. Perkinsville
   Up for a 6:30 Mass with all eight children including Hilaire, who howled when his mother and father went to communion. The family had to go in two batches to the communion rail. Not much chance for feelings of devotion with a squirming restless baby, but what an act of faith, what will to receive, to worship.

Dave had been working for a neighboring farmer in exchange for plowing and harrowing on his own place, and is already well sun-burnt. There was the big job of spreading manure on the field too. But all days are full days in the country.

## May 8
There is a new book out about Shackleton and his Antarctic adventure, which from the *Time* review belittled him, and spoke of the senselessness of his project, regardless of the fact that his spirit has inspired and enlivened and strengthened explorers ever since.

From the standpoint of cold reason, many of the adventures of the heroes of fiction, tradition, and history seem meaningless and futile. Everything has to be studied in the light of the times past, present, and future. Taken in context, in other words.

## May 9
Tamar and I were talking of enmities in families, the love and hatred so close together, the painful struggles between brothers and sisters, the jealousies, the desire to hurt. In a big Irish family there is a struggle over every marriage, and breaking away from the family to marry is a most terrible and painful thing. And then in Tamar's case there is a struggle because David's ideas on Distributism strike at the foundations of their life, their jobs, their city existence. They would not be so scornful of the land, voluntary poverty, books, ideas, if these concepts did not upset them, make them unhappy and resentful.

Woke early this a.m. thinking of going on with my novel now that my jail experience has included the detention floors of the jail (to write of Monica's experience). The trouble with the CW is that one is so busy living that there is no time to write about it.

This morning Tamar took the five older to catechism at 9:30 and Dave and I had a good morning's talk about books and publishers. Hilaire follows him wherever he goes and when David is bringing back empty pails from watering the cow, Hilaire, 20 months old, carries one almost as big as himself. If David carries wood, Hilaire does, too.

All were working in the garden and it was a pleasant sight. Nickie likes to throw rocks so he threw 60 of them out of the garden.

Outside the crimson tulips, narcissus, and daffodils, pansies, and grape hyacinths are all in bloom, and in the woods trillium dogtooth violet, and many varieties of violet. "I like God," Maggie said.

May 10

Today Dave and Tamar to 6:30 Mass. The children are all sleeping and I up for my hour of Office with the sun pouring down outside, and larks singing in the sky. I don't know if they are song sparrows or meadow larks, but their song is piercingly sweet. The boys fished all day until 7 without eating even. It worries Tamar to death. They leave at 9 for catechism, having eaten a few pancakes and a glass of milk. Then nothing else all day. They talk of nothing but fishing—how many trout they catch—8, 10 to 12—and have to put them back because they are undersized. Nickie brought one to cook and he and the dog shared it with much enthusiasm. Eric brought in three and they were delicious.

May 11

The latest craze: can-can skirts with hundreds of yards of shoddy net decorated with ribbon. Johanna has one, Becky and Sue want them. They are fascinating, frothy, flowery, lovely for a dance if they were made and used more modestly.

May 12

Article on Confirmation in *Worship*, May. See also Baptism in Bouyer's *Liturgical Piety*. Cardinal Cushing said once to me, "You are one of those whose confirmation 'took.'"

To the appointment with Dr. Edward Hartung. He said "water on knee" and drained it, showed me exercises for muscles of feet and leg, and pills. Immediate results for the knee.

May 17. Mary Hennessy's First Holy Communion.

When I called Tamar she said Mary had a beautiful day for her first Communion. A beautiful Pentecost.

June 2

Della was very tired last night, very pale. I slept there because Franklin had flown to Chicago for conferences at University of Chicago Press.[183] We got up in leisurely fashion at 8. I read Thurber on Ross, editor of the *New Yorker*. We went to noonday Mass at the new church on Park and 38th St. I had resolved to spend one hour daily before Blessed Sacrament in thanksgiving to Sacred Heart, and yet have not started.

---

183 Della's husband, Franklin Spier, worked in the publishing industry.

June 17

Chas. B. in court [*charged with aiding in the escape of a deserter*]. Judge Noonan—very pleasant. Suspended sentence. He has Blessed Mother on his desk.

June 19

[Elizabeth] Gurly Flynn spoke.

A very hard day working on ms.—the two agitators. Arguments with Ammon. Anna Vacar's letter. I felt it was cruelty on my part to show it to him. I must take him as he is.

June 23

Fritz Eichenberg took me to dinner and told me of a Japanese artist's woodcuts, who works with incredible speed, filled with joy of creation.

Fritz also spoke of artist's exhibition at Museum of Modern Art—abstract, huge canvases. They get $6,000 for such a piece of work. One given a $10,000 grant from the Ford Foundation. He had to give them two pictures, grumbled he could have sold more. Such art is reflection of emptiness and despair of our day. Fritz is illustrating *The Possessed* with work which will endure, if war does not blot us out, through the ages. He advised our painting our house front and putting up a shrine.

June 25

Prayed especially last night for a priest since we had not had Mass for 20 days, and St. John the Baptist immediately came to our rescue. Father Koch showed up at 10 p.m.—who could expect a priest at that time in the country? Prayed the Mass, offered the Mass beautifully and clearly.

June 26. Montreal [retreat]

We are here to wash our hearts and minds and souls clear and free, so we can "put on Christ." Father Lesseur gave the first conference in French and I could not understand a great deal of it. Enough certainly to know that wherever he said Jesus, Father Brennan used Christ, or our Lord.[184]

---

184 In "Retreat," August 1959, Dorothy provided a long description of this retreat, sponsored by the Secular Fraternity of Charles of Jesus (Charles de Foucauld). "How far one's vocation will take one, is always a mystery, and where one's vocation will take one. But I believe it to be true that the foundations are always in poverty, manual labor, and in seeming failure. It is the pattern of the Cross, and in the Cross is joy of spirit."

June 27

Arose at 7:45, and now it is 4:30 and I am sitting on a long concrete and steel porch reaching the full length of this E-shaped seminary for late vocations which is used also for retreats. It is a completely still day, heavy and warm. The prairies stretch all around, mostly brought under cultivation. In the distance, trees, fields bordered by some trees.

The last conference was on Prayer, on practicing the presence of Jesus, finding him in the Eucharist, in the Gospel, in each other.

June 30

Tonight I began to worry about my coming "engagement" and to feel I am too old, presuming to try too much, inspired by pride to be a part of the Little Sisters in the secular institute. To keep up their practices—the two-hour adoration a day (for this retreat). The one hour other times. I keep the other religious practice pattern, Mass, Communion, Angelus, spiritual reading, and often half an hour of Adoration. Also Rosary and Compline.

Could not sleep until one, then awoke at 5. A beautiful sunrise. So wrote to Claude Gervais, saying how incapable I felt, that it was presumption and pride too which made me want to join the secular institute.

N.D. Meditation

It is a very close still day. Very silent. Only an occasional song of a bird. These days are very hard. I am so used to being the Martha. It is the 5th day of an eight day retreat and I have never made so long a one before. The silence, the not doing anything would not be so hard if it were not attended by so many small physical discomforts, such as glasses which do not fit properly, always sliding down one's nose. A pew in the chapel made for very short people and straight-backed. I am jackknifed into it. A too tight girdle, made more tight by my own slackness—due to lack of exercise. Too short and too tight stockings (a donation to the poor). Occasional hot flashes, even at my age, 61. Pains in the back, in hips, knees. All these contribute to tension. St. Teresa of Avila says one should be comfortable at prayer! The walls of the chapel are white and glaring and hard on the eyes. And here, among us eight, there is Dixie [MacMaster], a prisoner for many years in her bed, lying on a hard rented stretcher, wheeled in and out of the chapel, condemned to a life of immobility, a constant example to us of uncomplaining endurance, and sweetness and patience, and of rigorous intellectual life and life of hard work. Which adds to my shame, at my own lack of endurance. God forgive me. I am an unprofitable servant.

How dull as ditchwater I am. I would like to get out on a brisk walk. St. John of the Cross and St. Philip Neri used to take their groups out into beautiful wild places to meditate. Last night I did not sleep until after one, woke up at five. Chapel at 7:15. Prime, Angelus, Veni Creator. Breakfast 7:30.... Such is the day, every moment taken with silence, solitude, waiting for God to speak, and he is silent.

One hears often how retreats, revivals, do just that. But my long experience has been that they are hard work, a feat in endurance, persevering. Sticking it out, in blind, naked faith.

I believe that Jesus Christ, true God, true man, is here in the Eucharist, exposed on the altar. Body, soul, flesh and blood, humanity, divinity. He told me so. "I am with you always, even until the consummation of the world."

Under the form of bread and wine, for my nourishment, lest I faint by the way, his real presence. I am fainting always, yet I know I will endure this journey, some of it steeper, stiffer than others.

I have been reading *The Inn of the Sixth Happiness*, a paperback Mary Roberts gave me about a small woman [Gladys Aylward], a household worker, who went to China as a missionary and learned the language and trudged thru the hills and mountains alone, lived with muleteers and peasants and children and with her Bible.

July 5. Montreal

Mass at 8 with Madeline, and breakfast until 10. Then to [Benedict Joseph] Labre House to find a meeting waiting for me.

The house looks bright and gay in summer. It is only 2 rooms deep, two stories high, and it serves so many people and is such a meeting place. *Unity* holds all together with articles about liturgy, the interior life, and containing news of other movements in the Church. i.e. Abbé Pierre, Emmaus, retreats, Little Brothers of Charles de Foucauld, pilgrimages, life at the house—a paper for the Christian Life, well written, well balanced.

July 6

Started early, 6 a.m. to leave Montreal. Received Communion at 7 at church near the Little Sisters and St. Benedict Joseph Labre House. We got to Tamar and Dave's at supper time and she had fried chicken, string beans, all from garden. The boys brought a trout for breakfast.

July 7

Today I should have gone to doctor for my shot, but forgot medicine. I feel so much better—it is unbelievable. Last time I was here I was enjoying the children and their agility and this time I feel active again myself. David has received an offer of $13,000 cash for the house on Staten Island and wants to hold out for $15,000. Tamar wants to sell. It makes for contention.

I have finished *Inn of the Sixth Happiness*, a wonderful story.

## July 9

Went to doctor today and got my shot of B-12 with Tamar, then to Ludlow for feed for the chicks. Tamar estimates it costs $50 to fatten the 150 chickens before she kills them all and puts them in the deep freeze.

David works very hard out in the garden—the sun too hot these days too. His mother seems quite content. She is a very inarticulate person—except very conventional things like her desire for David to get a job in Washington to be near her.

## July 11

A sad and angry letter from Marion Shindell, pointing out my failures and my "unapproachability." How I need to make a new start. Love and poverty.

## July 14

I have been getting some writing done on the Retreat book since reading [J.D.] Salinger's latest story—a strange technique of starting and stopping.

## July 31

The fire department and health department after us again. The deed is being transferred to Beth [Rogers'] name. I wrote my will Thursday—Marge and Paula witnesses.

## August 1

To [Fellowship House] to speak and there were only a dozen there, not too interested.

Tamar and Dave have sold their Staten Island house. Also Mrs. Hennessy is leaving next week. Girls are there.

## August 5

After dinner I met Ammon at 5th Avenue playhouse to see "Modern Times." He started his fast today. Hard to sleep in town, what with traffic, gas fumes, all night.

August 6. Transfiguration. Press

Met Deane at 9 o'clock Mass at Old St. Patrick's and we breakfasted together. Got to printers at 11 and Beth was already there. Some argument with Bob over his idea of a cell on the loft, and over Stanley's poem, and Ammon's review. I so dislike being put in position of censor. But, in general, the day went well.

August 7

Signed over farm to Beth [Rogers] today. Now the headaches of answering summonses and making repairs is hers. She is 25 years younger and can take it, thank God.

August 8

Spent last night with Sister Peter Claver, at her sister Agnes' apartment on Waverly Place. We walked past the jail to go the bakery and prayed for the 590 women there.

In the afternoon I went to the office where everyone was happily mailing out the paper. Only Larry and Jim Callanan were both drunk. A.J. Muste came to talk of Art Harvey to Ammon. Ammon likes Art because he is an individualist anarchist and hates organized religion, and because he fasts with him. But Ammon is being paid back because Hugh [Madden] is going in to picket with him on Monday.

August 10

Don [Luigi] Sturzo died yesterday and there were columns in the *Times*. I am writing about this great man for the next issue.

Bob Ludlow said he was greatest Christian sociologist. There will be much written about him. *Cross Currents* will write an appreciation of him and of course many others. How I wish I had been more faithful keeping a diary to write about such a man. Someone said he reminded them of the noble priest in Silone's *Bread and Wine*, but he never retired. He met each duty as it came, fearless, outspoken, understanding, trying to give guidance in the world of men. He was not one who thought in terms of how many "souls" there were in his parish. He thought of their needs, the kind of society suited to man and his freedom. I hope others will go and find out what kind of a village was his in Sicily, how the people lived—worked—how he came to take part in public affairs, start a cooperative etc.

He looked like that famous picture of Cardinal Newman, sitting, frail, dignified, scholarly, with noble, austere profile. Did Danilo Dolci know this valiant man? Really know him with his heart and mind? Peter first told us of his work, of his writing—and when I mentioned his book *Italy and Fascismo* at a college talk I gave, I was labeled a Communist sympathizer, because I was opposing Mussolini and his program. Then as now, Catholic students were on the side of anyone opposing Communism. They could not conceive of a third course—it was either-or, Hitler or Stalin, Mussolini or Stalin, fight fire with fire.

Tuesday, August 11
*Liberation* [magazine] 6 p.m. about Khrushchev's visit. Bayard [Rustin] and A.J. Muste. The *Liberation* talks were all about mass action and I was not inspired, nor particularly in sympathy. Roy Finch, Dave McReynolds, Dave Dellinger, A.J., Bayard and various others including 2 women. Hugh [Madden] is Ammon's shadow, following him two or three feet behind, barefooted, bedraggled, and thin. At noon he kneels on the pavement and pounds his bare knuckles while reciting the Angelus. Sleeps at loft and wakes others at 6 by pulling their toes.

Thursday, August 13
Hugh has been picketing daily, two or three feet behind Ammon, kneeling on the pavement for Angelus, pounding his knuckles bloody, asking people on the street for money to buy coffee, otherwise fasting. Wanting everyone to take a vow of chastity, wanting to organize a rickshaw business in Central Park, etc.
His record is of 20 years at sea and 2 years in the Trappists or vice versa. Ammon is very patient. He said if it were not for Hugh, it might be five others worse. Cut off the head of one tyrant and then others grow in its place. Just the same, when asked by Hugh, Ammon said he did not want him to go over the fence with him at Omaha [missile base].

Sunday, August 30
Russian Mass at 10:30. A long quiet p.m. talking to Bronnie Warsaskas. His name is originally Bronnuis. Jonas came in with him from the Lithuanian Church near the Holland Tunnel. They sat at lunch raving about their Lithuanian sour rye, which Bronnie said his mother used to fry in butter for them for breakfast. He is a real craftsman, a lover of Eric Gill and Peter Maurin, most of whose book he typed out to carry with him since it is out of print.
One can scarcely count the things he has done for us while here this summer—putting up banisters, handrails, replacing all our broken windows with plastic glass, putting up floor and framework for tents for the kids camping over the weekend. He is a furniture finisher and knows woods and how

to handle them. He can cane chairs and transform old desks and pianos, etc. into things of beauty. He talks about "caressing" the wood. It made me think of Father Menasce who wrote once that Americans were obsessed by sex because they found no outlet for creative impulse in their work. A strong man, forced into celibacy by the death of a loved wife, pours himself into his work.

Monday, September 7
    4:30 recording—television—[Mike] Wallace program.

Tuesday, September 8
    Mass at 9 and a funeral Mass after. Mike Wallace's office called. Has to be done over again.

Sunday, September 13
    Henry Street was crowded—sidewalks jammed. Demolished houses and new projects all around. It was a beautiful day and everyone was out. Many drug pushers in neighborhood, Paula said. Her purse was so heavy I suddenly thought she either had it full of silver or was carrying a gun. Up to Della's for supper—Franklin morose, but cheered up talking about Haiti and his painting trip there. Marge called. Forster in to see me—said doctors disagreeing—perhaps not so serious. Perhaps an operation on Thursday.

Tuesday, September 15
    To Tamar's. Bus left at 7 and I arrived at 3. I can always sleep on a bus, the smooth driving has a hypnotic affect. Tamar very worried about Dave, his physical and mental health.... . My heart aches for him and for her.

Thursday, Sept 17
    To dentist at 12:30 and got wisdom tooth pulled. David got 5 out—very hard. He was most miserable at the end of the day. Could eat nothing, though we had chicken for supper. My pain was gone in an hour or two, but he is worse.

Friday, September 18
    When Dave and Tamar went to pick up Mel at Springfield, the boys brought in the cow and wood. They have had to do all the work Dave normally does. Little Hilaire valiantly carries logs as big as himself and dumps them in a long, neat row in the kitchen for the boys to bring downstairs to the cellar.

Saturday, September 19

Arose at 8—David's jaw worse and Tamar with heavy pain in her chest. We did too much yesterday in the house and garden. Digging potatoes, washing, cooking.

So much sorrow, sickness, homelessness in this country. Three dams being built around Springfield and many homes destroyed. We are bearing a little of the troubles of the world which we escaped during the war.

Monday, September 28

Hectic day. Noonday Mass at Holy Crucifix and to office and weeks' accumulation of mail—blew top because Judy [Gregory] could not handle Helen Wing.[185] If they know I am in town, difficult situations are saved for me. "They insist on seeing you." Reminded me of, "What makes Sammy run?" Always see the man at the top! With a little tact and friendliness they could find out what is needed, how they could help—Deane, Judy, and Pat [Rusk]. The latter useless around the office, very willful. Bob says Deane and Pat are the most argumentative women he ever met—disagreeable. They always disagree with him, Deane identifying herself with me, and Pat on her own. How long, O Lord, how long? How I hate factionalism. I am for Peter. I am for Paul, or Apollo, or Dorothy!

*In* The Long Loneliness *Dorothy described the circumstances of her parting from Tamar's father, Forster Batterham, after her conversion in 1927. Three years after their separation, Forster had found a new companion, Nanette, with whom he lived for the next thirty years. Yet he and Dorothy continued to see each other from time to time, and she had occasional news of him through Tamar. In September 1959 Nanette contacted Dorothy to say that she was dying of cancer. Dorothy had a reputation for caring for other people; would she care for her? At once, Dorothy responded to this plea.*

*Forster and Nanette were living in a bungalow on Staten Island, near Peter Maurin Farm. There, along with Lily Burke, Forster's sister, Dorothy faithfully accompanied Nanette during her final months. It was, she conceded, an unusual arrangement, but everyone took it in stride. Before her death in January 1960, Nanette asked to be baptized.*

*Dorothy never wrote publicly about this story.*

---

185 In "On Pilgrimage," September 1959, Dorothy relates the story of Mrs. Wing and her troubles, so typical of the destitute in the City.

Tuesday, September 29
Forster and Nanette have moved to another bungalow. Lily [Burke] is spending the night with me here [Peter Maurin Farm].

Wednesday, September 30. St. Jerome
Very rough seas. 70°. Most hectic day. Lily stayed overnight. So no quiet hour in a.m. Slept until 7:30. Breakfast at Nanette's. Then Lily and I to shop at A&P. She went into town. Then to visit Nanette for an hour.

Thursday, October 8th
Lily came down tonight. She is so devoted to Forster, such a creature of duty, loving to serve, to be of use. It is good we are having such weather so she can have a dip in the water each day. She is working for some firm that ships books to Communist China 4 days a week, half time, and gets two dollars an hour. Also she does volunteer work for the Marxist library. She is convinced we will have a socialist society and is devoted to her cause. I do not speak of religion to her, nor to Nanette, though I did once have time alone with her to talk of my mother's death, how beautiful it was.

These are such days of quiet, of waiting, and it may be 2 months as the doctor said, or a year, who knows the days of man? A lovely letter from Helene Iswolsky telling how at the end, her brother welcomed the priest. She too agrees I should just be here, praying. I do not do enough of that—so many distractions. Some days I get many letters done, but no regular writing.

Friday, October 9
Swimming still. Sent ms. [*Therese*] to Fides. Since I stayed up last night reading Lily's book, *To Make Accord*, until 2, I felt not up to much today. Much time is taken up just being with them: Nanette, Forster, and Lily. Very beautiful fall days—no letters done. No writing.

Saturday, October 10
How hard it is to be faithful even to the smallest rule. I left the beach at 2:30 and had time to rest at the apartment. I was short with Deane—regretted it after. It is hard to be always pushing someone off. We made our hour in the chapel and went to bed at 9:30.

Tuesday, October 13
Much colder today and it was hard to work. How time is frittered away. I finished one baptismal robe for Mary and Roger [O'Neil's] baby. Now I work on one for Sheila [Dugan]. Also knitting. Nanette's nurse comes at 11. We get

up at 8—breakfast, dishes, a little talk; Forster hears the news, and reads the news sometimes aloud.

## Wednesday, October 14

What with late breakfast—the morning goes. To the doctor's, which took from 4 to 6:30. Dining at Evelyn's and more talk. Bed at 9:30, the day is gone. I should be writing review of Danilo Dolci's document. Silone and [Carlo] Levi have done it much better. Pseudo-scientific—unemotional, unsentimental, but it is loaded. His bitterness and lack of understanding of religion shows all through. No Gandhian spirit. I hate to write a review which is critical. "If I believed the world were going to end tomorrow I would still plant a tree today."—Luther.

## Friday, October 16

Office all day—letters. To Della's for supper, and she and Franklin are getting nicely settled and she is enjoying shopping around for secondhand books. Fritz Eichenberg called and we met at Grand Central and talked till ten. He has finished illustrating *The Possessed*. Franklin said his illustrations for *Crime and Punishment* and *Brothers Karamazov* are having top billing. He gets so little pay—no royalties, just outright pay. Publishers are terrible.

## Sunday, October 18

Father Riordan's communion breakfast at nine at St. Vincent's Hospital on Staten Island. Arose at 6:30 in town, took ferry, and bus and arrived at 8:45. Met good doctors, a score, good response. Father Faley is very feeble—very thin, his black eyes staring out of a very thin face—never complains, only speaks of discomfort. But he shifts his position constantly and is under morphine all of the time now, every four hours.

## Monday, October 19

Lily went into town at 3 and I came down to the beach at 7, driven by Jean Walsh last night. Forster awakened me early, weeping that Nanette could not get up, so I rushed down. She was dizzy, felt bilious, could eat nothing. When the nurse came she told her to drink more liquids, but she tried eating some soup. I wrote letters all morning, after breakfast and dishes.

## Tuesday, October 20

Up at 6. Read until 7:30, then to Nanette's to see Lily off to work. She came down last night, sat up until 12 with F, playing scrabble. Then today her 2-hour commute to New York to begin her job at 10. And she is 70. I am ashamed of my lack of vigor. I made breakfast and Nanette said she felt better and ate a little. Dishes, and I wrote letters until the nurse came at 12.

Letter from Ammon via Father Casey asking messages be sent to Vivian, telling her how he missed her. Also declining to study Church history and protesting Mariology. Expects no change in Church. I wish he would read lives of heroes of Church. He is one on the natural level.

### Thursday, October 22

Last night I could not get to sleep. I had stayed up until midnight, working, reading, and said the Rosary looking out the window at the heavy swells crashing up on the shore. It was four before I got to sleep, and at seven awoke. Whether or not to go away, to go on to Tamar, to make my trip now—what to do, preoccupied me. How much presumption there is in my attitude of trying to be with Nanette, giving in to F's clinging attitude.

### October 22. Friday

This a.m. Nanette said, "Since I have so little time to live, I must get out a little."

Lily came down at 3:30 and I went into town to go over mail, etc.

David called that Tamar had been in the hospital, gall bladder, appendicitis, they did not know. Anyway, they did not operate, and after tests she came home Wed.

Thurs, the offer of a bridge tender's job, but crazy hours—7-3, 3-11, 11-7 stuff, disrupting home life. Besides he could not drive, no one goes to work that way, etc. Sat. Tamar drove the children to catechism in the rain. So they have had a hard time. Flu also has weakened her. She has had a hard time this summer.

### October 23. Sat.

Worrying so much about Tamar and David and their attitudes.....

I know they are both worried about jobs and the sale of the house, etc., so there is that tension.

Two very good things. 1) At least D and T are suffering, not complacent and content. They see each other's faults and are solidly Catholic so they'll stick together and work it out. 2) The children being so many take care of each other, and of themselves. They are never at a loss for something to do, since there is so much work they value their free time and enjoy it.

Today learned David had called from Perkinsville that Tamar had been in the hospital, so decided to go tomorrow. Pouring rain in the city tonight.

F weeps over N's state—"Why did it have to be her?" he protests—like a child, "It isn't fair." They have been together since 1929, 30 years, and she is like a child, mentally, serving him, housekeeping, shopping, intent on his every move, but keeping him very much at her level, a completely physical one, spectators and commentators, hedonists. And now life and suffering have caught up with them. My heart is wrung for them, for I cannot help but see clearly his cowardice in his clinging to Lily and me. One would think he is taking up where he left off with me, or rather that I had always been with him, as Lily has. I am part of him. Selfish and cowardly as he is.

Sunday, October 24. Perkinsville

An exhausting trip from 8:30—12 hours—and when we got there no beds made up, no meal made, no house cleaned, a demoralized household.... On the one hand I can see all their faults ... And yet my job in life is to see Christ in them, serve Christ in them, love Him in them, love them to folly. Nevertheless, I urged David on to job hunting (he has been trying) and lent them $450 which they will repay when the Staten Island house is sold.

October 25

Forster was reading aloud to Nanette this morning while I did the dishes all about Asheville, North Carolina, which is his home town, and I listened with interest to the story of the weaving done in the big industry set up there by the Vanderbilts originally.

He told us also of how he convinced his family that religion was unreasonable—I can see him as a sixteen-year-old, the only son of the family, arguing passionately against hypocrisy and ritual, and convention and organized religion. They used to spend all their weekends on the mountains around Asheville, going on hiking and camping trips. Later they bought land and built a cabin at the foot of one of the mountains and lived there summers. They knew the family of Thomas Wolfe, and lived down the street from them, and Forster roomed with Fred at Georgia Tech the years he spent there. "He was a wild one and I could not keep up with him," Forster said. "The sister sang in a cabaret. They were very ordinary people, really, but everything they did seemed wild to the neighbors."

To me Thomas Wolfe is like a Niagara of words and is filled with great vitality and love of life. Since I am spending all these days again with the Batterhams, it will be interesting to read the series of Thomas Wolfe, beginning with *Look Homeward Angel* and going on through the others which, though they seem to deal with different heroes, are all really autobiographical in a sense.

I was reading parts of *The Idiot* again, those parts about Hypolite and his fierce rebellion against death. Wolfe too has a series of stories about death in a paperback edition which I once had. Perhaps it is still in the library.

## Monday, October 26

Men want maidservants—want to settle with another in isolation, many of them. What to do, be submissive? Give in to selfishness? We need to make a study of the Martin family [*family of St. Therese of Lisieux*] and their activities.

## Thursday, October 29

Finished copy for paper and mailed it in special delivery later tonight. Visit from Ed Lahy, pilgrim to Washington, very intent on his interior life and naively wondering why people do not appreciate it when he says he will pray for them at shrine of Immaculate Conception at its dedication. Only 22 and a fine attractive fellow, junior at Holy Cross. We gathered wood on the beach, he and Johannah, and I discussed a philosophy of work, manual work, and its necessity. He kept holding to the primacy of the spiritual, and necessity of someone's praying, and I tried to emphasize man's duty to earn his living. Fasting would make it easy—minimum amount needed for food, but he refused to get my point and held up St. Benedict Joseph Labre as a model while he tucked away bread, cheese, and sausage with a healthy boy's appetite, upholding that it was work to beg.

## Friday, October 30

Lily down tonight and we played Scrabble, and Lily insisted on doing the meal and dishes. Stanley brought my radio, mail. I got in an hour of reading in the early morning and most of the Office during day, but I am constantly on call. Certainly it is hard to go without daily Mass.

## Saturday, October 31

Staying in bed this a.m. trying to shake the cold. Sick in the night—vomiting. Meals simple enough, soup and a kipper for supper and cereal before bed time. One never realizes how disturbed one is by the tragedies bearing down on one, like family troubles, Marge's, Nanette's, how tormented people are.

Hugh Madden came down from Spring Street to see about renting the store for breadline. I said Bowery, but not Spring Street. He was angry and said he would get the hell out then. He is another [Steve] Hergenhan, wanting to throw this and that one out. I felt too sick to talk to him and so failed again.

Impatience—a refusal of suffering, my own particular kind that goes with the work.

### Sunday, November 1. All Saints Day

A beautiful day on the beach. Mass at 11, lunch with Lily, Forster and Nanette and bus at 5. Rosary and Benediction at Old St. Pat's, and Deane came over to the apartment for coffee and bread and cheese. She is in a heavy mood. As soon as I got in, Beth called about George Clements's body being found in the woods off Woodron Road. He was always like a dried-up little gnome with his hunched back. He had been missing since last March and when found was just a dried-up little skeleton which fell apart when moved. A 12-year-old boy found him.[186]

### Monday, November 2

Press. High Mass at 8 at old St. Patrick's. Much overset and I'm not too happy with my contributions to the paper this month. Sense of pressure after visiting Tamar and trying to write Danilo Dolci review. I always have to do much correcting on proof sheets. Supper at Della's where all was peaceful. Did not go to office at all, Deane in a mood. Wrote a long meditation.

### Tuesday, November 3

Bob drove me down with typewriter and electric heater and we went to farm first. All we hear on radio is news of [Charles] Van Doren's confession and television deceit.[187] We had dinner at Evelyn Olwell's and constant discussion. Nanette loves Evelyn, probably as her only real woman friend. Lily was commenting that Nanette never had a single woman friend all her life. Charles Butterworth's illness. He says it may be his heart. He is preoccupied with it because of his desire to serve.

### Wednesday, November 4

Cloudy—mild. I woke at 6:30 and have an hour of prayer and reading before going over to Forster and Nanette's for breakfast. Usually they have everything ready, but it is company they want, and the radio and newscasts,

---

186 In "On Pilgrimage," December 1959, Dorothy described the death of this long-time, yet reclusive member of the CW family: "I cannot remember whether it was fifteen or twenty years he was with us, getting older, quieter, more bent than ever… It was a grave shock to us all to find that George had wandered off like a sick animal to die, covered over with leaves, hidden from the road, merging with the earth, overlooked by the mushroom hunters who scour the woods spring and fall, and finally found by a schoolboy playing in the woods one Sunday afternoon."

187 Van Doren, scion of a distinguished literary family, was the focus of a quiz show scandal.

plus my presence begins their day for them. But these last few days there are indications that they are not so afraid to be alone together to face death: it is a terrible thing to hear him say, "She will drive everyone away with her temper and then we will be left alone together to sit looking at each other."

## Thursday, November 5

I left right after breakfast to go to the city and it was a leisurely trip to 23rd St. to the Bernard Baruch School of Business at City College. They reacted with hostility to both pacifism and our ideas of non-violent resistance.

## Friday, November 6

This morning at ten George Clements was buried in our CW plot in St. Joseph's cemetery over in Rossville and there was a beautiful requiem Mass with the absolution in English and the epistle and Gospel also. Father blessed the grave after the Mass, and there was a good group there.

It was good to see Julia Porcelli's stone for Catherine Odlivak, with its Madonna and child carved, then painted, and the green vine on one side. We talked with Mr. McGinley, the undertaker, of bringing Peter [Maurin's] body to rest there in our own plot, and he will start proceedings at once. It costs $100 to open the grave and $225 for the funeral. It will cost much more, twice as much to bring Peter here. But I am so happy it is underway.

## Saturday, November 7

All last night it rained and it was very cold. Lily said she had not been able to sleep at all, on that porch at Nanette's, so tonight she came here to sleep, and we talked a long time. She spoke to me of this affair Nanette had had, and Forster had countenanced, with a younger man, who lived with them here on the beach and moved with them to Florida. It is all part of his absolute rebellion against responsibility, family, religion, tradition, as far as he himself is concerned.

He is completely selfish and a coward, Lily herself says, but she loves him dearly and never leaves him, she says, without feeling guilty. We talked of religion and death. I ended the evening playing Scrabble with Lily and Forster, while Nanette lay there on her couch, in the deepest sadness.

## Sunday, November 8

62 years old today. Presents—mushroom book from Stanley; stockings from Forster and Nanette; knitted hat from Lily; snuggies and candy from farm. Austin came down with ice cream and cake.

I had dinner with Forster and Nanette and Lily and it was the only meal all day what with superabundance of cake and pie. Nanette made a California fruit pie, 5 fruits, very delicious. She is a dainty and adept cook. Lily finds herself calling her Tamar.

I told her I was going to hang a St. Teresa medal on her and she does not object. She was more cheerful today. I was invited to Eileen Egan's for dinner, but did not go. Agnes Boulton O'Neill Kaufman telephoned last night. Wanted to drive by today but did not. Gray day.

Monday, November 9
Tonight Evelyn and I went to novena and afterwards to the farm to get the St. Teresa relic for Nanette.

Wednesday, November 11
Forster went to St. George for bandages and Nanette in a foul mood. Letters in morning. Stanley brought down encyclopedias and a quiet evening spent with them while I read about Algeria and Tibet.

Thursday, November 12
Arose at 6:30. Read Lauds and Cassian and *Imitation [of Christ]*. Letters after an 8:30 breakfast with Forster and Nanette. Very distracted by news and talk. Nanette very animated.

Stanley and I went into New York. New York University, Thomas More Club of law students, where we had a dinner meeting. Very good group, at least polite, but I wonder how much they understood. Anyway they wish future meetings to discuss poverty, pacifism, and punishment (abolition of capital punishment).

Friday, November 13
Thinking of answers to [Mike] Wallace questions in television interview as to why not follow the "pleasure principle" rather than the cross. I said "On the natural plane, the seed must fall into the ground and die or it remains alone. It is the law of growth. It is also the law of love, which always brings suffering." I should also have said, "We are born into this world in suffering—crying out—and we are in the process of being born into the next life—we are already living in eternity, we have begun to live the life of grace."

When we talk of the joy of suffering—"in the Cross is the joy of spirit" (*Imitation* Book 3 chapter 12)—we are accused of being "necrophiliacs," as Harry Sylvester called me, when he did not like John McKeon's review of his book, *The Golden Boy*. A priest also who reviewed my book insinuated that there was something morbid in my love for the poor.

Strange criticisms. Other jibes—when Bob drove the city car to the baptism, the godmother said, "I thought you were doing without cars." When after waiting from 6 to 12 to break my fast, I said I was starving, Anne Marie spoke out, "I thought from your article about the Carthusians you were going to begin a fast." And she began talking about her hunger during the occupation of Paris. Emily, when she came to live with us, was much disillusioned. "When you quote the early Fathers 'the coat which hangs in your closet belongs to the poor,' I thought you lived in beautiful poverty and simplicity, and you certainly have more than one coat and dress." The other day after a conversation during which I chattered to a friend she gave me a reminder of St. James' epistle on the dangers of the tongue, and I realized I had been complaining. "Whenever one goes out amongst men, he returneth less of a man." (*Imitation*)

Saturday, November 14
Confession. Rainy but warm. I drove Nanette shopping and she is not strong. Lily is here so I was free to read *The White Fathers* by Glenn Kittler. A fascinating book. Martyrdoms still going on in Africa.

Monday, November 16
Holy Cross High School, Flushing. Mass at 8 and breakfast with Deane. Too much talk. She reminded me of St. James—the tongue is a danger. Thank goodness on the beach there is less chance to talk. A long trip to Flushing—then a bus to the high school and I arrived in time for 40 minutes in chapel. Swank school. Boys indifferent. Brother John Joseph confessed himself mortified, but probably blames me for not inspiring them. I was reminded of the girl who died of cancer to whom I sent Father Jerome Murphy, who saved her soul. Her husband, a fellow traveler. The nuns an obstacle, talking of his "intellectual obstacles" and calling Father Jerome "unintellectual."

From 3 to 6 traveling to beach and found Forster had left Nanette alone again. When Lily and I are gone, he goes too. He cannot be alone with her. Or it was blackmail to make her stay with them.

Tuesday, November 17
A hard day. Forster did not leave her side all day. The workmen are busy putting in hot water.

Wednesday, November 18
Charles and Beth down. Charles will have to have an operation, perhaps, on his heart.

Friday, November 20

Forster walked to Great Kills for the paper and home along the beach. Dug space in garden for chrysanthemums, gathered wood on the beach. News today of 6 more mothers, 2 killed, 4 injured by teenage drivers at 60 miles an hour, one of the boys killed. Another tragedy, a whole family wiped out by two boys in stolen car. It makes me happy to give up use of cars; aside from driving Nanette twice a week, a dying woman's need, I do not take the car out at all. Oh yes, I did take the children to confession last Saturday—a most rainy night.

Saturday, November 21

This week I have been returning to the Prayer of Jesus which is the only possible one under the circumstances and which enables me to pray while I am with her while conversation, radio, discussion of day's news is going on. Even at night—trying to say the Rosary with the proper intentions, by the fire, I could not get through three decades without interruption. Settled quietly in one place, one is available, one cannot get away as in the city. It is good, more natural too.

Monday, November 23

To town, and a dull day. Smog and damp. Police had been in because of mob of hungry ones at the door whom Hugh had locked out.[188] Judy was busy at mail—Deane at telephone. Much fatigue from overweight and too much clothes. Much walking. Said Jesus Prayer all the way to town.

November 23

Fr. Russell. St. Patrick's, S.I. Too soft a voice. Such very bad delivery, such mumbled words, jumbled up, that he is very difficult to listen to. Very technical theologically—hard for the men who sit politely, quietly—God bless them.

*Providential love of God...* His voice wanders off, trails away. He mutters, laughs, uses slang in paraphrasing story of St. Francis. So much good wasted.

---

188 "As usual, the works of mercy become dangerous. One night, the food being exhausted and all fed that the loft could hold, Hugh Madden, our rancher-seaman, locked the doors downstairs, whereupon a crowd formed of those who were still coming. One of the neighbors called the police, and the squad car pulled up, and more people gathered. It is always hard to explain what we are doing. Why should individuals feed the hungry? Why are we not under the shelter of the Catholic charities? Are we an approved group? Have we a license to run a dining room?" (December 1959)

Whatever I do of myself is bad and fails. When I invite anyone to speak in town, Bob has already invited someone else better. Once even when we could not call off conference we had a double header…

I have ceased to try to listen, it is so irritating, I can only think, at any rate we are sitting in presence of Blessed Sacrament. Patience, patience, which means suffering.

"Blessed be this God! Here were servants of His that trusted in him, and defied a king's edict, ready to put their lives in peril so they might be free men, worshiping no God but their own."

We might say this in regard to the NY state edict. We will not worship that god which is a god of war. We will not endure that our God, our loving Father, be used so. This false god is not the God we worship, but a God of peace and light and truth and love. We are not, it is true, putting our lives in peril, but we are ready to risk our freedom, which is more precious than life. (It would be ungrateful to God, who bestowed it unless we regarded it so.)

Tuesday, November 24

To Forster and Nanette from 8:30 to 11:30. I wrote letters part of the time. The nurse came and left to work at my desk. Back from 5 to 8 and Nanette said she hated to see me go. We have so little to talk about it is hard to be there, but Lily is bearing the greatest burden from Friday night to Monday.

Wednesday, November 25

Nanette has been having a very hard time—not only pressure, but pain all through her. She lay there and cried pitifully today. There is so little one can do, except just be there and say nothing. I tried to talk to her—telling her the history of Ammon to distract her. I told her how hard it was to comfort her, one could only keep silence in the face of suffering, and she said bitterly, "Yes, the silence of death." I told her I would pray the Rosary for her.

Thanksgiving, Thursday, November 26

We went to the office to see Karl Meyer who was just released from federal prison in Pennsylvania. He had served four and a half months.

Friday, November 27

Wrote my article today. Went to Della's at 5 and left at 7:30 to get to meeting. Carmen Mathews there and she will read to us some Friday evenings around Christmas. Maybe the Christmas in *War and Peace,* maybe a Tolstoy story—"Where Love is, God is." A real crowd, and we always have room, thank God.

Sunday, November 29

Association Charles de Foucauld. Epiphany parish. We studied the constitutions of the lay fraternity Association Charles de Foucauld, and made our Holy Hour.

Monday, November 30

Still cold. Mass 8:30. Went through mail and then to the Island, going first to Great Kills where I got a record player for $20 for my French lessons, not to say symphonies also. Stanley brought down the 9th Beethoven, but it was very scratchy. The French lessons really are something—a great help to hear the sounds. Then with the Jerusalem Bible and daily readings and some attempt to translate, perhaps I'll get somewhere. What with Father Boylan speaking about bringing Jesus to Nanette by daily Communion, I am going to use the car for Mass. Aside from using it for Nanette I have not used it for 2 months. There are daily accidents with many deaths, what with teenage drivers.

Wednesday, December 2

Mass this morning at 9. Jonas down, Stanley. Between Stanley and Forster, great rivalry over making and keeping up fires. Smoked all day, chimney askew.

Monday, December 7

Very much disturbed about David's condition and am going to Perkinsville tomorrow to see them all.

Saturday, December 12

All day in bed with nausea, some flu bug as everyone says. Tamar says they all had it on Thanksgiving Day. As long as I lay still I was alright. I read *Mansfield Park* with great enjoyment and started *Sense and Sensibility*.

Sunday, December 13

Laetare Sunday and an improvement in dialogue Mass at St. Mary's Springfield. The nuns are too brisk, Confiteor too fast. But definitely you can hear low voices joining in. The priest says Mass perfectly.

Pat says, "Everyone at the office says, 'Dorothy, Dorothy, Dorothy and you can't do anything.'" I tried to comfort her by saying they use my name as a club. "Dorothy won't like it," meaning they do not want to decide. She said spitefully, "I used to think so too, but I wonder." Pin pricks.

## Monday, December 14

Judy [Gregory][189] said, "It is a pity Bob will not spread out the jobs this way. He tries to do everything himself. We get along so well while he is away." Bob is visiting a friend at Fort Detrick and picketing or rather "vigiling" there. There had been another scene with Gurdotti over a drunk barging into his undertaking parlor during a wake. "At least you might keep a man at your door to keep the bums moving," Gurdotti said. I had told Bob to do this, but he disregards it—willful. Power corrupts.

## Tuesday, December 15

Today I was sitting at Nanette's writing letters while Forster was in St. George doing some errands. Looking up every now and then to gaze out at the water, I suddenly saw Anne Marie [Stokes] and a priest, soutane flapping, beret, gestures and all, walking along the edge of the sea, conversing—walking five steps, stopping to talk, walking a few more. It was Abbé Alfred Berangeus from Algeria in exile, sentenced to 10 years in absentia because he had ordered a Colonel in the French army to repent or leave the Church, because he had ordered 80 hostages shot as a reprisal for the death of one French soldier. He is on his way to Mexico, having just visited the Pope. He stayed for supper.

## Saturday, December 19

Visits during month—from father and son of the little family which lost the young mother with cancer. They came to me before her death all of them and told me and the little girl looked at me and said, "My mother is going to heaven." What courage. What faith and hope. To be facing that great moment in our lives which is sure to come. We are all under sentence of death, and it may be "sooner than we think." Though the *Catholic Digest* this month carries an article from *MacLean's* reprinted on how scientists are beginning to believe that life can eventually be prolonged to 200 years. Certainly the desert fathers lived into the nineties and hundreds, and the Trappists do to this day. But that is the disciplined life. Giving up their lives they save them.

---

189 Judith Gregory was a Radcliffe graduate and a dedicated editor. "When Judy is in the city working at St. Joseph's House, she keeps her nose buried in desk work. She sits there answering the mail, sending out papers, and filing orders for books and pamphlets—and carrying on the most heated discussions on anything from politics to religion with any of the college crowd who happen to drop in." (*LF,* 148)

Wednesday, December 23

Nanette very bad, suffering from nurse's ministrations, her three-way irrigations. Nanette says she is continually wet, flowing from colostomy. She cried pitifully, hating her decay, wishing she could commit suicide, go back to the hospital for a few days, etc. It was a hard day, though we started out well making mince pie, etc—anything to distract her. I did as many letters as I could, and prayed, since there was nothing I could say to distract her, or help her.

Thursday, December 24

Caroling at Women's Prison. 19°. Russian choir. Stayed on Island. "The Savior of the world shall rise like the sun, and come down into the Virgin's womb like a shower upon the grass, alleluia."

Afternoon, Nanette not so good. Called doctor about going to hospital.

Friday, December 25

Carmen Mathews reading. It was so wonderful to wake before light and watch the dawn break while I read Matins, Lauds, and Prime for the day. What with some quiet yesterday the house was neat, it was not cold. Stanley had gone to midnight Mass and awoke long enough to tell me as many as 75 had been caroling the second stop.

I went to the 9 o'clock with Tom Olwell, a good sermon for the children, shopping for baby foods after. When I got back, Nanette in a turmoil and Forster very disturbed. Her legs, even her face is swollen on one side and she is very weak. Lily got down at three and Pat [Rusk] drove down to take me in, but I am still hoarse with cold and it is very bad under foot. So I will stay down and work on my copy for the January issue.

Called Tamar and she and the children all well, but Dave is not well at all.

Saturday, December 26

Lily did not come until 12:30 last night—Forster doing his best to keep her and Nanette frightened at the thought he was afraid she was dying. I get so impatient at him and his constant fleeing from her, his self-pity, his weeping that I feel hard and must fight to overcome it. Such fear of sickness and death. I think it was Father Faber who said, "Do not add one straw to the burden another is carrying."

I do not pray enough. As soon as I remember to meet this with prayer, it is better. Lying in bed with a cold today I was constantly visited by Forster and then by Bob and Bronnie complaining of Hugh and Keith and their madness. Bob came to me to say I was the only one Hugh would listen to, evidently wanting me to throw him out. Mr. Minas used to say "When everything goes wrong in the house, look to yourself—how have you contributed to it, brought it on? What can't be cured must be endured," which goes for me too.

## Sunday, December 27

Mass at 12. Nanette is very low—face swollen on one side badly. Also legs. She is very fearful. Lily standing by. I came in to New York and spent afternoon with Della, Forster hanging pictures, fixing table.

Right after supper I came back to Cleveland Place apartment. Coughing all night. Much fog and rain. We never talk of ourselves. I was thinking of my conversation with Forster. We talk about Nanette and her condition, and of the news of the day. When he talks about her, he weeps and I feel as though I were bolstering him up, urging him on to courage and perseverance. When he reads aloud to us from the *Times* he is calm. She will no longer let him turn on the radio to listen to the news.

She is in a way hostile to everything he loves—flowers, plants, birds, the sea, and now she can no longer share his interest in the news. She is concentrated on a fight with death, a struggle, day to day, for life. She longs for it to end, but she says herself—"I am strong-willed and stubborn. No one can help me, doctor, psychiatrist, hypnotism, drugs. I am alone. No one knows." We are all Job's comforters—no one knows another's pain. Forster feels this too. We must not add one straw to the burden on the one hand, and yet on the other, we must be like surgeons, cutting out ruthlessly what they want, whether it be cars, drink, or drugs.

Food, warmth, shelter, clothing, beauty, yes—ourselves most of all—to be available to men. But in the CW there are so many, and each one wants it all, your time, your love, your attention. "You are never here." This is my suffering, my failure, and my cross.

Rejoice.

## Monday, December 28

Cleveland Place. Try to be quiet. Visits from Deane, Charles, Tom Cornell, Frank, and Tom, and of course Pat who is always quiet and unobtrusive. I failed—greeted Charles with impatience, the boys also; to be present, to be available to men, to see Jesus in the poor, to welcome, to be hospitable, to love! This is my need. I fail every day.

Tuesday, December 29

Day of Recollection. Read Père Voillaume until 11. Up at 5:30, Mass at 6:15. Breakfast at 7:30. Prime at 8:30 and for the last two hours, I have been in the chapel. The first hour of adoration, contrition, thanksgiving, and supplication—ACTS—and sleeping a little too. When I sit with folded hands or kneel, the time passes slowly. This is our taste of the desert. Father Weigel, S.J. says what we need is austerity, presence to men, presence to God. Père Voillaume, building on Charles de Foucauld's teaching, says, 1) Poverty 2) Contemplation 3) Desert 4) Charity.

# PART IV

# THE SIXTIES

With the 1960s Dorothy's pilgrimage reflected the preoccupations of the time—poverty, racism, revolution, war—with all that decade's competing spirits of hope and disillusionment. She hailed the Civil Rights movement, the emerging practice of active nonviolence, and a bright season of renewal in the church. But as the specter of Vietnam began to dominate the political horizon, the Worker maintained a clear and prophetic witness.

The first protest against intervention in Vietnam was staged by the Catholic Worker in 1963. Later, in October 1965, David Miller of the Catholic Worker staff became the first young man to burn his draft card in public after Congress declared this a federal offense. Others were quick to follow his example.

As members of the community began departing for prison, Dorothy prayed that their sacrifice would help bring peace. With the daring witness of the Berrigans and their associates, there began to be talk of a Catholic Left in America. But Dorothy's enthusiasm for such efforts was qualified by a fear for the direction of the anti-war movement. She perceived a growing sense of despair in the young, a frustration and eagerness for fast results. Many were questioning the "relevance" of such undramatic efforts as the Works of Mercy. They rejected the personalist revolution of Peter Maurin, rejecting, too, the faith that was the basis of her own radical vision. In the noise and tumult of the times, she clung to those things that were central to the daily practice of her faith: prayer, the sacraments, the Works of Mercy.

Even the Catholic Church was caught up in the spirit of renewal and reform. Dorothy welcomed the Second Vatican Council, and made two trips to Rome during this period. She had long embraced many of the central themes of the Council: liturgical renewal, study of scripture, the role of the laity, ecumenism, the rights of conscience, and respect for other religions, particularly Judaism. It would be several years until the church began to catch up with other aspects of her vision: "the preferential option for the poor," the principle of solidarity, and the challenge of Gospel nonviolence.

*But as the 1960s wore on she was distressed by a casual disregard for tradition and the widespread rejection of authority. She was saddened by the defection of priests and nuns from their vows; she was disturbed by the liberal attitude toward sexuality and a growing disregard for church teaching on marriage—principles on which she had staked her own conversion many years before.*

*At a time when her radicalism was resonating as never before with the younger generation, she found herself, curiously, upholding the value of tradition.*

# 1960

This year I must strive for gentleness and listening—less talking, no passing judgments, no impatience. God help me. Judy [Gregory] says I am more choleric than melancholic! Mike: sanguine, slightly better.

"The real transformation of society will come only in love, in work, and in stillness."—[Gustav] Landauer, 1907

Resolutions: Less criticism. Never to complain of others.

January 1. CW in 28th year beginning in May

Since Tues Dec 29 Jean Walsh has been with Nanette.[190] Lily came down Thurs, yesterday, and I the morning before after my Jesus Caritas meeting at Graymoor. Forster in a sad state. Resolutely refusing to spend time with Nanette. Nanette in a sad state all day, legs swelling badly, also stomach. The doctor has come only once to see her since early Sept. Later in the evening she cried out she was losing her mind and screamed continually. Jean and Lily finally calmed her.

January 2. NY

Warm and raining tonight. Nanette cannot believe she has cancer since Dr. refused to tell her or let others tell her. "If it were malignant why don't they use radium? If it is a high infection why don't they use antibiotics? Why don't they give something for the nerves?" And she screams out that he has been lying to her, everyone has been lying to her. It is inexpressibly painful to hear

---

190 Jean Walsh was a nurse who joined the Worker community soon after meeting Dorothy Day. She recalls: "Nanette was a sweet, sweet woman—beautiful and childlike. And stylish, too... There would be Dorothy and Forster sitting there, and they'd talk and look out at the water. Nanette was so innocent and so uninhibited. I remember one day Nanette was all excited, telling me that when she got well, she was going to give all her clothes away and her jewelry and live like Dorothy did, like Jesus." See Rosalie Riegle, *Dorothy Day: Portraits by Those Who Knew Her*, 114.

her despairing. And Forster keeps running away. He would like to go in a coma and escape it all.

January 3
   Mass at 11. Coming to the Loft, some hardboiled eggs were thrown at Judy and me. Potatoes have been thrown at Hugh, ice at a visitor, stepping out of a cab. Health and fire department noting violations. Always trouble. But men are being fed, poor disordered people have a place to stay. The work goes on. The undertaker very disturbed at our poor men every time he has a wake.

January 4
   Mass at 8. Went from CBS to ferry by bus. Drove to farm to pick up Beth to drive to St. Vincent's. She told me of Mary Lathrop's[191] pulling Tom Cain's beard and how he has not appeared from his room since. How he almost killed dear soul [Arthur Lacey][192] for threatening to shave him.

January 6
   Today Nanette very low indeed, her skin clammy, her nose cold, and suffering much pain. For the first time she had a needle. She had been taking Demerol only at night, a tranquilizer 3 times a day.
   Tonight for the first time Jean [Walsh] stayed overnight and Forster slept at Evelyn's. Mary Lathrop is staying at the cottage, cleaning, doing mail. She is a dear. Stanley down chopping wood.

Thursday January 7
   For the first day Nanette kept to her bed too weak to move and Lucille, Jean and I stayed with her. We said the rosary together and at eleven, Lucille baptized her. She had said many times she was sorry for sin, had asked God's

---

191 In *Loaves and Fishes* Dorothy described Mary Lathrop as "a lively young woman who looks eighteen rather than twenty-eight, slim, beautifully built, with the strong legs of a dancer... We were in the loft on Spring Street when she first came to us. If she felt like running from end to end of the place, letting out Indian war whoops, she did it... But she could be as gentle and appealing as she was outrageous and boisterous." Soon, as related below, she attracted the interest of Ammon Hennacy.
192 Arthur J. Lacey, a slight, gentle man, was a familiar CW fixture for many years, serving as general courier, concierge, delivery boy, and eager source of gossip. Dorothy described below (Dec. 12, 1961) the origin of his nickname, "Dear Soul." He went by other names, including "Haberdasher of the Bowery" (for his work in the clothing room) and "The Bishop," on account of the oversized cross he wore over his baggy suit. Hearing him thus introduced, visitors were often uncertain how to respond. But he quickly resolved any doubts by presenting his ring to be kissed.

mercy, had kissed the infant of the Little Sisters, had venerated the relic of the Little Flower. I got to bed at 4.

### Friday January 8

This morning at 8:45 Nanette died after an agony of two days. The Cross was not as hard as this, she said. People in concentration camps suffered like this, she said, showing her arms. She died peacefully, after a slight hemorrhage. She had a slight smile, calm and peaceful. Lily came by eleven, and she and Forster and I went to the funeral parlor. He wanted a cremation. "It is finished. This is the end. I want no praying over her." He referred to our praying some of the Office of the Dead before we washed her, or rather they washed her.

### January 11. Press

Called Della and Lily and Forster. I was very unkind to him yesterday, refusing to see him. He hangs around Olwell's like a lost soul. Also he has to gather together his things, his binoculars, clothes, fishing equipment, etc.

### Tuesday January 12. Bus to Perkinsville

Mary [Lathrop] took me to the bus and Della met me there and we had a good visit. A comfortable ride and Tamar and Becky and Sue met me, all gay laughter. Bedroom all neat and readied for me and house even too warm... .

### January 13-14. Perkinsville

As usual in winter the outflowing pipes from sink are frozen and the tubs must be boiled out. Tamar is surrounded with beauty. But oh how hard life can be with the children—poor Eric having to care for Hilaire at night and Sue, Martha. It is hard on them. Becky is difficult, David is 46, and Tamar is pregnant again. The physical certainly wears one down. Tamar says she has nightmares all the time, the last one about an injury to Maggie. I dreamed too of the work and people's attitudes to me, of praise and blame. Only prayer helps keep a balance. A good talk with David today, but he is overcome by a sense of futility.

### Jan 14

Leaving New York by bus to go to Perkinsville, Vermont, one can go at seven or eleven thirty and when I take the late bus my sister can see me off and I can have a visit. We are companions since childhood and give each other diaries for Christmas and share the same tastes in music and literature. This year Della gave me a set of Jane Austen.

Bus riding always reminds me of Dickens and his stagecoach rides—not *Pickwick* but *Barnaby Rudge* and *David Copperfield*. Last time I was in Vermont I spoke in Fr. Cosgrove's parish in Chester at the Grange Hall, a town place but only Catholics were there. There is a study club and discussion group and some very interesting people. Allan Sheldon introduced me and as we stood in the wings of the little stage he made the sign of the cross before we started. This holy sign always impressed me as a child. I can remember how when I was ten or eleven, going swimming once with my brothers inside the breakwater, just over the Illinois Central tracks in Chicago, I saw for the first time children making the sign of the Cross as they dived into the water.

There are no more Catholic Worker farms in Vermont, nor houses of hospitality but we have a great number of friends of the Catholic Worker, subscribing to the paper and contributing to the work.

Tamar, now going on 34, met me at the bus stop with the two oldest (girls) of her 8 children, and all were laughing and joyful with youth and with the little adventure of being out at 8:30 on a cold, icy night. It was ten above zero and the roads were slick, but Tamar is used to driving under all conditions. Eight-thirty is past the children's bedtime. Becky and Sue, 14 and 13, go to their rooms with the rest, but to read or study. It is still light at 5:30 now and the days are getting longer.

The Hennessy house is on the Weathersfield road, between Weathersfield and Perkinsville. The house is white clapboard, very large with a wing with 4 gables over outer kitchen, woodshed. Wagon shed, and the barns. They have 3 cows, 2 rams, which were brought to them as pets but which are now beginning to butt. There are two pigs and a steer has been slaughtered and packed away in the deep freeze which is also full of vegetables. There are apples in the cellar, and carrots and squash. The chickens occupy one of the gabled rooms over the barn in winter. They are laying well now.

Five roosters hanging around the back door in the sunlight terrify the children and rightly so because they attack with beak and claw and the two and four-year-olds are no match for them.

My visit was a short once since I arrived Tuesday night and left Friday noon. But there was time to bake and try out some recipes from the country cookbook with Tamar and talk with David about Distributism. He spoke of recent attacks on agrarians and other CW positions.

"It is always Eric Gill and Chesterton they are attacking and they also disregard all the pronouncements of Pope Pius XII."

He reminded me that I had borrowed one of his precious copies of *The Pope Speaks* in which there is a good bit about craftsmen in an industrial society.

Tamar showed me her latest spinning wheel, the old fashioned farm wheel at which one stands, drawing out the thread and turning the wheel by hand. It has all its parts, is well balanced and spins beautifully fine thread. It is easy to learn on, far easier than the small wheel and foot treadle one. "Men make their millions by the machine," Peter Maurin used to say, "but they spend them on hand-made things."

Tamar has her hand-woven curtains at living room and bedroom windows, two hand-woven blankets, the wool for which she dyed herself, linen towels, linen tablecloth, and various other pieces of cloth put away for future use.

Setting up the loom is the hard thing—making the warp and setting it up on the loom. Once she said she set it up at four in the morning when one of the babies had waked her early and she could not get back to sleep. Doctors have called knitting and other such crafts tranquillizers. Certainly it is tranquilizing to see beautiful curtains and drapes and blankets in one's home, the front of the house.

What it does too is restore the sacramental aspect of things. One gets a feeling and a knowledge of materials, of God's creation, and becomes co-creator, in fashioning wool from a fleece and towels from hemp and flax and to plant a bed of flax is to see a most heavenly blue mass of flowers.

There is no Catholic school in the country and the church is in the middle of town, a six-mile drive from home. Some icy days the roads were impassible, but most of the time Tamar gets the children to catechism Saturday morning and the entire family goes to Mass Sunday. There is not a day of the week when a mother can relax and "sleep in," as the saying is.

January 20. Sandstone[193]
At 8:15 we drove out to the prison. Ammon was nicely dressed in new shoes, suit and overcoat and with $30 was released. The warden and his boss of the educational dept. both came out to greet me. Sandstone was used as a mental hospital from end of war until last Aug. Walls yellow, ceiling coral, green base.

January 22
Missed Mass as I could not sleep thinking of Fr. Louis [Thomas Merton] remarks in his article on Pasternak in *Thought*. Wrote all morning On Pilgrimage.

---

193 Ammon Hennacy served six months at Sandstone Federal Prison in Minnesota for trespassing on the Omaha missile base.

February 7. Fargo

Mass at 9:30. Another at 11:30. Both crowded and coffee and rolls served after. Newman Club buildings well laid out. Chapel plain and beautiful. Dinner meeting. Good but students much amused by interference. Deaf mother with daughter whispering loudly everything I said. Talk until midnight—literary, Hart Crane, Malcolm Cowley. Allen Tate, Kenneth Burke, Mike Gold, O'Neill, etc.[194] Train at 1:50. Had time in station to read Matins. Very uncomfortable car on train.

February 8

Riding thru Wisconsin on the Great Northern, it is 40 degrees, and too much heat in the car. I had hoped for leg rests such as I had enjoyed before on these trains. But it was a battered old car, seats broken down, close together, and I could have had my ankle crushed when a heavy man in front of me reclined suddenly so that the seat came down on my foot.

But there is the Vista Dome, and it is pleasant to sit up there and see the palisades, the fields with scrubby weeds and underbrush coming up thru the snow. And the miles meandering along, filled with islands, dotted here and there with fish huts on the ice which cannot be used because of the warmth.

I picked up *Main St.* yesterday by Sinclair Lewis and Gopher Prairie remains the same and in a way the people too, money making, getting ahead, oblivious of the ugliness of their small towns. How different is New England. The Middle West remains the same year after year, and the dismal ugliness of its towns is depressing.

February 8. Chicago

Sleeping—unable to read, knit, but I could write on train. Arrived in at two. Nina [Polcyn] met me.

Ammon to dinner. Bob and Terry came in after. Disturbed at chancery officer, Msgr. Burke's temper tantrum on phone over picketing of Federal Court over Eroseanna Robinson's jailing, Cook County jail.[195]

February 11

Gordon Zahn,[196] Karl Meyer for dinner. Called Fides Press. Mail came yesterday accepting THERESE which may now be out in the Fall. Worked on

---

194 All these writers had figured in her earlier life.

195 Eroseanna Robinson, a social worker in Chicago, was arrested and imprisoned for a year for refusing to file tax returns. While in jail she fasted and was forcibly fed.

196 Gordon Zahn was a pacifist scholar who served as a c.o. during World War II. Karl Meyer was now in Chicago, where he had founded St. Stephen's Catholic Worker house.

the foreword again and then the typewriter ribbon failed and I must do letters by hand.

February 27. Seattle

A good loafing day with visits to St. Vincent de Paul market down by the canal, a long alley along the water front with stalls and books and plenty of space along the docks for second-hand furniture and fixtures. A cold wind but a sunny day so we went on to the farmer's market down by the harbor. Sue [Spier, *Dorothy's niece*] and [her husband] Mike are living in the Walling-ford section near the university, an apartment open and sunny, with windows looking out over the canal and boats and the city on the other side. We talked till 12, about Alaska and expeditions and research and work and ambition and science and man's part in it.

February 28. Seattle

Up at 8:30 and to Assumption church for 10:30 high Mass, and Sue waited outside for me, reading. I prayed for her and Mike most specially—I love her as my own. My only sister's only daughter, so close to me. She is a good teacher.

February 29

Mail from Charlie and Stanley. All seems well at home except that $2,000 is needed to make house suit building and fire inspectors. Appeal needed. Too much reading. Henry Miller and D.H. Lawrence. Enough of that stuff.

March 4

The meeting [at Washington University] was on a houseboat. Several pro-claimed themselves atheists before meeting started. All had had wine and there was one most talkative young man who, as I was leaving, started reading aloud from [Allen Ginsberg's] "Howl." Aside from only S asking questions, the meeting was good. Left at 11.

March 16. San Francisco

Good meeting. Jerry Brown, governor's son.

March 17

Berkeley. To Bro. Antoninus [*poet William Everson, formerly of the Oakland CW*] who spoke of self-hypnosis, sanctity, beats, and fame.

March 21. St. Benedict

Santa Clara. Had a good day, letters, walk downtown, visit to Newman Club chapel, donated by Clare Boothe Luce. Read Lanza del Vasto's[197] book—made notes on Vinoba [Bhave]. *Encounter* has article about [Jayaprakash] Narayan, coming leader, communitarian.

March 24

Sister Josepha, Maryknoll, gave me a picture of Fr. [Charles] de Foucauld. Mr. McCullogh wants a picture of Xmas cover [by] Fritz—leather jacketed boys. I keep coming on pictures of Fritz's cut out and tacked on walls of offices, slum centers, missions, Mike Gold's house, etc.

April 4. Albuquerque

Here in Albuquerque there is a beatnik place called the Grave. Boarded up, it is sinister and mysterious. No liquor is served but coffee, so the young can go in. Baptist friend of Kathleen's went in and, according to his report, there was a cross on one wall with a monkey hanging on it.

On another was a picture of Christ and Mary [Magdalene]. But she was naked. The Baptist took out the Cross saying it was sacrilegious and was brought to trial for it.

Could it have been that it was a writhing, tortured Savior, such as the Puerto Rican ones I have seen? Once a bishop criticized Ade's drawing of Mary Magdalene as too naked, her thin robes revealing her body too much.

Catherine says people have lost all sense of sin. They do not try to keep the commandments. "If you love me keep my commandments." We all wish to love even more than we want to be loved, tho it is true love brings its response. (But we have all known unwanted, unhealthy love and its oppressive persistence.)

April 6. Albuquerque-Oklahoma City

Left at six a.m. St. Vincent de Paul man drove me to station. Texas all day. Very hot. Green just beginning to show. Catherine packed me a good lunch.

Arrived at Oklahoma City at 10:30 so tired I fell asleep at once. 3:50 Mass. All Oklahoma pretty flat.

---

197  Lanza del Vasto was a French pacifist and disciple of Gandhi. With his wife, Chanterelle, he founded the Community of the Ark. His book, *From Gandhi to Vinoba*, described the work of Vinoba Bhave and Jayaprakash Narayan, who tried to carry on Gandhi's nonviolent social revolution in India.

April 9. St. Louis

Wrote 18 letters yesterday. Wrote Forster and Della. I will not see him.
Not to try to make order where people do not want order. Leave them
alone but love them.

Double thinking, double motives. *The Idiot.* A help in prayer. Also to counteract sense of futility. "Why am I doing this?" Self-analysis to be avoided.

April 13. St. Louis

Very rheumatic today, breathless. Fr. [Joseph] Becker in auto crash on way
to pick me up to go to Rhineland. Not injured. He returned to get another
car so we started later. On the way on Rt. 70 the hood flew up—most terrifying. Fr. talked wonderfully on the Incarnation and Redemption on way
home.

April 17. Easter. St. Louis

Mass began after midnight, blessing of new fire at 10 last night. In bed by
2:00; rain, but could not sleep. A hotel is a dismal place to be on a holiday.
Up at 6:30 for 7:30 Mass when the children made their first communion.
Solemn high Mass, church full as it was last night, but this morning it was
like an aviary.

April 23. Detroit

Visited Bon Secour Hospital nuns and spoke to them. Very warm group
and gave great help to house in out clinic. Very warm.

Such patience and fortitude in bearing the pain of little Brian's crippled
condition. His head is so beautiful, of a little 8-year-old boy, his body that of
a baby. Deaf, dumb, blind, no mind.

April 27. Dostoevsky

His spiritual help. About love. Fr. Zossima, Ivan Karamazov. Attitude toward children. "The world will be saved by beauty" in *The Idiot.* What is
more beautiful than love? Gospels. *Crime and Punishment.*

For those who do not believe in God—they believe in love.

April 28. S.I.

Day at beach writing On Pilgrimage. It takes so long to write so little.

May 2. Press

Bob, Marty, Arthur and I at printers. Execution of [Caryl] Chessman at 1
p.m.

May 3. Air Raid Drill

No jail sentence this year. A great rally, 700 perhaps, mothers and children, many others. It was impossible to clear the park so Mary O'Neil and Sheila stayed with their babies. They did arrest 28 at random, no leaders. Tonight listening to music of Weber. Wonderful Masses this a.m.[198]

May 6

9:30 trial. In court all day. All got 5 days.

Ammon picketing all night. Deane moody.

May 8. Sunday

Spent the day utterly exhausted at the beach and at seven Beth picked me up to go to the farm where Fr. Becker was hearing confessions. Too tired to think of anything but my impatience, resentments, and speaking ill of my neighbor, repeating his faults. Our young parish priest on hearing such a confession advised me to read again the encyclical on the Mystical Body, remembering that we are all members one of another and what we criticize in another is our own fault.

Slept like a log. We had been in court all day Friday and it had been so terribly moving to see the young ones on trial. I do not mean our friends who had demonstrated against the falseness of civil defense, who were students, artists, actors, and had full lives, but all the young adolescents picked up on various charges. One can never hear in the courtroom—everything is transacted up there in front of the judge and even the charge read aloud is so hastily read that it is impossible to hear. But the young fellows, with their narrow sloping shoulders and soft undeveloped bodies, being held, unable to pay bail.

The suspense of the entire week, the going to press on Monday, speaking on radio Monday night, demonstration on Tuesday with the expectation that we would most surely be arrested as we had been these last six years, and then the overwhelming number of mothers and children and students in the City Hall park, and the terrible emotional strain of presenting our case over and over again to the reporters. We went all the way uptown to the trial which did not take place. Instead there was a trial at Center Street and there all were released for sentencing Friday. Ammon is in his element on these demonstrations, but I am utterly exhausted.

The sermon this morning was wonderful. Father Becker spoke of the Mass as being not only a memento of Christ's passion and death, but his resurrec-

---

198 The numbers that turned out for this year's annual civil defense protest indicated a significant shift in public opinion. An editorial in the *N.Y. World Telegram* said, "Yesterday's test can be called meaningful and successful only if a potential enemy's plan is to drop marshmallow puffs on N.Y. City—and to advertise in advance what time they are coming."

tion and ascension into heaven and that this should always be kept in mind. All the Gospels for this month after Easter are taken from the Last Supper, that triumphant and happy time of the last discourse—and then not much longer Jesus was prostrate on the ground, begging that if it were God's will the chalice of suffering should pass from him.

In talking to me out in St. Louis Father posed the question—are we to think of God as a just judge, demanding that a penalty be paid for the Fall, were we to emphasize the fact that Christ redeemed us by his sufferings, paying the penalty for us, paying our debts, this being exacted by a stern Father? Or were we to think of original sin as a turning from God to creatures, and Christ coming and taking upon himself our humanity in order to win us back by his love to the Father, knowing that men would, being what they were, put him to death on the Cross, rejecting him, but afterward accepting Him. That his triumphant entry into heaven brought our humanity, in His, back to the Father, reuniting us to the godhead. But taking on our humanity, he enabled us to partake of his divinity. The full circle had been made, Christ coming down to earth, returning to the Father, with our human nature, so that now body and soul, flesh and divinity, he is there in Heaven to which we also will go.

Today he did not speak of this juridical aspect of the redemption, nor of the emphasis on love, the aspect of Jesus Christ, his life, death and ascension willingly undertaken from love. Fr. Becker spoke instead of our being taken up with Him and how we shall be changed. When we were conceived in the womb, and that moment was only the united egg and sperm which is no more to all appearances than a blob of jelly, and when we compare what we were then to what we are now, it is an unbelievable difference. But that is as nothing to compare what we are now to what we shall be.

May 9

Slept till ten. Still very tired. Peggy [Baird] came at noon. She left carrying food, money, basket—looking very frail. They are broke, so he is not drinking. She has a lump in her breast. And ah me—having finished an article on Hart Crane, she is doing one on me. And yet how little she knows of my life.

May 11

John 4:7. "Beloved, let us love one another. Love springs from God; no one can love without being born of God and knowing God. How can a man who has no love have any knowledge of God, since God is love?" St. John of the Cross says, "Where there is no love, put love and you will find love." The hard work of loving. That is our CW work. Learning to love, exercising our love so it grows strong. And exercising our faith too. Natural and supernatural love.

"No man has ever seen God. But if we love one another, then we have God dwelling in us."

### May 13

Words of hope. When there are so many children and there is such bad example one must trust in the power of the sacraments and in prayer. They have all been baptized. There is a strong power at work. We must pray mightily that they overcome the world. "Letters to my grandchildren." So many things I would like to write "if God spares me." What an expression. Rather if I have the time. Now I am 62. I think of that often.

### May 15. Perkinsville

Bus at 4:30 at Charleston and a long tiresome trip on a Sunday in crowded bus. My ankles and feet very bad after wearing bad shoes all week and on my feet at Tamar's.

Mass at 11 with the children. Tamar and Dave went at 8. He told her his mind is a torment to him.

Three days of very crowded life with the Hennessy children in Vermont.

Whole world in turmoil, what with spy plane shot down over Russia, our submarine fired on by Cuban ships, etc. threats, hostility, etc. Summit conference, K driving around in great car while we are down to small ones. Emulation, envy, greed, hatred, the world.

Here it is too of course in microcosm. But in general a very happy visit.

### May 18. S.I.

Harper wants me to sign a contract by June 1 for [book about] last eleven years.

### May 27. Retreat

Too much activity. Last night and today, cleaning and no letters. No article written for June issue. Just started one and it was time to go in to N.Y. 3 p.m. Dinner with [Della] and [Franklin] and they were unhappy. F requesting prayers. My head ached. My hour a heavy burden. Weighed down. Beth and Frances, D and F, Tamar and David, John and Peter, so much suffering. Stanley in commenting on it said we must keep ourselves unspotted by world's suffering. Impossible. Bed at 10. Awoke at 2.

**June 1**

Today the first strawberries and radishes from farm. I cooked the green tops, baked bread and biscuits for shortcake. Andy and Hugh down painting. Hugh not eating but speaking.

Finished going over Peter Maurin's *Green Revolution* which will be out in Sept.

**June 7**

I felt impelled to write to Karl [Stern] about my troubles and suddenly thought—they have enough troubles. Why add to their burden.

The other day when writing my article and appeal I threw away my article telling of all our troubles and thought "this is not what our readers want—to be tortured with tales of broken families, men beating their wives and children, etc."

I will write happily of June and its beauties. Of course if you do this you get a double share of complaints from all around you who try to make you see how bad everything is. Still you cannot help but help others by your own repose and joy if you try to maintain it.

**June 19**

So little time. Sow time to reap time, Fr. Roy used to say. One's spiritual life takes 3 hours a day at least.

My "hurt feelings" at Peter Carey's criticism that I had been responsible for Slim's condition boiled over at breakfast. Resentments muddy the heart. I'll need a long time in purgatory. I have learned by long experience how to avoid conflict with my own family—why can I not learn with my CW family?

**June 28**

Tonight Johannah [Hughes] graduated from H.S. All the girls wore strapless very low dresses and looked as tho they were just coming out from under a shower. Bob babysat. I baked cherry pie for Jimmy. Deane cleaned lettuce, etc. All very peaceful.

**July 1**

All day it rained and the children had to stick to the porch. The girls did not mind but Eric was homesick.

Boat purchased for $35. Jimmy wants to call it Admiral Day, and I Guardian Angel. Great distress. Finally concession. Admiral Day's Guardian Angel.

July 9

Catherine Ann [Hennessy] born 4:30 a.m. at Springfield Hospital. Called David after 8 a.m. Mass. We go to Vermont tomorrow. Great excitement.

July 11

If God wanted me to be someone training others he would give me the grace. Also he would hide my faults from those around me as St. Teresa said he did hide hers. (I am not comparing myself to St. Teresa.) But it is true that very often "they have eyes but see not" one's virtues, but only one's faults, which is good for humility.

July 13

Up at 6:30 to pray, read, write letters until 8 when Myrtle came to wash blankets and help change around beds. Ankle very sore from driving the 49 Chevy. If I ever had a good car I'd be on the road always. Flat tire also. Roger, Myrtle's brother, came and fixed it. To psychologist who says David must learn to drive.

July 14

Tamar coming home from hospital.

Reading in Encyclopedia about interest and usury. If we cannot write the letter to make our point we will turn money over to [William] Horvath. Or if we send it back and they return it.[199]

July 15

Studying matter of interest on loans and usury. Eric Gill says 2 great problems, usury and war.

July 17

Baptism of Catherine Ann. Jim and Ann Hassin godparents. Everything went off beautifully. Mass at 9:30. Tamar's car had a flat, which Eric fixed.

July 20

Day of recollection at Weston Priory. Sat at garage until 11:30 having starter and tire fixed. Got to priory at 12:45 and received.

---

199 Dorothy was faced with an ethical dilemma. After seizing the house on Chrystie St., the City of New York had recompensed the CW for the value of the property plus an additional $3,576.39 in interest. As a matter of principle, the CW had always defended the medieval ban on usury. Dorothy weighed various alternatives—returning the money or perhaps turning it over to a cooperative housing project in Harlem.

July 21

Fr. Cosgrove's brother was there and did not speak to me. How hard it is to talk of these truths, about Christ's teaching—peace, war, work, man and state, etc. They get so angry—as theologians. I too can see all sides—all problems involved. But Jesus' teaching is there. Even his apostles could not understand. We see thru a glass darkly. "Come and pray a while." He multiplied loaves, walked on water, but their hearts were blinded.

July 24. Ammon's birthday

Russian Mass. Breakfast at Automat with Ammon and "The Idiot" at Translux. A Soviet film. First half of book shown. Excellent. Power of money. So stirring. I went back to office and read up in Cath encyclicals on interest and usury and composed letter to city to return interest.

July 25. Press

Bob [Steed] and I making up paper. I wrote letter to city treasurer, which we will print in Sept issue.

*In the September issue, Dorothy published an open letter to the Treasurer of the City of New York, under the title: "This Money Is Not Ours":*

> Dear Sir:
> ... We are returning the interest on the money we have recently received because we do not believe in "money lending" at interest... We do not believe in the profit system, and so we cannot take profit or interest on our money... Please be assured that we are not judging individuals, but are trying to make a judgment on the system under which we live and with which we admit that we ourselves compromise daily in many small ways, but which we try and wish to withdraw from as much as possible.
> Sincerely yours,
> Dorothy Day, Editor[200]

July 28

Today the car is being repaired at garage. Mass at 8. Chas B[utterworth] and Ralph Madsen drove me back. Two letters from Della telling me not to come up. Rather offensive to pride.

July 29

Spoke tonight on present state of CW and read letter to the city about interest. Quite a crowd. Called Tamar and she had just driven David to a new

---

200  See *SW,* 294-295.

job, night clerk at Windham in Bellows Falls, 40 a week and board, 6 day week, 2 12-hour shifts.

July 30

Up at 6. Mass 7. Had breakfast with Ammon and then in downpour drove upstate. Roads flooded with tropical storm Brenda. Slow leak in tire. Got to Otis by one and lunched and slept. Franklin and Della had office company. Bed early and good rest. I must keep quieter about rats, drug addicts, poverty, slums, etc, when out in company. People do not want to hear about these things.

July 31

I am praying my *Therese* will cover these costs. I am so happy David has work tho it leaves a heavy burden of farm work on Tamar and children. But it is good for them, the children. Certainly I am happy to be occupied with daily chores, washing, cleaning, cooking, putting food away for the winter. It is all "on the side of life."

Tonight at 8 I spoke and the priest seemed so against our ideas. It was hard for him to think of leaving the 99 to save the one. It seemed as tho we were minimizing the goodness of the 99—as tho we were judging them. We must emphasize vocation more.

Aug 4

Reading in Mark, Jesus' multiplication of loaves and fishes. The Lord always sees to it we have what is needed. I should not worry about tending to Tamar and Dave's roof and chimney. The ceilings will fall if we do not. There was one chimney fire already. It is a wonder that the crisis comes now when we have the money to have work done, instead of a year ago. Family is important. I must read Mother [Elizabeth Ann] Seton who had such loving care of her family. And Therese, "Be not solicitous." I must work the harder.

August 7

Such bad news, Congo, Laos, mutual spies, Cuba and Cardinal speaking at the Eucharistic conference about the menace of communism and need for preparedness and that devout men make best soldiers.

Four million unemployed.

August 12

Rewrote [review of Jane Addams] and sent it to Mary Lathrop to type over and send to *Times*. "Best I could do" in 600 words (Hans' phrase).

Sick in bed Tuesday with a cold. And now looking forward to getting away. Teresa and Mama Hennessy are here, and more than ever, Becky and Sue sit and do nothing. Clothes, movies, only the life of the senses, not even that of the mind, let alone the soul, preoccupy them and they look so desperately unhappy all the time. Dull, bored, resentful.

Is adolescence such a disturbance of the body that it affects the mind? They read Westerns, scarcely listen to radio which they used to love, or ball games, for which Sue still has some enthusiasm.

It was a mistake to give so much time here this summer. I've quite outworn my welcome.

All this because of Becky's "Why don't you hire a servant?" when I asked her to get some bowls for dessert.

They do nothing, literally nothing, and Tamar is the indulgent parent. I will be glad to be gone.

August 15. Randolph

Left this p.m. at 2:30 when the rain had just started and was sad to go. My heart is so tied up with them all. I worry about Becky. I worry about anyone who is not happy—on the way to being happy.

August 18

Stayed last night at shrine. St. Anne's shrine is beautiful. Little Sisters, Montreal.

Well, I feel entirely different. Becky was about to be unwell—and next day she was different. What an unhappy age, and if we are resentful and unloving, we older ones, who is to help them? "Christ is patient, is kind, etc." I read over I Cor 13.

"When we are judged we are being chastised by the Lord that we may not be condemned with this world."

These things are a lesson to me to show how much pride and meanness there is in me. As St. Vincent said, "You have to love them very much to make them forgive you the bread you give them."

August 21

Karl [Stern] is writing on Tolstoy for *Jubilee*. He was interested in Ammon's article on anarchists but protested my allowing A. to criticize the church or print his report of doing it.

St. Jane Frances de Chantal. Sacred Heart Convent in Montreal

Our retreat began last night after supper and now, Sunday at five p.m., the silence is upon us. There are eight of us. Fr. Joseph Brennan is giving the retreat and he will arrive tonight. He is a scripture scholar and has studied in Rome, Jerusalem and North Africa and is now teaching in the seminary in Rochester. The retreat will last for eight days and there will be six days of "Sessions."

The silence is complete as to human voice, but the church bells are clamoring all around from various churches and it must be for Benediction. They rang at three, three-thirty, four, four-thirty, and now again. It has rained steadily for two days and now the sun is out and all is cheerful and beautiful.

Today how did it go?

I woke at 5:30 but did not get up for an hour. I had coffee, read in Butler the life of St. Jane Frances de Chantal until 8 when we met in chapel (the chapel of the martyrs) for Angelus, Prime and Veni Creator. There was a dialogue Mass at 8:30 and breakfast at 9:30. Later I made my hour of adoration from 11-12. Again Angelus, Veni Creator, and scripture reading for meditation. Lunch 12

It is very beautiful here, listening to the wave made by the boats splashing against the rocky breakwater.

There is a paved walk all along the river and an iron railing to lean on. The sun sets over the water and across the river is the Ile Jésus. We are on the last street on the north side of the island of Montreal, easy for a stranger to find.

Peaceful grounds, a lovely orchard, lawns, a vegetable garden, space, cleanliness, community, worship—what with my life in the slums, with people, this is a desert to me. And would be to a great many of the poor, too, since it is not their vocation to live in a convent.

The Little Sisters of Jesus have a larger apartment upstairs that extends over the entire house and I imagine both felt glad of the presence of the other at first. However, once you settle down in a slum and know your neighbors you feel safe, safer indeed than in a "respectable" neighborhood where you know no-one, and are really closed off from others.

Where people live so much in the streets there is community of a sort.

Yes, to be alone is to be in a desert. To be silent, to be concentrating on the spiritual is to feel off-balance, so I write as a relaxation of penance. For these retreats are penance, are strain, are loneliness, partaking of what Conrad called "the horror of infinity."

First Conference. Pray for union, that the message of Brother Charles [de Foucauld] be known.

Seek Jesus in Eucharist, in reading Gospels, contacts with one another, still small voice. Say nothing, do nothing without looking at Jesus first. Follow

him. Order your lives, rooted in him, built on him, overflowing with gratitude In Him...

Meanwhile, I listen, as tho fixed to the Cross, aching, stifling, while Elias
travels from Carmel to Sinai, fleeing, while Matthew jumps up from his tax
table (the kind Jesus overturned perhaps) and prepared a banquet, a farewell
to his past life, a feast for Jesus, an invitation accepted, and Peter fished, and
jumped into the sea from the constraint of the boat and Zacchaeus climbed a
tree! All physical activity being gestures of spiritual impulses.

Retreats are hard. If women could help prepare meals, wash dishes, mend
and wash and iron vestments, it is much easier on them. That is why our
retreats at Maryfarm were so good—everyone had work to do to keep the
retreats going. Also, if there are not too many people and some of those are
strong, painting, carpentry, digging, cultivating, harvesting and canning went
on.

To remember the past is also to prepare for the future—so it is not vain
nostalgia (and there is a need here to mortify one of the interior senses, the
memory), but a recounting of past joys and benefits which brings with it a
swelling sense of gratitude. "My lines are fallen in goodly places."

Manual labor—the joy of it, the need of it, in measure of course and according to one's strength. Not the deadly repetitious tool, nerve-racking in its
monotony, which nevertheless can be endured if it is not too long in continu-
ance.

Bob Stowell said he would willingly work at a machine three days a week if
work could only be so divided that all would take their share. Or one could
go to the harvest or sweep the streets or work in a cannery.

Fr. Pacifique Roy was attached to work. Probably that was why God sent
him to us, to us who were so inadept, if there is such a word. He was first up
and last to bed.

August 22. Retreat

It is not that a retreat drags. There is never enough time to do what one
wishes to do, on the one hand; then too one feels out of one's element, almost
hypocritical, playing a part, aspiring too high. It is as tho the devil keeps whispering, "You are a liar, you are not a good member, a faithful member, you do
not keep the rule."

August 24

The Eucharist was moved from small chapel to large church—and more
nuns are here, only a few sing. Nonparticipation is stifling. The nuns all little
so seats low and uncomfortable.

August 25

Books—*Monastic Piety* by Louis Bouyer. *Diary of a Country Priest*. The day is so broken up I get no writing done. No note taking even. I can only work in my own environment of CW and home. Only breathe there. I have been long away this summer, this entire past year, what with beach, trip, Tamar, and this retreat. I hope to stay home this year and write.

August 26

"What is CW for?" someone asked a girl staying with us. "To take care of the wounded," she said. That is what Catholic Worker houses are, our farms. And I am essentially a housekeeper. In a book on radical literature of the 20s, reference was made to an early book of mine. Its conclusion was, "Women were made for husband and children, a home, a family, the first unit of society." It was not tired radicalism, but true wisdom I had attained.

And Jane Addams, Maria Montessori, Madeline Slade were doing just that—working for families, if not their own. "The family" again. And ours are hospices for the wounded, the rejected, the lost (from families).

August 27

Father Brennan asked us to read the Epistle to the Colossians in relation to obedience and my testament has a little foreword giving background material. The Colossians "claimed for angels a very high place of honor, and boasted deeper knowledge of Christianity, insisting on Jewish observances and a false asceticism." In it St. Paul, who was at that time in chains himself, tells slaves to obey their masters, "whatever you do, work at it from the heart, not for men." And he goes on to tell "masters" to give what is just and fair to their workers.

Much as Ammon hates such a verse, I could not help but think of his work by the day for the army captain out in Arizona—heavy, hard work in the field, a wage slave if there ever was one, yet how he gave an honest day's work always, not to build up the estate for this army captain (his master) but in honesty, to earn his daily bread.

I am writing these things down now as I think of them. I want to guard against niggardliness—that is the word which comes to my mind as mean and stingy, but it is a funny word and I must look it up. I mean about food. When you are the housekeeper and constantly see one or another person, sometimes adult, sometimes child, constantly taking more than their share—for instance, drinking 2/3 quart of milk when there is only 1 quart for 6 people—or three bananas out of eight which were intended to serve 8, or 2 pieces of meat when there is not enough to go around. And when you know the bitterness at poverty that goes with the greed, it is hard not get impatient.

1) Peter and the eggs.[201]

2) More faith in our heavenly Father is needed. Father, give us this day our daily bread. He will certainly give us what we need. One does not have to be so watchful over the supplies. Food is a physical and a psychological necessity.

I began to think of this when my sister came down and brought hamburgers and there were only enough for one each and she was so upset to think she had not brought enough—that we had to watch our helpings.

Peter's solution is the immediate answer. "If there is not enough to go around, I will do without. This involuntary fasting perhaps is of more merit than voluntary, as having less self will in it. At least that is what St. Angela of Foligna says. But it is easier too—more spontaneous, less dread.

There is a delightful smell of beeswax about this convent. Just as I was reading some notes of Père Voillaume about the psychological effect of odors, and smog and other slum smells.

August 28

A day of silence; the last day of retreat. No conferences from a priest but a reunion in the evening. Very wonderful weather.

September 1

Reading *Waiting on God*—Simone Weil (letters to Fr. Perrin). Another book, "a long study of the reciprocal duties of the individual and the state," *The Need for Roots*, written for French provisional government in England.

September 7. N.Y.

Mass 9. Got copy ready. Then to printer. Read galleys. Jacques bad but needs encouragement. He tries to outdo A. in criticism of hierarchy.

To Barnes and Noble for *Fontamara* [Ignazio Silone] for Ammon and on to Medical Center to see Deane who is standing up under the operation wonderfully.

September 8

Resolution. We women around the CW must be more companionable with each other.

---

201 Reference to a dispute at Maryfarm over eggs, which prompted Peter Maurin to announce that he would forego all milk and eggs for the summer. See August 10, 1938.

September 12. Press
Hurricane Donna—driving rain, high tides, electric off. To the printer at
7.
Finished *Heart of Darkness*, Conrad.

September 28
Today all day at beach with Ammon going over his book.

October 11
Walter filing and throwing away valuable letters which fortunately I re-
trieved—the one about the Pope blessing Eichenberg and us too. Letter written by Abbot Augustine.

October 21
*Therese* arrived.

November 4
Carmen Mathews read "Ivan the Fool." Mary sang. Very good. Loft was
packed, many young people and beatniks. Coffee and sassafras tea later.

November 24. Perkinsville
Thanksgiving. Wonderful day of rest and feasting. David is so much better.
We have much to be thankful for.

November 25
Left Tamar's at 8. Arrived in N.Y. at 8. Then Ammon and Mary [Lathrop]
announced they wished to be married.[202] Talked till two.

December 8. Immaculate Conception
Mass at noon. At four went to Della's where she started in on birth control
so I left and went to S.I. Oldsmobile had to be fixed. Transmission, cars most
expensive.

December 13
A gloomy letter from Tamar about their poverty. Compared to others they
have so much. Mary Lathrop called to say she had broken off her engage-

---

202 Dorothy described this short-lived engagement in *Loaves and Fishes*. Soon after, Ammon
departed New York for Salt Lake City, where he opened the Joe Hill House of Hospitality, and
thus began a new chapter in "the Book of Ammon" (the title of his autobiography).

ment—had been to Confession. So much discontent all around. Deane, the girls. Everyone wants so much.

## December 14

I feel as tho I fail people constantly—they come expecting to find a solution and there is no easy solution. They are all in trouble. They come to get help, not give it usually.

## December 25. Sunday

It was a good Christmas except at the close. Helene Iswolsky, Larry Evers and Jonas were our extra guests. Larry coming down at 4, walking up icy Bloomingdale Road with all his clown paraphernalia. After breakfast he put on his show, catching us all in passing, in the hall—clown tricks, bird noises, shell game, Punch & Judy, etc. He also had a bird and a mouse and he left with a kitten and homemade bread, some money. Helene said it was like a medieval player arriving on a holiday. She brought me also news of Jacques Maritain—he is now in Princeton, to sell the house in which he, his wife and sister-in-law who was also his secretary, lived for so many years.

Within the last year both have died and she says he wrote her, sending a picture of Raissa [Maritain] on her deathbed, and told her he was going back to France to spend his remaining days with the Little Brothers of Jesus at their Toulouse center, or adjacent to them. Helene always brings us such beauty, such loftiness of thought about life and man. I had just been reading about Herzen and Proudhon and the influence of the latter. I had wanted to talk to her about Herzen but with so many people it was hard. We had both sat up wrapping presents together for our S.I. household of 25 and only casual conversation can go on with such occupations.

Our dinner, which Hans cooked, was enormous, ham and turkey, turnip and mashed potatoes, dressing, cranberries, celery, lettuce—a loaded board, and too professional, almost. A job. Our household of the poor—living like kings and we with them. A disturbing thing—this richness of life in the midst of the hunger in the world. But in general people are used to the best in America. After the war, people returning from Europe were overcome when they saw our pushcarts on Mott St. loaded down. In general the poor who know food and like to prepare it, live well and graciously. Italians, Puerto Ricans, poor Jews, all live well, and their kitchens smell delightfully. Feasts are truly feasts with them. Deane has the ability too to make a meal of black-eyed peas (with garlic, celery and salt pork, and cornbread on the side) a feast indeed. This morning her good cinnamon bread and coffee were so good.

After dinner, gifts given out, and alas, Molly's box of candy disappeared, but she had an apron and a sweater.

Slim and Molly as usual cleared away and did dishes and then pleasant rest until more guests, Ann Marie, Beth and Frances arrived for further feasting. And of course all day music from Stanley's FM set upstairs, and Deane's borrowed FM set downstairs, and when they were silent, the hi-fi set George Cooley gave us with all his magnificent records when he decided to strip himself. [*Missing text*]

December 27

Ed Forand said he intended, God willing, to stay for life. Also Stanley, God bless them both. So good.[203]

# 1961

2/16. Balmorhen, Texas. Thursday after Ash Wednesday

Coming west on Rt. 190 from Fort Stockton on the way to El Paso, you come on thousands of acres of cotton fields, some owned by great companies, others by individuals. You are past the desert ranches with their cattle, sheep, and goats (wool and mohair). So there are cotton gins.

The people and the homes they live in. They are of great dignity, noble in bearing, and their homes are hovels, mud huts or small trailers in which they eat in these seasons when there is no work. Today they are out gleaning—picking the cotton.

Why each member of staff is important.

Ed Forand—(connection with Fr. Hugo, Fr. Murray); his suffering, his dedication, ex-army.

Ralph [Madsen]—(his ideals, interest in family, community, manual labor).

Ed Turner—(for his patience, silence, fidelity, his great love of Peter Maurin).[204]

---

203 Ed Forand, "ex-Marine, a good journalist, who gets up at four in the morning to beg a crate of vegetables from the market, and who drives the car and shares the cooking...," was still living at the Catholic Worker twenty-five years after Dorothy's death. Stanley Vishnewski remained at the Worker until his death in 1979.

204 "Ed Turner ... walked out of the Army to become a conscientious objector and served two years in prison for his beliefs... He not only teaches and writes but is doing research on Peter Maurin and his teaching." (*LF*, 150).

Feb 24 Friday

Spanish motto in Pecos priest's house (on one of his plates): "It is good to do nothing and having done nothing, to sleep." Some days are like that with me. Today I thought of a title for my book, "The Duty of Delight," as a sequel to "The Long Loneliness." I was thinking, how as one gets older, we are tempted to sadness, knowing life as it is here on earth, the suffering, the Cross. And how we must overcome it daily, growing in love, and the joy which goes with loving.

Feb 26. Day of Recollection. At Balmorhen Lake, Texas

A warm sunny day. Not a cloud in the sky. Many are fishing at the lake but we have gone past them and there is complete silence, aside from an occasional call of a bird.

My heart is wrung by the suffering in the world and I do so little.

There was a picture in *Newsweek* of a dozen starving babies in the Congo, one tiny little one with his face in his hands. Terribly, terribly moving. The only consolation is that God will wipe away all tears from their eyes. But woe to us who caused those tears. We white ones ….

It seems to me that one of the happiest lessons in the gospel is that of love. That we are told to love one another and to show that love by giving. And that love becomes more like that of God when we see Jesus Himself in those around us, as the apostles did on Mt. Tabor, when the celestial light faded, and "they saw only Jesus," most loveable. They loved, because he first loved them, and even in those three, there were the sins of the world—they would deny Him, desert Him, at the end, and the weak of faith and greedy of the first place, while he was still with them.

He taught them about love, about loving. The prodigal son, the sick, the leprous, the privileged, the tax-gatherers, the sinners, those in prison—in other words, loving the unlovable, naturally speaking.

Some people think the most important task of the Catholic Worker is peace, to clarify thought about modern war, man's freedom and the use of force; other people go deeper and say voluntary "poverty" is the answer; others say "Providence."

But truly "Love" is the reason for it all. "Love your enemies, do good to those who hate you, bless those who curse you, pray for those who calumniate you, and to him who strikes thee on one cheek, offer the other also, and from him who takes away thy cloak, do not withhold thy tunic either. Give to him who asks of thee, and from him who takes away thy goods, ask no return."

So here we are begging again, for the Catholic Worker family, which is made of the lame, the halt, the blind, for the mentally afflicted, for all those suffering the long loneliness which is life.

Our need is especially great now, as we are forced to move again, after being a little over 2 years on Spring St. We are going back to Chrystie St. again, further down into the East Side, with the Bowery on one side, and a Puerto Rican section on the other. God is good. We seem to have found a landlord who will put up with us, and we have signed a 2-year lease at $250 a month. That is for office, clothes rooms, bread line. The rents for sleeping quarters continue, and the editors share their slum quarters with others.

It is a mystery to me, and always will be, how we keep going—these 28 years, with nothing in the bank, and debts piled high. But we survive, and since where love is, God is, and God is Life, we can truly be said to truly live.

## March 22, Wed. [Tucson]

Woke up at 5 a.m. and went to the 6 o'clock Mass, a high Mass sung by the Benedictine Sisters of Perpetual Adoration on Country Club Road in Tucson.

The hosts we receive at Communion are extra large—like the one for the monstrances—and they have special permission to receive them and those who communicate in their chapter. The Lord remains with us for two hours, it is estimated.

## March 23, Yuma

We left yesterday at 10:30 and arrived around six at Yuma stopping in a comfortable motel—$6 for the two of us, Alberta Bicson and I. Smell of orange blossoms in the heat. It was 85 degrees here in the shade and it must have been 100° in the sun, driving all day. The desert is incredibly rich and fertile wherever there is irrigation and the contrast between arid desert on one side and cultivated orchard and truck gardens on the other is startling.

The highway we came on is well frequented by trucks and is double lanes highway most of the way. In Yuma as in Tucson there are air bases and the sound of jet planes is an ominous overall nerve-wracking accompaniment to daily life. No silence of the desert here.

We stopped at a wayside park for lunch of tamales and avocado pear, and of course we carried a can of water.

The Negro attendant of parks drove up while we were there and told us of his 18-year-old son studying to be an engineer "so he won't have to work as hard as I do."

I told him I thought his was an honorable occupation, more so than that of men who worked at the missile plant in Tucson. Four thousand are occupied there, and the prosperity of the town is built on war. They are digging 18 huge holes around the town to launch rockets, and one of the Quaker students suggested that part of the widespread Easter demonstration could be to have a shovel battalion go out to make the gesture of filing them up.

March 30. Holy Thursday. St. Andrew's Priory

I got here just before Mass at 5:30 in the chapel, which was once the barn. There is a beautiful (and expensive) simplicity about it all—but not near big enough for all who come to the Benedictines for nourishment. The Mass was beautifully sung and since there were 14 students from Loyola in L.A. there was the Mandatum or washing of feet.

*Mandatum novum do vobis,* "a new commandment I give to you, that you love one another as I have loved you."

"I have given you an example that you also may do likewise."

When the Mass was over, and the altar stripped, the procession left the little chapel (it seats only about seventy-two people, and with lighted tapers we went out into the dark and a high wind that immediately put them out. "The alter of repose" was so small, only six could enter and then it was so crowded that we all stood outside while the last of the pangina lingua was sung.

Supper was a paschal meal with lamb and green herbs, and unleavened bread and wine, and we three women sat in a room apart and read the story of the Last Supper, which we ourselves ate.

Compline at 9:15, and then bed.

Good Friday, March 31

I did not try to get up for Matins and Lauds today but slept till 8 and skipped breakfast, making some coffee out of the tap water.

I spent an hour of adoration, an hour reading in the sun and rested again after a lunch of soup and stewed peaches from the monks' own orchard.

Reading *Seeds of the Desert,* here in the desert, those chapters on prayer.

Père Voillaume quotes: "Listen to these wise words of Gandhi's: 'Whether you wet your hands in the water basin, fan the fire with the bamboo bellows, set down endless columns of figures at a desk, labor in the rice field with your head in the burning sun and your feet in the mud, or stand at work before the smelting furnace, as long as you did not do all this with just the same religiousness as if you were monks praying in a monastery, the world will never be saved.'"

At three the services began—the reading from Scripture, adoration of the Cross and the Mass of the pre-sanctified. The little chapel was crowded but not uncomfortably so, with the 14 young men from Loyola, some neighboring families, and the Grail and Catholic Worker represented by the three women.

A late supper and it seems so strange always to be waited on by a great and learned monk. But that is the Benedictine tradition and rule. Work and Pray.

Compline at 8:30. Everything is admirably simple.

April 1. Holy Saturday

We keep the vigil in silence, Eileen and Miss Rodriguez and I and now after Matins, Lauds, and Prime in English from the short breviary, the breakfast. I had a short interview with the Father prior, who was in St. Andrews in China.

Being men of peace—of prayer and work, these monks seem to understand our position of nonviolent resistance to Communism and to capitalism (that is, the industrial capitalism of our day). Here are these monks—exiles from China, where they suffered the loss of all earthly goods, imprisonment and finally banishment.

April 24. Santa Rosa, N.M.

I had so stupid an argument with a chancellor of a western diocese. We started with Cuba, and I said part of the resentment of the people is because the Church or churchmen were on the side of the rich. "What proof of that have you?"

"The poverty of the agricultural workers in California and no condemnation of growers by hierarchy."

"You should see our poor, the Indians," he said. "You have seen nothing yet."

Péguy: "The sinner is at the very heart of Christendom. No one knows more about Christianity than the sinner. No one unless it is the saint. And in principle they are the same man."

Graham Greene: "The greatest saints have been men with a more than normal capacity for evil, and the most vicious men have narrowly evaded sanctity."

Greene's work proclaims that mankind, in Cardinal Newman's words "is implicated in some terrible aboriginal calamity."

April 28. Air Raid Drill.[205]

Saturday May 13. Detroit
It is a wonderfully bright day after a long spring, in fact no spring at all.
Yesterday [Arnold] Toynbee spoke at Ann Arbor and said that just as there were no longer religious wars, so too wars between nations will cease. He condemned the kidnapping of Eichmann and the invasion of Cuba as examples of the gangsterism of modern nations.

May 14
Bob Steed went with Dave Dellinger to Washington to picket and fast in front of CIA building to protest invasion [*Bay of Pigs invasion of Cuba*]. Got ten days in Washington jail. Is selling paper on streets now for carfare, sleeping at Maryhouse or the beach.
Big news this week is mobbing and beating in Montgomery, Alabama of Freedom Riders. Jim Peck beaten at Birmingham. Now all riders Negro but all arrested in Jackson, Mississippi. Attorney Gen backs down, asks for "cooling off" period.

May 16
Was a very long drive, and by resting an hour I was able to drive [David] home to Perkinsville, and would probably have lost my way if I had not. Tamar not too well, gastritis or something—due to worry as much as anything, over finances, what with David getting only $40 a week and board and room. He looks very sad.

May 18
Hilaire is a manly 3, four in late August. He can manage the cow better than Becky who is 16 and who is not a lover of cows. But of course all the children can milk. Becky can bake bread, and sew a fine seam. Hilaire came striding in yesterday after following the neighbor's horse and wagon spreading manure all morning. He begins unloading his pockets of eggs—11 of them, in rear pockets and side pockets. No wonder men don't have to carry bags with such pockets.
I produce a little catechism every day for the two littlest. Martha is 5. "Who made you?" I asked her. "God made me," she said. She used to say Mommy and Daddy, recognizing their co-creatorship. "And why?" "Because He likes

---

205 Dorothy was out of town for this year's largest and final protest. Over 2,000 people flouted the law; about 40 were arrested, receiving varying sentences. It was the last time the City ever attempted such an exercise.

me," she answered. The children always say, "Like," not "love," and very earnestly too.

But when I asked who made the lake we were passing, they were dubious. It is the result of a dam they saw in the process of being constructed, and men seemed to be creating water where only a brook had trickled before.

### May 24

Exhausted today and could not go in to N.Y. or to farm. Community takes it out of me. In what does our poverty consist? In toilets out of commission in town, dishwashers who wipe their noses on the dish towels, people who are mental cases.

### July 4

Della and Carol over in afternoon. Then to 38 St. for dinner and Franklin and I watched doubleheader ball game. I with my arthritis in feet and knees and he with his leg, enjoying the graceful movements on television.

### July 6

Came back in to N.Y. after refreshing overnight stay. My arthritis very bad, sudden sharp pains in feet, knee, and hip. Have to have cane or umbrella along. Clam chowder with Stanley. He is such a help and companion too. Long letter from Deane in doldrums. Stanley good there with advice.

### Friday July 7

Reading *Satyagraha* [Gandhi] at meeting. Letter from Gertrude Power with check with $2,000. Deo gratias! How good God is. And his friends.

### July 9

Controlled my tongue till night when I scolded Jean Morton for having guests until 2 a.m.

### July 12

Stanley has finished 55 pages of "The Wounded Ones" (Loaves and Fishes). He needles Bob [Steed] at table. Such sufferings.

### July 19

Mass at 8. Worked on book and Stanley came in to bring typed pages and took entire ms. to Harpers. Then to Golden's for my reading glasses. For 2 weeks I have been taking Vitamin B complex and for last four days have not had to use a cane.

July 29
Left farm with Stanley at 8 for Fr. John Monaghan's funeral. Cardinal, bishops, monsignors, ACTU, Sisters, John Cort, George Donahue, all there. Letter and poem from [Thomas] Merton.[206] Letter from Jack English.

August 2. Press.
Drove in to printer arriving by noon. My article on Cuba disjointed. Time I did nothing but lecture.

August 7
Stayed at the beach last night. Called Tamar and she told me David went to the State hospital today. I will go up to see her, Friday. But she says she is relieved. He is really trying.

August 13
Sharon Farmer's first Holy Communion on farm. Jim Forest spoke in grove.[207] At Tamar's I was exhausted with Sat work and rested all day reading.
I'm reading Pearl Buck, *Letter from Peking*. Light but interesting. Tamar is wonderful—no self-pity. She has not been getting enough sleep.

August 14. Left Perkinsville
Very cold last night. Investigator came this a.m. at 9. Very nice. I called Tamar later; she said no lien on house but a survey of personal property to see if there is enough to take lien on. $40 a month for each child, and something for her. She feels the tension. Distributism versus welfare state. But Dave kept going 17 years without it. I must write the history of his jobs.

---

206 A letter from Thomas Merton was not an everyday occurrence. The Trappist monk and author of *The Seven Storey Mountain* was at that time the most popular Catholic spiritual writer in America. But increasingly he felt compelled to address the social issues of the day, particularly the problems of racism, peace, and nuclear war. For several years he relied on the CW as one of his primary vehicles. Beginning with an ironic anti-war poem, "Chant To Be Used in Processions Around a Site with Furnaces" (July-August 1961), he contributed a steady stream of essays until the Trappist censors forbade any further publishing on issues of war and peace. This initial poem, written in the voice of a death camp commandant, ended with the words: "Do not think yourself better because you burn up friends and enemies with long-range missiles without ever seeing what you have done."
207 Jim Forest, a recent convert, had joined the CW after being released from the Navy as a conscientious objector. Dorothy soon recognized his literary talents and put him in charge of editing the paper.

August 20
    [Allan] Hoffman speaking. He considers himself a Zen Buddhist, I think. A very attractive boy. He told the judge he did not believe in Divine Providence, so that judge gave him 90 days in the Civil Defense case April 28. He spoke of the presence of an angel while he was waiting in line at Riker's Island. Fr. [Philip] Berrigan, Josephite called and he and Fr. Wayne of Xavier Univ are going on a Freedom Ride tomorrow under CORE. Truly ecumenical.

August 22
    Headache. To office at 5. Called Tamar and she had been to see Dave. He said the ward he was in was like CW—6 men.

September 1. Retreat. Mt. Savior
    90°. Could not sleep with the heat last night. Up till 2 reading "My Desire." Crying of a woman in the neighborhood. Spanish. It sounded first as tho she were reciting a long dramatic poem. Up at 6:15.

Sept 2. Mt. Savior
    The conventual Mass here is at 7:30 and the monks were reciting one of the hours as we arrived.
    When Janet B came this morning and was asking about a schedule, about hours when the Blessed Sacrament was to be exposed for adoration, I told her of Fr. Jos Woods and a conference he once gave in which he said, "The Blessed Sacrament is to be consumed, not just adored. He is our life, our food, and we do not adore our food as such. We might as well adore the altar."

This morning when the kiss of peace was given, it was given deliberately, not a perfunctory, nor self-conscious embrace. The monk placed his hands on the shoulders of the monk to his right and bowing first, slightly, bent his cheek to the cheek of his brother monk so that they touched, so that human love and tenderness was expressed, sublimated by Christ's love. Mind, body and soul are all integrated in such worship.

September 3
    Ammon this month says if we do not print his stuff on Mary, not to print it at all. So for the first time he will not be in. I should send him Camus quote:
    "I have always drawn my hope from the idea of fecundity. Like many men today I am tired of criticism, of disparagement, of spitefulness—of churl-

ishness, in short. It is essential to condemn what must be condemned, but quietly and firmly. On the other hand one should praise at length what still deserves to be praised."

September 15

Meanwhile our bills—Bernie $2,200. Taxes $1,200. Garage, hardware. I spoke to Ralph months ago about charging but he cannot conceive of going without. This generation, which grew up during depression. The war benefit generation. How terrible to think of our prosperity being based on war. Another reason to go to Jackson on a Freedom Ride. To do penance, to be poor. Meanwhile, dear Lord, pay our bills by Thy divine providence and forgive us our indulgences, conscious and unconscious. To learn to do without, to strip ourselves!

September 16

Beautiful weather. Thank God. "The Lord of the heavens and the earth, and the sea and the fountains, and the rivers and all creatures and may health be given us." Prayer of Tobias. And last Sunday, "In Thy loving kindness, O Lord, purify our souls. We beseech thee and quicken us to a new life by thy sacrament, that in both the present and the future, even our bodies, therein may find relief."

September 17

No use saying I do not worry. Others have more faith than I do. No matter how broke we are, people do not stop coming, nor do they go away. Sometimes, I feel like saying, "Those who don't have to be here, please go away." But they would just look helpless and say "Where else shall we go?" Fernando says, "No one ever loved me."

I hear that many times a month and feel like saying where there is no love, put love—we all need to learn that. Of course sometimes it is hard to love people. Fr. Hugo said you love God as much as the one you love the least. So all our life is a practice to learn to love God. The first commandment. St. Vincent de Paul.

October 6

To Tamar's. Lovely weather. Arrived at 6:30, sun still shining on the house which faces south and has 4 windows facing west. Very cheerful in these darkening days. Boys chopping and splitting wood. All very cheerful and helpful. Becky especially, changed for better.

November 18

David left hospital. Went to Washington. I telephoned Tamar—all is well.[208]

Dec 12

Arthur Lacey brought my mail down to the beach at nine-thirty at night after he had "paid the men in" on the Bowery.[209] Charles Butterworth who has charge of the house in N.Y. and all its finances gives him the money, and the cost is ninety cents or a dollar a night. We patronize the Salvation Army hotel, the Majestic, the Sunshine, the Cunard, and Uncle Sam's (where Peter Maurin used to stay before we had a house of hospitality).

The Association of Catholic Trade Unionists sent down a Puerto Rican last night who brought to 14 the numbers put up. Always more than ten dollars a night, three hundred a month, not to speak of our rents on apartments and furnished rooms which make up our decentralized house of hospitality. When I count all the violations in the buildings we are occupying I am appalled at the corruption, blindness, partiality, bureaucracy of the building department of N.Y.

Arthur J. Lacey, or "Dear Soul" as we like to call him, because he once had the maddening habit of saying tenderly to those he was trying to help, "Have you a problem, dear soul?" does indeed help a great deal. He gives out men's clothes whenever we have clothes to give, and runs innumerable errands between farm and city, and beach and city, dropping little tidbits of gossip on the way. He is the grapevine of the CW right now. I scolded him for coming out so late, but do certainly appreciate his coming out with mail and messages as he does several times a week.

Dec 25

"The brightness of your glory has made itself manifest to the eyes of our mind by the mystery of the word made flesh, and we are drawn to the love of things unseen thru him whom we acknowledge as God, not seen by men." From the preface in the Christmas Mass.

"What have I on earth but Thee and what do I desire in heaven beside Thee?"

It is joy that brought me to the faith, joy at the birth of my child 35 years ago, and that joy is constantly renewed as I daily receive our Lord at Mass. At

208 David Hennessy had not done well since the move to Perkinsville. His physical and emotional health deteriorated to the point that he was unable to support his family. Eventually he and Tamar separated.

209 Aside from permanent or short-term "guests" in the house of hospitality, the CW regularly paid for a number of beds in cheap hotels or "flophouses" on the Bowery.

first I thought that following the prayers of the Mass would become monotonous and something for the priest to continue day after day, and that that was why people were silent and bookless. Some Quakers going to Mass with me once said, "Now I know what the Mass is—it is a meditation." But it is an act, a sacrifice, attended by prayers and these prayers, repeated daily, of adoration, contrition, thanksgiving, supplication are ever new. One or another emotion may predominate, but the act performed evokes the feeling of "performing the work of our salvation."

Christmas Eve and Christmas this year I went to the 11 o'clock Masses, at St. Thomas and was moved to the deepest gratitude that we have two such good priests in our parish. That is the greatest gift the Peter Maurin farm has ever received. We were included in the greeting in the parish bulletin, as the "largest family in the parish."

Dec 28. Snow is falling

Feast of the Holy Innocents. From early morning till late at night the house is riotous—Tamar's nine and two guests, an eight-year-old and a 15-year-old. This morning they were out sledding after a hasty breakfast and now they are in again racing up and downstairs. The furnace fire went out and Eric is downstairs struggling with it. The fire in the kitchen stove and the Franklin stove in the living rooms are going good. The teenagers have their radio on, Nick and Margaret talking loudly and playing Monopoly. There is perpetual motion and perpetual sound from Mary H., Martha, Hilaire, and Louise, their guest. The house is in a turmoil of caps, coats, mittens, galoshes, scarves, toys and if anything is ever found again it will be thanks to St. Anthony.

A goodly amount of spun silk and a great deal of cotton thread for the loom had come in at Chrystie street and Tamar wove a silk scarf and is going to set up the loom in cotton to make some material which she can afterwards dye. Weaving is her "tranquilizer."

Knitting, generally, is mine, tho I never get beyond scarves. I have made socks for the children, and once in a while achieved a good pair for an adult. One monstrosity I made which would match nothing and was due to be ripped out was seized by Anne Marie [Stokes] as an amusing gift (together with one of her own perfect ones) for a worker priest. I hope by now some friendly soul has re-knit it for him.

As I washed and teased wool for the comforter I finished last night during the days I had visitors at the beachhouse I thought of God's good news and the sacramentatality of things.

Our pastor said in his Christmas sermon, "On the one hand shepherds, sheepherders, and on the other hand, angels."

# 1962

Wed Jan 10 [Pittsburgh]

Slept at Strassers until 9, Erica drove me to Duquesne chapel where there was a Mass beautifully participated in by the students.

Later I went downtown a few blocks to Kaufman's to buy wool stockings, a present from the Strassers, a great comfort in this zero weather. Also a pull-down over-the-ears hat, a crocheted black wool. What fun to spend money on some clothes when one is used to hand-me-downs from the clothes' room at the Catholic Worker. Women never cease to be interested in clothes, no matter how old they get.

Eric Gill wrote a good deal on the subject of clothes but the most moving was his meditation on Christ being stripped of his garments.

The Duquesne meeting was sponsored by the Pius X society and was very crowded, as all the meetings have been at Albright, St. Francis, St. Vincent's, Seton Hall, and Mt. Mercy. The questions are all about war and the state.

After supper, we went to see Bishop Wright. I had thought just to "pay my respects" but he was home and welcomed us all most affably. We saw his collection of Joan of Arc statues, pictures, manuscripts, etc, which he has been collecting since he was 14. He knows so many people we know, and asked about the trip, where I had spoken, where I was going, whom I would see in Chicago.

We did not talk of pacifism, anarchism, communism, Cuba, Spain, nor of the Holy Father and his great messages to the world, nor of the coming ecumenical council because of which, in connection with which, Bishop Wright flies to Rome monthly. But it was a pleasant two-hour meeting and I am grateful indeed to the Bishop for his friendship and help.

A seaman, John Givens, brought me a statue of Joan of Arc years ago and someone around the CW (where we hold all things in common—in theory) walked off with it. Bishop Wright gave me another and I shall treasure this figure of a girl and her sword, who died for conscience (and for the Church).

Jan 14. Evanston

The train from Pittsburgh was filthy, stinking from the men's room, no drinking water, no water to wash with in the ladies' room. We left at 11:30, got into Union Station at 7:30. One walks miles in a vast station (with heavy suitcase), waits interminably for a cab, etc. I list these inconveniences to point to the discomforts of our luxury-loving, efficiency-minded "civilization." Busses are far more comfortable and convenient as far as I'm concerned.

Karl Meyer's St. Stephen's House of Hospitality is on W. Oak St. in one of the infamous tenements owned by Winkles, a Scrooge-like figure of greed and infamous exploitation of the needy. Karl pays $70 for the long narrow apt. on the first floor which was once a tiny store and apt. Karl sleeps in the store; the next room was the meeting room last night. Forty came.

When I got there after a day of rest at Nina's, Erica Enzer, who was one of the first to practice civil disobedience at the Omaha Missile base, was with Bob washing walls and floors and moving boxes of newspapers and such like down in the basement. Erica is a non-believer, and a warm and loving soul, serving Christ in His hidden guise, tho she denies Him. And how many there are who say Lord, Lord, and do not recognize Him in his poor.

Certainly Karl is in closest touch with the destitute.

How much work is being done on all levels, housing, interracial justice, against the usury of the loan companies who suck the blood of the poor and force them into destitution.

And the work for peace, about which we write so much. Karl is working at the bottom, sharing most truly the hard life, the life of poverty, and manual labor of God's least.

There was a midnight meeting at CBS. Everyone was very serious and courteous and no one would dream that any of the positions the CW took and which I had the opportunity to express were at all controversial. The only hint that I was not all-conformist came when the football celebrity replied to the question as to how educational football was by saying that football taught one sportsmanship and gentlemanliness, as was evidenced by the present company in listening to me.

February. Work camp

Much trouble all during February with beatniks—Jean [Morton] and Jim [Forest], [Ed] Sanders, Nelson Barr, Bob Kay, Ellen Paulson.[210]

March and April issues made up by Bob [Steed], and I gathered the material.

Spoke Feb 21 Seton Hall in Patterson, very hostile. Feb 27 at Harvard, March 1, Woodstock, Md. March 2 N.Y. Univ Newman Club, March 9 in Montreal at St. Helen's for Nazareth House. Met Cardinal Leger, who asked me about the juridical position of the CW. When I explained our lay free-

---

210 Dorothy applied the term "beatnik" rather broadly. See below, March 2.

dom, our investigation of disputed questions, he called us "John the Baptist groups."

## February 27

Jean Goss and Hildegard Goss-Mayr.[211] A most beautiful and dedicated couple. Eileen Egan gave us supper and a score crowded in to hear them. He spoke French and she translated. Most effective.

## March 2. NY University

Jean Morton, Nelson Barr, Bob Kay, [Allan] Hoffman, [Ed] Sanders all asked to stay away from CW. In their mimeographed publication they have shown hatred, contempt for the very sources of life itself, and have defaced in every way the creativity within them, a blasphemy and a horror from which one can only recoil with fear and disgust at this breath of evil among us.[212]

## March 4. Perkinsville

So that both girls could get to Mass I stayed home with the little ones and read Matins and Lauds, and prayers of the Mass aloud, and Hilaire just listened. Katy babbled joyfully, holding a book, imitating me. In the afternoon Tamar made a banana cake, very good, and Sue made fudge. A happy birthday. She got a nice letter from David. She shows a deep and compassionate understanding of his troubles, thank God. No bitterness or anger.

---

211 Jean Goss and his wife Hildegard Goss-Mayr were Catholic pacifists (from France and Austria, respectively) who played an enormous role in raising the consciousness of the church on issues of war and peace and the rights of conscience.

212 Dorothy alluded to this purge in the July-August issue of the paper: "The crisis was a moral one, not a simple one of techniques, or emphasis, or choice between two goods. A group of beats or those desiring to follow the life of beats, descended on us. This lasted some months. They came, they went. My criticism was that they despised the life forces within man, that they were nihilistic rather than pacifist, that their contempt was directed against the very body of man, that temple of the Holy Spirit and that all the four letter words they used so glibly (and so reminiscent of our prison days) was to express this contempt, this hatred—not only of the square, of the bourgeois around them, but of the life force in man himself. Also they lived and moved among the poor as though they were not there, taking their meager housing space, pushing in to table at the CW to get their share of the food, and so living that they disregarded the affront they offered the simple, reticent, decent and modest men among whom they lived." Jim Forest, though not part of this group, felt that Dorothy had been indiscriminate in her ire, and so resigned from the CW as a gesture of solidarity. He provides a less euphemistic account of the affair in Rosalie Riegle, *Dorothy Day: Portraits by Those Who Knew Her*, 154-55. The crisis had been provoked by Ed Sanders (later a founder of the rock group The Fugs), who produced a broadsheet entitled "F— Y—: A Magazine of the Arts," in which he mischievously thanked the Catholic Worker for use of its mimeograph machine. Years later, the memory of this incident could still arouse Dorothy's anger.

March 5. Perkinsville

Today received word of arrest of Jean Morton, Jim Forest, and others (Nelson Barr, Ellen Paulson) for their sit-down at Atomic Energy Commission. Their non-violence is violence too considering the little magazine.

Friday March 9

Two things we have to learn—not to judge others and not to mind others judging us. To endure conflict between charity and common good, authority-freedom, state vs. personal responsibility.

Fear and trembling, meekness, yet faith in God's powers to correct gives sureness. (Mike Wallace: How can you be so sure?)

April 3. Becky is 17

Bright and sunny. To N.Y. at 5 with letters, clothes, etc.

Bad news of Jim [Forest] going to marry Jean [Morton] outside of church. Wrote [Thomas] Merton.

May 3. Princeton. Prof. [Karl] Barth of Basil

Audience cramming the Princeton chapel.

Barth is hoarse. He is speaking of "this solemn power which takes possession of one." He speaks a little like Peter Maurin, in his emphasis, earnestness, voice breaking now and then. He looks young for his 75 years, grey, not white, ruddy, healthy skin, steps a little hesitant, he must be helped up the pulpit steps. He makes little jokes, which the audience appreciates inordinately. For instance, criticizing expression Holy Ghost, he said it reminds one of spooks (general murmur of laughter). Spirit is the word, a holy word, the Lord and giver of life, who proceeds from the Father and Son, and with Father and Son is adored and glorified, Lord of Covenant.

He dwells in men. He is that atmosphere in which men can live, move and speak. There are men known by him, called by him.... (Anne Marie very restless, bored, stirring, rustling like a bush). His hand trembles as he turns the pages. ... Anne Marie yawns, examines her fingernails, rubs her eyes, sighs, nods her head, gives every indication of trying hard to keep awake.

The problem of the last-eleven-year book—what to call it: Loaves and Fishes, no. Love of God, Love of Brother. All Men are Brothers—? I am trying to round off my last chapter, "on a note of joy," Mr. Sammis [free-lance editor for LF] said. On a note of love, I am thinking.

May 9

Went to press today. Printed appeal a month late. Also Ed Forand, Chas Butterworth, Deane, Judith, Karl, Lou Murphy—a good list, and Thomas Merton besides.

Since Jan I have written no On Pilgrimage what with working on my book and it has drawn the others out.

June 8

To Dorothy Tully to sign will. Judith [Gregory] is responsible if Chas and I both die. Then to lunch with Chas. Long talk about married state. Then to farm, delightful day.

June 23, Saturday

Damp, cloudy. Could not go to Mass because my underclothes washed last night were not dry. Went at one to picket U.S. Mission to U.N. for Bill Worthy, arrested for coming into the country without a passport.[213] Then to Della's. Franklin just home from hospital after 3 months. My heart aches for him. And for David H. Tamar has not heard from him for a month. I called her last night.

To office at five. I am always getting involved in problems and forgetting people who are waiting to talk to me. The fellow who wanted to sing to me one of his compositions and tonight a man who had lived a long time in China and wanted to speak at CW.

June 26.

CBS, Chrystie St.[214]

July 4. St. Sisoes, hermit

"Let us lay all our cards on the table."

That is not a very good title because it partakes of the spirit which most discussion of money engenders.

Personally I like to know what work people are engaged in, how much pay they get, how much rent they pay, and so on and so on But I have been brought up in the convention that talking about money is bad manners, is too personal.

---

213 William Worthy, foreign correspondent for the *Baltimore Afro-American*, was prosecuted for the "crime" of traveling to Cuba without a passport and then returning to the U.S. (September 1962 CW)

214 CBS was producing a television documentary on the CW.

If your interest in people—all the people you encounter—is personal, you like to know everything about them, as Ignatius wrote to Francis Xavier, even about the fleas that bite them. "Tell me every detail," St. Ignatius implored in their long correspondence.

The Catholic Worker has always been frank about money. For instance, the first issue cost $57 to print; 2,500 copies. Now we print 75,000 at a cost of . . . .

Our grocery bills—rents, were public knowledge, because we begged so much of our help.

Really, we felt it was an exchange of goods, rationalizing so our pride did not suffer. We wrote articles, cooked meals, shared what we earned "outside," gave our best to the cause, the Catholic Worker, the house of hospitality, the farm, without pay. We all worked according to our ability and received according to our need.

These are grand phrases. Of course there is the matter of vocation and the need that goes with it. I need a typewriter to write articles, carfare to travel, to point out a few discrepancies. Critics can always find the flaws in our lives, our inconsistencies, our subtle hypocrisies, our complacencies. The wonderful part of community is that these are so consistently pointed out to us, it makes, if not for humility, then for a certain hardness. As St. Paul said, "I do not justify myself."

This is sort of a companion piece to the account of our wealth and expenditures which follows.

It is a sad fact of human nature that avarice, which builds up wealth, is accompanied by envy—two most unlovely vices. Lust and gluttony seem playful and superficial in comparison, attractive in their early stages, and more easily redeemable by the natural disgust of satiety. But is there ever any end to envy and avarice?

I am reading Cassian's conferences on Avarice and they frighten me. We suddenly are acquiring so much, and how hard it would be to lose one "estate." Because we have now become. . . .

*By the summer of 1962 Dorothy was planning a new adventure —a month-long trip to Cuba. For some years she had followed the progress of the Revolution, and now, in the midst of rising Cold War tensions, she wished to experience the situation firsthand. She went as a journalist, to see and report on the process of social reform and the state of the church. But she also went as a pilgrim, to express her solidarity, to seek "concordances," to "see Christ" in the Cuban people.*

Aug 8
Validation of passport arrived from State Dept. *[for travel to Cuba].*

Aug 9.
[Bill] Worthy found guilty in Miami. Sentenced later.

Aug 10
Sent passport to Czechoslovakian embassy. Had already sent pictures and application.

August 24
Bought ticket. $80 one way, tourist. $158 round trip. Garcia Diaz line. I will be under Spanish law on boat. Rules and regulations amusing about firearms.

August 25. Sue's birthday
Havana shelled last midnight from 2 yachts. Students from Miami blamed or claimed credit.

August 28
Wrote Cuba article for Sept. CW [*"Pilgrimage to Cuba: Part I"*]. To Third Ave. for suitcase and transistor with Stanley.

August 29
Woke up this a.m. to find a man asleep on floor of hall. Chas says this happens each morning on Spring St.

August 31
Chas de Foucauld said, "Once I believed there was a God I saw no other course than to serve Him."

Sept 1. Annual Retreat
Mass at 8. Most beautiful surroundings. Low tide and I collected shells, very large mussels.
Two "lights" which came to me in my life for which I shall be always thankful. One at 16: that I could earn a living by manual labor, housework, and so honorably could obtain my bread. I failed to remember this when I asked St. Anthony to send me a job writing!

Second light at 26 when I realized that the pleasures of the intellect would grow, that the delights in the search for God would never end—at the beach.

## Sept 2

Up at six. A still foggy day, very close. Great clamor from crows, great murmurings among starlings, laughing gulls. I can sit on balcony overlooking water. The smell of the sea at low tide. Boats were out clamming last night. It is good to sit out here in early morning and think and pray about my coming visit to Cuba. To me, the issue is always that of nonviolence as well as man's needs on this earth where God put us to work out our salvation. How are we to achieve some measure of justice, striven for because of our love for our brothers. In the case of Cuba, the means used were guerrilla warfare, the overthrow of Batista, the putting down of counter-revolution by executions and imprisonments. What are to be the attitudes now?

I am talking to myself as I write this, and my first thought is—I go to see Christ in my brother the Cuban, and that means Christ in the revolution, Christ in the counter-revolutionary. But to both sides, being violently partisan, such an attitude will be considered reasonable by neither. The fervent Catholic in U.S. feels that a loyal Catholic must hate everything Fidel stands for, must hate Marxism-Leninism (without understanding in the least what that "pernicious doctrine" is).

Muriel said to me last night, "If you could only see Fr. Tomas Matachos who is in prison in Havana—terribly tortured and mutilated."

That gives me one assignment—to inquire about torture, which the Castro government claims it has done away with. This attitude generates fear, which in turn leads to that teaching of self-defense. A man has a right to defend his life and a right to give it up... Then too last night Fr. Foley, one of our best priests, said in talking of evil in the world, "communism is an example." If he had said hatred and fear, the hatred of God and man's religious nature, and the attempts to crush it in the name of man's liberties, I could understand him. But what if this hatred of religion has stemmed from seeing religion used by big business—"I took God into partnership and so I prospered." These are the actual words of a steel magnate who hired armed guards to shut down striking steel workers. As long as the profit motive is the predominant one, and not the common good, religions should have a hard time getting along in the capitalist system too. In *Osservatore Romano* some years ago, the leading editorial writer said Capitalism is a cancer on the social order. And *Blackfriars*, the excellent Dominican monthly had an issue, "Who baptized capitalism?"

The thing we should all remember is that in Cuba, the job the revolution is undertaking is to build a social order more in accordance with man's needs. And to do that all revolutionary movements are devoted to tearing down (in order to build up, they say) and the force the movement requires to give impetus to the little way of hard toil is fed also by fear and hatred of the enemy. "We must do these things, build up the economy in order to *show* them we are right and they are wrong. If we do not arm ourselves the invader will come and take away our land."

The first job of the Christian, it seems to me is to grow in faith in God—in His power, in the conviction that we are all held in the hollow of His hand. He is our safeguard and defense. This faith, we must pray for, does away with fear, which paralyzes all effort. Fear of losing a job, of hunger, of eviction, as well as fear of bodily violence, and the blows of insult and contempt. Let us respect each other as well as love each other.

I do not want to play down martyrdoms, but to keep in mind always, "Father, forgive them for they know not what they do." God loves all men. "God wills that all men be saved." But we have that great and glorious gift of free will, which distinguishes man from the beast, the power of choice, and man often chooses evil because it has the semblance of the good, because it seems to promise happiness.

"Behold I am sending you forth as sheep in the midst of wolves. Be ye therefore wise as serpents and simple as doves." This is the text on which Newman preached his sermon "Wisdom and Innocence" and which led Kingsley, the Protestant, to accuse him together with all Roman priests, of deceit, cunning. Newman had written the sermon as a Protestant.

I know that we Catholic pacifists are always judged as using quotations from great men "out of context." I do not understand that objection. The missal gives many examples of this practice. For instance the communion prayer.

Then there is that commentary of St. John Chrysostom, "I have sent you as sheep among wolves." "As long as you remain sheep the Lord is with you. But when you become wolves, the Lord Jesus is no longer with you."

And yet St. John Chrysostom himself was a wolf in his diatribes against the Jews, which could incite the wolf pack to pogrom.

Prince Kropotkin, that noble anarchist and Personalist, whose great book, *Mutual Aid,* influenced Maria Montesorri, wrote another book, *Conquest of Bread,* in which he talked of the difficulty, once a regime is overthrown, in building up a new economy.

Certainly this was one of the difficulties in Cuba. And the Communist had for scores of years—for generations—been working on just this problem. They felt assured that their program worked out in their own countries would not work out in Cuba.

We of the U.S. made the vacuum by withdrawing all help and imposing penalties besides. So the Communist, who had opposed the revolution before, stepped in with technical aid, machinery, and their Marxist-Leninist philosophy.

September 5. Sailing, Guadalupe
Up all last night till 4 with Greta's coughing. Mass 8:30. Then proofs, packing, and Louis Amter called in his tiny car and took [Stanley] and me to Harborside pier in Jersey City where we had lunch and waited. The boat sailed at 6:00 instead of 5 and dinner right after. 12 sea gulls followed us and these other freighters. No one was allowed on with me and I had to go on at 3:30. Rough wakes, rolling seas. Bed at nine, almost sick. Tourist class is main deck.

Sept 6
Up at 7. Feeling very ill. Mass at 7:30. Breakfast. John's seasick pills a help. Weather warm so it is good sitting on deck. Many children, noisy, stay up late. I am reading Spanish phrase book. We are off Carolina now.

On board boat, Guadalupe
Little flies biting the ankles, drawing blood. Cloudy, bursts of sun, white caps but only mildly rolling compared to last night. Yesterday the ship seemed rusty, dirty hulk, dear tho because of her name. The color of water has changed—deep and beautiful blue.

Just met the two young girls from Canada and England on way to Cuba to work there and see what is happening. They are pacifists, members of Com of 100. One was reading Marxism by C. Wright Mills, his last book.

There are 3 Masses every morning, 6:30, 7:30, 8:30. Breakfast is at 7:30, large cups of not-hot-enough milk and coffee and very good bread and little rolls.

3 p.m. broadcast from Carolina—someone or other in Washington says we of U.S. should not be trying to settle the Cuban problem thru OAS, but by setting up a government in exile, arming Cubans and looking forward to another invasion.

One of the young Cuban women going back looked at me wistfully—asked if I thought there was going to be trouble.

Sat. Sept. 8

Dear family—Stanley, thank you for your faithful loving-kindness, seeing me off and sticking by Della.

The boat is packed with children, babies, 4-year-olds, 8-year-olds, a few teenagers, and many young people going back to live. Some are going on a visit, and have visited relatives each year, some have made yearly visits before going back for good.

No drinking, no luxury, the ship is old, well-scrubbed each day—no hot water, one shower, no soap, one towel, poor food, fried in much oil, many beans and potatoes and macaroni—all put in soup, leftovers, I am sure. All very formally served, however.

Yes, there is a picture of Franco, a large one, under the clock in the dining room which never runs on time.

There is a chapel, very small, into which 18 people cram themselves for Mass each day. Ladies all wear veils, big ones, like Deane's, not like my square one. The chapel is in the center of the boat and we sweat there. The corridors of the first class seem to be air conditioned.

I have a cabin (for 2) alone with a porthole open all the time. But outside the door there is a lounge full of children—noisy, crying, one or two of them at all times. On the deck it is the same. Mothers are always with the children, however—one member of the family is always responsible, so the noise does not worry me, as it does not worry them.

I have done a lot of sleeping, in my most enjoyable privacy, and my cold is almost gone.

They say we will be in Havana Sunday morning, so I will be able to go to Communion on the boat and to Mass later in Havana. One of the girls at our retreat expressed surprise that there could be Masses in Cuba.

It is beginning to be very hot. I am going bare-legged and barefooted when I sit in my deck chair. Women are modest, but casual in dress. Most of the men so casual you might think them members of the crew. Very few English-speaking.

A number of families from Spain on their way to Mexico City. (I am jotting down things as they occur to me.)

The sea is very calm, in some places truly like glass, in others with tiny ripples like watered silk. Sky filled with little fleecy clouds which are reflected in the sea. We have passed Florida and the Keys, I guess, because I see no more land. Tomorrow at six we land at Havana. I heard there is no breakfast served tomorrow. I am glad I have my instant coffee. Even with cold water it helps to wake up.

The girls—Mary and Carol, avoid me, tho they sought me out at first. I wonder if it is because they think I am pious, or because they think I am counter-revolutionary because Catholic. I imagine anyone from the U.S. is suspect and a Catholic doubly so.

I keep thinking of Fritz Eichenberg's story about his giving all the Russian novels he illustrated to Khrushchev, and how he was received. He had gone to considerable expense to get all the Heritage editions of Tolstoi, and Dostoyevsky for which he had with great agony done the woodcuts and because it was a time when K. was most unpopular (perhaps the shoe-banging at the United Nations), he wrote that he would like to present them to the Moscow University Library. Perhaps it was to the Russian Mission to the United Nations that he wrote. He received a note after his presentation of the books which were suspiciously received. He said both American and Russian officials acted as tho he were carrying bombs as he appeared with the books. Later the note came inviting Fritz and Mrs. Eichenberg to meet with K. formally. He arrived and was greeted first with thanks, then with truculence, "Why do you people—" K wanted to know, "treat my country so?" And he proceeded with an outline of history, the U.S. opposition to the revolution, dating back to Archangel in 1918.

"I felt," said Fritz, "that I was meeting with the representative of a deeply humiliated people."

Fritz as a Quaker and a Jew is a man of deepest sympathies and has suffering in his bones.

I too felt the humiliation inflicted on the Cuban people by our non-recognition, by our diplomatic break with them. I felt it at the 26th of July party at the General Assembly lounge at the United Nations, and I felt it before at the reception of Dr. Garcia, permanent ambassador of the Cuban Mission to the U.N. and of Dr. Raul Premebles, the alternate ambassador.

September 9

Arrived Cuba, 7:30. Landed at 4. Customs and immigration. Hotel Regis, Charles Lopez. Found restaurant, rice and avocado, café. Inner room—air conditioned. $3. No water.[215]

---

215  Dorothy's diary from her Cuba trip is mostly filled with shorthand, journalistic notes. A full description of her activities and reflections is contained in the series of columns she wrote for the CW: October 1962, November 1962. See also "A Revolution near Our Shores" in *Dorothy Day: Selected Writings*, 298-311.

September 10

Dr. Ortega and a good interview. Supper with the Joneses and afterwards to the Chaplin theater to hear Castro who did not begin to speak until almost 12 and continued until 1:30. I got home at 2:30 or nearer 3. It ended with the singing of the Internationale, all the young people joining uplifted hands and swaying from side to side.

Sept 11, Tues a.m.

Yesterday was a full day. In the p.m. a young doctor, who had lived and practiced in N.Y. came and we talked for hours. Dr. Ortega—educated in N.Y., practiced there for years. He is heart and soul in revolution. He is against euthanasia, abortion, and birth control. The subject came up in relation to Church and politics. They are teaching—want to graduate 100 doctors a year for all rural sections.

Everything is being coordinated—health. They begin with providing shoes for all children so parasites cannot enter the body, hookworm, etc. Now it is gastroenteritis and all the restaurants have huge signs with pictures of babies and appeals to all gastronomical workers to cooperate and go to schools and be clean about themselves and utensils.

Saturday, Sept 15

Yesterday I went to Mass, to ministry, wrote. Then to Bishop's palace, great residence. Waited to visit. No luck. One young priest saying Mass. One old with cigar. Porter amused, indifferent, lolling.

Sunday, September 16

Last night there was a block meeting like civil defense, discussing problems of stealing in neighborhood.

Mass at St. Augustine's. Full church.

Monday, September 17

Big new wooden church in Santiago just above bus station, beautiful architecture, all glass windows in front so we could look in but locked. On outside some notices, pasted on building. 10 priests in Santiago. Taxi driver said 20 churches, Catholic. He went often but not every Sunday.

To Cobre—an hour or less by bus, to mining town. Shrine where I talked to Sister Mercedes, very friendly, also priest. Bought pins and medals.

Then to town again and bus to Guantanamo.

Base is 40 miles from Guantanamo. Prosperous little town. Shops, filled with clothes. Lines wherever meat was sold.

September 19
[William] Worthy sentenced to one year yesterday.
To Capri Hotel to visit [Robert and Mabel] Williams and girls. They want to keep vigil at Guantanamo but I am here to write, not to embarrass governments. Williams told me story of his escape to Cuba—a wild adventure story. I took notes and will try to write it tomorrow. Mabel and I went later to Habana Libre to see the shops and books and I got "Dostoevsky lived here." In evening we talked about the church and Cuba.

September 26. Guantanamo
Beautiful to awake on high hill overlooking this old city. Sisters of Social Service run a hospital there and I talked to Sister Mercedes, young and happy. They run a hospice, large and comfortable. Footpaths to mines and Chas wanted to follow them. Lovely bus ride. Then awful lunch.

September 27
All day at the school and interviews with teachers and visits to granja. Very large. On bus baby pig in basket, chickens, bananas.

September 28. Manzanillo
This was called a red town in the past but the church was open in the square at 8:30 and I went in with half dozen. Everywhere we were followed, as "Russ" pronounced rooso and cynical refused to believe we were North Americans. We left Camilo Cienfuegos at 10, having gotten up at 5:30 with the children. Saw the director. I thanked God for Charlie and his inquiring mind, constantly interviewing. We were sorry to see a dozen people waiting. In p.m. to Manzanillo and fisherman's village and coop, an unforgettable scene on the bay.

Sept 29. Manzanilla. Feast of St. Michael
Got reservations on special bus, "equipado con motor Sovietico," as it said on the back. Little jeep busses are called polikelos, after the Poles who sent them. The Chekas are the guns most milicianos carry.
All day Chas Horwitz was sick, writhing with cramps and pain in bones.[216] The church on the Plaza was half full, at least this morning at the second Mass. It was already very hot, over 85°. The people are beautiful, thought-

216 Charles Horwitz: "a graduate of the University of Chicago, who had worked at teaching in one of East Harlem's schools for the past two years, aimed to stay for a year and teach in Cuba, but on the day of our return he was picked up by security police and deported"—as Dorothy suspected, because he asked too many questions and sought out counter-revolutionaries. (October 1962)

ful, serious, and yet suddenly breaking out into gaiety. The fishermen were especially gay when we talked to them. "Now we live like the rich," one said laughing, pointing up from the shore to the little city of fishermen.

Two thousand children in fisherman's village, they said, and little boys seem to go naked up to the age of three. The campaign against parasites and infections has meant that all these naked little ones go around with shoes, their bodies brown with sun, a beautiful coffee color. But there are all shades of color here from ivory to black. "Do you like people of color?" one Negro woman asked me. And she added that I looked like her mother despite my being one of the "pink people," as G.B. Shaw said once of people of our color. My identification: press card issued me, and required by the dept. of foreign affairs, describes my height, weight, eyes, and type—*rosado*, which must mean my complexion, since my hair is grey.

Sept 30

All day yesterday Chas was miserably ill with gastroenteritis, prevalent here too in Santa Clara. If we had known how sick he was we would have stayed in Manzanilla where the hotel was comfortable

All night rioting in Oxford, Mississippi. Two killed, 50 hurt over registering of James Meredith [at the University of Mississippi]. News came in very clearly over radio which [Stanley] and I picked up on Bowery.

October 1

Mass at Iglesia Pasca, the oldest church in Santa Clara, and met Fr. Joseph, whose gentle happy face reminded me of Fr. Roy.

October 2

Everywhere vultures hovering over the fields, the villagers, waiting for carrion. Again the matter of food. One day there was the scandal of vulture meat being found in croquettes, a bit of feathers, perhaps. People shuddered. And yesterday the story of a man killing (murdering) horses and dogs and selling the meat. What a craving for meat. In all the kinds of beans sold, there is protein, black beans, brown, white, etc.

Sent telegram to Fidel Castro about imprisoned priests.

To Silesian church of Our Lady Help of Christians. To Mass. Crowded. Many boys, confessions. In bus station in Santa Clara one small boy said Church is good, the other "the priests are thieves." Then home to Casas, slept. Dinner at Jones and Chas called, said he could not go to dinner because he was in custody. We all went in rain to see if we could see him but he had to spend the night at the old Jesuit school.

October 4. St. Francis

Charles not released but deported today to Miami. He probably talked too much to Cubans in Miami—his inquiring, thorough mind. Too bad. He wanted to stay a year. Already had a job with school of architects.

October 5

This is the boat that took out 200 priests to Spain. It seems larger than the Guadalupe and more luxurious. We were delayed in leaving because 2 others, the only ones leaving Cuba, did not have their papers straight.

October 6

Today news that Fidel has agreed to begin release of the prisoners in exchange for food and medicine. There was a rumor the other day.

All day today I was ill and slept. Calm seas, very hot. Thank God for air-conditioning. The swimming pool is full all the time—it holds only a dozen.

October 7

Mass at 7:30 and the priest preached a long, loud sermon on the ecumenical council.

October 8. Mexico

Up at 8 and bathed and breakfasted on an American breakfast. Then late to a high requiem and to the docks. The heat unbearable, soaked to the skin at once. Took bus to Mexico City.

October 9

Mass at San Fernando's 8:30 a.m. Then wrote first Cuban article about Castro and the meeting on education and religion. It took all morning until one thirty.

October 10

Saw [Diego] Rivera mural at Palace. Marx-like God teaching peasants. Cortes hideous. Rivera saw only the enemy.

To Mass at 8. Supper and then a meeting. I spoke. Prayer in common.

October 13

Fr. [Don] Hessler offered Mass here at 7:30 and after breakfast we went first to the Shrine and then to an Indian village in the desert. A church, falling into ruins, a desolate yard filled with roughly dug out and stone covered graves, a little school, a well, a few houses. We watched the Indians making adobe, spinning.

October 14

Mass at 11:30. Marie Pepper called for me and we went to Shrine of [Our Lady of Guadalupe] and sat for an hour and a half before the marvelous picture. Two pilgrimages, one a small village with drums and trumpets, another huge one from a slum of Mexico. Benediction, rosary, litanies, hymns, there is nothing like it anywhere in the world.

October 15. St. Teresa. Cuernevaca

Up at 5:45. Alan MacDougal and Marie Pepper came for me at 6:15. I had been ill during the night and dragged myself out but the drive down was beautiful. Mass at 8 a.m. To Fr. [Ivan] Illich's school, closed between terms. He not to be found and we left cooling our heels, the secretary not even taking trouble to tell us. Much criticism of coldly intellectual atmosphere and coldly insulting action.

*Dorothy had hardly returned to New York when the Cuban Missile Crisis brought the world to the brink of war. For ten days the world braced for the possibility of a nuclear exchange. Like many other historic events, this drama receives only passing notice in Dorothy's diaries.*

October 22

Crisis—[*Soviet missile*] bases in Cuba.

October 25

A.J. Muste called and wants me to speak at Community Church Nov 12 on Cuba. He and Lawrence Scott going to fast for a week beginning next Monday.

December 4

Lunch with Betty Bartelme at Macmillans. She wants a book and I suggested my book of requiems. She took part in UN rally of 11,000 during crisis.

December 5. Press

To the printer on bus. Got there before Tom Cornell and made up paper myself getting rid of all the overmatter. Martie Corbin in—told me of Roy Finch labeling me a Communist, quoting my letter in the *Daily Worker*.

December 6

The appeal not out yet and the paper coming in today, Chas said it was because we needed $600 in the bank to pay for stamps. So last night I sorted opening mail and there was $500 and with $100 from Bob Steed we got it all out today. The check was not even made out right but the bank cashed it at once, anyway.

December 12

War Resisters [League] wants me to accept their annual peace prize. They are a secular group, accepting all. Among them A.J. Muste, Bayard Rustin, Dave Dellinger, Ralph DiGia.

December 14

Great victory. [Lower Manhattan] Expressway defeated. Ed Forand, Charles, Jane Jacobs, every organization, political and religious, worked together.

December 16

Tom to farm and we went over all material for the CW for next month. Martie [Corbin] has consented to edit and cut articles for us.

December 23

Sister Peter Claver at the farm all day. She came with Charles in time for dinner. We made the outdoor stations.

December 29. Chicago. Karl Meyer's wedding

My baptismal day. Leisurely rising, then downtown to have a hair wash, the first since Cuba. Then lunch and the wedding. There was a big crowd, mostly non-Catholic, from the peace movement.

# 1963

February 8. Maryhouse on the beach

There is a good fire going in the kitchen, but I must look at it again. Stanley is staying overnight. In the winter doldrums for weeks.

For the last two weeks I have been in town going to my Spanish lesson every day. Jan 30 the War Resisters' dinner where I was given an award, citation, scroll, for the CW. Speech by Evan Thomas. Norman Thomas, A.J. Muste, Bayard Rustin, Dr. [Ed] Gotlieb, Ralph DiGia, etc. were there.

On Thursday to Eliz Mayer's to meet [W.H.] Auden and Eichenberg. The latter is illustrating *Resurrection* by Tolstoi now. Then to train to Boston. Mass at the station, then to Deane's school for the blind at Newton Corners, an easy trip from South Station. St. Paul's school is beautifully located but right now they are crowded indeed. A remarkable place. I spoke to the faculty, then to the students. Judy Gregory called for me and I went to Cambridge where she shares an apartment with two young women.

A letter from *Esquire* asking me to be in a group picture of those who took part in "literary and artistic renaissance of the 20s and 30s." I did not take part in it. I prefer the youth of today.

Sat. 2/10/63
Ps. 104-45
"And they took what the peoples had toiled for, that they might keep his statutes and observe his laws."

These words are applied to the exodus of the Hebrew people from Egypt, on their way to the promised land. These words remind me of the Cuban people and the expropriation of lands, and refineries. "They took what they had toiled for."

When Castro offered to reimburse the owners, with repayments over a long period he took their own estimate of its value—the estimate set for tax purposes.

Traveling by bus one sees fence posts painted bright orange. These are nationalized lands, Marjorie Rios says.

There are so many questions to ask. I should like to write Castro directly. Or Maria Sanchez, his secretary. I should like to ask, "Is it true that one of your men in the Sierra Maestra led others in the rosary every afternoon? This is said of the man you appointed head of the great mental hospital whose grounds I drove thru. We went to visit him but he was not there then."

I would like to know also if there were chapels in those new buildings which were being erected. There seemed to be a slow-down of work on them, as well as on other building operations I saw in Sept. But this might have been because of the military buildup, occasioned by threatened invasion. Thank God it did not interfere with the emphasis on schools and classrooms which were omnipresent. It was very impressive to see barracks turned into schools in every town, and classes going on in the shops of the Havana Libre.

Now that I am studying Spanish intensively I would love to return to Cuba if I could get another visa.

Another question:
There was a story in the *Sat Eve Post* last week of Donovan and his final interview with Castro. Did he or did he not read aloud to him the St. Francis

peace prayer? And did you make the response that those too were your aims, tho you took different means to attain it?

Continuing as you are on the works of peace—honesty, truth, justice, pursuit of wisdom, health, I do believe that you wish these things. If only there could be a man strong enough to lay down his arms and devote his entire energies to the pursuit of peace. Then truly that would be an exemplary road. In turn that would be a revolution that would be an example to others, to all over the world. Even to make this attempt—this gesture, even if it failed— would be a beginning of peace.

"Make known His work among the nations."

Wherever there is truth, justice, love—there is God, and his work. "The unknown God," maybe.

*In April and May 1963 Dorothy joined a group of fifty women on a pilgrimage to Rome. Their intention was to express their gratitude to Pope John XXIII for his work for peace, and to urge him to an even more radical condemnation of the instruments of modern war. The women left Rome exhilarated by the knowledge that their message had reached the Pontiff. In less than a month, however, came the news that Pope John was dead.[217]*

June 1. Eve of Pentecost

The Pope is lying in his agony on his iron bed—probably very much like all the beds we got from the Sisters of St. Francis when they closed their home for the aged poor on E. 6th St. He had four hours of consciousness and the papers said he talked to the "parade of cardinals who streamed to his room." He talked at length with the prelates, expressing hope for peace, for the ecumenical council. "With death a new life starts," he said. "The glorification of Christ."

His brothers and sister there, he mentioning each by name.

July 2. At Della's

Yesterday I made so many resolutions about writing, while I was at the ten o'clock Sat. Mass and sat right down to the typewriter when I got back.

My best time for writing is in the morning after Mass and I will have to get up earlier. The noise of traffic on Kenmare is such that I am worn out, and last night an air conditioner in the apartment upstairs kept me awake.

Today the atmosphere very heavy. Rain threatens. So often one is overcome with a tragic sense of the meaninglessness of our lives—patience, patience,

---

217 Evidently, Dorothy's travel journal has been lost. But she described her trip in her column for June 1963. See "Servant of Peace," *Dorothy Day: Selected Writings,* 162-65.

and the very word means suffering. Endurance, perseverance, sacrament of the present moment, the sacrament of duty. One must keep on reassuring oneself of these things. And repeat acts of faith. "Lord, I believe, help thou my unbelief." We are placed here; why? To know Him, and so love Him, serve Him, by serving others and so attain to eternal life and joy, understanding, etc.

So it means study, and St. Thomas said the more we learned of the life around us the more we studied, the more we knew of God thru his creation. So—read, study, write, especially since by writing one is aiding others. When I write "I," the other reads "I." We each of us are unique, yet so alike too.

N.D. [July] 1963. Retreat

I must renounce my over-much speech, which tends to be gossip. Today I announced to Peggy that I wanted to choke Ed Haas who has been going around giving his manuscript (about his way of life, I suppose) to everyone to read during retreat.

So many things to disturb one. Sitting by the beautiful old cherry tree I see it is all gashed and stabbed and bleeding. And John F. tells me that the other cherry and pear trees are the same way.

We need doctors, psychiatrists, spiritual directors. Once when I went to see a woman we were caring for in the mental ward, the doctor asked me what was my interest in her. Was I a relative? I said, not wishing to enter into a discussion of our work—"She is my sister, isn't she, since all men are brothers." He looked at me keenly and said, "You know, religious mania is one of the worst forms."

Another time Cecilia Hugo said, "Why does this movement attract all the crazy ones?" We do have a goodly share of wandering monks, and Ed is one of them, dressed in denim and a cord abound his waist. I feel resentfully—if he wishes to be a pilgrim, let him continue on his way—not stay in comfort for months and months.

But my attitude should be—if people are slightly mad how much more attractive it is that they should be mad for God.

Read *Eternal Husband* by Dostoevsky last night. He always makes me accept more.

My God, my Father, I want to thank You for this retreat and ask You to bless Fr. Casey most abundantly with blessings piled up, heaped up, pressed down and running over.

Help me now to respect Your way with others. Help me, St. Benedict Joseph, to walk a pilgrim in the world, as far as I can, and do all in Jesus' name, bringing Him on to picket lines, meetings, encounters, confrontations. May He increase and I decrease.

*In October Dorothy traveled with Eileen Egan to England, where she had been invited to speak at Spode House, a Dominican retreat house. She visited various Pax Groups, met Muriel Lester, the British pacifist who had played host to Gandhi, and visited the graves of Karl and Jenny Marx in Highgate cemetery.*[218]

Nov. 13

For the last two nights we have had the great privilege of talking to one of the dozen or so worker priests who remain in the apostolate of the sea with the permission of their bishop. There are 7 bishops in France who practice this principle of subsidiarity, in other words, using their own judgment as to whether or not they will permit their priests to remain as workers.

These are the forerunners of the new order when bishops will have authority to make practical decisions like this for their dioceses.

Jean Picharon is a Breton, a slight man with a quiet, strong face. His face lights up every now and then, giving some intimation of a happiness within. That it is a hard-won happiness is indicated by the settled gravity of his mouth and eyes.

For seven years he has been a steward on the French line, working 12 or 14 hours a day, seven days a week, for $100 a month. It is a dollar an hour overtime. There are tips too and I thought of the placard in Cuban restaurants—"a tip crushes the heart of the worker," or some such slogan.

Ideally speaking, this is true. Practically speaking, they need the money. It was out every month, there are eight days off, and after Caribbean cruises the ship is laid up for a while. Pay goes on. It is only now I begin to see the suffering of this life.

I myself suffer from the stifling atmosphere of these huge palatial ships like grand hotels, where every sense is sated and stifled. I have had a sense of claustrophobia in the air conditioned cabins, black as pitch until one pushes the button that transform by well-concealed lighting fixture the black into light. The sad attempts of people to have a good time, to dance, to flirt, to drink and smoke, and see movies and play games, and somehow pass the time, kill the time, every second of which is so precious.

It is now 9:30. We have watched the shore, the docks, waited an hour for breakfast, eaten, cleaned out our cabins and now are waiting this last two hours in the smoking room. At least 500 tourist class passengers are standing on one side, waiting. At least I can use this time to jot down these thoughts

---

218  Again, the journal from this trip has been lost. (See "On Pilgrimage," November 1963)

while they are still fresh, about Father Picharon, and the stifling atmosphere in which he lives.

Yes, his is the harder way, harder than to work on the docks, or in a factory, or in the engine room, where he would be a worker among workers.

As steward he is treated by the passengers as a servant, no, worse than a servant, as an appendage of the ship, a creature to give service, who is abused, treated with contempt. Despised, and himself put in the position of despising others, if he does not constantly discipline his thoughts.

He, a priest, ordained to bring God down among us, to give the most precious gifts to man, is asked instead for the most tawdry gifts. He has offered himself, a sacrifice, giving up this ability to dispense spiritual riches, giving over his body to menial and often meaningless tasks, sacrificing the delights of the interior senses. But no, he told us he is translating St. John's Gospel and his epistles again from the Greek. O beauty ever new!

I suddenly had a deep discernment of Father Picharon's intention in living as he does when he returned a copy of a paper we had loaned him which told of the recent Pax conference at Spode House in the Midlands, England.

He returned the paper which contained also a picture of me and a statement I had made about being confused with a woman of the streets I was trying to help.

"Poorly dressed herself," the account in the paper said, "she was taken for a destitute woman and kept waiting in a queue for eight hours.

"'It was most salutary,' she said. 'You must suffer with the poor to be one of them. I learned then what it is to be despised.'"

Jean Picharon's face lit up as he passed me the paper, tapping the last line. "That is what it is—to be despised."

Charles de Foucauld and his Little Brothers of Jesus always emphasize this idea of "abjection." To seek the lowest place, which shall not be taken from them.

I felt then that I had been given a great light—not only about Father's vocation as worker priest, but for myself, too. I too must accept this being despised and criticized and accused and berated by "the friends of the family," with whom we live, and react in gratitude and love, despising myself for my hurt pride, my resentments and loving those who show me to myself. "O Lord, let me know myself, that I may know Thee!"

*By the fall Dorothy had discovered the site for a new Catholic Worker farm in Tivoli, New York. An old mansion overlooking the Hudson River, it served as the CW Farm until the late 1970s. Dorothy hoped to call it "Maria Beata," after an inscription carved on a cornerstone of the main building. But this name never stuck. Instead it was known simply as "Tivoli."*

December 13

The reason we want this new house, Maria Beata, on the Hudson is because it is on the river, by a stream of living water, a torrent!

The water which Jesus promised the sinful woman of Samaria, if only she wanted it, stood for Christ Himself, and the Holy Ghost.

This is one of the reasons why a place by ocean, bay, or river is so fascinating—always that symbol before us.

December 14

Paul [Bruno] used to work in the flower market up in the thirties (where Mary Lathrop used to beg pounds of flowers every day) and he said he worked from 4 a.m. to 4 p.m. until he could not stand it any longer. I don't know when he came to us, but he is with us at least four years. He is Italian and he loves to cook, but with his irascible temper we only let him two nights a week. Every now and then he threatens people who irritate him, holding aloft a big meat cleaver.

But every night he gathers together all the leavings on the plates of the eight or so people who come for our evening meal and saves them in long cartons (much wider than flower cartons). Then three nights a week he disappears down the street. "He is going to feed the cats in the park," some say. "He is feeding the pigeons on Cooper Square." "No, the police chased him. He goes to Union Square and feeds them there."

But last night Chuck Frassinetti told me, "He takes the subway to the Pelham Bay Station, gets out and walks two miles to a deserted part of the beach where he has built himself a little shack, and there he feeds the seagulls. When they see him coming they fly around him and welcome him. Then he gets undressed, takes a dip in the sea, and dries himself at the big fire of driftwood he has prepared, gets dressed again and comes back to Chrystie St."

"What? In this 20 degree weather?"

"Yes, he does this winter and summer. I went with him once, Jimmy and I."

The longing for beauty and space, light and moving water, the desire for healing, for well-being, that there is in these men amongst whom we live for so many years and yet know so little.

Dec 16

A beautiful white Israeli ship going into the Kill van Kull—white seagulls coasting, a freighter going out, a ferry coming in, and we too, on a ferry, marking time, waiting the passage of this traffic of the sea, to get out into the cold bay where a wind, 25 knots in gusts, makes pathways in the bay. A bright cold day.

# 1964

January 27
Becky [Hennessy] arrived tonight for a few days' visit, not too cheerful over her studies. She is staying at Marge's. Mary is working 5-9 at A&P.

January 28
The girls toured Greenwich Village, bought records and ate at crazy restaurants. Then to Johannah's to dinner. Becky hates the city. She is determined to keep at college. Tamar will be pleased.

January 31
In town, 10 a.m. Betsy follows too—working with Msgr. [Ivan] Illich in Cuernevaca.[219] Says he suggested my name for observer at Council! Nonsense. Told her I had learned—or rather confirmed my vocation at my Peace pilgrimage last year. Also she spoke of CIA money to missionaries.

February 1
Considering selling beach houses to get down-payment for Beata Maria.

February 5. Press
Mass at 8:30. Press day with Monica Ribar and Tom [Cornell],[220] Martie [Corbin] and I. To rest a few hours, then to Trinity Church where I spoke to an uncomprehending group. My electric typewriter stolen.

February 7
Scott Nearing and his granddaughter and [her] husband.[221] Why are non-Catholics and non-religious people so good—so much better than R.C.'s?

---

219 Ivan Illich was a prophetic priest and social thinker. He ran a language school in Cuernevaca that became a point of entry for many North American missioners working in Latin America, and a center for creative thinking about the role of the church in society.

220 Tom and Monica were married later that July.

221 Scott Nearing and his wife Helen were life-long radicals who achieved fame, late in life, for their books on "simple living."

February 12

To Mt. Kisco to Cenacle. Fr. [Philip] Berrigan, SSJ giving retreat. Chapel full, good private rooms. Sally and I said all our aches and pains came out and got worse when we were on retreat.

February 22

I just finished *Morte d'Urban* [J.F. Powers], a truly wonderful book.[222]

February 24

Agreed with Walter [Kerell][223] to sell beach houses for $13,000 to be vacated in June. Then I could not sleep all night—these radical changes—consolidations—necessary but so much work. Centralization. But since the N.Y. house pays all the bills, very necessary. Also it is with future in mind—retreats, people, besides all the crowd at the farm.

February 25

To only have these things settled, I think—then I can begin to be more detached and more spiritual. Why not begin now? But then unless I press lawyers, keep these things in mind, nothing gets done. Or so I think.

February 29. On Pilgrimage

A mixed up evening but very interesting. I got home at 11 to find Kathie, the baby, 2 young men, Barbara, Nicole, Eleanor, Ann, Monica—the latter searching thru the house for some empty beds. The gas heater and gas radiator were on, and I suppose the atmosphere, to them, was warm and cozy. I stormed around like a mother—not that it did any good.

And then the place where I am, cold, unheatable because the gas flow is meager, cluttered and dusty, Marie's newspapers and magazines piled high—what compulsion is there for her to collect, collect, collect? How I long for another newspaper strike when we are free of all this. Now she brings in 2 shopping bags a night, God knows what all besides papers and magazines, and the room gets fuller and fuller so there is scarcely a passageway thru. And there is always an odor in the rooms. My room is both dirty and cold and I have not the energy or strength to clean. My bones are stiff with cold and

---

222 Dorothy described *Morte d'Urban* as "The story of a priest of good will, who didn't have sense enough to put off the old man, who tried to make friends with the mammon of iniquity, and so the Lord took him in hand and did it for him, by means of a bishop's golf ball and a loose woman's slipper." (March 1963)

223 Dorothy described Walter Kerell as "a convert, exercising his creative urge all over the place—writing poetry, painting each one of the file drawers a different color, or designing African masks on horseshoe crabs to place above the editors' desks." (*LF* 150)

I am tired with the weight of clothes I put on to keep warm. I will look for a sunny place in the neighborhood and see if I can move and be alone for a while. At least that way, "out of sight, out of mind," I can leave the young people alone, not worry, and *get some work done.*

Regardless of my love for the country the city stimulates me, and between hours and days of writing, I can get around to see what I need to see, hear what I need to hear, of all that is being done in the little island which is so fascinating and so productive in the long run and which so stimulates others when we write about it in the paper. Involved in too many problems at home, one is apt to lose sight of the hopeful and joyful.

## March 23

Finished moving into Mrs. De Ruyda's apt. Went over to supper at St. Joseph's house.

## March 25

Up early in my sunny room, reading Karl Rahner, S.J., "Christian Commitment." So inspired that after Mass I wrote the article for *Dialogue.*

## April 26. *[Sketch of flower]*

White shades of pink, yellow centers, 9, 9, 6 petals per flower. 8 leaves, 4 flowers on some. Very fragile, growing around trees on Wood Rd. Are these anemones?

We have now visited the two young priests at Red Hook. Fr. Dornbrowski and Fr. Monaghan. Fr. Kane at Tivoli; we will go to the Brothers of the Christian Schools at Barrytown for Mass at 6:30 tomorrow. Today we drove down Wood Rd. to the Carmelites, and I was there in the chapel as they recited Matins.

## May 31. Retreat

Sometimes as a lay person I have been irritated that priests underestimate the capacity of their penitents for the spiritual life and gave the minimum in instruction. Sunday sermons were very brief, anything but meaty, not even milk for babes, I often thought. After all, milk is strengthening, nourishing food. For example, a group of us went on a picnic on Pentecost Sunday when I was visiting in Seattle. We took a long trip by ferry to some island where we intended to go to Mass, then have a picnic breakfast afterward. The priest at the Mass scarcely mentioned the feast of Pentecost when the Holy Spirit descended on the disciples and they received the gifts of the Spirit. No, he mentioned that the following Sunday was Trinity Sunday and if the members

of his congregation did not make their "Easter duty" by then, they were guilty
of grave sin.

"Easter duty" is the one reception of Holy Communion a Catholic is
obliged to, if he is to consider himself still a "practicing Catholic."

I could not help but think of the early Christians in Acts.

June 13

Finished Bouyer's *Newman* and it helped me a lot. Resolution to read more
studiously and purposefully as a cure too for melancholy and discouragement. Newman read 12 hours a day! Marty Corbin gives such an example.

June 16. Perkinsville

Very chilly tonight and we have a good fire in the dining room at Tamar's.
Tamar is busy planning to take a 4-months course at Brattleboro, practical
nursing school, to be followed by another 8 months at Springfield Hospital.
The first 4 months she must live away from home, and I have offered to stay
these four months—a hard prospect.

June 22

Started out this morning at 9:30, delivered Eric to his job at the filling station and continued to Bellows Falls where Gerry Hardy lives. Fr. Miller came
in after and a most animated conversation about the liturgical movement
proceeded. He hated the Rosary, quoted Karl Rahner as saying it is doubtful
if our Lady ever appeared at LaSallete or Fatima, etc. thanked God we were
done with the prayers at the foot of the altar, never had said a requiem Mass
except at funerals, etc., etc. Mr. Hardy and I became quite reactionary and
unliturgical for a bit.

July 2

Mass at Red Hook.

An engineer came across the CW last week on the street at St. Agnes Church
and read it and visited Chrystie St. They sent him here. He has been helping
with plumbing at Chapel House all day and will stay the week, I guess.

Read Suso's *Pilgrim* this morning. The weight of the world is on me when I
awake, and until I get to Mass. Problems—whether or not to take insurance.
With faith in divine Providence we should not. Study morality of insurance
companies. Their ownership of farmlands, investments, etc.

"I am naught, I have naught, all I want is Jesus and the Heavenly Jerusalem."—Suso.

July 24

Fr. Casey's retreat ends. Confessions. He reminded us of martyrs and confessors. "Confessors, those who confess His name," thus glorifying him.

The word *glory* is a beautiful one. How many children are so named without realizing what it means. My grandchildren at Christmas standing before me singing "Glory," their sweet little mouths open, their eyes so serious.

*For the next four months Dorothy spent most of her time in Perkinsville, Vermont, caring for her grandchildren, while Tamar was in Brattleboro, studying for a course in practical nursing.*

August 30

Tamar to Brattleboro at one p.m. Thompson's School of Practical nursing.

August 31

Martha is 9 and has her own missal. "Of course I can read it—the epistle and gospel. Katy can have my baby missal... That man that reads is showing off how fast he can read. No wonder nobody says anything. No wonder everyone keeps quiet! They shouldn't let him."

We pray at odd moments—when we think of it. "Dear God don't let Nicky get hurt at football... Dear God, dear guardian angel, take care of Maggie." (She was bicycling to Springfield with Rhonda. It was 8 miles away on a well-used highway. The bicycles are too small for her now that she is eleven. She was away so long that day that we all sat in the glider under the black walnut trees and said a decade of the rosary.)

September 2

Two calls—*Jubilee* and the *Michigan Catholic*, to reprint my article on Cardinal McIntyre.[224]

September 3

"Don't sweat the small stuff, Granny," Becky says when I fret over whether the car is running right. Just paid a $25 garage bill. Tonight she was talking of

---

224 "The Case of Cardinal McIntyre" appeared in the July-August issue. A priest in Los Angeles had petitioned Rome for Cardinal McIntyre's removal, citing his autocratic style and the prohibitions he had placed in the way of Catholics working for social and interracial justice. Characteristically, Dorothy addressed this controversy in a personal and somewhat indirect manner, reviewing at length her relationship ("shall I say friendship?") with Cardinal McIntyre, and how, through Peter Maurin, she had discovered the great freedom that exists for lay people in the Catholic church. She ended by urging Christians to follow their consciences. "One must always follow one's conscience, preach the gospel in season, out of season, and that gospel is 'all men are brothers.' This teaching is contained in all the work of the Confraternities of Christian Doctrine. It just needs to be applied."

someone with a "warped gourd," meaning a crooked thinker or perhaps just someone who did not see eye to eye with the teenager. The rest of the children batted this expression around all evening until she declared she would bring home no new insights in language when she has Christmas vacation. She cleaned yesterday and today and she does a thorough job of it. I brought 2 loads of clothes to the laundromat, which is the nearest thing to the village.

I love the fresh sweet smell of clothes dried in the open air. Nicky in being tackled today got a few sprained muscles on his leg and groin. Up at 6:30. My turn to take Rick and Nick to practice. Chicken for supper. What appetites! Martha learned to ride a bike today.

September 5
Drove to Tivoli to Fr. Hugo's retreat.

September 13. Sunday
Beautiful weather, cold at night but the fireplace adequately warms the house. We had to wait for an hour for Tamar's ride. Much traffic because of curiosity seekers—cars driving in to see the scene of yesterday's tragedy. An old man, refusing to give up his farm under the right of eminent domain for the highway going thru did as he threatened to do, set fire to 3 buildings and is supposed to have perished in the flames.

The children getting themselves filthy in the attic looking for old bottles which Maggie sells for a few cents. Tamar has found old papers and account books back to 1844. She saved me a little Shaker bottle which had held valerian.

September 14
Cardinal McIntyre collapses at opening of Vatican Council. Later it turned out to be exhaustion from lack of sleep and the heat. The Protestant theologian Oscar Cullman also fainted.

Reading in "Letters of the Saints"—St. John Chrysostom's letter to an agitated woman about the state of the world. And that of several other saints announcing imminent end of the world because of its evils.

On top of this, Khrushchev came out with announcement that the Soviets had discovered a weapon that would end all life on the planet. How newspapers love such headlines. There is an end of this world for all of us anyway. And certainly the Lord can take care of this too.

September 16

Dreamed last night of writing speech for [Elizabeth] Gurley Flynn's memorial service at Community Church next Tues. They called me up about it and I told them I would write a letter.

September 17.

Up at 5:30. It is wonderful to have this quiet hour in the morning.

September 18

It is hard to write or think when the record player is blaring with "Devil Woman."

Every morning I wake at 5:30 or 6 to have an hour before I get the kids up for school. Six children rushing thru breakfast, making their lunches, washing, brushing up, make for tumult. To be heard over it is impossible, so I must be content with making the sign of the Cross on each forehead and a plea—"Say a little prayer as you go down the road. Just thank God, or say Jesus, I want to love you." Evening prayers are only for the three littlest. Hilaire rushes downstairs to his bed, but if you go there afterward, he will say them then.

Fr. Hauser S.J. once said to me, "Omit worry about the children at this age. The senses certainly predominate. It's only natural. They are absorbed with growing and learning. The only thing is prayer—with faith."

I'm always getting back to that personalist position—"Only God and myself." Looking after my own duty to praise, thank "at all times, in all places" the God who made me.

We always have the example of Peter Maurin, living the life of poverty, doing his own job, convinced of the importance of his message and so realizing his own importance as the bearer of it and yet humble enough to accept rebuffs and contempt.

And his patience—his seven years at Mt. Tremper, his 16 years with us.

St. Therese wrote that if the Lord could pick out anyone less than herself to make a saint he would have done so.

September 21

Sex, overemphasized because of lack of activity in life of ordinary man. Also lack of tenderness and love. He is ashamed to express love, save thru the roughness, almost the brutality of passion, which stirs some hidden depths within him, some force in him, mysterious, deep, profound. He wishes to be taken possession of. It would be by some idea, ideal, great love.

Second best is to be possessed, even for the moment of orgasm, by some force greater than himself. Creative force, life force.

Sept 22
Wrote a paper to be read at Elizabeth Gurley Flynn's at Community Church. N.Y. Tom Cornell will read it.[225]

Sept 24
Wrote *Commonweal* article. Feeling very dull about writing, but money so needed. Tomorrow Stanley will copy it.

October 20
Eric and Nick are now dandies—combed hair, wet foreheads for me to kiss as they start off for school. Tight pants, fancy shirts. Eric is very generous to Nick, who is growing fast (almost 15) and loans him his clothes. Nick never washes them, but Eric does, washing his own pants and shirts.

October 28
Last night Peter Reynolds, one of 5 boys in his family, had gone hunting and came in to supper. He and Eric try to outdo each other in cursing and after a pleasant supper with Nick, Mary, Maggie, Martha, Hilaire and Katy they rushed in shouting, more cursing because they did not get anything. I went to my room and slammed the door and left them to get their own supper. Pete is 13 and Eric 16 but of equal size and noise.

I wrote letters and mended but thought afterward that if I had prayed more that day I could have controlled myself.

November 4
[Lyndon] Johnson elected.

November 17
Anniversary of Ammon's baptism. Wrote him.

---

225 Elizabeth Gurley Flynn, Secretary General of the Communist Party of the United States, died in Moscow on September 5, 1964, at the age of seventy-two. Dorothy's message, "Red Roses for Her," appeared in the November 1964 issue. See *SW,* 144-47.

December 13

The time of my stay here is drawing to a close and it has been a very happy visit, all four months, tho hard too of course. Made harder by the fact of an immense correspondence that I cannot keep up with. Always leaving me with a feeling of great uneasiness at neglecting so much of my duty.

Peter Maurin never answered letters. But then he did not write personally, as I do, and so did not leave the door open to lettter-writers with their problems. It is hard for me to escape the nagging feeling that I must answer every letter with questions addressed to me. This is nonsense of course.

But the fact is that life with 7 children (and their friends) and cooking, shopping, washing, etc. takes all one's time. The constant demand for attention, the constant bickering—where the 4-year-old not only wants exclusive attention but wants all the toys and games. "I'll take all," little St. Therese said.

# 1965

Tivoli, Friday, January 1

Mass at 9 at St. Sylvia's—Fr. Kane. A dull grey day, very cold. I telephoned Tamar and she was off but must work this weekend at the hospital. All work, no training. Also the pay has not come through. The children all fine.

Stanley and I took a walk around chapel near site of the stations which George is putting up with help of John.

Tivoli, Saturday, January 2

To laundromat at 8:30, already crowded. So to church to pray for Tamar and children.

Tivoli, Sunday, January 3

Keeping a diary helps to clarify ideas, keeps record of reading, as well as happenings. One's memory is always faulty—not just age.

Tuesday, January 5

Very melancholy—miss my grandchildren. Very cold and desolate on Kenmare St.

Wednesday, January 6

At 4:30 went up to Eileen Egan's. Eileen and I had dinner. Then to movie. "My Fair Lady." A very good cure for melancholy. Theme—man's capacity to change.

Thursday, January 7

At St. Patrick's the altar is facing the people—pews roped off to keep everyone up near front, instead of being lost in that vast old cathedral.

Saturday, January 9

Slight cold, generally disorganized feeling. Reading *Herzog* [Saul Bellow]— very good indeed, feel very much as he describes himself in his description of his life in the country—unable to write. Had such a hard time getting On Pilgrimage done—letters. One gets to hate paperwork. I was so happy at Tamar's with the definite job of meals, dishes, laundry—the purely physical things.

Opera—"Don Pasquale"—indifferent.

Sunday, January 10

Snowed all day. Mass at 11:30. Sermon on Holy Family. I was late because I was cleaning Peggy's room. That household job made me feel better. I am so sick of my obligations—of my writing. Manual labor is absolutely essential. I can understand the appeal of Saul Bellow's *Herzog*. We are so many of us in that disorganized state. Desk piled high with letters, writing, etc. Loss of balance.

Monday, January 11

Last night a carload went to Marist College to see "M," a German movie. Arthur Sullivan babysat, with firmness. Children went to bed. In my room reading. Loraine Freeman came to talk about her children and complain of racism here—Hans, Alice, *Daily News*. When I see the constant failure around me, I think of myself as Emma. Rita wanted to know once why I spoke with literary allusions. It helps balance me: Dickens and Dostoyevsky help me more.

January 14

St. Ephraim: O Lord and Master of my life, grant not unto me a spirit of idleness, of discouragement, of lust of power, and of vain speaking. But bestow upon me, Thy servant, the spirit of chastity, of meekness, of patience and of love. Yes, O Lord and King, grant that I may perceive my own transgressions, and judge not my brothers, for blessed art Thou unto ages of ages. Amen.

O God be merciful to me a sinner.

Reading *Herzog* by Saul Bellow. He says semen absorbed is said to be creativity increased. Virginity, celibacy, a martyrdom, so considered by Fathers of the church, because it is putting to death the natural in man, the good "natural." "You are dead and your life is hid with Christ in God," St. Paul said. God has made the barren the mother of many children. So priests are truly fathers of many children bringing them to birth in Christ. If they direct the intention. It is absolutely necessary. Varya Bulgakov years ago told me how an actress can make her voice heard to the last row in the theater because she has directed her intention spoken to the people in the last row.

One must *intend* to be heard. How necessary it is to know these things, to consider these things.

There are so many priests who are highly nervous, suffering men, in their prime, and usually everyone says they are working too hard. That may be true, but Peter Maurin would say they did not do enough physical work. Baron von Hügel speaks of the necessity of living on three levels, physical, mental, and spiritual to relieve the tension.

Also Gerald Heard once said that there is a great hunger for tenderness and love expressed in our lives. People are afraid of being considered sentimental if they speak so.

Watching adolescents—or young people up to twenty when there is a small child in the family and see how much loving and petting that little one gets. Also parents are not afraid to express themselves so with the little ones and neglect to show love to the older children.

Priests lead too sedentary lives and their study is too one-sided. If we only had a few revolutionaries amongst them—more in fact who study deeply the problems of our times, as Fr. Tompkins did, or Fr. McCarthy in New Mexico, and Fr. Ganey in Fiji Islands.

All over the world men seek guides, whether a book or a leader, a teacher. In India, a guru, [among] Sufis, a staretz, a spiritual advisor. If we are faithful in seeking we will find one. "Seek and you will find." If we will pay attention to those whom God sends our way, He will continue to send more. Again a paradox, seek and yet not seek. Seek as tho you were not seeking, that is. If you find one, be quite content with him, until another comes along. This is "abandonment," not sloth. This is trust in God, to be content but always discontented with one's state. To be loving, grateful, uncritical of God's direction of me, even if I see with my human critical faculties the limitations of my advisors.

Feb 2. On train[226]

Snowing in N.Y. again and not so cold. Clare Bee, Ed Forand and Walter Kerell saw me off. My sister had provided me with sandwiches so I had supper on the train. It was dark and gloomy when I left, in more ways than one.

Then I woke up in North Carolina, with its ocher and red and green cover crop on the fields and brilliantly green pines, tho all other trees were bare and the sun shone over all.

Reading the Psalms for Matins and Lauds in Fr. Frey's Psalm book I was comforted. I carry also in my purse a small New Testament, *The Problem of Pain*, a paperback by C.S. Lewis, "On the Invocation of the Name," a pamphlet on the Jesus Prayer, and some letters from my friends in Natchez, Mississippi telling me of the terror there, the hate calls on the phone, the threats of bombings, etc.

I need the weapons of the spirit, which I carry in my bag.

I am very conscious of myself as an outsider, going into a situation, but I go not to speak, to demonstrate, as I did in Danville, Virginia, two summers ago, where I was invited by Mother Teresa [superior of the Society of Christ Our King]. I go just to be with my friends who have visited us in the North and who have helped us. Of course we will talk about the war going on in our midst.

Besides, this is my country, all of it, not just North or South. My father was born in Cleveland, Tennessee, just across the Georgia border, and my grandmother in Rome, Georgia. My mother's people, men from New England and New York State. I probably love New England best because of its beauty. I am passing, as I write, row upon row of Negro shacks, the size of corn cribs, and fields of junked cars and the earth over and over is wounded with erosion.

All these things hurt. Of course I am surrounded by the squalor of the Bowery, and the moral squalor too of the beatniks who in their arrogance outdo the Bowery. Why is sin looked upon as attractive and "natural" in the young and revolting in the old?

February 5. Conyers [Georgia, Trappist monastery]

Spoke to monks in crypt. Very friendly. Fr. Abbot and Jack [English]. Jack certainly needs prayers. Sick in pain, a compulsive talker, living in the infirmary, smoking, occasionally drinking, "hanging on by his toenails," as the saying is.

---

226 See "On Pilgrimage," February 1965.

February 9. Gadsden

Today took bus at 3:30 a.m. and arrived tonight at 5:30 at Natchez. In Jackson was met by Father Bernard Law, editor of the paper. Had met him at Harvard Catholic Club.[227]

February 14

Today in bed. Bit of flu. Reading *Augie March,* Saul Bellow. Extremely good, novel of Chicago. Finished the *Moviegoer* by Walker Percy.

Visited cemetery, fine mansions, generally opened for pilgrimage, and sat by the river. Went to 5:30 Mass—fine young priest, good sermon. Margaret told me of "incidents" by Klansmen or White Citizens Council or Americans for Preservation of White Race members. Garage man cracking bullwhip across from Fr. Morrissey's Negro church. Undertaker called out and beaten. Mayor's house bombed. Betsy threatened for letting colored help in her restaurant use white toilet.

February 21

Tonight Malcolm X assassinated in N.Y. Demonstrations here in Austin for and against war in Vietnam. Press gives no mention of it.

February 23

Last night hateful utterances on radio by Gov. Paul Johnson of Miss. Pray for his conversion.

February 24

Spoke tonight at St. Mary's, Our Lady of the Lake. Birchite material distributed by head of Young Republications.

March 23

Left at 8 with Pat Rusk[228] for bus—she to St. Louis, and me to Minn. Same bus to Cheyenne at 8 in evening. Desert wastes all day. All this night to Omaha, cigar-smoking men, drinkers, old and young, many small children, one ill, very crowded, snowed all night.

---

227 Father Bernard Law later became the Cardinal Archbishop of Boston.

228 Pat Rusk had been an airline flight attendant before discovering the Catholic Worker. She remained a faithful member of the CW family for the rest of her life. An obituary in the CW (April 1999) described her as "a complicated person with a need for simplicity and certainty, which sometimes made her seem contrary."

March 25. St. Cloud

Jimmie Lee Jackson. Rev. James J. Reeb. Mrs. Viola Liuzzo. The latter killed the night of the March [from Selma to] Montgomery. Requiscat in Pace.

March 27

Jim Palmquest came and fixed the furnace which is without grate and unplugged kitchen sink. Such kindliness. Three more inches snow and zero weather at night. Drove to Burkes, a flat tire on the way and a passing motorist helped us fix it. Arrived late. But not too much so for the movie which they show every 2 weeks. Tonight was "Life" [*Ikuru*], a Japanese film—profoundly moving. Man dying of cancer and his struggle for a place for the poor—his search first for life in dissipation—a Sasha-like Mephistopheles—then in service. Talked to students.

April 4. Ossining

Got into Harmon at 8:20 and found Della waiting. First to her place and then to Mass at 11 at St. Augustine's church. Quiet leisurely Sunday.

I had been praying [Franklin] would be led to Scripture. Now as editor at Rand McNally he has had to read St. Paul, a biography! Pray, pray without ceasing.

April 6

To Tivoli finally. A wonderful day with everyone sitting out in front awaiting me.

Eileen, Howard, Jim, Tom. Necessity to consult laymen in rewriting Schema 13, Church in Modern World.[229] "Layman's touch was sadly lacking from the draft document."

April 9

In bed all day. I should have gone to Philadelphia to LaSalle but could not. Too many demands. I will need to be fresher when I go there to be able to handle it. But felt very guilty nonetheless. The first time I had to break an engagement in years.

April 10

Frustrations. Robert who takes out fuses and shuts off lights, hot water, etc. Also turns on and off water in cellar. These retired ones always feel they know a great deal about household engineering.

---

229 This was the draft for *Gaudium et Spes*, "The Pastoral Constitution on the Church in the Modern World," which addressed social issues, including war and peace.

April 12

Went to office for supper. All well. But Ed wishes to not be responsible for house. Wants Clare to "pay-in," distribute tobacco etc, at night. Tom Cornell over, with 16-page article. Mine was 7 pages travelogue.

April 13

Enormous amount of material for April issue. Tom Cornell's article too long, but newsy.[230] Much cut. He will be offended. But it will help reinstate him and counteract gossip. Monica very sick—spent evening with her.

April 14. Press day

Marie collecting again and in terrible temper at being asked to get rid of papers.

April 16. Good Friday. Tivoli

Mass at 3 p.m. Father gave a conference at 10:30.

Napped. Nightmare that Maggie was injured up in a field. Reading van Zeller—approach to Calvary. Very good on discouragement, failure, exhaustion and so on.

April 20

Warm and lovely day. We sat out in sun all morning and rested. All the ice on the pond melted in one day. This is Easter week and the house is in fearful disorder.

April 21

Awoke at 5:30. Usual expression over failures, inefficiency, incapacity to cope. Dom Hubert van Zeller's book, *Approach to Calvary*, invaluable, teaching one to accept this discouragement which he says will increase with age. But I must learn to contain myself, to do my own work which is writing, correspondence, and the constant study, meditating on both natural and supernatural life. But women, we see the burdens of others, and how little one can do to lighten them. No matter how we try to change things, clean things up, make order, it essentially remains the same. It is hard to keep from heaviness of heart. One must just keep going and my work is *to write* and I am neglecting it. New resolutions. Will I ever learn that it is only myself I can work on and so much needs doing there.

---

230 "The Berlin Wall, in Selma, Alabama," April 1965.

April 24

Woke up with the words in my ears, "Live your *own* life," not Tamar's, not the children's, which is too exhausting. Women are that way, unfortunately, especially about their own. Need for more detachment.

April 25

Letter from Ammon telling me of his marriage before a justice of the peace. How to write about it.[231]

As to "living one's own life"—doing one's job such as writing, when I got back Mary showed me some quotes from my book in *Temoignage Chrétien*. Then a letter from Brazil about how my Cuban articles were translated there and appreciated. So, I must write.

April 26

Oh God, how to write about a great and good man who has fallen, who has fallen from grace, who has left the life of the Church, who has put himself outside, and not from some high and lofty principles of conscience, but from a weakness which we have all *[?]* about for years, a weakness for women. He has left the Church not for conscience sake but for the romantic, sentimental reasons, because of vanity, because of a picture of himself which he has considered, evidently incomplete if he cannot prove, at the age of seventy-two, that he can still charm.

Of course it was from loneliness too, from a desire for family, desire for a son, proof of virility. Virility of ideas, of the spirit...

---

231 See "What Does Ammon Mean?" June 1965. Dorothy's long article is mostly a review of Ammon's dedication and commitment to the cause of peace and his determination to live strictly by the demands of his conscience. Only toward the end does she express her sorrow at his abandonment of the Catholic church. Writing with great tenderness, she speculates that "Ammon is on his way to going through another conversion in his long and adventurous life, and I do not mean a conversion to another faith but a return to and a deepening of his understanding of the Catholic faith." She repents of her own failings and the example of other Catholics who failed properly to inspire him. In light of these failures, "we can only pray that God will give him further light, that another conversion, that is, a turning to God and a return to his own strong mission, will come about, and that he will begin to see the Church in perspective, as founded by Christ on the Rock of Peter and enduring to this day in spite of the tares among the wheat—in spite of the scandals." In his self-published autobiography, *The Book of Ammon,* Ammon gave his own account of his disillusionment with Catholicism: "Whether I left the Church or the Church left me depends upon how you look at the question," he wrote. He had only become a Catholic because of Dorothy, he said. If she had been a Quaker or a Mormon he would have embraced those faiths. Still, he called her "the best ever," a woman with "more integrity about what is worthwhile than any two radicals or Christians I have ever known."

May 1. St. Joseph's

Woke at Brandeis Faculty Center at 7. Read Therese (also prayers) till nine. Wondered why I was there. Too much speaking. Fr. Troy has little sense of hospitality. No breakfast. No goodbyes. Just on my way.

May 6

I consider the loss of faith the greatest of disasters—the greatest unhappiness. How can one help grieving over friends and relatives. How necessary to pray without ceasing for them.

May 8

Spoke at Manhattan United Church Women at Riverside Church at their annual luncheon. A.J. Muste there. Also my dear godchild Jean Kennedy who is doing social work in neighborhood. She has two sons, priests now.

From now on all my spiritual reading and reading in theology must center around Newman, who has begun now to influence our day. [Louis] Bouyer is admirable. His book tremendous about Newman.

May 15.

Memorial Mass for Peter Maurin at 10. Dear Soul [Arthur J. Lacey] officious, father mixed-up, also Joe, trying to do everything the old way, including the gospel. Father did not come to breakfast. I started at once, not too much at ease, Frank and Joe asking for money to finish outhouses and Marty refusing. He is offended with me anyway. I wonder if he is as unforgiving as most of the Irish.

May 16. Perkinsville

Hilaire's first Holy Communion. A not too crowded church and all went well. Monsignor Nolan offering the Mass. Tamar was off today. She was telling me how all came to the rescue when a baby was born with a cleft palate, calling in a mother who had refused to see her child the first few days—then the wonders performed by the operation. She will go anywhere now to reassure a grieving mother. It certainly is only a sample of the professional and personal goodness Tamar has found. Suddenly it occurred to me why she runs down "religious people." It is because they did not match, or rather surpass, these naturally good ones, as they should. Also it is some more of her revolt against poverty, which means a shabby home, plaster falling from walls and ceiling, unpainted floors, and poverty in physical energy to keep clean… It is a fallacy to think the more people there are the more work is done. The more work there is to do, rather, and many without the knowledge or training or strength to do it. And without the direction.

### May 18

Nothing is more depressing than to read *Time*. More and more one is driven to accept the Little Way. Silence, quiet, peace, acceptance.

One has such a constant sense of failure, uselessness, inability to cope. Then at night, going to sleep in sadness suddenly remembered Van Zeller, [*Approach to*] *Calvary*—and remembered to accept the suffering as work, as spiritual weapons. Chas de Foucauld and Therese both made so much of "littleness"—the "least place," which no one can take from you. "The grain of sand."

### May 20

Tamar has so much homework, papers to write, etc. and feels frantic about getting it done. She went to the doctor Monday and he put her on a bland diet. No ulcer yet but irritation. No raw fruits or vegetables. She loves her work—both at hospital and at home with children, but it is too much. She dreams of everything being half-done—going to hospital half-combed, half-dressed, etc.

### May 25

Tonight to see "The Lower Depths" in a Japanese film. "Ikuru" ["Life"] was better but this suited my mood tonight, gave me a sense that we were indeed doing something about such misery. One needs reassurance at times.

### May 26

Read Franz Jagerstatter all p.m.[232]

### May 27

I received letter from Lanza del Vasto about coming to Rome in Fall and fasting with Chanterelle [del Vasto] and ten other women in a Roman convent.

---

232 In the June 1965 issue Dorothy reviewed Gordon Zahn's *In Solitary Witness: The Life and Death of Franz Jagerstatter*. This was an account of an Austrian layman who was executed for refusing to serve in Hitler's army. Published during the Vietnam War, Zahn's book became a great source of inspiration for Catholic pacifists, especially young men facing the draft. (In 2007 Franz Jagerstatter was beatified by Pope Benedict XVI.)

June 3

Confession. I'm trying to be regular once a month before 1ˢᵗ Friday. The only way I can remember. My lack of charity to Deane. Priest at Holy Crucifix always available and good counseling. Still, one cannot give the intimacy or human love that Deane demands, and she always feels it.

June 28. The Vigil of Peter and Paul

"We pray you, Almighty God, that You suffer no disturbance to shake us, whom You have founded as on a rock, on the confession of your apostles." The epistle is about Peter and John going to the temple at the 3 p.m. hour of prayer, and their encounter with the lame man who had to be carried to the gate every day by his relatives so he could sit there and "beg alms."

We had a woman like that at Precious Blood church in New York on Baxter St., a woman with a cancerous face who used to be at the door. If it were not in a slum she would not have gotten away with it. It is against the law to beg in N.Y. As it was, her poor family were enabled to help her at home and feed and clothe her, and people giving her help could say, "There but for the grace of God go I." She was bearing their burdens of bodily ills. She was Christ-like in that if in nothing else. (They said of Christ also, "There is no beauty in Him. He was a worm and no man, an outcast." In other words He did not go in for self-defense, for standing up to the other fellow.)

Peter cured the lame man who was looking for a handout, for money. Peter said, "Silver and gold have I none, but what I have I give you."

He, fastening his eyes upon him, said, "Look upon us." And this gaze of Peter healed him and Peter took him by the hand and lifted him up, and his feet and soles received strength, and he, leaping up, stood and walked and went in with him into the temple, walking and leaping and praising God.

How I wish I could walk and leap and be free of pain from this crippling arthritis. But the Lord leaves me with it and it goes on. And I reflect that after all I am 67 and the pains of age are in me to be accepted.

We must be pruned to grow, and cutting hurts the natural man. But if this corruption is to put on incorruption, if one is to put on Christ, the new man, pain of one kind or another is inevitable. And how joyful a thought that in spite of one's dullness and lethargy one is indeed growing in the supernatural life.

July 4

Spent day at Della's until 5 when I went to Maryknoll Cloister which is only ten minutes away. Spoke to Sister M. Irene Sullivan to whom we owe so much and then to the community which is large for a cloister. A very quiet Fourth.

July 12

Sloth is man's besetting sin. *Acedia.* Cassian would say avarice.

July 14

To see Peggy Spier and children. Lovely picnic. Children swam and boated. I sat in swing and read *Time* on Ho Chi Minh.

July 16. N.Y.

Meeting tonight of Young World Federalists at office. Young people with us.

I had meeting with John Coster [attorney] and Ruth Collins [real estate advisor] at Muni. Bill sent me excerpts from Jan Myrdal, *Report from a Chinese Village.*

July 18

To Russian Mass (Mary has been staying over Friday and Sat nights) and again that glorious sense of worship. "Prayer sung is twice said," St. Augustine. Carol Jackson spoke of birth control. She sees one part only. Not authority and freedom.

July 21

Speaking at Immac Conc College, Troy NY before American Franciscan Soc for Vocations. Got there at 12:30. Meeting at three so had an hour in church. Talked from 3-5 including questions, and do not feel I gave them what they wanted at all. God forgive my presumption. Talked of Pope John's diary and of his early training. Tried to talk of Poverty and Peace. No questions on peace. Only on poverty.

July 23

Drove down 9-12:30, an easy relaxed drive. But very hot. To St. Teresa's, a good meeting, then to our own meeting. Jacques Travers on Simone Weil—a good presentation. Nicole [d'Entremont] handed her story in. She and Chris [Kearns] will be on masthead.

July 31. Pax

A most wonderful day. Jim Douglass in the morning.[233] He is a true leader, his life, his thinking, his writing, his teaching at Bellarmine College in Kentucky inclines me to trust him absolutely when he says, "Come to Rome," where he will go for the opening of the Council.

I had already said yes to Chanterelle del Vasto—to the fast. Janet Burwash gave me the money at once—$500. God bless her.

August 2

Up at 7, finished the Franz Jagerstatter review, Mass at 8:30 and Pat and I went to printer. Martie and Nicole came later. A hard day. Martie insists on proofreading as well as makeup. Very thorough. Train at 6 to Della's. Called Tamar. She is getting on well.

August 25. Perkinsville

"Eve of Destruction"—radio, latest record.[234] The Hennessy record player is not working and they miss their favorite songs, Roy Orbison and Elvis Presley, etc.

The children do dishes and help clean—go to dump and laundromat but are pretty disorderly with it all. Becky gets discouraged when first in home and then settles down to enjoying housework. She likes being a waitress. Is mentally lazy right now.

August 28

Paul VI exhorts whole world to penance and prayer for Council. Fathers will walk in penitential procession, bearing relics of True Cross from Holy Cross in Jerusalem.

August 30. Tivoli

Spoke to Peacemakers [conference] at 10 a.m. Wally Nelson in charge. Last night drinking in the mansion. Mike Sullivan, etc. Peter said they confined themselves to one room. Worker and scholar conflict I am sure.

---

233 Jim Douglass, a lay Catholic theologian teaching at Bellarmine College in Kentucky, was one of the most eloquent writers on the subject of war and peace. He was among a small group of pacifists who went to Rome during the final session of the Council to lobby for a strong statement on nuclear war.

234 "Eve of Destruction"—an anti-war protest song released in 1965 by Barry McGuire.

August 31

When I woke up in the morning I wonder why I am going to Rome. Then when I think of the fast for peace, my mind is settled again in its resolution. It makes more sense than any word or encounter.

September 1

Eric [Hennessy] came to N.Y. from Atlantic City where he was visiting his father, a sad experience. I am glad they love him, the children, and want to keep close to him, and that Tamar never utters a bitter word about him.

*In September Dorothy embarked on another pilgrimage to Rome. She planned to join a group of international women fasting for ten days to support the Council Fathers in their deliberation on the subject of war and peace.*

September 3

Boarded at noon. There are 35 bishops on board and many priests. One cardinal, Sheehan of Baltimore. So many priests seeing them off it was hard for our group to get around. Each morning I receive communion from a bishop. This boat goes on from Naples to Genoa. Met Bishop [Marcos] Mc-Grath of Panama. He is Holy Cross and said he met me when he was an undergraduate at Notre Dame.

He spoke of Schema 13. They have dropped out [conscientious objector] clause in deference to Italian authorities, but disagrees there—it should be restored, he says. They have not enough time to study issues of war and peace, he said. Should be another session. Have not had time to consult nuclear physicists and military men! Seems to think I am soft on communism. "My experience is different from yours," he said. "I have found they will present any amelioration of condition but keep things stirred up to provoke violence." But that is usual tactic in whole trade union movement—to ask for more than they expect to receive, so they will get more. Pope John asked for "trust," to be wise as serpents and gentle as doves. Bishop McGrath who is tall, handsome, young and very serious was more concerned about the contraception issue, it seemed to me. He took however my literature, James Douglass' articles, Thomas Merton's, and today I will give him *Reconciliation Quarterly* with its fine articles on church and state and last issue of *Jesus Caritas* with Yves Congar.[235]

---

235  The July-August 1965 issue of the CW was a "Special Issue—War and Peace At the Vatican Council." Dorothy had received funds to mail a copy to each of the assembled Council Fathers. It featured a banner headline with the words of Pope Paul VI: "We are responsible for our times, for the life of our brothers, and we are responsible before our Christian consciences." The lead article was by Jim Douglass, "The Council and the Bomb." Another long piece

September 6

Fr. Cormier and Fr. O'Hanlon have been so helpful in helping me translate some of the passages in the document, "The Church in the Modern
World." Those on war, deterrence, and conscientious objection. The latter is
very strong. The new document is very long, gathering together the opinions
of many bishops and including them all so it sounds as if they were working
two ends against the middle. But it is to be debated in the council and comes
at end of a very long document.

September 8

This morning I saw Bishop McGrath again. He will concelebrate at 5 p.m.
and leave the boat at Gibraltar to go to Madrid to speak. He told me to let
him know where I was staying in Rome so he could get in touch with me. He
is in close touch with Cardinal Suenens and Mrs. Peter Grace who are working together in Rome and have meetings at their house there. I really do not
want the behind the scenes meeting but perhaps James Douglass would profit
by them. I want to write of the processions on the feast of the Holy Cross
which will open the Council.

Now at 1:30 we are seeing land for the first time since Friday. Probably
the white cliffs of islands. We are passing them and do not approach closer.
Lovely hot weather, not too breezy.

There is always, in talking about the work, a subtle self-aggrandizement.
One may not intend it, yet there it crops out to humiliate one; perhaps it is
good to have it come out in the open, unintentionally this way, without self-
probing for faults, sins of pride, etc. For instance, speaking of the new role of
nuns, and being asked my opinion, I told of Sister Judith of St. Catherine's at
St. Paul who said the sisters want to give up their expensive-to-man hospitals
and work for wages in the municipal and state hospitals, if necessary, even give
up their garb but not their community life; their religious life. This would be
true charity, a giving of self, and would work a transformation in the mental
hospitals for instance. As it is there is little charity left in Catholic hospitals
as the city pays for all free cases. And I brought out all the CW did to give
unquestioning help to convalescents released from Catholic hospitals.

September 9

Gave Bishop McGrath *Fellowship* to read. Very interesting issue on Italian
c.o. Also church and state.[236]

---

was by Gordon Zahn. Thomas Merton's essay, "St. Maximus the Confessor on Nonviolence,"
appeared in the September issue.
236  See Dorothy's detailed account of her trip to Rome in the October 1965 issue.

September 10
    Rome at 3:30. To Notre Dame center.

September 12
    Frank McDonald called for me to go to Mass at St. Susannah's, the Paulist
Church here. Good sermon on the Sermon on the Mount.

September 13
    Council opened with Mass. The Mass was tremendous, sung. I could have
wept at the Sanctus. Concelebration. After to press room with Fr. Richter
where I met Bob Hoyt [*The National Catholic Reporter*], and John Cogley.

September 14
    Slept for an hour. Then to meet Jim Douglass and to Lateran church to
await the procession. Two or more hours on our feet. I forgot to bring chair!
Tremendous crowd. Prayers, clear and loud over system as perfect as any I
have ever heard. An orderly and quiet crowd, some women reciting rosary
aloud. Blessing relics of True Cross.

September 15
    Much conversation about birth control. Bishops more concerned about
this than war. Archbishop Roberts[237] spoke of natural law and conscience.

September 18
    Lunch with Cardinal Tisserant, secretary, and Jim [Douglass]. Last eve-
ning Dick Carbray called up and gave me directions.[238] He had arranged a
meeting with His Beatitude Maximos, who received us at ten o'clock at the
Salvator Mundi Hospital. He is terribly impressive in robes of office with his
ever-present archbishop and another priest, all great big men, huge. We had
picked up Archbishop Roberts at his Pensione earlier. His Beatitude expressing his firm desire the Council speak stronger for peace and then his doctor
cut short the interview.

---

237 Thomas Roberts, an English Jesuit, was appointed Archbishop of Bombay by Pope Paul
VI. He was an outspoken proponent of nuclear disarmament, and a good friend of the Catholic Worker.
238 Richard Carbray, an American pacifist, was part of the peace lobby in Rome.

September 22

Seeing Fr. [Bud] Kieser at 4:30.[239] Got English copy of Schema on Church in Modern World and Fr.'s questions about poverty. Back to Notre Dame Center, where Vince [McAloon] told stories of Padre Pio.

September 23

Breviary. Job, Tobias, Raphael, and much inspired to write today. Mass at St. Mary Major—such devout congregations. I missed rosary so shall read Pope John's encyclical on Rosary and say mine.

September 24

4:45 interview by Vatican radio. Fr. Kieser, Paulist, making shows in S. Calif. Programs called Insight. Panel discussion at 3—then to Vatican radio for broadcasting interview. A good talk on war, private property, of which much discussion at panel.

September 25

Up at 7. Mass at 8-9, then to American Express where I stood in line with Bishop Furlong and while we waited for checks to be cashed we talked of Cardinal Hayes, Cardinal Spellman, the military ordinariate, solders, conscience, nonviolence, anti-clericalism, and music. We ended on a most cordial note.

September 26

Meeting Lanza del Vasto.

September 27

Meeting at Cardinal Suenen's headquarters. Very crowded. A few spoke. Frank was wild over his contact with Pope. Taize brothers there being greeted by Pope Paul.

September 28

Six a.m. Mass with Jim Douglass, Gordon Zahn, Dick Carbray, Meeting at FOR [Fellowship of Reconciliation] office—Hildegard and Jean Goss.

September 30

Visited exhibit on nonviolence at Unitas, Mass at St. Agnes at 5. As usual rosary, litany, benediction too. I had been to St. Anselm's to see Abbot Butler

---

239 Father Ellwood (Bud) Kieser was a Paulist priest who would later produce a film about Dorothy Day, "Entertaining Angels" (1996).

of Downside.[240] He said he would make an intervention stating Christianity did not need defense by armed force. He was much interested in Farm column. And took last two copies.

## October 1

Awake at 6. Got cab, then waited for Barbara Wall[241] and Eileen [Egan]. Enjoyed sitting watching St. Peter's and bishops arriving. Long walk around inside of St. Peters. All confessionals filled with bishops. I went to Syrian rite Mass, sung. To Cenacle with Eileen. Shantidas[242] prayed with us in garden. Then a planning of our day, for prayer, silence, a lecture at 5. Abbot Butler said he would remember me at Mass.[243]

## October 2

Our schedule. 7:15 Mass daily. Meditation and prayer in common till 9. 9-12 silence and free time, reading. 12-2 garden. 2-4 silence. 4 meetings. 5-6 in chapel. 7-8 meeting and prayer.

## October 4

Such pains in my legs from hip to ankle that I cannot sleep. I took what they call a purge but it did not work. Chanterelle is in bed ill. We sing morning and night prayers with her. The St. Francis Prayer after the Our Father and the beatitudes. We all kiss her good morning and at night her and each other. It is the custom in the Community [of the Ark].

## October 5

When this day's finished we will be half thru and all of us better than can be expected. It is certainly suffering, tho. At 4:30 Eileen, Dick Carbray, Barbara Wall came with papers and to tell me the debate had opened on the parts of the Schema relating to war and would go on for some days.

---

240 Dom Basil Christopher Butler, OSB, Abbot President of the English Benedictines, was an influential participant in the Second Vatican Council.

241 Barbara Wall was a representative of the British organization Pax.

242 "Shantidas"—Servant of Peace—was the name Gandhi bestowed on Lanza del Vasto.

243 Dorothy provided an account of the women's fast for peace in the November 1965 issue. "As for me, I did not suffer at all from the hunger or headache or nausea which usually accompany the first few days of a fast, but I had offered my fast in part for the victims of famine all over the world, and it seemed to me that I had very special pains... It was a small offering of sacrifice, a widow's mite, a few loaves and fishes. May we try harder to do more in the future."

October 7

Yvette [Naal] told us a great deal about Fr. [Dominique] Pire and his schools of nonviolence in Belgium.[244] Another year I will visit them, perhaps.

October 8

Aside from hammock bed and weighty covers, I have been most comfortable. Letters from Deane who is fasting (her 5th day) and Tamar and Maggie. I have managed to write about 20 letters and have piles more. So much reading to do about Council.

October 9

I am reading William Dean Howells, *Roman Holidays and Others*. It is delightful. The best travel book on Rome I have seen. His feeling for people. Thank God for this little library, a scant 4 shelves, but good. I have read *Nicholas Nickleby* again.

October 10

Abbot Butler came this morning at 11 and gave a little talk in such slow French I could understand it. He said the Holy Spirit listened to prayer and fasting, penitence, and we were a little Council. When he left he said to me, "You see you came at the right time. I saw you at the beginning and now at the end." He spoke of Newman too but I did not catch that. The day passed quickly enough. At 5 our fast ended but it was not until 6 that the sisters were able to prepare enough fresh fruit juice for 20 women. Grapes, pale green, pears, tomatoes, etc. and we were refreshed utterly. Then at 7 a pale tasteless but hot vegetable broth. For the first night I slept well, without pain. No visitors except some of the community today.

October 11

Mass at 7:15. I stayed downstairs with the extern members of the community who had lived with us, shopped for us, stamps, wool, paper, etc and had tended the exhibit in the rear corridor (an out of the way place) of the Foyer Caritas. The exhibit was first rate—good pictures, explanations, text beautifully prepared in Eng., French, Italian, German, and plenty of literature. Much talk, some farewells, a lunch of tasteless farina, made with vegetable water, and thin like gruel, and then Eileen and Barbara Wall called for me at the Pensione and I slept while they went to say farewells to Barbara's friends.

---

244 Dominique Pire, a Belgian Dominican, won the Nobel Peace Prize for his work with refugees.

October 12

Today Archbishop Roberts had his press conference at 4:30, a triumphant success, crowded with journalists and friends. Dick had gotten 86 signatures but still the A. could not speak. So he delivered it triumphantly to the world. We were all so happy. Earlier E and I took carriage and had a most wonderful drive around Rome with a good cicerone.

October 14

Mass on board ship each morning at 7:30 and 8:00. An Ave Maria pilgrimage all very devout, kneeling uncomfortably between theater seats in auditorium. They are cabin class. We are third.

October 15

A very small selection of books, but I have read Flannery O'Connor's latest and a very good introduction referring to Caroline Gordon's help to the young writer—what a generous person she is.[245] Now I am reading Katherine Ann Porter's *Ship of Fools* and a life of Walt Whitman.

October 20

Today the purser, who knew the CW in California years ago, came to visit me. He had sent me a bottle of wine the day before. I will bring to Tamar. He is a Jugoslav—his family have owned orchards and farms in Calif. And we talked about Peace and the land with little agreement. He told me of a former shipmate, an ordinary seaman who ran a little library of Catholic books on board ship, and who had quite a clientele among the seamen, who also got the CW, so that he kept being reminded of it over the years.

October 21

Very warm today and has been. This is first calm, sunny day. Thank God no headache. I've been to Mass each day, but nothing seems real or vital on such a trip, not religion, nor my work. I am suspended, it seems, on my own—not used to this idleness.

Reading Flannery O'Connor—two devastating stories of do-gooders.

---

245  Flannery O'Connor's *Everything that Rises Must Converge* was published posthumously in 1965.

October 22

Foggy morning which delayed arrival at Verrazano Bridge at 11. *Times* reporter, waiting to talk to me about David Miller. There had been and still was great furore.[246]

October 25

Meeting at 5 Beekman [War Resisters League] to discuss draft card burning. Chris, Tom, Pat, Kathie and David Miller there. A.J., Brad Lyttle, and many others. Ned O'Gorman, Anne Marie—Tom Cornell says he is burning his. Chris drove me to Tom's house to dinner after and Tom at another meeting. Got home at 11, could not sleep till 2. Terry Sullivan, Kathie, Salome, all disturbed by my homecoming. And I am too impatient with them.

October 26

Interview with ABC in front of Kenmare—to St. Vincent's to see Ursula McGuire, who is very ill indeed, paralyzed from the hips down. Doctor cannot understand her illness unless it was something she had in Africa, while she taught there. The Maryknoll Sisters visit her and her family.

October 27

David Miller appeared in court—his trial postponed until Nov 22. A very good story in *NY Times* Sunday.

Deane called last night. After my speaking engagements to which I am already committed, I will take no more engagements for a time and write more.

October 28

Picket line at Federal Building. A.J. [Muste] there. Great opposition. Threats of violence. Many bystanders and such a crush of press and radio, television, it was impossible to burn cards. Two were ready. Tom [Cornell] and Marc Edelman.

October 29

Confession today. I will try for weekly instead of monthly. St. Andrew's. Read St. James letter at lunch. David got 30 days in Syracuse today. CORE demonstration some months ago. Tom Cornell called. Draft card burning—4 of them, in Union Square November 6.

---

246 On October 18, Catholic Worker David Miller became the first person arrested for burning his draft card after Congress passed a law making this a specific crime.

November 6

Demonstration in Union Square. 5 draft card burners. A.J. Muste and I spoke. My first time speaking in open air.[247]

November 9

Early this morning Roger LaPorte burned himself to death at U.N. Tonight a blackout. Failure of electricity from Ontario to N.J. All New York in dark. A strange and terrible day.[248]

November 14

11 a.m. Mass at St. Patrick's old Cathedral. In church bulletin, a "hip-hip hooray—USA parade to endorse U.S. Vietnam policy."

November 24. Perkinsville

Last night I dreamed my aches and pains all left me and I could walk freely without fatigue and wandering around the Vermont hills. A delightful dream.

Early supper and T and kids to see Elvis Presley.

---

247  Dorothy's remarks at that demonstration appeared in the November CW: "I speak today as one who is old, and who must endorse the courage of the young who themselves are willing to give up their freedom. I speak as one who is old, and whose whole lifetime has seen the cruelty and hysteria of war in this last half century… I wish to place myself beside A.J. Muste to show my solidarity of purpose with these young men, and to point out that we too are breaking the law, committing civil disobedience, in advocating and trying to encourage all those who are conscripted, to inform their consciences, to heed the still, small voice, and to refuse to participate in the immorality of war." Meanwhile, counter-demonstrators on the other side of the Square chanted "Moscow Mary! Give us joy. Bomb Hanoi!" And "Burn yourselves, not your cards!"

248  At dawn on the morning of November 9, Roger LaPorte, a young volunteer at the Catholic Worker, sat in front of the United Nations, doused himself with gasoline, and struck a match. "I am a Catholic Worker," he said to hospital workers. "I did this as a religious action. I am anti-war, all wars." He remained alive for thirty-three hours in Bellevue Hospital. His death was a terrible blow for the CW community, and for Dorothy as well. LaPorte, a former seminarian, had been volunteering at the Catholic Worker for only a short while, and he had discussed his plans with no one. Nevertheless, Dorothy was blamed for encouraging this "suicide." Thomas Merton, hearing the news from his hermitage in Kentucky, felt it was a sign that the peace movement, along with the rest of the country, was "going nuts." He sent an urgent telegram asking to be removed as a sponsor of the Catholic Peace Fellowship (though he later repented this decision). Dorothy felt keenly judged. In this light, her response was telling.

In the November CW she wrote a reflection, "Suicide or Sacrifice," in which she acknowledged the church's prohibition of suicide, but preferred to see Roger as a "victim soul," who had taken on the suffering of others in hopes of easing their pain. Yes, it was a "sad and terrible act, but all of us around the Catholic Worker know that Roger's intent was to love God and his brother. May perpetual light shine upon him and may he rest in peace."

Strangely, that day, which had begun with Roger's small flame, ended with a great power failure that turned out the lights in New York and most of the eastern United States.

*The year ended on one positive note. On December 7, 1965, the Council Fathers in Rome approved the "Constitution on the Church in the Modern World" (Gaudium et Spes). It contained the strong affirmation of the cause of peace that Dorothy and the "peace lobby" had been advocating. One line, in particular, stood out: "Any act of war aimed indiscriminately at the destruction of entire cities or of extensive areas along with their population is a crime against God and man himself. It merits unequivocal and unhesitating condemnation" (G.S. 80). It was, as Eileen Egan pointed out, the only condemnation issued by the Council.*

# 1966

January, Epiphany Thursday, Tivoli

I spent New Year's at Tamar's in Perkinsville and we were able to get to Mass both New Year's and Sunday though the roads were very muddy, due to the thaw. The worst mud, Tamar said, in the eight years she had spent in Vermont. Now on this feast of Epiphany, Becky is with me in Tivoli, and I lie in bed early morning reading Bouyer's *Liturgical Piety*—his chapter on Advent, Christmas, and Epiphany which stresses our new birth through death into eternal life, which makes me think of Agnes Sydney and her present slow dying in our midst. She is 86 and we have known her these past 30 years, off and on, since the time the Catholic Worker was housed at Charles Street back in '35. We all love her and one still sees in her the mischievous, pleasure-loving girl who married a barge captain and when ashore "flung roses riotously with the throng," celebrating with her husband freedom from the confinement of their water-bound life.

Age has tamed her, as it tames us all. Now she awaits death—her appetites are leaving her, one by one—all her little comforts are being stripped from her, and she looks wonderingly and even sadly (but with calm acceptance) at the great unknown life into which she will soon again be born. Like a babe she sleeps more and more each day, tho she obediently gets up mid-morning and late afternoon to sit by the window "for a change."

And we all, day after day, contemplate thru her our last end which we cannot realize. I am amazed at the amount of material I am finding about death which will, pondered prayerfully, lead us to look forward, if not joyfully, then with a vision illuminated by faith, to this greatest of all adventures.

"Eye hath not seen, nor ear heard what God hath prepared for those who love Him." But do I love Him? The only test is am I willing to sacrifice present happiness and present love for Him? I have done it once, and thereby kept them. The thing is, one must keep doing it, day after day, beginning over and over, to count all things but dross compared to the life of the spirit which alone is able to bring joy, overcome fear—"Love casts out fear." "I know that my redeemer liveth, and in my flesh I shall see God my Savior … I believe—help Thou my unbelief." Most of the time I am as sure of these things as I am of my own life. And as for those periods of desert and doubt, there is so much in the line of inescapable duty that one can work one's way thru them. Maritain has a beautiful article in the *Jesu-Caritas* bulletin of the Little Brothers of Charles de Foucauld.

God respects man and gives him the tremendous gift of freedom, not wishing the love of a slave. He allows man even to sin, tho he knows man will turn as to a parent and blame Him, "Why am I born? Why did He let this happen to me?" I started thinking of this yesterday, that if God respects man and his freedom, so must I respect Him, by not judging—by leaving him to God, who alone knows and understands him, whom He has created. We must not judge, but always try to love.

Had no chance to write my meditation yesterday, what with driving Becky to the bus in Albany, so it is not too clear in my mind now. The martyrdom of community. Last night as I read in the chapel the lessons of Matins for Epiphany, Arthur comes in to ask me for a battery for Agnes' radio. It was 8 p.m. "He only did it to annoy because he knows it teases."

While at Tamar's I read *Pigeon Feathers* by Updike—a beautiful tribute to faith, but there was a malicious thing in the *New Yorker* about a man whose wife went on a civil rights demonstration. I am writing now on the last day of the month, reviewing in a way the reading I am doing these winter months, especially on these days, these last two weekends when we have been snowed in and the winds are icy and rattling the windows and singing thru the trees.

To live in a community of 25 to 30 people, house-bound in winter, to avoid cabin fever, one must be something of a hermit too, and in the country one can have a room of one's own. Mine looks out now on the snowy expanse of the river and the feathery line of trees along the shore. There is no color anywhere today—even the evergreens look black—all is uniformly gray. And one would feel gray and hopeless in mind and soul too, what with our renewed bombing of North Vietnam, were it not for our vision and the hope imparted by this reading. Right now I am reading *John XXIII* by Father Balducci.

February 22

Feast of Peter's [Chair]. He was given by Jesus the Keys of the Kingdom. What he binds on earth, is bound in heaven, etc. A practicing Catholic is one who goes to Confession, receives Communion at Mass, not necessarily weekly or daily—by rule of the Church, annually. This yearly Communion called "one's Easter duty" is considered so vital, that if one does not make it, he is not considered a practicing Catholic. Indeed out of communion with the Church—excommunicated, as it were, by his own will, not by formal pronouncement of Pope and bishop.

In what way does the priest possess authority? Certainly he has the authority to forgive sins—we believe that and so we go to Confession and feel there that we are confessing as tho to God himself, our sins and when he gives absolution, we believe that he has restored health to our sick souls and that if we keep on taking the remedies proposed, we will be safe and sure of "resurrection of the body and life everlasting."

The remedy he gives us is our bread of life—the greatest gift we can receive here on earth—our daily bread to strengthen both soul and body. And in penance, prayers are recommended and almsgiving—a way of life, a way of showing love for God and brother—father and brother, the family, the community. So herein lies the priest's authority. We go to him for what only he can give, due to his calling, his training, his love for his work. We go to him as we would go to a physician to remedy the pain of our bodies, and surely the pain of our souls. The sickliness of our spiritual life is a real illness. We accept the authority of the doctors as such even if we go from one to another seeking remedies. And it is so too we should understand the authority of the priest, and respect him for his function, and be grateful. What does it matter if he does not read Camus or Dostoyevsky—listen to Mozart, or Bach, or Beethoven—that his tastes, background differ?

We do judge him for not having an understanding of social and rural justice, national and international justice, because this is in the field of morality. The very healing he confers on us, the medicine, the food he gives us—and only he can give those particular supernatural helps—makes us expect more from him. "Physician, heal thyself." And yet the power he possesses by virtue of his ordination does the work, not he. We must not judge. But how can we explain the faith that is in us? "Flesh and blood have not revealed it to us"—in spite of our always citing "authorities," spiritual writers, thinkers, philosophers, etc.—"but my Father who is in Heaven." Faith, more precious than gold, is a gift. We cannot give it to each other, but certainly we can pray God to give it to others. Péguy wrote: "When we get to heaven, God is going to say to us, 'Where are the others?'"

We must not judge the Church by the man, by the human element. I must pray for priests, pray for conversions, and I must not seem in my writing to be telling others what to do—but I must be speaking of myself, for my own peace of soul. Not trying for conversions to the Church, not proselytizing, but leaving things to God, who wills that all men be saved, and can give His divine life thru any channel. "Catholics must be pretty bad, pretty weak to need so many helps—the saints, Mary (a Blessed Mother as well as a Heavenly Father), outward signs, etc." Yet incarnation, grace builds on nature. It would not get very far, what with our poor weak human nature. Unless we build on a rock, as our Lord said, our house will fall. And that Rock is Peter. Upon this Rock I will build my Church.

In the Matins for today, February, there are as usual three lessons with the Responses after each one. After the reading from the first epistle of Peter there is this response verse: "If you love me, Simon Peter, feed my sheep." "Lord you know that I love you, and will lay down my life for you. If I should die with you, I will not deny you, and will lay down my life for you."

It is as tho this versicle were put in here to remind the People of God how weak and unstable Peter, the Rock on which Christ built his Church, could be. As indeed all the apostles were, even after sharing Jesus' human life thru three years of public life. They only knew him for three years, after all—they might have justified themselves. Even after his resurrection, his coming to them and eating with them, they were asking about the earthly kingdom. But just the same, they clung to him, listened to him, and after his ascension—his finally leaving them as far as his bodily presence went—they followed his teaching in staying together in prayer for nine days. The Church calls this the first novena. They prayed together for nine days, awaiting the promise he had given them, and then on Pentecost, what a surge of the Holy Spirit engulfed them. They were like new men, new born, born-again Christians, reaching for the new life, the life of Grace.

Just the same, we must always remember Peter's betrayal. Peter the human, beloved fisherman, the ordinary man who had great desires to do extraordinary things such as walking on the water, who did not recognize Jesus on the beach until John said, "It is the Lord."


On Pilgrimage—February

We are supposed to go to Press the second Wednesday of the month, but somehow we have been later these last months than usual. The paper comes out mid-month, and since we mail it from Chrystie Street and our little band of helpers from the Bowery neighborhood are most leisurely (unassisted as they are by the young people of the staff), our readers receive their paper at the end of the month, or beginning of the next.

Stanley, who was away on vacation with his family in Baltimore, got the January copy just as he was leaving Baltimore, February 15. January issue carried an appeal to our readers to send us some sheets for our farm guests—the house is full all winter and in summer three houses are full. By the third week in February, half a dozen packages of sheets had arrived—one of them from Dan Herr, editor of *The Critic*, ordered straight form Marshall Field—delightful colored ones. I have a bright blue one on my bed right now.

Killing two birds with one stone, I am hereby thanking our generous readers and indirectly rebuking our New York staff for not getting the paper out. We cannot blame delays on the post office since the sheets arrived, parcel post, in such good time. There was time in the life of the CW when the staff itself took hold and got the paper out in three days or four. If we went to press Monday, the paper arrived Tuesday. It had to be mailed out by Friday or there would be no space for the Friday night meetings. Now, on a three-story, falling apart loft building, we have so much space the paper can linger around for two weeks before it gets out. But come summer we hope to have a new house of hospitality, smaller and more manageable. Scattered as we are now, between Spring Street and Kenmore and Chrystie, we do not know where people are, or whom we are housing.

There is a story appearing in the *US Catholic* this month which speaks of the ups and downs of the CW movement and it is certainly true that there are ups and downs, but everyone who has ever been close to us would differ as to which years or decades have been the best. As far as I am concerned there have been storms and calms in every period, and some times have been especially hard, humanly speaking.

Thomas Merton recently pointed out that these times in the new era of world history, when the whole world is in agony, there is a gigantic struggle. (Constant interruptions—visitors, telephone, and members of the household made me lose forever what Thomas Merton was getting at.)

April 23. Chicago

Dinner with Saul Alinsky[249] [with] Monsignor John J. Egan—hereafter to be called Father Egan, who is now in Presentation Parish.

He has two assistants, a resident priest who is a teacher at Quigley seminary, and there were two other priests from Mother Cabrini Parish nearby. Father Paul wore a housing button, similar to CNVA [Committee for Nonviolent Action] button which is a naval symbol meaning Nuclear Disarmament. Three BVM nuns also joined us at table for coffee, and Catherine Connelly, secretary to Father Egan. Father Lester Schmidt, a Glenmary priest, was there in slacks and sweat shirt on his last day and night of a week on skid row where he had been wandering homeless (all skid row hotels filled) living on the

---

249 Saul Alinsky was a Chicago-based community organizer and the author of *Reveille for Radicals*. Dorothy wrote, "To me [he] represents the man of vision, one of the truly great of our day, in a class with Danilo Dolci and Vinoba Bhave. Thank God we have some heroes today in the social field whose vision illuminates the hard work they propose." (May 1966)

inadequate diet of the men on small pensions or unemployment insurance, or just plain penniless. Why shouldn't a priest have as rigorous training as a Marine? Called THE PLUNGE—started a year ago by Episcopalian men and women—student venture.

May 18

Meeting at Loyola College with Dr. Nicholas Varga of history department as chairman—a very silent man, but of much peace and friendliness. Perhaps I talked so much I did not give him a chance. Most of the students friendly, but only two committed to pacifism as far as I knew. But if we had two in every college! What leaven!

But leaven is not good for a permanent diet, except as one takes brewers yeast to repair damages to the body. The host, the manna, is unleavened. The matzo, the tortilla also. An older man in the audience, evidently in the habit of getting up and being leaven, perhaps, getting a rise out of everyone else, shouted out something at me when I mentioned the Cardinal Mindszenty Foundation. Later when he rose to present from a paper he held in his hand a list of objections to my talk all of which reflected the *Wanderer*, St. Paul, Minnesota, point of view.[250] A number of sturdy, one might also say burly, Jesuits rose and stood around him in most intimidating fashion. We had to insist on his right to be heard and it gave me a chance to answer him, and to try to clarify my own statements.

May 19. Ascension Day

Breakfast with Father Phil Berrigan after our wonderful Pentecost Mass. We talked about Father Roy and the parish work.

Woke up this morning in a pleasant back room looking out on a backyard with azaleas in bloom and honeysuckles lush over a little fence. Green everywhere with new little trees planted.

May 21

To farm at 9. Always on my return after a month's absence, complaints.

Nicole [d'Entremont], Terry Becker, Diane [Feeley] arrested in Armed Forces Day counter-demonstration. Fifty taken in civil disobedience—sit-in on street.

May 22

Spoke at farm, in the library. The chapel looks beautiful. Marist Brothers and Christian Brothers there. I spoke of our trip in the Midwest, of our

---

250 *The Wanderer* was a virulently reactionary Catholic newspaper.

meeting with Saul Alinsky, Cesar Chavez[251]—men of vision. The encounters with people of the Mindszenty Foundation—men of fear. One cannot stress enough the dangers of fear. St. Peter said "deliver me from fear of their fear." Psalm "deliver us from the fear of our enemies."

May 23. Perkinsville

The high school students are debating the war in Vietnam. Here I am surrounded by teenagers as soon as I arrive. Maggie will be 13 in August, but she is already a most responsible all-around worker in the family; Mary is 15 in July; Nicky 16; Eric 18. Of the neighbors—Pete Reynolds is 14; Ricky Foley 18 and already enlisted in the National Guard; John Bullard 16 or thereabouts. Susie who was home last weekend is 19 and will begin her third year of nurse's training in September. She is now interested in Aldous Huxley and mysticism, and the work in mental hospitals. So we have in our midst discussion of new morality, war and peace, and man and his soul. Could one say the new theology? In other words, they think, besides going to school, taking apart and putting together cars, hunting, and fishing.

May 24

Glanced at Camus' journals. He kept complaining about his memory—said he should keep a journal, a diary. I keep resolving—especially on my travels. I forget so much—people, ideas, etc. I will try again.

An old house like this is covered with built-in homes for the birds—as I write two are feeding their young with the insects and grubs from the butternut tree by the house and the ancient apple tree down by the garden. Tremendous activity of birds, barn swallows, blue and orange.

Tuesday May 31. Pentecost week. 10 p.m.

A rainy night on the bus on my way to New York. I had to leave my car in Manchester, Vermont, because it broke down, badly I am afraid.

All my presents were in it, a big wooden bowl from Tamar and two small salad bowls, a soapstone griddle, a pot of catnip to plant and a box of odds and ends.

It was a wonderful day, however, after an all but sleepless night. It was not only that I was in pain with both sciatica and arthritis but fretting about B

---

251 Cesar Chavez was the founder of the United Farmworkers Union. In the decade to come Dorothy would form a particularly close bond with Chavez and his cause. The UFW, she believed, was a social and religious movement, building community, fighting for justice and the dignity of the most victimized of all workers, while educating the public as to the power and meaning of nonviolent action.

and T and their future, so I put on the light and read Dickens' *Bleak House* until 3:30.

We were to go to Gerry Hardy's for a Mass in his home, and to begin with Tamar had a flat tire so Becky and I went on without her. Fr. Miller appeared at eleven, happy and full of life as usual, and he being late, Tamar was able to catch up with us.

We talked a great deal of course about war in the world—the suicides in Vietnam of Buddhist monks, nuns and students, of Roger LaPorte. The seminarian had been a classmate of his at Barre, Vermont and knew him as we did as a normal, lovable, hardworking young man.

Mrs. Hurd has two sons in the merchant marine, young officers on freighters and tankers bringing munitions and oil to Vietnam.

One, after 5 trips, had been flown east to Baltimore where he was shipped out to Africa by the same line. One of the boys after witnessing the famine victims in India went back on board boat and cried all night. He is only 23 and it was his first experience of the sight of destitution. I could not help but think of Father [Lorenzo] Milani's defense of himself against the charges made against him of advocating resistance to conscription for war, saying even those who cooked for troops, contribute to war.[252] How involved we all are, with the hidden taxes we pay for war, even when we make the gesture of refusing to pay income tax, so much of which is used to finance wars. We are all exploiters, as Orwell writes in one of his essays. Workers who consider themselves exploited are in fact the exploiters of others. I remembered the general strike in Belgium when the workers revolted against the austerity regime brought about by the loss, or the giving up, of the African colony, the Belgian Congo.

One of the most stirring statements and the most radical Pope Paul has made is his calling for a new economic order— and I thought: Garibaldi served the Church well when he fought against the Papal States and relieved the Church of her hold on Italy. Who will rise up to work out a just and wise solution to the money holdings, the investing on industry (how much of it is exploitative). The money power of the Church which is an occasion of suspicion and distrust, if not of actual scandal in the eyes of the world.

Which reminds me of Seymour Melman, Professor at Columbia, who has written several books recently on the problem of converting a war-time economy into a peacetime one.

It is sad that so many are profiting by the war. Communities fight for government contracts, even for manufacture of napalm and noxious gasses, not

---

252  See "Dom Lorenzo Milani: A Priest-Teacher on Trial," January 1966.

to speak of bombs, planes, helicopters, trucks, and all the armaments that go into the devastatingly expensive wars.

How many countries do we arm, to keep the peace, as they say. What insanity! If we are coming back to this always it is because Peace is the most important cause of our time, and because too I have spoken to convents of nuns who have never considered these things—who do not know the gasoline jelly that napalm is, a fire that burns the flesh from the bone, who know nothing of the gasses which are being manufactured.

How can they use those tremendous powers of prayer which they possess if they do not know—if they do not "form the intention," if they do not know what they praying for, if "they pray amiss," thinking of an impossible victory by force of arms.

June [10]. Friday
After the hail and rain, thunder and lightening, awake to a blue cold day with sudden showers. Hans brought breakfast. Read in my '65 diary. Had pains in my hip last year also. Encouraging since I thought only this year. But they are worse. Cannot bear weight on one foot—cane a most real necessity. Went to bus station last night without it to pick up Bill Cannon and could scarcely get home.

Stanley got hate literature about me due to an article he wrote about Birchers being Communists. He is so mixed up about CW and Communism.

June 16
Woke this a.m. with the feeling very strong—I belong to Someone to whom I owe devotion. Recalled early love and that joyous sense of being not my own, but of belonging to someone who loved me completely.

June 22
We went to grave [of Joe Cotter]. Problem of drink. The mourners accusing others of no grief and now Joe Ferry receives his check and more money for liquor. Alice wants to apply for total disability benefits, all for liquor and medicine to kill her pain. How to handle it? As a family does with patience, but when there is violence, as with Jack, they have to go. Jack is at Chrystie St. and has been of help. The hardest thing to bear is when John and Jack glorify their drinking as "being with the poor, the sinner."

June 24. Tivoli
The retreat ended with a colloquium. No one agreed with Father [Hugo], tho they like and admire him. Deane, Marty, Tom, etc. Detachment is re-

jected. New morality, new theology "since John XXIII," but they do not read John XXIII. Yet when I spoke of a sense of failure Fr. encouraged me and spoke his admiration and agreement with the protests and civil disobedience and jailing of the young ones. I was much consoled.

### June 26

Up at 5:30. Hans was already down cooking. John F. told me Hugh [Madden] was back and staying in his cave under the drive. The hole he dug inside of the hill will be used for burying trash. I was afraid he had taken off. He will go on a pilgrimage to Canada later.

### July 6

Marty has translated Abbé Chaigne's criticism of the Council's pronouncement on war as self-contradictory and unsatisfactory to both sides. We will publish it in our July-August issue. "Frankness and Freedom in the Church."

### July 8

Today I drove down from Tivoli with John McKeon. We lunched at Kenmare Street and at 5 went to Mass at Nativity Church, which was hot in the glare of lights which they turn on too generously. The church has all its statues still, its artificial flowers, but it has too its altar facing the people, and the liturgy is English.

I stayed for a good hour afterward since I had to speak at the Friday night meeting which was crowded even tho the night was terribly hot. Phil Maloney was chairman, Tom Hoey faithful and so serious in his desire to serve. He is not yet 18. There were many Fordham students. I spoke on anarchism as opposed to Communism and Capitalism, the need to study it, the recent books on the subject, methods being used now to combat evils by direct action. Protests, voluntary poverty, by refusal to work in war industries, refusal to pay taxes, the proposed withdrawal of moneys from Chase National and National City Banks to aid the cause in South Africa. Voluntary poverty, willingness to suffer jail for civil disobedience, most potent weapon against war.

Whether my driving made him nervous, I don't know, but he [John McKeon] talked of women all the way down. Peggy—she spoke of breaking her heart over Jack J. who is now drinking night and day on the Bowery. "Can you imagine this at 70?" she asked. Since she is now 78, it astounded me and touched me. Showing her capacity for love and for tenderness, which goes on with the years, even increases. "Does it ever end?" he said to her. He has that quality with women of sympathy, which brings out truth and honesty. They know his sentimentality, his Irish-ness, but know it will never be used against them. Lily Burke, when she was dying at 72, had the delusion that she had given birth to a child. She had a tumor on brain and was lying in Mt. Sinai Hospital. There were twins she told me, and the other is not born yet. Isn't it wonderful that a woman of 70 should conceive? She was so conscious of her age, and of her love for the imagined or real Negro she wrote about in her "To Make Accord." Both Peggy and Lily were women who constantly served others, loved people in general, loved life, made you feel their terrible vitality, their sexuality.

July 10

Mass at 11 and at 4. Very good day. Problems: squatters on Roger LaPorte Farm and on ours. Here the Rice family and there the tenants. So much fear and fleeing from the little way, the discipline of work.

July 16

Students did not like my talk. Not enough about Vietnam. Too much non-violence and pacifism.

July 20

Trouble now. Maxine wanting baby baptized in Barrytown. More antagonism to Fr. Kane. I am so glad to see the great happiness of the girls with their babies and they are to be congratulated for keeping them when priests, social workers, and all are opposed—but they should not flaunt their independence in the face of Fr. Kane, by whose kindness we have the Blessed Sacrament here.

July 24

Ananda Ashram. A good weekend crowd. Young beats sincerely interested in Buddhism and yoga and old people interested in peace and health. But not agreeing with CW stand on war and means used to bring peace.

July 25

Stayed at Della's all day so she could visit Tessa and go shopping. Franklin and I had a quiet day, both of us writing—he a book report.

Finished *Problem of Pain*. A wonderful book. Spiritual reading.

July 29

Kinds of poverty—mortification of senses, in this case of smell. P empties his chamber pot off the back porch and the smell rises up to my window right above him. Senility. Old Mr. O'Connell used to do the same at Easton. To endure filth in these surroundings is doubly hard. Not to have the strength to remedy the ill. To close the window in 90 degree weather!

Terry Sullivan sentenced to one year for burning his draft card. He pled guilty.

## July 31. Pax Conference

Awoke in great misery of spirit. Last night the food ran out. More than 200.

Mary Lou Williams and a singer, her nephew, and his accompanist, all arrived after food gone. All we had were toasted cheese sandwiches.

Karl Stern[253] played. Mrs. Douglas Campbell recited poetry, then jazz concert and incomparable Negro singing. But I feel old and totally exhausted today. (This is the way I felt at 7 a.m. But the day want well. Conferences, Mass, tho Deane would not receive, and many staying over, about 25.)

Mrs. Delacorte, leading film actress in Hungary. Mrs. D contributed a thousand to mailing peace issue CW to all the bishops of the world before last session of the Council. She came to visit me at Kenmare and was quite horrified at the place and wished that her publisher husband's money could help out. But I was flippant, suggested putting Marie Langlots in charge, who had lived 2 years in subways and knew destitution. Also I said, "This is how writers live, while publishers live on Park Ave." I am ashamed of my tart tongue. I am not really bitter but irrepressible. Perhaps bitter for the poor, not myself and my meager rewards for writing. For instance, I am offered 75 pounds by John Todd in England for a pamphlet.

## August 2. CW school

This morning Karl [Stern] spoke wonderfully—never heard him better, on ambivalence, on violence. What a brilliant and holy man. About acceptance of mystery. Library was crowded. Many young people with problems. Pat's seaman Communist friend full of questions about fear of God, about God.

Then the yogi came from Ananda Ashram, 3 of them. Dick Haines, two young men, a Polish "expert," and the Indian poet. A wonderful afternoon. We learned much. But self discipline and practice we all lack.

## August 4. CW school

This morning Stanley spoke out under the trees—very good, Helene said, more serious and less romantic than last year. I stayed in my room and wrote,

---

253 Karl Stern, a German-born psychiatrist in Montreal, was a close friend of Dorothy. He wrote *Pilar of Fire* about his conversion from Judaism to Catholicism.

under Pat's pressure, another chapter in "All is Grace."[254] She left at noon for
N.Y. taking a chapter on Fr. Lacouture with her. I certainly get all upset when
I am not getting any writing done.

## August 7

Mass at Russian chapel—very beautiful today, and the blessing of first
fruits, celebrating Transfiguration. Maritain says this incident is to give us
some knowledge of heaven.

Many demonstrations—thousands as compared to the few score we used to
be. The present most unpopular war.

## August 10

Our circulation mailed out is 87,000. We print 90,000. Of those more
and more single copies, bundles 20,000. Keith keeps accurate track, getting
better acquainted. He will not live in same house with women, he says. Every
woman is looking for a man, he said, and he needs to be protected. He is a
monk—a hermit in the world. Very devout.

## August 16

Ruth Collins called about the new house [on East First Street]. Contract
ready to be signed.

## August 18

Finished comment on [Erich] Fromm book and sent it to [Joe] Cunneen
[editor of *Cross Currents*]. 11:15 Mass at Christian Brothers and had lunch
with superior in charge of the retreat of novices. Not much of a retreat.

## August 20. Westport

Berkeley Tobey[255] died two years ago, aged 86. He had taken an 8th wife—
former sec of [Theodore] Dreiser. Berkeley was pall-bearer of Dreiser.

---

254 At this time and for some years Dorothy worked on a book called "All is Grace," which
would tell the story of the Retreat movement and the priests and spiritual advisors who had
played a role in her life. She never finished it.

255 Berkeley Toby occupies a particularly mysterious place in Dorothy's biography. In 1920,
on the rebound from an unhappy love affair, she married Toby, a founder of the Literary Guild
in New York. The relationship lasted less than a year. As she wrote to a friend, "He took me to
Europe and when we got back I left him. I felt I had used him and was ashamed" (Miller, *Dorothy Day*, 143.) She described the European trip in *The Long Loneliness*, but never mentioned
her marriage. As she often said (quoting her mother), "least said, soonest mended."

August 28. Tivoli. Peacemakers[256]

Bob Swann—Gandhian movement. He argues for village economy. Another is all for city economy and machines, mechanized farming. Another talks of lack of refrigeration and food spoilage.

Discussed case of Suzanne Williams, 17, arrested in demonstration at Electric Boat, Groton, Conn., on occasion of launching of the Will Rogers, the 41st Polaris sub. She grad from [high school] in June. Works with Boston Committee for [Nonviolent Action]. Others got 9 days, or $25 fine. She got 30 days, then 60 days for contempt of court. She is fasting, 8 days, in Boston, vigiled, 24 hours a day, conversed with crowd. Aug 6-9. Now fasting again. Vegetarian.

Such quiet, gentle discussion, endless. Richardson family trying to live in area. Try to break from migrant cycle. Not accepted by local Negro community. White farmers annoyed at losing workers, trying to find housing for them.

Wally Nelson exploded at Vivian Rosenberg for taking too mildly the rules of one large grower of no visitors on the property, in the excuse of protecting migrants from gamblers, loose women and liquor. Nelson called it slavery, when families were so ruled by bosses. He wanted to test the case. There are about 20 or 30 cabins there right on the highway. Loraine opposed this as not wanted by the migrants. Nelson said many slaves were afraid of freedom. There is no organizing on the East Coast—no disturbances since the Seabrook Farms strike in the Thirties.

August 29

Joe Zarrella arrived this a.m. Stanley and I picked him up and we had breakfast in Red Hook and I went to the bank to notarize the 2 summons I had from Cambridge, NY, where I went thru a stop sign and at 45 mph instead of 30, in the village.

Mass at 11:15 and much discussion with Christian Brothers and Carmelite priest on pacifism. If we can only spread an interest in nonviolence and such books as Fr. [Pie] Regamy's, which is just out *[Non-Violence and the Christian Conscience]*.

September 4. Peacemakers leave

Next year they will come again on the 19th of Aug. Never were so peaceful and considerate a group, young and old, and I enjoyed the sessions I attended. Not much chance to talk to individuals, our own company is so heavy.

---

256 Peacemakers was a pacifist movement founded originally by former World War II c.o.'s. . They favored nonviolent direct action, such as tax resistance.

Pat kept after me to write all evening so I did 4 pages. Work, work as Chekhov said.

## September 5. St. Joseph's Feast

Today, Labor Day has been named St. Joseph's feast day to take the place of the May 1 day (for U.S.). Went to Mass at St. Sylvia's at nine o'clock.

## September 6

Drove into town today. Had dinner with Tom Sullivan at 6 in Chinatown and Pat came down after I had left her to take care of visitors. Jack English is leaving the monastery and will probably come to Tivoli. I asked Tom's advice and he said to invite him. Tom is the same, a rock, steadfast.

## September 8

Mary's Nativity. The year the atom bomb was dropped, Jane O'Donnell and David Mason, Elinor and I and a few others walked from Mott St. house near Canal all the way to Mother Cabrini's shrine at 208th St. We left the house at midnight and arrived at the shrine at 6. I was 48 then and still strong. Could not do it today.

## September 9

To 36 East 1st St.—new home to meet the architect to go over the house floor by floor. Owner there, impatient of delays.

## September 23

Jim Wilson will be up for sentencing in 2 weeks. He dreads jail. A difficult disposition. Seminary, college, community, all given up.

## September 25

[Allen] Ginsberg sent poem for Bob Steed. Bob says Mary L. reminds him of Tragic Muse of Henry James.

## September 27

Theories. Why people leave Church now. Pope John's great and trustful gesture, opening windows. Catholics have been so complacently apart, as a whole, No contact with outer world. Gerry Griffin used to say we at CW were protected and talked of getting out in the world, meaning perhaps the world of earning one's living, too. One is so well cared for and comforted in the church in spite of all our criticisms. CW had more contacts than most what with Peter Maurin's emphasis on Common Good, with believer and unbeliever, Protestant, Jew, etc.

Tamar for instance was surprised to find how good people are, how many serve regardless of religion, and begin to see how mediocre, how *bad* Catholics are, how sunk in complacency, when having faith and the sacraments they should be so much better. What good has it done them? Etc., etc. So without having studied their own religion, they lose faith in it. Compulsory Sunday Mass, compulsory holy days, compulsory fasting. They have never been taught the motive which Fr. Roy so stressed, the supernatural motive which makes each act in life full of meaning, nourishing, growth. They have given grudging service, no joy in it, no obedience, since it was compelled, so they throw off their chains, as they think, and "all is permitted." Ivan [Karamazov]: "Since there is no God, all is permitted." Satisfied flesh, in youth, satisfies conscience. Senses stilled by content for a time. Conscience is also stilled for a time... So, "my conscience tells me I am all right," so regardless of denying the Sacrament (of matrimony) (in S. and P's case) they continue to receive the Host of the Mass, if it pleases them, if they have "felt" it, maybe contact with others. They have turned so to others with human love, to their brothers, that it has become a light which has blinded them—temporarily, one hopes. In our group of young ones, they find love in each other, somewhat in the poor, those of them who serve the line for instance. But only those they *see* around them. They give up Confession but receive. They "feel" they are right, so they are right.

Meanwhile, they despise the old, who have made such a mess of the world, and with the old—the ancient Church itself. They want to rebuild the Church in the shell of the old, as Terry said.

## October 5

Drove up on Monday to Rochester and stayed with Eloise Wilkin. Disappointing meeting at seminary. They did not know what I was talking about in relation to war and peace. Vietnam and our government, the role of chaplains. They are all blinded by medieval notions of defending the weak, protecting people from communism, the (truly) gallant bravery of chaplains under fire, etc. They have not heard both Pope John and Pope Paul's cry for dialogue, finding concordances with Soviet Union, with Communists. They will readily shift to the Party Line, in this case, our government's, that the evil is Peking Communism. Already one sees it in the diocesan press, the editorials (Providence *Visitor*).

It is hard to be treated so coldly.

On the other hand the students at Rochester U., both Newman Club and other organizations, were warmly receptive.

### October 18
A great sense of relief at making a decision, no more speaking except the McGill one. Bed and rest today and tomorrow.

### October 19
Bed rest and reading a strange story of a girl in a mental hospital (*I Never Promised You a Rose Garden*), which Judy [Gregory] gave me. She also gave me quotes from Simone Weil, and from Thoreau.

### October 20
Letter from a cousin of Fr. [Camilo] Torres.[257] I am reading too—*Liberation*, Marjorie Hope, "Revolution in Colombia."

### October 21
Reading Simone Weil essays. Very interesting on Languedoc civilization. Also her ideas on obedience. None left now except to the state. The concept lost. Must write on this in retreat book.

Must get entire score of Wagner's Ring in secondhand stores on Second Ave. They have old librettos. Simone Weil likes Wagner. Karl Stern does not.

### October 27
Wrote first article for *Ave Maria* [Advent Series] today, what with rewriting, revision, and having it copied it will be Sunday before it is mailed.

### November 10
Went to Red Hook dentist and he pulled the one tooth causing all the trouble.

### November 14
Telegram from John Cort, Jane Marra [of the Boston Catholic Worker] died—to be buried from the Cathedral in Boston, Wednesday.

### November 15
Arrived [in Boston] at 6 and called the Corts, who told me where the funeral parlor was and after supper at bus station I went there and met Arthur

---

257 Father Camilo Torres was a Colombian priest who joined the guerrillas and was killed in combat in 1966.

Sheehan, Catherine Ahern, Ignatius [O'Connor], [John] Kelly, the relatives, etc. A beautiful service led by Fr. Francis from the Cathedral. Reading from Old and New Testament, thrilling. "These bones shall rise again."

## November 19

I wrote letter to Tamar and wrote on last of four articles [for *Ave Maria*]— Obedience. What impossibly grand concepts I had chosen in my attempts to simplify my job. Marge typed the last one on Chastity the day I left for Boston.

## November 20

Did not get to Mass today what with this constant cough-cold.

Pat is typing my notebooks and doing a wonderful job, invaluable. From them I have gathered material I needed for the appeal, for instance, and which will save me also for the pamphlet on the Works of Mercy. She is a good writer herself and her letters make a book in themselves.

## November 22

Today at noon the man from the internal revenue dept came and I signed a statement that I received no salary, filed no return.

## November 27

Vietcong proposed ceasefire—Christmas and New Year's proposed.

## November 28

Letter from Anna Louise Strong dated Nov 21 saying she interceded for Bishop Ford.[258] No reply but she'll keep at it. Also writing about Red Guards.

## November 30

A most beautiful sunset at 4:15—purple and red and gold and lemon color. Snow promised and a damp cold feel in the air. Tom Cornell just called. Lanza del Vasto coming here.

Finished C.S. Lewis letters today. A most moving and fascinating account of a man of letters.

(Helene hurt by my brusqueness, my petulance. Must keep away from people when I'm under the weather.)

---

258  Probably Dorothy refers to Bishop James E. Walsh of Maryknoll, who was imprisoned by the Communists in China and released only in 1970. Bishop Francis Ford, another Maryknoller, who died in a Chinese prison camp in 1952. Anna Louise Strong was a radical journalist, whom Dorothy knew from her early days in New York.

December 2

This cold began Nov 13 and has hung on since. I have felt old and very tired. And when I consider the del Vastos—vegetarians, not a cup of coffee or tea, and so hardworking and disciplined a life, I feel ashamed.

December 3

Lanza del Vasto and Chanterelle came at 7:30. Discussion.

December 4

"May the God of patience and encouragement enable you to live in harmony with one another... so accept one another as Christ accepted you for the glory of God." I wake up needing this. Too much company.

December 16

East Side Dr. closed. Subway to printer. Pat, Jack Cook, John McKeon, Tom Hoey and Jim Wilson on masthead. Pat started it by teasing Marty to put her on. John on being called said "a signal honor."

Too-long center article by Merton. After all we are a layman's paper, for workers, not for men of letters.[259]

December 20

We skidded coming down hill from laundromat. Tonight for supper a young man and woman and 3-year-old child from Woodstock with 16- or 18-year-old boy they wished to leave with us. Marty said no. Then the young man told of his LSD "trips," the necessity of a guide, etc.—glowing, amazed, "I have come further—I have understood more, I have learned to accept myself. I can go much further." And all in an instant this realization. Rita brought up the report of alcoholics cured and he said yes, it was because they realized why they drank. "Released from the womb," was one of his expressions. I quote *Cloud of Unknowing* to him, and St. John of the Cross. He acknowledged St. John as a master, said one must learn to achieve this state without drugs, but that the drug had opened up the possibility. But he spoke as tho he had achieved it. He was interested in the hermits, George and Joe, and Keith.

See the 4th chapter of *Cloud*, on Time, and use of it. "To comprehend Him is incomprehensible to all created knowledgeable powers."

"2 principal working powers in the soul, a knowledgeable power and a loving power." To the first "God is evermore incomprehensible."

---

259 "Albert Camus and the Church," December 1966. Dorothy was inconsistent in her disapproval of long articles by priests; she was evidently still stinging from Merton's response to Roger LaPorte's death.

"And to the second...He is all comprehensible to the full... and this is the endless miracle of love, the working of which shall never end, forever He shall do it...endless bliss, and the contrary is endless pain."

Saturday, December 24. Perkinsville

From my $400 from *Ave Maria* articles I gave Eric $200 for his school dues, $50 to Sue, and $10 each to Becky, Mary, Maggie, $50 to Nick, $5 to Martha and $3 to Hilaire and one to Katy. Nick had worked all summer and earned $300 which he has received in installments from Adams, a builder on a very small scale. N does not want to go to college but wants to work with Rick and Larry.

When I got to Tamar's and found mail awaiting me I was so confused with the hubbub that I burned an important letter from Elizabeth Anscombe, an English philosopher teaching at Oxford. I had not read the letter. She had sent a check (for the work, probably).

Sunday December 25

Every car was covered with snow as we woke up this morning so no one got to Mass. Everyone talked of midnight Mass but the snow was already high and no snow plows out.

December 26

House is warm—it is beautiful and white out. For recreation reading C.S. Lewis, as portrayed by his friends. Most interesting note. C.S. Lewis, so informed by Williams, found he could take on his wife's pain.

December 27

When I cannot sleep at night I read Matins and it always helps. Certainly life with a bunch of kids is a constant effort—to pray, to live, to understand. When religion is thrown out the window, everything is permitted, as Ivan said.

December 29

Still more snow all day, But Nick and Eric went skiing today at 7 a.m. Peter and another boy. The last three out drinking beer. Eric and Nick came in and fell asleep, left Peter in the car asleep. He could have frozen to death. The light woke me up from the bedroom and I got them up. This was at 2 a.m. Read Matins, drank sanka and went back to sleep to awaken to "mercy meek and mild, God and sinners reconciled" running thru my head. I remembered how I had alienated Jim Montague by harshness when he went out bar hopping on his way to returning a borrowed chalice at Easton. And yet naturally speaking, one would claim it a duty. Prayer is more powerful and trust in conscience.

# 1967

Sunday, January 1. Perkinsville

A strange New Year's day—Sunday, and we could not get to Mass. Just as on Christmas, ground covered with slippery snow. Tamar working took my car and the boys the station wagon to go skiing. The boys are in such a state over school and war. And everyone exhausted with the long vacation.

After Jim Hughes's death a year ago and Al Uhrie's 6 mos. ago life seems very uncertain for the young. One can only pray.

January 3

Drove down from Tamar's. We had visitors recently from Puerto Rico who said that the archbishop, the first Puerto Rican one, offered to say a Requiem for Don Pedro Campos, when he died last year. There are 20 men still in prison for the shooting in Congress and Lolita Lebron, who is spending her time in the women's Federal prison in West Virginia as in a convent or hermitage.[260]

January 6. Epiphany

Wept all morning over state of world and the house. Mailed review of *La Vida*. I will never write another book review. Not a fast reader—they taken an immense amount of time, an unnecessary amount. People talk so much about the meaning of life and the work is to grow in love, love of God our destination, and love of neighbor, our first step, our continuing step, our right road in that direction. Love means answering the mail that comes in—and there is fearful amount of it. That person in the hospital, that person suffering a breakdown of nerves, the person lonely; far-off, watching for the mailman each day. It means loving attention to those around us, the youngest and the oldest (the drunk and the sober).

---

260 Don Pedro Campos was a leader of the Puerto Rican Nationalist Party and a long crusader for Independence. On March 4, 1954, Lolita Lebron and three Puerto Rican men unfurled the Puerto Rican flag in the visitors' gallery of the House of Representatives and then opened fire on the chamber, wounding five lawmakers. Lebron herself apparently fired into the ceiling: "I did not come to kill anyone," she said. "I came to die for Puerto Rico!" She was released from prison in 1979 after receiving a presidential pardon.

January 7. Tivoli

Yesterday what started me off was the array of bottles ranged along the hall in front of each door. The malice of Whitey or Ursula, whoever did it.

Mrs. Willis, John's teacher, came for the day and disclosed the fact that real estate men are trying to get property because of an atomic reactor to be built along the Hudson. They want riverfront property. Might offer more than we paid for it. Which may mean my feeling about this place as being too much for us, far from Easton, voluntary poverty, etc, is a true one. It may mean looking for another place, on a bus line (we pay $100-$150 a month to garage) so we can get to and from NY for the paper, as needed.

January 10

It gets so that when I see a priest without his collar and staying with us I wonder whether he is on his way out of the church. So much rebellion against the comfort of convents. Going out into world to see and relieve poverty and the returning to comfort. But the rigid discipline, voluntarily undertaken, enables them to do so much work. In school and out, visiting hospitals and teaching children reading twice a week. How many externs are doing as much. They are all afraid to bear the burden of criticism which they will get, out or in. And they want the appearance of poverty, not the secret practice of poverty, mortification.

January 11. Press

Mass at 8:30. Subway to Bronx, printer. Marge [Hughes] on masthead, next month Bob Gilliam. Too much solid copy, not enough [illustrations], quotes, subheads.

January 12

Visitors all day. Tom Cornell with Xmas present from Monica and Koinonia cake. Read Harrison Salisbury's vivid dispatches about Hanoi all evening.

January 13

A long day of letter writing. We are catching up with Xmas mail, Pat [Rusk] and I, and Stanley who wrote 1,500 letters up at the farm. Thanks to constant writing I have very bad arthritis in my fingers again. But I don't feel it typing.

Early to bed and reading Leslie Dewart's *Future of Belief.*

In the *Commonweal* we were termed medieval socialist. I prefer Martin Buber's term Utopian Socialists.

Reading *Homage to Catalonia*—Orwell on anarchist accomplishments.

January 14

Reading Luke 16 in the morning. "Until John came, there were the law and the prophets; since then the Kingdom of God is being preached and everyone is forcing his way into it. Yet it is easier for heaven and earth to pass away than for one dot or stroke of the Law to lose its force."

January 15

This morning Mass at ten at Good Shepherd chapel in Croton, a 3-minute drive and I enjoy going there. The participation of the people is so easy and natural. One cannot conceive of the old silent Masses, often a half hour of dreaming and distraction. Now there is adoration, contrition, thanksgiving, and supplication, the ACTS, as Fr. Wendell used to say, expressed in the confession, Confiteor, the repetition of the litany, Lord have mercy, Christ have mercy (Kyrie)—the Glory to God (Gloria) and I believe (Credo) and so on thru the Mass.

Franklin gave me a handwritten copy of *Fables of Aesop*. I had never seen such a use of calligraphy in bookmaking. Very attractive. It would be good Sunday work to copy some of the Gospel out, as Tamar did once during the year she spent at Ade Bethune's, a copy of the words of Christ at the Last Supper, which she bound in sailcloth and gave to me. So many of my treasures are taken from me when one's room is used, continually, in one's absence by visitors and "ambassadors" as Peter Maurin called "the unworthy poor." The "ambassadors of God."

January 17

It is this knowledge of the reality of *conversion* that fills one with peace and hope in relation to those about me, relatives and friends—and strengthens my life of prayer. All on God's good time. I do not want "a thousand to fall at my side and ten thousand at my right hand, and it shall not come nigh" me. As Péguy said, when we face God he will say, "Where are the others?" Heaven is a banquet too (as well as a bridal couch) and as at Emmaus, "They knew Him in the breaking of bread." I think that even *now* we know Him in the breaking of bread together.

January 18

SEX. Paul Goodman said once, according to reports which came to me, that my attitude toward sex was blasphemous—that he liked everything else about the CW.[261]

I believe, as do Jews and Christians, that God is a personal God, who created Heaven and Earth (the formless waste) and all they contain "in the beginning." All that he created was "good." It is a continuing process. "He sends forth wind and rain from their storehouses." He breathes life into the animal world. He is Creator. Man and woman are co-creators. In this lies their great dignity. Sex is in its pleasure, its joy, its "well being"—the image throughout the Old Testament of the beatific vision—the nearest we come to God. Sex is a gigantic force in our lives and unless controlled becomes unbridled lust under which woman is victim and suffers most of all. When man takes to himself the right to use sex as pleasure alone, cutting it away from its creative aspect, by artificial birth control, by perverse practices, he is denying "the absolute supremacy of the Creative Deity."

This according to Bouyer and McKenzie is "the original sin" which brings in its wake (the sin of Adam) the disorder of the world.

(Of course it is "the leap of faith" which enables me to write this.)

Origin of sex in second chapter of Genesis. Curse of man is concerned with the fertility of the soil. Woman's with childbearing.

Martyrdoms having to do with purity—Maria Goretti, Martyrs of Uganda.

St. Augustine, "Love all men each as tho he were the only one." "As if."

January 22

Speaking. "Journalists should make history, not just write about it." They should be students of history, to find out how things were, where mistakes, what led to the chaos today, so as to make present different; to make future different. For instance Calif missions and present agricultural situation. Describe paper. Ecumenical.

I make notes like the above and then do not know what I am trying to say. I will have to write out clearly. But so often I am interrupted. I must fast more from sleep.

---

261 Paul Goodman was an anarchist writer whose books, including *Growing Up Absurd*, had a great influence on the counter-culture of the 1960s.

February 1

Eileen Egan sent me St. Augustine on prayer. Fr. Hugo who has been writing on St. Augustine has been transferred to a small church 45 miles from Pittsburgh. I shall certainly go visit him there when the weather clears up.

Called Maryknoll about Dr. Sister Mercy, to visit Agnes since no doctors make house calls.

Mr. Murray of Catholic Charities of this area (Poughkeepsie) who reproved us for not being more voluble in sympathy for our soldiers. Our hearts are breaking for our soldiers.

Interesting news in *Times*, "only soldiers give blind obedience, difference between soldier and priest"—a priest of Colombia working with the people.

February 2

John McKeon is writing about Colombia, anniversary of Fr. [Camilo] Torres's death. Warm out so called Tamar—she sick with cold, not working. Eric left school. Working with Rick now. Thank God the boys love to work. Eric refuses to ask for exemption from military service because of his mother dependent. She is not paid this week, so I sent her the hundred Kenedy sent me for my introduction.

February 5

Annual meeting of Pax at Marymount College. No nuns. Large crowd. Dr. Dorothy Dohen spoke on Nationalism and American Bishops. Cardinal Spellman had many precedents. John Geis there. Also character not connected with us, glad to say. Every meeting has them. Dickens-like women and men.

February 5. Notes[262]

Who were these 23 young people who went into [St. Patrick's] Cathedral at 10 o'clock Sunday Mass late in January, all with signs folded up under their coats, and at the offertory, after the sermon, got up from the front pews where they had been following the ritual of the Mass and displaying their signs, started to walk down the center aisle? The signs read "Thou shalt not kill." And displayed pictures of a Vietnamese child.

They were not an organized group, but "just people who knew each other,." According to one newspaper account at least 10 taught in fields of chem., psych, music, and language. They included faculty members from NYU, New School, Fairleigh Dickinson, Brooklyn and NY Community Colleges. For all

---

262 See "On Pilgrimage," February 1967.

but 2 a first arrest. The others for previous demonstrations. Bail set $500, trial Feb 9.

Women held in H of D. Judge's innuendos—in question, as in case of one previous arrest. How can one respect law and order?

Why do I defend them? Why—because two of charges show harshness, compounds the injury. A respectful protest. They must have gone out with fear and trembling. One cannot go into a great Cathedral without a sense of awe. Instinct to worship God, Truth, Love, the Unknown God. Transcendent. Unity which should be unanimity of purpose, to love, adore, praise, thank and glorify God and beg His help, not just power and glory. God knows how conscious each is of his weakness, his powerlessness.

Regardless of what they felt, I felt drawn to defend them against harsh, immoderate charges, and they asked me to. Legal defense means money, lawyers, will be appointed if they do not have their own, so I permit my name to be used as sponsor.

Who is not scandalized, injured, and I too. Injury to one is injury to all. These are my children too, my grandchildren. Having so many grandchildren, I love …

February 6. St. Dorothy

For my name day, Mrs. de Ruyder bought goodies, cheese and olives, yogurt, ham and tomatoes and Louis Dragha brought in onion rolls and bagels. Pat bought me a pair of rubbers—very good, non-skid soles. And in the evening Mary Lathrop a Japanese doll.

February 7

Tom Cornell took us to court, going thru snow hip-deep. All were at the trial, A.J. Muste (Tom fetched him too) who asked me again about going to Hanoi. Mary pleaded guilty and got a 60-day suspended sentence.

A.J., Pat [Rusk], Brad [Lyttle] pleaded not guilty and no lawyer wanted and trial postponed till March 6.

February 8. Ash Wednesday

Today began a three-day fast imperfectly observed. For breakfast coffee and oatmeal, no milk. Lunch, rice and tea. Supper cornmeal mush and molasses! One cup of prune juice. Fasting really meant none of that delicious stuffed pepper brought down to us by Mrs. Vaccaro, 3 of them, and enjoyed by John McKeon, de Ruyder, and Jack Cook.[263]

---

263 Jack Cook, a draft resister and CW editor in the 1960s, has written two books about his experience at the CW: *Rags of Time* (New York: Beacon, 1972) and *Bowery Blues* (Xlibris, 2001).

Mass at noon, crowded with men from police dept as usual in Lent. Long lines for ashes afterward. People love these ceremonies, so casually dropped by the young protesters today.

February 11

A.J. Muste died this afternoon after pains in his chest this morning.

Last night A.J. had been at a meeting on Riverside Drive, Council of Churches, where Dom Helder Camara spoke and tomorrow there was to be a reception at Muste's for Bishop Camara who had been invited to speak at Cornell and Princeton. Tuesday I had spoken to A.J. at the trial of the group who had protested the bombing of civilian areas of Hanoi (Dec 15). He had received a suspended sentence of 60 days. After the protest he had gone to Hanoi and only returned a week ago.[264]

February 13

Community Church, David Dellinger (and A.J. was to speak) memorial meeting.

Another interesting meeting here in town. Msgr. [Ivan] Illich, Fr. Dan Berrigan. Betty Bartelme and others about Latin America. Fr. Illich's article in *America* is most stimulating and true and we must ask to reprint it.

February 15

Could not sleep till 3. Pains in my chest. Up at 8:15 and got to 8:30 Mass. Talked to Bob Gilliam about the desire on part of Phil and others to fast two weeks at National Shrine. They do not get to daily Mass, do not give up cigarettes or beer or anything else in Lent and it looks more like a jaunt.

Trying to read about A.J. for an article in the *Commonweal*.[265]

February 17

Agnes very much worse tonight. Dr. Ann Veronica sent her sleeping pills but she struggles terribly against sleep. I stayed in her room. For a while we thought Agnes was dying. But how hard it is to die—what hard work for

---

264 See Dorothy Day's obituary for A.J. Muste in the February 1967 issue: "The thing that marked him especially was his relationship to the young. He listened to them and they listened to him, well 'over thirty' though he was. He never judged the young, nor criticized them. He criticized the social order and by his writing as well as by his actions, tried to bring about a change in that social order... He truly worked to make that kind of a world where it is easier to be good."

265 "A.J.," *Commonweal*, March 24, 1967. See, *Dorothy Day: Writings from* Commonweal, 158-62.

some. A long labor, a long struggle to be born into eternal life. She received communion yesterday from Fr. Guerin.

February 18

To Christian Brothers at Barrytown to Mass. Three guitars and good singing. To lunch afterward, and only remembered late that I had not asked Deane if she wanted to come. But with a hard night with Agnes and just making up my mind the last minute I did not think she should have a grievance, but she did. She did not come to supper and came down only to express her displeasure to me.

February 19

Mass at eight-thirty. Fr. said the Gloria instead of the Creed. The new liturgy confuses him. He is a gentle soul and I like him, even tho he is begging for money for an epistle stand now.

February 20

Peter left for N.Y. When people go I always think too late of all I have neglected to do for them—of all I forget to do, just in little ways of showing interest and loving kindness. It is wonderful how young and old (Peter is 18) turn to Peggy [Baird], who is always calm, equable, un-judging. "She has something," Kay says, speaking of the way men are attracted to her. Her continued enjoyment of life for instance as epitomized by the bottle of wine by her bedside. Her enjoyment in books and flowers, and nature. She is a Colette. But she prays too. I love to hear her join in, "Pour forth we beseech Thee O Lord, Thy grace into our hearts."

And how easy it is to take care of anyone so loveable as Agnes. No virtue in it. Only virtue is to love the unlovable.

February 22

Finished my article on Muste for the *Commonweal* and Marge copied it, with 4 children in the room and television; just before supper. Spent an hour in chapel. But cannot get to Mass. Roads muddy, and slippery.

Agnes ate cereal, soup and eggnog today and also hot milk. She can only sleep in snatches and the room is filled with her breathing.

February 28

This morning when Agnes woke up she said, "This is the life of Reilly." Just because of the comfort of a wet washing and a hot cup of coffee. She had a good night for the first time in 2 weeks. Last night she had taken Milltown instead of the sleeping pill which evidently made life a nightmare to her so that she was in and out of bed continually, falling asleep between words, between the snuffbox and her nose! "This would be no time for one to be crossing the Bowery and Houston," she said another time.

## March 3

To Della's for the day. Clear, sunny day and warm. Very tired from too little sleep at night. But coffee pulled me together so we had a good visit. Franklin very much interested in Emma Goldman's book with its story of the free speech fight in San Diego.

Drove back at 4 and it was still light at six. Found Luigi raging because Bob [Stewart] had called him a no-good bastard. He swore to kill him on the anniversary of his wife's death, March 27. He is an ex-prizefighter and now a carnival hand, tending "the big wheel."

## March 4

Mass at 9 in Tivoli.

Tamar's birthday. Telephoned but she and all the kids had gone to the movies, all but Nick. The boys all await the draft as a great ordeal. At least all the boys in service have heard of conscientious objection. Tho it does not make them esteem them—jail's nothing to what they have to pass thru.

Opera today—"Magic Flute"—delightful music, but too complicated a story.

## March 8

Fast in Washington planned by [Jack] Cook, Bob [Gilliam], Phil [Maloney] , Chris [Kearns], and Paul [Mann].[266] Two weeks. David Miller's imminent arrest. What are future plans of CW? Peter Gaffney asks. To continue to work for the kind of a society where it is easer to be good, a decentralized, personalist in the Mounier sense, kind of society, where man will grow and use his full capacities.

## March 9

Sitting in the chapel at 5:15—distracted as usual, this time by Hans and Luigi drinking. Hans walking up to village in slush, then the woods, with empty bottles, in danger of falling, cutting himself, breaking a limb.

---

266 Several young men from the Catholic Worker undertook a fast at the Shrine of the Immaculate Conception as an act of protest against the Vietnam War. Most of them were soon on their way to prison for draft resistance.

Agnes did not sleep well last night. Had coffee at 3:30. Wanted to share it and visit. I'm sure it is death at night she is afraid of.

## March 15

Snow all day. Up at 5:30 and reading of scripture in dining room. To my typewriter upstairs and wrote on Works of Mercy all morning. And after lunch and rest, on All is Grace. Community takes so much time, meals, conversations, etc.

Reading. Mauriac, *Life of Jesus*.

## March 17

Up at 5:45. Then everyone at breakfast at 6:45. So to my bed again to read and Agnes full of tales of Niagara Falls. Her throat is so thick it is hard for her to talk. A tranquilizer at night, a back rub—it is little we can do for her. She wants to want things like lobster, orange soda, lemon pie, a piece of corned beef, a bit of coffee cake, but in general food, the labor of eating, appalls her.

## March 21

Not much work or writing being done these days—plain fatigue. Helene keeps working—a very disciplined person. I get some letters done—and the appeal last week. My contract came from Harpers. I hate to sign it. Feel so incapable of writing. So unclear in thought.

## March 22

Up at 5:45. Reading [Fr. John] McKenzie [*The Power and the Wisdom: An Interpretation of the New Testament*] on the New Morality of the New Testament, which all young people interpret today as permitting all. Free unions multiply.

Birth control, abortion, free love—all in the name of love. It is not only youth. Felix [McGowan] and John McKeon are no longer young. The hunger for human love, how beautiful in marriage and in renunciation, too. But it is always to be respected, even in all these free unions, even in all these sad searchings, of a Paul Goodman or an Ed Sanders.

Shouted at children tonight for their noise. Great quiet reigned afterward.

## March 25

A long day. Yesterday there was much time spent in chapel and since there are windows on three sides, no matter how grey the day the outlook is always beautiful. The river is clear of ice now. Today an empty tabernacle. Tonight the services, the vigil started at 10:30, a long service.

And then the festive feeling, which we could not help but feel all day, was irrepressible. Everyone stayed until after one. No children here for this service.

Clarice [Danielsson] came and wept because she could not receive communion with us. We were wishing she could be baptized at once. "Look, here is water!" We were reminded that the Ethiopian was baptized by Philip with very little instruction. That came after.

## March 26

This morning before ten I set out for Ossining to visit Della and arrived by 12:30. A beautiful sunny day. My doing without meat an embarrassment to me and those I visit, who provide legs of lamb, roast beef, etc. But Della, always resourceful, brought out shad from the deep freeze, caught by David last year, and it was delicious.

Slept and read. A wonderful hour, "The Messiah," from Denver with the Mormon Tabernacle Choir. Most moving. Then later the Smothers Brothers, some of it amusing.

## April 18

At Tamar's. Eric to trial today at White River Junction for cracking up the car. Tamar appealing to draft board for exemption for him on ground of her dependency. He hates to go but would rather go I fear because all his friend are going, one by one.

## May 20. [Catholic Peace Fellowship] Meeting.

Meditating on a tree. To plant a tree. Sasha said there is a Russian saying that if one plants 3 trees one has saved his soul. He may have made it up. I think of the tree (hemlock) which I have nurtured in my room all winter. It is two feet high. I see a place from the chapel window where I can plant it that no one will disturb, near the old outhouse Hugh put up for the swimmers.

The constant sense of futility that dogs us. But some saint said—it is told of many in answer to a question as to what he would do if he knew he were to die in one hour—or 24 hours—(our life being destroyed by a nuclear bomb), "I would go right on doing what I am doing."

So I will plant the tree.

Martie spoke this morning on Pacifism. About 500 people showed up for the meeting. He brought out the reason for most Catholics upholding gov. position on Vietnam is that they think this is essentially a religious war—in the minds of most people—between Christianity and Communism. Catholics know of the mystery of iniquity, the evil in the world, the propensity to evil in their own selves. The violence, this evil is incarnate in Communism, they think. It is the old legend of St. George and the dragon.

Wars are based in hatred—hatred of evil and that evil is incarnate to the simple in Communism. What it can lead to is the McCarthyism of the 50s in the U.S., the slaughter of half a million people in Indonesia, in the guise of wiping out Communism. And now the hideousness of this long drawn-out, undeclared war in Vietnam, in Southeast Asia.

June 19

Drove to farm. Stopped to see Agnes. She has been so noisy at night that other patients could not stand it and she was transferred from room to room in the month at Northern Dutchess hospital. Now she has to be transferred to Hudson State hospital, so I had to sign the papers, with much grief. How we have to choke on our high idealism which judges those families who put their old people away because they cannot deal with them. Certainly no one at the farm could take the constant care, and she was most demanding.

June 23

Stopped at Hudson State Hos to see Agnes in the large ward with old and senile. Heartbreaking to see all this.

Abbie Hoffman spoke on Hippies, and the girls went. All came over after and much discussion as to relevance of such protest. Sue said, "They do no harm," and Mary, "But no good either." I felt in view of blood and guts spilled in Vietnam the soldiers would like to come back and kill these flower-power-loving people. The word becomes meaningless. Middle-class affluent homes, they have not known suffering.

June 27

Bob Gilliam arrested by FBI.

July 15

Reading St. Teresa of Avila, *Interior Castle* again. It is hard to realize I have not read her for 35 years! She will be my encouragement now in writing "All is Grace." If the Lord wants it, it will be done.

August 6

Reading Martin Luther King's latest, *Where Do We Go from Here?*

Forster called at 9. Just wanted news. Talked to Tamar too. Invited him up.

## September 5

Conversations with Murph D. and his wife—on their way west. About the hippies planting a tree, burning money—dressing as Indians, discarding worldly values. About the Hopis in New Mexico and indeed all over the country, going to the land. Catherine Reser had sent me a clipping about the "communes," a number of them about the state—10 or 12. Perhaps 200 across the country. It will be interesting to see what happens in the winter.

## September 8

Rev. Jim Drake, right hand of Cesar Chavez, speaks at the meeting with Julian Balidoy, a Filipino, and Nicholas Valenzuela. The others stayed home and rested.

Up at the farm, Placid went wild last night, screaming fire thru the house, trying to throw Jackie off the roof "to save her," and running screaming thru the home. He finally jumped off the roof of the library room. Margie who is in the apt. said he ran to her saying he was burning in hell. They had to call the state troopers to bring him to the hospital, Hudson State.

## September 11

Visit from Mr. John Demboskey, town clerk of Osborne Estate about selling farm. I said I would for $200,000!! Hoping such a fantastic price would settle matters. But he seemed so sure I was frightened later. Probably a temptation of the devil. Or an opportunity to try for a more village-type of community. But I am too old to start again and I decided I would do nothing myself—let the others decide. Search, find, move, etc., etc. Whereupon Marty says, "I thought you said"—men are maddening, and women talk too much—think out loud, change their minds and are equally maddening.

## September 12

Got news of Hugh [Madden's] death Sunday night at 8:00. Killed instantly.[267] A policeman from 5th precinct reported it to us. Got telegram from

---

267 Hugh Madden, a "holy fool" even by CW standards, was struck by a car while bicycling his way toward the Shrine of Our Lady of Guadalupe in Mexico. "He was a spare, gaunt figure of a man, with a little goatee on an otherwise clean-shaven face…One might be astounded at the picture of Hugh at first, but somehow the aspect of a man doing penance shone through." Why penance? "For the napalm, the bombings in Vietnam perhaps. Because we are all guilty. God help us." ("Requiscat in Pace," September 1967; *SW,* 151-153)

Andy Gundelfinger, Berkeley, that body was at Johnson Memorial Hospital at Arlington.

September 13

Up at 6. Mass at nine which Fr. Kane offered for "Hughie," as he called him, affectionately. Only Kay, Arthur, and I were there. Body will be shipped up to Poughkeepsie and buried from St. Sylvia's. "Our God is a God of deliverance, and the Lord God gives escape from death." (Matins)

September 16

I saw Father [James] Groppi [*civil rights activist*] of Milwaukee on "Meet the Press," or "Face the Nation" program and he was strong and hard answering questions about his role as youth director of NAACP and leader in the marches which are going on in Milwaukee all summer and are still going on. He is following Rev. Martin Luther King's line in his fight for an open housing law—made far more clear what he meant when he was asked a sentence about self defense. We will exercise that right to defend the women and children on our march, he said. He asserted the need of black power—refused to condemn Rap Brown.

In answer to a question about obeying his superiors (who have already upheld him) if they told him to stop, he said he would answer that question when it happened, but that he would at all times follow his conscience. Thank God for these young, strong priests.

September 20. Press day

Drove up to printers. Truly an agricultural workers issue. Also I.F. Stone on Israel. Always conscious of material left out. Fr. Groppi for instance.

September 23

Started to write the appeal when Jim Canavan brought me word Peggy was very sick, in much pain. Called Dr. Schiff but could not reach him so called the volunteer ambulance service and took her to Dutchess Memorial at Rhinebeck. Went to see her at 4 and she wanted a mystery, jelly beans, foot warmers, and a comb and brush for her long, still-brown hair, bedroom slippers. The last thing she did before being put on the stretcher to ambulance was to give me 5 dollars for ice cream for the family.

September 24

It seems to me I have always had a sense of an immanent spiritual world. As a little child of 8, it was from reading the Bible, and going to a few Methodist services with a little friend next door to us in Oakland, Calif. The beauty of nature brought this to me. At the same time I remember passing a note to a little boy in school saying "I love you," and the teacher keeping us both after school and probing us both to find the wickedness that my simple words were not meant to convey. I had merely thought he was beautiful. A year later, when we had moved to Chicago after the earthquake of 1906 and I began to attend St. Mark's church with the minister's daughter, who was also named Dorothy, I remember the same admiration for a boy in the choir whose name was Russell. He sang beautifully and he looked like an angel.

In California I remember children who talked dirty and one little boy especially. We had been making tunnels through a field of thistles. Sometimes we found what we liked to consider rooms in those sheltered recesses among the weeds. It was like living in a green sea, a shallow sea with sunlight sifting through, with the odor of the earth, and the hum of insects and the drowsy heat all around us. In one of these rooms, this one boy, he might have been ten or so, wanted to "play house," mama and papa, but this was an intrusion on my happy mood and I rejected him. I believe that many times children have advances made to them, by older people too, and their own innocence of evil keeps them from judging or being frightened.

Even before this Chicago and Oakland period, when we lived in Bath Beach, I remember two incidents when as a child of six I encountered men when I had wandered away from my brothers who were fishing in a creek when I wished to explore, but no harm came to me. Even before I ever heard of guardian angels, I felt secure and protected, without fear, and knowing I was so protected. "Sensuous spirituality, more sickly than dangerous"—O'Brien.

St. Therese of Lisieux used flowery language of her day to cover the hardness of her teachings. She had the severity with herself of the Spanish mystics.

The doctrine of Lacordaire that all loves are the same—that for mother, sister, brother, a man and a woman—all may become perverse, a turning from God and a turning to creatures. God is a jealous God. Must go thru the joyful and the sorrowful mysteries to reach the resurrection.

Paul Goodman has termed my attitude toward sex as a blasphemy. He probably means what Maritain calls a "Manichean blasphemy," when he criticized a statement of Mauriac.

Remembering—In Connor Cruise O'Brien's analysis of Bernanos, *La Joie*, he describes how Chantal, in an ecstasy, perceives his state (the state of the unbelieving priest) as that of Judas and offers up her life for him. This offer is immediately followed by her rape and murder by the chauffeur Fiodor. "The priest, when he sees her body, loses his reason and regains his faith."

Two instances of this: Fr. Judge and Fr. Roy.

Victim souls.

Roger LaPorte—to die for love.

I have always prayed for an increase of love and surely this prayer is granted, "Ask and you shall receive." Surely to love people with faith, hope, and charity, not to judge them (tho this does not prevent us from judging the situation) is not to love them in sickly sentimentality, but to know them, and see in them that reflection of God which is in every man. Such knowledge is not scientific, not the result of questionings, probings. "Holiness is silence," Mauriac says. But it is intuitive.

When Roger LaPorte died and I was interviewed by radio and television, as to CW responsibility; when I once had to be rescued from bodily attack at a meeting at N.Y. University Catholic Center for my so-called responsibility, I felt a hostility on the part of the young people around me, Roger's peers in age and education and background. "She did not know him, she was not his friend," they seemed to be thinking. "What right has she to speak?" I speak because I am listened to. I write because I am read; I am asked, so I must give what I have to give. What little knowledge I have to give.

Let these young ones too write what they have to give, let them share their richness and abundance. They were his companions. They broke bread with him; only the midnight before he immolated himself, "They knew Him in the breaking of bread," as it was written of the two apostles.

*In October Dorothy traveled again to Rome for the International Congress of the Laity. She was one of two Americans (the other was an astronaut) invited to receive Communion from the hands of Pope Paul VI.*

October 15. St. Teresa[268]

This morning I received Holy Communion at the hands of Pope Paul, an overwhelming honor of course, since only about 150 were chosen from all over the world, out of the 3,000 delegates, auditors, consultors, experts, etc. Donna Myers told me of this yesterday at a large general meeting in the Pius X auditorium, while I was listening to Gallant speaking, and his words were so exciting and I was so concentrated on his message that I did not realize Donna was trying to tell me something important. So many people come up

---

268  See "On Pilgrimage," November 1967.

to greet you or tell you they heard you speak in North Dakota or Oregon, 10 years ago, that I kept saying, "Wait, I must hear this man—sh-sh." But finally it sank in. "You are one of two Americans chosen from the American representatives to receive Holy Communion from the hands of the pope. Tomorrow morning," she said, "and you must go and pick up your special ticket."

All tickets issued are of a different color—mine was purple. Eileen's and Marguerite's entitles them to a seat at one of the Tribunes. We got there early and it was a long wait in a crush of people before the pope arrived. We privileged ones were herded into a fenced-in enclosure, our passes carefully examined, and every now and then during the course of the Mass we were counted (like prisoners) by three ushers. We sat on the same kind of plank benches we use for our waiting soupline at Chrystie St. We also waiting to be fed. A beautiful African woman, wearing her native costume, let it slip from her shoulders during Mass and the usher rushed in and draped it back over her shoulders, supplied a white chiffon veil to a girl without a head covering and then began counting us to see no outsider slipped in. At the end, as we were ushered out to stand 2 by 2 on the side of the great altar, he suddenly found there were not enough of us, after all his and two others counting, and rushed to the sidelines which were still inside the barricades, and dragged 4 more up to fill our ranks! It was scriptural, "go out into the byways—."

October 19

Mass at 7:30 at Jesuits. Dinner with Dorothy Coddington, Gary MacEoin, and Eileen, Tom Cornell, Fabrizio Fabbrini who spent six months in jail for teaching c.o. to his students. Underground cells, 9 inmates, eat, sleep and toilet in one room. No work, no exercise. Lost job. This is voluntary poverty. He has a teaching job now. Dorothy told wonderful stories of her visits to India—the schools Gandhi set up, children become self-subsistent at ten. At 16 go out and start schools. Then her trip to Danilo Dolci near Palermo. Groups—teaching—they clean their streets, the dams built will revolutionize agriculture. We must go there.[269]

---

269 Dorothy described this dinner party in "Danilo Dolci's Sicily," December 1967. "My idea of a good dinner party would be one at which everyone took turns to talk about his latest interest." Two days later Dorothy and Eileen Egan traveled to Sicily to observe firsthand Dolci's nonviolent campaign against the power of the Mafia. "It is not just the things envisioned and already accomplished, but the fact that Dolci carries to all he meets on his extensive trips these ideas of love and brotherhood, this 'little way' of nonviolence.'"

October 23

Tonight we had dinner with the Silones[270] in Piazza Carlo Goldoni, a restaurant usually very quiet, but tonight very noisy. He is deaf in one ear and
I in one, and my placing at table was bad with 2 tables full of noisy young
Americans, one Italian family with 2 babies, and one large party of Italians.
It was uproarious. Ignazio wanted to know more about Peter Maurin, his
background. He knew Marc Sangnier's "Sillon." Wanted to know whether I
was a practicing Catholic. Surprised at the real hostility of a bishop of Philadelphia or Allentown. He talked at length about Dolci, his early promise,
but he liked neither his campaigning against Mafia—tho he emphasized that
it showed great courage—nor his marriage with a peasant woman. A socialist gesture, he thought—a lawyer in the Abruzzi had laughingly suggested a
similar one—to marry his cook. It was the thing to do. "Was that why you
married me?" Darina asked. "No, I was an unfaithful socialist."

November 1

We drove out to the airport with Mrs. Silone. Dorothy C also had come to
the hotel to see us off. It was a momentous day for me, my first flight and a
good day to begin this new way, for me, of traveling.

Darina Silone's warm presence and our talk together kept me so engaged
up to the moment of flight that I had no time to be nervous. The plane was
a small one, Alitalia, and I was jammed in between a priest and an Indian.
Eileen was across the aisle further up in the plane. I had thought the plane
half full of priests, but it was the English group of Christian Brothers returning from the canonization of St. Benild, of their teaching order. I felt much
at home, what with the Brothers being our near neighbors and friends.

In 2 ½ hours we were in London, and greeting Chas Thompson and John
O'Connor who had driven out (a two hour trip from London) to meet us.

It was 2.30 in the afternoon when we arrived but it was dark when we
arrived at the British Museum and parked under some dripping plane trees
whose yellow leaves dappled the pavement. While John and I had a conversation in the car about Fr. John J. Hugo and his book, *Applied Christianity*,
which John said he had read twelve times with profit, Chas and Eileen went

---

270 Ignazio Silone was the author of one of Dorothy's favorite books, *Bread and Wine*. See her
account of this dinner in her January 1968 column: "I am grateful indeed for the writings of
Ignazio Silone. In a meeting in Switzerland not longer after the Second World War, he said that
those writers who sold their words to governments in the persecution of a war were as guilty of
profiting by the war as the men who remained at home to work on the instruments of death…
… As far as I know, Silone is not what is generally called a practicing Catholic. I certainly did
not presume to question him on the subject. But I do know that his writings bring to us the
Christian message and my heart is warm with gratitude."

around the back to check on some hotels. The place they found—one can recommend it unreservedly, a warm and homelike place.

November 13

Today the day before we fly home, I am thinking with intense gratitude of the time I have spent in Rome, in Sicily, and here in England, how kind people have been, what a joyous exchange of ideas and interests and what a good traveling companion I have had in Eileen Egan. It has been work and holiday for us both. She has been teacher and guide, as has Marguerite Harris who was with me as far as Rome. She went on about her own work to Lausanne, Switzerland. Both of these women speak Italian, French, and Spanish and in Marguerite's case Russian. They are indefatigable students and workers, women of the world, as well as women of the Church, serving her in incalculable ways.

We are just back from Spode House, Eileen and I, where we attended the Pax annual retreat with Chas Thompson, John O'Connor and Barbara Wall, who are most active in Pax work in England.

December 3. Cambridge (Mass.)

Mass at St. Paul's in Cambridge and beautiful Gregorian for the Gloria and Credo. The choir even more beautiful than Sistine. Church packed at ten and eleven.

Went to Judy Gregory's in pouring rain and not icy, thank God. We talked all afternoon about her friends and more personal matters. Bed at nine in a bad cold.

December 6

Today we went to Press, our Dec. issue. It is worth staying in town to be able to get to Mass each day. Peace and joy and strength too! But I was a wreck at the end of the day, walking and climbing stairs. At the little restaurant across from the press, Mary Kae began telling me about the Washington demonstrations [*the march on the Pentagon*] and it helped me write my On Pilgrimage.

December 7

3 p.m. to see house. I stayed hour and watched Cardinal Spellman's funeral Mass on television. Mass at 8:30. Could not sleep last night.

200 arrested today in demonstrations.

December 24 [Perkinsville]

Mass at 11. I hope the snow holds off until I get back to Tivoli. As David Spier says, the only solution is work, and not judging others. But this throwing aside the sacraments, the skepticism, the dissipation. A sense life only, not even an intellectual life. But it is their age—they are so young and Tamar must live with them, with their interests. It is her bitterness about religion which hurts.

December 25

Mass at 11 at St. Mary's. Children all up at 7, a great hubbub.

A sad day with no one else going to Mass, and Eric not even unwrapping his packages and leaving us for the army Jan 2.

December 28

To me the cult of the saints is a most fascinating study—the beauty of holiness shines out thru them and illumines history. One feels their influence still, in the memory of them, in the places where they lived. The fact that Ignazio Silone also came from the Abruzzi makes this place, these saints interesting to me. The stories may be mixed with mythology, the Greek influence is strong there, maybe mixed with the crudest superstition, but these legends, myths, fables, fairy tales, are to be studied and should lead not to contempt of "the people" but a deeper love for them, and a desire to work for and with them. They have much to teach us with their patience, endurance, hard work, and if their celebration of the saints is to be criticized for their accompanying drinking and gambling, dissipation—to me they are more open, colorful and meaningful than those of N.Y. night clubs. At least our festas, our feasts in little Italy in NY are in the open, under the sun and stars and everyone participates.

I shall pray to these saints of the Abruzzi, for Ignazio Silone, whose work is of such nobility and beauty in this arid day.

December 30

Yesterday feast of Thomas Becket whom I have always found it hard to admire—his luxury, pomp, struggles with King Henri II over benefices, taxes, etc. Next only to the king in pomp.

# 1968

**January 1**

Still snowing. I missed Mass. Tamar had to work. Cooked—baked pies.
Eric's last night home.

**January 2**

Today Eric went to Woodstock to the induction center. Nick and Brenda
and Tamar went with him. I did dishes. Editor of Templegate called long distance and asked me to write introduction to a little book on Camilo Torres,
5,000 words. By month's end.[271]

I fear greatly for Eric, that he will break down as his grandfather did in First
WW. [Forster] had flu, collapsed, did not recover and spent the time of the
First World War in the psychiatric ward. He did not begin to recover until the
war was over. Eric, I'm afraid, cannot break away from home, one reason he
gave up college.

Father Plante gave me very good spiritual direction in confession. To pray
for others, not to be concentrated on my own relatives, and God would bless
my own too. He has learned that himself—loving his own family dearly. How
much suffering goes with that love. St. Therese knew it.

**January 7**

Plan of Torres article. Priests in Latin American and their tradition of participation. Wrote to Fr. Berrigan too.

Problem remains—how to make position of nonviolent as colorful, heroic,
as that of guerrilla fighters.

**January 11**

Bishops' letter published today. Very good. Reading Rosemary Haughton's
*The Transformation of Man*. An inspiration. Carried same message as bishops,
only incarnated in incident and human encounters.

**January 14**

Reading about Bolivian revolution and Colombia.

**January 15**

Betty [Bartelme] dreamed I was climbing down into a cesspool and was
trying to keep me from it. Reflected her attitude toward CW. "Judge not."

---

271 Dorothy contributed an introduction to John Alvarez Garcia, *Camilo Torres: His Life and
His Message* (Springfield, IL: Templegate: 1968).

January 16

Dreamed I slept on living room couch and a little crippled child on the other one. The child was awake in the night and I was praying aloud so he could hear. The child, Ben's age, crawled over to me and tried to get into bed with me and he was very cheerful and happy. It was still night so I persuaded him to get back in his own narrow couch.

January 18

News about Maryknoll priests and nun suspended.[272]

January 21

Meditation. How little sympathy the well person has for the sick! One needs to experience this oneself to realize and to remember.

January 25

*Twin Cities* publisher, financed by Schick, getting out pamphlet against me by Fr. Lyons. Persecution can be an occasion of pride.

January 26

Helene [Iswolsky] in New York. [Alexander] Kerensky dying. He is 86, she thinks. Anne Fremantle's book, *Pilgrimage to People*, arrived. Inaccurate and superficial but she is a terrific writer. Much about Cuernevaca.

February 18

Farm conference on Peace. Tamar arrived.

February 25. Della's

I drove up at noon. Mass at Tarrytown. In the evening Smothers Brothers had Pete Seeger on, singing his controversial song, "The big fool said to push on."[273] He is a fine person, loving people, a ballad singer, close to present and to the past. He traveled over Russia singing, he loves the Hudson, the Catskills, the region in which he lives.

Franklin gave me *Death of God* and Paul Tillich. He had had to do a resume of another like book for Rand and McNally.

It is so hard to reach those you love the most—your own family.

---

272  In 1968 three Maryknoll priests and a nun were expelled from Guatemala and suspended from Maryknoll as a result of their clandestine meeting with guerrillas.

273  On "The Smothers Brothers Comedy Hour" folksinger Pete Seeger caused a stir by performing his song "Waist Deep in the Big Muddy," a thinly-veiled critique of Lyndon Johnson and the Vietnam War.

April 1
Chris [Kearns's] trial. Refusal to report for civilian work. About a dozen of us there.

April 2
Chris accepted the deal proposed by the judge. To give up his plea of not guilty, plead guilty and accept probation, 6 years suspended sentence. He had to stand before the judge and say that no threat or deal had been offered him. A tragic day. He had started it so well, chose jurors, questioned them, made intro speech, "religious" objection and so any conscription interfered with his religious beliefs. Said he would appeal, etc. I was sick with headache. Slept 3 hours when we returned.

April 4
Martin Luther King shot.[274]

April 7
Mail all day. Two pages on Dr. King's death for Garvey at Templegate.

April 9
Meditation. Martin Luther King ceremonies. Those who went—crowds—saw nothing, heard little. Multitude. "What is it all about?" Meaninglessness at times. Yet such great events as death of a man must be clothed with pomp, ceremony to keep one from feeling agony of briefness of life, agony of death. Impelled to go, yet got nothing out of it—no uplift, fatigue, loneliness, isolation. Yet perhaps one moment stands out with a sense of grandeur of man. What you desire first, the experience and glimpse, he has attained. He has entered into glory.

Christ is betrayed. King is betrayed, and his agony goes on until the end of time. We inch forward, gigantic effort to attain what? God.

---

274  Dorothy responded to the death of Martin Luther King in the April 1968 issue. "Martin Luther King died daily, as St. Paul said. He faced death daily and said a number of times that he knew he would be killed for the faith that was in him. The faith that men could live together as brothers. The faith in the Gospel teaching of nonviolence. The faith that man is capable of change, of growth, of growing in love... Always, I think, I will weep when I hear the song, 'We Shall Overcome,' and when I read the words, 'Free at last, Free at last, Great God Almighty, Free at last.'"

April 12. Good Friday

Drove to Tivoli with Bill and Dorothy Gauchat.[275] Bill told me of his healing. He had been very ill and before taking trip to El Salvador to see Helene Marie, Peace Corps, who was in hospital, had a checkup. They found one lung x-ray dark. Took blood tests and bone marrow biopsy and found cancer. Gave him 3-6 months and reluctantly allowed him to go on the trip. On way back stopped in Mexico City, got a guide to take them to Guadalupe. They had just a flying visit, up thru crowds of Indians, approaching the Shrine on their knees, adoring, petitioning. Such a rushed, crowded visit. D and B going in blind faith, never even thinking of a healing, or making a petition. Then on their return, Bill went to the hospital again and everything had cleared up. No trace of cancer. All doctors mystified. Bill afraid to speak of it. People look askance.

Easter Sunday, April 14

At the farm. Up at 5:00 and reading *The Power and the Wisdom*. Chapter on the death of Jesus, the saving act of Jesus. It is tremendous. I thank God for sending me men with such insights as Fr. [John McKenzie]. Always when I awaken in the morning it is to a half-dead condition, a groaning in every bone, a lifelessness, a foretaste of death, a sense of "quiet terror," which hangs over us all. A sense of the futility of life and the worthlessness of all our efforts. It is, as one of our retreat masters said, as tho we rowed a fragile bark at head of Niagara Falls and all our efforts are to keep from going over into the chasm below.

I turn desperately to prayer. "O God make haste to help me. Take not Thy Holy Spirit from me." And there is always Matins or Lauds, those magnificent psalms, the official prayer of the church, prayers which thousands, tens of thousands are saying each morning all over the world. And I am saved.

This consciousness of salvation comes to me afresh each day. I am turned around, away from the contemplation of the world of sin and death to the reality of God, our loving Father, who so loved us he gave us his son, Son of Justice, who became sin for us, sharing our human condition, bore the penalty, our death, and showed us the resurrection. He overcame it.

Thru this turning around, "all the way to heaven is heaven" to me, as St. Catherine of Siena said. The sun has risen, the air is warmed, the birds are singing outside and I go outside to sit by the dead-calm river, which flows by,

---

275 Dorothy and Bill Gauchat were part of the Catholic Worker movement from the early years. Bill was a founder of the Cleveland Catholic Worker. He and Dorothy later founded Our Lady of the Wayside, a "home for children no one wanted," in Avon, Ohio.

the tide carrying bits of driftwood, the only thing indicative of motion, of progress toward the sea.

And from quiet terror, I go on to quiet joy at God's goodness and love in giving us Jesus to show us how to love. The testimony of our hearts shows us the truth. We experience, no matter how briefly, the sense of salvation He won for us. Assassinations, wars, the lying and treachery of man, even the best of men, what with his capacity for evil, fades out in such blinding flashes of light.

The saints, who renounced themselves, who did penance, who starved themselves with fasting, who scourged themselves, kept vigil, were burnt by heat and paralyzed by cold but felt only joy at such sharing of Jesus' Passion.

And what woman is there who does not and would not willingly suffer for love of man and love of the child which comes into this world with cries and with blood.

April 20
I was on verge of tears all day and did not go to office. Might as well get used to idea of two more months at Kenmare. So we all cleaned house all day.

April 24
Pouring rain all day. Tel strike on, cannot reach Tamar. Student strike at Columbia over gym at Morningside Park.

2nd Sunday after Easter—April 28
When one is 70, there are many glimpses of the quiet terror. There is not much more time. I have had two letters this last week from people over 90 whose handwriting is still clear and steady, who still have the spirit, the joy in the gift of life. On the one hand, I shudder at the thought of the holocaust ahead. Will I live to see this desolation?

My mother said when she was dying—"Do not pray I live longer. I have seen earthquakes and hurricanes, two world wars and I've had enough." She did not say it but her oldest, her dearest, her pride and joy, had disappeared during WW2, not to be found until war was over, and until after her death. She said another time, "Do you really believe we will see those we have known in life—your father, for instance?" And when I said yes, I do believe, she said, impatiently and almost petulantly, "I don't know whether I want to see your father again." I laughed with joy at her frankness. "You will know him as you first knew him, and you will love him as you loved him then," I told her. What assurance! But I felt no shame at this presumption. I was sure.

It is only now that I wonder, Were there others that she loved during those long years when she was raising us five? Perhaps she loved our young family doctor in Chicago who died of blood poisoning a few years after we met him. Were there others? Did every now and then that wave of sexuality wash over her that brought with it an exquisite and shattering joy at the beauty of a face, a character, or even at the pure masculinity of a friend or acquaintance, the exchange of a glance, a touch? In Hebrew scripture men and women "knew" each other and this knowledge can be contained in a meeting of eyes, a sudden flash of understanding. How little we know of our parents, how little we know of each other and of ourselves.

But do we want to know ourselves when once we have glimpses of the demonic in the sudden flashes of hatred and rage that also on occasion have swept over us, when we have seen the blind hatred and rage of others which we would not see so clearly if it were not a reflection of something in our- . selves.

### May 1
Mass at 8:30. At office, mailing paper. How separate we all are, no celebration.

### May 2
Voluntary poverty as most radical, revolutionary measure—resistance, transcendence in technological age. Impossible without God.

### May 7
Paul Muller talking to me of revolutionists in New York—Kropotkin, Ho Chi Minh, Trotsky, exiles here. Perhaps many new potential leaders. Treat all with respect—listen—who will be leaders? Study history to know what has passed, work in present so as to make future.

### May 8
"Transcendence in Life Today." To speak as a practicing Catholic means faith, or a desire for faith.

3 strikes against me in a discussion like this. I'm a woman, a Catholic, and my language itself, called to contribute to a symposium of philosophers, psychologists, social scientists, who have a language of their own. My language may also seem to be filled with Catholic jargon. And yet probably half the 90,000 circulation of the CW is non-Catholic, [this] indicates that it is un-

derstood by non-Catholics to a certain extent. I'd like to call this, "What Do the Simple Folk Do?" using the words of the popular "Camelot" song.[276]

What do they do to satisfy the cravings and longing of the human heart when it is not too stifled by overwork and too many luxuries at a time when they lack necessities. To me transcendence and life go together, two sides of the coin. Man is a creature of body and soul—he is educated, brought up to maturity by all he learns thru his senses. The exterior and interior senses, which means not only the 5 senses but the interior senses, memory, understanding, and will (as St. T of Avila called them). That is why the sacraments are outward and visible signs of an inward...

## May 11

Got back on Friday night to hear Eric had called. He is on leave for 12 days. Transferred to Ft. Benning, Georgia, for more training on guns. Sat up until 3 in case he should come to Tivoli. Called this a.m. to find him in Perkinsville. Got in at 4 a.m.

Recent bomb tests in Nevada have brought predictions of a terrible earthquake in California.

## May 12

Malcolm [Cowley] and Muriel came on hearing of Peggy [Baird's] wanting to become a Catholic.[277] They must have thought she was dying or senile. She is fine, gets out to her garden still. She is getting to Mass daily. Malcolm and I had words over Lily. I am not very tactful.

## May 17. Tamar's

Eric tells tales of basic training. Forced marches, scrubbing, waxing and polishing barracks, pushups, running. Allowed to sit, not lie down. Can sleep standing up, or leaning against one's fellows three at a time.

Cruelty. Fellow forced, for untidiness, to get on his knees and crawl around proclaiming he is a pig. Ricky, National Guard, said it was worse—he was kicked by the sergeant as he passed. Fellow beaten to death, his head banged against washroom wall until he died. Men, boys, standing around had to take it. No protest made. Are we ready to interpose our bodies, be beaten, take these blows, ransom these captives with our own blood? Too many instances

---

276 Dorothy's talk, "What Do the Simple Folk Do?", was a contribution to a symposium on Transcendence," sponsored by the Church Society for College Work. It was first published in the CW in May 1978. See: *SW,* 173-79,

277 Malcolm Cowley was Peggy Baird's former husband.

these days of people standing by while torture is being inflicted, while murder is being done. We stand by, witnessing it on television.

Only love is strong enough and O God, let us grow in love so we do not fear (and do not fear pain!).

"I would crawl thru sewers to avoid pain," C.S. Lewis wrote, and Fr. Hugo quoted. The instinct for cruelty, those demonic depths in man which lead children to inflict pain. Our distorted natures. How children watch another child being punished. In *David Copperfield* watching beating.

Rebel and Indian yells—also in "War and Peace" movie. Long sustained shout of men going into battle which blended with music. Kill, kill, kill—shouted over and over with utmost viciousness. The attempt to stimulate murderous hate. The use of speech. Take a word, love, breathe it, speak it, sing it, murmur it. Jesus is honey in the mouth and a cry of gladness in the heart. "The world will be saved by beauty," Prince Myshkin.

But we do not want the world saved. We want to destroy world we did not make and remake it to one's image.

Pierre [in *War and Peace*] running away after shooting his opponent in a duel, stumbling thru the snow. Pierre horror stricken, staggering about the battlefield in his incongruous civilian clothes.

*On May 17, Fr. Philip Berrigan, his brother Fr. Daniel Berrigan, and seven lay Catholics—the "Catonsville 9"—were arrested for destroying draft files with homemade napalm. It was an historic event which was widely covered in the CW.*

May 21

[Cesar] Chavez sec, Miss [Marion] Moses found me.[278] We went to Time-Life building, beautiful fountains. We all had coffee or diet cola and talked for two hours. He would not commit himself on Vietnam war. His oldest son 19 going for his physical. 8 children—youngest 7, wife Helen. Eileen brought him a Gandhi plaque in mother of pearl on black marble.

June 1

Peggy [Baird's] reception in Church.

June 5

Robert Kennedy shot.

---

278 Marion Moses, a nurse, was inspired by her work with the United Farm Workers to become a doctor. Later, living in New York, she became Dorothy's personal physician.

June 16

*Soul on Ice,* Eldridge Cleaver. Robert Coles reviews in *Atlantic.* Says he is full of Christian care, Christian grief and disappointment, Christian resignation, Christian messianic toughness and hope.

June 19

David Miller—3 years. Demonstration in front of Foley Square Court. Taken to West St. Detention.

June 20

Pat Jordan, OFM seminarian.[279]
Dan Kelly sentenced to 3 years.

July 1

Sitting by the sea at St. Alfonso Retreat House, Long Beach. Very hot even at 12:30 am. The sea fills me with such joy. My conversion came about when I lived in Raritan Bay, 1927.

Ps. 92. "More powerful than the roar of many waters, more powerful than the breakers of the sea—powerful on high is the Lord. Seas and rivers bless the Lord—you dolphins and all water creatures bless the Lord."

July 21

Jim Douglass is in jail, 15 days for obstructing a convoy.

July 29

Noble language about peace and love. The air is full of it. See Merton's paper for Pax on Ulysses!

August 9

Jack Cook spoke on Che's diary. Very good. Very hot. Electric fans, hard to hear. Mass at 6 for victims of Nagasaki and Franz Jagerstatter.
Walked for Biafra victims.

August 10

Joan Baez tonight on Second Ave. She did not begin until 9:15. Packed house, which sang with her very softly and well. Not a hippy crowd. They

---

279 Pat Jordan, a former Franciscan, became a managing editor of the CW. He was arrested for refusal to cooperate with the draft, but the judge, apparently impressed by his statement to the court, "sentenced" him to continue working at the Catholic Worker. He and his wife Kathleen (whom he met at the CW) later lived next door to Dorothy's cottage on Staten Island.

could not afford it. Two slept on our basement floor. Ten came from Free Store to pick up clothes.

## August 15

Peggy wants to go to the hospital, wants anointing. Thinking about the loneliness of death today I suddenly thought how when I was traveling rather fearfully thru the clouds on my first air flight I was not lonely. It was too thrilling to be up above the clouds, in the sunlight. I thought of those I left behind, but also of those I was going to see, and it will be the same at death. I will look forward to seeing those family and friends who have gone before me, besides innumerable others, the saints, the writers like C.S. Lewis, etc. We will know and be known.

## August 19

Started out from Tivoli at 10:00. Arrived in Washington, D.C. just before dinner. No time to rest or think over my 3 minute talk.[280] Thank God. Fr. Bob Hovda told me about the 3-minute acceptance of an honor. I had it all written out, so I put it out of my mind. Rev. Andrew Young had coffee with us. A handsome man. Calm—a great sweetness. The story was that when he was asked if he was for black power—held out his arms helpless, indicated he was on both sides. His hour or more speech was profound. Hope for a nonviolent rev.

Let[281] me in turn pay my tribute to Liturgical movement—first to recognize the need for "personalist and communitarian revolution," to use the phrase of Emmanuel Mounier, whose book *The Personalist Manifesto* was translated by Peter Maurin and Fr. Virgil Michel published in 1934 or '5.

It was the Liturgy which led us to both an understanding and joy in prayer that revolutionized our lives. It was the Liturgy that brought us close to Scripture, with its new translations and commentaries, so that the hard sayings of the gospel became for us truly a sword which pierced the heart and separated us all too often from family and friends. Who can doubt that Father Phil Ber-

---

280 Dorothy accepted an award from the annual Liturgical conference. "I had accepted because I welcomed the great privilege of being with Rev. Martin Luther King, who was to give the opening address. What a tragedy had occurred since that invitation came!" ("On Pilgrimage," September 1968)

281 This is a draft of Dorothy's acceptance speech for her award from the Liturgical Conference.

rigan in prison at the Federal penitentiary at Lewisburg is praying and reading scripture now truly as perhaps never before.[282]

It was love of brothers, of men conscripted and dying in Vietnam and in how many other countries armed by us that drove him, impelled him to that revolutionary act (symbol) by destroying draft records. It was a nonviolent act in that it was directed against the symbols of man's enslavement today—not against man—and it was at the same time the violence of our Lord Himself when he overturned the tables of commerce in the Temple.

The words of a Fr. Hovda in the Liturgical bulletin were violent, crying out against the investment of Vatican funds in luxury housing when the poor in their desperation are burning down slums—their own slums, mind you, not the houses of the rich, making themselves homeless as a warning of the fire to come.

### August 24

Selma, Alabama, 7 a.m. We stopped at this historic spot for breakfast. The more I think of it the more I wonder at and admire the tremendous demonstration which took place there. Priests, nuns, and laity, the thousands who gathered for that historic march, will never forget it—will look back on it as a peak experience. Now, a few years later people are apt to denigrate it, to be a bit ashamed of their own enthusiasm and to feel they had thought it then bigger than it was. But it was a tremendous pilgrimage, it was embracing hardship and contempt, hurt and exhaustion.

### August 27

These profound truths! You have to do it all on your own at first, in blind faith before you see results, before you get anywhere. Looking at television last night. Fannie Lou Hamer, sitting at the [Democratic Party] convention, one of a delegation, half Negro, half white, I could only think how she had suffered, beaten in prison, alone, on her own, following her inner voice, the Spirit. Charles Evers, Julian Bond—the struggle they have to go thru, the overcoming of fear, of discouragement. Marge Baroni, too, I thought of her, her constancy, her daily work in this poverty program, fighting the discouragement in others—keeping the vision alive of a country where men are brothers and can live like men, holding their heads high in the knowledge that they are sons of God—made in His image and likeness.

---

282 On October 17, 1967 Father Philip Berrigan, one of the "Baltimore Four," was arrested for pouring blood on draft files.

August 29

Wind bloweth where it listeth and I have often sat and observed this on the two old butternut trees in front of Tamar's house. One little clump of leaves would start trembling as tho a tiny hand were stirring them or an invisible one. And John, our seaman farmer, who loves every inch of soil and what grows out of it, said to me once, "I often wonder where the wind comes from and where it goes." (He also makes "meditation spots" around the farm, a clearing or a bench.)

August 31

On this trip I've been reading [W.E.B.] Du Bois and have had glimpses into the history of "black folk"—during Civil War and after.

September 4

I keep thinking how little we know of our history. The Cherokees here— the Choctows of Miss. Ammon has always paid attention to the Indians. All our unknown brothers. And how much we have missed of beauty. "The world will be saved by beauty," Dostoevsky says.

September 14

Met Eileen at Waldorf for layman's meeting where I spoke ineffectually on our CW experience of Freedom in writing and demonstrating as laymen, and of the courtesy and frankness due the clergy.

September 16

Visitors all day. An Italian priest, "Why did not the New Catechism include the Trinity. Do you agree with this?" I looked it up and indeed find no mention of the Trinity. "What do you think of Camilo Torres?" "Tell me all about the Catholic Worker." He kept pushing aside the paper—the back issues, the articles on our aims, and kept pressing me on what was my, *my* position, until I finally rebuked him and said I did not like interviewers ignoring all who made up the movement and concentrating on a "personality."

September 18. Press

Jack has his column ready. Deane a good one. Mine uneven, written in patches. Coming back to violence at the house and all our problems it was hard to write.

Adolph at Rogowsky [*CW printer*] was pressing for funds. "I have nothing to do with the money," Marty said when asked to answer the phone calls from the printer. (When the children were little Nick used to say, "Not me." And Mary used to say "Not me too.")

Arthur at the printer to proofread. He likes to talk and is lonely. Jack and Marty unresponsive, positively rude. Paid no attention to him. I was embarrassed for him and furious at them. "If I pretended I was not bored I would be a hypocrite," I suppose they argue.

September 23. Perkinsville
Each day I wake at six and now it is dark. A letter from Eric—he is now in the Rangers (not Special Forces, or Green Berets).

September 24
"There is nothing new under the sun." "Men have always warred, at home or abroad." Christianity is 2,000 years old and a thousands years are as one day.

It is part of age, the depression which comes with age, to realize so keenly the horror and suffering around us. What early Father of the Church said that if we could sit on a mountain top and see the misery and evil in the world, life would be unbearable to the sensitive. Thru radio, television, all modern communication we do just that. So many try to drown out the sound of man's screams with the frantic music, dizzying lights and colors. Speed, and rushing from one end of the world to the other, to try by words, by reason, to bring repose.

It is a time to study history, to study the lives of great men and women and to realize we begin with ourselves.

With all the tumult going on now against the church, the "institutional" church, it is as tho adolescents had just discovered their parents were fallible and they are so shocked they want to throw out the institutions of the home and go in for "community" as a salvation to all their own pressing problems, including the children that are arriving (if they are) as a part of the ever-recurring problem of marriage. They call them "young adults" but it seems to me they are belated adolescents with all the romanticism that goes with it.

They are trying to throw out all the wisdom of churchmen and philosophers in their emphasis on "the world." "Romanticizing the secular," one Protestant writer accuses them of. Disregarding the primacy of the spiritual they think to begin with the secular which is so much an important part of the job of the layman. (To make the kind of society where it is easier to be good, as Peter Maurin said.)

The trouble is Americans want too much. Yes, they (priests) are men of desires, as Daniel was, and so are beloved of God. But why do they want to be laymen too and do the work of laymen. They want everything—the good, physical life, food and drink, comfort for the flesh, including wife and children, and a home to shelter their loneliness, and they want too to be in on all the demonstrating which is going on today—to play the prophetic role as well as the priestly.

Yet reform in the church has always come about not thru the mob, mob action, revolutionary action, which without prayer and penance means violence. Jesus Christ showed the way. Scripture, the gospels, show the way. Prayer and fasting. Penance, acknowledgment of our personal sin, which is part of the sin and disorder of the world. Whence come war and strife among you?

I love the story of the two hermits of the Desert—"Let us have a quarrel." And the other, the uncritical Father who on going into an untidy cell exclaimed, "How this monk must be absorbed with the things of God!" and on going into an orderly one, "What peace in this soul."

But what means so much to me, such stories and the lives of the saints who so influenced their times, and lived in such peace and joy—do not reach people today. Nor the Gospel either, tho there is much talk of "Jesus and Buddha," put on a par.

People need to be rediscovering the Gospel. They have to find them thru people who find their joy in them, and who accept the crosses of this life as preparation, as the inevitable in the way.

Reading St. Lutgarde by Thomas Merton, written before he wrote *Seven Storey Mountain*. Also Acts, Chap 20, Paul being chained and flogged speaks in terms of the law, which applied to him as a Roman citizen. I must reread and retell this in more detail in light of happenings today, "respect for high priest," for instance. The hard contempt in which the opponent is held is a sin against love. If we must love our enemies and if our worst enemies are those of our own household. The hundreds walking out of the Cathedral when Cardinal O'Boyle read his pastoral message. The *Commonweal* arrived with its double-page ad of a mother and a starving child, and the allusions to the Pope's encyclical *Humanae Vitae*; the scorn of a woman reviewer of two women's books heaped on a priest for his "pious" ideas and the scriptural language "with which he clothed his ideas."

September 25

Today Tamar and I visited the Foster museum at the top of the hill and found a copy of Ruskin, the *True and the Beautiful*, and found the beautiful quotation on the "Duty of Delight."

Dan Berrigan called about the Milwaukee burning of draft cards records. Twenty took part, 5 priests.[283]

## October 3

Had to write draft on CW now for [John] Coster. Then read letters from John. He says tax officer is now convinced that I am not a "pacifist activist," but I am. If to gain that $50,000 legacy I have to deny conviction I will drop it at once.

## October 4

I must write on obedience. ... my statement on McIntyre, Spellman, clarify my need for church.[284] Obedience—respect, love. My uncertainties. God's will. Others will do it better. God raises up what He needs. Perhaps I stand in way of saints.

## October 5

Visiting Christian Brothers. Mass and lunch. Brother Augustine. Discussion on obedience and conscience.

They brought a card for me to bring to David Darst.[285] What soul-searching is going on. Probably more vocations from these acts of disobedience than harm done.

## October 6

Reading *Ramparts* on its smart-allecky article on Catonsville 9. Contempt for liberals, for priesthood, for church. Melvilles [Thomas and Marjorie] pre-

---

283 The Milwaukee 14, arrested on September 24 for burning draft files, included Mike Cullen, director of the Casa Maria CW house in Milwaukee, and Jim Forest, former editor of the CW and a co-founder of the Catholic Peace Fellowship.

284 Possibly this refers to Dorothy's essay, "In Peace is My Bitterness Most Bitter," published in January 1967, which responded to the role of New York's Cardinal Spellman as an enthusiastic supporter of the Vietnam war. "I have often thought it a brave thing to do, these Christmas visits of Cardinal Spellman to the American troops all over the world... But oh, God, what are all these Americans, so-called Christians, doing all over the world so far from our own shores? But what words are those he spoke—going against even the Pope, calling for victory, total victory? Words are as strong and powerful as bombs, as napalm. How much the government counts on those words, pays for those words to exalt our own way of life, to build up fear of the enemy... As to the Church, where else shall we go, except to the Bride of Christ, one flesh with Christ? Though she is a harlot at times, she is our Mother.... Love is indeed a 'harsh and dreadful thing' to ask of us, of each one of us, but it is the only answer." See *SW*, 337-39.

285 David Darst, a young Christian Brother, was one of the Catonsville 9. After their trial, and before reporting to prison, he was killed in a car accident.

sented as not non-violent. An attractive picture of [Tom] Lewis, Dan [Berrigan], and David Darst.

## October 6

Baltimore trial. 3 or 4 sets of jurors. All looked alike, except two had Negroes. So far all had no feelings about selective service, pro or con. "Is there anything in your experience that would keep you from making a just decision?"

Do they believe in God?[286]

## October 31

CW with Fr. Hugo's first article arrived air mail.[287] It looks good. I pray it does good and gives meaning to the life of many.

President Johnson spoke tonight, ending all air and artillery strikes. Comments were skeptical.

## November 1

How wonderful to think of a cessation of shooting in Vietnam. I cannot believe it is true. Irish missionary, Fr. Pat Dundon (from Brazil) says Latin Americans regard Che Guevara as a saint

## November 2

Only cease fire is in North Vietnam.

Reading Dorothy Sayers intro to Dante's *Inferno*. Picture of our time. A must. Reading is oil that keeps lamp burning.

## November 14

"Nip things in the bud at once," says Stanley. "If we did not have so big a place," I say, "people would not move in on us." "We never should have bought it," S. says.

But people come more and more to our doors—workers and scholars, the lame, the halt, the blind—all sinners.

But God has given the increase. He has given us the means, the place, the surroundings to work in. When we had no space in S.I. we had greater problems overrunning us—which we were quite inadequate to handle. We went

---

286  In her OP column for October 1968, Dorothy wrote about the Catonsville 9 and Milwaukee 14 cases: "These men, priests and laymen, have offered themselves as a living sacrifice, as hostages. Next to life itself, man's freedom is his most precious possession, and they have offered that, as well as the prayer and fasting they have done behind bars, for these others… we can only thank God and try to add our prayers and sacrifices."

287  Fr. John Hugo, "The Plan of Salvation," November 1968.

away and left our problems. Now we have a new set. We did not solve them. Nor can we solve them. "Without Him we can do nothing." "In Him we can do all things." We need to pray more—to bring these problems to our Father, to ask Him to send the Holy Spirit. We need to listen to the words of Jesus which the Holy Spirit will help us to understand.

"A mistake ever to have gotten this place," Stanley says. But we are a family. What would a family do? What they too often do—throw their problems out, as so many of our old ones have been abandoned. They are thrown out, never to go back. Agnes would not forgive her two daughters, ever. How many times should we forgive? 70 x 7. The righteous (self-righteous) must forgive—the sinner must forgive those who reproach. How many times I have sinned, been forgiven! I remember reproaching Jim M. for wandering from bar to bar with a borrowed chalice in his possession which he was supposed to return. He never forgave me. Helen, his wife, forgave him 70 x 7.

On the one hand Jesus had no place to lay His head. He fed the multitude but He did not do it every day. But He taught. He taught hospitality, love. "Inasmuch as you have fed and sheltered one of the least, you have done it to me." So we know we love God, or want to love God.

And what about sins. "Let him who is without sin cast the first stone." Even tho I know my sins are forgiven, I remember them—must never forget them. We love ourselves so much that we are never revolted by our own sores—by our own stink of corruption as we are by those of others. "Knowledge of salvation thru forgiveness of sin." This gives me peace and joy. I have no power to judge or forgive, considering my own past. I cannot help people by condemning them, by my cold disapproval, my silence.

But I have no power to control smoking of pot, for instance, or sexual promiscuity, or solitary sins.

November 23

Called Tamar. Maggie answered. Eric telephoned. Finished his course—has his stripes as a Ranger. Will get apartment off base with a friend and be home for Christmas. Perhaps he will not go overseas but teach.

November 27

This afternoon I read Abbie Hoffman's *Revolution for the Hell of it.* A terrifying book, bitterness, hatred, hell unleashed. The fruits of war, materialism, prosperity founded on a slave class, whether black or white. Sex and war. "Knowing war" which began in 1914 and the drugs which enable them, the young, to endure, with an illusion of courage, and the fantasy which sublimates the horror around them, and which also acts unpredictably like the drug which [Robert Louis] Stevenson foretold in *Dr. Jekyll and Mr. Hyde*. God help our children, our Marys, our Erics.

## December 1

To freely give is an expression of love. That is the explanation of the "penny a copy" of the CW. One cannot get a second class mailing permit which means cheaper mailing rates unless you show a paid circulation. What happens is that our work of hospitality in the city and country is paid for also by our readers who send a dollar for a subscription or five dollars! Love is an exchange of gifts, St. Ignatius said. One could meditate all day on that.

*On December 10, Thomas Merton, the Trappist monk and a frequent contributor to the* Catholic Worker, *was accidentally electrocuted after speaking at a conference of monks in Bangkok.*

## December 17

Wrote column this month—also Thomas Merton obit.[288]
The day turned beautiful.

## December 18. Press day

Sick in bed. Lots of mail. Visitors. Chuck Matthei[289] and Pat Rusk. Chuck is an amazing person—nonviolent, non-cooperating but not provocative. A normal, sturdy, attractive human being. Served a month sentence for hitchhiking (resisting an officer, thrown in for not cooperating). He is going to see Susie Williams in Alderson, W. Va.

## December 19

Norman Thomas died today.[290] The priest who said Mass seemed to think him more important than Thomas Merton. Norman was 84. Had just had a birthday with his children and grandchildren around him. He had written me lately from his nursing home, saying he was sorry not to answer our appeal,

---

288 See "Thomas Merton, Trappist, 1915-1968," December 1968. Dorothy quoted at length from recent letters from Fr. Merton in order to contradict rumors that he was contemplating leaving his monastery.

289 Chuck Matthei was a young Peacemaker who lived from time to time at Tivoli. Dorothy admired him tremendously for his courage and consistency. He was, she often said, "a young Ammon [Hennacy], but without the ego."

290 Norman Thomas was a leading pacifist and a perennial presidential candidate for the Socialist Party of America.

but nursing homes expensive. I am so glad that I walked on that picket line with him (hospital strike) a few years ago. A noble soul.

# 1969

January 4

All day letters. Pat tried to find *Penny a Copy* at bookstores for David H.[291]

Fr. Dan Berrigan witnessed or solemnized the wedding [of Hersha Evans and Jack Cook] which was an "anarchist Christian" one. Large crowd, also from Tivoli, including Wesley and Mary H. most indecently dressed. Music and readings from Kierkegaard. Hersha is Presbyterian. How youth is attracted to CW. Beautiful sunny days, but cold.

January 7

Reading *City of God*—how barbarians spared churches and Christians! *Look* on Hanoi.

Necessity for people themselves to change. Quit worrying about Popes, Cardinals, Bishops, structures, institutions.

Peter Maurin long since spoke of building up new institutions within shell of the old. Follow Scripture. A great day for Scripture study during this last century. (Little Flower could only read certain parts of Bible.)

"What's new?" Peter brought us what was new then in the thirties. [René] Bazin's *Charles de Foucauld*, before even Père Voillaume as a seminarian was reading it and with other seminarians was pondering.

Peter stressed work of laity. "To make kind of social order where it was easier for man to be good." The terrible simplicity of these ideas.

January 20

Inauguration Day.

January 21

News from Ruth [Collins] of Internal Revenue writing to CW movement, why no returns filed?

January 27

Send Gandhi calendar to Chavez, Dolores [Huerta], Mrs. King.[292]

---

291 *A Penny a Copy: Readings from* The Catholic Worker, edited by Thomas C. Cornell and James H. Forest (New York: Macmillan, 1968).

292 The War Resisters League calendar for 1969 celebrated the centenary of Mahatma Gandhi's birth.

January 30

Fr. Dominique Pire, OP died in Belgium.

February 1

Deane briefly stormed at table. I must tell her the compliments her column received. New resolution: Be kind, be kind, be kind, and you will soon be saints.—Ruysbroek.

February 2

Little upsets. Last night Deane: "You don't know all that goes on around here!" Indeed I do. Every one makes haste to tell me. I am weighed down with complaints. Tonight, Emily's wrath: "Why is not Loraine's baby mentioned in CW? And she is a Negro and so sensitive!" Then Fr. Jack came in drunk. "Why didn't you visit Peggy?"

The children racing around until 11. Bathrooms deluged with water. We are a little sample of chaos, with our luxurious world of cars, self-indulgence in food and drink. "The fire next time." Or perhaps Nixon and Internal Revenue.

February 3

Tonight a call from Walter saying the prostitute we prayed for last Fri had been in touch with the "junky priest," thanks to Sister Francis. We must keep praying for Mary, Jack, and this girl, not to speak of Holy Church and ourselves. I believe in conversion.

Yesterday was the beginning of the preparation for Lent and I will take as my Lenten stint, beginning now, the rewriting of this book, "All is Grace."

The title really means "all things work together for good to those who love God."

God, the unknown, the un-nameable. Man can and did give a name to all things under the sun but he could not name God. Naming all the beasts of the field, the plants, the stars, meant a sort of mastery over them. We can call Him Father, as Jesus taught us. We can know Him thru Jesus, His Son, our Redeemer "who took away the sins of the world."

That last phrase comforts me, and I need to be comforted. We are the offscouring of all, as St. Paul said.

To live in the midst of alcoholics, many of whom steal to satisfy their craving—and to have an alcoholic priest visiting us, and a drunken prostitute living with us who has been in and out of mental institutions and jails, always released over and over, always returning, plying her trade, are so hard, so desperately hard to live with, especially for one "having authority," as the saying is.

But we are not to judge. We are to forgive 70 x 7. We have the parable of the prodigal son told to us by Jesus Himself. Of course he returned to his father because he was hungry and tired of his job of feeding swine. But who knows whether he did not get bored at home and get some more out of an indulgent father and wander off again. Maybe that was why Jesus preached 70 x 7. And told us not to judge.

And as for turning the other cheek—what to do when a drunken priest chases an irritating fellow member of our community down the road with a knife, and another priest, a schismatic, took a gun to threaten some Negro boys who were robbing our cherry trees.

My only comfort is that we are living in the midst of war, race war, class war, and all the things we talk about have to be tested and worked out, and we have to learn patience, learn love, and above all learn freedom.

One of the reasons I want to write is not only to get the help for myself which comes of writing about things, but also to try more and more to see them in the light of faith.

When I think of this or that alcoholic priest, so fallen from so high estate, so filled with self-justification, so well-dressed, well-fed, driving the latest model car, enjoying all the luxuries and comforts of a modern rectory, in a wealthy suburb—I can only forgive him for his banal talk and most boring presence by suddenly seeing him as a victim soul. I'm sorry I have to use these old fashioned expressions but I do not know how else to speak of it. He is suffering for the vast accumulation of self indulgence and luxury of the priests and lay people who "can take it" and don't let it drag them down. Whenever I see or hear of these well-stocked bars, I cannot help thinking of the cost of liquor and tobacco, and remember Fred on Skid Row, too much the thieving drunk, the brawling drunk to have in the house. Another victim.

Not that we do not know that wine gladdens the heart of man and should also be taken for the stomach's sake. We have always allowed Hans and Peggy, not to speak of John, their tippling, and strive for patience and understanding.

Right now we have a young former Methodist with us who has been in India and is returning in Sept, working his way on a wheat ship. He and Daniel, our Saskatchewan hermit, are fasting for a week. That is a Gandhian tactic.

I will fast from speech, but not too obviously, God help me.

War and violence soon to dominate the scene right now, and the Church too is beset by war, a sort of guerilla war.

Feb 4

I woke up at 7. Often I find that I have started praying before I am really awake, just as I fall asleep praying. Lord Jesus, have mercy on us sinners—over and over. Usually I am praying in a state of desperation, certainly not peacefully and confidently as I should. That is to say, these days. So I come back to praying for myself. But it is the misery of waking to the thought of a drunken priest in our midst. Oh God, have mercy on Fr. John. Pope John, pray for him. The priest's name is not John, but there are so many Johns. I'll call him that and be praying for all priests with their well-stocked bars. "Don't be Jansenistic, Dorothy." "Don't be prudish."

But he is depraved besides. I'm in despair over drunken John and whorish Mary, who said, "I may be depraved but he is worse." (Tolstoy said to Gorki, "I have whored a great deal in my youth." As we all have.)

I must read Osee, or Hosea again. God's mercy and loving-kindness, forgiving all, generous to all.

Sin is attractive in the young, and to the young. "The call of the flesh is so strong then," an old priest said to me. But what if this perverted priest is fifty? No, it is not so attractive then.

I must ask Péguy to pray for all sinners in our midst, especially me, so wanting in charity. I must read again "God Speaks," in *Eternal Verities*. That wonderful poem about the Our Father.

Today is the feast of St. Andrew Corsini, a dissolute of Florence nobility who, as his mother dreamed while pregnant, turned from wolf to sheep in a sudden conversion.

Pope John XXIII, pray for our priest here. St. Andrew, pray for him. Péguy, pray for him.

I read for two hours, my only time of utter quiet. Mail arrives at 9:30 and at eleven there is a Mass in our small chapel where a scant ten or twelve are present.

Our good priest—silent always in the face of the "human misery around us," a gentle silence, not a critical one, comes in from the sacristy with the holy water. And he sprinkles us with this to cleanse us from sin, presupposing that we are not guilty of serious sin, and that we are sorry for our sins of omission and the constant small sins of uncharitable speech and thought.

There used to be "prayers at the foot of the altar."

Priest: I will go up to the altar of God.

People: To God who gives joy to my youth. Why art Thou sad, O my soul, and why dost thou disquiet me?

Hope then in God who is the health of my countenance and my God.

And so on.

One of my young friends, unhappy in love, who began to go to Mass for the first time voluntarily, was struck by these words. The priests had just begun to use the vernacular, a great advance in the life of the lay person. We had, not so long ago, speaking of time in the life of the church, not been allowed to use missals with the translation of the Latin ritual of the sacraments. In the time of St. Therese of Lisieux, who died in 1897, she was not permitted to read the Bible in its entirety. She seemed to know by heart what she did read however.

"And now," my young friend said, "just when we were understanding and being comforted by what we pray—-half of it is being taken away from us."

## Feb 5

Feast of St. Agatha. It is the season of Septuagesima, preparation for Lent, but the church still directs the priest to say these Masses of the saints instead of the Church seasons. This grim season there is a hunger for penance because the sins of the world, the wars going on, weigh so heavy on us, especially when I think of my grandson on his way to Vietnam, a Ranger, a staff sergeant at 20. They are certainly picking babies to fight their wars. A boy of 20 cannot get a license to marry without his mother's permission, he cannot sign contracts, vote, etc.

I write "they." The government, the men in power. Peter Maurin wrote that we should stop saying "*They* don't do this, *they* do that," etc. "Be what you want the other fellow to be…" In this case a firm refuser. We must say "we," when we pay taxes, and always look for better jobs, higher pay, a higher standard of living. We sign, we accept a social security number, we are branded like cattle.

Daniel, a French Canadian from Saskatchewan is staying the winter with us and God knows we need him. He has lived as a hermit, has built log cabins to live in the wilderness—he is a practicing, devout Catholic, and he is gentle. Right now he is fasting, as Gandhi fasted when there was sin in his midst. Dan is fasting for Fr. J who was drunk all day yesterday and sat up until one with Mary H, who said "I know I'm depraved, but Fr. J is more depraved than I." He was quiet, but she kept the house awake with her noise.

What remedies do we have except prayer and fasting?

I fast partially, from meat now these 2 years, and now this Lent from breakfasts when I can. I was constantly on my feet in chapel this morning.

"Where sin abounds grace did more abound." Mysterious words. But there are saints in our midst, hermits, pilgrims, and thru these little ones, the spirit of nonviolence will grow.

A conviction of this brings joy. True joy which no man can take from us.

Meanwhile, on the natural level, what to do?

One rule is sure—do all with love. But how can you put out into the cold, the bitter cold, a girl who has been in and out of hospitals and jails?

Last winter, a 14-year-old girl from a small town in Ohio came to the East Village in New York with a boy, was lured away from him and taken to a slum tenement on Mott St., a few blocks away from us, and given drugs, raped, and thrown down an air shaft to die. Or perhaps she jumped.

Another girl from a wealthy Conn. family was also murdered in an East Side basement. Thinking of these things, I decide to do nothing. I must talk to her again, however.

But there is the priest. I told him not to come and use our place to hole up in and drink. I reminded him he went to the Trappists to protect himself from temptation and for 8 years was sober and became a good priest. (He was the late bishop's confessor.)


Feb 6. Feast of St. Dorothy

I looked at myself in the mirror this morning and saw again the lines around my mouth. "You have thin lips," Pat said the other day. I often look at people's sad and ugly hard faces in the subways and buses and think how people lose the beauty, the freshness of youth. Not necessarily. But certainly among the poor.

Ill-fitting girdles and corsets and brassieres, not to speak of shoes, or too short or tight stockings, keep one in a state of discomfort. I read the other day of a description of an old demonstrator and the cruel young reporter spoke of "ill fitting dentures." All these things, and also continued pain from arthritis, and various other troubles twist the face into an ugly grimace.

Worry, sorrow do not enable the countenance. As one gets older, the more knowledge we have of the sins and tragedies of the world build up in the memory and unless wisdom brings the practice of silence one can be weighted down by suffering, so that the heart is literally heavy and literally aches, and breathing is impeded. One "cannot draw an easy breath."

Once when I knew Katherine Ann Porter in Mexico City and she was renting a "little hoose" as she called it, I was amazed to find her bringing many mirrors for it. "They mean windows, and reflections," she explained. She was and is a beautiful woman and I often thought how wise she was. It is good to suddenly come upon a reflection of one's self, serious, somber, hard with thought, and I remember how I once met an old and tactless friend unexpect-edly and as he came up to me, he laughed and wanted to know what I was mad about.

One must guard one's expression, for the sake of others around one. One of our friends has a face like a tragic mask one moment, then is filled with a joyous mirthfulness the next. Unfortunately, the tragic mask predominates most of the time.

Irene Mary Naughton used to quote Ruskin on "the Duty of Delight" and when I traced the passage I was delighted to find that he urged us to find solace in the beauties of nature instead of delving into our interior.

Chekhov says to find it in work, which is a cure for all ills and a relative of mine whose son is perhaps a thalidomide baby says his only comfort is in work when he becomes despondent.

In the Cross is joy of spirit, Thomas à Kempis says. I'm glad to see him listed with Hilton and Julian of Norwich and Ruysbroek and the author of the *Cloud of Unknowing*, in the Penguin edition of the latter's book.

Modern man, of religious instincts, appalled by the materialism and luxury of the West, finds it in Zen. This morning I started Thomas Merton's book on Zen. A beautiful book. How we will miss this man of God. He set us an example of hard and steady work.

On Pilgrimage, Feb.

Maritain said once we are given many intimations. Transfiguration. Wed-ding feast. Joy unutterable. But that we are still on the way. Dante, C.S. Lewis, *The Great Divorce*, Angela of Foligno.

You will see Him as He is—and others too. A frank, open soul once said, "I don't know whether I want to see my husband again!"[293] (Indeed he had wronged her on occasion and his last days of cruel suffering made him rage a lot.)

Feb 8. John of Matha, redeeming captives

Before the Second World War we had a German friend in Toronto who offered himself to Hitler to redeem the captives and who knows how many others?

Edith Stein, the philosopher, Mother Mary, the Russian woman who ran a house of hospitality in Paris.[294]

---

293 As Dorothy indicated elsewhere, the "frank, open soul" was in fact her mother. See Janu-ary 16, 1968.

294 Edith Stein, a German philosopher and convert to Catholicism, became a Carmelite nun. She died in Auschwitz in 1942 and was later canonized by the Catholic Church. Mother Maria Skobtsova was a Russian émigrée in Paris who became an Orthodox nun, combining her love

"Victim Souls," a designation which sounds ridiculous to the modern mind sickened by false piety, but Fr. Pacifique Roy had offered himself. "We may not really mean what we say but God takes us at our word," he said wryly not long before his death.[295] And Father Judge, the Minnesota priest who offered himself for his parish because several children in his parish had committed suicide.

This last year there have been 3 suicides. B.J., John, the ex-Jesuit, and a young boy in his early teens. What long drawn-out agony—what despair, and how we must pray for them now.

To offer one's life for another is the highest form of love, a noble act, but how many of us would do it? We might turn out to be romantics like Lord Jim (Conrad). We are filled with fear but have little courage. Especially when we are alone and faced with terror. If there are others around who expect us to protect them—who depend on us, who look to us for example—then we might offer ourselves up.

Father Vawter, C.M. has written about the book of Genesis and explained for me what was formerly inexplicable, such as the ages of the patriarchs, or the two accounts of creation. Archaeology and other modern sciences have done much to shed light on Bible history. And Fr. John McKenzie has made us understand how the Jews stood out as God's people who alone retained and returned again and again to God, the one God, the infinitely Other, the un-nameable. Adam, Man, named all the beasts, the plants, trees, stars. He named them, knew them and is gradually taking possession or dominating even the moon and the planets—and he is also trying to destroy all [that] God, the Other has made.

But who can succeed against God? Last night I was reading, or rather mulling over Doughty's *Arabia Deserta*, with his tale of barren desert wastes and cities abandoned, evidences as indeed there are throughout the world, in Indochina, in Yucatan, in Peru, of prehistoric civilizations.

It does seem that at different periods of history God "wiped from the earth man who he had created" in Genesis by flood. "The end of all creatures of flesh is in my mind: the earth is full of violence because of them."

And now again the earth is full of violence. And there is talk of prophecies of earthquakes and tidal waves wiping out California and the East coast.

Catholics have so long been looked on as the credulous, but just as the very young flee from the horror of the war in Vietnam, the starvation in Biafra and

---

of God and neighbor in a manner very similar to the Catholic Worker. Because of her efforts to rescue Jews she was arrested by the Nazis and died in Ravensbruck in 1945. She was canonized by the Russian Orthodox Church.

295 In *Loaves and Fishes* (128-134) Dorothy described Father Roy's final sufferings, and her belief that he had offered himself as a "victim soul."

the slow dying of countless millions thru famine and dispossession of land and home, flee to horror movies, so too the young are fleeing to the land.

"What would you do if you knew the world was going to come to an end tomorrow?" someone asked St. Ignatius.

"I would go on doing what I am doing now," he said calmly.

So that is what we are doing.

I think I have always read looking for the serious themes that draw men to noble deeds, to self-sacrifice, to a greater love of others. Even the most frivolous literature. I began to realize the seriousness implied in the word "duty" for instance in a love story I read when I was fourteen. It was about a nurse who was working in the Klondike and there were two men in the story, one a hero, one a villain. The villain came down with pneumonia and she was called upon to nurse him and just before the crisis, her fiancé, the hero, was severely injured and she was called for but she would not leave her "duty." Somewhere in our family the words "bounden duty" came into us, and we liked the phrase and used to use it often. I would tell my sister it was her "bounden duty" to make us a cake or remind my brother it was his bounden duty to shovel the snow off the front steps.

When my first grandchild used to chase the three pet ducks, I said, "Becky thinks it her bounden duty to chase ducks," whereupon she added the phrase to her chasing—calling "bounden duty," as she shoved them around the garden. But the one aggressive male leaped on her once as she fell and pecked her back with his bill so that it was covered with welts when we rushed to her rescue. We heard no more of this form of "bounden duty."

February 9

Blizzard. All day it snowed and there was howling wind. Called Mary Hennessy. Eric called from Lewis air base to say he was flying Thurs to Vietnam.

Feb 10. St. Scholastica's day

I am writing this long Lenten diary as a bounden duty, as a form of discipline, and also to approach many subjects which I feel I must speak about, as a woman, as a Catholic. I cannot remain in silence (silence means consent) when there is a guerrilla warfare going on within the church.

The things I want to say are hard to say, hard to write, and I'll have to approach them over and over again from every angle, as it strikes my mind at the time, as it is brought to my attention by events.

A woman cannot help but be distressed and concerned about sexual morality. It concerns her too closely. About birth control, about authority, about obedience, about sin in general, which brings about so much unhappiness. Unhappiness in women and in children.

Feb 11. Feast of Our Lady of Lourdes

Franz Werfel's *Song of Bernadette* is the best account to my mind of the apparitions of the Virgin to 14-year-old Bernadette. Today I'll say the Little Office of the Virgin and of course we have the Rosary at night.

"All my life I have been haunted by God," Kiriloff said in Dostoevsky's *Possessed.* I try to trace back to my first religious instincts.

There was Mary Manley who lived with us at Bath Beach. We were six. Mother, father, two brothers, my sister, and I.

I shared a room with Mary and she was a good Catholic. She told me in after years that she took me to church with her on Sunday but I stood up in the pew and gaped at the congregation. I remember nothing of this. When I was seven I began to read the Bible, in Berkeley, Calif., when we had just moved. We lived in a furnished house, and I found a Bible there in the attic where my sister and I played. My mother and father never went to church. He had been brought up a Congregationalist and Mother, an Episcopalian.

We children were taught to "say our prayers" at night, "Now I lay me down to sleep. I pray the Lord my soul to keep. If I should die before I wake, I pray the Lord my soul to take. And bless mother and father and help me to be good."

Being bad meant calling my brothers names, and hitting them when they teased me. My mother washed my mouth out once with soap and water for the name calling. I never felt guilty about sex tho my brothers and I had laughed about it a great deal when we were respectively six, seven, and eight. Later when I was about ten I came across some bitter reflections about sex in a de Maupassant story or essay, a set of whose books were locked away from us. His complaint was that the exalted feelings of sexual love were unfortunately connected with those organs which had to do with the plumbing of the human body.

My deep-set guilt feelings as a very young child seemed to be over deception and theft. I had stolen a nickel from my mother's purse, at five, for ice cream and again had sold a schoolbook at ten for candy (a little girl I played with always had money for candy) and I was immersed in gloom until I had confessed my fault to my mother.

But my childhood fears were concerned with the awfulness of God and I often had a nightmare of a monstrous being, beating a batter in a huge bowl, a noise which got louder and louder until I woke up to find my mother sitting beside me, holding my hand for I had cried out.

Was it after the San Francisco earthquake that I had this dream or before? I do not remember, except that it was in California that I dreamed.

We moved from Berkeley, the house of the Bible, to Oakland, where we had a home of our own with garden and brook and a sunny kitchen and near the hills where my brothers and I rambled after school up to an orchard of apricots.

There was a Methodist family who lived next door and I played with a little girl who gave me a pious book about a holy child called Birdie and under this influence I began to go to Sunday school occasionally. I never felt I belonged. No one else in the family went to church, and none of us children were baptized.

And when our parents went on vacation we were left to the care of a young woman who lived in a slum not so far but that she could run home in the afternoon, taking me and my sister with her. I only know it as a slum because the rooms were tiny and papered with comic strips and full-page pictures of handsome youths and beauties of the nineties (this was 1905), with bulging bosom and protuberant buttocks and bustles to accentuate them. This was no pious household and the girl and her friends indulged in lewd remarks and gestures.

Playing in a field of high weeds and thistles, we used to make tunnels enlarged here and there into green caves thru which the sun filtered so it seemed we were playing under the sea, and in these playhouses, ever expanding, and known only to a half-dozen of us, another child, a little boy, wanted to caress me, but I avoided him, sensing something "not right," but not deeply concerned about it, nor shocked. (Later, at twelve, there was another child, a dirty-minded little girl, who read and recounted all the sex crimes her mother talked about with others and which she read of in the scandal sheets of the daily press. Because she had good manners Mother thought her a nice child but I knew her as a "whited sepulcher." But before this there were other children on 37ᵗʰ St. in Chicago—the Harringtons and the Barretts—who told me stories of the lives of the saints and heroes of the child that roused me to emulation. I heard for the first time of devotion to Mary, the Blessed Virgin, and learning that Heaven was populated, I ceased to have that dread nightmare of a Presence which left room for no one except in the silence of the grave. "One is one, and all alone, and ever more shall be so," as the song goes.

One day, I saw Mrs. Barrett at her prayers, kneeling by her bed at ten in the morning, in the bedroom off the kitchen, and suddenly the grandeur of that act of worship—- [*unfinished*]²⁹⁶

---

296 In *From Union Square to Rome* Dorothy related the story of how one day as a child she burst into her neighbor's house looking for her friend, Kathryn Barrett, and came upon her

Feb 14

Since I have to speak tonight at the Methodist Church in Red Hook, I awake with gloom pressing down on me. After my morning prayers, the 7 penitential psalms, picked up Martin Luther King's *Strength to Love*—a paperback—and began reading some of his sermons on fear, on prayer, and so on. They warmed my cold heart.

When I was 14 I read Wesley's sermons which I picked up in a secondhand book store on North Clark Street in Chicago. Perhaps it was because I had just read *Adam Bede* and the *Mill on the Floss* in high school that I turned to these sermons, as of that period and background in England.

But I have to keep going back again, when it comes to reading. When I was 12 I broke my arm in three places, tripping over my brother's feet. In addition to the Sherlock Holmes, and Rider Haggard that Aunt Jenny, my only Catholic relative, sent me from New York, I had the books a playmate of mine, Lenore Clancy, gave me, the Tom Playfair books. I had read Frank Merriwell and Jack Harkaway and Horatio Alger but here was religion cropping out again in the most unlikely places. Tom Playfair went to a school run by priests and could speak Latin! I was in my first year of high school and had started to study Latin and was fascinated by the pursuit of wisdom.

I remember very little about the books, a glimpse of poverty in Alger's story of bootblack boys in New York, a sadistic scene in Jack Harkaway when our "hero" nailed the ear of a "native" to a door for eavesdropping (it was in Malaysia), but Tom Playfair had a mystery about it—the mysteries of the Mass and "serving the altar."

But I must go back further—once again—to a year or so earlier. One must not forget the Elsie Dinsmore books and how in the following of principles (she would not perform on Sunday on the piano for her godless father's guests) she all but lost her life. Her passionately loved father had punished her by making her sit on a high piano stool on a hot humid day until she fainted and falling off struck her head. "If the wound had been an inch nearer, I would have lost my darling," the repentant and converted father cried.

I found nothing unhealthy in the fervent love between father and daughter, which has often been criticized in discussions of children's books as approaching the incestuous. I can imagine children starved for love becoming obsessed by the desire for it. In our quiet reserved home we were sure of the solid affection of our mother and father, tho he was reserved and shy with us.

---

mother kneeling in the bedroom saying her morning prayers. "All through my life what she was doing remained with me.... Mrs. Barrett in her sordid little tenement flat finished her breakfast dishes at ten o'clock in the morning and got down on her knees and prayed to God." (*FUSR*, 26)

Last year when I attended a crowded conference at a big hotel in Washington, I stayed for a few nights at a tourist house across the street where I found in an open bookcase in the upstairs hall an old copy of one of the Dinsmore series. She was a happily married woman and lived on a large plantation with Mr. Travilla, her father's friend, with her father, her former slaves and all her children. The Civil War was over and their next-door neighbors were Northerners who also ran a plantation. Other neighbors and impoverished whites had by now joined the Ku Klux Klan or its equivalent and were plotting to burn and destroy the neighbor's property and person if he would not consent to go back North. A time came when the neighbors took refuge in Elsie's home and she and her old Negro Mammy planned the defense. In the kitchen the servants were making soap and there were boiling kettles of lye and grease brought to the upstairs balcony of the old Southern mansion, and poured down on the mob rushing in to break down the doors. This tactic and the guns of the men-folk scattered the screaming assailants who staggered or were led blindly away from the mansion. Napalm of the 1860s!

So there was violence and brutality in the Harkaway and Dinsmore books of my day. But Elsie was supposedly a Christian!

## February 20. Press

McKennas in Boston have given up nonviolence.[297] Freedom to kill that brutal policeman. To force another human being not to go to Vietnam by bombing an induction center. Read Berdyaev's *Dostoevsky*. In training it is kill kill kill. To defend Eldridge Cleaver it is kill kill. To defend poor kill kill.

## February 24

Here are troubles at the beginning of Lent. By writing about them I can see next year how they have been resolved, how conditions have improved, how God has dealt with them for us. Right now I am exhausted with them and see no way out.

But perhaps I should start commending ourselves—it will make me more balanced in my judgments.

---

297 Kathe and John McKenna were founders, in 1966, of Haley House, a CW community in Boston. Kathe McKenna remembers this encounter well: "Now John and I were not pacifists at the time. And we were going to talk about that, about our anger and our...even if she was there. We were prepared for the worst, because we knew that she tended to be rather adamant about pacifism... After it was all over, we were drinking coffee and Dorothy came up to us and said in her wonderfully stiff, warm way: 'You must feel very strongly about what you believe.' And she just smiled and left it at that. What she identified with was not our beliefs as such, which clearly clashed with hers, but with our struggle." (Riegle, *Dorothy Day: Portraits*, 70.)

We are taking care of at the farm two epileptics, one with a very bad ulcerated leg which smells to high heaven. He himself seems unconscious of the offense given others and continues to sit in the dining room by the stove to which we come so many times a day for tea or coffee. He will not go to doctor or clinic. He is one of those who have been put off Medicaid. There is Slim who, if we had not taken him in 30 years ago from the breadline (he was 17), would have spent his time in the streets or in a huge mental ward, like live storage.

Daniel-Rops, in his *Life of Jesus*, says that everything in Galilee that takes place there, the Sermon on the Mount, the calling of the disciples, the marriage feast of Cana, is marked by tenderness and charity. Jesus knew there the happiness of childhood, of being loved and understood.

The savage and harsh land of Judea—the harsh prophecies, reference to the divine wrath, the other side of the gospel is there. Eleven disciples came from Galilee. Judas from Judea.

I want the farm at Tivoli to be our Galilee.

I woke at Tivoli this morning at 5 to depression, worry, our inability to be harsh—to handle the unwanted ones, the squatters, the lunatic, the drunken. We are all constitutionally unable to "move people on," especially in winter when they dig in. Reading Lauds and the little hours brought reassurance. We want to be a Galilee, not a Judea, with its unloving righteousness, as Daniel-Rops pictured it.

"Thou hast heard the voice of my pleading when I cried to Thee…Take courage and let your heart by strengthened—all who hope in the Lord." Ps 30:23-25.

February 25

Snow and ice. Tamar in Vermont reading *Soul on Ice* and *Malcolm X*.

Kay working on files and archives. Heard from Dr. Miller.[298] Book taken by Herder and Herder. He will move to Florida in June.

Copying Fr. Merton's last two papers from Calcutta.

February 26

About miniskirts. One of the reasons I like legs is because mine are failing me. At 71 one should not be surprised. Franklin [Spier] and I like ball games. He is crippled. We like to see these leaps out into the field—these runs for

---

298  William D. Miller, an historian at Marquette University, and later Florida State University in Tallahassee, was the author of *A Harsh and Dreadful Love: Dorothy Day and the Catholic Worker Movement* (New York: Liveright, 1973). He helped transport some of Dorothy's papers to the Catholic Worker archives at Marquette, and later he published *Dorothy Day: A Biography* (New York: Doubleday, 1982).

bases, etc. The legs of girls are of course attractive, and I remember with nostalgia the legs and slim hips of a boy in high school when, at 15, I was stirred to passion all one winter and went to all the basketball games.

One should love the human body, which has served us well. Long slim legs, stout fat legs, and youth in general is beautiful. As for age, old Italian women—women like Kathe Kollwitz, Elizabeth Mayer, friend of Auden and Britten, these women too have a special beauty. Sleeveless dresses, miniskirts. Bikinis are so plentiful. Of course all my granddaughters wear them. I do not care particularly for nudism. Children and new schools—7 or 8-year-olds. "Look at whose-its vagina!" The pride of the young at learning these new words in sex education classes then. I do not see how.

I write because I am tired of all these cries of complaint. When people are looking for Truth, everything comes out in the open, rather childishly, like the little boy in the "progressive school."

We'll always be returning to reticence and silence and a delicate sense of the inviolability of each and every human being. That silence and delicacy I have always found in the confessional, for instance. (I have only met one priest in my life in whom I sensed an unholy curiosity.)

Peter always said to study history to get perspective on the present. Remember the tights of men in Dickens novels—leotards you might call them. Or the codpieces—such styles of hairdressing for men! The hippies have contributed color, as well as head-bands and beads, bare feet, monk robes, capes, etc., to the garb of men. Men have always worn shorts in summer.

March 15
Meeting with Danilo Dolci at Algonquin.

March 16
War—Buddhism. Our increased knowledge of other men, and thru them, of God. Ecumenism. [Abraham] Maslow speaks of psalms as irrelevant today. Yet Buddhist and Hindu Scriptures, thousands of years older, are relevant to the young. Books in 8th St. paperback store. The Search. "You would not seek me if you had not already found me" [Pascal]. Time. No time with God. Seeking is finding.

May 15. On train
The coach I am in is almost full. There are a score of Indian children on their way home to Montana, and just now passing thru the car a dozen boys of draft age, just on their way back from Fargo, I think, where they had been undergoing their physical. They looked somber. Somehow Pres. Nixon's

peace talk last night does not carry conviction. There has been other talk of withdrawing troops from Vietnam and then a few days later denials of such talk.

Money, a topic of vital interest to man. Like sex or food, it can be made subject of intense interest. How to get it, how to spend it. Men at highest level—enormous salary, enormous expenses. Tales of corruption in high places always involve money. [Abe] Fortas takes retaining fees to protect a client and is disgraced publicly. Disgraced and discredited.

Dwight Macdonald wrote once that a foundation was a large body of money surrounded by people, all of whom were trying to get some of it.

Foundations are tax-free, and the less powerful are now being investigated.

When gangsters, now called Mafiosi, are being convicted it is often on charge of evading income tax—not on charge of extortion, murder, blackmail, drug trafficking, white slave traffic.

The love of money is the root of all evil.

Whence come wars among you? Each one seeking his own.

People are secretive about money—how much they have, where it came from, inherited, earned? How closely it is tied up to work—hard work, work that is for the common good.

What are students learning in colleges and universities? To work for the common good, to contribute to the common good, or to get the degrees which will entitle them to enter ever-higher fields of learning and recompense.

What vast fields of knowledge there are which relate to man's need for a good life, for the food, clothing, and shelter man needs to lead a good life.

"A certain amount of goods is necessary to lead a good life," St. Thomas Aquinas writes. How much goods? How much land does a man need? What do men live for?

These are questions which preoccupied Tolstoy and about which he wrote so much.

What was the attitude of Jesus toward money? (Judas was the one who held the purse, who betrayed him for money and then threw the money away. He was playing for greater stakes—power, world domination perhaps.)

"Take no thought for what ye shall eat or drink or wear. Your Father knows you have need of these things. Be like little children. Trust. Ask and you shall receive. If a child ask for bread will his father give him a stone? If he ask for fish, will he hand him a scorpion? Take no money on your journey. Do not lay up for yourselves treasures on earth." Do you need money for paying taxes? And here Jesus does something fantastic, like something out of a fairytale. He doesn't tell Peter to go to Judas to get the money. He tells him to go fishing and open the mouth of the first fish he catches and take out the coin he will find there and pay the tribute "lest thou should offend them."

Render to Caesar the things that are Caesar's but the less you have of Caesar the less you have to give him. Jesus was living in an occupied country. At the moment it was peacetime, a Pax Romana. It was Law and Order, Roman law and order, with a standing army to keep the peace. Jesus was not concerned with joining the resistance. He was laying down principles that made for true peace. They could take it or leave it. He forced no man. But he did try to arouse in man that hunger and thirst for "living water," for the abundant life, for the joy that no man can take from you, for the "unspeakable gift" which so many have caught a vision of and have tried to communicate to others.

All this ruminating is because the Catholic Worker has been left $55,000 in a will. People are so cautious and secretive about money that I cannot write about the other legatees, just about ourselves. There were many claims to the will. Servants, friends, isolated missionaries were all left gifts, furniture was given to museums, pets were given to friends to care for, together with money to support them, and the residue of the estate was to be divided between 5 Catholic institutions, charitable institutions, of which we are one.

And now it is a question of taxes to be paid on this inheritance. Are we, or are we not a charitable institution? There was no question about the 4 others. They were accredited institutions, money that came to them could not be taxed. Accredited by the State. The State agreed that money for the poor was exempt from taxation. It was holy. It was on another plane, another level, on another dimension. You entered another realm when you dealt with this money. You dealt with a fairyland. You had gone thru the looking glass like Alice, or thru the wardrobe like the children in the C.S. Lewis stories.

But we—the lawyers of the State decided—were living in *this world* as well as in the next. When we acted as tho all men were really brothers, as though "all the way to heaven is heaven" because Jesus Christ had said "I am the Way" and we were trying to "put on Christ" as St. Paul advised, and "put off the old man," and really act "as if we loved one another," "as if" our brother, our loved one, was the man on the Bowery, Skid Row, or prison, or prison camp, or battlefield; "as if" the Chinese, Soviets, North and South Vietnamese, Cubans, are truly our brothers, children of one Father, one Creator, maker of Heaven and earth, the moon and stars which we are exploring now—Oh God how wonderful are all Thy works.

What *is* man that thou art mindful of Him?

Thou hast made him little less than the angels. Thou hast put all things under his feet.

But unless you become as little children you shall not enter the Kingdom of Heaven.

Yes, we were left $55,000, and there is more to come, the lawyers tell us.

For a long time we did not believe in the $55,000. It was like *Bleak House*; it was like the Circumlocution office. We knew all about the law's delays, and we were not going to be deceived into believing we would ever get that money. We were not going to ruin ourselves with vain expectations. (I am quietly influenced by Dickens. I would rather be a McCawber than a Mrs. Jellyby.)

So we were quite content when the government, the state, the lawyers of the Revenue Dept. decided we were not a bona fide charitable institution, or perhaps we were only partly that, but also we were a pacifist-activist group.

Was not Holy Mother the State supporting (punishing or rehabilitating) three of our organization, our institution, "our family" in federal prisons? Three others of these enemies of the state have recently been released. Jim Wilson, Bob Gilliam, Tom Cornell. Past offenders, Karl Meyer, Ammon Hennacy, Deane Mowrer, Pat Rusk, Nicole d'Entremont, Dorothy Day, all have spent time in jail.

Can these possibly be bona fide "charitable works"? Never have people who worked for charity been like these. I do not wonder the State is confused.

No wonder the State, the men who make up the State, who are on the side of the State, who are the "here and now" men, do not understand. We too see in a glass darkly. We see in a mirror what manner of men we are—made in the image and likeness of God, and go away and straightaway forget what manner of men we are and how we should try to act, to behave. "Yes, we are trying to do good," the State tells us sorrowfully "and how can we take care of all this business for you if you do not pay your taxes? You cannot build bricks without straw."

"All these poverty programs, this war against poverty, this war against aggression, costs money. We go to the ends of the earth to defend you against the aggression of your enemies. We launch satellites in order to bring you news of the enemy. We hide nothing from you. You know where your tax dollar goes. Down to the last detail you are informed. We know any move of the enemy, even to the last manhole installed on a Moscow St." (Some gov official said this recently.)

And do they know about our Minute Men [missiles] which dot the vast plains of Montana, hundreds of them?

Undoubtedly they do, we have spy ships on sea and in space and so have they, and so also we must have more money for ABM sites all over the United States. We will spare no effort to defend you. So we need more money, more taxes to take care of you.

It is in vain that we—CW people—talk of works of mercy. Jesus called the nations before him, "Inasmuch as ye did it to the least of these my brethren, you did not feed them, you destroyed their crops, their fields, you prepared poisons, deadly germs, nerve gasses, you burnt them and the clothes off their backs with napalm, you destroyed their villages. You did not feed the hungry, clothe the naked, shelter the homeless. You did the opposite." But these are the enemy! They are all my children. More, made in the image of God, all under the cape of heaven is mine. I built the earth to be inhabited, not to be depopulated and destroyed.

How can these men understand when we see thru a glass darkly ourselves? And yet we know too that we have seen "a great light." If even in the visible world men have accomplished so great feats, have worked out so great a vision, why have we not developed our spiritual capacities? While I write men are encircling the moon. Last night I looked at pictures on television sent to us from the cabins of these ships in orbit. Perhaps I was seeing what was not there, but it seemed to me these men were under terrific tension, strain, risking their lives each moment, their capacities stretched to the breaking point. To me there was infinite pathos in those faces. And what reward? The State showers praise and honor and glory on them, the world acclaims them, even the enemy, the world loves and honors them, and yet none of this, we know and they know, will satisfy. Our hearts are made for Thee O Lord and find no rest until they rest in Thee.

When the astronaut read the words of Scripture, "In the beginning, God"… he must have known, uttering the holy words, that peace the conquest of moon and stars and the world below cannot give.

Such light is so bright, we cannot endure it long. Seeing Jesus transfigured, the 3 apostles came down from the mount and went on arguing as to who would be first in the Kingdom and when would their earthly kingdom begin. But when the promised Holy Spirit descended, they began to live in that other dimension, a world in which the promise of "blood, sweat and tears" would lure them more than gold and honor.

God help us! In our perversity we seek it even in war, in the gigantic and senseless slaughter that is going on now, not only in Vietnam but in Israel, Nigeria, Biafra, we think we are doing right. Especially those who are not there ennoble it with their pens, their speeches. Yes, Holy Mother the State thinks she is trying to remedy the suffering at home and abroad, and she needs to tax us because after all, we are the State, and our duly elected representatives have so legislated for us, committed us, levied on us taxes by which these programs enable the theater of action to go on. The tragedy, the comedy continues. We are all a part of it.

We are all guilty. So we all deserve punishment. We crave penance. Paying taxes is penance but not the kind of penance we want. We are so perverse we wish to choose our own penance. So we chose not to pay these taxes. Yes, we understand that these tax dollars also go to wage war against poverty, so they think. But we do not believe in the nationalization of the poor. We do not believe in State ownership of the indigent. We believe in voluntary poverty and the personal practice of the works of mercy. These are old-fashioned terms. Charity means love. Love presupposes justice. In the scriptures the just man is the holy man, the holy man is the whole man, the man of integrity, the integrated man, the man who works and lives by the sweat of his brow, not on someone else's sweat, not on credit cards, not by cheating and being cheated, and repaying the cheaters by cheating again. But we have not earned this money by sweat, though certainly we have worked at all kinds of work these 36 years of the CW existence. We are trying to build a new society within the shell of the old, with peaceful means, with nonviolence. Long before Marshall McLuhan wrote "the medium is the message," Gandhi wrote that the means become the ends. Truth needs constant restatement. We believe we need to work with our hands and this writing is manual labor as well as mental, just as washing dishes, preparing food for the hungry that come each day to be fed, cleaning up, building, repairing, sewing, etc., etc., require manual and mental labor.

We have worked, we have prayed. A priest said once manual labor is hard, mental [labor] is harder, but spiritual [labor] is hardest of all to learn.

Oh, the tedium, the ennui, the disgust, the rebellion that comes to deter us from the exercise and strengthening of the spiritual faculties. Yes, we have worked. There has been lots of suffering too, frustrations, discouragement, hopelessness—all of which is *sin*, or a temptation.

In patience you will possess your souls. Patience means suffering and suffering is spiritual work, and it is accomplishing something tho we don't realize it until later. It is a part of our education, our pilgrimage to Heaven. By it we keep in mind that all the way to Heaven is Heaven. Heaven is within you. The kingdom is here and now.

So joy and suffering go together, pleasure and pain, work and rest, the rhythm of life, day succeeding the night, spring following winter, life and death and life again, world without end.

Holy Mother the State must submit to my discursive way of explaining what makes us do what we do. Once Cardinal McIntyre, when he was bishop in N.Y., said to me, "Do not write such long letters," smiling as he said [this]. Personally he was always very kind to me, a woman, a laywoman. (Not much was to be feared from, or expected of a woman. And a convert, besides.) I was trying to explain our point if view. We were never called to task about pacifism or anarchism. The words did not seem to frighten them as communism did.

They did worry about our attacks on capitalism.

"Sooner or later you will have to take that word 'Catholic' off of your masthead," Msgr. Gaffney said. "Of course the Church is committed to the capitalist system." I wished I had a Dominican magazine, *Blackfriars*, printed in England to show him, with that headline, "Who Baptized Capitalism?" He would have brushed it off, Irishman that he was, coming from an English order priest and he himself an Irishman and a diocesan priest. That is still another war, between order priests like Jesuits, Dominicans, and orders and secular clergy. There are vestiges of it still all around us.

I was called to the Chancery office another time about a retreat Fr. Fiorentino was about to preach to us. He was another Savonarola, or St. Bernadine, and was a fiery enemy of self indulgence, advocating a strict asceticism which would have wrecked the capitalist system in no time. Abstention from liquor and tobacco, from movies, telephone and radio, from unhealthy recreation. (Montana is a recreation state. Recreation is a billion dollar industry. N.Y. is a summer festival.)

"Examine your conscience as to recreation," he would tell us. We would rather say, as to *work*. He also harped on immodest dress. Lust in marriage. Once he said to a woman having a fifth child, "Not much self-control there!" No wonder they burned Savonarola…. I saw a church once in the neighborhood of Pittsburgh, with an Italian pastor, which had a stained glass window of Savonarola. I would have preferred one of Garibaldi who purified the church by wresting from her the papal states.

We have encountered far more trouble when we have attacked *money* in these 36 years.

When I visited [the] Archbishop during the steel strike in '35. he said, "I hear you've been visiting the strikers at their headquarters." Where could he have obtained this info? Spies, informers, in the ranks of the strikers. Associations of steel men, coal operators hired Pinkerton men who in turn hired spies, etc. "That headline in the June 1937 CW, 'Cops murder 10 pickets in Chi Strike,' certainly smacks of class war," he said, but smilingly, almost as tho he meant, "Communism endorses class war, foments it, and so you can

be accused of communism, doing away with private property and godless-
ness. So of course businessmen suspect you. We know you are good Catholics, you people at the Catholic Worker, mindful of the needy and the poor,
but remember, Christ said, 'The zeal of thy house has eaten me up,' and he
also said, 'the poor you'll always have with you,' so watch your step."

He did not say this of course, but when I knelt to receive his blessing and
to kiss his ring (those were the olden days when we were taught manners)
he gave me a little slap on the cheek as bishops do when they confirm you.
Did that mean he was confirming me, us, in our mission to do away with
war, change the social order, abolish capitalism, overthrow the State (nonvio-
lently)? There had been a Slovak Benedictine priest accompanying me the day
before to the headquarters of the newly formed Steelworkers Union. He had
been visiting the men in hospital, wounded by the goon squads hired by the
steel magnates, indirectly of course. He had visited their families—there was
no war on poverty then—and collected clothes for their children. After his
visit with me he was transferred to a house of the order in Denver.

It was John Cort who wrote that class war headline. "Cops murder 10 pickets in Chi Strike." He is now head of a poverty program in Mass. He was head
of the Peace Corps in the Philippines, labor organizer of newspaper guild,
arbitrator, editor, ran for office once and gave up politics at once.

He was a graduate of Harvard when he came to us, had become a convert,
God knows how or why, it is always a mystery, and came to us after hearing
me speak. He worked with us in N.Y. when we were running our house of
hospitality on Mott St., shared a fifth floor tenement dormitory with striking
seamen, out of work longshoremen, teamsters, gandy dancers, linemen, all of
whom had lost their identity when they landed on the bottom of the Bowery,
the Skid Row, and were not only bums, derelicts, freeloaders, who would not
work if they had the chance, but would drink the clothes off their backs and
steal, cheat, lie and perform every abomination for the price of a drink. Or so
they were generally regarded. The unworthy poor, the hopeless cases. But to
John they were other Christs. His compassion transfigured them. Sometimes
he groaned at the thought that he was helping run a flophouse instead of
organizing labor for a better life. But he actually had a wide experience with
us. It was postgraduate work.

Neither he nor many other young men who worked with us really agreed
with the extremist stands of the CW. They would not be considered pacifists
now, but selective c.o.'s if they were of the age to be c.o.'s. How many there
have been, these young men—the successful, the honored, the illustrious
ones: Robert Ludlow, Michael Harrington, John Cogley, Tom Sullivan, Gerry

Griffin, Joe Zarrella, Dwight Larrowe, Chas Butterworth, Martin Corbin, and how many more.

And now so many in jail, in prison, all of them following their vocation, all so different, the mature and the immature, the flawed.

As to how many of these have a whole view of what the CW is trying to do—they all look to the wise and balanced program of Peter Maurin and agree there must be a new synthesis of cult, culture, and cultivation. But all differ as to emphasis. It is all very good for the monthly paper, *The Catholic Worker*, but rather confusing to Holy Mother State in an approaching trial. It will come to that, I expect, and maybe even courts, imprisonment, confiscation, suppression, and the end of the movement. All the more reason for me to keep on writing this most rambling account which is the only way one can write in a busy life. I am an occupied person, and my life is full indeed. I am a pilgrim in this world and a stranger. I hate the world and I love it, because God made it and found it good, and He so loved it He gave His only begotten son. And I love people because they are His and there is some reflection of Him in all of them.

Yes, we were left $55,000. It took more than a year of investigating to prove to Federal Income tax people that we could not be considered tax exempt. The deceased's lawyers had to pay the tax under pressure and are now appealing the case, to force the State to return the $30,000 tax to the 5 legatees for whom the deceased intended the money to go. I do not know whether the 4 other recipients of this windfall are involved or have protested at their association with us. Our lawyer, a member of the Association of Catholic Trade Unionists which John Cort founded with several other union members back in '37, says no. They are too rich to bother. They need the money too little. They are too sure of the charity of the faithful keeping them going. So he says. But with revolution on the way, they should not be too sure. The Church is too respected, too tied up with the State not to suffer for it.

June[299]

Talked to Fr. David Duran of Corcoran California, who said the Mass for Robert Kennedy, which began the meeting last night, the first anniversary of his assassination. I read the epistle, "The life of the just are in the hands of God and the torment of malice shall not touch them. In the sight of the unwise they seemed to die but they are at peace."

The memorial eulogy was by Paul Schrade, regional director of UAW who was one of the others who were shot with Kennedy, he the most seriously. Took 3 priests to distribute the Communion while all sang. De Colores began

---

299  See "On Pilgrimage," June 1969.

the Mass. O Maria was communion hymn and Nosotros Venceremos concluded it. Bread was blessed and distributed after the Mass, each breaking off a piece, and passing it on to his neighbor.

After the Mass, there were many introductions and many speakers, with 3 bus loads of Canadian labor leaders from all over Canada, bringing greetings. Banners and greetings hung about the Filipino Hall where the Mass and meeting were held.

"Taste and see how good the Lord is." And "I am the Bread of Life," were the two long colorful banners hanging on either side of the altar.

Larry Itliong and Cesar [Chavez] chaired the meeting, and Juanita Brown, who with her husband is in charge of the worldwide boycott of grapes, was the interpreter. She is a beautiful young woman and with lively charm in her translations brought out the best in all the speeches.

The best part of my being called to speak was the view of the packed hall, with Filipinos and Mexicans standing all around, and there they stood for 4 solid hours, not moving except to applaud—a rhythmic applause which increased in tempo to a crescendo and was accompanied by a stamping of feet and shouts of *VIVA!* which shook the hall and then died down just as quickly as it had flared up.

June 17

Went to Dr. Moscow and had all 7 teeth removed. He gave me what he called "analgesic," a gas which he said was tranquilizing and even euphoric. I felt no needles and the extractions did not bother me, tho it seemed as tho he were breaking down a stone wall.

June 27

Dentist, N.Y. stitches out.

Mark Silverman came to see about an apartment for [grape] boycott leaders. We found one at same building with Little Brothers. $61 a month. We will pay it. Reading *New Yorker* profile of Chavez.

July 9 [1969?]

We certainly live in no ivory tower. If there are any problems that our readers write to us about, we have them too. What is hard is that they envision us as a beloved community, a group of Christians. Like the early Christians, so devoted, so peaceful, that people can point to us and say, "See how they love one another."

I remember two instances when friends have come for a long visit and have said that our farms, our houses, were not at all as they thought to find them from the way we write in the Catholic Worker. One young woman added, "It is even better than I hoped for." The other thought that we idealized the surroundings too much, and were surprised to find such poverty and destitution around us. Such as in the Harrisburg house which was in a solidly black neighborhood where some of the houses still had outhouses in the rear, and no running water so that the tenants had to go to the firehouse to get them to turn on the hydrants at certain times during the day so that they could get water. (This was in the Forties.)

As I write, I suddenly remember an architect who came to visit us on a Sunday at the Peter Maurin Farm and was scandalized at the good Sunday dinner we sat down to. He ate it and enjoyed it, but as he left, he commented on the fact that we lived very well, far better than he expected.

I am moved to ruminate on these things upon my return from a two-months trip to be overwhelmed by complaints of the old for the young, and the young for the old, in two of our communities. The complaint of the old is that the young have been caught smoking "pot" and going on "trips" with LSD, not to speak of a few beer parties and loud singing and shouting at all hours of the night. I take it that the acid parties are quiet. City and country, the story is the same. Each accused the other.

It is summer time and I do not mind asking people to leave us. Some go without being asked. Mutual suspicion leads to an atmosphere of silence and hospitality, some of which of course is directed to me. Where is our vaunted hospitality? Where, indeed, is our religion? Was not Christ Himself surrounded by publicans and sinners, did they not feel attracted to Him? And did He not say, Judge not? "Why are you seeing the mote in your brothers' eye and paying no attention to the beam in your own?"

In the bitterness of my heart I can only say that He was not supporting them, providing a place for them to hang about and pervert others. He Himself had no place to lay His head. "The foxes have holes and the birds of the air their nests, but the Son of Man has no place to lay His head."

While I was at Mass this morning I remembered the story in the Old Testament, where Abraham stood before the Lord: "Suppose there are fifty righteous within the city. Wilt thou then destroy the place and not spare it for the fifty righteous who are in it... O let not the Lord be angry, and I will speak again but this once. Suppose ten are found there?" He answered, "For the sake of the ten I will not destroy it." And the Lord went his way, when he had finished speaking to Abraham.

But the story goes on to tell how the city, all the cities thereabouts were destroyed by fire, but Lot and his two daughters were saved. The sons-in-law who scoffed and remained, and the wife who looked back, were also destroyed. I started to think of this story and related it to our household not because of the just men to be found there, but because of the poor and the suffering and the mentally afflicted who can scarcely be held responsible. There are so many, epileptics, hernia cases, those out of mental institutions, besides the children, and the aged. Right now there are the seriously ill, and those who have endured cancer operations and in one case an operation for tumor on the brain.

Will He not save the city for the sake of these?

But certainly the life of Lot and his two daughters, living in a cave, is not anything to look to nor to understand. There too is incest and drunkenness.

One had better not try to seek comfort in this way, but to find comfort instead in binding the words of Jesus to our hearts. "Judge not," and try to cultivate a holy indifference as to what is happening and what is going to happen. Our stand is clear, both by example and by the words we have not been able to prevent, we set our faces against these disorders that are around us, and we profess with our [prayers] our need to seek guidance and help when we go to daily Mass and Communion, and turn again at seven in the evening to rosary and Compline. Without prayer we could not continue. As breath is to the body, prayer is to the soul. Without it we are smothered by the cares of this place, which seems sometimes like a camp of refugees.

I remember too, for my comfort, the words of a German doctor, who had somehow escaped from Germany after imprisonment by the Nazis, who after coming to treat a few of our old alcoholic women said, "The only thing you can really do for them is to make them happy." I guess the only way to do that is to strive to be happy and at peace oneself, remembering that lovely phrase of Ruskin, "the duty of delight."

No Date

Mass this morning at eight-fifteen and as usual there were only the dozen very old Italian women who have taken to greeting me with much warmth when I go to that Mass instead of the 5:15 in the afternoon. Perhaps it is the kiss of peace which has done it. The young priest, Fr. Dillon, comes down from the altar and clasps the hands of each one of us, smiling and we in turn turn to each other and clasp hands. Only at this morning Mass there is a variation, it is in the small chapel and the room is so small it is easy for each woman to touch all the others, not just one next in the pew or behind them. It was all very heart warming.

We are reading in the book of Genesis in the epistles, and this morning it was about the Fall. There in the garden of paradise was the tree of the knowledge of good and evil and the tree of life. There are two accounts, in chapters two and three, and the first account mentions the two trees. It reminded me of a story Helene Iswolsky began her lecture to us which was about Tolstoy, Dostoevsky, and Soloviev. She said that there as an old Russian saying that in a field where poison grew there was always to be found the antidote. And here it was again. The fruit of the tree of the knowledge of good and evil, was offset by the tree of life. They ate of the fruit of the first tree, but already (there is no time with God) there was the tree of life and when we eat of that tree we are healed. That tree is Christ.

I was saddened last week when a former nun told me she was tired of going to Mass daily. She had been doing that for fourteen years, and no longer felt it necessary. So much routine.

One could only point out that breathing was routine, and eating was routine, and many a time we had no appetite, food even seemed disgusting to us. We go to eat of this fruit of the tree of life because Jesus told us to. "Do this in remembrance of me." When we take to heart literally the humanity of Jesus as well as his divinity, and remember how he died for us, laid down his life for us, took upon himself our sins, then we should simply obey his commands. He took upon himself our humanity that we might share in his divinity. We are nourished by his flesh that we may grow to be other Christs. I believe this literally, just as I believe the child is nourished by the milk from his mother's breast.

Besides, man's first duty is to praise God, to adore him, to thank him. Even the unbeliever can say, O God, if there is a God, have mercy on me, or us. And how can we do this adequately except through his son. When we have received Communion, then it is Christ himself who can adequately praise and adore.

Daily I feel how constantly I fail in love, in kindness, and when I am being careful to guard my tongue, and at least *want* to love the sinner, then I find myself shrinking away in contempt. Didn't Jesus himself say that anyone who offended one of these little ones should have a millstone tied around his neck and be cast into the depths of the sea. I have not "put on Christ" so I must not, as he himself demanded, pass judgment. How hard it is.

No Date. "For Helene"

Of course the church is corrupt! "But this corruption must put on incorruption," St. Paul says, so I rejoice as I have in my short lifetime seen renewals going on, or read of them, and see the excitement, the joy of this sense of renewal. Certainly I knew when I became a Catholic that the church was a human institution and at first I had a sense of my betrayal of the working class, of the poor and oppressed for whom I had a romantic love and desire to serve. But just as I in my youth sought them out, lived in their slums and felt at home, so the Lord was seeking me out and I could not resist Him. And I found Him in the Church, in the Sacraments, life-giving and strength-giving, in spite of the American flag in the sanctuary, the boring sermons, the incomprehensible and mumbled Latin, the Sunday Catholic, the wide gulf between clergy and laity, even the contempt for the laity which I often felt, and even heard expressed, the down-grading of marriage by religious.

"The sexual act itself is a sacrament," I said once to a seaman who had expressed surprise at the chastity of a fellow member of our community. "I've heard it called many things," he said, "but never that," he commented.

How much criticism I could have written over the years of Church, priests, religious and laity too. They were a world apart from the life I had lived up thru my first 25 years.

But I read the lives of the saints, and knew that the renewal they brought—over and over, the St. Benedicts, St. Francis, St. Dominic, St. Vincent de Paul, St. Isaac Jogues, etc., etc., etc.—was not just a thing of the past but was going on, over and over.

In the labor movement there were all the unsung and unknown "saints" who had suffered and died pursuing justice for their fellows (the just man was the holy man in scripture, and the "holy" man is a "whole" man and strives for the kind of life for all where it is easier to be good).

I saw the cross all around me in the failures, the sufferings of those strikers, and how the seed dying bore much fruit, and so I had faith in man, too, and his capacities as well as in God whose image we are. [*unfinished*]

## July 15

Letters all day. To dentist at four and he carved off those bumps in jaw—6 of them. He is skillful with the needle and chisel but his helper this time was not so with the cold spray in mouth.

## July 22

I went to church last Sunday at Croton—Holy Name of Mary Church—and the old pastor being sick we had a vigorous sermon by a young, or perhaps middle-aged, priest who spoke on both epistle and gospel. Everything I read and hear recently accents the work of the Holy Spirit. "Whosoever are led by the Spirit of God, they are the sons of God... The Spirit himself giveth testimony to our spirit, that we are the sons of God."

It was so rich a sermon, I cannot remember how he linked it all up but he brought out my favorite themes. "Where sin abounds, there grace did more abound."

Adam fell, mankind went astray, but Jesus Christ was born and we are the richer by that Fall. What a great mystery. The worst has already happened and been repaired (Julian). What great good can come from the present technology so slanted to destruction rather than life, poison gas, air pollution, nuclear power? Who knows. "Do not fear, I am with you always."

The evangelization of the earth? Will this war perhaps bring us closer to an understanding of Buddhism, Hinduism? All nature, all the world seems to be groaning in this new birth, this new era, this *aggiornamento*. "Incarnations are bloody," Ed Willock once wrote. Wish we could find that quote.

August 16

Story in *Times* about Rock Festival at Bethel [*Woodstock*], most favorable. "A well-behaved half million young people." All farm teenagers went.

Sunday, August 17

Mass at Holy Name of Mary in Croton. Hard to sleep with my new teeth, irritating. Mary Callanan says "Keep them in, keep them in." So I'm doing it.

August 18. Tivoli

Mary, Maggie, Martha, Adrian and all the other teenagers back from Rock Festival. They had had weekend of rain. Sounded like a nightmare to me.

August 19

Having them at least under one roof—the hordes of them; it means they are not at bars, hangouts, etc. But movies, late movies, open air movies, devour their substance...

A problem. If the Lord wishes us to continue this way, we will. Anyway, we will start trying to sell the place and get smaller. The squatters are more of a problem than the young.

September 2

Dreamed of [my brother] Donald last night as tho he were still alive. He was in a motor boat. We were on the water but not with him.

Night before I thought of him, how he died. His indigestion. My own caused by Jeannette's apple pie late at night. Dreamed of Stanley, a room full of people.

September 14

Last week finished 1ˢᵗ volume of Orwell's notebooks edited by his wife Sonya and another letters, book reviews. Many on the Spanish Civil War. He was
a subsistence gardener, and for years lived by running a little store, profits
from which paid his rent. When you have done wrong, go out and plant a
tree, he wrote. Must find exact quote.

September 15

Bob Fitch—living on Pete Seeger's Clearwater—photographer, visited.[300]
He had pictures of Chavez and M.L. King. He spoke with deep interest in
Ralph Abernathy whose phone he gave me in Atlanta. Great faith in his abil-
ity. Also Andy Young.

No Date

Reading Documents of Vatican II. Vast erudition, references in footnotes,
not only to other documents but to Scripture, to Fathers of Church, Acts of
the Apostles, etc., etc. Fascinating reading—presaging many directives, many
problems, such as authority and freedom—we are heady with freedom, in-
toxicated with the fresh air of the *aggiornamento*—but love solves many of
these problems, and also the very circumstances of our lives, the situations
we are put into because we exercise that very freedom to do, to act. We go on
learning every day of our lives.

Take the problem of our Catholic Worker family for instance. It seems always to be growing. We are, to use the words of a Council document, "members of an earthly city who have a call to form the family of God's children
during the present history of the human race."

October 1

Ann Upshure [*Peacemaker*] visiting. She is 80—full of vigor, a joy to have
around. (I'll never forget how a few years ago at PM farm she kicked off her
shoes and danced to parts of the 9ᵗʰ Symphony. She reminds one of a D.H.
Lawrence heroine, perhaps one of the Women in Love. She will always be in
love with life.

Peggy [Baird] Conklin too, enjoying each day—her flowers, her cats, her
books, the company that drops in to see her.

To list them all. In keeping a notebook it is good to look back on in moments of suffering when the Cross seems unendurable.

---

300  Bob Fitch, a "movement" photographer, took a number of famous photographs of Dorothy Day.

Reggie is gone, taking every tool, a truckload, to help Skippy. There is more left behind, he says, but it may be a junk pile he accumulated over the years. Stanley says people come to CW with a shopping bag and leave with 3 truck loads. He outdid them all.

After his departure he left a legacy of a stream of wild visitors who tried to take over. They brought trailers and trucks. Marge and Stanley valiantly dissuaded them.

Off-scouring of all.

The dung applied to barren fig tree. That is us.

No Date

The kind of controversy going on in the Church today is certainly resulting in "clarification of thought," to use a cliché which P.M. did not hesitate to use as a prime necessity in any program of action. "Wisdom is the most active of any active thing." Mortimer Adler quoted this one.

Authority and freedom, man and the State, war and peace on the home front as well as abroad. These are great issues today and include the problems of poverty and race relations.

My concern is that the controversy be carried on without violence.

To me nonviolence is the all-important problem or virtue to be nourished and studied and cultivated and my reading lately of articles by Stan Windass has brought me much light and joy.

"Language can as validly be used to repel threats as to assert dominance as can fists and guns," he writes in a recent Pax bulletin from England. "Judge not that ye be not judged," is the title of the excerpt and is part of "A Blow for Peace," one of a Where We Stand Series published by Darton, Longman and Todd. The ideas in this have dominated my thinking for the last six months.

October 13

Reading Stan Windass, these days, my only aid when I worry about Tamar and the children and my own struggles over judging. Merton's *Contemplation*, new book.

October 15. Moratorium[301]

I went to UN with Bob Steed and walked to Cathedral. Enormous peaceful crowds. Candlelight. Rabbis, priests, ministers. Legs aching and sciatica worse.

---

301 The October Moratorium was a day of nationwide anti-war protests. It was followed in November by another, larger demonstration.

October 18

Jeff and his friend played at Bard tonight and Peggy and Emily went in tattered finery—as tattered as they were. The mad search for distraction and pleasure—movies each night, or a lecture.

But if saved from depression or alcoholism? It seems sense of guilt at not working and praying postpones the cure. Acedia even if one works. Walking for recreation. Nature tours at farm. Very good.

October 19

Mass at ten. Sermon on eschatology in science and religion. The world will come to an end. The fear of the young. A good sermon but ending with condemnation and ill concealed disgust at the youth "orgy of sex and drugs" at Bethel. No compassion for the young.

[October 1969]

I have fallen in love many a time in the fall of the year. I mean those times when body and soul are revived, and in the keen clear air of autumn after a hot exhausting summer, I felt new strength to see, to "know" clearly, and to love, to look upon my neighbor and to love. Almost to be taken out of myself. I do not mean being in love with a particular person. I mean that quality of in-loveness that may brush like a sweet fragrance, a sound faintly heard, a sense of the beauty of one particular human being, or even one aspect of life. It may be an intuition of immortality, of the glory of God, of His Presence in the world. But it is almost impossible to put into words. The point is that it is general rather than particular, tho it may come as a reminder, this flash of understanding, of recognition, with the reading of a particular book, or hearing some strain of music.

It is tied up in some way also with the sense of hope, and an understanding of hope. How can we live without it, as a supernatural virtue, "hoping against hope," during this dark period of violence and suffering throughout the world?

I am bold in trying to express the inexpressible, to write of happiness, even of Joy that comes, regardless of age, color, or condition of servitude to us all. Regardless of failures, regardless even of the sufferings of others. If we did not have this hope, this joy, this love, how could we help others? How could we have the strength to hold on to them, to hold them up when they are drowning in sorrow, suffocating in blackness, almost letting go of life, life which we know with a sure knowledge is precious, which is something to hold to, be grateful for, to reverence.

This is the point of war protests, of a strong faith in the doctrine of nonviolence, the evidence of its continuing efficacy throughout the world.

It is the spiritual weapon of the little ones, the weak, the powerless, the poor.
In some obscure way, an inarticulate way, the young have grasped this. They
are not listened to, they have not the words. The few are trying to express it,
the Dave Dellingers, the Eugene McCarthys. It is enough for the young that
these men are on that platform trying to codify this newfound faith in nonviolence, betrayed over and over by those who lose faith and, inspired by the
success of a Castro and the suffering and failure of a Che Guevara and Camilo
Torres, they want to lay down their lives (always *that* is expressed, rather than
being the instrument of taking the lives of others). No, in the young—that
hope is expressed, that fearlessness in the face of those who discourage, who
point out the futility, the unsuccess.

Three experiences this month brought me this joy in the continuing nonviolent struggle, not to say revolution.

One was the Moratorium. "We have had enough of war."

Secondly, the reading of Solzhenitsyn in the *Cancer Ward*, for instance, and
the consciousness that on the other side of the world the struggle is going on
in spite of the fact that Solz. has already suffered 12 years imprisonment in
Soviet Russia for his thought and writings, and is liable to suffer more.

And third, the Pentecostal prayer meeting I attended at Ann Arbor, where I
glimpsed what "eye hath not seen, nor ear heard." Grow in spiritual life—St.
Thomas—go forward, or backward. No standing still.

Meditation: From this day on I am going to ask for the Holy Spirit and
wait. I will be growing, of this I am sure. Maybe it won't come until the moment I die.

But how wonderful if we could be "surprised by joy," to use the title of C.S.
Lewis's book. I have heard of witnesses who said, "When he or she died, at
that moment a look of surprise" came over their faces, "surprised joy which
was wonderful to behold."

At any rate, we are told to ask by Jesus, and so tenderly—not just ask and
you will receive. But, "if you ask for bread will he give you a stone, or a fish,
a serpent?"

November 1. All Saints Day
5:30 Mass. Beautiful weather. Vivian Gornick, *Village Voice*.
Forster called.

November 2

Mass 10 a.m. Rainy and raw. Finished *Cancer Ward*, Solzhenitsyn, started *First Circle*. "This then is perfect joy."

Read Merton on ecumenism. Refers to Taize eliminating vows. Monks on land, foresters, game wardens, ecologists, farmers.

November 10

Reading Raissa Maritain, children's book on St. Thomas. "In the greatest dangers he remained calm, making the sign of the Cross, and saying, 'God came in the flesh, God died for us.'"

November 13

As a result of the *Village Voice* article, an editor of Deus-Newman books wants a meditation book from me. "The Dailiness of Grace," struck him. So Stanley is doing it and signing the contract. There will be $500 down payment, half to Tamar. He is doing all the clerical work, and choosing. Something I could not do.[302]

Carmen Mathews liked the picture in the *[Village Voice]*. No one else did. Homefolks interpret it as harsh.

December 12

I spoke at the meeting about Bill Gauchat's miracle and Mrs. Donald Demarest's, his healing of cancer and her child's of polio. Then on to Peter's 3rd step in a program, to the land. A good audience and more and more are interested in community. Some left their names to be kept in touch with. One, a wife of a minister, Lutheran, bored with life and husband and children. She irritated me. God forgive me. I'm full of class war with people like her and Clara. They have so much, are selfish.

December 13

More of the same. How lacking in sympathy and loving-kindness I am. But to hear again of two mothers of three, ready to leave their children and go away with other men than their husbands. They know so little about love. The fragility of it, how it can evaporate, turn to bitterness. And how hard for the children in such a confusion of parents.

December 25. Perkinsville

A.J. Lacey called. 9 turkeys contributed to CW. Fr. Berrigan sent a young man, "very gentle," a poet.

---

302 Dorothy Day, *Meditations*, ed. by Stanley Vishnewski (New York: Paulist, 1970).

Listening to Handel's "Messiah" while Bobo howls. Clouding up, another storm on the way. Mass last night at midnight, again today and I am deprived. Isaiah 38: "In peace is my bitterness most bitter."

December 26. Snow sleet

Truce violated 80 times in Vietnam.

Eric called 9 a.m. at Kennedy airport. Last flight in. It is now 7 a.m. Everyone went to bed at 2 and Eric and David and friend arrived and great excitement.

December 27

All cars are immobilized. So now Eric and 4 cronies are shut in his room drinking beer and Jim looks lost and desolate. Also the girls. "Nothing to do, no place to go, no milk in the home."

# PART V

# THE SEVENTIES

With the 1970s Dorothy's travels expanded to take in a wider circuit, including Russia, Ireland, and an around-the world trip with stops in Australia, India, and Tanzania. She remained vitally engaged in the struggles of her time—first standing down a threat from the Internal Revenue Service over her refusal to pay federal incomes taxes, and then, at the age of 75, being arrested for the final time after picketing with the United Farmworkers in California.

A heart attack in 1976 finally curtailed her travels. She was steadily slowing down, letting go, increasingly content to let the "young people" take on responsibility for the paper and the houses of hospitality. Still, there were major projects. With help from the Trappists at the Abbey of the Genesee, she bought an old music school on East Third Street which served, after refurbishing, as a shelter for homeless women. With the closing of the farm in Tivoli, Maryhouse would become her final resting stop.

She marked the passing of old friends and comrades, from Ammon Hennacy to Stanley Vishnewski (one of the original and most loyal of Catholic Workers). But young people continued to take up the work. She was delighted to see renewed interest in decentralization, ecology, and other aspects of Peter Maurin's "Green Revolution." After the protests of the 1960s, she delighted in this constructive work of building "a new society within the shell of the old."

From her window on the second floor of Maryhouse she surveyed the activities in the world beyond. Though her writings in the paper were increasingly confined to short snatches from her daily log she spent much time recollecting the friends and books that had influenced her in her youth. She even contemplated writing a final book that would go over her life one more time, recalling the events and incidents that had turned her heart to God.

# 1970

Jan 14. Kansas City

This a.m. woke at 6:30. Prayed first 15 psalms, after each psalm reciting, "Eternal Rest grant unto them." Thinking of my immediate dead as well as Biafra, Vietnam, Israeli, Arab, and then suddenly the soul of the woman who left us $50,000 and others who have left us money ($500 recently because of our work against conscription and war).

*News of Ammon Hennacy's sudden death on January 14 at the age of 76 came as a terrible surprise. Writing of Ammon in the CW, Dorothy wrote: "He literally would have liked to give his life for the obliteration of wars and all injustice from the face of the earth. He would have welcomed being shot as Joe Hill was, that labor martyr for whom he named his House of Hospitality in Salt Lake City. But Ammon's death was a triumph just the same. His first heart attack came to him on the picket line on his way to the Federal Court Building in Salt Lake City. He died suddenly a week later... He died protesting the execution of two of the least of God's children." (February 1970)*

Jan 15

Joan [Thomas, *Ammon Hennacy's wife*] telephoned—Ammon died yesterday. Heart attack. Picketing, fasting, he weakened his heart. Autopsy showed his heart's collapse. On plane now, Frontier airline—K.C. to Lincoln, Nebraska to Denver, to Grand Junction, to Salt Lake, 10:30-4:30.

No one at airport. Joan distraught. I took a cab away out high above downtown section and went to an address given me. No one home, kept cab waiting. Got address of mortuary from children of the house, and went from the beautiful background of snowy mountains downtown again. There was a great group there.

Jan 20

It was the day after we went to press in N.Y. that Ammon died. Joan did not notify us until the next a.m.

Fr. Kaiser said the funeral Mass.

Msgr. MacDougall from the Cathedral telephoned me a few days later and told me Fr. Winteret, the chaplain of Holy Cross hospital, had talked often with Ammon during his week in the hospital and had had a long talk with him the night before his death.

I did not ask and he did not volunteer what they talked about. But both Msgr. McDougall and Fr. Winteret too called me later to tell me A. had received the last rites of the church while he was still alive, surrounded by nurses and doctors, "and the sense of hearing is the last one to leave," Father Winteret said.

Ammon had collapsed on the picket line the week before, and was taken to Holy Cross hospital. We were not notified until Tues morning by letter, which was reassuring, so when a telephone call came two days later... The funeral followed twenty-four hours after the call so none of Ammon's out-of-town friends could attend. However, his first wife, his two daughters, and their husbands did arrive and I was happy to have a little visit with them.

Ammon died as he had lived, collapsing on the picket line after climbing the long hill to the capital building. He was picketing in protest of the impending execution of two men who were to be put to death by hanging or shooting on Feb 5. There is a third choice—by decapitation. Mormon law forbids the electric chair or gas because they believe blood must be poured out in atonement

Ammon had spent a lifetime upholding the sacredness of life, opposing all wars. The CW printed the story of his imprisonment during the First WW which included 9 months in solitary confinement in Atlanta Penitentiary. It was there he read the Bible and "saw so great a light that it blinded him," as one priest not too sympathetic to Ammon said to me later.

Feb 18

Finally last night wrote about Ammon for the Feb CW.[303] It was very hard to do—his attitude towards religion and the institution of the church. I felt I had to be truthful and face up to what always hurt me in Ammon—his deep distrust of the church as being on the side of the State, and his contempt for priests. He could never speak of them without the prefix f—g. All this went well with the Protestants with whom he felt always at home. He was baptized a Baptist and accepted conditional baptism and confirmation in the Catholic Church, but his marriage "out of the Church" lost him the friendship of Fa-

---

303 "Ammon Hennacy—'Non-Church' Christian," February 1970. "One of Ammon's favorite quotations from Scripture was: 'Let him who is without sin cast the first stone.' But I must admit that Ammon was a great one to judge when it came to priests and bishops and his words were coarse on many an occasion, so that it was hurtful to me to hear him, loving the church as I do. But there's that love-hate business in all of us, and Ammon wanted so much to see priests and bishops and popes stand out strong and courageous against the sins and the horrors and the cruelty of the powers of this world. But we cannot judge him, knowing so well his own strong and courageous will to fight the corruption of the world around him."

ther Casey, who could not forget J's past history. It is a male world and just as men will stick by each other, as Fr. C did at first with Ammon, so the priest sticks by the priest.

I spent days trying to write about Ammon for this memorial edition of *The Catholic Worker* and do not feel now at all satisfied.

As Hans always says after cooking for a big crowd at the farm, "It's the best I could do—I did the best I could," shrugging off the praise which nevertheless delighted him. How we all need it.

For how many days now we have been waiting on the jury's verdict in the Conspiracy case in Chicago, and how shocking a trial that has been.[304]

First the chaining and gagging of [Black Panther leader] Bobby Seale to his chair in the courtroom and finally his sentence of six years for contempt of court. How terrible a situation we are all in with respect to the black. What a breakdown of all order and how helpless Judge [Julius] Hoffman showed himself in the face of the violence and contempt of Bobby Seale. The judge from the beginning showed himself not impartial but from every account prejudiced, fearful and contemptuous of the defendants, and they in turn returned hostility for hostility and contempt for contempt so that from all accounts the courtroom seemed charged with it.

There was no possibility of introducing an atmosphere of "love of brother," "love of enemy," into that courtroom. No good to remember "where there is no love, put love and you will find love." They were all on the rack, judge and defendants and witnesses and bystanders (it was a small courtroom). Could there ever have been a chance of mutual respect? It seems to me love and re-spect go together.

From all published accounts it was five months of deadly boredom lit up by fires of hatred and contempt again and again so that the tension grew un-bearably. The climax came finally with the judge handing down sentences of contempt to defendants and attorneys alike. Unbearably goaded, the judge was getting even.

It seems to me that all who were listening in were taking sides or in conflict themselves, trying to overcome their own wrath, and the whole procedure was tied up with the war in Vietnam—the horror of our being there, and the helplessness of the young in the face of the increased and ever increasing momentum of the State and the military.

---

304 The "Chicago 7" (or 8) conspiracy trial was one of the most unusual courtroom spectacles in American history. An unlikely assortment of pacifists (including David Dellinger), New Left radicals, Black Panthers (Bobby Seale, later removed from the case), and Yippies were charged with inciting violent protests at the Democratic Convention in 1968. The cultural and politi-cal divisions present in the courtroom reflected wider fault lines in American society.

The charges of conspiracy themselves came about after the shocking scenes in Chicago at the Democratic Convention. I have myself been at enough demonstrations, parades, marches of protest these past years to know that in all of them were groups, carrying inflammatory slogans on their signs and pigs heads and how there were always heard the shouting of four letter words which by now have lost all their meaning. I myself cringe before such words, because of the contempt and hatred they express and involving the perversion of the act of creation. To use such a word is to drag the sacred and the beautiful into the mire. The love of God for man and man for God in the Song of Songs, in the book of Hosea is compared to the love which involves both mind and soul and body, and implies an act, a physical act which results in the miracle of creation. Looked at from a natural or a supernatural aspect it is an astounding thing, and its sublimation has resulted in masterpieces of music, literature, art, and architecture. There are also the small tendernesses that are so much a part of love, of all loves, the tender love that makes so much suffering in this world endurable.

It is hard to talk of these things. What I am trying to say is that the use of the word coarsely or humorously applied to the sexual act, is calculated to enrage. There can even be said to be an element of the demonic in it.

Of course the press, the radio, the television screen, catches all the violence in word and deed and when violence in word leads to violence in deed as it did yesterday where 200 police confronted 2,000 or more demonstrators who were protesting the conspiracy trial and the Black Panthers Trial at Foley Square.

Feb 25

Ammon meeting at Community Church.

Reading Harvey Cox, *The Feast of Fools*. Good to read as Spring is breaking. We need festivity to "enlarge our experience by reliving events of the past." "Fantasy is a form of play that extends the frontiers of the future." "Together they help make man a creature who sees himself with an origin and a destiny."

We've talked of a philosophy, a theology of work. Too much.

When Peter Maurin spoke of his synthesis he envisioned dancing, singing, miming, costuming. Too much celebrating at Tivoli. Too much fantasy. Dreams of beach houses, farms on mountain tops, caves for hermits, etc.

Feb 28

Arrived in Detroit. Lou Murphy, our CW there, took me to Bon Secours Hospital. Chinese doctor took cardiogram. Another x-rays and Dr. Henderson of Grosse Pointe, internist and cardiac man said, "This is a case of heart failure," which startling words meant that water in my lungs, hardening of arteries, enlarged heart and so on were responsible for the pains in my chest and shortness of breath which makes me sit gasping for 5 minutes after I walk a block, or have to hurry, or am oppressed by haste, urgency, etc.

I say to myself, in relation to making new ventures, going on trips, etc., "Lord, I want to do your will. If you do not want this please prevent it." I used to add, "even if it takes a Mack truck." But I've quit saying that since I do believe God takes you at your word.

We used to say the Angelus before lunch and dinner at Maryfarm. We still say grace but cold soup brought about the change from involuntary to voluntary praying. (Grace is short and the unwilling can wait outside the door the moment it takes to say it.)

But as an example of asking God for something without realizing what it entailed, the prayer ending the Angelus goes: "Pour forth we beseech Thee O Lord, Thy grace into our hearts so that we to whom the message of the Incarnation was brought by an angel, may by His passion and Cross be brought to the knowledge of His Resurrection."

"Do we really know what we are asking for?" John McKeon said once. Passion and Cross.

"Do you know what you are asking for?" I asked Peggy [Baird] Cowley, who always said the grace with us, tho she was anything but "religious." "God takes us at our word."

"I do mean it," she said stoutly. (She is a tiny wisp of a thing, but I like that forthright, determined-sounding, old-fashioned word.)

Right now she sits in a wheelchair or lies in her bed surrounded by cats, plants, flowers, books, candy, wine or whisky, and is a picture of contentment. In and out of the hospital she never utters a word of complaint, a word of criticism of others. She accepted the faith which Fr. Jack English instructed her in a few years ago.

Does God mean, by my present troubles or rather illness, to indicate that I should give up the projected trip around the world, to Australia and back, projected and to be paid for by Australian priests, and the Central American one, by Fr. Leo Neudecker's invitation? I am afraid it does mean just this.

And staying home does not mean I'm sedentary. The farm at Tivoli, the house of hospitality in New York, and visits to my very dear sister nearby will mean at least closeness to home base, and the time to go on with my book, "All is Grace."

This does not mean I will not take occasional speaking engagements. This is a necessity in our work. One engagement paid for a new boiler at the farm.

A new roof is needed there too, before ceilings begin to fall down and the house to disintegrate. Of course occasional "windfalls" as Agnes, our barge captain's wife, called her $37 a month from the government, may mean the engagements won't be necessary. It is up to Him. Two mortgages to be paid off on the N.Y. house by 1972. One for $14,700 and the other for $7,250.

But here is the real reason I do enjoy traveling and speaking. Msgr. Charles Owen Rice has a school in Pittsburgh which his parish is supporting for blacks. I want to visit and learn more about it—how it is run.

There are Montessori schools now—and Neil schools (Summerhill), many in this country without Neil to guide them. In Boston 3 volunteer teachers man a free school and teach 36 children.

When I learn about these things I write and speak about them and become in a way a referral agency so that other people, other places can do these things—and trust in God and other human beings for cooperation instead of State or Foundation. If it proves itself, the aid is forthcoming and State and Church are instructed as well as enabled to aid.

March 7

I come back to mail about meetings (Australia, Central America). But Jim Milord's letter is a stab in the heart—the bitterness, hatred of the Church poured out, and to think that this venom has been piling up in him—this poison he is spewing out, from some terrible wound. It is appalling when to me my faith, my feeling that the Church is Christ on earth, is my joy, my delight, my solace.

I feel when I receive such a letter as tho I were reeling under heavy blows. And appalling to have cast away something he has had all his life, which sustained him in all his work, his marriage, his children. I cannot bear to read his reflections on the Indian situation because it drains me of courage. I feel so unutterably alone when I see people like Ammon dying "outside the faith," rejecting the sacraments which Christ left us which do so strengthen and sustain us, which so sweeten the way.

"What have I on earth but Thee and what do I desire in Heaven beside Thee?"

"Hope then in God for He is still the health of thy confidence and thy God."

It is of course depressing to come back from my week in Detroit and Boston, where Judy, Mary, and others have lost or (for the time being have rejected) the faith. It is of course a temptation to abandon work—my own conviction that one must cry out constantly against man-made human misery and injustice and to cry out too against all war—class war as well as the war in Vietnam, the Arab-Israeli war.

God have mercy—

Christ have mercy—

God have mercy.

"I shall not die but live and declare the works of the Lord."

### April 21

Left Tivoli farm at 9:30 and arrived at First St. at 12:30. Drove Ramon Rodriguez in. He told me about the life of [Puerto Rican Nationalist] Lolita Lebron, mother of two children, one of whom, a little boy, was drowned. Her brother turned state's witness after the shooting into the Senate (the House) in 1954. Three men injured, one seriously.

She shot at the ceiling, one testified. Her brother said she aimed at the men on the floor. She got 50 or 75 years. She has been in prison since 1954. She leads there at Alderson the life of a religious. We have been writing to each other for some years, and I am planning to go visit her.

### April 22

All afternoon with Pat Jordan getting ready for press tomorrow. We are early for once; 12 pages. Spring appeal. Chris [Montesano's] draft statement. Ammon's [essay on John] Woolman on front page.

### May 26. St. Philip Neri's day

At Tivoli. Last week Ron and Eliz Gessner left. No word from them. A terrible restlessness in people today, fleeing from place to place. I'm afraid Tamar gets bitter at the young couples and larger families living off the CW and she is always so concerned for money for food. But I would not have her living off the CW, money sent for the poor.

Tamar is rich in that she has a house and 25 acres and all the family are in good health. It was beautiful weather while I was there, she was putting her garden in—had peas, potatoes, cabbage, carrots, beets, lettuces and onions all planted. I only hope the deluge of rain we have had does not wash away the garden here as there.

"Think of it—we are made for heaven and yet we have to be perfect before we get there. It is too hard," Pat Rusk was saying. "I don't believe what Catherine of Siena said, 'All the way to heaven is heaven.'"

## June 3

This afternoon Frank Donovan[305] treated Pat and me to seats for "Man of La Mancha"—a two-hour entertainment.

## June 5

Last night Gordon Zahn spoke on army chaplains. A well-ordered, understanding, reasonable talk. He is a true pacifist, and is reaching people who have never thought about morality in war. Men must have the chaplains he says, but the chaplains must know the soldiers' rights, what the Council, the popes, the bishops have taught about c.o.'s so they, the chaplains, can help a man to gain his right as c.o.

## June 8. Tivoli

All this a.m. sat in sun, basking in the beauty of the river. Always too much casual conversation, so I can neither read nor write when I set out. It is Stanley's birthday and I hope we will have strawberry shortcake for him. We are giving him a fan for his room, where he works, because it is very hot in summer.

Story of Saphira and Ananias was read tonight in the chapel after Compline—a puzzling story. But I connected it with the lack of honesty of us all, our cheating, withholding—calling oneself a pacifist—or a Christian, without a right to it. We are in fact violent people, lacking in courage, quite willing to accept the help of police if we need it. More humility needed. We are not yet nonviolent in the true sense. The bishops endorsing the idea of selective conscientious objection shows them wiser than me, trying honestly to give guidance.

As I write about people here, it is a prayer. Jean Goldstone, our "engineer," is dying in Bellevue. A great soul. Very Jewish, very sad at having accomplished so little (as he thought). While Ruth Collins was getting our headquarters at 36 East First rebuilt from the shell it was, he went there every day to be on hand to check contractors, electricians, plumbers, deliveries, etc. A most faithful friend to the CW.

Jesus, Mary, and Joseph, be with him in his last agony. St. Therese pray for him. I had just finished praying this before the shrine in my room at the farm, when Mike Sullivan walked in with one beautiful red rose in a glass jar for

---

305 Frank Donovan, a Bostonian with refined talents and a limitless capacity for work, was an employee of the United Parcel Service when he began volunteering at the CW in his spare time. After taking early retirement he joined the CW fulltime, serving as general office manager and, eventually, as Dorothy's primary *aide de camp*. As she wrote toward the end of her life, "The Lord has given me a son in my old age."

the statue of Therese. She will hear us, she who is spending her heaven doing good upon earth. Sometimes I feel very close to "the dear departed," as the Irish call them.

How many we have to call upon. I carry on converse with them—for instance Chesterton and Belloc. "You were a bad influence on D.H., glorifying drinking and good cheer as you did, for one who could not take it; your example meant a broken home and fatherless children and intense suffering and the frustration of noble hopes; and Eric Gill, you emphasized too much the pleasure principle, and now young people trifle with life forces and become jaded and weary and lifeless. The severity of the sex code in the New Testament on the one hand and the counter emphasis on the marriage feast to which the beatific vision is compared, if lived up to, would only exist and purify the joys of body and soul and make known the delights and desires, cleansed and purified by abstinence. "The best thing to do with the best of things is to give them up to the Lord." (And note that fleshly pleasure if not isolated from mind and spirit is not here labeled sin, but called "the best of things.")

The best of things; the taste of heaven on earth, marriage, wherein all joys are purified in the most natural and supernatural fashion, in the "nature of things," pleasure and pain going together. I've so often thought of the "dark night of the senses" which mothers go thru, bearing children, nursing and rearing them.

## June 14

Jean Goldstone died last Wednesday at Bellevue. He was 66. There will be a memorial service for him.

## June 18

Indochina conflict—that is what radio commentators call it now. Fires and fire bombings on East Side. Nihilism or indifference, both are saddening. I was ashamed yesterday at my state of discouragement. Sciatica, constant pain, makes one querulous, critical, discouraged. It is hard to start learning holy silence at 73. It would cover a multitude of sins. I always preached to myself about the necessity of the Cross, failure, pain and heartbreak as a prelude to the glorious mysteries. Peggy [Baird], dying at the farm, is an admirable example of bravery and composure. She never complains. "I did not know it would take so long," she said to me. All her motions are slow, deliberate.

She is surrounded by her beloved cats, flowers, books, and bits of candy, fruit, a bottle of wine or whisky to sip at during the day. Marge sleeps in the next room and she says at night she sometimes groans in her sleep. She has a bell and rings it when she wants her coffee in the morning.

I can never forget that it was Peg who told me with good common sense to buy that little beach bungalow rather than fritter away the money I got for the movie rights to that very bad first novel I wrote back in 1922 or thereabouts. It became for me a hermitage, a place to read and think and contemplate, and resulted in my conversion two years later.

It was she who first gave me a little statue of the Blessed Mother. There were long periods, years and years, when I lost track of Peggy. One period of twenty years, I believe it was, when she was married to a newspaper man and lived in Washington, D.C. and in Atlanta, Ga. It was after his death of a heart attack that she returned from the South to Greenwich Village and married again and got in touch with me, coming to live with the CW at Peter Maurin Farm, she and her husband, when he was out of work. On his death about seven years ago, she returned to us for good. Once when I was traveling she wrote me a letter thanking me for not "trying to convert her."

Once I noticed how she joined in the Angelus which we used to say before meals (when we were a smaller group and more like a family than a hospice). I quoted John McKeon to her, something he had once said to me. "Do you mean what you say when you repeat that prayer?" "Pour forth, we beseech Thee, O Lord, Thy grace into our hearts that, by His passion and Cross, we may be brought to the glory of His resurrection."

"God takes us at our word," I told her, this time quoting Fr. Roy. (How much we owe each other! How little originality we have, except perhaps in presenting a synthesis, in trying to apply an idea, a principle, to our own lives.)

"I really mean it," Peggy said firmly, and I rejoiced in my heart, and loved her for her words.

People have said to me, "How wonderful Peggy has you people to care for her now," but I think, how wonderful to have such an example of uncomplaining endurance, of appreciation of God's beauty, of faith in His loving kindness and mercy.

Peggy does not go in for spiritual reading. One is much more apt to find James Joyce's *Ulysses* or a detective story, or some poetry in her hands than the lives of or writings of the saints. She did not read Péguy's "God Speaks" to understand God's mercy.

How different we all are. I am sure if she read my books she would or probably did say, "It wasn't like that at all." And for her, those 15 days we spent in jail together when I was 20 and she was 28—those years on the beach, those months I stayed with her in Greenwich Village, meant something entirely different for us both. We both found our way to God thru different paths. We are each one of us unique, as Hugh of St. Victor said, and God's love for each one of us is unique. That was a revelation which came to him, he said in one of his writings. As I remember it, the soul complained to God, questioning His love for His creature. "You love everyone, and I want to be loved, I myself for myself." And God answered him in a revelation, "You are unique and my love for each one of you is unique."

I do believe in a personal God, because I too have had revelations, answers to my questions, to my prayers, and if the answer fails to come, which is usually the case because God wants us to work out our own salvation, I have that assurance God gave St. Paul and he passed on to us, "My grace is sufficient for you."

And what is grace? Participation in the divine life. And that participation means for me light and understanding and conviction, of course only occasionally, but strong enough to carry me along, to lift me up out of depression, discouragement, uncertainty, doubt.

My sister and I comfort ourselves with a line from T.S. Eliot's "Cocktail Party": "Wait," said the psychiatrist, "wait and do nothing."

My mother used to say, "When you are in the dumps, clean house, take a bath, dress up, go downtown and window-shop." Everything passes, St. Teresa of Avila says.

How beautiful a thing that Peggy found God. She announced that she wished to receive Communion with us, and Fr. John went over the creed with her—the Baltimore Catechism, which he considers is for learning, while the New Dutch Catechism is for reading. She had been christened a Presbyterian when she was born, in Babylon, L.I., so in our new ecumenical era she did not feel a repetition of the sacrament was necessary. She is no longer able to come to the chapel but Fr. Andy [Crusciel] brings her the holy bread.

June 20. Shirley Beach, L.I.

Pat [Rusk] in one of her silent moods has walked down the beach. Silence would be good—even 3 hours straight of it were not that it began, as it usually does, when I have refused one of her suggestions—this time to take two ferries and a round-about way home from our 4-hour afternoon drive. As it was we had a most interesting drive along the truck route 25. A beautiful sunset. Also a great cross of white clouds with what to me was a clear figure of a robed Christ, the face visible for a moment. The southern sky is all mother of pearl now.

More unemployment ahead is announced at every newscast today. But the dear Lord has sent us another gift, $10,000 from a reader of the CW now in a t.b. hospital. It was, he said, an inheritance he did not earn, fruit of the work of the poor, and he wished us to use it for them—our soup line, the old and the ill who live with us. It will last us thru the summer.

June 21

The antiphon for the Benedictus today is "You have heard that it was said to the ancients, 'You shall not kill,' and that whoever shall murder shall be liable to judgment."

Are killing and murder two different things?

For 20 years I have welcomed the beautiful collect on this day. It first struck me when I had an experience of healing. It was immediate and it filled me with gratitude. I say it always with great faith as to its efficacy.

Whenever there is an outburst of drinking in the house I have to keep reminding myself of the solid virtues and hard work, most of the time, of those who are offending.

Government checks, pitifully small tho they be, pay rent on the Bowery. Rents have gone up there too. The Salvation Army charges $10.50 a week, for a tiny monastic-like cell, for instance, and requires the money be paid weekly. It is a clean and orderly place. Other hotels require nightly payments of $1.50 and many are decent places. We used to patronize the Union on Hester and Bowery, and Fr. Joseph Woods, who did not hesitate to stay there (houses of hospitality are always packed to the door), said the only objectionable feature was the noise, the groans, coughings, retchings—the crying out in the night. Those sad night-hours, sleepless hours of regret, foreboding, and despair. No wonder our friends and fellow workers take to drink. St. Teresa, when she grabbed her castanets and danced said to her disapproving sisters in religion, "We must do something to make life bearable." Her most famous saying was "Life is a night spent in an uncomfortable inn."

Many of those uncomfortable inns on the Bowery are giving way to studios for artists as rents go higher and higher in the city.

July 10. Tivoli

Eric drove down from Vermont with me yesterday. How silent my grandchildren are. Yet interested, observant, still searching. Sue too. The baby Tanya is adorable. Mike Scahill, just back from Cuba cane-cutting, says Tanya was the name of Che's friend in Bolivia. Farm is so crowded—70 people—that little chance to think or work or even write herein, to put down notes of impressions.

Peggy very low. Under codeine. Utmost patience in suffering. Peggy lay there last night in a delphinium blue bed jacket, her hair combed and tied back with a ribbon, reddened finger nails, and somehow this "vanity" was not repulsive, standing as she is at the gates of death, but a testimony of her love and gratitude for life. She is doing something, accepting the ugly, hideous, repulsive business of dying with dignity, even honor. Sister Death, St. Francis would say—loving all the little things of life, kittens, flowers, the little presents of sherbet, brought to her. But she murmured to me once, "I did not know it would take so long." Dying is so hard. What a purgatory she is going thru. I pray I meet my end with the same dignity. [306]

Things I wish to write about:
1) Outhouses. Sex and elimination and life and death. De Maupassant.
2) Giving away an onion. Julie and de Ruyder. Will and rubbing Peggy's feet.
3) Interview with Chavez on community.
4) Pope John and concordances.

July 12
[Maryknoll] Bishop [James E.] Walsh released from China hospital prison, having served 12 years of 25-year sentence.

July 17
Another little ailanthus tree died. Paul [Bruno] feeds his 2 extra cats on top of the fence—they are afraid of the dogs—and they knocked over a wooden tray he had balanced on top of the fence, and it cut down the little tree. I am afraid the second one is also doomed.

*In August Dorothy undertook her most extensive pilgrimage to date—literally around the world. Traveling with Eileen Egan she went first to Australia, then Hong Kong, India, Tanzania, Rome, and England. A highlight of the trip was her visit in Calcutta with Mother Teresa, who presented her with the cross worn by the Missionaries of Charity—in effect, recognizing Dorothy as an honorary member of her Order. Her diaries are very sketchy, mostly filled with notes. She provided a more complete account of her journey in the September, October-November, and December 1970 issues of the CW.*

August 4
(I kept a travel diary which I can scarcely decipher. I try to write too much and find it unintelligible. I must try again.)

---

306 Peggy Baird died on September 23 while Dorothy was traveling abroad. She wrote more about her old friend in the October-November 1970 issue.

August 5. Honolulu

Slept well last night at expensive Holiday Inn. In the afternoon drove for an hour around Honolulu, Waikiki beach, and thru tourist and night club area—then thru older parts, and saw a beautiful palace and a banyan tree, many, many trunks, monkey pod trees, also. I would have liked to sit under that banyan tree to pray.

The old cathedral was beautiful and open on all sides, a dozen praying, a man cleaning.

Hippy communes on other islands. 50 nationalities, many languages.

August 9

It's like autumn, clear bright weather. Mass at 10. 11-4 discussion. Leaders in peace work. Ride around beautiful beaches. Surf shells polished stones.

Up at 6. Reading scripture. At night and early morning yesterday reading *Sal si Puedes* by Peter Matthiessen. A truly beautiful and inspiring book about Cesar Chavez. Today discussions on peacemaking attitudes, Eileen on Satyagraha, and I on Ammon Hennacy. What we do with our aggressions.

August 19

Up at 6. I must walk down the yellow roads with a flashlight to the little chapel where we had a requiem Mass for Peter and Ammon last evening at 5. They say the Office here, the Rosary and other prayers.

What an oasis this is, this farming commune and how Peter Maurin, peasant and teacher, must rejoice from heaven over the sight of it. A beautiful day.

August 25. Sydney

More and more one sees students thinking in terms of "honorable occupations." Earning their living by the sweat of their own brows instead of someone else's. Manual labor.

August 29. From Hong Kong to Bangkok

Singapore. One does a lot of praying on a trip like this, where the power of man is so manifest in conquering the earth and the air—when space and time mean nothing. One travels from Hong Kong to Calcutta in 4 ½ hours flight time.

But the power and the peace of God! "All that may be known of God by men lies plain before their eyes, etc." He has given them the senses to see, the mind to discern and understand, and yet how much baffles him. An aborigine, whose father comes from Afghanistan, told me of seeing the desert of Australia rolling in waves like the sea, like the surf coming in.

I thought too of typhoons, as we were directed to fasten our seatbelts because of turbulence. The power and the peace of God. Both reflected in his people.

August 30. Calcutta [India]

Mother Teresa came in their ambulance, bright blue, no springs. Over rough streets, thru slums like those of Naples, Palermo, Hong King, only multiplied by millions. Nothing gets better, only worse.

August 31

Last night Mother Teresa warned us there would be a general strike and probably violence today, so to stay in, no sightseeing.

Abdul Magid, Moslem who prepares our food came in this a.m. and told of two bombs thrown in market by CPI (M) because market not observing general strike.

Gandhi said that the change in the life of the poorest and weakest man in the village is the measure of the economic development of the country.

September 1

Mother Teresa was expecting us at 9:30. We went to children's home, clinic mother and child, feeding station, babies abandoned. Both Eileen and I talked. Then on to Brother (Father) Andrew, S.J. who went thru his novitiate in India. We talked there to the brothers, about 50 of them. Brother sang hymns for us before we left. Mother pinned a cross on my left shoulder as both sisters and brothers do.

From there to Nirmar. Kalighat district. We saw a burning ghat, ashes, then thrown in the tributary of Ganges. The real Calcutta, all Hindu. The house of the dying was full, 85 women, 75 men. In two wings. It used to be part of Temple of Kali, the pilgrim's hostel. I have seen individual cases like the ones there, Agnes, Mr. Breen, etc., with us, but never so many. All sidewalk cases of the 24,000 and more cases, 11,700 have lived to be discarded. To go to this hostel and help feed the dying is a pious act by some Hindus, also students (non-Catholic).

September 4

All day yesterday and today the streets are so flooded we cannot get out. Worst rains since 1959, 100% humidity and hard to breathe. Schools, offices, r.r. stations, airports, not functioning to any great extent.

The glow of the invisible world, so movingly described by Newman in one of his sermons, is all around us in this land of the poor, the lepers, the rickshaw drivers. The curse of colonialism is all around. Disrupted village life, trade, buying and selling, profit, made the acquisitive society.

How to remedy such evils of the past as our slave trade in North and enslavement in South? Colonialism here? Seems insoluble under present social order. "The misery of the needy and the groaning of the poor" here is worst in the world.

The violence here, from refugees from Pakistan, from students, is a crying out for recognition of the poor man, as men, as people, God's children, made in His image, whom He loved so much He gave them His only begotten son to redeem them, to share their sufferings, their humanity.

Sept 5

Up at 6:45. Prayed for an hour in the dark and thought of Deane [and her blindness].

Probably no chance in getting out until Monday. If then. This is surely the monsoon season. They wade thru water up to their hips and yet carry our umbrella! Our street is flooded even into doorways, but rickshaw men are working, an occasional high car or jeep gets thru, a few bicycles.

Sunday, Sept 6

How can one write as I did yesterday? Only blind faith, naked faith.

Sept 12. Bombay to Tanzania.

Sept 14. Dar-es-Salaam

Reading St. Francis de Sales. Resolutions: to get on with the book. I must write it at home. In midst of my own surroundings. Be more faithful to mail and visitors.

Sept 24. London

To Pulborough via Victoria Station to meet Barbara Wall and visit Donald Attwater. Donald Attwater is most happily situated in an old stone house some miles from Pulborough station. Donald has been losing his sight for the last 3 years. But he is still writing and his life of Eric Gill will be reviewed in

a later issue of the CW. He is well known for his tremendous work with Fr.
Thurston— *[Butler's] Lives of the Saints,* which is a monumental work of historical research. Peter Maurin used to say we should study history by studying
the lives of the saints. Vinoba Bhave in a recent article in *Sarvodaya* recommended that children should be taught about the lives of saints and heroes.
Penguin books include Attwater's lives of saints and lives of martyrs.

At 7 we went to War Resisters International where about 50 guests heard
me on Tanzania, U.S., and growth in working toward new social order.

**November 3** *[typed]*

I certainly cannot be accused of being a neo-Platonist. My conversion came
about over the years, through the knowledge I gained through my senses. I
was a very small child when I first held the Bible in my hands, and tasted a
little, through my eyes that read the words, the power of Scripture. I felt that I
was handling something holy. Later on Thomas à Kempis, a great mystic, but
not in much favor these days, said that the Church rested on two pillars, the
Scriptures and the Eucharist, and certainly for many years, almost for centuries, the faithful have been deprived of the Scriptures. Certainly I knew when
I was very young, perhaps seven years old, that "all that may be known of God
by men lies plain before their eyes"; indeed God himself has disclosed them.
His invisible attributes, that is to say, his everlasting power and deity, have
been visible ever since the world began, to the eye of reason, in the things he
has made. There is therefore no possible defense for their conduct; knowing
God, they have refused to honor him as God, or to render him thanks.

I owe great thanks to God that he gave me an appreciation of his beauty
so young. Certainly I thank my father who always saw to it that we lived as
near as possible to a park or beach, in all our wanderings around the country.
I remember the beach when we lived in what is now known as the Bay Ridge
section of Brooklyn. I went there with my two older brothers and I went there
alone even before I went to school. I walked through the swamp near Fort
Hamilton and remember the enormously tall grasses and the path we made
thru them to the rivulet where we caught eels.

I have never gotten over my love for the sound of water, little waves lap-
ping on the beach, retreating through the heaps of small stones and shells.
On other days there was the strong sound of breakers pounding on the beach
and the smell of the salt spray. I remember the taste of the seeds I nibbled,
the hearts of the thistle burrs which we ate, and the taste too of salt from the
shells and stones which like little animals we liked to lick. All senses were engaged, sight, sound, smell, taste, and yes touch because the feel of things gave
us sensuous delight.

I am sure that it is because the Church is so alert to Man, as body and soul, because she believes in the resurrection of the body and life ever-lasting, that I became strongly attracted to her when I began to catch glimpses of her later.

Even the garishness of her beauty appealed to me and still does. Stained glass windows, statues, flowers, and pure bees' wax candles, incense, the organ and the choir when they have them, all these appeals to the senses contribute to devotion and the sense of mystery and awe. I enjoy even the feel of a rosary between my fingers, whether it is a wooden Indian one, an amber Moslem one, or a Russian woolen one, or our own Roman Catholic variety. To finger it, to let all my distractions turn to prayers for the people I am thinking of, even these distractions come from repeating the mystery to be meditated on. Last night when we prayed the joyful mysteries, I was thinking deeply of women, and of the pregnancies of two of my grandchildren, and the women's liberation movement.

I may not believe that the Blessed Mother appeared to St. Dominic with a rosary and instructions on how to say it, but I do know that rosary beads have been common to the poor and illiterate since history began. We do not have to believe in private revelations, though some of the devotions which have grown out of them have brought us comfort at times. I affirm, however, though in jest, that I too have had revelations in my life.

When I was sixteen and went to college and got jobs as a babysitter and for a time worked, was overworked indeed, for my board and room, my feeling of being exploited was overlaid by an exultant feeling that I could indeed always, and forever while on this earth, earn my own living. Even grandmothers and great grandmothers are worth their salt, as the saying is. The other revelation came ten years later. A young man who took me out to dinner, looking at my hands, which perhaps were a bit toil-worn, announced that he could always tell a woman's age by her hands. I began to feel old. I brooded on this for a day and suddenly while reading St. Augustine, had a marvelous sense of this truth, that no matter how old one becomes there was always a possibility of an increase of knowledge, through books and people, and the world around us. It was my first sense of the meaning of the words of St. Paul, "This corruption must put on incorruption." This is the old translation, of course. But it meant a lot to me.

## November 5

Yesterday afternoon Mike Vogler and his wife came to see me. They have been working in apple orchards all summer in northern Vermont and are now on their way south to find some place to stay where his wife can have her baby in March. The cost of having children is exorbitant and I'll write more on this later. What I want to write about now is the terrible urgency young people have to live, to savor life, to be so grateful for it and to feel it is so great a good that they are willing to bring new life into the world, to take this terrible risk, not only for their own joy but for the joy of the child so that he too can be grateful for life, in spite of all the threats which hang over head. Because together with this determination to live, there is also a fear, a horror living with them always.

The two of them sat at the table in the dining room eating our good homemade bread and grape preserves, the former made by Laura and the latter by Andy, and drank the leftover coffee from breakfast, and at the same time talked of the amount of nuclear weapons stored up, each one the equal to so many tons of bombs and so on and so on. They had all the statistics of death, and the realization of what was happening in the world meant, for Mike, that he had to spend two years in prison in Arkansas rather than cooperate with this evil, to make his protest against participating in this evil. He refused induction into the armed forces and so went to jail. His sentence finished, he came out to take up life and work, and that work too had to do with life rather than destruction.

But this fearful and so complete knowledge, as they had memorized statistics, all but cast a gloom or rather did cast a momentary gloom over our meeting. I say momentary because conversations at our home are always so interrupted that no topic is completed. On this occasion other topics were natural childbirth, when to begin with doing the exercises, and whether the insistence on early practice was not just for the psychological effect, and so on. And of course I told how during the Second World War everyone urged women to have their babies at home and call in a midwife, something so impossible to do today, at least as far as the midwife is concerned. I was glad to be able to introduce them to Will and Laura and their two-year-old Johanna who was born in a big room here overlooking the river with the husband assisting and no one else knowing what was going on. The rest of us were all at Mass down under the trees which center the big lawn.

I much prefer to be participating in this kind of talk, of life, rather than death, and am inclined to feel that there is too much talk of the other.

But what attracted me so much about these young people is that they were going about the business of living, and they could not help radiating love and joy.

This morning in my reading, in a book which came in to us for review about the prayer of the spirit, the emphasis was on Jesus' prayer in the garden. He knew that he had been betrayed and that the mob were coming to take him and that the penalty for what they accused him of was to be a horrible death suspended from a cross, and he was "sweating blood." Meanwhile the three apostles he had chosen to take with him slept. Peter, James, and John, the leaders, the first indication of collegiality in the church. Thank God that an angel from heaven visited him and brought him strength. And with strength and resolution there is always joy, so mysterious is the life of the spirit. He had prayed to be delivered, "Father if it be Thy will, take this cup from me, yet not my will but Thine be done."

"Why are you sleeping?" he asked the others. "Rise and pray that you may be spared the test."

These young ones who are going to jail are not sleeping and they have a constant realization of the death that is working in the world. Their joy is that they are on the side of life.

As for me, I pray that I be ready to go to jail as they are, and since I have had to face the authorities and some very brief periods in jail some eight times, and never for more than twenty-five days, I cannot boast. My confrontation with the state will be because of a refusal to file [tax] "returns," to give any accounting to the state of my income from writing or speaking, to sign any papers as to being a non-profit organization. Aside from occasional telephone calls and a few visits there has as yet been no crisis for me.

Without the sacraments of the church, primarily the Eucharist, the Lord's Supper as it is sometimes called, I certainly do not think that I could go on. I do not always approach it from need, or with joy and thanksgiving. After thirty-eight years of almost daily communion, one can confess to a routine, but it is like a routine of taking daily food. But Jesus himself told us at that last supper, "Do this in memory of me." He didn't say daily, of course. But he said, "as often as you drink this wine and eat this bread," we would be doing it in memory of him. And this morning I rejoiced to see those words in the Gospel of St. Luke. He said, "How I have longed to eat this Passover with you before my death!" The old Douay version has it, "With desire, I have desired to eat this pasch with you before I suffer."

Desire to me always meant an intense craving, a longing, a yearning which was a joy in itself to experience.

With all my faith in his words, "This is my body, this is my blood," which was perhaps more understandable to people of that age who knew more than we do about human sacrifice, I do believe that we know Christ also in the breaking of bread with others, as the disciples at Emmaus knew him when they sat down in the inn and ate with him. At the Catholic Worker we feel it daily in the meals we serve and the meals we share. I suppose that is the reason for the long endurance of the Catholic Worker. Thirty-eight years now the paper has continued and the work goes on, and has led many others to this sharing.

# 1971

*Dorothy's diary skips from November 1970 to May 1971.*

May 9

This last month I've been in New England, Worcester, Boston, Perkinsville, Orange, Pittsfield, then Syracuse, Orwell and home thru Binghamton.

Today I wrote my On Pilgrimage column, 3,000 words. It was an all-day job. I think vitamins are helping me, also a chunk of cheese for breakfast! Sally Appleton's husband Joe Weber told me about the energy derived from that.

Frank Lonergan brought me an azalea for a mother's day gift—also cream puffs for Julia who has been sick all week.

Our ginkgo tree is planted, out in front of 36 E. First, St. Joseph House.

May 11

Elizabeth Corrigan, wife of Bishop Daniel Corrigan, visited. He has retired as dean of Rochester Colgate Divinity School and goes to Denver soon. She told of their trip to Rome. Met Fr. [Pedro] Arrupe, General of Jesuits there. He asked about the Berrigans. Bishop Corrigan praised him to the skies—said he was an inspiration. Hence the Superior General's recent visit to Danbury Federal Prison.

I was so happy to visit Mrs. Berrigan [*mother of Daniel and Philip Berrigan*] in Loretto Home in Syracuse last week. A tiring day. Got little done. Puttering about as I usually do before a trip, cleaning up my desk, taking care of a few letters. Frank Donovan, who will be on our editorial staff from now on, will take care of my mail.

June 5

Karl Meyer in jail in Chicago. His letter for June issue. He got 2 years on 2 counts, to run consecutively, and $2,000 fine [for tax resistance]. Gov is worried about growing tax refusal. Karl's letter is wise and practical. But what suffering. He has "lost his faith," he said. Not even a "non-church Christian" like Ammon

I shall say the Creed and Memorare daily for him on my old knees.

June 20

The last two days Jean and Hildegard [Goss-Mayr] conducted a seminar for Pax members in the clubrooms of Nativity Church. It was very good indeed. One of the best meetings we have had for years.

Last night I called Tamar. Bad news about J. What impossible problems are arising. Heartbreaking for Mandy, and seemingly insoluble. Heartbreaking literally. My heart is literally heavy in my heart. My heart literally aches, pains, hurts. What to do? What to do? Pray, yes. Watch and pray. But what steps can be taken before lives are ruined. "Wait and do nothing," the psychiatrist says in "The Cocktail Party." "Least said, soonest mended," my mother used to say grimly. Talking does not mend matters. Neither does precipitate action. Hasty action. "Nip in the bud," is another saying. Wait and see.

The morning with a young man who says he is losing his faith—he cannot go on. Again, least said soonest mended. I think he has been talking about it for a long time to whoever will listen. So little we can do to help another, but just listen, sympathize, reassure. People have to live thru their inner crises alone. We can pray. That is the important thing: to leave it in God's hands. He loves them more than we do.

June 24

"God wills that all men be saved." 2 Peter.

Yesterday, thinking of our S.J. seminarian and the priesthood, I thought how great their faith must be in the sacraments (of penance, especially), in men themselves, to go on working at their vocation, bringing "knowledge of salvation thru forgiveness of their sins."

Hope and faith—how they are tied up together. And love—which desires the best for others. Not an emotional love, a self-gratifying love, but a love which surpasses dislike—that dislike occasioned by dishonesty, and offenses like drug pushing and sex irregularities, in other words corruption, impurity. Dislike is a mild word—hatred would be better. How to hate the sin and love the sinner! Our God is a consuming fire in what he expects of us—the impossible. Yet he has promised, "I can do all things in Him who strengthens me." Not achieving holy indifference, but to bear in peace the suffering, to overcome fears as to the outcome of all this, to know that he can bring good out of evil, that "all will be well." (Julian of Norwich)

June 26, '71 [typed]

I awake in the morning with all the problems around me pressing me down. Always in my life I have found that with writing about them, putting them down on paper, I can lift the burden from my heart. I have done this innu-

merable times and end up by losing these diaries, these meditations. Partly
my own fault, partly the fault of the way we live, when my room is used by
others while I am away traveling or on a speaking trip, my papers seem to
become public property. My books also. I have lost all my autographed editions by famous people like Maritain and Eric Gill, and now Erik Erickson
and Joan Erickson, Robert Coles letters disappear from my files just as many
other letters do.[307] Both Ammon Hennacy and I (I suppose he was copying
me) wrote down the names of those who wanted my prayers in our missals
and read them over in prayer, asking God's help for them. One of my friendly
enemies in our house of hospitality in New York used to say often, "You know
just who is bugging Dorothy by the names written down in her missal or
breviary." Ammon used to say, "I read over those names right after receiving
communion in the morning because that is when I feel God is close to me."

God is closer to us than the air we breathe. Certainly I feel his closeness
when I turn to Scripture for my morning prayer. Thank God for the short
breviary which we use in city and country, these few of us who say Vespers
and Compline daily. There is never a time when it is not balm to me for an
aching heart. Thank God for the old missals too, and I hope the new missals
are out soon.

For some weeks now my problem is this: What to do about the open immorality (and of course I mean sexual morality) in our midst. It is like the last
times—there is nothing hidden that shall not be revealed. But when things
become a matter for open discussion, what about example set, that most powerful of all teachers. We have with us now a beautiful woman with children
whose husband has taken up with a seventeen-year-old, is divorcing her and
starting on a new marriage. She comes to us as to a refuge where by working
for others in our community of fifty or more, she can forget once in a while
her human misery. We have another case of a young married woman whose
husband thinks it is his duty to befriend young girls (the latest only fourteen).
People have not been loved enough. Parents do not give their children the
love they crave, the attention they want.

In the slums there are always old and drunken prostitutes, well into their
sixties, who come to us for food, or to lie down on one of our benches in the
storefront which is made into a dining room, and sleep for a while before they
go back at night to the streets, to the empty buildings which house "jungles"
of men and some women. If we have three of these women in New York, now,
there are of course many more. They can be looked upon with horror and

---

307  Robert Coles, a psychiatrist from Harvard, was the author of *Children of Crisis* and many
other books. Dorothy admired his compassion and moral sensibility and his respect for poor
and working people.

compassion, or amusement as though they were characters in "My Fair Lady." What will become of them? How far are they mentally responsible? As long as they keep to the slums they have their freedom, but once they are ill and helpless, they are shunted off into our huge buildings for mental cases, houses of dead storage, as Fr. Duffy used to call them.

We have one young one, drunken, promiscuous, pretty as a picture, college educated, mischievous, able to talk her way out of any situation—so far. She comes to us when she is drunk and beaten and hungry and cold and when she is taken in, she is liable to crawl into the bed of any man on the place. We do not know how many she has slept with on the farm. What to do? What to do?

Our communes, as they are now called by young people (if they are not termed collectives) or agronomic universities or farming communes, as Peter Maurin called them, are microcosms. Each is a little world where we have all the problems, all the suffering there is outside our doors, outside our gates. It is our job to see how to handle it.

I know Peter Maurin, our leader and our teacher for so many years, was sadly disappointed with the lack of success of these ventures, which I, as a woman, had to initiate. "Man proposes and woman disposes," he said once. I considered of course that I was putting some flesh on his dead bones of thinking. It is one thing to dream of Utopias, it is another thing to try to work them out.

We must make the kind of society where it is easier for people to be good, Peter used to say. But how to make it? It was he himself who brought out into the open that wonderful statement of Jesus Christ as to the works of mercy (in Matthew 25), feeding the hungry, clothing the naked, etc. And how to do it with the poverty we all endured in the thirties. By the practice of voluntary poverty, he says. If you give what you have, with no thought for the morrow, the Lord will constantly multiply the loaves and fishes for you. And we were to live in beauty as the birds of the air and the lilies of the field.

And here we are, not one of us without a heavy burden of suffering, our own and that of our children and our children's children.

If it were not for Scripture on the one hand and Communion on the other, I could not bear my life, but daily it brings me joy in this sorrow which is part of our human condition, and a real, very real and vital sense of the meaning and the fruitfulness of these sufferings. Thomas à Kempis, a mystic not at all in fashion now, says that in the Cross is joy of spirit. Jesus said, "Take up your cross and follow me." There is no one living who is not bearing a cross of some kind, and if the crosses of others look to you to be unbearable, so that you find yourself suffering for them as well as for yourself, then I am lacking in faith. "My grace is sufficient," God promises us.

We talk so much about our freedom. And then "Why does God implant in us these instincts and then punish us when we satisfy them? God made all things to be enjoyed. Enjoy, enjoy!" Meanwhile men are dying by fire in Vietnam, by plague and famine in Pakistan and India, to cite a few holocausts that are going on. Men are dying trapped in a water tunnel in the mountains of California, in mines in West Virginia, murdered "in cold blood."

Accent on sex? Jansenism, Puritanism, Manicheism. I do not know what they are talking about when these terms are so freely bandied about, but I do know that sex has to do with life, in bringing forth life, as war brings forth death.

*N.D.*

When I left home the few who gather to say the rosary and Compline in our little chapel and listen to some readings were finished with the *Little Flowers of St. Francis* and were beginning *Pilgrim's Progress*—the story of a journey.

I was setting out on a journey too, with a group of 54, a peace pilgrimage which started for me at Kennedy airport, where I met others who had started from Sacramento, Palo Alto, as well as the Midwest. The only one I know was Nina Polcyn, who had been previously to Poland, the country her grandparents came from to settle in Wisconsin, Milwaukee, where I first met her years ago…

*In July Dorothy set off for another trip—this time to Eastern Europe and Russia. Traveling with her friend Nina Polcyn, she had the thrilling experience of visiting the land of Chekhov, Tolstoy, and Dostoevsky. She visited the grave of Jack Reed and "disrupted" a meeting of Soviet writers by expressing her admiration for Alexander Solzhenitsyn. She described her travels in the July-August, September, and October-November issues of the CW.*

Aug 19

In the Hudson River book much talk about how the early explorers found the country so fragrant, the delicious odors could be overwhelming even far out to sea.

The odors at the Greyhound bus station in Albany today were so atrocious, it sickened me, also a young woman waiting for her friend, who kept changing her seat, but found the odor came from the huge pillars-like cigarette ash. Coming home from the spotlessly clean cities of Eastern Europe it was very oppressive. One poor little man was cleaning the toilets. I suppose he was held responsible for the whole place. People are either overworked or unemployed.

Mail from Robert Coles and *The New Republic* with his review of *Varieties of Religious Experience* [William James]. We seem to be thinking on same levels.

## August 31

Karl Meyer's letter, which came last week, gave me much joy. I'm happy that he loves the Arthur, Camelot legend, his continuing search, finding Christ in others, in his attitude also toward his wife.

## Sept 2

Waking up and reflecting on our utter failure. Only God can help us. Psalm 142 is my cry for help and Isaiah 16:10-14 is my comfort. And Ephesians 2:10, "We are God's workmanship, created in Christ Jesus for good works, which He prepared beforehand that we would walk in them."

## Sept 12

Today Karl Stern called to say [his wife] Weibe died. She had had two heart attacks and a breakdown in the last year. A gentle, beautiful creature. As beautiful as Greta Garbo—more so. A craftswoman. I must go up to see Karl later. He said not to come to the funeral Wednesday.

## Sept. 14

It is hard to live with the sense of guilt and grief and horror which we all feel this day, which in the calendar of the church is the feast of the Holy Cross. The riot at Attica is over with 28 prisoners and 8 guards dead.[308] We are left with Christ's words.

"What you have done to the least of these, that you have done unto me."

"The Lord whose kindness endures forever, and his faithfulness to all generations" will not forget them now.

The great mystery of man's freedom, which means also to choose good (God's will, as far as we discern it) or evil—so often in the guise of good, is now made clear to those who died at Attica. They have their freedom now, the prisoners whose prevailing complaint was: We are imprisoned and forgotten. We demand to be treated with respect, as men, not beasts. To the guards,

---

308 A prison uprising at the Attica Correctional Facility in Attica, New York was suppressed with deadly force. Ten hostages and twenty-nine prisoners were shot by State Troopers in the retaking of the prison yard.

the hostages also, shot by their own brothers, how hard, how terrible a thing is Christian religion—to forgive your enemies (as you wish to be forgiven) and so many of them "of one's own household"—to remember that the last words of Christ, in torture on the cross, were "This day you shall be with me in Paradise" and "Father, forgive them for they know not what they do."

We possess the freedom to believe, to choose to believe this highest and hardest of all roads to walk. Or we have the freedom to hate, not only the sin but the sinner, and pick up those same weapons, bombs, guns, or the words which inflame, incite to violence.

To even *speak* of nonviolence in this time when a sudden realization of man's sufferings in the prisons of our country reaches us, is so hard, that it means in a way doing violence to all one's *natural* instincts. But man is more than the *natural*. Each least one in Attica as in our own Bowery surrounding is possessed of body and soul, no matter how limited his freedom is, and Christ died for *the least* of these. We hope against hope, we believe and beg God to help our unbelief, and "in pain is my bitterness most bitter…" Such scripture phrases in all their obscurity come to us when we too are imprisoned by our own helplessness, "outside" as we are.

Our Lady of Tenderness, comfort them. Christ, hear us, mercifully hear us. God help us, make haste to help us.

Sept 17

Ruth Collins [*CW real estate advisor*] and John Coster [*CW lawyer*], 5 p.m. John Magee wants to give us $20,000 but wants us to be tax exempt. He is going away on a 3-week vacation right now. I'll go see him later when he comes back. It would help us make a first move from Tivoli.

Internal Revenue agent has been going over the matter of our taxes, our income with John and is going to bring it to court. I have to begin preparing a statement—the Pa. court case may come up in December. Meanwhile John and Ruth both approve of selling the farm at Tivoli and decentralizing.

Oct 4. St. Francis

"I have to, I got to, I'd better," Tanya says as she goes thru my picture postals, throwing them around mischievously. What beauty, what joy children are. She is two and a half—seems to be able to say anything. Coming on a photograph of Hans [Tunnesen] she said tenderly, "Only one Hans," something she had heard someone else say.

How one's heart aches over children. It was the same with Tamar—then with her children, and now with the great grandchildren. One can only say "to love is to suffer." The sight of infidelity, broken homes, adult unhappiness is cruel for children. Dostoevsky understood this when he wrote of "the sufferings of one little child" in *Brothers Karamazov*. Ivan's bitter words, his rejection of God. Portuguese saying, "Take what you want but pay," says God. But it is not only oneself that pays, but the children—the little ones. To see one child go around wailing for its mother—having already lost a father.

Oct 28

Yesterday at Catholic Relief Services in the Empire State Building. Mother Teresa was there with some of her sisters, whom she brought over to start a foundation in Harlem.

Fritz Eichenberg has been illustrating a life of Erasmus, or a book of his. Now will work on Tolstoi's childhood. He sent us many of the originals he had of pictures he had done for us. He called from Rhode Island.

Mother Teresa said to Andrew Young, "Tell me something good of Harlem. We have heard only bad." And when he finished speaking, their hearts were stronger, their faces lit up.

Nov 8-14. San Francisco

The happenings of this week and their significance. Thirteen churches, 8 of them Catholic, offered sanctuary to any sailor on the aircraft carrier Coral Sea. The city of Berkeley, in an unprecedented action, followed suit, thru its duly elected city councilmen.

But the Coral Sea sailed yesterday, bearing its instruments of death, and the war goes on. The Constitution sailed from San Diego. Two more aircraft carriers are scheduled to follow. With all the talk of withdrawing troops, the war goes on, is extended even into Laos and Cambodia.

The Coral Sea sailed with approx 4,500 men, 35 men AWOL, one third of crew signed petitions against sailing. Three officers resigned their commissions. One sailor took sanctuary. Many just failed to show up. The media—news radio and television—played it up, then pointed to the week's events as demonstration of the hopelessness of the entire situation, the inability of the American people to do anything to stop this terrible war, the longest in history, in spite of the fact that all polls show that the majority of our people are sick at heart—sick, afraid of the retribution piling up for us.

But to me it showed the capacity for hope and faith that there is in man, not to be extinguished.

The more it is expressed in such actions as these the more it will grow.

These actions, these demonstrations, are the discipline, the exercises that will make it grow. So often it has been the image of a battling city that the country has seen. Students and police on either sides of the barricades (an adolescent romantic dream of revolution). Violence combating violence, wars to end wars. But these gestures, this week, have been demonstrations of nonviolent action, nonviolent tactics. If the world sees in this only futility, only folly, it is nevertheless a part of Jesus Christ's "folly of the Cross," as St. Paul put it—a failure, which nevertheless was followed by resurrection, a proclamation which is still reverberating around the world. If people despair of Xtianity, as they look around them and see people at war, and widespread poverty and injustice, one can only remind ourselves of the age of the world. And Christianity is only 2,000 years old, and a thousand years are as one day in the sight of God.

We are only beginning, each of us, to practice the folly of the Cross, of trying to live as tho we were brothers, and according to Christ's teachings—his last command.

# 1972

Saturday, January 8
Allen Ginsberg came in tonight with Gary. Attended Vespers. Ten in the dining room sang mantras, some of which involved us all—Hare Krishna went into Jesus, Mary, then Virgin Mary, then a litany asking prayers for all. He had a tiny little accordion-type piano which he got in India. He was there 18 months and returned recently to work with the refugees from East Pakistan, now Bangladesh. We've all sung better since he was here. I mean the hymn to the Blessed Mother at the end of vespers.

*In January Dorothy traveled to California to visit the headquarters of Cesar Chavez and the United Farmworkers in La Paz. She provided a long account in her January 1972 column.*

Sunday, January 9
Worked all day on January copy. My visit with Cesar Chavez and how his place was guarded at La Paz. When I slept I had such bad dreams, like a gangster movie, I turned on radio news as soon as I had said my prayers to see if anything had happened to him. Thank God no bad news.

Monday Jan 10
A woman sent in $8,000 from Florida. I wrote we were not tax exempt but she said it was a gift from the heart. We are going to give away to Farm Workers, pulpwood workers, Haley House [Boston CW]. Chris [Montesano's] house in San Francisco, and [Ammon] Hennacy House in Los Angeles.

## Feb 2

I am reading Pope John XXIII's letters to his family. A great comfort. A strong spiritual comfort. Today the last day of the Xmas season it is still necessary to me to use the missal and the old St. Andrew's is a treasure, an encyclopedia. That and the "Prayer for Christians," an interim Breviary, leaving out the old Latin words, "matins, lauds," etc. and substituting morning, midday, and evening prayer. Expensive—around twelve dollars. It is well bound and printed and has "readings," Scripture from the Fathers, and from the 2nd Vatican Council. Invaluable.

## Feb 3

I spend my days praying in the depths of my heart for our young people. Turning to reading (Pope John, Archbishop [Anthony] Bloom, Psalms, à Kempis) reaching out for help in all directions. "The sorrows of my heart are multiplied," I am afraid, and my only courage is Christ. There is an element of the demonic in the air we breathe these days. Letters come daily from parents who flee the cities with children (eleven-year-olds) to escape, and evil is everywhere in the guise of sex and drugs and words!—"beautiful," "love," "the new family," etc. Much lying and deceit, self-justification—an arrogant taking over, a contempt for the old people, or tradition.

They demand support, other people's work, to enable themselves to keep going. If refused, the ugly face of hate and violence is revealed, to subside into silent pride, arrogance once more. "We know what we are doing. We are building a new order." What a parody on what many others are trying to do.

Self-discipline, self-denial, voluntary poverty, manual labor—washing the feet of others—they taunt us with all these things, blind to every need around them outside of their own circle, their own age group. They accuse us of every failure to cope with drunkenness, insanity, and violence. "You have thrown out this one, that one. Where are the blacks, the Puerto Ricans? There is no democracy here." My heart aches for them, they are so profoundly unhappy. Their only sense of well-being comes from sex and drugs, seeking to be turned on, to get high, and to reach the heights of awareness, but steadily killing the possibility of real joy.

O God come to my assistance, O Lord, make haste to help us. Lord, hear my prayer, let my cry come to Thee. In Thee have I hoped, let me never be confounded. All I have on earth is Thee. What do I desire in heaven beside Thee?

And that "they" should have Thee, find Thee, love Thee too, those You have given us, sent to us, our children, our flesh and blood. May they cry out for the living God. "No one comes to the Father but thru me," you have said this, Jesus. Draw them, I beg you, I plead with you, so that they "will run to the odor of your ointments," that they will "taste and see that the Lord is sweet." Let them seek and find the way, the truth, the light.

Yesterday only tragic mail. A letter from that teacher in Canada, trying to flee with her twelve-year-old, already corrupted children.

The two letters about Jack English's third heart attack, and Bill Gauchat's cancer operations, are not tragic in the same sense.

Pope John: *Letters to His Family.* "Everything has its value, illnesses, crosses and tribulations, provided they are borne in a spirit of faith in our Blessed Jesus, who suffered for us and has promised us his consolations and blessings..."

"Everyone is working for the good of the family, some working in the fields, some praying, and some offering their sufferings. Suffering draws down upon us the greatest blessings."

"Silkworms—a great deal of work for little profit. Still it is always something."

Pope John, pray for my family, especially my granddaughters.

Feb 13

Pouring rain today. I stayed in, resting—feeling exhausted. Sorrow, grief, exhaust one. Then tonight the prayers, the rosaries I've been saying were answered. *[Name crossed out].* And the feeling that prayers are indeed answered when we cry out for help was a comfort in itself. I had the assurance that they were answered, tho it might not be now.

I would not perhaps see the results. "Praised be God, the God of all consolation. He comforts us in all our afflictions and enables us to comfort those who are in trouble, with the same consolation we have had from Him."

Cor 1:3-7. Suffering draws us to prayer and we are comforted. Or at least strengthened to continue in faith, and hope, and love.

Feb 17

Today I came back from Phil. where I spoke at LaSalle College (Christian Brothers). Demonstrations—ashes (for Ash Wednesday) at Federal Building, tax building, etc. Draft cards burned for ashes. Liturgy in the basement chapel. Very beautiful.

Contract signed with Curtis Pub. Co for *Long Loneliness, Loaves and Fishes.* Sent more On Pilgrimage to them. For paperback in Fall.[309]

---

309 In honor of Dorothy's 75th birthday in November 1972, Curtis Publishing Company issued a three-volume mass-market paperback set consisting of *The Long Loneliness, Loaves*

Friday Feb 18

What a tremendous strength comes from the Mass. Lent started Wednesday. My fast probably will be giving up newspapers and television. Not reading.

Rites for the Sick. This sacrament used to be called "the last rites." Now "its proper grace...gives strength to the sick person. This grace endows him with God-given peace of soul to bear his suffering. It also effects the forgiveness of his sins, if this is necessary. And if God so wills, the sacramental anointing can even effect a total restoration of physical health."

Christ's words on the Cross.

Both Matthew and Mark report only "My God, My God, why hast thou forsaken me?"

Luke reports: "Father, forgive them for they know not what they do... This day thou shalt be with me in Paradise. ... Father, into your hands I commend my spirit."

John: "Mother, here is your son...Here is your mother. .. I thirst.... It is consummated."


Feb 21

I had been harried and worn out all day yesterday by the consciousness that we were inundated by an ocean of unemployed and unemployable, black and white human beings, searching for food, warmth, comfort, momentary surcease from suffering. If you have ten volunteers working at the Catholic Worker, each one multiplies the load in the vain attempt to help, to satisfy one or another need. With the pressure of some most serious problems, I went to bed aching in soul and body, sleepless for hours, keeping an involuntary vigil. (I comfort myself by St. Angela of Foligno's statement that such sleeplessness, loss of appetite, and suffering are not a willful asceticism that has little merit, but since it has no element of self-will and means patience and endurance, it is more pleasing to God and more profitable for souls.)

I see however that much confusion is the result of our willfulness, everyone seeking his own solutions, a refusal to exercise authority, a refusal to exercise obedience and humility. As it is, each brings more into the house, into the evening meal, than we can feed or house.

For instance, they saved ten plates tonight for those who were at Mass. But so many extra had been let in—former houseguests— that Rufus and others coming in also at six had no dinner but bread and coffee. Even tho we cook for ten more than we expect there is still not enough. The cold winter, the

---

*and Fishes,* and *On Pilgrimage: The Sixties* (a compilation of her columns). Unfortunately, the company soon went out of business.

lateness of the month, the New Way group coming in (because they like our atmosphere) all make our evenings chaotic.

I thought how little [St.] Peter Claver could do for or with the shiploads of African slaves brought over to Central and South America.

This morning I read Chekhov's "Peasants" and again was shamed by the contrast between their lot and our own. He saw too, in the "House with the Mansard," how important it was for people to "have time to think of their souls, of God, and to develop their spiritual faculties."

"The one thing needful," according to Scripture.

Chekhov puts these words into the mouth of a young artist, who calls on the young intellectuals to "take on themselves a share of their labor." "If all of us, city and country dwellers alike, everyone without exception, would agree to divide among ourselves the work which is expended in satisfying the physical needs of mankind, each of us would be required to work perhaps two or three hours a day, no more."

But how hard it is for men to find work now; for the old and injured it is impossible. Also for the young and unskilled.

There is always work on the land of course but a great lack of self-discipline and self-denial, to keep ourselves at it. We always have more important things to do!

Feb 24

How suffering drives us to prayer. I mean mental suffering, caused by the sin of those you love. But it seems that to love is to suffer. One must constantly recall the necessity to grow in confidence in God. The word means "with faith." *Con fide.* An opportunity then to grow in faith. Confidence, trust, trust in one another too. Trust that prayers will be answered. Maybe not as we want but as others need it to be.

Thinking of St. Peter Claver again. We can no more set the world right than he could. Our desires are very modest. As Peter Maurin said, "To make that kind of society where it is easier to be good." Our home, protected as we were by a good father, and by poverty (not destitution) was good. I look back on it with happiness.

But with all our theorizing and efforts and communicating thru writing about the efforts of others—like Vinoba Bhave, Cesar Chavez, Charles Evers (I mention only those still alive)— we know that we will never solve what St. Paul called the mystery of iniquity. Fr. John McKenzie writes of Job and this mystery beautifully in *The Two-Edged Sword.*

To love is to suffer. Perhaps our only assurance that we do love God, Jesus, is to accept this suffering joyfully! What a contradiction!

March 9

St. Catherine of Bologna. She was aware that the origin of her faults, past, present or future, was in herself. She used to consider herself too as the cause of all the faults of her neighbors, for whom she felt a burning charity.

Sunday March 12. Grey, rain, cold

"I consider the sufferings of the present to be as nothing compared to the glory to be revealed in us. Indeed the whole created world eagerly awaits the revelation of the sons of God. Creation was made subject to futility not of its own accord, but by him who once subjected it; yet not without hope."

"Salvation is from the Jews," St. Paul said long ago. In them, thru them, I am always finding the Messiah. The sayings of the Hasidic Fathers have often saved me from despair. Like that saying Elie Wiesel quotes in *Souls on Fire*: "I am much more afraid of my good deeds that please me than of my bad deeds that repel me."

I say saved me from despair, because there is the joy of recognition, a real encounter with truth in such a saying, a joy that urges and liberates.

March 25. Saturday at Tivoli

Forster called. He will be 78 this week. "Fighting off death," he said. I wonder if he wakes in the night sometimes, appalled by a glimpse of nothingness, of not being, of loss of all the beauty he has known. I do pray for him every day. And so does Nanette, his deceased wife.

Phil Berrigan case closing soon. Defense rested. No witnesses. Marches, vigils, protests in Holy Week.[310]

Sunday March 26

Last night to St. Sylvia's to 5:30 Mass. She was the mother of St. Gregory. Since receiving the Baal-Shem-Tov citation at the little synagogue in N.Y. at a Friday night service, I think of our Sat. evening Masses at 5:30 as "ushering in the Sabbath" and we should say first Vespers for Sunday. But I was thinking of yesterday, Sat., as the feast of the Incarnation. A time to say the

---

310 While serving his prison sentence for the Catonsville 9 draft-board raid, Phil Berrigan was indicted along with six others on a broad range of conspiracy charges, including an unlikely plot to kidnap National Security Advisor Henry Kissinger. The Harrisburg Conspiracy trial came to a conclusion during Holy Week in 1972. Berrigan and Elizabeth McAlister, a nun whom he had secretly wed, were convicted of smuggling letters in and out of prison. The jury was deadlocked on the other charges, and the case ended in a mistrial.

Angelus, morning, noon and night, and remember that March 25th was the day the Church celebrated because on that day Christ took on our humanity so that we could share in His Divinity. O man, dust thou are and unto dust thou shalt return. "Yahweh God fashioned man of dust from the soil. Then He breathed into his nostrils a breath of life, and thus man become a living being."

We had a wayfarer who accepted our hospitality for a few years who used to kneel down and kiss the earth on that day (March 25) each year, because Christ in putting on our human flesh which came from the earth, had made that earth holy.

But the Mass last night was Palm Sunday. Passion Sunday Mass. It was said at St. Sylvia's with dignity, with solemnity, in bright vestments and six altar boys, entering the church and coming up the center aisles in procession. There was good reading of prayers and the Passion of St. Matthew.

Wednesday in Holy Week. Mar 29

Did my washing this morning. Mass at 11. Wrote Fr. [Theodore] Hesburgh and Jon Erikson, the former about the Laetare medal and the latter about his pictures.[311] I had started to write Fr. H. about our tax situation but sent a short one-page letter instead. His letter was full of loving-kindness.

We sent pictures to Curtis Books for publicity. Jon Erikson's.

Easter Thursday, April 6

If I had not suffered from heart failure this past month or so which caused me to cancel all engagements which had suddenly piled up upon me (a trip around the world is less taxing to health of mind and body) I would not have had time to read *Souls on Fire* by Elie Wiesel. It has of course been widely reviewed but I must add my own comments, my gratitude.

The joys and sufferings of the Jews! I knew nothing of Jews until I lived with a Jewish family on the Lower East Side when I was eighteen. And then too how little I knew. Ritual about food gave me a sense of the sacramental. I had rented a tiny hall bedroom for $5 a month with a separate entrance next to the toilet in the hall, used by two families. My window was on an air shaft. (We were on the third floor of a 5-story building.) When I came home at two a.m. from my work on the *Call*, a Socialist paper, I often found a plate of food

---

311 Fr. Hesburgh, President of the University of Notre Dame, wished to present Dorothy with the prestigious Laetare medal. The citation of the prize, which she later accepted, recognized her long commitment to "comforting the afflicted and afflicting the comfortable." Jon Erikson was a photographer whose portraits of Dorothy appeared on the covers of the Curtis volumes. He later collaborated with Robert Coles on a book about the CW.

by my bedside with a note from one of the children (the parents knew only Yiddish) explaining, "no milk or butter, if I had meat," etc.

I began to know the Jewish people then in the breaking of bread, as I was later to know Christ. I began to "go with" Mike Gold, not long after, and he wrote a play "on the airshaft" (his mother's apartment on Chrystie Street had rooms in the airshaft common to tenement apartments). I used to go with him to the Provincetown Playhouse on MacDougal St. in Greenwich Village and often since have been called a Villager. But I despised the arty atmosphere, the liberal mind, as opposed to the radical, and always associated myself, then and now, with the Lower East Side. The West Village was Italian and Irish and "Bohemian." East Side was Jew, Pole, Ukrainian, Russian. I was steeped in it and still am.

Elie Wiesel brings back to me that feeling of the joy and sadness of the Jew. I found the Messiah in the Jew. One might say living there brought my conversion to Catholicism closer. Since there is no time with God, I am living in both past and present. As I sit up here in the little chapel of our farm at Tivoli where we have the Blessed Sacrament, and read the sayings of the Hasidim as part of my prayer for the Jews, suffering as they are today in Israel, always on the verge of war, geared for war, suffering also in Soviet Russia, which I visited last summer. I could protest, while I was there, at the treatment of Alexander Solzhenitsyn at the Peace Center, at Friendship House, and to those members of the Writer's Union whom I met. But I could not write about the brief contact Nina Polcyn and I had with the problem of the Jew in Russia. We did not wish to involve friends in further trouble.

The mystery of suffering. My reading this morning helps me to deal with my own sufferings over our turmoil in which we live, our tragedies, our frustrations, our sense of futility in the face of such failures.

Here at the Catholic Worker houses around the country, here at the farm, "we have here no abiding city." We must be content with our vocation, which, if we follow it, will mean we will die to self and put on the new man. With the wonderful liberty of the children of God, which St. Paul writes of, we learn constantly to respect man's freedom. We can have no control, no power over others, only over ourselves, and that is a grace, a gift, which we must continually pray for.

"Where there is no love, put love and you will find love." St. John of the Cross. "You love God as much as the one you love the least." (Probably a paraphrase of "Whatever you do to the least of these you have done to me.") "Be what you want the other fellow to be"—Peter Maurin. "Wash the feet of others…serve"—Jesus.

"If anyone takes your coat (book, money, time) give him your cloak too."
"If anyone slaps you on one cheek, present to him the other." "He who takes
the sword, perishes by the sword." "Give to him who asks and do not ask a
return."

There is neither justice nor right order in all of this. One would think Jesus
one of the Hasidim. How close the Hasidim are to Jesus!

Peter Maurin too longed for order and justice. A world "where it was easier to be good." He talked about the "Thomistic doctrine of the Common
Good." But he lived the folly of the Cross. He gave himself to all, would talk
for hours and listen, too, even to a madman who came in one night and spent
the night in talking. No one else would listen to him. We, the younger ones,
thought, "If we listen he will come back again and again, we will never be
rid of him." But Peter recognized the dignity and the tragedy of each human
being and treated each with respect.

I realize, as I stay quiet here at Tivoli, that my talk of common sense and the
folly of do-goodism, our lack of recognition of our own limitations and capacities, of our own immediate duties, falls on deaf ears, and now the young
ones, of whom there are plenty, thank God, continue in their folly in trying
to deal with the destitution of the Bowery and slum around us. They fail.
Peter failed. Other young ones come who try to follow Peter and hope to
succeed where he failed. And perhaps when they get their sense of direction
and go on to study to develop their own vocations they have grown so much
closer to Christ so that they will persevere in what they can do and leave the
rest to God.

To grow in faith in God, in Christ, in the Holy Spirit, that is the thing.
Without Him we can do nothing. With Him we can do all things.

He will raise up leaders who will know how to combat the secular, or rather
how to integrate the spiritual and material, so that life will be a more balanced
one of joy and sorrow.

Right now Marge [Hughes] has tried to deal with an unbalanced veteran,
WWII, who is full of mischief, turning all our books backside to the wall,
closing all windows when they are opened and opening them when they are
closed, stealing and hiding things like a magpie and sleeping always on the
living room sofa instead of the bed he has been given, breaking our statues,
tearing down our shrines. In a veteran's hospital, a man is only taken in who
commits himself voluntarily and he can sign himself out whenever he wants
to (which is a good thing, of course). James always goes willingly but never
stays for more than a day or so.

*In 1972 the Catholic Worker received a letter from the Internal Revenue Service stating that the CW owed $296,359 in fines, penalties, and unpaid income taxes for the previous six years. Dorothy was determined not to pay any money for war, nor would she apply for charitable "tax exempt status" for the Worker. "It is not only that we must follow our conscience in opposing the government in war," she wrote. "We believe also that the government has no right to legislate as to who can or who are to perform the Works of Mercy." Once again, she faced the prospect of going to jail or being put out on the street.*

Sat April 21
  We go to press May 4, and I must begin to write about our tax situation.[312]

June 8
  Last Sunday Frank Donovan paid $250 rent for the location in the Spanish camp of a small bungalow or shack ($1,500).[313]

  "It is religion itself—prayer and sacrament, and repentance and adoration, which is here, in the long run, our sole avenue to the real."—C.S. Lewis
  Christ's blood was the price of our salvation. If money is the blood of the poor, as Leon Bloy wrote, then we, here at the CW, are offering our blood for our brothers, suffering in Vietnam and for our country and its leaders, guilty of shedding that blood. (All men are brothers. This is fratricidal war.)

Thursday, June 29. Feast of St. Peter and Paul
  Monday at 9:30 of this week we met with Mr. Hunter. Assistant Attorney General, Mr. Oscar Olean, John Coster, Ruth Collins, Pat Jordan, Ed Forand, Walter Kerell. Very conciliatory meeting. Ruth will type her transcript of it. Call Ruth
  Tomorrow I go to Pax meeting, then hopefully to farm, to Perkinsville for 2 weeks.

*In the July-August issue Dorothy shared this good news:*

> Dear fellow workers in Christ,
>   Good news! On July 11 we received absolution from the U.S. government in relation to all our tax troubles... In a conference in late June with William T. Hunter, litigation attorney from the Department of Justice, one of

---

312 "We Go on Record: CW Refuses Tax Exemption," May 1972. See *SW,* 311-314.
313 This cottage on Staten Island would provide Dorothy with a retreat and escape from the City in her later years. Eventually, after her death, it was destroyed by developers.

the Assistant Attorneys General of the United States, we reached a verbal settlement couched in more human and satisfactory terms than the notice we later received.

"They" were willing to recognize our undoubtedly religious convictions in our conflict with the state, and were going to drop any proceedings against us... I think Mr. Hunter shared with us the conviction that we would continue to express ourselves and try to live the Catholic Worker positions as best we could, no matter what steps were taken against us by government...

Yes, we would survive, I thought to myself, even if the paper were eventually suppressed and we had to turn to leafleting, as we are doing now each Monday against the I.B.M. Wall Street offices, trying to reach the consciences of all those participating in the hideous and cowardly war we are waging in Vietnam.

## July 20

I saw "Uncle Vanya" and "Fiddler on the Roof." Wonderful. One of our readers sent a check and said spend some of this on "wine and roses."

Check for $750 came from Popular Library (Curtis).

## July 21

Fr. A. used to omit the creed when he offered Mass and was much criticized by Emily. (She used to speak up when she could not hear his low voice in the chapel. "Are you only speaking to the young ones?" she complained.) Now we are saying the creed. Is it that he is particularly sensitive?

For instance, he also leaves out "It will (the bread) become for us the bread of life...It will become for us our spiritual drink." Is he thinking of St. Paul's harsh words—"whoever partakes of the body of Christ unworthily" (1 Cor 11)? But who is worthy? Father Plante also used to quote St. Paul often and sadly when he stayed at the farm. As to priests "with problems" who come to stay with us, who are we to question them? We are only too grateful for the Masses they say in our little chapel, in our living room, or out under the trees. (I have seen young people, long alienated from the Church, begin by being present afar off, approaching nearer Sunday by Sunday, until suddenly they are closely present.) I can scarcely breathe for fear of frightening them away. Like wild animals they approach, warily, fearfully. And how right they are. "It is a fearful thing to fall into the hands of a living God."

"Wisdom is the most active of all active things." This comes from the book of Wisdom, an apocryphal book in the Protestant Old Testament.

I had some glimpse of this when I had what I like to call a revelation, the second in my life. The first one, I tell it to show how materialistic, how selfish, how rooted in pride my inspirations, my revelations are, was when a sudden burst of happiness came over me at the discovery that I could earn my own living! I was seventeen and a freshman at the University of Illinois, working for board and room. I had to give 4 hours a day for that board and room, and I got 20 cents an hour for ironing clothes, or scrubbing a kitchen floor, or babysitting. I can still remember the exultation I felt. Exaltation, I might say. I had got hold of a profound truth. I had found a "philosophy of work," a phrase which Peter Maurin liked to use years later. I had never heard of St. Benedict, *orare et laborare*. Thomas Mann discoursed learnedly on this great truth in an essay, a very good one, in a Communist magazine, *Masses and Mainstream,* on Chekhov and his philosophy of work—a fascinating literary study. This discovery of mine, this insight, gained thru experience, led me to shirk my required studies and spend the next two years, aside from earning board and room, writing and dreaming with friends, two such diverse friends as Rayna Simmons (written about in Vincent Sheean's *Personal History* under her married name, Rayna Prohme) and her fiancé in these college years, Samson Raphaelson, story writer and playwright.[314]

My next great insight, or revelation, came ten years later, roughly speaking, as I read St. Augustine's *Confessions.* I was 27 and the day before I had had lunch with a young man whose advances I had repulsed, whose feelings I had somehow hurt. He had said to me, looking at my brown, un-manicured hands (I was living on a Staten Island beach), "I can always tell a woman's age by her hands," a remark which rankled. I was 27. My insight came, suddenly as I say, by the waters of Raritan Bay, reading. "No matter how old I get," I thought, with intense joy, "I will always have the torrents of pleasure promised in the Psalms, that come from reading, from study, from the association with great and noble minds."

No matter how old I get (and I am 75 in Nov 1972, this year), no matter how feeble, short of breath, incapable of walking more than a few blocks, what with heart murmurs, heart failures, emphysema perhaps, arthritis in feet and knees, with all these symptoms of age and decrepitude, my heart can still leap for joy as I read and suddenly assent to some great truth enunciated by some great mind and heart. This writing, the occasion of it, is reading an old 1951 copy of the *Sewanee Review* with a review of books on Hindu philosophy—Aurobindo by Wheelwright.

---

314 In her first memoir, *From Union Square to Rome,* Dorothy devoted a chapter to her college friend Rayna Simmons (or Prohme, her married name). Rayna later became a dedicated Communist. Around the time Dorothy was entering the church, Rayna was dying in Moscow. Her memory remained very present to Dorothy, especially in her final years.

July 25

Two quotes on chastity in the little book of excerpts from Thoreau. This week I have become a vegetarian again. I fasted from meat for two periods of a few years each, and it is in that spirit that I fast again, except for fish. God help me keep this spirit, this recognition of need for penance. For health too. Much summer flu.

July 29. St. Martha

Frank Donovan is retiring from his work with U.P.[S.] and will work full time with us.

Jan [Adams] across the street working hard on IBM leafleting.[315] We bought a mimeograph for $100. Hand turned.

Tues noon two officials—IBM lawyer and purchasing agent—visited us to talk over why. Peter Cunneen, who has been helping Jan with the project, Henry, who will be leaving soon to help get out the *Peacemaker,* and Jan, and a few of us sitting in. The lawyer also a member of Clergy and Laity Concerned. They attack Honeywell and ITT on war contracts issue, and themselves are earning this living (at expense of others dying) at IBM.

Demonstrations going on at IBM Poughkeepsie and other places.

August 2

Cool and quiet but getting hotter again. Trouble with Anna. She accuses Mickie of ransacking her purse. I remind M. that I have been accused for years by Catherine Tarangel, even to the extent of threatening letters from lawyers. And she and Steve side with Catherine, who is one of those women described by Leon Bloy in his book, *The Woman Who Was Poor.* A very strong and strange similarity, even to the fire which consumed Catherine's poor son, a few years ago. We have had her on our hands since 1950s.[316]

"To love the unlovable." "We love God as much as the one we love the least." "Inasmuch as you have done it unto one of the least of these…"

Life gets harder.

How hard it is to down the violence in our own natures—to "be present" and suffer and have faith and hope. To keep an appearance at least of calm

---

315 This protest focused on the sale of computerized weaponry to the U.S. military for use in the war in Indochina. See Jan Adams, "Catholic Workers Vigil IBM," July-August 1972.

316 When Catherine Tarangel died the next year, Pat Jordan wrote her obituary in the CW: "Catherine was one of the most unforgettable persons who ever dawned these doors. Not only was she a landmark of endurance, she was the embodiment of the Gospel widow who would let no one have peace until her wishes were satisfied. And in all candor, her wishes were never satisfied."

confidence that "all will be well, all will be very well." Must read Julian of Norwich again.

August 7

My ailments for these last two weeks. Sore throat, coughing at night, retching spasmodic, dry—very disagreeable. And always when I fine-comb my hair a few lice in the head. "What am I doing about it?" Combing constantly seems more effective than periodic poisons.

Long talk with Sister Donald. Gave her "Jesus Caritas" to read. After long questioning I finally understand what she wants. "To live poor." She is very quiet, loves her community, has no intention of leaving it, has no delusions about being able to do very much except by beginning with herself. No sentimentality and no judging. Two exponents of the sentimental approach to our work were in yesterday—M and T. Hard to keep them out. They at least are persevering. If they refuse to go—to give us up—we may be stuck with them. But that may be God's will too.

All budgets have been cut for hospital care, custodial care, and the streets are alive with not just drunks and drug addicts but with these saddest of all victims of our war economy, the "insane." The disturbed seems so inadequate an expression. The plain, stark unequivocal word insane seems fitting. Jesus said, "The poor you have with you always."

Thurs. to printer. Talked to Adolph. Decided once for all not to switch printers. Photo-offset is cheaper and good too, and the hand-setting and old machines seem to be obsolete but they are hanging on and we will too. We have been with them since 1933! They let our bill go as high as $10,000 many a time and it was they who once sent us a bill "pray—and pay!" They are like companions in this work of ours.

August 15. Sunday

In Nov Curtis or the Popular Books will bring out [On Pilgrimage] 1960s, together with [Long Loneliness] and [Loaves and Fishes] and I am reminded of how inadequate, how tormented those columns of the 60s are. There is a sort of travelogue of my trip to Cuba in 1962 and I wonder if I even mention the crisis in my Oct O.P. Perhaps because after visiting Cuba I could not believe the Cuban people would let themselves go the whole way—that is, bring on WWIII and risk seeing the destruction of the entire people, and yet it would be in character for them to be ready for annihilation rather than come under the yoke of the U.S. again. Certainly Fidel Castro was angry at Khrushchev for withdrawing.

That time and those three men deserve a better portrayal than I gave them. I must read Khrushchev's memoirs. More about Kennedy and Castro.

Aug.—

Well, I have just been to Mass, I have just "received," I have just "celebrated the Eucharist," as one is supposed to say now. No more Catholic jargon in this post-conciliar period. But we replace the old way of talking which used to delight me with its mystery, with its perhaps inexactitude of expression, with new jargon.

I will say now that one of my preoccupations during Mass was this notebook I had in my bag, which carries my knitting. I was resolving as I had many times before just to keep at that book which I am under contract with Harpers to write, keep at it from day to day, disjointed tho it may be, or seems to be, until it is finished. It will be my last book. I have written a dozen in my life, ten published and several unpublished, but now that I am 75 this will be my last. Of course it will be about myself, my life, people, books, events, family. After all, I can only know myself, try to, and I'm greatly reassured by the words of Ignazio Silone, one of my favorite writers, who said he was only writing one book in his lifetime. I had read those words of his 20 years ago, and now he has repeated them in his last book, *The Story of a Poor Christian*.

On Pilgrimage, Sept 1972

Since the Fall of 71 I have been a stay-at-home rather than a pilgrim, tho I go from New York to Tivoli, back and forth, and to our little refuge on the beach on Staten Island. I've had probably a half a dozen visits there this summer and all the young people around the CW have enjoyed it this summer, including two young newly married couples, the Jordans [Pat and Kathleen] and Montesanos [Chris and Joan]. I've been down with Stanley, Pat Rusk, Johannah and Rosemary Morse. Frank paid $250 yearly rental for the land and $1600 for the house which can scarcely be described by any other term but shanty or shack right now. No toilet or bath, only a kitchen sink. But Fall is only beginning, a beautiful season.

Sept 22. Tivoli

I wish I felt better so I could relate better to all that goes on here. Never before in the history of the CW have we had so many mental cases. Yesterday a young boy came, a novice for 2 years in a society of brothers. He had been in a hospital, had had shock treatments and was in a daze. Later in the day a young man working in a mental hospital in the Bronx came in with a half dozen other young people in the same state but not yet out of hospital. He is married and lives across the river in an old farm house with wife and 2 small children, drives to the Bronx (3 hours away) each day and takes a number of his charges on trips. Never stays very long, just enough to have cookies and coffee or tea. It is so sad to see so many dislocated young people. But how good to see work like his. How many marvelously good people there are!

Sunday, Sept 24

Just beginning to wake early and feel better, tho an itch tormented me into waking. Part of poverty—this business of lice, mites, ringworm—a constant battle for cleanliness, with all plumbing equipment breaking down.

Population 72, this weekend at the farm. It is truly a school of living, a school of nonviolence, but the longer I am here the happier I feel about it, or rather the more I am convinced we are on the right path. Insanity is a problem in our era. In the thirties, depression and drink; in the forties, war and "prosperity" (full employment); in the fifties, fear, cold war; in the sixties, drugs (and violence); in the seventies, "insanity." One can call it many names, alienation, withdrawal, depression, nervous breakdown—we have them all, together with the troubles of the past decades. Fear and hopelessness are always there to be fought. One way is to quit reading the daily press and listening to radio, looking at television. And yet there is a therapeutic element there. "Everyone's problem is no one's problem." Seems to me there is some kind of a proverb or aphorism like that. Perhaps Silone wrote it in *Bread and Wine.*

"Chickens come home to roost" is another. Our government started abortion clinics in Japan after WWII to solve the population problem (only 50 Japanese allowed annually to enter US at that time) and now we are overwhelmed with the horror of abortions. The poor feel this murder of the innocent is being forced upon them. I have heard the educated black speak of genocide when he refers to birth control and abortion.

The enormity of the drug problem and the senseless violence of our streets. War and fear is in the air.

Sept 27. Tivoli

A still breathless day. Fog on the river and the fog horn at Saugerties Lighthouse across the river has recently replaced the bell which we loved, and the new sound reminds me of Gene O'Neill's plays and New York harbor.

Hans Tunnesen who has known many a harbor tells me that Albany is a "port," an inland port, and has a harbor as deep as that of Bayonne, N.J. for the great oil tankers and barges which pass our house at Tivoli. The channel is very near to shore. It is thrilling to see the big ships looming up and passing us

silently. Strange. The larger the ship the more silently it moves thru the water.
The barges and tugs are noisy. And the freights on the Penn-Central tracks
are noisiest of all. River traffic is cheap, compared to train and truck traffic.
How sad that all our waterfronts are ugly and inaccessible, not places where
you can sit out in an open air coffee house.

The Bible has always meant much to me, since I was a little girl. It was the
Word, and so was *Christ* to me. I came across it by myself, not by example of
others. Certainly not from my parents, tho my mother taught us the simple
prayer, "Now I lay me down to sleep." I never remember seeing my mother
or father read the Bible, tho I found out later that my father always carried a
Bible around on his travels as he followed the races from Belmont to Saratoga
to Kentucky to Miami to Cuba.

But to speak of religion, to bear one's soul was as bad as to bare one's body.
Might as well strip naked in front of others. But now it is the fashion to strip
naked as it were, and to display all one's blemishes as well as one's beauties.

Perhaps there is something therapeutic about it—for one's self as well as for
others. If you love people you want to communicate with them. Silence may
be golden on occasion but it may be wounding too, isolating oneself from
others, isolating others.

Also, "Least said, soonest mended," our mother used to say. I can see that
when one is surrounded suddenly by scandal, tragedy, silence is golden. There
is a living silence, an understanding silence. Wisdom often comes in this way,
a healing wisdom, which can be communicated later on.

When I was a girl in high school I heard of a writer called Marie Bashkirtseff
who was supposed to have written her memoirs, which were very revealing. I
never came across a copy—so never read them, but I remember thinking "I
will write that way when I get older." Perhaps I was combating the loneliness
of adolescence then in my desire to communicate.

Oct 2. Feast of Guardian Angels

Eileen Egan is a model worker. Takes much of burden off me. Will go to
Danilo Dolci meeting on Oct 9 and give CW message and check for contribution to his new school in Sicily.

We must also contact Lanza del Vasto next week. I'll write him.

Jim Peck, War Resister. Thank him for the money he sent from sale of his
wife's jewelry.

One realizes one's awful helplessness. One knows too the bitterness of Ivan
Karamazov's sufferings over that one little child—and Stavrogin's despair (and
suicide) over his sin against one of God's littlest ones.

October 31

Curtis books came. I liked the makeup, covers, but Pat Jordan said they at First St. were not too enthusiastic over "blurbs," type, and cutting up of pictures. I'm only too happy to have them in paperback—*The Long Loneliness, Loaves and Fishes*, and *On Pilgrimage: The Sixties.*

November 1

Wrote to Nina Polcyn, asking help for Tom Cornell, also Bill Miller, about James Finn's projected "biography" and history of CW. Also Robert Coles' book. What a year this has been. "They're fattening us for the slaughter," Marge says. I prefer to think of all this "success" and awards as a nine-day's wonder. Everything passes. Better to be ignored. The philosopher said when applauded, "What have I done wrong now?"

November 17. St. Elizabeth of Hungary

I resolve this morning that if this darling saint who went fishing to serve the poor, and sewed for them, and accepted the brutal scourge of Master Conrad, her "director" (she was a lay Franciscan) I too will accept John Stanley's brutal letters and his hatred of me because I am not the perfect uncompromising Christian he wants me to be.[317]

Of course there is much truth hidden in his mad frenzied words. So I shall read them. He may be God's instrument, his hammer and chisel to work on me, as I must be working on him.

When he worked with us at Newburgh, Maryfarm—I loved him. We all did. He worked hard, he served others. But we were all too flip about calling attention to each other's faults. (We are always laughing at each other around here, but we like to think, excusing ourselves, that it is our sense of humor, which we count as a virtue—pride again). But our laughing at another's desire for perfection, and head-on collisions with a stubborn old alcoholic priest was evidently a cruel thing in his case and began this "feud" one might call it. There is an Italian saying, "The best is the enemy of the good." J.S. wants perfection and will not settle for less. And he hates me because he sees all my faults.

This is the month of November, the time in the church to remember the dead. I will read the Office of the Dead each day, remembering not only loved ones but all those in my past life in whose sins I have shared.

---

317 John Stanley was a former Trappist who came to New York and gravitated to the CW. At first he venerated Dorothy, but eventually, after becoming disillusioned, he took to picketing the Worker and handing out leaflets denouncing her hypocrisy.

Mary Therese, a beautiful black girl who lives across the street from us in New York, comes in often, drunk usually, more or less. Last time I saw her she sat and held my hand and quoted Scripture to me for half an hour. "We are *all* sinners, and always will be," was the refrain. And she went on in St. James' words, "He who says he is without sin is a liar." Sometimes her words were perfectly clear, sometimes she reverted to baby-talk, sometimes to gibberish. But she had studied the New Testament, she told me once, while she was in an alcoholic ward, out on "the island," and was baptized a Catholic. Whenever a priest says Mass at our place, she is there. Uncontrollable, sometimes she preaches also but stops after a few moments.

There are occasionally other disturbances. But when I am there I always, beforehand, close my eyes tight and pray intensely, "Dear God, let us have no disturbance," and my prayers have most literally been answered. They are silent at times, devout, even the priest has remarked it.

The Office of the Dead is beautiful and finding an old English-Latin breviary, I am praying it this month, this beginning of my 76th year. One should by now spend more time preparing for death.

At the end of Lauds there is the antiphon, which always makes me think of, and pray for, Mary Lou Williams, who set it to music, who composed stranger (to me) music for the Mass. "I am the Resurrection and the Life; he who believes in Me, even if he die, shall live; and whosoever lives, and believes in Me shall never die."

What a promise! I heard it sung in a Harlem church some years ago, and again at some of our Peace meetings here at the farm where she brought other black musicians and played for us.

When I write out these quotations from Scripture or mention "the Holy Name" in my writings, I always will capitalize it. It is not the style among many Catholics to do this now. Perhaps they wish to emphasize His humanity, which is beautiful to do. But both the great Teresas underwent a fresh conversion at the sight of a statue, a picture, which suddenly emphasized Jesus' humanity.

And today Alexander Solzhenitsyn complained in one of his essays at this habit today of using lowercase in referring to our Lord and Creator.

This by believers, I presume. Come to think of it, it seems to me that it is "religion" that is always referred to in their propaganda, rather than, specifically God, Jesus.

And isn't it hard, even for us, to use these words seriously? Don't they in a way embarrass us Americans, as though we were suddenly exposing ourselves, laying bare our souls? To get back to the point, I must myself use capital initial letters.

I have a bad habit of rewriting on some occasions official prayers of the church, such as that for the dead in general.

O God, Creator and Redeemer of all the faithful, grant to Your departed servants the forgiveness of all their sins. May our fervent prayers obtain for them this favor of Yours which they have desired so much. This we ask of You, Lord Jesus.

Certainly of these old associates of mine whom I remember with love and pain, Eugene O'Neill, Mike Gold, Wally Carmen, Berkeley Tobey, Lionel Moise, to make but a beginning of such a list—of the famous and obscure men and women which I will continue as I go thru this month's writing—none of them could be called "servants" of the Lord, nor did they expressly desire as far as I know "the forgiveness of sin," a word which in those days too, (the 20s) had lost all meaning.

It is good to *read* prayers, the psalms, for instance, penitential, or any of the psalms of the Office as a matter of fact. Even what you don't understand begins to sing in your mind, beautiful exclamations like, "O Lord, I have loved the beauty of Thy house, the place where Thy glory dwelleth...I will lift my eyes up to the hills from whence cometh my help... Our help is in the Name of the Lord... O Lord Jesus Son of the Living God, have mercy on me, a sinner."

## December 3

Today I'm listening to the 4th movement of the Oratorio, a mother's lament for her dead child. I'm lying on my bed, radio beside me, books, letters to do, having finished one of Dominic's good lunches. I have appetite, enjoy the beauty of the river which I can see from four of my five windows, which let in plenty of cold but such beauty. "The world will be saved by beauty." [318] At the same time I cannot go downstairs; my nerves are on edge—children, adults, noise, conversation, even tho the sounds are happy ones. My nervous exhaustion is still with me, which takes an outlet in uncontrollable tears. Stanley says when he returned from the hospital after his heart attack he too was affected with tears. I have had it a few times before after flu. Maybe it is more that than nerves.

Perhaps it was Saturday night's movie, which Marcel gets from the Red Hook library. It was about El Prado, art, music, dance. The pictures of Goya, the change from one type of painting to another. The horror and fear, agony of those howling, screaming, open-mouthed faces, appalled me. And suddenly Sally began throwing her shoes at the screen. Yet she had painted such

---

318 A line from Dostoevsky's *The Idiot*.

faces on a birthday card to me last week with the caption, "Welcome to the nuthouse."

All this made me go to bed weeping, and Sunday wake up weeping. It is Monday p.m. but I will bestir myself and go down to supper and Compline.

December 20

Fr. Phil Berrigan released from prison. 1,000 at Danbury to welcome him.

December 21

Mass at 1:30 or so at St. Joseph House, First St. Only Frs. Dan and Phil who looks wonderfully strong. Only our CW family there. Everyone so happy.

December 25. Christmas

Bombing continues on Hanoi.

# 1973

January 1

A beautiful sunny warm day—over 50°, I am sure. I took a walk, made a little terrarium in a glass dish with mosses and tiny plants. Johannah said she had one in the city last winter with a turtle. There are 2 little mice in my room. Very bold.

January 2

Maggie arrived today to look for work. No jobs in Vermont, where they are either snowbound or icebound.

January 3

A beautiful Mass today. Introit! Maggie spent a good part of the day with me, lengthening a warm skirt for me, practicing on the autoharp I got for Christmas. Stanley and I drove to RR Express with packages for the archives. To bookshops—had not seen my paperbacks. Bought Walker Percy's *Love in the Ruins*. Only 62 people here (15 children), 6 puppies, 4 dogs, 4 cats, chickens, rabbits. And mice in my room! When they rustle in the wastepaper basket it sounds like rain on the windowpane.

January 4

Deane wrote the best [column] she ever did—discussed her blindness (as poverty). Her keen sense of beauty of nature. My own not so good. Two quotes, brief. Just an indication of my recovery from a long flu, a plague of some sort, and accompanied by frayed nerves, which caused me to sit and weep. Thank God I am better now. It took me all day to write the little I did and half dozen letters.

January 5

Bob Fitch arriving at eleven. (Marge put him in Ed Turner's room next door. So I found him poking his head in my room while I prayed in bed.)

January 7

I must learn Holy Silence. But how hard to write (the story of my childhood) with 60 people around.

January 9

Mass. Speak Lord for Thy servant heareth. To listen more. More silence. St. John of Cross. Overmuch talking.

January 17

Margie took Hans [Tunnesen] to hospital tonight or rather ambulance came. She and Andy stayed until 12. A Korean doctor in residence. Everyone likes him. Hans very bad. He only consented to go because I kept telling him he was only 2 years older than I.

Set of Merton tapes. First time I ever heard his voice.

January 19

Train to NY. Mass at one at Holy Family. Fr. Dan Berrigan. Demonstration in Dag Hammarskjold Plaza after. Eileen spoke.

Hans Tunnesen died last night at 10 p.m. peacefully, with Vivian closing his eyes.[319]

January 27. Ceasefire [in Vietnam]

Did some writing today. House is packed to Mass of thanksgiving for the Ceasefire tonight at St. Sylvia's.

January 31

Fr. Voillaume and Bro. Roger visited us from 9:30 to 12. Took bus at 2:15—just made it with peanut butter sandwiches for lunch.

---

319 Hans Tunnesen had remained with the Worker ever since the seamen's strike in the mid-1930s. See "Hans Tunnesen," February 1973.

I do not observe people to describe them enough. I do not listen enough. Perhaps because they are always telling me their troubles. Does it comfort them when I tell them my own?

February 6

This a.m. had good talk with Cathie—wrote her a long letter about suicide and abortion, prayer, salvation. So tragic a case, what suffering.

February 15

Stanley and Marge to lunch. She brought my mail. She is not well, yet available night and day to all 65 in the house. I come back and evade Earl, Larry E., C. Tarangel, Joseph—the drunken and the mad who bother me!

February 19

Cesar Chavez, St. Paul's 6 p.m. Hall packed. Our farmworkers came down. Barbara, Jeff Rudick. 50 loaves of bread baked. Also we baked 3 hams, 10 lbs. each. Many reporters and television men. Cesar early but busload of farm-workers late. Great oration for the California crowd.

February 20

Ecumenical meeting. Cathedral of St. John the Divine. To speak from the pulpit of a Cathedral with Coretta King and Cesar Chavez would have been better if I could have seen the people I was speaking to. I was too exhausted to go to lunch, so walked to Broadway and bus down.[320]

February 23

Wrote Mrs. [Abraham] Heschel.[321] Refused degrees, Marquette, George-town, speaking at commencement in Calif. Giving an interracial retreat. My voice is hoarse. In [Bill] Moyers film it is tired; I look exhausted. Time to rest—not to talk. Too busy in NY. Too many who want to visit.

February 25

William James: "I am against bigness and greatness in all their forms, and with the invisible molecular moral forces that work from individual to indi-vidual, stealing in through the crannies of the world like so many soft rootlets, or like the capillary oozing of water, and yet rending the hardest monuments of man's pride, if you give them time. The bigger the unit you deal with,

---

320  See "Chavez, Workers Step up Boycott," March-April 1973.

321  Rabbi Abraham Heschel, author of many books and a prophetic champion of peace and civil rights, died December 23, 1972. Dorothy particularly admired his work on *The Prophets*.

the hollower, the more brutal, the more mendacious is the life displayed. So I am against all big organizations as such, national ones first and foremost; against all big successes and big results; and in favor of the eternal forces of truth which always work in the individual and immediately unsuccessful way, under-dogs always, till history comes, after they are long dead, and puts them on top."

From a letter to Mrs. Henry Whitman in the course of comment on G. E. Woodbury's *The Heart of Man*, especially the paper on "Democracy" in the *Letters of William James*, Vol. II, p. 90.

## February 26

Bad radio news—delay in returning prisoners. Fighting continues in South Vietnam, Cambodia, Laos. Violence and massive weaponry. But Cesar said from St. John's pulpit there are daily small nonviolent acts to counter the violence. Power of the spiritual forces incalculable. Beyond our knowledge. St. Paul says, pray unceasingly. Since I read William James quote on television, inquiries came by mail and phone, where is it from. (Modern Library edition of his letters. Must copy it and reprint in O.P.)

## February 28

The need for solitude. I stay at the farm not just because flu, a cough, a fading heart, arthritis, age, ties me down from the travel I love. But because of the overmastering urge to write. Here I can. I can be alone in the midst of others whom I love, who are my family. Solitude is a real necessity today. The poor in cities are not alone. Distractions. If we have to have "the poor always with us," as Jesus said, let there be communes—better, agronomic universities. The commune is the answer to a universal loneliness (Jane thinks). But without God it is a delusion, a snare. How afraid we are of God, to have "Him alone," lest having Him we shall have naught.

## March 1

Patrick O'Connor will receive Christopher Award for me, my *On Pilgrimage: The Sixties*. Spent day in bed, reading. So good to be alone and quiet. New girl, Mary Jo, and a little boy Joshua are in next room. Delightfully tidy. She is a "lover of beautifulness" and both very quiet. He plays and makes his noise downstairs, outdoors.

## March 2

Reading Attwater's *Dictionary of Saints* (Penguin edition). Fascinating. Birds singing. We will undoubtedly have a few blizzards in March but have had a week of spring. Heresies. (Like Sherlock Holmes, I like to retrace my thoughts. Lack of interest in Dominic. Looked him up in dictionary. A loveable gentleman. How had I come to associate him with Inquisition? Went to Languedoc to combat heresy.) Looked up all of them listed in front glossary and found many of us are tinged with one or another. Fr. Hugo said "one could go to hell imitating the faults of the saints."

March 3

Finish article with "heresy is overemphasis of one aspect of the truth." Fr. Hugo has been accused of most of them when he was merely complimenting his retreatants by expecting much of them in way of study, self-discipline, etc. Some went to extremes and swung as a pendulum from acceptance to total rejection.

March 4

Tamar's birthday. Telephoned.

Jan Adams here proofreading *OP 60s* and doing letters, refusing honorary degrees. 5 offered. Fairfield, Georgetown, Marquette, Brown.

Reading Teilhard de Chardin *On Love*. "Knowing"—word used in scripture for love's consummation. *Knowing* as heaven (St. Augustine's conversation with his mother at Ostia). This little book of quotations stimulates thought. The possibility of loving all!

March 5

C.S. Lewis remarks about death, its hideousness. The attempt to surround it with some dignity shows man's irrepressible attempts to defeat it, oppose it by surrounding it with pomp and glory. John Kennedy, Martin Luther King (find out details of Malcolm X). On the other hand—the hideousness of burying thousands of dead in wars—the common man. The unknown soldiers, an attempt to make it up to them. We too in "waking" try to "make it up." Remembering my parents' quarrel. Make it up as a phrase, "Let's make up."

March 6. Strange experience of being penetrated by God

Sat all morning with Mike [Sullivan]. Thought he was going to die any moment. Such struggle—to breath. In *Time* there was a story about what a dying person most needed was someone holding his hand. But there were not enough hands to go around. So I sat and talked and prayed. Finally he came to enough to go to hospital. Ambulance men, six of them, were very helpful.

March 7

The old are wounded too but more used to bearing it.

Mike Sullivan, 65, died today at Northern Dutchess hospital. So much work to do and the old ones, like Hans and Mike who did so much of it, are now gone.

How joy and sadness mingle in such a place as this. And also how little we each know of the sadness and loneliness of each individual. "We are the wounded," Mildred, who was young and beautiful too. "This place is for the wounded," she told Helene Iswolsky.

March 8. St. John of God

Mike was "waked" tonight at White's funeral parlor in Rhinebeck. Mr. White reminds me of a Dickens character. Those who love Dickens will get the implications. The wake—where is it practiced still? Here in the country perhaps it is more often practiced. But certainly young people, surrounded, living in a time of war as we still are (Cambodia for instance) are repelled by the laying out of a corpse in his best suit, in a coffin, with his friends around praying the rosary. But we did it for Hans, for Mike. Simple souls want it. It insures them, they know, of that half hour of prayer, concentrated solidly on them.

March 9

Mike Sullivan buried today in our little cemetery connected with St. Sylvia. Peggy Baird is there and Mary Hughes and her baby who died at birth, Larry Doyle, Agnes Sidney, Joe Cotter, Hans Tunnesen, Hugh Madden.

The fact that this may be the last year of my life should make me faithful in keeping this diary.

March 10

I get despairing about our slum-look around the farm, which I would like to call St. Isidore, since he is patron of farmers, and because it would remind me to pray daily for our Isidore [Fazio]. He would hate me for praying for him. People, many of them around us, are repelled by my pieties. (I am reading just this a.m. Rabbi Heschel's *The Pious Man*. He died a few months ago, may he rest in peace.)

We are not really a farm but an agronomic university, which is what Peter wanted to call it.

March 12

"Dear God, 'make it up' to Rabbi Heschel *for all* the *sufferings* of the
Jews."

I have no delusions about this CW farm. It is lighting a candle. I love the
beach more, but alone there its suggestion of vastness terrifies. It is not good
for man to be alone. I can be a hermit here, in my room, in the chapel. In
the large family we have, much suffering here. Unrequited love, forbidden
love (the young), epilepsy, brain tumor, emphysema, drink, madness, old age,
youthful delinquency, the suffering little children (Sally with her Goya-like
paintings). Slim in his jungle, Dan in his terraced shack, some have been in
mental hospitals, some in jails, etc.

March 16

Tony Equale is back after his 60 or 70-day bus trip. Mass today. "A priest
is a priest forever according to order of Melchizedek." I asked him no mum-
bling prayers he made up himself. Might as well have Quaker silence. Also
why not the drop of water in the wine—our humanity. That prayer is so
beautiful. And bread even before consecration is holy. We are one body in
Christ. A great mystery.

I have committed myself to try to start a women's house—mothers and
children too. How? Where? St. Ann help us. Next warm spell must go to
N.Y.

March 17

The house is jammed. I pay for my self-indulgence in music by the nausea
I feel on hearing coughing and spitting of Marcel every morning.

All times are eternally present with God.

March 18

Michael Mok went "out of his mind" today. Sebastian Opfer said he meant
no harm, but it was disconcerting to have him rush into my room and fling
himself on me when I was just awakening from a nap, lock himself in with
me, after he threw out Stanley who had followed him down the hall, and
playfully kick Pat Rusk. Insanity is the bitterest of our tricks. He had seen so
much suffering as a reporter in Vietnam, Biafra, Middle East, etc. Highway
police again took him to Hudson State. He had been drinking too.

March 19

Everyone has "given away an onion." Gruschenka story in *Bros Karamazov*. Jim Ryder who comes in "off the road" and always with a bottle. I re-

pulsed him mildly—his effusive greeting. "Peter Maurin started these places for people like me." I repented my lack of charity even before Marge told me how he visited all the halfway houses in Albany, Schenectady, Graymore, etc, and brought news of this one or that (and good cheer in the way of a bottle). Orwell says "plant a tree as penance and note it in your diary."

### March 21
Saw [Forster] all afternoon; he in a very comfortable room with one other man, a longshoreman who had a Trappistine niece. He had 3 visitors all of whom knew the CW. He is 78—sight and hearing perfect. C.S. Lewis says that at our age an ailment goes or is terminal. Must get exact quote. A good one. But I expect that when pain strikes we will rush to a doctor to alleviate it. F. is well covered by insurance. Hospitals now charge a fortune—$100 a day.

### March 23
Lunch today with Maisie Ward[322] who confessed to a love of mystery stories as I have since reading Conan Doyle at 12. Meant to go on to St. Vincent's but [Forster] called to say he was going home. Fr. Lyle [Young] spoke tonight.[323] I did not go. The city tires me so. Social engagements too.

### March 24
Spring day. Gangs of children over roofs, fences, thru the houses. Rita wondered once about my always referring to books. I told her it helped my perspective. "All times are dangerous times," St. Teresa said. The mob of tormenting kids in *Bros. Karamazov*, for instance… the drunkenness of Sonya's father in *Crime and Punishment*. Tonight one quarrelsome woman, Eleanor, who hates blacks, "I've been raped by seven of you," she says. And Toby—a Melville character, dangerous, throwing his arms around me and crushing me.

### March 29
AIM [American Indian Movement] still holding Wounded Knee.

### March 30
Women's Lib was topic of Barbara Deming's talk. She was superb. A clear, beautiful mind and heart. Physically she is beautiful too, but her voice is dif-

---

322  Maisie Ward and her husband, Frank Sheed, were the publishers of Sheed & Ward.
323  Fr. Lyle Young, an Australian priest, worked in prison ministry, and regularly said Mass at the CW.

ficult to hear at a meeting such as ours. I met with her afterward in our new reorganized office which seems so quiet and spacious now, thanks to Earl (recovered with his two-year drunk), shelves and a new desk built, painted. Everything spotless. Books, Fritz Eichenberg's cuts.

We are blessed with brilliant and noble women these days. Ruth Collins, Rita Davis, Carmen Mathews, Eileen Egan, Rose Morse, Hannah Arendt, Marge, Rita, Clare, and my own Tamar and children, Helene Iswolsky, and Deane, Caroline. All interesting, mature, helping others, and not problems. Deane is growing steadily. Anne Perkins is another. I feel myself tottering beside the strength and goodness of the young girls around me—tired and uncharitable tonight to Mary Dilworth and Yvonne, with the women problems I confronted on my return from the beach.

## April 7

Getting ready to go anywhere takes thought, planning and time. Della's this weekend, and then Tamar until Sat. Tamar, thank God, never makes me feel as Pat does. We have a very comfortable time together, relaxed, doing things, walks, books, crafts, etc. She is wonderful and I learn much from her.

I did not get away until 2:30, but escaped a rush of visitors. Students in groups. Stanley shows his slide show. But too much light talking. Talk of Church today always ends up making Deane mad and threatening to leave the Church.

## April 9

"Our dear sweet Christ on earth," a phrase used by St. Catherine of Siena when she was admonishing Gregory XI.

## Tuesday April 10, Perkinsville, Vt.

Yesterday, driving up the sun shone—brisk weather. Weatherman foretold snow and we woke up to find the ground white this morning, and the skies heavy with more. By noon inches had fallen. Wet heavy snow which sun could melt in a day.

Always, arriving at my daughter Tamar's, I feel completely relaxed.

## April 12

I would give up all the beauty of Tivoli and live in the vilest slum to save Eric and Nicky all the despair and unhappiness they are gong thru. And that Tamar is going thru because of them. It is right for us to love our families, but oh the heartaches.

But it is the cross, the saving Cross. We cannot have Christ without His Cross.

No Date: Passion Week

Letters: Fr. Hesburgh. A letter of thanks. I'd like to begin it with: "I am so grateful I can be bought with a sardine," St. Teresa. "It is not a sardine, a small fish, you have given me but a whale of a present—the Laetare medal." But that would be flippant—lacking in respect, insulting, deflating to all who prize such honors. I am guilty of uncountable sins of the tongue. If I could only learn more silence. If I could only recognize my "wise cracks" for what they are before it is too late, and the mischief done.

Here Lent is almost over, a scant ten days left and I have achieved nothing in the way of self-sacrifice, "putting off the old man" to make room for the new, to grow in Christ, to put on Christ, to be Christ to others, to find Christ in others.

Every day I say, "now I have begun."

Repetitious prayers—their efficacy. In jail—lights out, the girl who sang the Our Father. Is my memory at fault, or did I myself sing it to a tune I heard (in my heart) as I fell asleep? I certainly remember the woman brought in and put in a cell and crying all the day—she had stabbed her husband, who beat her frequently, using the knife she was cutting bread with for supper.

April 17

Wrote intro to [Dorothy] Gauchat book, *All God's Children*—how her work grew. An impressive book. Stanley typed it and mailed it from Grand Central as I arrived at noon for Mass at St. Agnes. My walking and breathing better.

April 19. Holy Thursday

Mussorgsky, Fyodor Chaliapin. 100th anniversary on WQXR.

Terrible and incredibly beautiful scenes of anguished remorse over death (murder) of his son (?). The horror of taking life. The love expressed. Suddenly the thought came into my mind of abortion and even tho our entire Prot pop has been taught that it was not "taking life"—"Life only began at 4 ½ months." Legal restrictions alone made women guilt ridden. Does the changing of laws—the Supreme Court decision—do away with this instinctive feeling of guilt? My own longing for a child.[324]

---

324 This is one of the very few references in any of Dorothy's writing, public or private, to abortion. Only in her autobiographical novel, *The Eleventh Virgin*, written before her conversion, did she describe her own decision to have an abortion after an unhappy love affair. The reference to her "longing for a child," is echoed in *The Long Loneliness,* a partial explanation of

April 20. Good Friday

No meeting. Mass awkward last night. The desire of Pat for beautiful liturgies. But we are in parish of the poor, large families. Good tonight. We
were all more together. Most of us from CW there. We could of course shop
around and find a Palestrina Mass at some Episcopal church, a Bach chorale
on Fifth Ave. But we are with the poor, the people. The disorderly. I found
it all very satisfying, tho not aesthetically. How far better than the long Latin
Masses, tho of course there was always a sense of worship, of mystery, at best,
and of acedie, at worst—a desire to escape, a feeling of stifling, not being able
to breathe in this dying-to-self supernatural atmosphere. Nothing to appeal
to natural—no stimulus for mind or food for benumbed soul.

April 21. Holy Saturday

We read John Tracy Ellis article in *Commonweal*. Extremely good. Gave
hope—enlarges vision on what is happening today in the church. The changes about celibacy are all to the good. If they would only allow the priest to
continue saying Mass—continue his ministry!

April 23

Dear God, our 3rd floor is like Ward #6. Please keep Anna and Julia from
violence. Help me to be peacemaker. Help me to help them in their fear and
suffering. Unto old age and grey hair forsake me not. I can do so little, have
such a sense of futility. ([Victor] Frankl, *Man's Search for Meaning*.)

April 24

Tonight I had drinks with our parish priests and scholastics. A very good
crowd. Cover story on Jesuits in *Time* magazine. Dean Brackley is the one I
know best. The poor are locked away from our churches, I mean the poor and
dissolute, like Eleanor and Bowery men who used to sleep in doorway, now a
huge iron gate there. I must canvas churches on East side.

April 26

Frank Donovan and Pat Jordan make up the paper every month. A thoroughly good job. Those who have been in seminaries or convents show the
training they have received, control of tongue (the perfect man? St. James),
the ability to work efficiently, both manual and mental labor. Sister from
College of St. Rose brought postulants or novices down once to clean "a truly
dirty place" instead of cleaning "to keep clean." Old saying, "Some clean

---

why her eventual pregnancy, while living on Staten Island with Forster Batterham, "filled her
with a gratitude so large" that only God could receive it. See also December 24, 1976.

to keep clean, others to get clean." We have learned from every Sister who came.

April 27

To *be* is good. I am grateful for life, to *be* in this world, frightful though it is today with wars spreading and expanding—Vietnam, Cambodia, Laos, Thailand. Mad and senseless, and seemingly headed toward catastrophe with Nixon as president—drunk with power, with no knowledge of fundamental Christianity in spite of religious services in the White House.

But we are more and more becoming world-conscious, conscious of our fellow man, Chinese, Russians, Malaysian, Indo-Chinese, etc.

Young people are studying more and more about religion—Hinduism, Buddhism, Confucius, Tao, Plato, etc. In other words, studying man in relation to the world.

These horrible wars, I think of as child-birth, bloody, accompanied with anguish of mind and body so often, but the physical function of child-bearing leaves its marks on mother and child.

Pope John told us to find concordances. Teilhard, whom I am reading, with the help of Henri de Lubac. "Faith in existence, faith in the world," is the starting point.

Ammon's favorite quote, "All things work together for good to those who love God."

This thought, these readings, this gloomy, rainy, cold April morning at Tivoli, are started by the offer of the Unitarian-Universalist prize—Toronto convention in June for best liberal religious writing of the year, *On Pilgrimage: The Sixties*. I am a Christian, a believer. How to or whether to accept this honor? Peter Maurin talked of his synthesis, his concordances, our meeting grounds. Karl Meyer's defection from Christianity (?) and my lack of knowledge of UU teachings, make me inclined to accept—to learn more. What a universal appeal the CW has in its simplicity.

Another concept of Teilhard—the Universal Christ, not Christ the King. (The word King always puts me off, as a product of the U.S. Then I learned from Dr. Karl Stern that he objected to Teresa of Avila always referring to "His Majesty"!)

April 30

"The influence and radiance of the Christian Revelation."—Teilhard.

Stayed all day, sunny and warm at our "dacha." Reading Solzhenitsyn's Nobel Speech. Beautiful.

What ugly corruption the Watergate scandal shows. Lying, bribery, forgery, theft, breaking and entering—what a power struggle. The nation shocked. [Rep. Bella] Abzug calls for a commission to impeach Nixon. He should resign.

May 1. Anniversary [of the CW]
Such drunkenness and noise in the house tonight that I could not stand staying downstairs for our 40th anniversary party. A vision of hell. Went upstairs and wept. Still not well tho I can walk without shortness of breath now. Am ashamed. Only disturbed others by my tears. Frank and Kathleen shocked as children are when they see an adult cry.

May 5
I am a mean impatient soul. Does me good to read [Dorothy] Sayers.

May 6. Mother's Day
Dorothy Sayers and Rosemary Haughton are two theologians who impress me. *A Matter of Eternity* (quotations from her writings). Very impressive.
Now a matter of conscience—can I accept the $1000 award from Universalist-Unitarian Soc. at Toronto in June? Must write Fr. Hugo. A reward for religious "liberalism"?
Mass was long and boring, God forgive me. Fr. Cletus slow and prayerful. Must talk to him tomorrow.

May 6. Kinderhook
Sitting on Della's east porch under the morning sun, listening to bird song, and basking in a windless day. The Peacemaker group and many CW readers who are not of them but wanting to learn more about them are having these two weeks an important conference in Peter Maurin house. The first week has been cold and windy, some rain each day. The children are enjoying it. Freedom from angry reproof and correction seems good for them. "Children are born to be happy," Castro says in one of his posters in Cuba.

Concerns
Problem of conscience. Unitarian-Universalist award. Do they take me seriously as a Catholic? Eyes that do not see, ears that do not hear. If they were awarding me for good works (concordances) yes. If for liberalism in religion, no. I am dogmatic. I believe in Divinity of Christ. Christ as God and Redeemer, Savior. True God and True Man. I believe in a Heaven and Hell. Resurrection of the body. Life everlasting. I believe with St. Augustine that

we are all members or potential members of the Mystical Body of Christ. In other words, that we are all members one of another, and that if the health of one member suffers, the health of the whole body is lowered. I believe with the IWW that "an injury to one is an injury to all."

Members or potential members of Christ? Since there is no time with God, we cannot judge others, their spiritual status. "It does not yet appear what we shall be," St. Paul writes. Am I a religious liberal? Can I accept this award? To be honest, I'm afraid not. The offer of it shows that the book *On Pilgrimage: The Sixties*, which would have been 1200 pages if all of those 100 columns, more or less, of mine had been printed, was not understood. Or, of course, that I do not understand the Unitarian-Universalist position.

### May 9

James Luther Adams—a Unitarian Universalist, a very noble man. A Christian Universalist. Never knew there were such. But I have written to Boston that I cannot for health reasons come to the banquet.[325] They had already said it was not necessary. Marty told me about Adams. Also about the prisoner, Martin Sostre.[326] How much work—even in letter-writing to be done.

### May 10

Have been working with Pat Rusk over mail—really catching up. I sent Dan Berrigan a Bonhoeffer book and he sent a check for $500. We sent $5,000 to Cesar [Chavez]. Dr. Coles's book is out about CW. First St. with Jon Erikson's photos.[327] Latter has been very ill. I wrote him.

I am most interested in Peacemaker discussions of Land Trusts which are growing all over the country. We are in effect one, since our land is in a holding corporation to be administered by the unincorporated Catholic Workers—those who are doing the work. We do not believe in voting officers or unanimous decisions. One would wait forever,

### May 14

Am eating right so I feel better but it is humiliating to be on or rather have extra fruit, cereal, yogurt, raisins for iron, etc. Veg diet is excellent. Peacemakers teach us much. They are generous, truly peaceful, hardworking, painting,

---

325 Dorothy received the Frederic G. Melcher Book Award *in absentia* at the General Assembly of the Unitarian Universalist Association in Toronto, May 31, 1973.

326 Martin Sostre was a black activist who spent eight years in prison on what he claimed were trumped-up charges. Amnesty International recognized him as a prisoner of conscience.

327 *A Spectacle Unto the World* by Robert Coles, with photos by Jon Erikson (New York: Viking, 1973).

cleaning, between long meetings. Young and strong. I love them. Chuck Matthei a natural leader, inspiring others, drawing them out.

May 16

Roger and Walter arrived at five p.m. with the typewriter and also Dr. Coles
and Jon Erikson's book. I loved it. Beautiful pictures of the family at First St.
and a text, and the word I liked was "ordinary" about people and their capacities. Must read it more leisurely.

May 21

"The joy of the Lord is your strength." Neh 8:10.

I am sitting here in Perkinsville in the hot morning sun after 10 weeks of
rain and cold and the sound of birds and the sound of rushing brooks fills my
ears and there are no other sounds. By my side my 3-months-old great granddaughter Kachina is sleeping. There is another great grandchild Sean Patrick
to be baptized Sunday at St. Mary's church in Springfield, Vt., 15 miles away.
It is early and Hilaire, Maggie, Martha and John (Becky's husband) are all out
planting, putting out the lush plants which have come up in the greenhouse.
It is still. There is no wind.

Cats, dogs, goats, chickens, the two steer up the hill, all have to do with
life, with being and becoming. The youngest member of this community is
Kachina, and the oldest is me.

May 26. St. Philip Neri

A delightful saint who used to kneel by his window looking out over Rome
and praying for her. He wished his followers to cultivate all their gifts to the
full, he opened an oratory of Sacred Music, "Nothing too high for him, nothing too low." He taught beggar women their prayers, children the lives of the
saints. A spirit of joy. The Rochester NY group came at noon. We talked till 6
about the house there. The usual problems, of young people and the freedom
in sex life which is a problem everywhere. St. Monica. St. Augustine wrote of
her, "It was You, God, who made her obedient to her parents, rather than her
parents made her obedient to You."

May 31. Ascension Day

A beautiful day. Sunny breezy. Things quiet, comparatively. We have
$25,000 from John Magee, $10,000 from Abbot Eudes [Bamberger] for
house. St. Joseph will have to find it for us.[328]

---

328  The money was for a new house for homeless women—eventually Maryhouse on 55 E.
3rd St. Most of the funds were a gift from the Trappist Abbey of the Genesee.

June 6

Mary Lathrop in bringing *NCR* [*National Catholic Reporter*] with pages on me with an interview which Stanley said was obtained by a fellow saying he was a student writing a paper for Columbia! More personality cult. Dwight Macdonald did the same thing with a telephone conversation (in *NY Review of Books*).

June 8

To supper with Eileen, Tom Sullivan, Gordon Zahn at Ratners. A good and simple meal but how expensive all is. Such a good evening. Tom epitomizes faithfulness, to me one of the greatest of virtues. Constancy, dedication. He is blessed in his vocation. Assist. Principal and counselor at a large, black school in Roosevelt, L.I. Fearless and constant. Every few months he takes me to dinner. Tonight he brought me Chekhov's Letters. $17.50!!

June 9

Last night Gordon Zahn spoke well, on aims of the Catholic Peace movement. Less attention to "alternate life styles," more labor for peace, for prisoners of war, exiles, etc. His whole heart is in it. He spoke of Franz Jagerstatter. Then he spoke of being Catholic, faithfulness and obedience and respect for the church. Not to call ourselves Catholics if we did not wish to abide by her disciplines. He is strong, a noble figure in the peace movement. A task for me to study his writings—call attention to them, build up esteem for him, and so imitation of his dedicated life.

I was mush impressed by his talk. Thank God for him.

June 10. Pentecost

 Woke at 6. Went back to sleep and dreamed of looking for houses, getting to Mass, very confused, but one picture stands out, a somber figure like Murphy sat by a crib and called my attention to the baby which I picked up in my arms. It was a little black child, but pale skin. He said, "It is dying," and I held it in my arms—it was like Tanya, and I felt such love and grief it woke me up. I've been reading the *Imitation* ever since, and thinking of the joys and tribulations of this life, and Phil and Liz and their love and suffering. Somehow it all goes together.[329] Such choices are presented us! But such suffering. Generations of suffering.

---

329 Dorothy was troubled by the marriage of Phil Berrigan and Liz McAlister, a former priest and nun, who had wed without obtaining official dispensation from their vows.

## June 15

"A breath of joy." Read in *Prayers of Christians*, which Bill Gauchat sent. Prayed for him and his family, my family, the young people here, that they would experience that "breath of joy" that "rapture of the spirit" here in this sometime hell, ugliness, noise, suspicion, anger, contention, and lack of brotherly love. That they would find their special vocations and pursue them. This is lasting joy and sureness.

## June 17

Sunny and bright. We all do too much talking. Stories of history of CW, stories of others' tragedies. I must stop. Must go to confession about this. More silence in my life. "I must decrease, others increase." Fr. Don Hessler said that to me a long time ago. Will I never learn?

Am reading with great delight *Once and Future King*. Another Christ figure (in that we are all supposed to be "other Christs"). Like the Idiot and Don Quixote are. "Put off the old man."

## June 19

We feel so powerless. We do so little, giving out soup. But at least we are facing problems daily. Hunger, homelessness, greed, loneliness. Greatest concern of the Bible is injustice, bloodshed. So we share what we have, we work for peace.

## June 20

A call from Joan Baez. To speak in California at her school for nonviolence and at WRL.[330]

Reading Chekhov letters. $17! from Tom Sullivan. His work during cholera epidemic. Dostoyevsky influenced my youth and gave me the insights for today (such work as ours). But Chekhov's stories and letters are a never-failing inspiration now.

## June 21

Joan Baez called a second time to come to Institute at Palo Alto July 30-Aug 5. Farm Workers will be there. WRL after that? I said I would go.

## June 23

7 p.m. Michael Cullen and Tony Russo, associate of [Daniel] Ellsberg, former worker at Rand [Corporation]. He [Cullen] looks so young to be father

---

330 The singer Joan Baez was a founder of the Institute for the Study of Nonviolence in Palo Alto, California, the site, that year, of an annual convention of the War Resisters League.

of four. My only advice to him was to accept deportation if it came.[331] "All things work together for good," even our mistakes, even sin, since God can bring good out of evil.

June 24. Corpus Christi

Up at seven and I had time to go to Mass at 9 a.m. Happily the Tabernacle was surrounded with flowers, altar cloth hanging in front, richly decorated, vestments beautiful, fitting the celebration of so great a mystery as God giving Himself first as Man, then leaving Him with us as Bread and Wine. Reading Book IV ch 1 in *Imitation of Christ*. How great Beauty, how great a remedy we have with us! Deo gratias.

Rosemary helped me with some letters at the beach. The beach always fascinates. I love Teilhard de Chardin because he loved stones! Horseshoe crabs are laying eggs all over beach. Profligate.

June 27

Coming out of Mass, Sister Eliz told us of Third St. Music School for sale. It looks *too good*. Henry broke down our tree again. Mike Kirwan unfazed, fit with a splint.

July 6

John Cort arrived and stayed until after Vespers. The same good, dear person. Ten children, one wife.

Five Carmelites, 4 in college yet, came for last 5 days, helped in clothing room but were not real workers. Our surroundings are a shock to people. They do not find the work worth doing. Talked to them an hour. At end of day was exhausted. Yet when I beg the BVM for strength I get it. I forget to ask. Where is my faith?

July 7

Reading in bed. *[Portrait of the] Artist as a Young Man*. That retreat! How cradle Catholics lament the guilt instincts they suffer from. Tamar too. All the more reason to write about retreat. About priests. Chastity and celibacy. Teilhard de Chardin. John Cort likes him too. John was frankly a virgin when he married. He shocked Joe Hughes by this admission. When I told Joe the act of love, the marriage act was a sacrament, he said, "I've heard it called many things but not that."

---

331 Michael Cullen of the Casa Maria House in Milwaukee, having served a prison term for his part in the Milwaukee 14 draft board raid, now faced deportation to his native Ireland.

July 11

A wonderful letter from Abbot John Eudes, offering to subsidize the house, selling superfluous goods. The price does not seem to appall him. I must write more openly of money, like Jane Austen. Write too about that $300,000 tax bill. Secrecy is wrong.

July 13

Anne Perkins gave me a Portable Viking of Chekhov. In one letter he said he would have to travel 25-30 days by carriage. The rest by steamer on deck or in a room writing letters. Even if he accomplished nothing, "Won't the whole journey yield at least 2 or 3 days which I shall remember all my life, with rapture or with bitterness?"

July 15

All summer I'm reading Chekhov letters. How could he write so many! He loved his family and friends.

A wonderful letter from Joan and Chris [Montesano] about the death of their poor crippled child (no skull).[332]

July 17

Cure for despondency, according to T.B. White in *Once and Future King*— to learn something new (about birds or fish, in this case). Napped an hour. Must be sensible. Forster called up and told of strange interview while he was in hospital again. A Village casual acquaintance about whom he knew nothing, Sylvester Rocco, approached him and wanted him to find out if we would take Gene O'Neill's son at Tivoli.

How we cannot get away from our pasts. F. wants his name spelled right in Miller's book, next edition! Sooner or later I must read it. I love Coles's book and naturally Bob Fitch's. Not vanity, but gratitude.

July 19. Tivoli, cool, beautiful

Sue is taking Kachina to specialist about a lump on her spine. The Montesano baby born with no skull! O the sorrows. Both Sue and John are brave and young and have some knowledge of the place of suffering, the meaning of their pain in this war-torn world.

Spent morning with Deane—her birthday. She suffers most because she is old, won't accept it. A rebel. She has been doing very well, studying Span-

---

332 The Montesanos were founders of the Sheep Ranch Catholic Worker farm in California. See Chris Montesano's article "Therese" (December 1973) about the death of their infant daughter.

ish, Braille, flute-like recorder, making a tape library—has all her columns on tape, but misses her friends, Clare, the Marshalls, Caroline Gordon, etc., had bad scare in dining room, "Lost control—was beside herself," she said. Wished they were blind, etc.

July 26
News our offer accepted for House [a former music school on East Third St.].

July 27
Sue says baby will be operated on Tues. Benign tumor on spine.

*Dorothy accepted Joan Baez's invitation to California, which afforded, among other things, an opportunity to picket with the United Farm Workers in Delano. As it turned out, this provided the occasion, at the age of 75, for her final arrest.*

July 30
Arrived at 2:30 Calif time. It is now late. Joan [Baez] came to sing all evening.

July 31. St. Ignatius
A long drive to Delano and arrived as meeting ended. Today many arrested. Also nuns attending Institute.

August 1
Up at 2 a.m. and picketed practically all day, covering many vineyards.

August 2. Day of arrest
Went from Park (up at four a.m.). Went to plum orchards, grape harvest there too. Injunction here. 8 groves united and many small groves. Selma, Sanger, etc. Large picket line, where pickets were supposed to be 100 feet apart, etc. Three (or 2) buses picked us up, 99 women (42 nuns), 57 men (2 priests). Brought to Caruthers 640-acre farm—can take 300 but 100 or so here. We occupy 3 barracks, 2 with riot fencing, which encloses yards. Allowed out 2 hours daily. Medications daily, mail, visitors, we keep our suitcases. Eileen brought mine. Fr. John Coffield my first visitor and Sean Burke, MM, and Sister Reina Paz.

August 3

One of the women who could not reach her family and was not allowed to phone got ill, presumed to be having a heart attack, and was taken to hospital in Fresno. Afterwards we found that after electrocardiogram she was put in County Jail, alone in cell. Poor woman. They are all so gentle. This violence has really taken hold. Maria Hernandez still ill. Flu is going around. One of our guards said she coughed all night. They are all doing extra duty. No overtime pay.

August 4

Eileen [Egan] has come three times, brought returning suitcase, stationary, has picketed again. What hours. Always a report on radio of strikers' violence. No talk of teamsters running down cars, pointed sticks. Police pay no attention to them. Protect growers and thugs. Talk over radio of National Guard! But women reserve guards are called and are doing double time. Constant medical attention. No complaints.

August 5

With such a crowd in prison there is little time to write or read. Fr. Coffield comes every day. Brings food. Kathleen and Pat [Jordan]. Big day tomorrow. Legal aid from union comes in, gives news, asks about complaints. I'm given one all-purpose vitamin a day. Also kelp.

August 6. Transfiguration. Hiroshima Day

Interview or visit from a grower's wife, Glenda. They own 40 acres. Second visit, Eugene Nelson, IWW, tried to interview me for [*Industrial Worker*]. but told him he'd have to wait until 8. He could not wait. Again, many visitors for the families and Sisters, priests. The Sisters and some farmworkers signed up for a night of prayer. It got cold tonight. I feel very rheumatic. No arrests made yesterday tho a mass picket line turned out. Tonight young legal assistant humiliated by guard. He looked like an El Greco painting. Many visitors tonight. Mass after. Very beautiful.

August 7

Mass in yard. Ecuador Bishop from L.A. Many priests from Fresno.

Maria Hernandez back from jail. Today no other strikers there. She is very upset, vomiting, sick. All fasters asked to give their names. Breakfast today, hot oatmeal, orange juice, all you want, bacon, toast. Other inmates very friendly.

August 8

This morning Joan Baez, her mother, and Dan Ellsberg visited and she sang the most poignant prison song. Her voice, her complete control of it, is remarkable. It tore at your heart. Very dramatic.

August 9

Dream of these beautiful smiling faces. Then before waking of John in trouble, baby brother.

Dr. Evan Thomas, brother of Norman, came, despite his 91 years, by barracks and sang for us all. There were many other illustrious guests. The only real humiliation and hardship in the experience was the fact that showers and toilets were all lined up openly in rows, and Mexicans are modest people. They got up at various hours to perform their toilet. I was remembering how I have seen women bathing in their dresses during the days I spent in Calcutta. They sat on curbstones next to hydrants, bathing in just the same way. The open rows of toilets was also a not too refined form of torture.

August 10

Today a most crucial day for reconsideration of teamsters. Much praying. This a.m. before breakfast all were on their knees beside the two long tables, praying the rosary.

August 12

Lawyers here tonight. Probation officer also. Said we'd be out tomorrow. Beautiful Masses each evening. Power of prayer.

August 13

All left at nine, sent right back to the Industrial Farm. Public defenders came. Mass meeting in park. Slept at Sisters of St. Joseph. Cesar welcomed us at Park—Helen [Chavez] and daughters also. Action moving to Delano now. Picketing now there as Cesar wants. [333]

August 14

Trials begin. Judge Harper.

Eve of Assumption. Month of importance. Death and Transfiguration. Hiroshima and Nagasaki martyrs. (Death is swallowed up in victory.) No time with God. On this feast Mary's resurrection meant her life sacrifice was accepted by God. Her assumption into heaven was not merely a privilege bestowed without relation to rest of her life. It formed summit of her sublime

---

333 Dorothy provided a better account of her time in jail in her column of September 1973.

redemption. Salvation embraces whole human being, not only his soul but
his body.

August 17

Today was to have been a day for a Mass meeting at Delano Forty Acres
but an early call notified us of a funeral instead, in fact of two deaths, Juan
de la Cruz, shot thru heart by high-powered rifle, and the other in Lamont,
an Arab boy from Yemen, Naji Daifulla. We drove from Fresno and arrived
to follow an already mile-long parade of mourners, and to hear the wailing
mourning of Muslim liturgy.

August 18

Picketing called off. Boycotting to go ahead, and fundraising. Cesar is confronted by a tremendous challenge, and many sorrows. Another Moses. What
patience needed.

August 19

I lose all track of time when traveling. Now I am in L.A. Ammon Hennacy
House, finished copy for Sept., thank God.

Sister Catherine [Morris] (Holy Child) is here at A.H. house 5 days weekly.
Fasting.

August 24

Mass at St. Basil's, to confession to Cardinal McIntyre. Many at Mass, great
and beautiful church often crowded.

September 1. Dallas

A marvelous day with Cath Pentecostals who alone had the courage to
do what they are doing, bring Mass and Confession to the Dump in Jaurez.
Meeting at an old school first—then, over border and the day in this utterly unbelievable place where 150 or so live on a volcano of refuse (for recy-
cling).

September 12

Judy [Gregory] went to Jaffrey N.H. to deliver her father's car. She is very
angry and wrathful over Women's Liberation. Really into it. It seems to bring
all anger to the surface. Sad. I am semi-retired.

September 14
Stopped at library. Got *China Diary* by Charlotte Salisbury. Very good.
Fritz wants me to go to China. Perhaps I've thought of a way to get a visa.
God guide me. We must find concordances, as Pope John says.

September 26
Pat Jordan, Frank and I to 120 Wall [St.] to sign a contract for Third St.
house. We are completely broke. Paid $20,000 down.

October 1. St. Therese
Telephoned Forster. Letters all day.

October 3. Guardian Angel
Auden high Mass 8 p.m. missed.[334]

October 5. Washington, D.C.
To Ed Guinan's house. School of nonviolence. [CCNV—the Community
for Creative Nonviolence, in Washington, D.C.]

October 7. Franklin [Spier] died.[335]

October 8
David [Spier] here yesterday and today. What a son! Glad Tamar has Hilaire to rejoice over.

October 13
Wrote Abbot [Bamberger] last week and heard from him immediately. He
sent $10,000 to make up for $10,000 we lent (gave) Fr. Lyle.

October 16. Passport, glasses
News of Israeli war very bad. [Henry] Kissinger gets Nobel Peace Prize.
Called Forster. He's very weak. Told me to call his lawyer if anything hap-
pened to him.

---

334 Dorothy had become acquainted with the poet W.H. Auden through Helene Iswolsky's
group, the Third Hour. She wrote his obituary in her column for October-November 1973.
335 Franklin Spier was her sister Della's husband. In "On Pilgrimage," October-November
1973, she wrote, "Franklin Spier was a dear friend who was always trying to find concordances
with me, though to all appearances we were miles apart religiously."

October 17
  Visited Förster. His mother came from Lancaster. Must re-read Brother Lawrence and do 2,000 word introduction for Mr. Garvey. $200.[336]

October 18
  Visited F. A bombing on 14th St. made me so late I arrived at CW dinner time, having missed Mass and late for visit with Anne Perkins We have delightful bookish conversations. This time about the biography of Florence Nightingale and the Crimean War out of which came abolition of buying commissions, the opportunity for women to go into nursing, and medical work in England, etc. And how God brings good from evil, etc. She borrowed Pope John's letters.

October 20. Beach
  It is 7:30 and I have been up since 5:30. So beautiful it is down here. I am trying to persuade F. to get a little house down here near us. I am sitting up on a cupboard so I can look out the high windows at the Bay and tide going out and hundreds of gulls, wheeling and circling, almost dancing in the air, settling on the rocky seaweed-covered rocks, finding a delicious breakfast evidently. We came after dark last night so I must enjoy today, going in tonight. There looks like a harbor seal on the big rock!

November 2
  Anarchist (Israeli) meeting at War Resisters. John Stanley and Isidore there. Not too hostile. Did not read flyer they distributed.

*In November Dorothy traveled to England and Northern Ireland with Jane Sammon. She described her trip in the December 1973 issue.*

November 25
  This morning 11 a.m. high Mass at the Cathedral. Beautiful choir. Congregational singing, the vernacular now. Mass, yet Credo and Pater Noster in Latin sung by entire congregation—tremendous organ. Full triumphal Bach Toccata and Fugue at end as organ voluntary. Bitter cold in house. Insanity of British for fresh air.

---

336 Dorothy's introduction to Brother Lawrence's spiritual classic, *The Practice of the Presence of God* (Springfield, IL: Templegate, 1974) was reprinted in the March-April 1976 issue of the CW.

November 26

Still in bed at 10:30 reading Chaucer's *Canterbury Tales*.

Plane to Belfast at 5 p.m. completely deserted streets; an autistic city, working men at war with working men: Prot-Cath. Broken windows, boarded up. Bombings and snipings daily.

November 28

I'm losing all track of time as I relax in the comfort of Dublin where I am comfortable for the first time at the hotel and have enough to eat without asking for it.

November 29

New people and beautiful new places. From Tralee to Donegal, and 4 miles past. Now, Friday a.m. I am catching up. Mike [Cullen] and Netty have found kindred spirits in Pat and Ulton, her husband, 3 children. What faith, what joy. But I am sure Netty has won it all by her patience and endurance. She reminds me of my own daughter and all she has gone thru. Mike has faith and vision, and being a family man, 4 children and another coming perhaps, is the apostle for our time.

December 6

CW out. Jan's story secular. "Hints"— I should not let myself be disturbed.[337] *Monthly Review*, not CW. We have so little space. My own story feeble. But generally paper is beautifully done. 2nd issue by new printer. I am still very tired.

December 7

Hildegard Goss-Mayr. Up at 5:30. Reading, prayers, saints, and how we learn from them not to judge the present day, and holy men's involvement with the state.

December 15

Reading [Eugene] Debs book on prisons.

# 1974

January 10

Finished O.P. column. Not very good. Uninspired, pedestrian.

---

337 See Jan Adams, "Inflation," December 1973.

January 11

Made tape for Gordon [Zahn] on c.o.'s I remember at Stoddard and Warner.[338] Bob Gilliam gave very good talk on c.o.'s—peace movement in general
in CW. Both Bob and Gordon ignore class war, race war, man-woman war.
(Women's Lib.) Good crowd.

Not to speak of worker-scholar war. He spoke of early 30s, "everyone for
peace." Communists and fellow travelers. Committee against War and Fascism. How we always had to separate demonstrations!

January 23

Struggling all week with introduction to Brother Lawrence. Neglect correspondence which is more important. That and O.P. for CW are more important. So little time. Necessary to eliminate.

February 28

Visited beach. Windy still. Man died on golf course. I remembered a priest
saying, "If we asked to be born from the womb we'd be reluctant—it is the
same about being born into eternal life." A strange saying but good, if one
has faith.

April 11

Archivist [from Marquette University] here all day, packing material, all
letters will be closed to public until year 2000.[339] All other materials, writings,
pamphlets, books, my articles, etc. open.

June 6

Jane Sammon and Kathleen Jordan came for overnight visit. Letters. Invita-
tion of Sister Donald to Carmelites in Bronx, also from Abbot John Eudes.
Both girls urge me to go. A sign, they said. But I have more silence on buses.
Religious make me speak. One reveals one's self by talking. Is mine empty?

June 7

Girls brought me my Oxford Bible. St. Paul's love of women shown in
Philippians. Very cold wind. Forster called.

---

338 Gordon Zahn wrote an account of Catholic c.o.'s in World War II: *Another Part of the
War: The Camp Simon Story* (Boston: University of Massachusetts Press, 1979).

339 According to a later understanding, Dorothy's diaries and family correspondence were to
remain sealed until twenty-five years after her death—November 2005, as it turned out.

July 10
   Mass at Huguenot for Forster.

July 16
   Tape of [Daniel] Ellsberg at Brown Univ on Solzhenitsyn. Lunch, rest, two heavy rainstorms. [Gulag] Archipelago. Comparable experience for Solzhen—Ellsberg.
   Faith in a man's power to write, speak.

July 20
   Forster left hospital.

August 8
   I came up last night, Pat Rusk driving me, and our two guests, Mary Humphrey and her oldest son John, who is retarded. A peaceful happy soul who shows he has always been loved and accepted by a large and talented family.
   The specialist's verdict last week was that my heart condition was indeed that of heart failure, which was what Peter Maurin suffered from and so did our much loved Fr. Roy (see his story in *Loaves and Fishes* and Peter's in *The Long Loneliness*). In their case, the heart had such difficulty pumping blood to the brain that they could no longer function, and had to be cared for like children for the few years before their death. They were both hard, hard workers, being indeed what they wanted the other fellow to be—that is, "servant of all." Using their great talents for the service of others. As today, even always, there were many "loafers living off the Catholic Worker and the hard, hard labor of others." That last is in quotation because it is the prevalent complaint when I arrive at the farm for a visit to hear also that other complaint, "You are never here!"
   When Kay Lynch and her 80-year-old mother were with us, Joe Cotter passing thru the dining room said to Mrs. Lynch, "Good morning; how are you today?" "No complaints," she answered. "You don't belong here, then," was his bright reply. I like to recall this every time I arrive at Tivoli because I am the receptacle of all the stored up frustrations of, especially, our oldest and dearest of fellow workers who indeed keep the place going, give the work continuity, and whom I look on with deepest affection and satisfaction. They have taught me many a lesson in faithfulness and they are also mirrors in which I see my own reflection.
   St. Paul implied or wrote (I cannot find the quotation now) that we see the imperfections of others because those others are a mirror reflecting our own

faults. I too complain ceaselessly in my heart and in my words too. My very life is a protest. Against government, for instance.

August 9

My godchild Johannah bitterly unhappy. God, make haste to help her.

August 13

At Della's. Inspiration to write Della a daily spiritual letter (would she read it?). I want her to have the same comfort I have each morning.

August 14

Dear God, help me not to judge people harshly. But men certainly take advantage of women more than ever these days.

August 22

Everyone under the weather. Fasting, naturally all day. B. constantly dropping by to see if he could help me. God help him. We are an "open ward" at times.

September 17

Reading *Poustinia* by C. de Hueck. Eugene Geissler asked me to write a blurb. Ammon's Joan Thomas also asked me to write a blurb, saying "Silence is golden but gold is you know what." Blackmail. So here goes. The book is not Ammon, it is Joan. Not A. as we have read him and heard him spoken of. There was never anyone quite like him. None has worked as he worked. No one was as courageous as he, long suffering, enduring and endearing. It is really a novel, not a Jungian interpretation of A, as Joan wrote us. A novel about J, not A.[340]

October 26

Eileen going to New Brunswick to receive ACLU award (to be presented to me by [Jules] Feiffer, cartoonist). Must write acceptance and apology for her to read.

October 28,

I must get to work. No more speaking. All cancelled. Eileen Egan took ACLU meeting at Rutgers last night. Bob Gilliam spoke on [Eric] Gill at one Friday night. Not as good as his talk on nonviolence.

---

340 Joan Thomas, Ammon Hennacy's widow, recounted his story in a self-published memoir, *Years of Grief and Laughter: A "Biography" of Ammon Hennacy* (1974).

At end he spoke of his simple Catholicism, not the same as today's "advanced thinking," and I took it to mean on the family, birth control, etc. He (Gill) was far more advanced than modern youth with their acceptance of birth control. Gill's *good* sensuality and his frank thankfulness for the pleasure, the joy of sex had a sound foundation.

November 19
Ruth Collins with "tiger's milk" and vitamins, a fine array of pills. My weakness and loss of weight is bothering me and others around me.

December 7
Forster called. 80 years old this week.

December 17. Retreat
Convent Corpus Christi. Dominican. Perpetual adoration.
Wrote O.P. for January. And more. Writing is Prayer. (*Prayer is a Hunger* [Edward Farrell]).

# 1975

January 1, 1975
John and Tessa [Day] visited last week, a lovely day. Brought books—Chesterton's autobiography, and two old volumes by Mrs. Jameson about saints and angels in art and sculpture. She was a widely traveled Englishwoman.

January 13
Fr. Lyle and Bishop Gumbleton of Detroit offered Mass. Anna talks and berates me continually. Nerve wracking.

January 22
Steady enough and cold these days. This is longest month. Wonderful silence. Time to think, read, study scripture. C.S. Lewis chapter on scripture in *Reflections on the Psalms*. Wonderful.

February 1. Staten Island
We are going to Holy Child church on Amboy Road now, the 9:15 Mass which is sung. Prayer sung is twice said, according to St. Augustine. Today the blessing of candles and of the throat. A good talk on sacramentals which "predispose us for the sacraments."

February 3

Finished OP. No heat at St. Joseph house. Oil ran out. Also office broken into and all the little envelopes of Bowery men's SS money taken—about $250 dollars in all. Before day was over one of our readers came in and brought gift of $250! God is good.

February 11. Ash Wednesday

Blizzard, sleet, and snow all day. No chance for ashes. Will fast from coffee.

February 14

I am trying to write 2 pages daily. Saw [George Bernard] Shaw movie on "tellie." He wrote 5. I write about 3 long letters a day. It is an act of humility not to write with carbons. But I write by hand.

February 18

Reading old letters to Della. Della is naturally a hermitess. She gave me a list of birds.

February 19

Reading and resting. Very good visit but no walks. In the shrubbery, no footpaths. Now housebound, learned much about the Talmud in the Rabbi detective stories.

March 8

Today I finished my March-April On Pilgrimage, some typed, but my bedroom was too cold so I handwrote it in the kitchen. Very inferior. Always so hard. Next month it will be this day-by-day account. People like diaries. I know I do... Frank came down to get the copy which he will type. They—he and Anne [Fraser] and Bill [Griffin]—can cut and otherwise correct. This month I wrote one article for *Newsday*, read proof on a taped talk given at Community Church when given Gandhi Award, and not so long ago a brief sketch about Auden for *Harvard Quarterly*. And letters, letters, letters. The CW correspondence is enormous. Mailing costs are enormous. And food, shelter, warmth, what we give away is enormous. "If we sow sparingly we will reap sparingly." So no use worrying about money. Our heavenly Father knoweth we have need of these things. Money for repairs on house.

March 9. Coldest day this winter

At Holy Child parish I've been to 8, 9:15, and 11 o'clock Masses and every one was a sung Mass, all congregation participating. Not a guitar Mass, organ. Deeply impressed. Poor boxes, a St. Vincent de Paul Society. This is personalism, not centralism and referralism, which is a run-around system. The poor, poverty, like garbage, "kicked around until it gets lost."

March 10

Some bitter cold days. But so many deaths. I must say the Little Office of the Dead for them all and go on reading Dante's *Purgatorio*, one of the 3 Penguin books Dorothy Sayers translated with such brilliant introductions. These are drab days. I try to discipline myself, keep a schedule, but it is hard. Easier surrounded by community, in a way.

March 19

Reading C.S. Lewis, *Reflections on the Psalms*. His writing is delightful, inspiring, sets me off on meditating. The cursing psalms he handles marvelously. While I was in town I read *Beyond Personality* (his talks over BBC). I get new insights into my own life always when I read him.

March 22. Beach

We went to 5:00 Mass and were late. Coming in at long Gospel for Palm Sunday. I have no strength. I guess I expect too much of myself. Do not relax. Always confronted by mail. Heartbreaking letters. One must answer. And pray.

April 14.

Letter from Paul Moore [Episcopal Bishop of New York] inviting me to be a canoness at Cathedral [of St. John the Divine]!

April 16

Last night Bill Gauchat died at a cancer home. What suffering! Came into NY with A.J. Lacey, my good courier. My room is now Frank's office, Susie Weimer's sleeping room, and mine. Two mad women on our third floor. Susan a little treasure, bless her.

April 17

Anne [Fraser] and I will fly out to Cleveland, 1 ½ hours! We both fear planes. Easy flight, crowded. David [Gauchat] met us at airport. Our Lady of Wayside. Everything so exquisitely clean and beautiful. The children are surrounded by beauty and peace.

April 18
Funeral Mass at 11. Most moving, and beautiful. We all wept.

April 29
I read for 2 hours and pray each morning. Reading Pope John's journals. Also "Pilgrim's Regress," by C.S. Lewis. Very good.

May 22
Arrived at Rochester, Bethlehem Retreat House at Our Lady of the Genesee. Supper with Abbot.

May 23
Read Silone. Retreatants all men. No women around. New church beautiful.

July 14
Left Della's at 11. Downpour of needed rain. Eunice Shriver telephoned about Sargent deciding to run.[341] And could I sign in list of supporters! I an anarchist. But "Pray for him." I like her. He is a daily communicant.

July 16
Mary Lathrop visiting. Helped move to larger room. Forster called about Maggie. He had not called for a month. Asked an explanation! Meanness about money.

September
"There is only one *The* Church, in America," Lenny Bruce is supposed to have said. I cannot remember who quoted this to me.
(I once came across a book by Lenny Bruce—shockingly vulgar. Yet funny, as a small boy can be who has a wickedly vulgar sense of humor, which scandalizes respectable, or should one say "refined" parents. At the end his humor bared his tragic sense of life.

---

341 Sargent Shriver sought the Democratic Party nomination in 1976, but lost to Jimmy Carter.

September 9

I awoke with a heavy sense of a problem nagging at my heart. It is early morning, just light. Having prayed briefly and pondered long, I must write now. It is a work which goes on no matter how feeble my rheumatic knees—as long as I can think and hold a pen. I must try to be brief. St. Paul, who wrote so beautifully, so warmly of love, said "Let these things be not so much as mentioned amongst you," so great was his repugnance to homosexuality and lesbianism, unnatural sex. And now in this perverse generation, it is proclaimed from the housetops.

I must set down my own insights which came to me after prayer. I only go into this because two of our [friends] have now written and spoken to me of their acceptance of lesbianism. Whether this means they are "practicing" it, I do not know.

I am always being confronted in mind and conscience with those words of Christ, "Do not judge." And also the words of St. Paul, "Let not these things be so much as mentioned amongst you."

But this practice of "unnatural sex" is now being proclaimed from the housetops in America. (Maybe I exaggerate!) Because my heart is troubled. Why do I have to deal with it, write about it at all? It has been amongst us before, i.e. homosexuality, and judged with horror and coldness by some in the CW movement and with faithful friendship which endured till death by many others. One of the latter brought to my attention a treatise on Friendship written by St. Aelred centuries ago.

My meditation this morning began with St. Paul, whose writings I love, whose words are scripture and holy to me and from which I derive strength and nourishment. (People use the word "gospel" truth.) There is no record of Jesus having taken up the subject. Of course He differentiates between love and lust and instinctively we understand Him. (I have never looked up the word lust in the dictionary.)

But how wide and beautiful is our understanding of the word love—love of children, love of one's brethren (man, woman and child), and how it warms and strengthens the heart. And how often it must be called into play—70 x 7! How great a thing is love, how great a force, a tidal wave, a Niagara, which can utterly destroy, or, harnessed, can supply us with light and warmth and indeed life itself, one might say.

So one can consider love, human love when not controlled. How control it without the grace of God?

Even in so-called "natural love," it must be controlled and, if not enlightened by grace, can become a "delectation in temptation."

I am sure we all know enough of love to know that first thrill of adolescence when we can exultantly say, "I have a friend, a bosom friend," the phrase used to be.

The sun shone brighter, unexpected beauty appeared all around us in all our relationships, in fact, we were in a way "in love."

I remember two occasions in life when this happened to me. I was 15 the first time, in high school, studying Latin and history. I enjoyed Latin, Cicero and Virgil fascinated me. I did my homework with zest. History bored me.

It was the custom in that small h.s., too small for study halls, for us not taking the course being taught in the room at that hour to sit in the backseats and study, concentrate on tasks for the next day while another class recited. We must have had great powers of concentration. But there was one girl in the history class I always listened to when she was called on by the teacher to "recite"—that is, describe some situation in the era the class was studying. I cannot remember whether it was ancient or U.S. history. The fact was, it was the girl herself who fascinated me. She was plain, even homely, stringy hair, poor clothes, and no style about her—but her face was transfigured with intelligence and to me at least seemed to glow. She was beautiful at such a moment—to me, that is. She was undoubtedly a very intelligent student. I loved her. My own studies became more interesting. I worked harder at my studies. She was in a way a model to me. I never knew her name or anything else about her but in a way she cast a light about her. A schoolgirl "crush" perhaps, to describe this feeling, which ennobled her in my mind and enlightened me. To me she was the embodiment of Sancta Sophia, and I never forgot her, even tho the next year I fell in love with a basketball star, a truly physical passion for his graceful swift strength and skill, as well as for his bright and knowing blue eyes set in his face. When I wheeled my baby brother in Lincoln Park after school I gazed on the beauty of the blue sky between the leafless branches in the trees and was thrilled with the remembrance of his beauty.

I had a glimpse of this love once again in the first years of my conversion, when I went to Communion daily for the first time since my conversion six years before. (In my ignorance I thought daily Communion was only for the devout.)

The girl that attracted me at this time was a tall Polish girl, who had a stately beauty, giving an impression of strength. Such strength, I suddenly thought, as the Blessed Mother had when pregnant she walked the hills of Galilee to visit her aged cousin Elizabeth. Such strength as a girl had who could bear a child by herself in a stable, and knew how to deal with it, endure the facts of her human condition, one might say.

How contemplation of that Polish girl deepened my faith, and love for Mary—a real love, a living love which has comforted me (which literally means, made me strong with her).

Once I was asked to write an article for the *Marianist,* a Catholic magazine which may not now be in existence, and wrote glowingly of this encounter, one might call it, and never heard from them again.[342] Nor did they return my ms. Maybe they thought charitably that I was an unconscious lesbian and "least said, soonest mended," as my mother used to say.

But it is the time now to say it, to write about it, because it is one of the problems of the day. Two brilliant women in our midst have recently announced to me in all "honesty" that they were publicly acknowledging they were lesbians and in coming to me in this way paid me the compliment of accepting one as a person who followed Christ's teaching not to judge.

But I do not narrow that important command of Christ down to small meanings.

One must judge what is right and wrong and if one considers oneself of the Judeo-Christian faith, one must remember the admonitions in both Old and New Testaments about unbridled sex, practiced today in every form and fashion.

I am sure the knowledge of how men and women mated was a shock to us when we were children. It was even revolting to suddenly realize that our parents shared the habits of dogs who were so immodest (one should write "public") in seeking after and practicing sex. A child is so literal, so unlearned, that it is hard for him to accept his human condition. But falling in love more or less in the guise of hero worship for the first time brings with it a new light on human and even Divine Love.

I mean that one must be grateful for the state of "in-love-ness" which is a preliminary state to the beatific vision, which is indeed a consummation of all we desire. "What have I on earth but Thee and what do I desire in Heaven beside Thee?"

It is this glimpse of Holy Wisdom, Santa Sophia, which makes celibacy possible, which transcends human love. Oh, if we could only grow in faith, hope and love, and the greatest of these virtues is love.

September 14

Canonization of Mother [Elizabeth Ann] Seton. Now I know why my sudden impulse to get to N.Y. Mass Sat evening for her at Nativity, and Sunday

---

342 See "I Write of a Maiden," *Our Lady's Digest,* September 1948, pp. 155-159. Condensed as "Dorothy Day, a Stranger, and Our Lady," *Catholic Digest,* May-June 1981, pp. 73-76.

morning Spanish Mass!! My memories of a Sister of Charity who pushed me along in my conversion. Sister Aloysia.[343]

October 29
Visitors. Dan Ellsberg. (Bob [Ellsberg] is 5th floor.)[344]

November 14
Tom Cornell called. Bob Ellsworth is going to help him!

December 24
Helene [Iswolsky] died Xmas eve.

December 29
To embrace a faith is to "kiss a leper." To make a leap, as over a chasm, from one world into another; or to plunge into an abyss—"underneath are the everlasting arms."

# 1976

January 1
Stanley gave me this [diary] for a Xmas present. It will be my early morning diary at Tivoli where I lie abed and read each morning.

January 2
Can't do mail except postals. Can't write intro to books, give interviews, or help people with term papers or theses. Write Marty Corbin for that. He doesn't answer letters but does see people.

Too busy to write now as we are starting, or trying to, a house of hospitality for women and children.

January 3
We are two years in April getting Maryhouse underway.

---

343 Sister Aloysia, a Sister of Charity whom Dorothy met on the beach on Staten Island, helped prepare her to be received in the Catholic church, a story recounted in *The Long Loneliness*.

344 I arrived at St. Joseph House in September 1975 and met Dorothy soon after. She called me "Bob," "Young Ellsberg," or sometimes "Bob Ellsworth." My father had visited her when she was in jail in California.

January 14

Second day in new house, Maryhouse, E. Third St. All day a fear and trembling over my talk at UN church. Bob [Steed] and Walter [Kerell] over to lunch. Mass at 12:15 with Maryhouse group working on talk to UN meeting, Cardinal Cooke present. I asked for a priest for Tivoli. Tomorrow must send a [subscription] to him.

Jane Sammon and her troubles with a disturbed suicidal girl. We agreed to call Fr. McNutt to study more about healing. Letters from Jan Adams and taking her name off masthead and a good one from Fr. Hessler with check and request to send the CW to charismatic groups.

January 15

Got nothing done. Visitors—Mary Lathrop, Bob Ellsberg, Bob Steed. Missed Mass. Between Bob S. and Stanley and Deane running down the farm and its immoralities I felt quite sunk. Jane and I agreed on prayers for healing. Very quiet street here on Third.

January 18

Saw Fr. Paret tonight. He went over the house. Then after Mass I spoke to him about conditions. First to let priest know. He advised me to write Cardinal's secretary. M. Lathrop typed letter for me ready to go tomorrow. Decided not to send letter. Frank [Donovan] advised against it.

January 19

Called Pat and Forster tonight. He is very weak. Visiting nurses come. What a good person Pat is.

Bob Ellsberg's "Bread Labor," this month in CW. Very fine.

January 20

Forster just called. Visiting nurse in daily. Must ask Helene to pray for him. A miracle!

January 22

Peggy Scherer came in tonight.[345] Met her after Mass. A list of all at farm who are united in wanting to sell and buy smaller farms, decentralize. We will talk tomorrow. I will suggest plans drawn up and consulting Ruth and Frank. Also perhaps lawyer.

From now on I will settle in N.Y.

---

345 Peggy Scherer came to the Worker via the Peacemakers. She became a mainstay of Tivoli, and later served as managing editor of the CW.

January 23

Bob Ellsberg, Jim Forest, Igal Roodenko all spoke—the former at great
length. Eileen chaired. Crowded and very tiring. Many standing. They had
expected Dan Berrigan. Could not sleep last night, fretting about farm. We
were there since 1964.

January 25

New young priest appointed to Tivoli from Beacon (gave Helene I. Communion).

Jan 30

Just when I begin to feel a sense of letting go, relaxing, giving over authority
to Anne Fraser, Peggy [Scherer] and Sister Ann and [Sister] Charity, the latter
came to me discouraged. So a.m. spent in encouraging her. We had laughed
at her for worrying that our chairs did not match. We are so insensitive to
others. I must be more careful.

February 1

Gandhi Award—Promoting Enduring Peace, Community Church.

Feb 4

Bill Miller called about Rockefeller Foundation grant to Marquette for our
archives. I told him that no more papers will go to them until we get letters
assuring us this will not be accepted.

Feb 9

For the last year I have been afflicted with mites, scabies, not noticeable but
with small scabs on back of neck and shoulders, have used all prescribed remedies, sulphur ointment, camphor, and a powerful lice killer, to be washed off
10 minutes after applying (bathing, washing underwear and blouses, scarves,
to no effect). A punishment for little sins of impatience, overmuch talking,
sloth, lack of charity, etc, etc.

Feb 10

Prof. Miller wrote terse letter giving up, as I asked him, writing my biography. Also pledging himself not to use any Rockefeller funds for archives or
his work.[346]

---

346 William Miller's *Dorothy Day: A Biography* (Harper & Row) was published in 1982.

February 13

Msgr. Leonard 1-3 p.m. A good visit. He says he knows the Cardinal will allow us a priest for Tivoli and the Blessed Sacrament for Maryhouse.

March 17. St. Patrick

"I, Patrick, a sinner, am the most ignorant and of least account among the faithful, despised by many... I owe it to God's grace that so many people should thru me be born again to Him."

Mary Theresa, a black woman who lives across from us on First St., came in one night and sitting down with me, held my hand and quoted "He who says he is without sin is a liar and the truth is not in him." She went on quoting scripture in a singsong voice and I felt great warmth and gratitude to her. One finds the voice of God everywhere.

April 12

Chuck Matthei visiting us on his way to Alderson, W. Va. to visit Lolita Lebron. I sent her my New Mexico crucifix, which Eddie Cahill gave me in the 50s—a bloody Christ crucified for our sins. Also a shawl and a short breviary. The Holy Week psalms, especially Holy Thursday, are so beautiful. Imprisoned 22 years ago for her part in an armed attack on the House of Rep, in Washington. After Attica she led and planned a prison strike which all joined in, occupying one building. Other leaders were shipped out to other Federal prisons. She was one year in solitary.

April 15

Eunice Shriver called to offer me the use of her Hyannisport house in summer. She is reading my books. Bedside books, she calls them. She is not a happy person. "Do you believe in heaven and hell?" she asked me. "Why?" Driven by some sense of duty and the responsibility which goes with wealth and her family's experience in politics. And what tragedy. A lovely, unspoiled family of children—I met Bobby Kennedy's and hers at supper. The boy at Yale, young, responsible—a sense of family. He read Solzhenitsyn, whom I so love and even reverence.

And how brave a family. With the violence of our day and kidnappings so prevalent, resentment of the rich so strong. I marvel that they do not live in fear. But they have faith—the Faith.

April 16

Visitors pour in. A mother and three young ones—no one knows who answered the phone and accepted them. They are not introduced to anyone when they arrive. Ginny and Florent excessively rude when rebuked. The farm becomes like a hobo village, on the one hand, and a concentration camp on the other. Bob T. calls many times a day on someone's credit card. The suffering intensifies. God help us. Only He can. To move or not? Sell or not? "Where shall we go? He has words of eternal life."

April 18. Easter Sunday

Somehow I began thinking about taxes today. Maybe it was because death and taxes is an old phrase, and today being still Easter time it is Death and Resurrection, Death and Transfiguration which fills the mind.

I suddenly, or rather my mind suddenly began to work on the problem of taxes, and deductible and undeductible taxables. Are the poor who come to our door "the undeductable poor?" I'm afraid they are. We get so many inquiries from our friends and readers as to whether the Catholic Worker, or me personally, or our speakers from the staff are tax-deductible that this became a point I think needs clarifying in our own minds, as well as our readers.

No, it is the undeductible poor—or is non-deductible the word? who come to our door. They are the old, the lame, the halt, and the blind. Some of us editors are all three, but still able to work, thank God, answering mail, some amount of housework, laundry, cleaning rooms, etc. The younger wield the mop, cook the meals, bend over pots and pans, and take out the garbage (not to speak of spraying of rooms and beds).

Manual labor balances mental and spiritual. The Opus Dei is all embracing. (Embracing is a meaningful word.) We must ponder on it as we clean up after our untidy or destitute brothers, repair windows broken, and mourn over three broken trees planted—one planted by Holy Mother the City in front of our "disorderly houses."

No salaries are paid. So no trouble about taxes there. People do not give us "fees" for speaking, but contribute money to the Opus Dei, not to the speaker.

Twice I spoke locally last month and got neither fee nor contribution! This then is perfect joy! as St. Francis said.

Royalties from books written? Any author can tell how pitifully small they are. Paperbacks bring in 1 ½ cents a copy! But I rejoice to see them kept in print, as *The Long Loneliness* was, for 18 years by Image books (Doubleday) and is now reprinted by Curtis (out of print now) and the *On Pilgrimage* books had one big edition printed by Curtis and now Popular Books will bring out the Thirties, Forties, and Fifties. Or so I hope. The Thirties is made up and soon to go to Press.

But my royalties dribbling in are surely non-tax-deductible. I'm at last one with the unemployed. I have no taxable income.

But I cannot say I have the bitterness, the undeserved shame and humiliation of the unemployed. There is always work around Houses of Hospitality.

## April 20

I seem to have lost a day. Tues. I came back—a quiet trip. They told me all their troubles. Tanya came and lay beside me. "I was thinking of evil," she said. She is 7. What evil? "If I could break an arm and a leg at the same time!" Her 7th birthday next week.

## April 27

Read 30s [CW issues]. 2/3 of it. So much vital stuff left out. Might call it "Life Goes On" while Hitler in Germany was massacring Jews and anti-Semitism was rife in New York and U.S.! And Spanish Civil War, conscription, oppression, steel strikes, sit-downs in autos, sharecroppers being evicted, etc. Unemployment, poverty, "Home Relief" evictions. A cheerful book, as tho "what can we expect from life in this agonized world." The account of the Thirties amazed me as I read it—so much taken for granted. Conscription too. All heading toward WWII... . As I look back I remember so clearly WWI because Sam [Day] was radio operator on a mine sweeper in the British Channel and Donald [Day] in Air Force in Pensacola. I was in King's County Hospital nursing thru the flu epidemic. Coming daily on the ward to lay out as many as five bodies of those who died at dawn, night nurses had no time to get them down to morgue.

## April 29

To New York again for Chavez dinner and meeting at Madison Square Garden. Felt Forum. Melanie singing. Rock? Benefit concert. Had dinner first with Chavez at 84 St. headquarters. He wants an editor for a paper like ours, written like my On Pilgrimage. They have presses at La Paz. Maybe L.A. groups can help.

## May 6

Age and weakness. Halting steps. Uncertainty in walking. Constant aches, pains, and temptations to complain. The flawlessness and obvious falseness of "dentures," of false teeth, the blemishes, knotty veins, hollow temples, thinning hair, shrinking flesh. Thank God for models such as Mrs. Lynch who *accepts*. "No complaints," she replies to Jim Canavan as he passes the time of day with her. "You don't belong here, then," he replies grinning. "Unto old age and gray hairs forsake me not," she doubtless prays daily. Other psalm verses to mind. "Let me sing of the Lord. He has been good to me."

## May 9

I must remember old age and weakness go together. Not complain.

## May 12. Perkinsville

Over stimulation. Books, people, three lives—mental, physical, spiritual.

Physical and spiritual senses need to be "mortified," subdued, disciplined. In this time of rapid change and crisis ("so little time")—denying oneself. Taking up one's cross, especially needed.

Best help for women is manual labor, but they get too much of it.

Having spent 2 ½ hours in reading I will get up, wash accumulation of dishes from a day of company among these pioneers, these young people, this school, which is Tamar's turbulent family. Then I will return refreshed, more balanced, (giving up one's life to save it) to my job—part manual labor, of writing the OP column for June.

How can I be grateful enough when I see how beautifully Roy [Lisker] has recovered and how much he contributes to our joy at farm with his violin playing, his play readings, his silences in the face of disruption, his healing us, as well as we healing him. Truly Mutual Aid.

Yes, the farm is not to be criticized and maligned and looked upon as an utter failure, as it often is. What suffering and degradation we have seen there and what heroic endurance, forbearance. Constant expense and failure of course. We are the offscourings.

## May 30

Peter O'Donnell died, falling or plunging into an airshaft of an old tenement on E. 11th St. and Ave. C. O God, what suffering in the world. Nicky is going same way as Peter. Destruction to self, drinking. I must fast more. Sisters here fasted over problems and it cleared. More prayer and fasting.

## June 3

Sasha Bulgakov called. Desperate, tempted to suicide, living with his mother, and this month the condition of Nicky, young Peter's death, makes me realize I must give up my casual glass of wine or jigger of brandy recommended by my doctor for my aged heart.

June 8

Richard Taylor, Philadelphia, came with group about demonstrating at Eucharistic Congress.[347] Quakers all. All morning I was exhausting myself. I tried to talk personalism—"Be what you want the other to be"—not pointing out his (the hierarchy's) "crime" of spending so much money, while ignoring our own state of security—how far we were from poverty (holy).

June 17

Chuck Matthei back to Alderson [W. Virginia] having worked a few days with strawberry pickers. Interested in starting a H of H there for visitors to prisoners. He is checking to see if Lolita Lebron got her crucifix. They treat it at the prison as tho it were a bomb sent by a revolutionary group.

July 4

We had to sleep with windows closed! Hells Angels down street and their block party.[348] Fireworks. They came from all around Eastern states. They barricaded the block with cars. Sister Valerie made conversations with them. We are praying for them at Vespers.

July 8

Roger O'Neil came with his 3 beautiful daughters. What a good man!

Our readers write so often about the loss of faith of their children. Prayer is the only answer. "There is no time with God." "Pray without ceasing." These are the only answers.

July 9

Ours is a loving community, thank God. Thank God. Sister says we need not one hour but two in the morning. Pray without ceasing for our children today

July 30

The meeting in NY was wonderful. [Film of] Thomas Merton talking to monks at Bangkok, the last talk before his death. I must pray to him for aid now, and patience, and "diligence" in my work.

---

347 Dorothy was invited to speak at the Eucharistic Congress in Philadelphia on August 6, the Feast of the Transfiguration—a date also remembered at the CW as the anniversary of the atomic bombing of Hiroshima. Dorothy was disturbed to discover that the Congress organizers had chosen this date as the occasion for a Mass in honor of the armed forces. A group of pacifists planned to protest.

348 Maryhouse, the new Catholic Worker house on E. Third St., shared the block with the Hells Angels motorcycle club.

July 31

Our dear pastor invited me to a little party in their patio behind the rectory! God forgive me—I am too distraught with this Eucharistic Congress assignment to accept.

Well, I should thank God for this suffering of mine. If I did more penance, I would be stronger. God forgive me if I scandalize others by my fears.

August 5

Today to Philadelphia. Eucharistic Congress. Not at all prepared. One must just go where asked. A few simple words. "Fear not," is a most important message.

August 6. Hiroshima Day

*Dorothy accepted the invitation to speak at the Eucharistic Congress in Philadelphia on August 6. She was assigned the topic "Women and the Eucharist." She used the occasion to speak of her love and gratitude to the church for teaching her and nourishing her with the sacraments. But then, with sorrow, she addressed the decision of the Congress organizers to schedule a Mass for the armed forces on Hiroshima Day. "Today, we are celebrating—how strange to use such a word—a Mass for the military, the 'armed forces.' No one in charge of the Eucharistic Congress had remembered what August 6 means in the minds of all who are dedicated to the work of peace… I plead, in this short paper, that we will regard that military Mass, and all our Masses today, as an act of penance, begging God to forgive us… Today some of the young pacifists giving out leaflets here are fasting, as a personal act of penance for the sin of our country, which we love."[349]*

August 12

Two things I want to write about this day. Rejoicing in the Lord, Ps 97, for instance. All Thurs psalms in short breviary. The need of communal midweek prayer meeting. Attraction of music lifts up the heart.

Let us go to local Pentecostal group. He visited us! But not underestimate the profound value of silence!

August 28

Read proof Sept issue. I feel duller than dishwater.

---

349 Dorothy's talk, "Bread for the Hungry," was published in the September 1976 issue.

Read paper later. Not so bad but Chuck Matthei took 8 pages. And Bob Ellsberg the back page and both places meant front page openings![350]

August 30. Albany

Press day. Bob E, first time editing.

Very cold out. Sick this a.m. and weak three days. Too much orange juice Stanley gave me. Much comforted by Maisie Ward's favorite author Caryll Houselander, *The Reed of God*.

September 2

Walkers' feed group left at 7 to get to Rhinebeck.[351] The Gandhian spirit, to spread the word, to meet up with others, a silent witness to suffering and a leafleting too. How little I can do these days but suffer patiently the innumerable small difficulties of aging. And always Prayer which is a joy. Psalms are always the joyful ones on Thursday, in honor of the Last Supper. Where else would we have room save at Tivoli Farm for so much joy and sufferings?

*The strain of Dorothy's appearance at the Eucharistic Congress weighed heavily on her. In September she suffered a mild heart attack, which greatly limited her subsequent travels and activity.* [352]

September 3

The crowd gathering. Evening meeting. I could not go with what seemed like heart attack—pain in chest and left arm and great difficulty breathing. Pulse fast, Sue said. F sent Tamar $250 to help repair a car. Vermont is terrible. How poor are harassed. Stanley called her. She said "stay in bed two weeks." Glad to.

September 5

Dr. [Leroy] Holbert came today to see about my heart. Bed for a week.

---

350 Chuck Matthei, "A Nonviolent Campaign: Shelter the Homeless," and Robert Ellsberg, "Bringing the New Day" (on Gandhian spirituality) did indeed fill most of the September 1976 issue. It was my first issue as Managing Editor.

351 The Continental Walk for Disarmament, organized principally by the War Resisters League, attracted both long-distance and short-term walkers on a march from California to Washington, D.C.

352 "I had a mild heart attack in September, pains in my chest and arms and a gasping need of fresh air. It is certainly frightening not to be able to breathe... My orders were—bed rest for four weeks here at Tivoli." ("On Pilgrimage," October-November 1976)

September 11. Tivoli

Bombing in Grand Central Station. Listening to Thomas Merton's tapes. Very good. Papers full of Mao's death.

September 14

Rev. Jasko from the Pentecostal church visited and prayed over me for healing. They are going to have prayer meetings in homes. Hope they can sing.

September 17

Dr. Holbrook and his wife drove me to Hudson Hospital for blood test, x-ray, electrocardiograph. Rain all day, could not sit out.

September 18

Tonight a good movie on the Hudson River and a long one on "Long Distance Runner." I sat near door and in the dark room two state troopers came in with one of our old time guests (reeking of alcohol but able to stumble thru the score or so of people to the dormitory in the rear of the house). The police stood there like two guards for a moment (perhaps till their eyes became accustomed to the gloom). Everyone went on munching our usual popcorn treat.

September 19

Today a glimmer of sun. Reading psalms. Joy is a beautiful word. The rejoicing psalms on Thursdays and Sundays.

September 24

"I do not for a moment question that affection is responsible for 9/10 of whatever solid and durable happiness there is in our natural lives."—C.S. Lewis.

How necessary to show affection for one another! And no criticisms, judgments. Jesus said he came not to judge but to save.

October 4

A day of correction and humiliation for me. Deane contradicted all I said about air-raid drills to Jean, and I reproved myself (after being offended at her for accusing someone of walking off with my relic).

October 7

Sat out all p.m. under a young maple which dropped its red, yellow, and green leaves all around us. I talked to visitors, got overtired. Reading aloud or talking are a labor, so considered in monasteries. I mentioned my fatigue to Walter, a frank and honest soul, and said I had talked too much. "Yes, you do," he said frankly. How good community life is!

October 17
Finished O.P. on death in Psalms (joyful).
Hail Marys end with "now and at the hour of our death." How happy that thought makes me.

October 19. Feast of Jesuit martyrs
*Sojourners* editors today?[353]

October 21
Chuck [Matthei] in prison fasting, non-cooperating in jail. Peggy is very concerned. Will try to see him.

October 22
Awoke in great misery. Board of Health threatening to close us. Letter from Della yesterday and a gift. "Love is an exchange of gifts." (Where did I hear that?)[354] What a joy to say the Gloria in happy moments and the Credo when in need of reassurance and the Ave too with its conclusion, "Now and at the hour of our death." The Eastern churches know the value of repetitious prayer.

October 23
"I have sinned exceedingly in my youth," Tolstoi said in a conversation with Gorki. I remember that often in my prayers for the young, and whenever people speak of my *Long Loneliness* as an autobiography. It is rather a story of a conversion. Aside from drug addiction, I committed all the sins young people commit today. I am glad we repeat the Confiteor every day at Mass. I am glad I know so many prayers by rote such as the Memorare and the Act of Contrition. They are no more meaningless than a beautiful poem is.

November 1. All Saints Day
Arthur Sullivan pulled a drunken scene, wanted to beat Dan Marshall for being in priest's room. I had an awful time getting him out. D. Corbin and Steve put him on train.

---

353 Jim Wallis, editor of *Sojourners*, visited the Catholic Worker and interviewed Dorothy for a special December 1976 issue of the magazine.
354 Dorothy frequently attributed this saying to St. Ignatius Loyola.

Fr. Plante confused in his offering Mass. Could not find his way around in the book, the new liturgy. Glad he did not want to stay. Just back from Mexico where he buried his brother. He had fled the mafia.

November 2. All Souls Day

Remember Gene O'Neill, Mike Gold, Lionel Moise, Mary Houde, Jimmy H., Ling Libby, David H's father, Ammon H., Mike Sullivan, Larry Doyle.

Arrived in time for 5:30 Mass. Our staff studying Ezekiel. Sis in Florida on a visit. Ann to house of prayer, Brooklyn. Great variety in life. The Sisters all take turns. Lay people, mothers of families, parents cannot do this. Always the same grind. I can understand now Gerry [Griffin's] anger at my "going" all the time. Damned if you do, damned if you don't. No days off, no weekends in the lives of a mother. But the Sisters *do* work hard. Always on the alert. They have common sense.

November 4

Reading [Henri] Nouwen's book on Our Lady of Genesee Abbey. Very humble man.[355]

November 5

Fritz Eichenberg with his new wife Toni. She is a beautiful, lovely person. I will certainly want to visit them in the summer on their island. He brought me a magnificent book, *The Art of the Print*.

November 6

Forster has been calling each day. More pictures ready![356]

November 8. 79 years old

Bob Steed brought a rose. D. Gauchat called. Also Pat Jordan gave me finger rosary. Frank gave me a check for Tamar.

Nov.

"I have sinned exceedingly in my life," Tolstoy said to Maxim Gorki once. This phrase comes to mind when fulsome praise comes my way. If I started to list my sins "which are ever before me," it would not be the "explicit" ones (or imaginings which left me burning with desire) but the deep shame I felt

---

355  Henri Nouwen, *Genesee Diary* (New York: Doubleday, 1976).

356  Forster Batterham had taken up the hobby of framing art prints, which he donated to the CW. From time to time Dorothy would send a volunteer up to his apartment to collect a new batch.

at "stealing" a nickel from my mother's purse to buy a soda or candy, which I lusted after at the age of 6. When I was ten I had to make another such confession, in Chicago. Both times it was connected with poverty—the worry over money which my mother had at that time.

My loose life as a young woman was like that of so many young women today, only there was no "drug scene" then. We drank; we were the flaming youth of the 20s, portrayed by Hemingway and Malcolm Cowley.

In my book *The Long Loneliness* I tried to write only of those things which bought about my conversion to the faith—a happy love affair, a love of nature, a truly good life in the natural sense, but that book is not an autobiography, as the word is used today.

What I am writing now, aged 79, is more a diary of our times, but of course one always turns back to the past to be able to deal with, to cope with, the events of the day.

Goya, the great artist crossed the Pyrenees on foot, aged 78!

Artists I love—Van Gogh, Goya, Kathe Kollwitz.

In this Oct-Nov issue of CW Susan [Weimer] has an article on Kathe Kollwitz. She usually writes the First St. column, which everyone looks for, but we like to follow Peter Maurin who said we were to work for a new synthesis of cult, culture, and cultivation.

November 13

"When I was a little girl," my mother used to say to us at the supper table, when we were eating something we did not particularly like (children are finicky). It was the beginning of some tale of her childhood, and storytelling is better even than being read aloud to. I learned from my mother to "make a point," as Peter Maurin used to say, by telling stories. It is often reported as "reminiscing," especially if I am making a point which is unpalatable to one's listeners.

November 15

When you tell things that have happened in the past they are incidents ruminated on, and their sting dissolved, and one might say digested, even a lesson learned, and one's life enriched accordingly.

November 20

So hard to have company, especially those one loves, when ill. "Unto old age and gray hairs, O Lord, forsake me not." "Bless these visitors—repair my weaknesses and sloth, complainings."

November 22

Managed to finish my Dec O.P. for CW. Stanley typed it for me. I have signed a rough paper making him my executor of all my notebooks, and papers, "archives." He is the soul of delicacy. An invaluable help to me. He is acknowledging all my mail. Better than any secretary.

Forster has been calling daily. Frank calls each night at seven.

December 3

Mass at 9:50. Reading Mike Harrington's *Fragments of a Century*. Very good. His analysis of giving up the faith preposterous. Otherwise a good book. What is he trying to say? He credits it to Pope John.

Telephone call from L.A. My attitude towards God! There? On phone? I had just come from Communion.

December 6

Dan Marshall's shopping day. He eats nothing but raw vegetables and fruit and nuts. Chuck also—no milk, butter, eggs, etc.

December 17. Staten Island [Mt. Augustine retreat house]

Sister gave me her room, God bless her always. Two large butterflies on the wall, symbol of the Resurrection (in Russia). Dining room and chapel packed—men, women, good ordinary people, finding joy in praising God. We are body and soul. Uplifting of hands, clapping, even dancing. Rejoice! This is the way of praise—Hasidic Jews, to this day continue this tradition of worship. "The spirit bloweth where it listeth." Laying on of hands. Some kind of healing always takes place. By eleven I was so relaxed I slept at once.

December 18

Awake at 6. Read 15 psalms.

December 20

My memory gets worse.

Trials of every description. I must flee to chapel.

December 21

Awoke depressed. Xmas a materialistic time. One can then strip oneself of all privacy, imitate the Suffering Servant. I'd like to sit and read, escape. But must use my regained strength, renew my faith. Eyes weak.

Lost my peace for a time. On verge of tears. Paperwork. Losing letters, misplacing checks. Need to be faithful to my hour.

December 23
Dan Berrigan's mother died.

December 24
My sense of guilt over promiscuity and abortion here, reminding me of my own sins. "Tomorrow the iniquity of the world shall be blotted out." Mother used to say when in trouble, "Tomorrow is another day." A fresh start. Without a morning meditation I could not survive.

December 26. Tivoli
A snow storm is upon us, the house is crowded like the inn where Christ was born. Besides our community of 40 there is an Italian mother and family of 6, not to speak of some unidentified ones who suddenly appeared.

Why do I start this year's chronicle on such a note? It was the enumerating that did it. That first census taken in the Bible led to dire results and was it not condemned by God?

We are not a community, a Christian or a religious community that is. We are an inn by the side of the road. We have no common sense. We do not say no. Or "be thou warmed, sheltered and fed," and not do it. God says yes to us. He gave us free will. At what a price! The suffering and cruel death—the Passion of Jesus Christ, True God and True Man, Who came to repair the Fall. "The worst has already happened and been repaired," Juliana of Norwich said. "Love God and do as you will." St. Augustine.

"Life is a night spent in a disorderly inn." St. Teresa of Avila.

December 27
Bob Ellsberg coming with copy.
I was insulting yesterday to Biddle, a ski enthusiast. Made him wash pots and pans. I am ashamed.

December 28
All morning with Bob E. talking of paper and next issue. Too long articles, etc. Deane saw him too. He stayed all night. I'm reading Chaim Potok, *My Name is Asher Lev*. Beautiful books.
Dan Mauk and Mary O'Connor arrested in Washington, D.C. demonstration.

December 29
For Jan 77 issue, "Remembering Ammon." Anne and Jane writing cards to Dan Mauk in jail. Trial? Charge? Lee LeCuyer on his way to sleep in packing

boxes so Washington will open up empty buildings to poor. Chuck Matthei. Berrigan's inspiration. Ammon's.[357]

Find beauty everywhere.

# 1977

January 1. Tivoli

Christmas was anniversary of Helene Iswolsky's death. Forster in intensive care at St. Vincent too. Now well, sending framed pictures, but must have operation for cataracts this month.

January 16

Anne Perkins[358] is reading *Jews without Money* [Mike Gold]. I found my old paperback, falling apart, held together with rubber bands, and began reading it. Looking backward at my own memory of the East Side.

My knowledge of socialism came from Jack London and Upton Sinclair's early books. (Both men lost their vision by success.) *Martin Eden*, which influenced I.F. Stone—was his masterpiece, as also his gold rush in Alaska stories.

Jews—Irish. Both persecuted. Rayna [Prohme] and Raph [Samson Raphaelson].

January 17

St. Aug on memory. 10th book [of *Confessions*]. Dredging the memory—beauty, mud and filth too. Everyone can say "Late have I loved thee." Also "Now I have begun." "No time with God."

January 21

Reading *Jews without Money* by Mike Gold. I pray for him and his brother George—Manny.

January 22

Writing early a.m. Anne Perkins had called me and told of reading Mike Gold's *Jews without Money*. Must ask Stanley to go to Workers Bookshop and ask for it. Also his columns in *Daily Worker*. His East Side and mine were not alike but he probably knew it better. It fascinated me. [His brother] George

---

357 Dan Mauk and other Catholic Workers chained themselves to the Pentagon as part of a disarmament protest. Lee LeCuyer and Chuck Matthei were involved in a protest on behalf of the homeless, organized by the Community for Creative Nonviolence.

358 Dorothy's friend Anne Perkins was a publicist and editor for Harper & Row.

Granich started Hunger March and I covered it for *Commonweal*. Prayed, and Peter Maurin came to me and made program of action.

Jan 22

Writing just becomes part of my prayer life, which begins at 6 a.m. (I am a morning person.) At night I read; I am self-indulgent and allow myself, since my mild heart attack, an intimation of mortality, a sip of brandy, or rather brandy and water, very warming to the stomach and easing to the nerves. This is the coldest winter since 1893. On one zero day we had no heat in the house. The furnace conked out.

Life at hospices such as ours is not a bed of roses. There is a great need of equanimity amongst us.

Remembering Peter Maurin. One of the psalm endings this morning is the 136th, with the refrain "for thy mercy endures forever." "For His steadfast love endures forever"—another translation, has not got the proper swing to it.

As I read it or recited it, I was distracted by remembering Peter Maurin's writing "To give and not to take—that is what makes man human." He liked to go to Columbus Circle or Union Square and attract a crowd by chanting that "Easy Essay" of his and have some of the young ones from the office (he was 57 then and was considered by all of us an "old one"). But the only one who would accompany him in his chant was Marge Hughes, who at 18 joined us. Three years after we began publishing and running a house of hospitality. Marge, then 18, would chant out bravely "That is what makes man human."

Copy Peter's *Easy Essays*. How he is held in esteem by the young today who recognize him as a prophet.

Feb issue

I hate my *Long Loneliness* being called an autobiography. It is more the story of a conversion. So much was left out of that book that I feel impelled to write another which will be much more of an autobiography.

Yet how to remember and write down the past without reading over the two books *From Union Square to Rome* and *The Long Loneliness*. To read them again is to bring back painful memories, and not to read them means vain repetition.

If I write daily, and profusely, and trust to an editor to prune and edit, what I have written would be rash and reckless because I only write because I should try to be honest and trust my own judgment. In a way it is like liv-

ing in the past and the present at the same time. I live now in what Peter
Maurin called a House of Hospitality surrounded by fifty women and nine
very interesting volunteers, some of them Sisters, nuns, and the lay workers,
brilliant young college graduates. (I myself am 79 so all of our "workers" or
"volunteers" seem very young to me.)

I rise early in the morning to pray, to read the Psalms. Sometimes it seems
more like browsing than praying. It is always the Psalms but sometimes it is
those in the Collegeville short breviary, or the new interim *Prayer of Christians*. I do not like the latter title. After all, Jews cling to the book of Psalms,
for *their* prayers. In Chaim Potok's books, so popular now, young modern
Orthodox and Hasidic Jews live by the Psalms.

When did I first hold a Bible in my hands? I remember it clearly.

It was in the furnished house we rented in Berkeley, California, where we
had followed my father, my mother and two brothers and four-year-old sister. I remember picking up the Scriptures from a desk in the attic of that
furnished house and holding it in my hands. It was my first contact with the
Book. (In this last year I read in a little book of scripture excerpts, that Jesus
Christ answered the devil who tempted him three times in the desert, "It is
written... It is written... It is written.")

These last few mornings I finished Frank Sheed's translation of St. Augustine's *Confessions* and was struck by Book X's analysis of memory. What a
ragbag of a mind I have, pulling out pieces of material to be used for this last
book I shall write—this Notebook.

The first time I entered a place of worship? Mary McCady, our little servant
girl my Aunt Jenny found for my mother took me to Mass once, she years
later told me, but I stood up in the pew and turned my back on the Altar and
kept surveying the people. (I was to do that for many years to come, over and
over.)

The first time I remember going to a place of worship was a little Baptist
church with a next-door neighbor's child in Oakland, California. There was a
children's library there and I was allowed to borrow a book about a pious little
girl called Birdie. I remember I wanted to be like her, as later in my early teens
I wanted to be like Ella in the *Wide, Wide World* and Fleda in *Queechy*, both
of which I read in my early teens with much profit. Both are very long stories
of the spiritual life of the two little girls they portrayed. Historically too they
are still of great interest, in the pictures they painted of both society and rural
life.

I especially remember *Queechy* and the impoverished heroine who had lived
in Paris and also on then fashionable Bleecker Street before the impoverished
family went back to the farm upstate near Albany. She visited rich society

friends in N.Y. City however, and I was struck by the anti-Catholicism displayed heartlessly by a frivolous society beauty who was vividly portrayed as a contrast to the holy young heroine. When one society woman commented on a shipload of Irish workers being imported, she said she wished the boat would sink on the way! Were they being imported to build the railroads of our country, or was it the Famine that made them come to these Protestant shores?

"Nobody but Irish washwomen and policemen are Catholic," a relative of mine commented once.[359] And he always carried a Bible with him on his travels with his own proud name in gold on the cover!

When I was 12 and read the Tom Playfair books written by a Paulist priest I was deeply impressed that the boys spoke Latin! I was twelve and just entering high school. I too began my study of Latin, but my six years' study gave me no proficiency in it. Caesar's Gallic wars were a bore, but I instinctively revered both Cicero and Virgil and enjoyed them. (Dr. Matheson at Robert Waller H.S. was a very good teacher and offered our class an extra period after school to take a course in Greek. But Xenophon did not entice me to continue Greek in college.)

I wrote of a pious Methodist girl in the LL but I spoke of going to Wed night prayer meeting with her.[360] I know I did mention [how she liked to] sleep close to me, and told me how she had slept "in the arms" of another schoolmate. She was pious, and I am sure she was as innocent as I was of lesbianism, but I was repelled and there were no more overnight visits. It was some emergency in her home which led to her visit because neither my mother nor father liked "outsiders" invading the privacy of our home. We were all great readers and spent our evenings devouring novels. In the Cottage Grove Ave. days mother read to us—Kipling or Stevenson, and told us stories of "when she was a little girl" in Poughkeepsie on the Hudson. I must have read Stevenson too—my father had brought two sets of books to replace our library, which had been sold with all our furniture after the earthquake. Those two sets were Victor Hugo and Stevenson. It was Stevenson I devoured. [*Not continued.*]

January 31

One only needs to set foot in the women's house to see how seemingly insoluble are our problems (Lena, Mary). Or to walk the streets of the Lower

---

359 The relative in question was Dorothy's father. (See April 11, 1977 and February 23, 1979.)

360 Dorothy did not in fact relate this story in *The Long Loneliness*.

East Side with its empty buildings. Every house should have a Christ room! The coat that hangs in the closet belongs to the poor.

February 6

It fascinates me to read of the deep spirituality of the Orthodox Jews in Potok's books. The devotion to scripture, the Talmud, the Sabbath.

February 15

Rudolf Serkin—Phil symphony orchestra. Beethoven. Piano Concerto.

Music glorious, ear phones allow you to have it any hour, anywhere. My dear sister, going thru a terrible siege of blood poisoning in one hand, many years ago, said she endured by recalling in her mind all the beautiful music she could, especially Beethoven's 5th.

We could not afford either piano or music lessons when we were children because of our traveling from NY to Frisco to Chi to N.Y. to Miami, my father's journalistic career as a sports writer. His mother's talent for music was inherited by my sister [as was her ability] to recall symphonies in her mind while she was enduring agony (there was no penicillin or those first so-called miracle drugs in those days).

I remember the first radio I had in the early 20s, constructed for me by Willy Green, a 12-year-old, out of a cigar box, a crystal and a bit of wire, an aerial and earphones. Manipulated properly, from my seashore bungalow in Staten Island, I could hear a presidential campaign, Saturday p.m. broadcasts, football, and miracle of miracles, symphonic music. That little radio was a miracle box. I could not understand it. If *this* is possible, anything is. Planting a garden, reaping a harvest ... Having a baby, the greatest miracle of all.

So I could take on faith the truths of Christianity, the Church, the sacraments. My heart swelled with gratitude.

Faith came to me just like that, and the need to adore.

I could not understand the mechanism of that little box with its crystal, set like a jewel to be touched by a bit of wire. It was a miracle to hear voices of people in conversation, a symphony orchestra playing Beethoven.

If I could not understand scientific truths, why should I worry about understanding spiritual truths of religion? I wanted to say yes, this is true.

February 17. Tivoli

There is very little secret drinking going on—a generally healthy peaceful atmosphere except for a feud carried on with the priest who is kind enough to walk the mile down here (and back uphill) thru snow and rain, to serve us. We have offered to drive him but he prefers to walk.

The feud came about because of some tactless queries of his. I have never quite gotten all the details. Questions about the blacks (two) in our midst, and a query about Jews and the usual "Could not these men get work if they wanted to?" might have started the feud. Two are maintaining it, filled with righteous wrath. I find any kind of wrath disruptive, factional.

March 1

At Tivoli they had an anniversary dinner for Fr. McSherry, in honor of his years of priesthood. I am glad they are sharing their gratitude for his daily Masses at farm.

March 4. Tamar's birthday. 51

Snow all day. Roads impassible. So at 4 p.m. we (Tamar, Maggie C., Nicky and I) had strawberry shortcake and whipped cream. Nicky is watching telly and Maggie is reading *Moulin Rouge*. Tamar is weaving a coverlet. I am reading *Solzhenitsyn* by David Burg and George Feifer. Also I have with me Penguin edition of Anton Chekhov's plays.

Also Solzhenitsyn lives in Cavendish, not far from here. Goes to town meetings.

March 5

It was a lovely birthday yesterday, tho the snow fell heavily all day. One must search for beauty in the slums. That sentence from John of the Cross pops into my mind—"where there is no love, put love and one finds love."

So, searching one finds it in the city, the suffering faces of the poor (as Kathe Kollwitz did), in the little trees struggling to survive, in pigeons on the roof across the street, on the rays of sun thru my windows. By craning my neck I can glimpse the deep blue of sky on sunny days.

March 6

Tamar goes on weaving. Becky's two, Lara and Justin, are in the tub, after a tumultuous visit this morning. Wails are thick. Car won't start, no Mass for me.

*NICK IS JESUS! NICK.*

Nick wrote those last few lines—those 4 words. He had a bad spell—where he got the gallon of wine, we don't know. He all but broke his knuckles banging the dining table. I could only keep repeating the Jesus Prayer and washing dishes while Tamar tried to calm him.

March 13. Susie's wedding

POURED RAIN. We all drove up in cars to Woodstock and up a high mountain to Fr. Francis, who is an archbishop in Old Catholic Church (schismatic), thru woods and windy rain-washed roads, up a muddy path to little church shut in by woods. Fr. Francis built church and rectory alone. Beautiful woodwork and carvings, his home behind it. Returned by 1:30 to a buffet feast.

March 19

Our faithful priest says Mass at 9. Walks down, refused rides. Deane refuses Communion at his hands and Peggy and Dan Mauk did not come to Mass. A sad day. However, Kathleen tells me to fast and rest. So I shall do just that.

A good day, reading Potok's *In the Beginning*. Makes one revere the Bible and the Jews the more. They are people of the Book. How can they see Christ in the world today when Christians behave as they do—wars of every kind.

March 21

Mass at 4:30. How I hate arbitrary changes in time and manner of worship! The *wisdom* of the church is challenged by it. Children look back with longing on things as they *were*. Change may mean growth but it hurts.

March 22

It is 7:35 a.m. Snow predicted for all day. Two priests and a sister were supposed to be driving down from Toronto. (I hope not. They want to discuss my *spirituality*. No privacy in this world today. It gets so everyone runs and hides when visitors come.)

March 28

Listened to Pentecostal Atlantic City tape and found it way too long. It needs editing. I wish someone would edit what I say; some sympathetic soul who is generally in agreement but sees my faults (verbosity, too diffuse). It is good for my pride to be thus humbled by having to listen to myself. My only consolation is the tapes reach some lonely shut-ins or invalids who need the sound of the human voice to comfort them.

April 1

Joe Fahey very good—is general secretary [Pax Christi] but talks too fast, packs too much material in his talk.

April 3

Fr. McSherry had Palm Sunday procession and 3-part reading of the Passion Gospel. Everyone was out in snow. Bob Ellsberg up. Read entire pages to Deane. She was happy.

April 7

Spiritual life takes up a lot of time (sometimes to the neglect of mail! But we do keep answering, however late.) Sow time to reap time. If you sow sparingly you reap sparingly.

April 10. Easter

A sad run-in with Fr. McSherry, indeed a trial! No Blessed Sacrament after Mass this Easter day—the altar tabernacle open and empty. Finally Fr. Peter who is staying with us (I did not know he was a priest), said Mass at three or so.

There are so many here I do not know them all (Fr. Peter for instance). My age, my unfortunate reputation, makes all but a few stand off from me.

April 11

Up at 5. At seven drove back to Tivoli. Ben does not talk to me. (My CW background and Catholicism intimidates my relations.) I'm closer to David [Spier] in a way than to others. A most sympathetic person. The Spiers feel the latent anti-Semitism in Catholics and Protestants. (My father's remark about his hotel in N.Y. "All right but full of Jews." And Catholics, "Only Irish washerwomen and policemen are R.C.") And R.C. retaliate in their own way.

April 12

Primacy of the spiritual. With our young right now: Activism—demonstrations, such as Seabrook [nuclear power plant]. But such whole-heartedness gives time also for reflection on our times, our powerlessness, yet strength…

The power of the Word. (Talk less and write more is advice for me, my advice to myself.) "The word was made Flesh and dwelt among us." Christ said "I am the Word." Recommended reminders—*Practice of Presence of God*. The Jesus Prayer. (Pray for [J.D.] Salinger. That he writes again. Pray for him, his wife, his family. We owe him a debt.)

April 17

Beautiful weather. Deane would not go to Mass with Fr. McSherry. So Virginia drove her to an evening Mass at Red Hook.

Tensions and irritations have led to heart pains which woke me in the night. Dr. Holbert and his dear wife came. My memory is so bad. I can't remember their first names. They are reading Dickens together. *Little Dorrit*. (So is Deane.)

April 20
Received Communion in my room yesterday and today.
Mother used to talk of "nervous prostration." I think that describes my sufferings which are not basically physical (or rather not seriously physical). Just great weakness.

April 21
Suddenly thought, "I have never prayed for Rayna." There is no time with God," as Fr. Zachary said once, so if I want her to be with us in Heaven, and with all those she loved, and who loved her, I begin now and will continue to add her to my prayers. I must call her sister.

April 24
Meditation on Death and Prayer. The Our Father and Hail Mary, "Now and at the hour of our death." It is good to have a long period of "ill heath." …nothing specific, mild but frightening pains in heart and arm. Weakness. Ebb tide. Ebbing of life. Weakness. Then some days of strength and creativity. "Wait and do nothing." Surrounded by loving kindness. Flowers, tulips, a rose, a picture, a book, food. T.L. Care.

April 25
Here in N.Y. I am more comfortable physically, more "private." So many volunteers. Dr. Yanovsky and wife solicitous. Brought much food.

April 26
I am feeling better physically. Ruth sent down vitamins and "tiger's milk," all made up when she heard I was "failing." Have gotten out to Mass this last week but my memory is bad. Can't remember day of the week for instance or whether I have answered letters. Stanley brought down unanswered mail.

April 27
A crowd from here going to Seabrook demonstration. Another group to go to Union Square to celebrate our anniversary.
Very depressed and nerve-racked all day. Slept 2 hours. Reading Chekhov helps.

April 28. Taxes

Water and sewerage and street lights. Honoring our community responsibilities while opposing the STATE (Caesar). "The less you have of Caesar the less you have to render to Caesar." Jesus picked up a coin (money) and called our attention to the image stamped on it. What to do with it. Sow it. Scatter it. Sow abundantly and we reap abundantly. Frank [Donovan] who has charge of finances agrees absolutely.

April 29

I wake up this morning feeling joyful and determined to write my NOTE-BOOK "religiously" each morning. Today it is joy thinking of "the man" and Tamar's conception on a morning in June at the beach. The picnic at the Tottenville circus with Peggy and Malcolm [Cowley, *when she realized she was pregnant*].

April 30

To Seabrook: Bob E., Dan Mauk, Gary Donatelli, Paul Loh, Terry (support group) left at 7:30. Seabrook crowd 2000. 1200 arrested. People went limp. Police gentle. People brought their own food. "Mostly Clamshell Alliance," well trained, 3 different places, down main road, by boat, and swamp.[361]

Today Stanley went to Union Square C.P. demonstration. He called and said many were asking about me.

May 1

Mass at 10 at Holy Child. Not a good sermon.

Our plumbing as usual a disgrace. We must get plans for Swedish outhouses.

May 8

Fr. McNutt's retreat. I encountered Chaim Potok in the Sister's room at St. Augustine which she had given me to sleep in. [*My Name is*] *Asher Lev* was the book and I rejoiced in a new author. These last months I have finished *The Chosen, The Promise, In the Beginning*. I was again living on the East Side and Cherry St. with that Polish-Jewish family. And meditating on the Jews. It has made me devour the Scriptures, the Psalms, with new intensity. Jean Walsh's gift of the new translation with all its footnotes and cross references made me identify more completely. "Spiritually we are Semites." Was it Pius XI? What

---

361 Thousands of nonviolent demonstrators, organized into "affinity groups," took part in a sit-in at the construction site of a nuclear power plant in Seabrook, New Hampshire. 1,414 demonstrators, including a group from the CW, were arrested on May 1. They were distributed among several National Guard armories around the state and held for nearly two weeks.

sins we have committed in not allowing their entry. Our deserts might have
bloomed by now.

## May 9

I love postal cards. This week Bill Griffin gave me one of birch trees from
New Mexico. A beauty. Mary Roberts at Cabrini Center sent me one of St.
Francis in Ecstasy by Bellini. Her note was as beautiful as her card. She is a
"lover of beautifulness" (a phrase I think is scriptural.)

Alone all day. Rose left last night. A sudden storm in the night. Very cold
all day with thunder and lightening. Vast dark clouds and a glaring lightning
flash with thunder. No rain. Read *Dr. Zhivago*. I must read again *Ten Days
that Shook the World*, Jack Reed.

## May 10

A television drama of an uprising in Taiwan made me think of Rayna
Prohme. If I only had the strength to write daily! My own story of Rayna at
Univ. of Ill. I pray for that strength, then I will write a little every day. "Faith
is the substance of things hoped for, the evidence of things not seen…If in
this life only we have hope in Christ, we are of all men the most miserable.
Eye hath not seen nor ear heard… the things which God hath prepared for
those who love him." What samples of his love in Creation all around us.
Even in the city, the changing skies, the trees, frail tho they be, which prisoners grow on Riker's Island, witness Him.

## May 11

In the beginning God created Heaven and earth. Looking out over the bay,
the gulls, the "paths in the sea," the tiny ripples stirring a patch of water here
and there, the reflection of clouds on the surface—how beautiful it all is. Yet
that offshore wind, keeping the tide low, is cruelly cold for May. Spring is bit-
ter-sweet.

## May 12

A letter came reproaching me for my love for Solzhenitsyn, claiming he was
a warmonger.

## May 13

Prisoners released at Seabrook.

May 14

Wedding of Mary [Lathrop] and Kevin [Pope] 11 a.m. Could not get in for it but prayed for them.

May 15

Still reading *Dr. Zhivago*—his last days in Moscow. Remembering Claude McKay, Langston Hughes, Wally Carmen and Rose [Carmen], Mike Gold, all of whom spent time in Moscow at this same time [of which] Pasternak writes.

And Donald, my brother, in Riga, trying to get into Russia and seeing all the refugees getting out. He starved there for a time living on $3 a week, until hired by *Chicago Tribune*.

And Diego Rivera in Mexico City and his telling me of the reprints in Russia of my story from *New Masses*, "Having a Baby. "Translated into many dialects or languages," he said. "Go to the Soviet Union. You can collect royalties," he said.

May 17

Mike Kovalak died last night, peacefully, at Mother Cabrini Hospital. A great shock to me. We had known each other so long. Since before 2nd WW when he left the Benedictine Monastery at Lisle, Ill. Mike was a son of a coalminer in SW Pa, I believe, who always had great love for his homeland, Russia. Mike had been failing for a long time. Always took his dinner plate up to his room to eat. He took care of the short breviaries, to bring them down after dinner to say Vespers. We sat on benches facing each other. Often some one (from too much drink), slept on a bench against the wall, while we prayed. He and Mary Lathrop used to take long walks when he got melancholy over his lost vocation. Now she is married last week, May 14, and he must feel he lost a companion.

May 19

Visitors. A.J. Lacey and Bob Ellsberg. His father in town. Bob felt his time in the armory was shattering. Crowding, uncertainty. It was primitive, tho awaiting trial.

May 23. Beach

Kassie Temple here to write a paper on Solzhenitsyn.[362] We had supper at Pat and Kathleen [Jordan's] outside. Fare on bus now 50 cents. Community expensive. Pat at St. Rose's.[363]

Rereading "Having a Baby." Thinking of Soviet reprinting. Still being Xeroxed for CWs having babies.[364]

May 25

Jesus Prayer. Thinking of [J.D.] Salinger.[365] There are sassafras trees in the yard. Thinking of Jonas who has cancer of the jaw. And of Mike Kovalak who was buried at Calvary this last week. Weddings, funerals, new babies, more great grandchildren coming. What a discipline a 2-year-old is! Into everything, yet unutterably adorable. Must be fenced in and watched every minute.

May 27

CW group from Seabrook spoke of imprisonment and demonstration at Seabrook. Eileen Egan came to beach, brought polished stones from Lake Superior. How beautiful is all creation.

May 28

Gene Palumbo telephoned this a.m. from Colorado. On retreat there. First time he had received communion in 14 years. He talked to Pat Jordan also. Joy!

Eve of Pentecost. My favorite feast. I was confirmed on the day at Holy Souls—adult. I felt indeed the Holy Spirit.

May 29. Pentecost

Woke up with great feelings of joy and gratitude to God for his great gifts of the Holy Spirit. And for friends like Pat and Kathleen.

---

362 Kassie Temple, a Canadian with a doctorate in philosophy, was one of the first volunteers to move into Maryhouse. She was an avid student of scripture, the work of Karl Barth, and Jacques Ellul. She remained at Maryhouse until her death from cancer in 2003.

363 Pat Jordan, former editor of the CW, was one of the first Catholic Workers to find work at St. Rose's Home, a hospice for terminal cancer patients in the Lower East Side. At one point almost a dozen Catholic Workers, along with Fr. Daniel Berrigan, worked there as orderlies or volunteers.

364 Dorothy's article about the birth of her daughter, "Having a Baby," originally appeared in *The New Masses*. It was reprinted in the CW in December 1977. (See *SW*, 27-32.)

365 J.D. Salinger's novel, *Franny and Zooey*, brought popular attention to the Russian classic, *Way of a Pilgrim*, and to the "Jesus Prayer."

May 30

How widespread the CW is. We print 93,000 a month. It goes all over the world.

May 31

I came to the beach, where so many years ago the beauty of creation plunged me into the faith, entranced me, and now I am, at my age, not boasting of strength but feeling healed in some way of a trembling of the nerves which I am sure overtakes young and old alike from too much activity of mind, soul, and body. I am sure many of the Seabrook demonstrators feel the same, and I am many scores beyond them in age.

June 1

"There is no time with God." Where? An Augustinian priest at O.L. of Guadalupe (14ᵗʰ St.) said this to me when I asked about praying for a suicide, or people who had already died without religion. (Someone hearing I had said this, thought I meant I had no time for God, too busy, and sent me a big book to study.)

"Judge not," Jesus said. "Consider all things but dung compared to love of Christ." St. Paul certainly went to an extreme in expressing himself. Fr. Hugo too did not hesitate to quote this. He ended his famous retreats with, "You are dead and your life is hid with Christ in God."

Look up photo of Mike Gold on beach. Quotes: "God wills that all men be saved."

We say "God's will be done," each time we say the Our Father, the Pater Noster, just as we pray for a good death when we say the Ave Maria.

June 5

Forster in hospital again. Kidney removed.

Jonas dying of cancer on neck. Dumchius is his last name. The young people visit the hospital—all works of mercy performed.

June 15

"All ye works of the Lord, bless ye the Lord." Singing to John as baby. A beautiful bird—mocking bird?—singing away. "Praise Him."

Waves pounding on beach, huge swell. Waters of Raritan Bay. Sea and sky meet on this humid day. Damp gets in your bones.

June 16

To N.Y. Mother Teresa and nuns.

June 17

Ps. 94 for Forster who has been calling often, after kidney removal.

June 18. Justin born (Jordans)

Reading *The Island*, a journey to Sakhalin, prison colony. Stanley lent me an atlas. I can follow Chekhov's journey by map.

Borrowed Orwell Vol IV from Pat. Mrs. Sheed said she wept on reading the last vol. that there was no more. Fr. Jack English gave me the set of 4 on one of his occasional lapses from the Trappists.

June 23

Mrs. Margaret Lloyd visiting. She brought in a precious bowl from Greece made from one rock (we are rock enthusiasts and she had lent me a library manual and map from N.H. Univ library which she is now returning). I have several small rock books which I can pore over. Staten Island is rich in rocks left by a glacier eons ago which had scraped them up in its ponderous and slow movement and left S.I. generously endowed with "specimens." Other specimens I delight in are horseshoe crabs, spider and rock crabs, pipe fish. They resemble tiny sea horses and we found one on the beach yesterday.

July 8

Marion Moses, whom I first met when she was a nurse and donating all her tremendous energy to the United Farm Workers in Southern California. In order to help them the more she has spent years and is now a full-fledged doctor doing her internship at Mt. Sinai in N.Y. She is specializing and studying the effects of sprays (chemical) and other pesticides on farm workers.

July 13

Blackout. 9:34 lights went out. Sweltering heat.

Continued martyrdom by pinpricks.

Suddenly I find [on] a slip of paper in my book the names Michael Schwerner, Andrew Goodman, James Cheney, [Civil Rights workers] killed in Mississippi 1964. True martyrs. We, CW people, "have not yet resisted unto blood," as St. Paul wrote.

July 14

4 a.m. lights went on. Much looting in city.

Away back in the thirties, when Peter Maurin was my daily guest, "indoctrinating" me with Emmanuel Mounier and his "Personalist Manifesto," he told me the story of Charles de Foucauld and the spirituality of this "desert father," whose Little Brothers now live in slums as well as deserts and are priests as well as brothers and earn their own living by the sweat of their brow, in factories or at manual labor.

They live in a slum yet surround themselves with beauty. Taking a grimy apartment in a miserable East Side tenement they first see that it is scrubbed and cleaned, bright and shiny, painted well so it will last, and then so simply and barely furnished that the crucifix and holy ikons light up the place. Peter Maurin gave me the life of Charles de Foucauld by René Bazin to read back in the early 30s. "This is a spirituality for our day," he said.

## July 17

President Carter in favor of neutron bomb. We need to pray without ceasing for peace.

## July 18

I am reading *Kristin Lavransdatter* again, which I read on Staten Island years ago. It was first printed in 1923 by Knopf and was reprinted over and over. The Nobel Prize edition came out in 1929. It was in 1926 or thereabouts that I saw it in the hands of my friend Frida, who lived next door. While she was reading it the beach house remained upswept, her husband and son unfed. I had never liked historical novels, but *Kristin* was great. As the years passed I recommended it to all the women in the CW movement and they were spellbound by it too. After the 2nd war started [Sigrid] Undset came to this country and visited us at Mott St. and told me she had been lecturing on my book, *Union Square*, on the night the Nazis invaded Norway. She made her escape by the skin of her teeth (she had been denouncing Nazism), and traveling thru Sweden, Finland, USSR and reaching the Pacific came to the U.S. and lived quietly in Mass. until the war was over.

"If a book is worth reading," said Martin Corbin, a former editor of CW, "it is worth reading 3 times."

## July 21

33 Jesuits defy terrorist threats in El Salvador. The government believes the church, peasant movement, and guerillas are same.

## July 23

Many cards, including Tanya and Sue, Deane, and 3 donors. Also Liz [McAlister] Berrigan. Mrs. Berrigan had told me before her death to "keep in touch." Liz is a lovely woman. Woke this a.m. worried about judging. "Judge not."

July 24

I have become to a great extent a hermitess. But a luxurious one.

Today all of "Tristan and Isolde" broadcast. Frank had a radio in the garden and heard it.

July 27

Bob Ellsberg down with mail and books. *Personal* conversation.

Doris to and from city. She drove Bob to train. I watched Elie Wiesel until 11 or after. (Polish Jews.)

Fr. Ingram encountered [Rayna] Prohme in Tokyo. Wrote for more info. Write Alden Whitman for obituaries of Vincent Sheean. He mentions Rayna as being greatest influence in his life.

July 28

Terrible news from Central America—Jesuits ordered to leave El Salvador. They stay, threat to kill.

July 29

*The First Circle*—in the field of experimentation in that book prisoners of the state are put to the task of trying to invent a way of identifying the human voice over the telephone. The hardships of the Gulag Archipelago portrayed by [Solzhenitsyn] are nothing compared to news accounts in NY *Times* of CIA activities, "a program of experimentation with drugs" tested on prisoners, etc.

July 30

Dan Mauk came down last night. Rained heavily in night. He is working four hours daily (with others) to save money to go to Mexico and Latin America. Went to Sears with Doris for dress (John Day's gift) but bought Narnia books and a gift for Tamar instead. Reading them myself. I love C.S. Lewis. His life—*Surprised by Joy* and essays are best.

July 31. Feast of St. Ignatius

Pray for priests, S.J.'s, in El Salvador in such danger from terrorists.

August 2

Since I cannot do any traveling these long months on the shore, not even to and from city or Tivoli farm, I am traveling with Chekhov to the Island of Sakhalin, a prison island he visited, making the long trip across Siberia.

August 7

The very energy of my desires to write, to keep up the chronicle of the CW and its workers, exhausts me! I keep thinking "at least I can write, the least I can do is write letters, because it helps other Houses to keep going."

August 11

To the beauty parlor, first time in years and years. It is near at hand, Hylan Blvd., and good, and not only got a wash but cut off six inches or so. In such blistering hot weather it is easier to handle. The cicadas have begun their singing, a sign of intense heat.

August 20

Wrote Liz Berrigan, whose sister died.

Dan Berrigan helps out at St. Rose's cancer hospital where Pat Jordan and Bill Griffin work.

August 22

Rain until 2 or 3. Then sun and I read introduction to Penguin's Chekhov plays. He stresses the essential loneliness of people. One good reason for House of Hospitality, for women especially.

August 29.

Reading "7 Women"—Anna Louise Strong very good. Mine awful! "3 liaisons"? etc., etc., beaten up by guard at Occoquan. Not true.[366]

September 2

Tom Sullivan called. He has been visiting Conyers as usual every vacation. What a faithful friend in life and death.

September 3

Woke in a state of depression. Late to 8 a.m. Will do my reading of Psalms now. And read Père Voillaume, Christian vocation.

September 8

A beautiful sunrise. Gulls on the big rock offshore. Low tide, sometimes one wakes depressed in September. Problems on every side. One cannot help but share them. The human condition. St. Paul wrote, "Rejoice! Again I say rejoice." Work. Clean a room, a desk, clean oneself up!

---

366 Judith Nies, *Seven Women from the Radical Tradition* (New York: Penguin, 1978).

September 11

Sick in bed. Missed Mass. Heaviness in chest. Took nitroglycerin pill. Slept, better in p.m. Tamar and I spent much time watching the street scene. Cool and clear.

Dr. Moses called by phone.

September 14

Pest control office called and they sent board of health man who investigated and found one woman made a pet of rats and fed them. She lived next door. She died and the rats are now hungry.

September 29

Walked over to First St. Very weak. Folded papers.

October 1

Spent most of day in bed. Went to 5:30 Mass. Forgot my cane. Could scarcely walk—weak.

October 4

My weakness keeps me from going over to First St. to fold papers, as Jonas and Michael used to do. We start, company joins us, and much gets done in a few hours.

October 8

Woke up, smothering feeling, result of [Hells] Angels zooming all night, tragedy of girl's death and fall from roof at Hell's Angels. Also story in the *Times* of 42nd St. trafficking in children.

Taken to Beth Israel by Frank and Marion [Moses]. Long exam. Machines galore. Attached by wrists to bottle of water dripping slowly. Everyone is fascinated by gigantic hospital apparatus. No wonder television thrives on it. The hospital scene. Drama of life and death. Machines enhance horror.

October 9. Beth Israel Hospital

Visitors, Tamar here, Frank, Tamar, Dr. Moses, Anne and Jane. Must be cold out. Coats and heavy sweaters.

Who gave me Roualt? He was intensively involved in the gospel stories—should be accepted as a valid expression of the religious orientation of our age. Only true religious painter of our time. The world, the judge, the prostitutes, the Passion story, the oppressed workers. "Nothing else is supernatural in this world but suffering. All the rest is human." (Bloy). Compare Orwell's story of a hospital in Paris—his suffering and loneliness.

## October 14

Dr. Marion Moses in Washington. Dan Ellsberg speaking tonight. Tamar and Forster here this a.m. F. bringing ice cream. Tamar stayed all day and knit a double sock. Sleeping as usual. Chicken for supper. Lots of fruit. All kinds of tests.

Bill here is $1,200 so far. We pay for living up to our principles. Naturally free care is necessary for the poor. But our "personalism"–our opposition to State responsibility as opposed to personal responsibility.

All things work together for good to those who love God.

## October 15

Forster and Tamar here every day.

How to live up to principles about the state. "War is the health of the state." "Render to Caesar." "The less you have of Caesar, the less you have to render to him."

Sis brings communion. Frank told of Ellsberg meeting last night. Packed house.

## October 16

Eileen [Egan] coming. Mairead [Corrigan Maguire] and friend came to visit us from N. Ireland this summer (from Belfast). She got the Nobel Peace Prize this year. How wonderful.

## October 18. Hospital

Forster came today and brought books and ice cream, just at lunch time! He seems well.

## October 19

Thank God for Frank, a truly voluntary poor man, never thinking of himself. Marriage has done it for the Jordans. Their family duties keep them tied. Frank seems to feel same way. Dedicated to CW.

Got home from hospital at noon. My memory is bad. Tamar has been having a good time knitting socks, and got materials too for rocking chair.

Article in *Progressive*. Hope it helps us pay our huge bill at hospital. Frank always says not to worry. All is well.

November 8

Article in *Daily News* for my [80th] birthday. Lionel Moise was first city editor,[367] also a friend of his, later c. e. of Chicago *Post* whose Huysmans books *En Route* and *The Cathedral* (and the Memorare prayer to the B.V.) started me frequenting R.C. churches. When I worked for Bob Minor on *The Liberator* when Chicago was center of C.P. in U.S. I used to sneak into the nearby R.C. cathedral at lunch time.

Cardinal Cooke telephoned me on my birthday!

Also a Mass at St. Joseph's for me.

November 12

$4,000 hospital bill. (Not covered by insurance or Medicare.)

Check for $5,000 came in today.

November 13

Tamar called at 8. Maggie Hennessey had her 2nd son, named Hickory (first is Oak!).

November 14

Went downstairs for Fr. Peter's Mass here at Maryhouse. First time down in ?

November 16

My memory has been affected in these last weeks. If I am not conscientious about keeping my diary I forget important things.

November 18

Round table discussion—Eileen, Bob, etc. Dr. Marion Moses back from Nebraska where she is giving attention to pesticide plants. She must testify before Congress about damage to workers in such plants.

Forster calls every day!

November 23

Tamar arrived this a.m. Much shopping for holiday.

Going to Mass at 5:30.

"Seagull" on television. Anne Perkins called. Harpers suggests another book. (Notebooks?)

November 28

Confession and Communion in my room. Have been receiving every day.

---

367 It was Dorothy's affair with Lionel Moise, after World War I, that ended in an abortion.

December 5

Could write nothing this issue, so they will use "Having a Baby."

Light snow falling. Peggy, Bob and Frank at printers. Girl named Julie [Loesch], Erie. Pa., attacking Cesar [Chavez] for receiving medal from Filipine dictator [Ferdinand Marcos]. Sent letter to Bob.

Deane sends word she is coming into town tomorrow. Everyone deserting Tivoli.

December 6

Received Communion early a.m. Dr. said I am in good shape. Made appointment next month. Much talk of selling Tivoli farm. Must find another place first.

December 10

Today read of Gene O'Neill's son a suicide in Greenwich Village, drug addict. His friends some years ago wanted him to go up to Tivoli, but he backed out. Gene's first son also a suicide, I believe.

December 11

Reading Little Office of the Dead for the O'Neills. Good article in *Times* on plays being put on now.

December 13

Eunice Kennedy called from Florida. Interested in Oct-Nov issue interview with Betty Williams. She is going to China (E.K.)—will bring me a souvenir of Mao. Wants me to have tea at Plaza.

Peggy just came in. Had been to visit Jane [Sammon] at hospital who had been stepped on by a horse, or some bizarre accident. There she met Tina [de Aragon] who had a back trouble (Tina did our Mary statue at farm.)[368] Peggy had been shopping for Jane who will be home tomorrow.

December 16

Miriam said she had had 4 years of depression! Has come out of it beautifully. I am a "pipsqueak," as Ammon used the term. Much tempted to depression.

December 19

Mass. Brother Peter. Went downstairs. Jane came to Mass in cast.

---

368 Tina de Aragon was the sister of Dorothy's sister-in-law Tessa. This renewed contact, after many years, brought Dorothy much delight.

December 22
Call from Tessa about report on Tina and her husband living in such physical distress on McDougal—in a rear house. Tina carved our statue of Mary (lignum vitae) at farm. Got very bad bursitis. Now both are ill. Cancer of spine? I must pray—pray.

December 23
Argument about accepting the military's check. I'm afraid we have a tendency to "holier than thou" attitude. I feel I am "on the shelf," invalided up here in my room.

December 24
Fr. Lyle [Young's] Mass midnight. Went downstairs for it. What a faithful friend.

December 25
Communion in my room. Stanley romping around house with Kassie dressed up like Santa (cotton beard).
Charlie Chaplin died at 86.
The girls managed that each in Maryhouse got presents.

December 27
Woke early, sunny 15° but house warm. Very active in mind, recalling how marvelously good our parents were to us. Must write story of my childhood.

December 28
Joe Zarrella and Gerry Griffin unexpected callers—was delighted to see them. They date back to the forties. Gerry drove an ambulance in Second World War in N. Africa, while they prepared invasion of Italy.

December 29
Little Office. Thinking of my conversion thru Huysmans. Sam Putnam who translated *Don Quixote* had a very good library. He was editor of Chicago *Post* when Lionel [Moise] and I were out there. I must always remember to pray for those in whose sins I shared in the early 20s.

# 1978

**January 2**

Mass tonight, Fr. Peter. Our beautiful altar covering was woven by Egyptian girls, away up the Nile and sent to us by one of the Grail girls. The women of Grail are sent all over—India, Africa, South America. I knew the one in central Brazil. She had been inspired by [Rayna] Prohme, whom she read about in *Personal History* by Vincent Sheean. I remember with sorrow our friendship, Rayna, Raph and mine in the U of Illinois and her disappointment in me when she tried to take care of me in Chicago when I was ill and living a disorderly life with Lionel Moise. The only good that came of that life was reading Huysmans' *En Route* from Sam [Putnam]. He and Lionel worked on the *Chicago Post* at that time.

**January 3**

C.S. Lewis's *Letters*. "A dear old man but the inexhaustible loquacity of educated age drove me ... to the Uni to recoup on a Guinness."

**January 6**

Ed Turner spoke tonight. ["Redlining the Big Apple."] T and J broken down on road. Frank had to send them $200 for repairs to get into W. Va. Frank is always performing miracles of "multiplying loaves and fishes." Nonjudgmental. T has two women, two babies. I feel the guilt of my early life, my own promiscuity.

**January 8**

Changes in liturgy, hard to find one's way around in *Prayer for Christians*.

**January 9**

"Scenes from a Marriage" [Ingmar Bergman]. Now writing this I cannot remember any of it. My memory is very bad. It will be on all week. Martin Corbin thought it a masterpiece. I found it dull.

**January 11**

Pat Jordan writing on Martin Buber and staying in town, so Kathleen glad of Jane's company. Started to read *Anna Karenina* again. What a genius Tolstoy!

January 12

Nasty letter from Alice Zarrella about Frank keeping me a prisoner. I answered it right away. I'm sure he was really hurt. He gave me an envelope with Alice's money in it. I'll try to get a Taize Bible with it.

(Apology came later in week.)

January 13

Snowing steadily all morning. Good letter from Peggy [Scherer]. She is going to Nicaragua.

January 14

We go to press Monday. Must write short paragraph. Awake at 6:30. Kassie arrives with coffee.

Quote from C.S. Lewis letters: "One must take comfort in remembering that God used an ass to convert the prophet. Perhaps if we do our best we shall be allowed a stall near it in the celestial stable." (I am thinking of myself, not Kassie.)

Reading *Anna Karenina* again. A masterpiece which I think—I'm not sure—Greta Garbo was filmed in many years ago.

Tonight went to dining room to eat (first time in weeks, what with my heart attack).

January 15

Woke up feeling so thankful for the parents God gave me. Want to write "Having a Family" as a follow up of "Having a Baby" in the last issue. No time to do it for this issue.

Psalms for the Third Sunday in *Praise Him, Prayer Book for Today's Christian,* edited by Wm. Story of Notre Dame (a family man, our good friend) are especially beautiful. Today pertinent for one who is ill.

Problem of Nella. Up all night in the bathroom, cleaning her face with cucumber pulp!

January 16

Problems, "CIA file," Bob's sending for it.[369]

---

369 With Dorothy's reluctant consent, I applied to the CIA and the FBI under the Freedom of Information Act for their files on Dorothy Day and the Catholic Worker.

January 17

Reading *Anna Karenina*, the tragedy of suicide. When a friend of ours took his own life by putting his head in a gas oven, I asked the priest at Our Lady of Guadalupe Church on 14 St. did he die in mortal sin, remembering Kirilov in *The Possessed* (by Dostoevsky). The priest said, "There is no time with God and all the prayers and Masses said for him after his death will have given him that moment of turning to God in penitence."

January 18

"The best is the enemy of the good." My brain, my memory is like a rag bag. I reach in and pull out of it the scraps that make up these columns.

The harsh judgments of youth! "Money from the military base wives," for instance. Youth is uncompromising. "Don't do anything if I can't do it right."

January 19

"Unto old age and gray hairs, O Lord, forsake me not."

Mary Lathrop Pope has a new job. In exchange for a dwelling place (rectory of old cathedral on 2$^{nd}$ St.) she and Kevin will be janitoring the buildings, cleaning snow off sidewalks, etc. She is getting her Masters degree in medieval art. She has done a mural of St. Thomas Aquinas and now must write a brief paper, a description of techniques, etc.

"The Duty of Delight." Ruskin

January 20

"Worst storm in a decade." Radio. Woke up to find my floor wet with snow, blew in. My window was only open a few inches. Not a car able to move on the streets.

January 21

All motor roads in area cleared. Worse in Manhattan for foot passengers. Thinking of Nina's and my trip to Russia.

Wrote Nina—did she keep a diary? We all should no matter how brief and factual—and to be careful in letters and diary not to err in charity and write things that may hurt others. I have been hurt by my brothers who were in turn hurt by my publicity, "air raid drills" arrests. Strange—in a family of newspaper people such as ours, nothing is more disgraceful than being involved in something which gets one's name in the papers!

When one illustrates one's beliefs by getting out on picket lines, putting one's body on the line—

Saturday, found a good old book in our library on Wagner. (This H. of H. used to be a music school. I feel its very walls are soaked in music.)

A long analysis of all his operas. Since Hitler it has been bad form to love Wagner! At the end of WWII at the death of Hitler, Wagner's music was played with the sense I suppose of the tragedy of the life and death of such a man as Hitler. A sense of the terrible aspects of sin and cruelty, a sense of the meaning of the words "a lost soul."

January 22

Langston Hughes and Claude McKay lived in corners in the Soviet Union. My room is so crowded that I feel I'm now living in a corner, what with Stanley V and Tamar and Katy spending so much time with me. Actually they are both having a vacation from duties at Tivoli and Perkinsville. It seems too long since I have visited either place.

January 23

Sun on tree. "The world will be saved by beauty."

January 26

Dull, gloomy day. Awake at dawn with such a feeling of gratitude to Fr. Lyle for coming thru the slush and the all but impassible roads to say Mass. There is always a crowd.

January 27

Frank gave me communion. What privileges our diocese and parish give us.

January 29

Woke early to hear car trying to get out of a snow bank. Much exhaust.

Reading a little of Lewis Mumford. Kassie went to Pendle Hill last night. That was where I met Eugene Exman, then religious editor of Harper's Pub. And he contracted for the *Long Loneliness*. Tina de Aragon telephoned. Cheerful (tho with the fatal illness, cancer of spinal cord).

February 2

Yesterday p.m. Stanley took Meg to see "Touch of the Poet," latest O'Neill play. Must read up in [Louis] Scheaffer's biography. Tamar gets out, walks and shops, and knits. Must write of my association with Gene and Agnes. He knew his genius and tried to protect it. Scheaffer's book is painful to read.

February 3

Woke up thinking of Rayna. Stanley brought me a book on China's revolution. Very cold in house. Bundled up in bed. I read Psalms and ruminate.

February 6

Ask Stanley to find me *The Idiot* by Dostoevsky. I want to read it because Tina, Tessa and Paula reminded me of the 3 sisters in that Russian classic when I first met them years ago.

February 7

Fr. [René] Voillaume [founder of the Little Brothers of Jesus] arriving last night. Word got around and all 3 rooms downstairs were full, library, chapel, and front office. Meeting afterward in library, jammed. In the thirties, Peter Maurin told us all about him. Now the Little Brothers and Sisters live near us on Lower East Side. Little Brother Peter says Mass at Maryhouse Monday nights, usually. Fr. Lyle Wed.

Heaviest snow I can remember since First World War. 1917. Walked the streets thru the drifts with Mike Gold before he went to Mexico where he probably met Borodin and went to Russia.

February 8. Ash Wednesday

Could not get over for ashes. Feeling weak. But Tina de Aragon with bone marrow cancer, and Chas Butterworth has leukemia. Must pray for both.

Our selling arms to Egypt and Israel. Sin and sickness.

Received Communion after Vespers. Snow heaped high.

February 9

First glimpse of sun on buildings across the street, 7:30 a.m. Reading St. Ignatius of Antioch on submission to bishops. Sis just brought my oatmeal and coffee. Sun on the pigeons flying past my window. Debate on obedience. Sis says she would move to another diocese.

News of Chas Butterworth's death came last night. Mary Pope had Kassie and Stanley to dinner and only knew of his illness. Shocking news. He was so *good*. I will pray not only for him and those he left behind, but ask him to pray for Tina, who also has cancer. And for me, so old and imperfect.

February 10

[Dwight] Macdonald speaker. ["Marxism vs. Anarchism."]

Received the host from Frank—what privileges we are granted! Marion Moses examined me and said my heart is strong and regular (so I must share more in the work). I am sure Charles B is praying for us all. Dwight wrote about me and CW for the *New Yorker*—was sorry I missed the meeting. He went to dinner with Bob and Eileen and Frank.

Friday night pastries. Frank brought me up two. I am self-indulgent and a bad beginning for a first week in Lent.

February 12

How one's mind wanders. Potok, Rayna, Raph. Stanley brought me *Personal History* by Vincent Sheean. One third of book is "Revolution" about Rayna Prohme, my dearest friend in college, when I was working my way and got ill from overwork and she shared her room with me and food. This chapter of the book inspired a girl at the Grail to go to the poorest in Brazil. To give her life to the poor.

February 16

Stanley not around all day. Feeling very weak and ill myself. But a visit to chapel, Vespers (after dinner in dining room) and Communion.

Looking at telly about whales.

February 18

Pat Jordan wrote on Martin Buber. Too long.[370]

February 21

Remembering Helene Iswolsky who is buried at Tivoli. Please pray for me, I am in a state. Want to weep.

February 23

Forster called.

February 24

Called Virginia Gardner. She stayed all afternoon. Still writing the life of Louise Bryant, who married Jack Reed (*Ten Days that Shook the World*), who fell in love with O'Neill also. He married Agnes Boulton and settled down to writing later. Jack died in Moscow of typhus. Louise later married [William] Bullit, Am Ambassador to Russia and died in Paris, a tragic end.

February 26

Went to Mass at 10 and was called out (or did he come in to get me?) by my brother John. Since I had gone last night I left with him and we had lunch

---

370  Pat Jordan, "Martin Buber: What is to be Done?" (February 1978).

together in my room. Tessa he had left at Tina's for a visit. They had been inseparable as young girls, coming to see me daily at the beach in Huguenot when John, my 18-year-old brother, courted and married Tessa. It has been a happy marriage.

March 1

Depressed over some of Feb. issue and the fact I had asked to see copy but no one showed it to me.

7-column article on Mexico. Dull. 2 col. on farmworkers by Marion Moses. Very good. Obit on Chas Butterworth, long but good. Martin Buber, long but engrossing, including one "Tale of the Hasidim." I remember my joy on discovering him.

After my more complete reading I felt better.

I want to go back to farm soon, now March is here.

March 2

Bob Ellsberg announcing retirement [as managing editor] soon.

March 3

Bob Gilliam speaking tonight. ["What Happened to the Church?"]

First meeting I've attended since my heart attack. Bob talked on church and tradition. Very good. My eyes and nose running. I found it hard to talk to people, yet I felt better than I had for some time.

Bob G. prefers traditional church. I too.

March 4

Try to remember Franklin's joke about memory.

Staff had a meeting downstairs. They will meet once a month or oftener to decide (what goes into CW) duties, etc. We never had a better group. Frank will stay home tomorrow. He has not been too well. Dr. Marion Moses examined me last night. Chest and heart ok. Head cold miserable! Dripping from eyes and nose.

March 8

Chains of thought. New missals (*Prayer of Christians*) in RC church (also Episcopalian), singing my baby brother to sleep with the Episcopal hymnal, i.e. "brightest and best of the sons of the morning." I told Anne Perkins how I wished I had an Episcopal hymnal, remembering the *Wide, Wide World* which I could read at 12, and was deeply impressed and became a better student and "manual laborer" (having a "philosophy of work," as Peter Maurin called it, because of reading that book). The new hymnal not the old, but Anne found one for me.

## March 13

Across the street from my window on E. Third St. is a sycamore tree with a few little seed balls hanging from it. When I first get up and sit by the window the rising snow at the foot of the street has made it a golden tree and during the heavy snows a tree white and gold, a joy to survey. I begin my a.m. prayers with thanksgiving.

## March 17

Paul Loh and Mary O'Connor. She announced her engagement as she brought up my oatmeal. I cannot write or spell. Jittery today. The above news is very happy news. They are both beautiful people. The wedding is in June.

## March 18

Cleaned one bookcase—discarding or passing on some books. Reading for the first time Miller's book [*A Harsh and Dreadful Love*]. Good.

## March 19. Wrote Dr. Miller

Last night Anne Fraser announced that she and Steve Kaune will be married in July. She has known him since Sept and is very happy.

## March 21

Short of help with Frank home sick for first time in years. It is nearly 11 and no one here with mail. Dr. Marion Moses says Frank must stay home for a week. He will come down for an hour tomorrow to delegate tasks.

Tonight started reading *Resurrection* (Tolstoy).

## March 22

Mairead Corrigan and Eileen.

Sharon's husband died—is at morgue. Burying the dead is a work of mercy. I gave my black rosary beads to put in his hands. They had been looking for a cross she had asked for. Gene Palumbo gave me a lovely set of beads, from where? He is one of the many young folks who live around our houses and work but give much time to CW. Did he give the new little icon too?

## March 26. Easter

Pope Paul will celebrate Mass on St. Peter's Square. Remembering the Council.

There is a long aftermath to a heart attack; of weakness of mind and will. But I now am able to get out to Mass around the corner at Nativity each day.

Easter night, March 1978
Perhaps I am over-stimulated by the joy of Easter—and the vigil and St. Joseph's House, Holy Sat. (First St.) or the two engagements that suddenly were announced this spring. When I traveled around the country visiting our various H. of H. I met so many young people who said, "I met my wife or husband at the CW!"

One vocation leading to or rather enlarging the horizons. I often think of Peter Maurin's simple program of "the Personalist and Communitarian Revolution." And his way of expressing himself by slogans to make a point, which I at first thought rather pompous, as when he talked of the "Thomistic doctrine of the Common Good." What were often thought of as catch phrases, he quaintly said, "They make to think!" (His own phrase, by which he meant he wanted men to stop and examine their motives, their meanings.)

Always to get to roots, that is what radicalism meant to Peter. "To make the kind of society where it is easier to be good." "Where there is no love put love and you will find love." "You love God as much as the one you love the least."[371]

I think of that telling statement and how Kay Brinkworth nudged me once as someone passed our dinner talk and muttered, "That is how much I love you!" I have quoted before the Arab saying which I found in *Arabia Deserta*, "Community is sword grass in the hand."

Tonight, however, when I went down to supper, I did not feel that way at all. I had a great surge of gratitude that God had sent us so many young volunteers to staff this large women's house of hospitality. How much work there is to do and how thoroughly they do it.

Tonight different ones were off early to visit the psychiatric ward of Bellevue where 5 of our guests had landed, to bring them little gifts and sweets. I too received a little gift with the fifty guests at dinner, for me a chair with a brilliant red heart hanging from it. I speak of guests, although I'm sure many will be with us for life. Their "ship" will never come in, but they have found a haven.

Who was it that wrote of "Our enemy the State"?[372] To be opposed to State is to be an anarchist. Kropotkin is the one anarchist I would follow and his

---

371 Dorothy frequently repeated these three quotations: the first from Peter Maurin; the second from St. John of the Cross; the third from Father John Hugo.
372 *Our Enemy the State* is an anarchist classic by Albert J. Nock.

books, *Mutual Aid, Fields, Factories and Workshops,* are visions of a new society "where it is easier to be good." Even those titles are what "make to think," as Peter Maurin put it.

Peter, the French peasant, became a Christian Brother in Paris, left the order (not radical enough), emigrated to Canada, homesteaded for a while, then crossed the border illegally and worked always thereafter at manual labor, in the railroads, in the mills. He liked also to think of himself as a troubadour, joining the groups in Union Square or Columbus Circle, which were the open air forums in the thirties.

"To give, and not to take... That is what makes man human," etc.

The Easter feast. Joy goes on. Our houses of hospitality may be filled with desolation and yet joy is here still. Easter Sunday I sat all afternoon in our long dining room which stretches thru the house, if one includes our capacious kitchen, and all the tables were filled all that rainy day with comings and goings, between the two houses. The one on First St. (St. Joseph's) and ours on Third St. (Maryhouse).

We had had the Holy Saturday night services at First St., one of the most joyful liturgies I have ever participated in.

Easter Sunday itself, there was no let down, but a continued joy as most of the women in the house sat and relaxed, even the busiest of them seemed relaxed. Some of the volunteers and staff visited the hospitals where we have "patients," Mother Cabrini, Bellevue, Manhattan State, etc. Somehow sharing in the suffering of others lightens the sorrow of the world. Sorrow and the joy of this season which lightens that sorrow.

Again, beauty will save the world. One of the girls who came in last night from visiting some of our patients said that Goya's colorful paintings lightened the psychiatric ward, which was cheering news.

I am not what is called a feminist, but I can see clearly how women are forced into being what, in the field of journalism, used to be called "sob sisters." Of course there have been great women journalists like Dorothy Thompson in the past and Abigail McCarthy in the present who can be called intellectuals (I use the word respectfully), that is, they took what I would call a "whole view of life." And wrote and still write about the political scene (and international scene). Peter Maurin talked about making a new synthesis of cult, culture, and cultivation—the very use of these 3 words "makes to think."

Not feeling very much like writing this month. I am asking our 3 members of the editorial staff who "make up" the paper at the printers to do as Peter always wanted me to do with his writing, that is, to reprint. Teachers have to repeat and repeat. We all repeat and continue to repeat in our lives and in our words, what we have learned. We ourselves never tired of hearing our mother repeat stories of "when she was a little girl."

## March 28

Tues night: More *Resurrection* of Tolstoy who gave all the royalties of this to enable the Russian sect, the Doukhobors, to emigrate to Canada. We (CW) were in touch with them by correspondence and I went to see them in Canada when I was on one of my long speaking trips. They went to jail rather than submit their children to compulsory state education. Our enemy the State.

Each one of us has a different vocation. Sis wants to return to Africa where she has worked in the apostolate before. I told her we would get her there somehow. All things are possible with God. We must abandon ourselves to Divine Providence.

## March 30

We have a wonderful group of young volunteers but how few there are who think of it as a life work. As Stanley V says, "Some come saying they have found their life work, and remain a few months (or days). Others, more tentative, speak of a visit and stay." We have become a large family indeed.

Comment of a reader on title "L.L." "Your life is anything but lonely." Another and another, over the years, has said, "I found my wife, or husband, at the CW." What an overwhelmingly large family we have.

## April 2

Woke up thinking of John, "my baby brother," whom I wheeled to the park every day, who was so difficult to feed, he almost starved to death. My mother "birthed" him at age of forty or over, and could not nurse him and when I would see Italian families picnicking in park, I'd wish we could feed him bananas and other foods as they seemed to do to their infants.

I always think of him as my "baby" brother because I enjoyed him so the first two years of his life. When I went away to college (Univ of Ill) and certainly could not afford to come home weekends, I missed him terribly.

## April 3. Press Day

Bob E. at a meeting planning a new Seabrook anti-nuclear demonstration.

April 6

Looking at the sunlit embellishments on the tenements across the street. Pillars, a red brick 5 stories, every window framed vertically by pillars topped by little wings, each floor different. 3 front windows, elaborately decorated with wings and cherubs, every floor different, fire escape painted black or green, somehow not defacing this delicately decorated frontage. This was part of the luxury houses of old N.Y., perhaps at the time of Mother Seton, our first canonized American-born saint, one of whose present-day daughters (of the order she founded), Sr. Aloysius, helped along my conversion in the 20s.

April 8

Dr. Marion Moses says I still have heart murmurs, whatever that means.

April 9

It is good to be eating downstairs again regularly at night. Good too to have men and women, so young and strong, helping us. (3 engagements). They hold each other up when tense moments occur, as last night (a woman who claimed to be a famous psychiatrist). She and Anna and I shared a table. There are many misers among the women, but one has no sense of real evil there. There was violence in this one.

April 10

Kevin, Mary and I are enjoying *Resurrection* by Tolstoy. They come after dinner and read a few chapters. The hero is giving away his land to the serfs in this installment, preparing to go to Siberia with Maslova.

Pleasant dinner. One of the young men gave me some beautiful postals. Stanley out book finding. He found one about Hemingway with reference to Lionel Moise whom I lived with in Chicago, a brilliant newspaperman who shared my love of Dostoevsky, which we read together. He fancied, even was a Stavrogin-like character.

April 11

Radio announces Ethical Culture Society (Sunday). Sexual and heterosexual relationship. Talks not conformable with Hebrew or Christian writings—scripture. However, Jesus said, "Judge not."

Cleaning my desk today, beginning to pull myself together. Dr. Miller called. He is a very silent person. Hard to talk to, but he wins one's confidence. He says we can have his book (remaindered). I must read it. It is painful to me to read stuff about myself.

April 12

Dr. Miller in morning, will take our archives with him.

I was very glad to see Bob [Steed]. He fasted once for 40 days against capital punishment. He loved Ammon. Also he held us together when we were evicted from 223 Chrystie. However, throwing out some of my books, like *Revelations of Anne Catherine Emmerich*.

April 13

Dr. Miller is so quiet and dignified a person it is hard for me to call him Bill. I *must* read his book.

April 14

Mary Gordon, *Final Payments*.

I do not remember what the above is about. My memory is bad these days. One reason for trying to keep a diary.

April 16

Went to noonday Huguenot Mass. No water in outhouse. Earl came over—may repair it. My brother John brought a new book on Gene O'Neill, by Arthur and Barbara Gelb. I had a 2 vol ed. with news clippings about his last days.

April 17

Mass tonight, Little Bro Peter. How happy Peter Maurin would be to know the Little Bros of Chas de Foucauld were saying Mass here. Went down late to supper and sat with a mad woman.

April 20

Fr. Geoffrey Gneuhs, OP will stay for summer. Last summer ordained.

Marc Ellis will have book published by Paulist. Research on Peter. Student of Miller.[373]

April 21

I will write about our beginnings for May Day issue and Mrs. De Bethune, Ade, Peter's philosophy of work. If it had not been for Tessa's Spanish hospitality I might not have met Peter.

---

373 Marc Ellis, a Jewish doctoral student of William Miller, wrote an account of his experience living at St. Joseph House, *A Year at the Catholic Worker* (New York: Paulist, 1979). He later wrote and published a dissertation on Peter Maurin.

Why write about one's self? It is expected of women to write feature stuff. When one writes "I," the reader reads himself or herself, i.e., "I am David Copperfield," "I am Little Dorrit," as I read.

May 1. Mass. 45th anniversary
New Seabrook action June 24, planning month.
Forster in hospital again, called.

May 5
Jim Wallis, *Sojourners* [editor], speaker.
Karl Marx's birthday (Eileen Egan and I visited his grave when we were in London years ago.)
Dan Ellsberg arrested at Stony Flats, Colorado—blocking uranium traffic.[374]

May 8
Bob Ellsberg and Brian Terrell leaving for Sandy Flats, Colorado.
Party for Peter Maurin's birthday. The dining room is so pleasant a sitting room with its red calico curtains, women sewing or playing solitaire, and "O.T. Mary" reading scripture. It is so good to be downstairs.

May 9
Bad plane accident in Pensacola, Florida. I still prefer buses for long distance travel (or ships).

May 10
Fr. Dan Berrigan, Mass tonight.
Bob Ellsberg, Brian Terrell, 14 arrested, [Rocky Flats,] Colorado.

May 12
Went to meeting tonight. Fr. [George] Anderson, prison chaplain, spoke. Women in house making nasty remarks about Frank treating me as a mother. Their hostility flows over to me. I recall prisons I have been in. Ugly in some ways but rewarding in others. A deepening understanding of the poor.

May 14
My heart attack took place last October 8, 1977. Hospital $350 a day.

---

374 *Rocky* Flats, Colorado, was the site of a facility that produced plutonium triggers for all hydrogen bombs. It was the site of a long campaign by nonviolent activists who tried to block the railroad tracks leading into the plant.

I was tied up to machines, needles in my arm. Hard to realize, to remember, so I write the info down here.

## May 17
Our new editor Dan Mauk, former Franciscan. Gave him little Franciscan Cross from Assisi.

## May 27
UN demonstration, Mobilization for Survival. Pat and Kathleen and children in for it.

## May 29
Augustine family both ill. Kathleen drops by to see them. I feel so helpless. Patience, patience! The very word means *suffering*. I'm glad I studied Latin. Being a journalist, I use many words and like to get at the roots of them.

Brian Terrell, Clearbrook County Jail. Robert Ellsberg, Jefferson Co. Jail.[375] Both demonstrated; at same time as Mobilization for Survival in NY at UN. I had planned to go but my heart "went back on me" and a deplorable state of weakness kept me on the beach. Where I can at least pray. "At least"! What an expression! Hard work, praying, and trying to subdue a rebellious spirit.

## May 31
Feeling sick and weak all day. Stanley walked in unexpectedly with two archivists from Marquette. All 3 filled kitchen. I was too ill to serve them and am afraid I was very rude.

## June 3
Death of Augustine. Pat Jordan told of another death at the cancer ward where he worked. (He leaves the house across the lane at 6 a.m. each morning.) In a 2-bed room, one patient set fire to his mattress while trying to light a cigarette and while Pat was putting it out, the other patient quietly died. I have been having supper each night with them. Last night Kathleen went to Mass and I stayed and washed dishes.

## June 4
I had wished to go to Auriesville again [Shrine of the North American Martyrs]. I first read of them in Edna Kenton's apt on MacDougal St. in 1917 I think. She had told Floyd Dell and another editor (Merrill Rogers, business

---

375 While fasting in jail, I received a postcard from Dorothy. It was an aerial view of Cape Cod, on which she had written, "I hope this card refreshes you, and does not tantalize you."

manager) of the old *Masses*, we could use it for the summer. I believe Edna K was writing about the [Jesuit] martyrs. When Rayna came to visit me she stayed with me there. Today's martyrs were brought to my mind by a book sent me from England.

## June 5

Press day. And I am not there! I wrote a very inadequate column. Just to show I am alive.

Christ didn't say "He who uses the sword," but "He who takes the sword" will perish by the sword." Rosemary called my attention to this.

I haven't my Bible, so cannot look it up now.

We are a guilty nation, threatening this beautiful natural world with neutron bombs.

## June 6

Rosemary and I at lunch are debating Scripture. The Pentecostal movement has made her an avid reader of Scripture. She is a living example of coordination, the active and contemplative life and the ecumenical life. She listens to PTL Club (Praise the Lord) on radio at 7:30 every a.m., and serves me breakfast in bed, mends the ridgepole of the roof with tar, listens to the 700 Club at 11:30, baby-sits across the lane with Hannah and Justin and doubtless will preach the baptism at the Jordans to them.

## June 7

Rose cleaned the outhouse and storeroom, washed some clothes. We heard Solzhenitsyn speak on television (Harvard graduation with interpreter). Very good.

## June 8

Damp and cloudy. Up at 8. My memory is bad. I forget the day of the week. No daily paper.

## June 11

Who wrote? "Doth it not irk me that on the beach the tides monotonous run? Shall I not teach the sea some newer speech?"[376]

Birds on road.

---

376 In the July-August 1954 issue Dorothy credits Sister Madeleva, the poet and president of St. Mary's College in Notre Dame.

June 12

Picketing American embassy. Demonstration at UN [Mobilization for Survival].

Deane coming down for it from Tivoli with Kathleen Rumpf? 30 were arrested from CW and arraigned and released and dates sent for some time in August. I had so counted on going but ill all day. Very quiet.

June 24. Seabrook

Somewhere this time in the month I went in town to receive an award, beautifully inscribed from Pope Pius XII for our work.[377] I was overwhelmed by this but it helped to recollect that it was in my name but the young women and men who were doing all the work—getting out the paper, running the H of Hospitality, etc. ...

June 25

Messages of sympathy from Mother Teresa of India who it seems is sharing my all but collapse with exhaustion.

(The award, or word of praise, to be framed later, was from Pope Pius and presented to me by Cardinal Cooke himself.)

July 6

Dr. Goldberg—heart specialist. (Reports all good but to be careful.)

Anne Fraser leaving on 10th for wedding trip, will bring me up to Beth Israel for checkup. Dr. Marion Moses (Mt. Sinai).

Tests at 11:30—heart, blood exam. Doris Nielson drove me in and out. But at 4:15 the Cardinal (Cooke) with Msgr. McDonough visited Maryhouse to give me a commendation from Pope Paul! How one dreads such honors when inactive, and a group of dedicated young women bearing the brunt of all the work. One feels like a figurehead.

July 12

House is crowded. How we accumulate things, comfort! My memory is bad. So I shall try to keep this diary to refresh my memory.

July 14

Oxygen delivered. Stanley, Tamar and I walked and sat on beach. Cloudy, damp, no sun. Complete quiet. Collected stones, a beautiful, colorful variety. Every day I am promising myself to walk a little more, to get my strength back. Templegate Press wants a new edition of *Therese*.

---

377 Pope *Paul VI* sent Dorothy a special greeting via Cardinal Cooke.

July 29

Proof sheets of CW July-Aug. Bob Ellsberg's story moving and impressive. Picketing Stoney Flats, Utah—lying on tracks to prevent train movement of nuclear parts of missile.[378]

August 1

Breakfast conversation with Tamar. Talking about Dr. Marion Moses (farm workers) mentioning sprays and her studies of them in Michigan. Tamar spoke of dioxin, widely used. In Italy several villages had to be evacuated. Eric came back from Vietnam with its poisonous effects—from his waist down. Government is denying it is causing this effect.

August 6. Hiroshima day. Pope Paul VI 1897-1978

Leafleting in front of Cathedral.

August 12

Sat and watched the funeral [of Pope Paul VI] all day.

Forster called and wants Stanley to make photographs of Pope's message to me. He saw collection of Mike Gold columns from *Daily Worker* and will send it to me as repayment.

No date: 1978

Tina—-Forster with flowers, visited her.

They both confessed that they had received Communion from visiting priest at St. Vincent's. She has cancer of spinal cord (great pain). He had just had a kidney removed. The priest was going thru the wards distributing Communion.

August 15

Memorare. Sam Putnam, Chicago city editor of one of lead papers (*Post* perhaps) gave me Huysmans to read—*En Route*, the story of a man going to a convent every evening for Vespers and hearing that prayer recited. I went from Chicago to New Orleans, lived in the Square between the Cathedral and the French market on the Mississippi River. No, it was Benediction with the Blessed Sacrament. This started my conversion. Having a baby by Forster B. finished it. I had her baptized, and had to give up a lover. It was hard, but most satisfying.

---

378 "Long Days, Dark Nights in a County Jail," July-August 1978, described my experience in jail.

August 20

Mass at Maryhouse 11 a.m.

Reading Attwater's lives of saints and remembering Anatole France's books read while I was going with Lionel Moise in early 20s in N.Y. Mike Harank gave me the paperback *Dictionary of Saints*. We have a set at Maryfarm, many volumes, compiled and researched by Donald Attwater, who was a friend of Eric Gill, a member with him in a community in Wales and in Ditchling, England.

August 25. New Pope

August 26

Pope John Paul elected. 267th pope. Shortest wait in history. Albino Luciano, a moderate. 65 years old.

August 27

Frank brought me Communion. Thank God for "the priesthood of the laity."

August 29

Tamar in Dartmouth hospital for operation on her hip bone. Hilaire getting married.

August 30

Telephone from Dan Mauk making up the paper. A discussion there about defending "the gays." Thank God, they consult me. St. Paul said, "Let these things be not so much as mentioned amongst you."

"Judge not," is our direction.

August 31

Called Dartmouth Hospital. Tamar had her operation! I pray God she can now be free of pain, in climbing those Vermont hills. She is in great discomfort now.

Sept.

If I did not believe profoundly in the primacy of the spiritual, the importance of prayer, these would be hard days for me, inactive as I am.

September 3 Sunday

Installation of Pope John Paul. TV. St. Peter's Square packed, standing for hours.

Went over next O.P. with Frank. (Very disheveled writing.) If I did not write, our readers will think I'm on my last legs.

September 4

Eating in yard with Ruth, talking of Raph and Rayna.

Gulls don't dive in water, but terns do, laughing gulls, Ruth says.

September 5

Supper outside with Stanley and Jordans. He brought me *So Little Time* by Barbara Gelb. She is a masterful writer. The tragedy of Louise Bryant. What she and Jack Reed went thru in Russian Revolution! I was working on the *Masses* then. Mike Gold, Maurice Becker, Hugo Gellert were my friends. Rayna spent summer with me. Raph was jealous of our friendship. She is featured in *Personal History* by Vincent Sheean.

September 8

Fr. Gneuhs talked on Peter Maurin. I read his book.

Letter from Peggy [Scherer], news of her travels. I succumbed to melancholy. My age, my "on the shelf, blueness, cold weather."

September 9. Feast of St. Peter Claver

Wrote Sister Peter Claver.

*Psychoanalysis and American Drama* (Samson Raphaelson). Does not mention "Jazz Singer." A book which I found down here at S.I. house. SR married Rayna Simons. I do not know her life between our college days and Chicago days and the account of her in *Personal History* by Vincent Sheean. He met Rayna in Hankow. She died in Moscow.

September 12

Awakened early by a cricket on my window sill. Thinking of Varya Bulgakov and "The Cricket on the Hearth" at the Le Galliene theater and the beach and 14th St. and the Maruchess family and Russia and the book Stanley Vishnewski brought me. *So Little Time* by Gelb, and Jack [Reed] and Louise [Bryant] and [Eugene] O'Neill and the Russian Rev. and the Provincetown players and Della and my "Masha" dresses from a Chekhov play ("The Three Sisters") and Tina and Tessa and Paula.

So! My mind in a turmoil and sleeping again and reawakening—sick.

September 13

Abortion trial, fictional, on television last night. Sick all day. Pat and Kathleen's wedding anniversary.

September 15

8:15 Kassie just brought me breakfast. I read my morning and evening psalms in the little Anglican prayer book and hymnal which Anne Perkins gave me—so much easier to find one's way around in. The words "ordinary time" put me in a state of confusion and irritation.

September 16

Read some of *Golden Notebooks* by [Doris] Lessing. She seems to make a religion of sex. It is of course fundamental, but religion transfigures it. "Love in practice" (Dostoevsky) is "a harsh and dreadful thing compared to love in dreams" is a half truth. Or rather, it (love) is a cross—transfiguration a necessity.

September 20

Evelyn Parker's baby due. A high school girl who said my OP (*Long Loneliness*) gave her courage to resist family's pleas she have an abortion.

September 29

A terrible shock this morning. Death of Pope John Paul.

September 30

House cold, a sunny day. A move going on to mix houses, First and Third, St. Joseph and Maryhouse. All our young women will want to be on First?!
Telephone from Rome, asking comment on Pope's death.

October 4

Pope John Paul I funeral. Pope only 34 days. Rained last 3 days in Rome, stopped now. Mass will be on television at 11. My eyes are worn out from watching tel.

No date: 1978

Peggy [Scherer] back [from Central America]. Sick twice with amoebic dysentery. Tamar also got that as a 3-year-old in Mexico. She brought me a beautiful little wooden cross on a fine chain. Also she sent me a purse while down there. However, she is the prime mover in the closing of the farm at Tivoli. Where shall we put all the people?

October 8

Up early reading *Kristin.*

Great discussion about sale of Tivoli. Peggy Scherer in lead, she being most efficient. Deane is staying down here at Maryhouse for some weeks. Taxes high at Tivoli. Also 3 houses make squatters a problem. John Filliger, our farmer since 1936 Seamen's strike and George our saintly hermit and pot washer since he came from jail at WWII. What to do with them? Pass them on to Fr. Lyle? Cold-blooded discussion about very important members of our community!

I can do nothing. An unheard voice. On the shelf indeed.

October 10

My column On Pilgrimage is culled from expanding the hints in this diary.

October 14

Papal conclave begins.

Tonight on tel "Chosen People." Elie Wiesel—he wrote a small book called *Night.* Others too. They are indeed God's chosen. He does not change.

Chaim Potok's books—*The Chosen, The Promise,* and *In the Beginning* are beautiful. All are beautiful, bringing to my mind the high esteem in which Jews hold their wives, mothers of their households. My memories of Cherry St. in 1917.

October 15

Very cold this morning but sunny. At 10:15 the house is still stone cold. Sometimes the hot water is boiling for an immediate hot drink, but nothing this a.m. worked. I am too thin. St. Therese said there was nothing she suffered so much as cold, and since then Carmelite convents have been heated in winter.

To have lived thru the Coughlin era is indeed to have seen something of persecution of God's chosen. Much talk of "international Jewish bankers" in Fr. Coughlin's "Social Justice" paper and radio talks.

October 16

"All things work for good to those who love God."

*Lohengrin* on tel last night. Tom Hoey gave us seats for opera. *Marriage of Figaro* last night. Deane went. I prefer Wagner, pagan tho he is.

October 17

Reading *Night* by Elie Wiesel

John Day called. Will drop by Sunday. Forster called.

Steve Kaune dropped by. His people were Finns. My brother Donald worked in Finland, covering Northern Europe, including Germany during WWII. Interned after WWII. US Soldiers stationed there visited Della often, bringing gifts from him. He was pro-German and an anti-Semite.

At 80 my mind is clouded. Born in 97. Am I now 83 in Nov?

October 18

Sick these days. Very uncomfortable. Plumbing bad on this floor. Overflowing toilet. One woman screaming at night.

October 20

Ask Stanley to find *En Route* by Huysmans, and *The Cathedral*. Also *Life of Garibaldi*.

October 21

Hilaire's and Erin's marriage. Call Tamar.

October 22

Sunday. The new Pope looks young and strong. A great delegation of Poles there. Nina Polcyn is a Pole and we visited Warsaw on our European trip, Warsaw, Leningrad, Moscow, etc. I sat at television until our own Mass.

October 25

Melancholy all day—closing of farm after all our Pax and Peacemaker conferences there. ... Steeped in memories. I am overcome by nostalgia for past and thought of a barren future. Each in his own and a little cabin in S.I. is Stanley's solution. He long since abandoned the sinking ship. He handles my remaindered books and with "offerings" he gets generously, buys me some of my old favorites.

October 27

Kassie and I went to hear Elie Wiesel speak uptown. I heard him on tel and read *Night*. Overwhelming writer and personality. Somehow serene, alive, tho he has seen so much of murderous death.

At exactly 8:05 a.m. the morning sun gilded the buildings across the street, creeping from grey over to red brick one. A lovely sight. Pigeons fly from the roofs—the ailanthus tree stirs in the cold east wind, the sky is a cloudless blue—and now one side of the ailanthus tree which reaches to third floor of the once-luxury tenements is all gilded, and the sun spreads rapidly around it. Young people are on their way to work, but children not yet on their way to school. I cannot figure out their nationality, Chinese, Japanese, Koreans, Vietnamese. I must ask Sr. Eileen at Nativity if she knows. My tree is now radiant with sun.

October 28
Liz Berrigan [McAlister] spoke last night.["Resistance and the Arms Race."] Missed her.

October 30. Press day
Nobody came by with mail or with lunch. A.J. Lacey had not brought it up. "He only does it to annoy because he knows it teases." Got it at night and in it a check for $10,000 from priest at Las Vegas. This issue too-lengthy articles by women.

October 31
Cold but sunny. 7 a.m. reading Merton's *Sign of Jonas*, remembering how a group of CW workers went on pilgrimage to see him. How Roger LaPorte immolated himself at the UN plaza and how TM wrote to urge me not to urge our young men to do this! Hard to forgive him this stupidity. Trappists have always been our friends. Jack English one of our editors died at Conyers Georgia, monastery. He was always a drinker and tho he ran away from the enclosure at Conyers he was always taken back. They were flexible. Bishop of Atlanta (I met him in Rome) told me soldiers from Fort Benning flocked to him (Jack). He converted my old friend Peggy Baird while they shared together a bottle!

November 1
Notes on last two days show my grievances! Must cultivate holy indifference.
Cardinal McIntyre once asked me "Do you see everything which goes in CW?" Then I could say "Yes." Now, no longer. I should rejoice that I am "just an old woman," as a little boy said at the Rochester H of H long ago. He said, "All day long they say 'Dorothy is coming' and now she is here and she's just an old woman!"

November 2
This a.m. early sun gilded the upper floors of the buildings across the street. Looking up I saw squirrels on roof edge! Always pigeons before!

November 5

Holberts coming. Arrived at 3 and I had to submit to an interview by Mrs. Holbert. She was here with her doctor husband, who, knowing I was cared for by Dr. Marion Moses, did not take my pulse. Dr. Yanovsky stays away altogether.

November 6

New floor started for women at St. Joseph's H of H on First Street. I'm sure only the most attractive will be welcomed. The old and demented, the feeble here. Someone said once of CW "the gold is rejected and the dross remains." Sometimes is my bitterness most bitter! I think the quote is "in peace is my bitterness most bitter." Don't know where I learned that. A strange quotation.[379]

November 8. My birthday. I was born in 1897!

Party in the dining room and many flowers. Eileen Egan gave me warm stockings for the coming winter.

November 10

The talk tonight was on Martin Buber by Pat Jordan, who went to Pendle Hill for a year (?) to study him. The depopulation of our farm at Tivoli goes on. A sad time.

November 12

A dull day, breezy, cold, could not sleep well last night, a head cold. Went to Mass last night at 5:30. Could not get myself together today.

Joan Walsh came in—may move to Rutherford. The closing of the farm was Peggy's idea—too many lame, halt and blind. Deane will come here. "In peace is my bitterness most bitter."

St. Therese, pray for me.

November 20

Trouble in Nicaragua, Sandinistas. I worked for a while years ago before CW for the Sandino group, sending medical supplies to Sandinistas, who were in the mountains.[380] The long struggle against our imperialism goes on still.

---

379 Isaiah 38:17 in the old Douay/Rheims translation. Dorothy used this line as the title for her column of January 1967.

380 In *Therese* Dorothy described how, at the time of her conversion, she had been working for the Anti-Imperialist League, which was supporting Augusto Sandino's struggle against the U.S. Marines in Nicaragua.

November 21

Horrible story of the mass suicides by cult, hundreds missing from Guyana camp (Jonestown). Family groups, dressed gaily colored clothes all but 3 dead from drinking concoction of Kool-Aid and cyanide.

"Heart of Darkness" by Conrad.

November 22

Help me, Dear Lord, to do my little daily tasks with "love and ease and discretion, with love and delight." (I do not know where that quote comes from. It just popped into my head.)[381] "The duty of delight"—is that phrase from Ruskin? Where did I get the idea that it is? Was it Irene Mary Naughton who first used the quotation (she said it was a quote) when she was one of our editors on Chrystie St.?

November 25

Cold in the head. Cold and windy. Mass at noon at Nativity. Felt low most of day over the terrible events in Guyana these last days. Read *Heart of Darkness* by Joseph Conrad. The *Times* mention that this S.A. horror reminds one of Conrad, whose story ends with "the horror, the horror!"

November 27

5 a.m. Disturbed women in recreation room talking loudly to herself. Told me to get out, none of my business, she said, as she burrowed around among her papers, scattering them all over the floor. Very disturbed.

November 28

Abbot John Eudes on his way to France visited us today and was delighted to see the House his gift had purchased for us, this old music school which is large enough for 50 women. There are always mattresses on the floor of the auditorium stage and library too. There is close cooperation between St. Joseph House on First St. and Maryhouse on Third St. and with the young men and women volunteers who earn their own rent money for little slum apartments. A few live in the houses, as needed, if they do not have school loans to pay back. "The less one has of Caesar the less one has to render to Caesar!"

Many of the young men are on night duty at the Rose Hawthorne cancer hospital too. The Quaker school a few blocks away also provides jobs for the girls.

---

381 These words are from a prayer of St. Bonaventure, cited in the Roman Missal of 1962.

November 30

Julia to hospital. She said to me once "I have enjoyed every day of my life." Poor dear, she has also been panhandler par excellence. Anna finally consented to see a doctor for her ulcerated legs. She has been suffering for years, getting up at night to wash out her bandages to be used again. The doctor at hospital said Julia probably had a stroke.

Sat a.m. the girl who "has the house" (they won't say "in charge") told me of Julia's maniacal struggles against going to hospital. Her bank books. She has "panhandled" for years. A miser, as so many women are of clothes and things too.

December 1. Fr. Dan Berrigan

Meeting packed to the doors. Fr. read Merton's poems—all said afterward it was a prayerful meeting—the best ever. And I could not attend, confined to my room! Dr. Marion Moses had supper with me and she examined heart and lungs etc. Thank God for the unceasing fight against the horrors of war.

December 3

Concert, "Salome." I heard it at old Opera House with Forster? Decadent music. Years ago the Johnsons were scandalized at my going to hear it.

December 9

Went to 5:30 Mass. Bad singing and standing around altar. Bad singing also at Vespers in the house. We are not spontaneous like our Puerto Rican fellow parishioners. No strong voices. We are Anglo Saxon. All the old women are obedient but me—I do not go up and stand around altar.

December 11

Tom Cornell visited me p.m. Had been in Nicaragua and conditions terrible there, papal nuncio on side of the dictator. He telephoned Rome about it. He will send me the FOR magazine, he said. Tom very ill, with dysentery.

December 12

Julia [Smith Moore] died in the night. Had the last rites (Fr. Geoff). Gave money she had in her closet to one of the women. A clot on the lungs. The girls did not call me, thinking it would disturb me. Her bank books—$36,000?[382]

---

382 See Lee Lecuyer, "Julia," February 1979: "Julia probably doesn't want to be remembered as a good, holy person. She will not be remembered that way here. But she loved life and longed for youth and its delight…. Her open selfishness and the basic mistrust it fostered, often prevented us from seeing the person beneath that callous appearance."

December 13

Jane Sammon came up to sit with me, knowing how long Julia had been with us, and fearing I would be "fearing death, perhaps." Jane is the most tender and sympathetic (the word means "suffering with" others) and has proved it by her feeling for Tina since they met in the hospital.

December 16

Stanley brought me 2nd volume of *Evelyn Innes*, by George Moore, read long ago. (Struggle between love and faith.) It undoubtedly influenced my conversion and separation from Forster.

Fr. Gneuhs book on Peter. It is so good to keep Peter Maurin's seemingly simple Easy Essays in mind—his repetitions—his sense of being a teacher, like "that is what makes man human."

Marge Hughes as a follower of Peter—a joyful cooperator. Many tragedies in her own life but a steadfast cooperator to this day, now working with the group in W. Va. A rare person who knows "the duty of delight."

John Day Jr. came in to visit while Tessa went to see Tina. They gave me lovely warm rose-colored robe, very cheerful.

December 19

We have such an attractive (physically and mentally) crowd here now in First and 3rd St. that everyone wants to be here. More stimulus in city. "Now is the winter of my discontent."

But it is good to have Deane here. I go down to the evening meal with her. What a valiant person she is.

December 26

I must get Stanley, "book finder," to search for the *Arundel Motto* [by Mary Cecil Hay]. Did he find *The First Violin* [Jessie Fothergill] for me? Kassie Temple brought up on *Anne of Green Gables*, a series. *Anne of Avonlea*. She often brings up my morning coffee. There was also *Rebecca of Sunny Brook Farm*. But Van Gogh in letters to his brother referred to *Wide, Wide World* [Elizabeth Wetherell]. It was my favorite too. Read it first when I was in first year h.s. in Chicago. Gave me a "philosophy of work, " as Peter Maurin called it.

December 28. Feast of the Holy Innocents

Pray for Berrigans—Pentagon demonstrations today.

# 1979

January 2

Cambodia and Vietnam war. Disturbance in Iran.

US recognizes mainland China. I must read the book I have on China by Han Suyin who was born and brought up there.

January 3

"Mourning Becomes Electra" on TV. Tamar brought a tiny terrarium (made with an electric light bulb?). Fr. Lyle brings the *New Yorker* to me every Wednesday when he comes as he does faithfully, rain or snow every week. Eleanor came to Mass tonight! She sends me little notes on pictures torn out of *National Geographic*. Frank subscribed to that for a birthday present.

January 5

Dan Mauk and Peggy [Scherer] getting out paper. Frank typing from my diary for coming issue. Did not like what Frank had typed so wrote a new column.

Victor Stier wrote a chiding note—one of our oldest friends—should listen to him.

Marion Moses came to supper to check my heart—says I should see Dr. Goldberg again at Mt. Sinai.

January 6

Woke up with two lines haunting me. "Duty of delight." And "Joyous I lay waste the day."

"Let those that seek Thee be glad in Thee, and let such as love Thy salvation, say always, the Lord be praised." From Wadell's *Desert Fathers*.

"Tosca" on the radio this afternoon.

January 8

Woke up this a.m. half remembering a dream in which someone said "This is the best country in the world." Wondering whether it was faithful Ed Forand, ex-Marine (service in Nicaragua) plus Tom Cornell's recent account of it when he visited me. He had just been there. My conflicting emotions! Result of Victor Stier's letter. He works for State Dept. Some embassy. Do not remember which.

**January 9**

Katherine Breydart gave cross to Dan Berrigan. He gave it to Bob Tavani, Xmas, and Bob sent it to me.

**January 12**

I have a bad cold. See nothing of Stanley. Since news of little Justin Haughton's death (struck by a car) last week he has not been in. I too feel prostrated. Grief is numbing.[383]

**January 13**

Terrific storm in Chicago. Mild here. But bad in Mid-West. My brother John came in while Tessa was visiting Tina, brought me *The Cathedral* by Huysmans. *En Route* started my conversion in New Orleans.

Borrowed *Dr. Zhivago* from Mike Harank. Becky [Haughton's] Lara (my first great-grandchild) is named from seeing the movie which was a great one. Best movie I ever saw—haunting, musical accompaniment.

**January 15. Press day**

Ps 49:3—"They shall give thanks unto Thy name which is great, holy, wonderful." The invocation of the Name—the Jesus Prayer. "Franny and Zooey" in the *New Yorker*, years ago. Salinger's article, his story, *Catcher in the Rye*. A little masterpiece which started many young ones praying. The Holy Name, "Hallowed be Thy Name."

**January 17**

Stone-hard baked potatoes for supper, cabbage overspiced, the usual chicken. I'm in favor of becoming a vegetarian if vegetables are cooked right. ... Another food grievance! Onions chopped up in fruit salad, plus spices or herbs! A sacrilege to treat foods in this way. Foods should be treated with more respect since our Lord left Himself to us in guise of food. His disciples knew him in breaking of bread.

What a hard job cooking here is. But the human warmth in dining room covers up a multitude of sins. Stanley is still a growing boy, can eat anything.

**January 18**

Asked Kathleen Jordan last night to bring me in *Wide, Wide World* and *Queechy* [Elizabeth Wetherell], my two favorite childhood books. She was having night off from Hannah and Justin. Will pray for all at Perkinsville in their sorrow. Rosemary Morse called telling of miracle of her Pentecostal

---

383 Justin Haughton was Dorothy's great-grandson—the son of Becky Hennessy Haughton.

group—a man's crippled leg lengthened! She wanted to go with me to beach house for a few days. Bitter cold.

## January 19

Fritz Eichenberg came tonight thru bitter cold, from Peacedale R.I., to give his talk and slide show. He brought me a beautiful book of ikons and a tiny book of animal Proverbs, *Wisdom from Beasts*.

## January 20

Ps. 100. O be joyful in the Lord.

Kassie or Marge bring me my morning coffee. I can say the above verse. My grandfather who fought in the Civil War used to have a glass of wine or whiskey at night, which he called his "O be joyful." Tonight Stanley brought me a half bottle of port before he went out to supper at Mary Lathrop Pope's home.

## January 21

Today we are having Mass in the house—Fr. Gneuhs. I love the 10:30 Puerto Rican Mass where the entire congregation sings so heartily. One of the priests tries to get his small daily Mass group to sing even tho there are only a dozen or so there! Yesterday noon was one of those Masses. Painful—but we try. If only those who have voices would sing louder they would cover up the failure of the self-conscious mediocre, who would be given more courage to try harder.

## January 23

Beautiful cards sent with donations. One comes from an Eskimo cooperative. With Xmas greetings in 3 languages, French, English, and I presume Eskimo. ("The world will be saved by beauty.")

## January 26

Peggy Scherer spoke tonight and showed her slides of her trip to Mexico. Did not get down. She will show them to me privately some time, as Stanley did his pictorial history of the CW.

My memory is so bad—old age is certainly trying. Also I am getting deaf. When, for instance, Joan Walsh and Tamar are talking quietly in the room by the windows, I cannot hear them.

Frank is too solicitous for my health.

January 28

$790 cost of Justin's funeral plus $125 for grave.

Movies on television are a great temptation but also a good distraction in time of sorrow, or bitter and ugly thoughts. "African Queen"—Katherine Hepburn. Story of a trip down a river from a jungle mission. Humphrey Bogart, skipper of mail on rivers. Unbelievable but interesting. Tamar and I enjoyed it.

January 30

Mini earthquake today in Brooklyn, S.I., N.J., and Westchester. Waiting for Frank to bring in the *Times* so I can read about it. Why was not Manhattan Island affected? What a thought! Unimaginable to think of those fantastic World Trade Towers swaying with a sudden jarring of what we have come to think of as solid earth beneath our feet! Yet I sat one day in a rocking chair 50 years ago, nursing my tiny daughter in front of a large mirror which hung from my wall in my beach bungalow in S.I. and suddenly saw that mirror begin to quiver as tho a train or truck, neither of which could be within miles of us, had suddenly passed the little house, making it tremble.

January 31

Elie Wiesel spoke on radio about the Holocaust and no one protesting. But the CW and *Commonweal* did.

February 5

One of my birthday presents last Nov was a subscription to the *National Geographic*. I love it not only for its texts (I can still be "on pilgrimage" while reading it) but also its pictures. I woke up this morning with a tune running thru my head—"He has the whole world in His hands, He has the whole wide world, in His hands." So why worry? Why lament? "Rejoice," the Psalmist writes, "and again I say Rejoice!"

February 7

Peggy Scherer and Dan Mauk will be managing editors of CW hereafter. (I will be listed as "publisher," I suppose.)

Just finished that incredible book *The Gadfly* by [E.L.]Voynich. I have an 1897 edition. Tessa and I wept over it years ago, at the beach house. Suddenly I have 2 copies of it.

February 9

Fr. Tom Berry speaker.

News of death of Allan Tate on radio, also of death of Dorothy McMahon, a very dear friend. Lucille, a nurse, one of the group, came East to help me nurse Nanette, Forster's woman, dying of cancer. She was a Polish Jew and talked to me about the faith. Lucille and I baptized her before her death and she smiled as she died. Lily Burke [Forster's sister] came in to see her and exclaimed, "She is smiling!"

She and Marge and Forster and I had a happy 3 months at the beach while Forster rented another bungalow down the little row of houses behind the Beachcomber. Forster was very happy with the arrangement! One understands bigamy.

He telephones almost every day now.

February 10

Anna, down the hall, howls in pain, hoarsely accusing me of stealing her social security card.

February 11

"Hell is not to love any more." Woke with this quote in my mind. Where is it from?[384] My memory, my memory!

February 15

Today we go to press. Peggy and Dan new managing editors. A very good team. Peggy, former head of the Peacemakers, and Dan a former Franciscan.

I must get a copy of the *Little Flowers of St. Francis*. "This then is perfect joy." We used to read one each night years ago after Compline at Tivoli farm. We also used to say the Angelus at meals which brought about Peggy Cowley's conversion. "May I by Thy Passion and Cross be brought to the glory of Thy Resurrection." Once John McKeon said, "Do we really mean it? We're asking for it." She said "I do!"

February 20

Discussion with Kassie on Camus and the *Plague* when she brought my morning coffee.

Frank brought up *Granma*, the Cuban paper. Front page, Message to Fidel from Pope John Paul II as Pope flew over Cuba on his way back from Mexico.

February 23

Michael True speaking on Flannery O'Connor.

---

384 A famous line from Georges Bernanos's *Diary of a Country Priest*.

Stanley brought me in an old copy *of Elsie Dinsmore* [Martha Finley] which I read when I was in 4th grade at 37th St. in Chicago. I liked the religiosity of it, began to read Scripture and pray before climbing into bed with my sister Della who complained of my cold feet. Tamar is like Della, has no interest in religion, thinks talking of it is like talking about sex—it is not done! To bare your soul is like exposing yourself. My father carried a Bible with him always, but my mother's only manifested interest in religion was Christian Science, which she tried to believe in, tho never attending any services.

When I had violent migraine headaches at 14 or 15 she had "treatments" offered for me by a "practitioner" across the street from us on Webster Ave. in Chicago. When I had played with Lenore Clancy in Chicago at age 12 I had wanted to become a Catholic but my Southern father said "only washwomen and policemen were R.C." and he bade me go to the Episcopalian church, which I did, and was formally baptized. When Tamar was born (out of wedlock, as the saying is) I was formally baptized a RC and left Forster, tho I still loved him. He professed atheism. Very difficult for some years for both of us. I had to go to California and Mexico to get away from him and so deprived him of our child Tamar, whom he loved and still loves. He telephones often, asking after our "progeny" (her 9 children and 14 grandchildren). She is more like her father, and professes no interest in religion. This natural world is enough for her. She has a deep, almost mystical love of natural world; she said, tho, "Do not worry—I believe in God."

March 1

Got a radio in time to hear Wagner's "Tristan & Isolde"—what voices. Forster, Lily and I heard all Wagner years ago at old Metro where it was easy to hang over top balcony and see all the tremendous orchestra.

March 3

Meeting of staff in office this a.m. I was not invited to sit in on it.
Opera—"Rigoletto" this p.m. Slept thru half of it.

March 7

"Studs Lonergan" by Farrell on television, coarse, harsh picture of RC family in Chicago. Knowing Tom Sullivan and John Cogley, I found it not true.

March 8

Reading *The First Circle* by Solzhenitsyn and when I finish it I will read *Day in the Life of Ivan Denisovich* and *Cancer Ward*. The latter sounds morbid but I found it inspiring. He has been called a "holy fool."

March 14

This p.m. Jacques Travers visited Deane and me, and brought gifts of flowers and vermouth. He is very much the Frenchman with his delicate attentions. Deane would not touch the latter, having long since "given it up" to help our weaker brethren. Fr. Hugo used to say "the best thing to do with the best of things is to offer them to the Lord—to give them up."

March 18

Stanley ate here, then went out with one of the young women. Television not working. "Get a new one," he keeps saying. Letters of Flannery O'Connor [*The Habit of Being*] in today's *Times*.

March 19

St. Joseph day. Mary L brought steak dinner, spinach, mashed potatoes, Italian gooey pastry! to celebrate. She had also brought a magnificent hanging of the Dominican St. Thomas Aquinas like a banner over my bed. A beautiful piece of work. Mass in chapel.

March 21

Fr. Lyle offered Mass. Frank's little ginkgo tree is growing and budding in a gallon can. A sign of hope, of perseverance.

Gene Palumbo brought Ernesto Cardenal to the Mass and they gave me an autographed copy [of his poems], of which Peggy will translate parts for me.[385] We used to have a huge poster of Che Guevara hanging in the office at First St. I remember Ernesto's visit on a Friday night when there were too many interruptions for a conversation.

Quarreled with Stanley for not helping Frank with manual labor.

March 23

Have Deane play her tape on liberation theology for me. Anne Marie Stokes visits her often. I think Deane is happy here at Maryhouse.

March 24

Peggy brought me a postcard, very fine picture of Wagner from the card shop on way back from the printers. Reading *Queechy* today. No letters done. "Joyous I lay waste the day."

---

385 Fr. Ernesto Cardenal, a Nicaraguan priest and poet, was a supporter of the Sandinista revolutionary movement. After the Sandinista victory in July 1979 he was appointed Minister of Culture in the new government, prompting the Vatican to suspend his priestly faculties.

March 25
Freedom of Information Act. Bob Ellsberg wrote for file on me. FBI.

March 29
Janet Ward and Kathy Clarkson brought breakfast (oatmeal ) and said they would demonstrate against nuclear submarine. Talked of difficulties of women in house.

April 3
My memory is so bad I cannot think who it was who brought me the little afghan hanging over my rocking chair nor the fruit salad (I ate it all yesterday!). Must ask Frank

Marion Moses called about Cesar but mostly about Harrisburg and nuclear energy and nuclear waste [*after the accident at Three Mile Island*]. "Pray as tho all depended on God, and work as tho all on ourselves." People have telephoned, called, praising Bob E. "He was right in Rocky Flats case."

April 4
Fr. Lyle offered Mass. Brought me *Memoirs of a Revolutionist* by Kropotkin.

Abusive letter from Paul [Bruno] at First St. Feeder of pigeons on our garbage and salvager of bottles and tin cans. A help really. He is quarreling with Dan Mauk.

Deane and I go to dining room to help fold the papers to get them ready for mailing. Dirty work with black pictures on front page.

Dan and some of the girls going to Groton to demonstrate against nuclear submarine launching.[386]

Bob Ellsberg speaking tonight. [Panel: "Why Catholics should not support the Salt II Agreements."] Sick all day. Only hot tea palatable. Feel as tho I had been poisoned.

April 7
Groton, Conn. 200 arrested of 3,000 protestors first [Trident] nuclear sub. We have a group there.

---

386 The protest was against the launching of the first Trident Submarine, the USS Ohio, in Groton, Connecticut.

April 8. Palm Sunday

Mass beginning with procession from back garden into auditorium. All the house. One of our guests gave me the *Little Flowers of St. Francis*—"This then is perfect joy." All the house is there.

My brother John here (Tessa to visit Tina) and he brought me books: *David Copperfield*, my favorite of Dickens; the *Imitation of Christ* by Thomas à Kempis and *Pilgrim's Progress*, which I have never read.

April 9

Up early at six. Volunteers plan to meet 3 times a day in chapel for Holy Week. 3,000 at Groton nuclear sub base. 6 CW. Gene, Geoff, Dan Mauk, Gary Donatelli, Janet Ward, Bob E. 200 arrested.

April 12

Dan preparing chapel. Mass in auditorium. Everyone taking turns keeping vigil all night.

April 13. Good Friday

Eileen Egan and I to Mass at Nativity—crowded at 5:30 with Spanish speaking. Supper in my room. Movie downstairs tonight. I am all mixed up as to time. Bob Ellsberg visited me in my room.[387]

April 15. Easter

Cesar Chavez visiting today. First at Riverside Church, Cathedral of St. John the Divine, and Corpus Christi. Dr. Marion Moses called at 8:30 a.m.

Telephoned Della. She is in a nursing home. Needs constant care with her arthritis.

April 19

Lena left by cab with literally innumerable plastic bags, filled with her loot from our clothes room—her collection from trash garbage cans. She will sleep in this debris. Her fat keeping her warm in the summer and Fall…

Radioactive iodine still leaking at Three Mile Island.

April 21

A gang going to Washington DC. My job is prayer. Sometimes I feel it is like a prayer wheel, mechanical. "His strength is as the strength of 10 because his heart is pure"? Pure in this case means single-minded. Our CW family has this single-mindedness. "It all goes together." Our program.

---

387 In this meeting I shared with Dorothy my desire to become a Catholic.

May 3

Barometer falling. Up early, reading John Cogley's paperback. Wrote Fr. McVey—Unity Acres—an apology. I had told him when he visited and spoke of his plans that "he was biting off more than he could chew." An old phrase of my mother's. I told him I should "eat my words."

May 6

I awoke at seven thinking of the thousands converging on Washington DC to protest nuclear weapons. Peggy and Dan staying home to make up May Day issue of CW. While I was downstairs, my bed was made up afresh with blue sheets. So many gifts we receive.

May 7

Stanley to hospital today.

May 8

May issue has Robert Ellsberg account of getting my dossier from FBI (Freedom of Info.) Very funny. They had come to see us at S.I. farm long ago.[388]

Long letter from David Spier about his visit to Della. Della and I miss each other. We were always very close, except when Tamar was having her family and Della had worked for Margaret Sanger (who started a birth control clinic in the early twenties and was sent to Blackwell Island prison. She was released in a few days—I interviewed her for the NY *Call*, the socialist paper I was working on then).

May 12

Reading *All the King's Men,* by Robert Penn Warren (Huey Long). First rate book. I had worked in New Orleans on the *Item*, feature stuff, human interest stories—for instance, the "taxi dancers"—a fascinating city. At that

---

388 My two-part article, "An Unusual History from the FBI," appeared in the May and June-July 1979 issues. The FBI files documented the government's efforts, over several decades, to comprehend just what kind of subversion the Worker represented. It disclosed that J. Edgar Hoover had recommended prosecution of the Worker on several occasions and, in the 1950s, had placed Dorothy's name on a list of individuals to be detained in the event of a national emergency. She was particularly amused by this assessment from the FBI Director: "Dorothy Day is a very erratic and irresponsible person. She has engaged in activities which strongly suggest that she is consciously or unconsciously being used by Communist groups. From past experience with her it is obvious she maintains a very hostile and belligerent attitude toward the Bureau and makes every effort to castigate the FBI whenever she feels so inclined."

time, living down near the river, I wrote about the Cathedral where I began to go to Benediction each night. When I was assaulted by the taxi dancers in a tavern, John dos Passos, the writer, was there. I had a black eye from a heavy cup thrown at me!... Got news of sale of *Eleventh Virgin* to Hollywood and came back to NY and bought bungalow.

May 13

John, my "baby" brother, born when I was 14, came by and borrowed *Kristin Lavransdatter*. Tessa was visiting Tina who has much pain (cancer of spinal cord.) Her illness brought about the reconciliation of sisters and she said it was worth it.

May 15

Stanley home from hospital. Looks fine.

Fr. Geoff got a car and took a crowd, including Frank, to visit Peter's grave.

May 19

The young people went up to Times Square recruiting station to distribute the paper and some people they encountered sent their greetings to me.

May 20

Frank at beach will bring in *War and Peace*. I like a good long book to live with for a few weeks.

May 21

Story of Pentagon Papers on television for 3 days. Bob Ellsberg's father brought the scandal to light.

Deane is going out on demonstration [to Shoreham, Long Island] with a crowd of CW against proliferation of power plants with their dangers. She brings me generous quantities of dried fruit and nuts.

June 3

Reading Flannery O'Connor's letters.

Big coverage NY *Times* at nuclear plant—all arrested, Deane included. All over country, demonstrations.

June 4

Write Della. Mrs. Holbert's writing to Cardinal Cooke to help with a fund so I could visit my sister!! Officious again. Must write her. If I felt up to it Della herself could help me.[389]

Still in jail, noncooperating, Deane, Jeanette, Janet, Gretta, Kathie, Mike H., Gary. 7 still in jail. Bob Ellsberg, Geoff, Meg, Bill Barrett back. 4 a.m. released.

June 8

Little patches of green pushing out thru cracks in the sidewalk. The sturdy ailanthus tree! My one large tree which just reaches to the third floor of the beautiful old building across the street. Fire windows on each floor, arched and pillared and decorated most beautifully, one greenstone with two red brick structures, six stories high. Beautiful little children live in the one opposite—they look Korean or Vietnamese or Chinese, I cannot tell which. The fire escapes serve as porches for the little ones!

June 14

Felt exhausted all day. Frank is right. Visitors are too much for me. Not even strength enough to answer letters.

June 16

Frank to meet Peggy [Scherer] at Marlboro across the Hudson from Poughkeepsie to look at small farm for sale. My mother was born there. Not too far from Newburgh.

June 17

Mother Teresa and Eileen visited.

June 19

Talked to Della on phone. I'm sending her Mother's two diaries, Florida and her trip to Riga. How she did know how to enjoy life! Even in 37th St. when she read to us as we ate an unappetizing meal at supper. In Florida it was racing and jai alai, and bridge parties. Aunt Jennie and I visited her there one winter and Cousin Clem from Georgia was on an island; we visited. Two hurricane shelters, one for blacks, and one for whites.

---

389 Dorothy was embarrassed to learn that her friends had written Cardinal Cooke soliciting money so that she could visit her sister Della, who was living in British Columbia—and that he had graciously contributed to this fund.

The other diary was her trip to Riga to see Donald. Della also went to Riga to get away from Malcolm [Cowley]. To flee temptation.

June 20

Deposit on Marlboro, new farm.

Samson Raphaelson called—author of *Jazz Singer*, about a cantor's son. He married Rayna Simons (Rayna Prohme when she was written about in Vincent Sheean's *Personal History*). She died in Moscow.

June 22

Stanley came down from Maryknoll and took all the girls but one out to breakfast. He has a peasant's feeling about money. He sells my books and keeps the money. But he persuaded a press in Ill. [Templegate] to bring out *Therese* again, and feels entitled. No Mass tonight. Raph: talked a long time on phone. Teaches at Columbia. Said he sent Rayna money in China and Russia. I'm glad they kept in touch.

June 23

Must ask Raph about Rayna. How she came to be in Hankow. Who was Prohme? Separated?

June 25

Monday night Mass. Tamar brought in wine and Frank dry vermouth. Della always served dry vermouth to Franklin and me before dinner. She loved to cook undisturbed in kitchen. It was an art with her. She must hate being waited on now.

June 26

Tina called, long rather strange conversation. She attributed her "conversion" to me.[390] Executions postponed in Florida. I had prayed all that Sat a.m.

---

390 Dorothy quoted Tina's letter in her column in the July-August 1979 issue: After receiving her prognosis in the hospital, she wrote, "for two hours, I was in mortal terror. Then, a thought came to me. Not an experience, just a thought of St. Teresa' wanderings along the roads of Spain. 'The mules are packed, they are kicking, the road will be very rocky, the destination is sure.' St. Teresa encourages familiarity. This descendant of converts, very female, very stormy, very valiant, does not want us to fall back from the quest in awe of greatness. She asks that we join her in all our failing humanity, since there is nothing to disturb or affright us except, perhaps, vermin in uncomfortable inns."

June 27

One of the girls gave me an Agatha Christie mystery. My favorites are the Amsterdam stories, the Boney Books and the Rabbi mysteries. The Talmud helps him solve crimes.

I am in my second childhood—I broke my arm at twelve years old (in Chicago) by tripping over my brother's foot. Mother was icing a cake, as she did every Saturday night and the doorbell rang and in rushing to the door I tripped over my brother's foot and broke my arm in 3 places! Our dear Dr. Lunn, a horse and buggy doctor, was telephoned for, came at once. I was laid out on the kitchen table, my mother administered chloroform and Dr. Lunn set the arm. My father, working nights on the *InterOcean,* came home at two bringing in his pocket an Oz book and a little white poodle. Thereafter my Aunt Jenny back in NY sent me a Sherlock Holmes mystery, one a week! Conan Doyle and Rider Haggard were my favorite writers when I was 12.

July 27

Tom Sullivan called. A book out—stories of converts, all of whom mentioned me as being an influence. He said he would send me a copy. It was reading *Sorrow Built a Bridge* that influenced me too. Many of our young men work at St. Rose's home for incurable cancer, started by Rose Hawthorne.

July 28

Tina called 2 times. In such agony with cancer of her spinal cord...I told her how we have Mass with her statue of the BVM carved in lignum vitae, the hardest wood in the world. She is having a hard time. But it "has brought about the reconciliation of sisters," she says. Her family gave an alabaster statue to us when we were at Easton farm. The Heaneys did not take it in in winter and it broke. One of our men (who died of tb later) built a fence and garden around it.

July 30

Dr. Moses scolded because of my lack of appetite.

"They" reprinted an old article of mine about "kissing a leper."[391] Like we reprint Peter Maurin's stuff. I feel like a has-been.

August 1

Dan in court. Deane, Jeannette Noel and Gary Donatelli. All pleaded guilty and released unconditionally. Same judge. They picnicked at Jones Beach, got wet. Pat Jordan visited. Told how they forcibly feed at St. Roses.

---

391 "Poverty is to Care and Not to Care," July-August 1979.

Tom Cornell and Monica visited. He wants to leave [Fellowship of Reconciliation] and return to CW. But we pay no salaries. They would like to be "family in residence" at new farm near Newburgh. He was a loyal friend when I was going thru a grueling time at Kenmare St. He and Monica are beautiful people. Two kids.[392]

### August 5

Demonstration today up the Hudson… Indian Point [nuclear power plant]. Crowd going from here. Deane very much a valiant leader. Jeannette Noel from Worcester visiting Trappists. She will ask prayers for me. They—all the Trappists—have always been our friends. Fr. John Eudes, Abbot of [the Abbey of the Genesee near] Rochester, gave us money for Maryhouse. They have new formation in South America and Africa. Pray for them.

### August 11

Felt too disturbed, mentally, physically, to go downstairs to Mass, but Fr. Gneuhs gave me communion. Stanley came up to supper. I could not eat. He brought some wine and Frank brought up brandy. I feel I should do without it, considering Nicky's weakness. However one "sun-downer," as mother used to call it, is a help. I sleep well. Put all troubles aside.

### August 12

Mass at 12 noon in auditorium. Fr. Gneuhs white robed [in his Dominican habit] and beautiful. He has written a book about Peter Maurin. Wish it could be printed. He joins in all the work, physical and mental and spiritual and body and soul. What blessings God sends us. Frank [Donovan] especially is a blessing.

### August 13

All arraigned again and back in jail. Refused to give names. Maureen (too young?) now in jail.

### August 16

Meg and Michael to be tried today. Marj Humphrey and Deane to attend trial. Buchanan where nuclear plant is. Jail at Valhalla.

Will get out Monday. Maureen fetched by parents.

---

392 After leaving the FOR, Tom Cornell and his wife Monica started a CW house in Waterbury, Conn. Later, they settled on the new CW farm in Marlboro, New York.

August 21

Anne Fraser Kaune comes on way to night duty at St. Vincent's to take my blood pressure. The other girls are learning to do it.

August 25

Eileen going to Poland for peace conference? Yesterday Charles Killian, most faithful on mailing out paper and coming to Mass, always—was drinking and Juan Hernandez killed him. Chas, bad when drunk, irritated him.

Jane and Dan Mauk went up to ward at Bellevue. Will try to see prisoner. We knew him about a year.

August 26

The priest who is saying Mass daily in the auditorium at Third St., Maryhouse, irritates everyone by commentaries during Mass but Frank says is helping in kitchen at St. Joseph House, cleaning slimy vegetables and fruits which we beg from market uptown.

August 29

Charles Killian funeral at Calvary in Queens. Enormous cemetery. 3 cars full.

September 1

Furor in Maryhouse. Janet Ward locked out of kitchen. Women howling for coffee and breakfast...nearly 11 a.m. now. No Frank yet with *Times* to satisfy my curiosity on Cuba.

September 3

Robert Coles advises Kennedy daughter stay at Maryhouse.

September 6

A quiet day. Mass on radio. Robert Kennedy's son picked up for seeking cocaine in Harlem, according to radio.

Soviet troops in Cuba. Carter may seek extra 4 billion for military.

September 7

Dr. Moses for supper. She says I must eat more. I am "cannibalizing"—what an expression! More peanut butter!

September 15

Great gathering of Hells Angels from many states on death and funeral of a leader. Much noise of motorcycles. Dostoevsky story, the onion. One of H.A. helped a family over the roofs when a fire broke out.

September 16

"God wills that all men be saved."

"Thy will be done."

The story of Lallah's son who committed suicide and how a priest at Our Lady of Guadalupe on 14 St. told me "There is no time with God." All the prayers you will say for him will have given him the grace to turn to God at the last moment. A rich reader in Milwaukee who heard this story wrote how sorry [he was] that I have no time for God and sent me a weighty book on theology to study.

September 23

Girls leafleted at Cathedral. Ammon would have been proud of them.

September 27

No Mass in house today. Frank and I went to noonday Mass at Nativity. As we returned two people, a couple, tried to break their way into house. Frank had to threaten a police call. They had caused much trouble in house.

Alexandra Tolstoi's death in *Times* today. I met her at Jenny Moore's house in N.J. and told her Helene Iswolsky was living with us. "She has fallen into very bad company," she commented. Bishop Moore is at Anglican Cathedral in N.Y.

September 29

Noonday Mass—a man with St. Vitus dance in front of me a few pews, his shoulders twitching and his arms. I prayed for healing for him… Coming from Mass met one of our guests in the entrance hall with a bunch of Padre Pio's pictures—prayers. I had made a pilgrimage on one of my trips to Italy to see this miracle worker (his father had worked in Brooklyn to earn money to put him thru the seminary).

I love the Italians and their popes. Frank arrived this p.m. with a color TV for my birthday, a week from now, Nov. 8.

Nina Polcyn called on phone. We are both excited over Pope's visit [to United States].

October 2

Practically all day given to watching television. Pope. A woman read the epistle. Every detail of trip here given. All day. Now at 9:30 [Yankee] Stadium Mass is being sung or chanted by some bishop or priest.

Deane and another had 2 tickets to Cathedral Mass. Mary dropped in to see. We heard the Pope, Message of Peace.

October 6

Dr. Marion Moses came tonight. We talked of Pope's speech in Chicago and the women's opposition to his "male chauvinism," not allowing women to give out communion (and on birth control), abortion, rhythm method, etc. She is a strong feminist. I am not, tho I can see all the problems.

I remember hearing my mother and her sisters talking about it when they thought I was asleep in next room, methods of bringing on an abortion by themselves.

October 8

No mail. Mass tonight. Katy Hennessy came to Mass. Cesar Chavez and his wife visited and Stanley took many pictures. Frank has an enlarged picture of me in my prison uniform, looking out a window at Tivoli. Where is the one of me sitting on my English traveling chair (I still have the latter, chair, in my room) between two police guards, at UFW picketing, mass picketing which ended in arrests?[393] Many nuns, also.

October 11

Castro at United Nations. Police guards everywhere. Mass at noon at Nativity. An exciting time, this month—Pope and Castro!

October 13

Got calls this month from Kennedy family about daughter working as a volunteer here. Also Gov. [Jerry] Brown of Calif. telephoned. I had met him many years ago when he was a student. He came with students to study migrant labor. I am not interested in politics or elections. "He governs best who governs least." "The less you have of Caesar the less you have to render to Caesar." (State aid, state schools, etc. we are used to. I remember in 1st grade at Bath Beach in 1904? we said the Our Father before our school day began.)

---

393 Bob Fitch's classic photo of Dorothy shows her sitting tranquilly on her "traveling chair" as she awaits arrest on a UFW picket line.

October 20

Will be glad to see Eileen Egan again after Pax meeting at Kansas City. Eileen represents Pax to me. Peggy, Peacemakers. Bob Ellsberg now [working] with War Resisters. I think a brave activist.

October 22

In *Times* story of imprisonment in Cuba, and the many political prisoners still suffering isolation. Sounds like Solzhenitsyn and a book published many years ago about Russia.

October 28

Everyone moving with van from Tivoli to Marlboro. Went to 10:30 Mass with Mary [Lathrop] Pope. All p.m. saw Tolstoi's "War and Peace" on television, very good, but of course book is much better. I read it again. Frank up at new farm, brought back roses from there. A quiet day. Tamar has difficult time. She needs to be here and good to have her. Mary L sent over Vermouth which we had with supper.

October 29. Anti-nuclear rally on Wall St. 1,045 arrests

Moving done from Tivoli to Marlboro. First Mass there yesterday. Lovely letter from Peggy giving news of first Mass at new farm.

Demonstration at 6:30 a.m. at Wall St. Deane, Beth, David [Beseda], Bob E. got arrested, latter to hold all day. Front page, 3 col lead in *NY Times*.[394]

October 30

Eunice Kennedy called, just a friendly call. Her brother Edward Kennedy will run for president and will declare his candidacy Nov 7.

November 8. 82nd birthday

My birthday. I was born in '97 according to my birth certificate.

My birthday presents piling up. My room a mess. My memory is bad so I like to write down details. Deane gave me 3 bags of nuts, also C.S. Lewis. Very good. Others, books, chrysanthemums. Mass tonight and afterward ice cream and cake for the house but I felt too nerve-racked to go down. A beautiful pen and ink drawing of new farm at Marlboro from Rita.

---

394 This sit-in at the New York Stock Exchange protested the immense corporate complicity in the nuclear power and weapons industry. It was timed to capitalize on the 50th anniversary of the Stock Market Crash of 1929, thus generating enormous publicity.

November 11

Received Communion in my room. Slept a good deal. Symphony on television. Tonight I'll read the *First Violin* by [Jessie] Fothergil again. An old time love story. Frank brought in proof sheets of Oct-Nov issue of CW. Very good, neat job. Symphony tonight. Opera this p.m.

Tel calls from Kennedys and Brown, Governor whom I met years ago before *Grapes of Wrath*. Met again in California grape strike years ago. Both young. My *Loaves and Fishes* paperback has a story of Kennedys who came to visit us on Mott St.[395]

November 12

Anna screeching down the hall. Her legs eaten away with ulcers. She will take no remedies. Sometimes I feel very much alone in the house. So many live outside. But Stanley is here in the house. Right now he is sick with flu. Holy Name Center priest and doctor visited him.

November 13

Stanley still not too good. We hurried supper, looked at telly as they call it in England.

November 14.

Stanley died.[396]

Tamar had just gone home to Perkinsville. We telephoned her and she came right back. Frank telephoned his family—"Stanislaus Visniauskas" was his family name. A Lithuanian immigrant family who came over to Brooklyn. His father a tailor. One of his brothers a steel worker now in Baltimore. "Little Waltie"—bigger than Stanley. He is godparent to one of my daughter Tamar's 9 children, Mary Hennessy. Mary came down from Perkinsville. A beautiful girl.

November 16

Awake for an hour, thinking of all Stanley has meant to us. He was like a big brother to Tamar.

---

395 Joseph and John F. Kennedy had visited Mott St. in the 1940s, as Dorothy recounted in *Loaves and Fishes.*

396 Dorothy wrote about Stanley, the longest-serving member of the CW, in the December 1979 issue, "A Knight for a Day." Peggy Scherer also contributed an obituary: "He was a Catholic, and a Catholic Worker; a writer, an archivist, a lover of walks and of food, of books and of puns, a photographer, and lecturer, and finally, a good friend. But more than any of these, Stanley was a man full of faith: his sense of joy, his love of life and his communication of these to others, came from his deep love of God."

November 17

Stanley's Mass—Fr. Joseph (Little Brothers of Chas de Foucauld). Fr. Lyle—our usual Wed night liturgy. Fr. Gneuhs, OP.

Waking up I confuse Stanley with Peter Maurin in my mind as to his Mass.

November 18

Waking up confused again. Seems like Stanley's Mass was on Sunday—church packed. His family had a plot next to one Peter Maurin was buried in. Beautiful coincidence.

9 a.m. radio Tchaikovsky. Stanley loved music. Tchaikovsky, Mozart, Chopin, etc. The funeral Mass yesterday seemed like a Sunday Mass.

Exhausted today.

Nina [Polcyn Moore] called. Frank and Peggy worked all day until nine. His coming up and telling me as he said goodnight made me feel useless indeed.

November 21

Up early reading Psalms. I am all mixed up as to time. Kassie Temple gave me my coffee, took my pulse. Gave me medicine. Still warm out. A mellow Nov., Tamar says. She just came in and had her tea. Like her father, Forster Batterham, she is very English.

Peggy wants Tamar to stay at farm at Marlboro. Tamar not very happy. Does not want to. She scolds me just as she used to do as a child.

November 24

How I miss Stanley. He saved my life twice. National Biscuit Co. strike and Biafra flyer.[397] Peggy gave me 3 pictures of Stanley. Also she cleaned the office, putting it in what order she could.

November 27

Losing my mind. Wake up not knowing what day it is until Frank brings in mail and NY *Times*.

---

397 "The first was during the National Biscuit Company strike when mounted policemen were called out to disperse a mass picket line [and] one of the police on a huge horse all but pressed me against a wall. Stanley got between me and the horse and its rider. The second time was when a crazed veteran, who had smuggled food into Biafra, Africa, and who went 'out of his mind' occasionally, stalked down the long hall at Tivoli, passed Stanley's room and came and there flung himself on my bed, burying his face on my shoulder to weep. ... Stanley was right there in an instant to place a strong hand on his shoulder and say, 'The dinner bell just rang.' This seemed to bring normalcy to a tense situation." ("A Knight for a Day," December 1979)

November 29

Crisis in Iran, who want Shah back (deposed). He had been operated on here. Gets worse every day (situation).

November 30

Sick all day. Ed Forand sends over *NY Review of Books* which seems like a procurer to me with its ads for male and female companions. But book reviews good.

December 1

Marion Moses telephoned. I'm ok to go downstairs again. My weight is 120 lbs, pulse 62.

December 3

Eileen flying to Oslo to be with Mother Teresa when she gets Nobel Prize.

December 9

Mass 11:30. Geoff, OP.

"La Boheme" on radio. Frank came up and reminded me. "La Boheme" was an opera which haunted my youth.

Mary Pope in this a.m. Wants to start a new order, leaving out of account she has a husband.

# PART VI

# THE FINAL DIARY: 1980

This *final diary from Dorothy's last year was discovered only in 2006 in the drawer of her bedside table, where it had lain undisturbed for more than twenty-five years. It shows that she continued, right up until a week before her death, to reflect on the events of her daily life, and to record the thoughts and memories that occupied her mind and heart. She was terribly weak. And yet, apart from a few short trips to the hospital, she was able to remain in her room at Maryhouse, visited by old friends, receiving Communion, listening to the opera on the radio, taking in the sight of morning glories on her fire escape, talking to Forster (who called regularly), enjoying frequent visits from Tamar (who was with her at the end), and still practicing "the duty of delight."*

## 1980

January 5
   Woken up late at night by Blanche, a little out of her mind, all packed to go out, to "escape." I sent her down to the dining room where many of the women sit up all night.

January 8
   Forster visited. Tamar had gone to visit him and they came back together, carrying boxes of pictures, two boxes full, mounted on boards, hangers and all on.

January 13
   No Mass in house today.
   "Siegfried" on radio. Reading *First Violin*. Good combination.
   Afghanistan and Iran crisis. Iran says "Send the Shah."
   "Solar power 30 years away. Nuclear power necessary." So they say. New farm near Indian Point.

January 14

Salty Wheatena for breakfast. I ate a banana instead.

January 17

I've been too weak and nervous to write for diary. Dr. Karl Stern said he could tell health by handwriting.

January 22

Tonight moved my bed facing windows.

January 28

Marion called from airport. On way to California. Tells me to read *Times* editorial on Hans Küng being censored by Vatican.

Mass tonight. Young man there who said he sang opera (including "La Boheme"). Another older man talked (extravagantly devotional), prostrated himself on floor on one side.

January 29

Anna howls in the night. Her legs are all ulcerated. She washes out her bandages in the night and uses them over again. She is 2 rooms away from me. Anna was my companion also when we had only First St. house. Still 9 women over there. Maryhouse full.

January 30

Draft registration for women?

January 31

Pres. Carter, "gloomy outlook about economy."

February 15

Editor of *Commonweal*—[Peter] Steinfels. ["Neo-Conservatism and the Left."] I'm sorry to miss our Friday meetings, especially this. The C. printed my first articles as a Catholic. Led to P. Maurin's arrival at CW.

February 17

Heard a lot of the "Ring" today and read the stories in an opera book.

Della called tonight with help of Sue. So good to hear their voices. Della's is very weak. I must send her the pictures, photos, I promised.

February 18
Make a packet of Stanley's photos for Della. At 8 p.m. she called and we had a good talk. Good to speak to her and Sue last night.

February 21. Press
Talked with Della on phone. She wants my books which have been published.
Will write her tomorrow about Dorothy Sayers and Josephine Tey.

February 24
No Mass in house today. All priests, Fr. Geoff Gneuhs, Fr. Lyle, and Fr. Joseph (Little Brother) busy elsewhere. I receive Communion in my room days when they are not here. Frank brings it up.

February 25
Things ("phrases") to remember. "Duty of Delight" (Ruskin?)
"Jesu, Joy of Man's Desiring." Lovely title for music.
"Romeo and Juliet"—beautiful music, tho not as beautiful as Wagner's "Tristan and Isolde."

February 26
Reading Josephine Tey's *To Love and Be Wise*. As good as Dorothy Sayers. Frank brings me ice cream every night. I cannot eat a heavy supper, so save my plate for lunch next day instead of the eternal soup.
When there is no Mass I receive the Host in my room from Frank. The Lord has sent me a son in my old age.

February 27
Jim Peck of War Resisters, where Bob Ellsberg is now working, wrote me a comforting letter. Eileen Egan, who has been sick, resigned from WRL and recommended Bob to take her place. Bob's parents wrote me when he first came to us, how happy he had made them by this choice of his.

March 2
Man called about a derelict, "not drunk and clean"! How did he get my private number?

March 4
Tamar's birthday. Telephoned her.

March 8

Dozen from CW and 2 Little Brothers went to Washington to demonstration, Pentagon. Twelve from here drove down in van. Episcopal church putting them up. One Little Brother of Chas de Foucauld (a priest) said Mass outside the Pentagon. A street Mass! I wonder what Chas de Foucauld, who started this order, would have said? I'm sure he was blessing the enterprise!

March 14

Three things happening at once tonight.
1. Meeting—Eileen [Egan's] cousin Fr. Jack Egan.
2. Return of Deane from Washington DC demonstration.
3. Dr. Marion Moses to supper and her researches.

March 15

Bill Callahan died. He was our first managing editor. Bill and I went to Washington DC to protest draft in WWII.

Everyone home from Washington DC Pentagon demonstration. They distributed many papers.

Anne came to cut my toe nails.

March 26

"The less you have of Caesar the less you have to render to Caesar." Jesus and the coin.

"Render to Caesar the things which are Caesar's and to God the things of God." "Whose face on this coin?" Jesus.

Foundation of our work.

Voluntary poverty and manual labor. Jesus and the coin, "Do unto others."

"Sowing and reaping." New Testament words of Jesus. "Sow sparingly and you will reap sparingly."

March 27

Woke up remembering that we go to press today with our miniscule 8-page paper (compared to the NY *Times*) and I think my usual wandering thoughts of what I could have written about myself, a woman born in 1897, a woman of long life, of varied experiences.

April 5

"Parsifal" on radio.

April 12

Tina called. We are all "dying daily," but she has the accompanying pain of cancer. Her beautiful carving of Our Lady which we have in the chapel here at Maryhouse, keeps Tina very close to me.

Transit strike ended. Very exciting to watch its coverage on television. Whole city moving to work on foot, thru heavy rain part of the time, moving over bridges from borough to borough.

David Spier called personally to tell of [his mother] Della's death. A most dear sister. We had been to see her recently.

April 13

Doris Harmon [Della's sister-in-law] came at 3:30 with her daughter Alice, told of a service at an Episcopal seminary near her house. How very kind of them all. They knew how close Della and I always were from earliest childhood, playing together, confiding together. I remember especially our first "childish" love affairs, she 12 and me 15. Two musicians lived on our street in Chicago, both young married men with families.

Armin Hand, head of the band which played in nearby Lincoln Park, Wed nights and Sunday afternoons, and Arthur Hand, who played violin in Chicago Symphony. I am sure he was conscious of my adoration as I always...

April 14

Cold, dull. Forster called—briefly, especially in speaking of Della's death.

April 15

Tamar called. Told her about Della's death.

April 16

Tina telephoned at 11:45, having just heard of Della's death. Just a brief call of consolation and understanding.

April 17

Only mail, John Givins, old faithful, still addresses me as "Dorthy" Day. He was and is a seaman still—Seattle now. Fought in Spanish Civil War. Name really Givonilovich. Years ago when he came back from Spain, he proposed to me and then to Eileen! Wanted to settle down. Now he is a retired longshoreman, after traveling entire West Coast, and is happily married with wife and children.

April 23

Kathleen Jordan visited bringing *To the Finland Station* by Edmund Wilson, which is, as he described it, about the revolutionary tradition in history and the rise of socialism.

May 1. May Day

First issue of CW in 1932 (?). Party in house. Papers distributed in the Square (Union) as in 1932. Dinner and meeting. Jordans there, children angelic. My day started miserably with a cockroach in or on my cereal. Weak and miserable all day.

Reviews in *Commonweal* of books by Michael Harrington and Malcolm Cowley. Della would have been interested in latter.

Every day I miss her. Only her devotion to Margaret Sanger and birth control divided us. How one misses a sister.[398]

May 10

150,000 Cubans coming in. Castro emptying his jails, his economic situation. 30,000 Haitians, more wretched have come. Reminds me of the mass movements of the Middle Ages—to the holy lands. A hysteria.

In my *On Pilgrimage* (my columns of 60s) I write of Cuba and how reformed it was from a "Red Light" district of the US (like 42nd St. in New York)—according to my young brother John Day Jr. who went there with my father for a month every year for racing.

May 11. Mass in the house

Anne Fraser in for breakfast of pancakes. Frank brought a rose for Mother's Day.

May 13. Press day

Paper looks very good.

Tonight Gene O'Neill's play, "The Iceman Cometh" on television.

---

398 Dorothy wrote of Della's death in the May 1980 issue: "Coming from a newspaper family, I usually do not find it a chore to set pen to paper to write my usual column... but this time it is hard, indeed, because I have lost my sister, who had always been my closest friend and confidante.... After Della's own marriage, she had three beautiful children, and, as she explained to me, 'We are true believers in planned parenthood and only had those to whom we could give five years of college, or even more for research.' When she went on to exhort me on another occasion that I should not urge, as a Catholic, Tamar, my daughter, to have so many children, I got up firmly and walked out of the house,' whereupon she ran after me weeping, saying 'Don't leave me, don't leave me. We just won't talk about it again.' So our friendship continued and I had many a happy visit with her over all these years, and I shall surely miss her."

May 15.

Pentagon demonstration. Deane and others to Washington to be sentenced.

May 16

Fr. [Henri] Nouwen speaker, teaches at Yale Divinity School, friend of Fr. Geoff who studied with him. ["The Ministry of Vincent Van Gogh."]

Nina Polcyn Moore here for visit. We talked of our visit together to Russia some years ago—mine financed by Corliss Lamont, a "pinko" millionaire who lived modestly and helped the CP in this country. Nina, having a bookshop at the time in Chicago and making money, came with me. She lives now in Minnesota.

May 20

Mt. St. Helen's [eruption], 5 dead, 29 missing. Like Italy volcano.

Ominous cloud of ash from volcano coming across nation.

8 a.m. beautiful music on radio; sunny day, pigeons flying by window, Hell's Angels zooming past. I am a sensual woman, ears, eyes.

May 21

Visit from Della's grandchildren. They wish to have a little Quaker-like ceremony as Della's daughter Sue did in her marriage, at the Quaker meeting house nearby.

But this time it will be here at Maryhouse. Wish they'd have it there now instead of our auditorium.

Tamar arrived tonight.

May 25

Mass in auditorium at 11:30 for Della—with her family and Doris Harmon present. After, dinner in her honor.

May 27

Mike Harank has planted morning glories in front of Maryhouse again. The strings for them to climb on go up to the third floor. Beauty!

May 30

NY Review of Books pornographic this week. Won't have it in house again.

May 31

"Tristan and Isolde." Opera.

Forster and I used to go standing room at top balcony, fascinating to look down.

June 8

Nina Polcyn Moore called. Also Forster, at supper time. I have no appetite. Apple heavily spiced with cinnamon, meat, mashed potatoes, and string beans, rawish.

Computer breakdowns brought us to verge of nuclear war twice today!!

June 10

Mary Lathrop Pope came in, just back from Paris. She is so young and strong. I asked her to make my bed, changing the sheets, which she did most efficiently. I am very fond of her. She and Kevin, who worked at Bread for the World, while she for Wall St. where they needed someone who had a knowledge of French. Saved their money for this trip.

June 13

John Cort speaking. ["Eric Gill, the Catholic Worker, and Socialism."]

June 16

A conversation on television on suicide. (Dostoevsky)

June 20

Dan Berrigan, S.J. speaker. ["Hope Against Hope: Resistance in the 1980s."]

July 9

Tamar here. Has Deane's room.

July 22

Tamar left for Vermont. I'll miss her.

July 24

Ammon's birthday. Would have been 87 years today.

"Their troubles were multiplied. Afterwards they made haste." (Where did this quotation come from?)[399]

July 25

Dr. Moses visited. She says my heart is fine.

---

399 Psalm 15:4 in the Douay/Rheims translation.

August 2
"La Boheme," radio.

August 3
Mass on television. Frank brought me Communion.
Forster calls every day: Do I hear from Tamar?

August 23
"Marriage of Figaro" was Sat after opera on radio. I prefer "Tosca" and "La Boheme" to "Figaro."
Reading Mike Gold's *Jews Without Money*, a battered paperback, its pages yellow with age, but you can still read the quotations from the NY *Times* review, enthusiastically recommending it. "It has the deep shadows of a Rembrandt picture and the high challenge of a Whitman poem." I must try to find another copy, bound and on better paper.
It reminded me so much of my first newspaper job on the NY *Call* and my meeting with Mike, whose name was Irwin Granich.

September 7
Mass on t.v. Wonderful for shut-ins.

September 8
Press day. Peggy and Frank did a good job. Dropped by St. Joseph in a.m. for Mass and they met Fr. Hovda there. Paper looks very good. It is 6:45 p.m. and finished a good summer tomato juice. But since canned, it has salt, not good for me. Alas!
Morning glories up to 3rd floor. Can see them grow each day! Mike Harank put up strong string like fishing line to hold them.

September 24
Tina called. Then Fr. Dan Berrigan. Then Eileen.

September 28
*Crime and Punishment.*
Exploring galaxies. Made me think of astronauts and my getting a recognition from the pope with 2 (?) of them [privilege of receiving communion from Pope Paul VI].

September 29

Much stuff on tel on nuclear missiles—how many launching pads in country. Guided missiles.

October 2

Reading *The Dream of the Golden Mountain* by Malcolm Cowley. A very good history of the times, those "parlous times" as the saying goes, of the Depression years. My dear niece sent me a copy of it after her mother's death and reading it now I found it a most interesting history of the Depression years. A far better book than *Exile's Return*, an earlier book.

That and Mike Gold's *Jews Without Money*, very stimulating. But I did not find the Lower East Side like that when I lived on $5 a week for the *Call*.

October 3

Speaker on ancient China tonight. I remember my effrontery at talking of Mao when he first came into power and reading a long story in *Time* when he first came to power. Chinese from all over NY City came to hear me. It was at Chrystie St., our old beautiful house.

October 5

Frank brought me up Communion this a.m. I walked a little in the hall—getting my "sea legs" under me, a family saying. My mother's forebears in Marlboro and Poughkeepsie were whalers.

October 8

Communion in my room. Took a little tour around Maryhouse. Much bigger than I remembered it.

October 11

Joan Thomas [Ammon Hennacy's widow] here today. Ammon's book—she still has 400 left. Her book, *Years of Grief and Laughter*.

This p.m. Jim Wilson, who burned his draft card (Tom Cornell, Roy Lisker burnt draft cards).

Roger LaPorte burned himself.

October 19

Mass at 11:30. Will go downstairs, God willing.

October 20

Fr. Lyle going to Australia, his home territory where they recently found a gold nugget as big as a man's head. There will be a "gold rush" there for sure.

Could not get down for Mass again.

October 26

My sister Della used to quote, "Had I foreseen what was to befall me, I would have rued the day." I do miss traveling as I used to—to all our houses, by bus. You feel you are really seeing the country as you speed along the highway, over plain and mountain.

October 28

My sister-in-law Tessa's sister, Tina de Aragon, is in St. Rose's Home. She will still be close to us all there, where so many of our Catholic Workers—at least eight—are employed.

November 8

My birthday. 83 years old.

November 11

Taken to hospital. Carried on chair downstairs.

November 14

Home. Stanley V. first anniversary. We still miss him.

Mass tonight at Maryhouse for special Stanley anniversary.

Moved myself into Beth Israel [Hospital] on First Ave and 16th St. My room on 8th floor. Faces South. Sun all day.

November 17

Not home yet! Tamar and Mary, mother of Forest.

Echo-test needed. Dr. Moses. Last straw!

Today Jane and Frank visiting. My ceiling at home cleaned up after flood by Frank and Dan Mauk, who gave me little panda bears.

November 18

Frank went home sick. Lay down much of the day. Brought in as usual yogurt ice cream, and chocolate nut cakes. Wish he would take care of himself. I love him like a son. The whole work depends on him.

November 20

Jane Sammon in to bring coffee. Frank—grilled cheese sandwiches at noon.

Kathleen Rumpf came down in van—brought corn husk doll. Cheese sandwich for lunch.

Rita Corbin at Poughkeepsie. Coretta and Martin John. Dorothy Corbin and Steve McGinn also. Sally has scholarship for Bard. Clare Danielsson, my godchild, lives in town of Poughkeepsie?

*Dorothy Day died in her room at Maryhouse on November 29, 1980.*

*A card inserted in her final journal:*

> "O Lord and master of my life, take from me the spirit of sloth, faintheartedness, lust of power and idle talk. But give to thy servant rather the spirit of chastity, humility, patience and love. Yea, O Lord and King, grant me to see my own errors and not to judge my brother, for Thou art blessed from all ages to ages. Amen." —St. Ephraim the Syrian's Prayer of Penance

This prayer I found years ago in a book called *The Humiliated Christ in Russian Thought* by Gorodetzky. It was the prayer of a political prisoner in the Czar's time. Also in that book was the story of a pious peasant or serf, a girl who loved dancing. An accident crippled her for life so she lay, a helpless invalid, but "rejoicing that she was counted worthy to suffer for our Lord." This story was in a volume of Turgenev, *Huntsmen's Sketches.*

# INDEX